EMPIRICAL POLITICAL ANALYSIS: RESEARCH METHODS IN POLITICAL SCIENCE

EMPIRICAL POLITICAL ANALYSIS: RESEARCH METHODS IN POLITICAL SCIENCE

FIFTH EDITION

JAROL B. MANHEIM
THE GEORGE WASHINGTON UNIVERSITY

RICHARD C. RICH
VIRGINIA TECH

LARS WILLNAT
THE GEORGE WASHINGTON UNIVERSITY

WITH CONTRIBUTIONS BY:
DONNA L. BAHRY
PHILIP A. SCHRODT

New York • San Francisco • Boston
London • Toronto • Sydney • Tokyo • Singapore • Madrid
Mexico City • Munich • Paris • Cape Town • Hong Kong • Montreal

Vice President/Publisher: Priscilla McGeehon
Senior Acquisitions Editor: Eric Stano
Associate Editor: Anita Castro
Senior Marketing Manger: Megan Galvin-Fak
Production Manager: Denise Phillip
Project Coordination, Text Design, and Electronic Page Makeup: Thompson Steele, Inc.
Cover Design Manager: Nancy Danahy
Cover Image: "Small People Measuring Big Shapes" © Warren Gebert/Stock Illustration Source, Inc.
Cover Designer: Joel Zimmerman
Manufacturing Buyer: Al Dorsey
Printer/Binder: The Maple-Vail Book Manufacturing Group
Cover Printer: Lehigh Press

Library of Congress Cataloging-in-Publication Data

Manheim, Jarol B.
    Empirical political analysis : research methods in political science / Jarol B. Manheim,
  Richard C. Rich, Lars Willnat; with contributions by Donna L. Bahry, Philip Schrodt.—5th ed.
      p. cm.
    Includes bibliographical references and index.
    ISBN 0-321-08614-7 (pbk. : alk. paper)
      1. Political science-Research. I. Rich, Richard C. II. Willnat, Lars, 1964– III. Title.

JA86.M35 2001
320'.072--dc21

                                                            2001029335

Please visit our website at http://www.ablongman.com

ISBN 0-321-08614-7

    5 6 7 8 9 10—MA—04

CONTENTS

Conclusion   368

Chapter 21

Writing (or Reading) the Research Report   368

Chapter 22

Overview   398

Appendix A

Statistical Tables   406

Appendix B

Ethical Considerations in Empirical Research   415

PREFACE

Over the years, we have all taught research methods to undergraduate and graduate students alike who, whether by choice or by administrative fiat, found themselves enrolled in courses that examined the nuts and bolts of the research process. And, over those same years, we have searched for a text that was readable but not trite, comprehensive but not overwhelming, sophisticated but not coy, and functional but not pedantic. We looked high and low, far and wide, down every aisle and up every stack, but we never found a text that was, in the end, teachable. We were thus drawn to the conclusion that we had only one alternative—to write this book.

The result of our effort, as we hope you will discover, is a book that balances the competing demands placed upon the author of an introductory text. It is, we believe, clearly and appropriately organized to reflect the various stages of the research process from conceptualization of the research question to interpretation of the findings. Each chapter has been planned around a series of substantive questions, presented so as to provide examples of the importance or application of the topic, enhanced with a series of research exercises to give the student practical insights into the issues raised, and rounded out with a list of key terms and an annotated bibliography suggesting both more advanced technical discussions of particular methods and places where these methods have been employed in the literature of political science.

In addition, the book is written at an appropriate level. We do not talk down to students, but we do write for them. We try to anticipate the questions a student might raise and to respond to them. We introduce necessary technical terms, which is, after all, a central function of a methods text, but we avoid unnecessary jargon. Specialized terms are defined in the glossary at the end of the book and are shown in **bold print** on their first significant use in context. We do not believe that one must be familiar with every technical term in order to grasp the essentials of the research process. We present detail and specify procedures, but we try to keep sight of the conceptual framework inherent in doing research.

Finally, and perhaps most important, this book is *comprehensive*. It introduces a wide variety of techniques, applications, and concerns important to political science research; their foci range from survey research to modeling, from the difficulties of comparative research to the opportunities of focus groups. And although we do not explore each of our topics to the depth that a specialized text might, we do provide sufficient insights into their workings and applications so as to meet the needs of the beginning researcher. We believe that having read this book, a student will both know and understand a great deal about the research process (not the least of which is how much more there is to learn), and we hope that most instructors will find that this is the only text they need to teach a complete methods course.

Despite these features, this book is not going to please everyone. Any undertaking of this sort requires the making of certain choices regarding what to include and how best to include it, and any such choices provide a potential source of disagreement. We genuinely appreciate the assistance of those reviewers who helped us through this task, both the first time through and in each revision, whether by agreeing with our choices (and thereby confirming our editor's wisdom in selecting them as reviewers in the first place), by disagreeing with our choices and arguing the merits of their cases persuasively (thereby improving the end product and earning our sincere gratitude). Without them the process would have been easier, but its result less satisfying.

In preparing this fifth edition, we especially want to thank David Ettinger of George Washington University's Gelman Library, who helped us to keep our treatment of systematic bibliographic search in chapter 3 up-to-date. Also, we would like to thank the following reviewers for their helpful comments:

Matthew M. Shousen, Franklin and Marshall College
Bruce Evans, Susquehanna University
UK Heo, University of Wisconsin–Milwaukee

Thanks, too, to Anita Castro and Nancy Freihofer for helping to make this new edition a reality.

We are grateful to the Literary Executor of the late Sir Ronald A. Fisher, F.R.S., to Dr. Frank Yates, F.R.S., and to Longman Group, Ltd., London, for permission to reprint Tables IV and VII from its book *Statistical Tables for Biological, Agricultural and Medical Research* (6th ed., 1974).

Finally, we want to thank our families, who, once again, have put up with our undoubtedly intolerable behavior as we came to terms with the fact that signing a publishing contract is not the same as turning in a completed manuscript.

With all of this assistance, the final product is ours. We are responsible for its weaknesses and for its strengths. We think it is a terrific book; we hope you will agree.

New to this Edition

- Materials from several chapters have been consolidated into a new section on qualitative empirical methods.
- Expanded and thoroughly updated coverage of new technologies.
- The ethical research practices in Appendix B have been updated to reflect source-level changes.
- New paperback format.

No one is entitled to the truth. . . .
Only what the evidence shows
and nothing more.

E. Howard Hunt

CHAPTER 1

THE RESEARCH PROCESS

I have seen
A curious child, applying to his ear
The convolutions of a smooth-lipped shell,
To which, in silence hushed, his very soul
Listened intensely; and his countenance soon
Brightened with joy, for from within were heard
Murmurings, whereby the monitor expressed
Mysterious union with its native sea

William Wordsworth, *The Excursion*

Curiosity and necessity are the primary motives underlying human inquiry. Either we seek to understand the world around us for the sake of knowledge, or we seek to understand it so that we may protect or better our lot in it. Whichever is the case, our knowledge often brings with it, at least potentially, a recognition of certain ways to improve upon things as they are. To put that another way, the more we learn about our environment, social as well as physical, the better equipped we are to manipulate, or adapt to, it. This is as true of our knowledge of politics as it is of other fields. The key to understanding and altering our political environment is, most simply, knowing more about it.

But this simple idea of knowing raises two far less simple questions: *How* do we know? *How should we use* what we know? The first is a question of method, the second, one of ethics and preference. In the first instance we are interested in obtaining and structuring knowledge or understanding; in the second we are concerned with the moral obligations that accompany it. Both questions require the exercise of judgment and both draw upon our experience, but each demands its own distinct kind of intellectual effort.

To decide how we know, we must set forth certain hard-and-fast rules for defining political reality. For example, we might define political reality as our experience with, and observations of, the political system. That seems straightforward enough. But what is the political system? What kind of observations are we speaking about? Have we witnessed all possible political events, or is our definition unduly limiting? Is political reality a product of the observer, as our definition suggests, or of the system itself? With a definition such as this, different observers, having had different experiences and perspectives, will arrive not only at different understandings of political reality but at different *ways of understanding* as well. The result might be a highly individualized body of knowledge with no mechanism for sharing it. The problem of deciding how we know, then, is a problem of arriving at a generally accepted way of defining reality, at a common language of inquiry, so that anyone who learns the rules or "speaks the language" can communicate on the basis of shared understanding with all others who have been similarly trained. At least in the abstract, if all of us can agree on *how* we know, then eventually we should agree on the higher-order question of *what* we know.

Deciding how we should *use* what we know is a different process. Here there is no need for orthodoxy or a common preference, though we still need a common language to permit communication and debate. Ultimately, deciding the best or most desirable application of knowledge is a subjective, individual activity. All of us have certain wants or needs that will lead us to value one outcome of applying our knowledge over another, and it is not necessary—though it may be desirable—that we arrive at some common value judgment. If taxes are lowered, middle-income people will live more comfortably but social services targeted primarily at the poor, the aged, and the infirm will be reduced. Should taxes be reduced? The answer, clearly, depends not on what we know but on how that knowledge is related to our own social position and value structure. Ideologies and political systems provide the means for structuring and aggregating the preferences of various individuals, but the decisions themselves are made by individuals one by one without resort to a common perspective.

Political scientists use some fancy words to distinguish between these two types of consideration. The first, that dealing with how (and what) we know, is termed **empirical** analysis. The second, that dealing with how we should use our knowledge, is termed **normative** analysis. Empirical analysis is concerned with developing and using a common, objective language to *describe* and *explain* political reality. It can be **quantitative,** based on statistical comparisons of the characteristics of the various objects or cases that are being studied, or it can be **qualitative,** based on the researcher's informed understanding of those same objects or cases.[1] Normative analysis is concerned with developing and examining subjective goals, values, and moral rules to *guide* us in applying what we have learned of that reality.

Carried to the extreme, normative analysis without empirical foundation can lead to value judgments that are out of touch with reality. Empirical analysis in the absence of a sensitivity to normative concerns, on the other hand, can lead to the creation of a fact structure in a vacuum, a collection of observations whose significance we are not prepared to understand fully. The object, then, in undertaking political inquiry is to draw upon both types of analysis—empirical and normative—so as to maximize not only our knowledge but also our understanding of political reality. Thus, although our emphasis in this book is on empirical political analysis, our goal is to develop, in addition to a facility with various aspects of empirical tech-

---

[1] On the relationship between quantitative and qualitative research, see Alan Byrman, *Quantity and Quality in Social Research* (Winchester, MA: Allen and Unwin, 1988). For an introduction to qualitative research methods, see Anselm Strauss and Juliet Corbin, *Basics of Qualitative Research* (Newbury Park, CA: Sage, 1990).

nique, an appreciation of the larger, normative perspective within which knowledge is interpreted.

In this context, we can see scientific research as a way of knowing and as a common language of inquiry. Scientific research is, to be sure, not the only way of knowing, but it is in many instances and for many purposes the *most effective*. People can know things through experience, but not everyone shares the same experiences. People can know things by keeping their eyes open, but they cannot be sure that through such unstructured observation they will note all or even a representative group of relevant events. Some people can even "know" things by seeing visions or hearing disembodied voices, and others may accept their descriptions and accounts as valid, but not everyone can be trained in visionary methods. Each of these ways of knowing serves a purpose and each has its uses, but none allows for the total sharing both of facts or conclusions and of the knowledge of how those facts or conclusions were obtained. Each allows communication, but none helps us reach a comprehensive, shared understanding.

Scientific research, meaning inquiry guided by the scientific method, does that and more. For not only does scientific research permit us to know reality and to evaluate the ways in which we know, but—because those ways are commonly understood by those trained in the method—it also permits us to improve upon our means of inquiry. Scientific research is a self-correcting, continuously developing way of knowing.

This is true because scientific research is *explicit, systematic,* and *controlled.* It is explicit in that all the rules for defining and examining reality are clearly stated. Nothing is hidden from view, and nothing is taken on faith. It is systematic in that each item of evidence is linked by reason or observation to other items of evidence. No ad hoc explanations are tolerated, and no carelessness of method is permitted. It is controlled in that the phenomena under analysis are, to the extent possible, observed in as rigorous a manner as the state of the art allows. Generalized conclusions are reached only after the most thorough and painstaking assessment, and caution (in the larger sense of exercising great care and attention to detail) is a watchword. Yet for all its constraints, or, indeed, precisely because of them, scientific research opens for those versed in its ways a whole new level of understanding reality. It is for this reason that the scientific method is applied to the study of politics.

As a discipline, political science has not always been "scientific." The earliest political scientists were trained in philosophy rather than in social science (which did not exist). Much of the earliest empirical work was interpretive and relatively unstructured, and even today there exist differences of opinion over what contemporary practitioners can or should accomplish. Beginning in the 1940s, however, and gaining pace from the late 1950s onward, the application of the scientific approach to describing and understanding political phenomena has come to predominate, at least in the United States, as more and more political scientists have become convinced that it yields important insights into the behaviors of individuals, political organizations, and governments.

In the context of our discussion, let us define scientific research as the "systematic, controlled, empirical, and critical investigation of hypothetical propositions about the presumed relations among [various] phenomena."[2] That phrase does not slip easily from the lips, but it is a relatively precise summary of the points at issue here. **Scientific research,** or for our purposes *social* scientific research, is a *method of testing theories and hypotheses by applying certain rules of analysis to the observation and interpretation of reality under strictly delineated circumstances.* It is these rules and constraints that we must learn if we are to gain and communicate knowledge in the science of politics.

Perhaps the best way to begin learning these rules and constraints is to ask ourselves, How does one go about doing political science research? As the question suggests, political science research is best thought of not as a set of observations or theories but as a *process* of gathering and interpreting information. This research process consists of six distinct but highly interrelated stages: (1) the formulation of theory, (2) the operationalization of that theory, (3) the selection of appropriate research techniques, (4) the observation of behavior, (5) the analysis of data, and (6) the interpretation of the results. These six stages provide the organizing rationale for the greater part of this book, and they are worth considering a bit more closely at this point.

The Formulation of Theory

The first step in undertaking political science research is the selection of an appropriate *research question,* and here we can readily see the importance of mixing normative with empirical considerations. What criteria make one research question more appropriate than another? While a number of such criteria come to mind, ranging from the personal interests of the researcher to the collective interests of society, most fall into one of two major categories. A question is worthy of research either because it fulfills a scientific need—that is, because its answer will further our theoretical understanding of some phenomenon—or because it fulfills a societal need—that is, because its answer may help us to deal with one or another of the problems faced by our society.

Although these two types of research questions, frequently termed **basic research** and **applied research,** are not mutually exclusive (asking one does not *necessarily* mean you cannot ask the other), they do frequently compete with one another. For example, should we study the hypothetical determinants of aggression under conditions of stress in order to develop a sophisticated predictive model of human behavior, or should we instead focus on the reasons riots occur and on ways to prevent them? Should we examine at length the decision-making processes of national leaders to help us understand leadership, or should we instead concentrate on identifying and avoiding the types of decisions that lead to war? Because too few scientific resources (money, time, and trained personnel) are available to study all potentially interesting or important research questions, there is often a conflict between the need to perform basic research—whose practical payoffs, however great, are almost always felt only indirectly and far in the future—and the need to

---

[2] Fred N. Kerlinger, *Foundations of Behavioral Research* (New York: Holt, Rinehart and Winston, 1964), p. 13.

use our scientific knowledge in the present for the immediate benefit of humanity, even though we may in the process delay or prevent the further development of our science. The choice must be made by individual researchers in accord with their own values.

Once we have determined the type of problem we wish to tackle and the type of contribution we wish to make, we then have to frame a more specific *research question*. Several considerations contribute to the making of this decision. To begin with, we must identify the aspect of the problem in which we are particularly interested. Once the excitement of starting the hunt has worn off, and until the answers to our questions are in sight, the day-to-day research can easily become tedious. At such times, the inherent interest of the problem becomes an important motivating factor, an intellectual snack that keeps us going until the main course is on the table. Since no research question can be answered adequately without hard work, one of the biggest mistakes we can make is to take on a task in which we have little interest.

Once we have selected a research topic, we must sift through the various elements or components of that topic to identify those that may be important to our research. We must draw on our powers of observation and reason and, especially, on past research—our own and others'—on related topics to identify the major factors that bear on the behavior we are seeking to understand. Perhaps an example will make this clear.

Let us imagine in the middle of the desert a town called Little America that consists of several miles of service stations and restaurants stretching from the exit ramp of an interstate highway to the edge of the horizon. One can do nothing in Little America except eat and buy gas.

Now, suppose we have decided to study the voting behavior of Little Americans in presidential elections so that we may explain why one person votes Democratic while another votes Republican. In this simplified example, the subjects of our analysis (Little Americans) differ from one another in only two ways besides their voting preferences: each is either an owner or a worker, and each is associated with either a service station or a restaurant. Each of these factors, which political scientists term *variables,* represents a characteristic of a particular individual. One citizen of Little America might be (1) an employee of (2) a restaurant who (3) votes Democratic, while another is (1) an owner of (2) a service station who (3) votes Republican. Since we wish to explain differences in voting behavior in terms of other kinds of differences among the voters, we must focus on all factors that might bear on a person's electoral preference. In this instance, we have only two to choose from: employee or owner status and service station or restaurant affiliation. Let us refer to these respectively as *socioeconomic status (SES)*—with ownership representing higher status than employment—and business affiliation. Is there any reason to expect that knowing either characteristic of a particular person will help us to predict his or her voting preference?

To answer that question, we must do two things. First, we must *think*. We must ask ourselves: Is there any *logical reason* to expect either of these factors to influence voting behavior? Second, we must consult the political science literature: Is there, in previous studies of this or related topics, any *empirical evidence* that one or the other of these factors influences voting behavior? In reality, there is little reason to expect the business-affiliation variable to make much difference in voting behavior in this instance. Differences may well exist between those associated with service stations and those with restaurants, but these differences are not likely to have much impact on presidential voting preferences. Few presidential candidates run on a pro-service station, anti-restaurant platform (or vice versa), and, other things being equal, this variable is not likely to help us explain voting behavior. The second variable, SES, however, is a different story. Since the Democratic party is popularly identified as the party of labor and the Republican party as the party of business, and since persons of higher SES are more likely than those of lower SES to vote Republican, we might well expect that employees will be more likely to vote for the Democratic candidate and owners for the Republican. Indeed, the research literature is replete with examples of precisely this kind of relationship. Thus logical reasoning and empirical evidence both point in the same direction. Our research question might then become, Does the SES of a voter in Little America influence voting preference in a presidential election?

In the real world, of course, people differ from one another on many more than two or three characteristics, but the problem we face in framing a research question is essentially the same. Because we have not the resources to measure every possible variable, we must choose, in a reasoned and informed manner, from the thousands of human (or institutional) characteristics, those few we expect will help us to explain whatever pattern of behavior interests us. We must try with the aid of both logic and literature to anticipate and identify the factors that might be related to this behavior. In so doing, we are not prejudging our results, as a first glance might indicate, but rather refining our thinking about the research problem to identify those avenues of inquiry most likely to lead to successful explanation. This process of refining our research question through informed selection is what we mean by the term *formulation of theory*.

The Operationalization of Theory

Once we have arrived at one or more research questions and the theory needed to direct our search for answers, we must progress to the next step, that of **operationalization**—the conversion or redefinition of our relatively abstract theoretical notions into concrete terms that will allow us actually to measure whatever it is we are after. It involves moving from the conceptual level (thinking about a problem) to the operational level (deciding how to solve it). It involves learning to think in *practical* terms.

Suppose, to continue our example, that we have a hypothesis—a statement of the answer we expect to find for our research question—that Little Americans of higher SES (owners) are more likely than those of lower SES (employees) to vote Republican in the next presidential election. This is in line with the findings of countless other voting studies and is a reasonable expectation in the present instance as well. But how do we find out for sure? We cannot simply walk up to a Little American and say, "Good evening. Are you of higher or lower socioeconomic status?" To begin with, the person we are interviewing probably will not understand what we are talking about, since *socioeconomic status* is a technical term with many variations of meaning. And second, even if we get an answer, we will probably not be able to interpret it. Suppose the respondent replied, "Yes, I am of higher socio-economic status." Higher than whom? How high? How does that person define socioeconomic status? Does it mean the same thing to the respondent as it does to the researcher? Once we have an abstract concept in mind, we must find a way to define more explicitly what we mean by that concept; then we must form our definition into as unambiguous a question or measure as possible.

The problem here is to make intelligent yet arbitrary choices among numerous shades of meaning. When we use the variable SES, are we thinking about respondents' level of income, occupation, or perhaps even subjective notions of which social class they belong to? Each might be a component of SES, but each has a somewhat different meaning, and each must be measured differently: What was the total income of your family last year? What is your occupation? Would you say that you consider yourself to be a member of the working class, the middle class, or the upper class?

In other words, once we arrive at some hypothesis or research question, we have to examine very closely just what it is that we mean by each phrase we use, and we have to translate that more precise definition into measurable indicators. We seek, in effect, the lowest common denominator of meaning. (Although not everyone would, for example, assign the same meaning to the term *socioeconomic status,* almost everyone would mean the same thing by *total annual income in dollars.*) In the process our concepts are narrowed and shades of meaning are lost, but because of this our thinking becomes much more precise, and our ability to communicate in clear, unambiguous terms what we have done is greatly enhanced. This process of translation and simplification, which we term *operationalization,* is *the single most important key to conducting meaningful research.*

The Selection of Appropriate Research Techniques

Once we have decided what we want to measure, we must decide how we will measure it. We must devise a research strategy, a plan of attack. Two considerations are of primary importance here. First, we must select a technique or a combination of techniques that will enable us to ask the particular questions—to measure the particular variables—that interest us, and we must do so in ways that are consistent with our operationalizations. We cannot, for example, measure the attitudes of individual voters by analyzing the content of newspaper coverage of a given election, because newspaper content may reflect the views of an editor or of those few people whose letters to that editor are published without necessarily reflecting the views of most voters. Moreover, analyzing news or editorial content does not permit us to differentiate among different types of voters, such as those of higher or lower SES. Thus content analysis would not allow us to answer our research question—that is, to test our hypothesis; survey research would be more useful. On the other hand, suppose that we wish to assess the coverage given by a newspaper to a political campaign. We might simply analyze the content of the newspaper itself, counting references to the candidates and so forth, or we might survey readers of the newspaper to measure what information they remember reading about the campaign. In the first instance we would have a direct measure of content from which we are forced to infer impact; in the second instance we would have a direct measure of impact from which we are forced to infer content. Depending on the precise formulation of our research question, one or the other or the combination of both strategies might be useful. The point is that the *appropriateness* of a given research technique is in large part determined by the particular problem we have selected for study.

But there is a second consideration as well, one that we might term *feasibility*. This is the stage of the research process at which we prepare to leave our ivory tower and actually go out into the real world. For that reason, we must assure ourselves that whatever method or technique we select can properly be employed under the particular set of conditions we are likely to face. For example, since there is no newspaper in our Little America (only service stations and restaurants), we cannot use content analysis even if we want to. Similarly, the most direct way to measure the level of tension between the leaders of Iraq and those of Turkey might be through a series of personal interviews with those leaders themselves, but such interviews are, to say the least, difficult to arrange. In each instance, we have to find less than ideal ways of measuring the key variables. A feasible technique, then, is one that will be maximally effective given the constraints of the research situation.

To summarize, we must find a way to measure those variables we wish to measure that will be (1) consistent with our working definitions of the variables and (2) practicable. We must be as scientific as possible, but we can be only as scientific as the circumstances allow.

The Observation of Behavior

The fourth stage of the research process involves actually carrying out the research strategy developed in stage 3. Many factors must be taken into account here, but two in particular are worthy of note. The first is the notion of generalizability, the second that of reactivity.

Generalizability refers to the ability to generalize or extend our conclusions with some confidence from the observed behavior of a few cases to the presumed behavior of an entire population. It is a concern we must take into account in selecting the particular cases (people, decisions, organizations, or nations) that we wish to study. The problem here is basically one of scale. If there are only, say, four or five occurrences of an event or subjects in a group we wish to study, we can examine each of those occurrences or subjects individually and make various general statements about them with reasonable confidence that our conclusions apply to all the cases. But if, as is much more frequently the situation, we have so many hundreds or thousands or millions of cases that it is impossible to examine each firsthand, we will have much less confidence that a study of a relative few of these cases, perhaps less than 1 in 1,000, will allow us to make accurate statements about the entire group. In such circumstances we must develop a strategy, often termed a *sampling procedure,* by which we can decide which few of those many, many cases we can study to come to conclusions that might apply to the entire population of cases.

In doing so, we must decide how many cases to study and how these cases should be selected, and we must try to estimate the representativeness of these few cases. The key to generalizability lies in selecting for observation those cases best likely to represent (be most typical of) the larger population.

Once we have selected our cases for analysis, we must exercise great care in observing them. We must avoid measuring political phenomena or behavior in ways that display **reactivity**—a situation in which either the person who is doing a study or the actual methods of the study somehow interfere with and alter the way those under observation would behave or think in the absence of the researcher. In other words, a danger exists that the act of observation may itself cause those being observed to change their behavior so that the results of the observation are misleading.

Probably the classic case of reactive observation was a 1939 study of the effects that changes in working conditions at a particular factory had on worker productivity. Over a period of more than a year, such factors as hours of work, rest periods, lighting, and methods of pay were varied for a small group of workers. But regardless of what conditions they worked under, whether long or short hours, few or frequent rest periods, or some other variant, this group of workers continually out-produced all other workers in the same factory. The most influential factor in their productivity, it turned out, was an unusually high level of morale associated with the fact that members of this group knew they were being observed and experimented upon.[3] This so-called Hawthorne effect, named for the factory where it was first observed, meant that no conclusion could be drawn regarding the relationship between working conditions and productivity, because the act of observation created a false reality, a work environment unlike the normal one.

Sometimes in undertaking political science research, we encounter similar, obvious examples of reactivity. An overbearing or unfriendly interviewer, a leading question, or a meddlesome observer can so damage the research situation that no confidence can be vested in its outcomes. As often as not, however, the process is more subtle. We might, for example, train the perfect interviewer properly to ask a perfectly good question yet still incur reactivity: *Q:* "Do you favor or oppose the president's economic policy?" *A:* "I'm in favor of it. I think it is a good idea." But how do we know for sure that our respondent has really given any thought to the president's economic policy before being interviewed? Is it not possible that the interview itself acted as a catalyst, in effect crystallizing the respondent's thoughts and creating an opinion where none had previously existed? This, too, is reactivity, but of a type that is much more difficult to detect and to avoid.

It is not enough simply to march into the field armed with a few questions and start looking around for answers. We must exercise great care in deciding how and where we shall enter the field and how and whom we shall observe. The best theory and the best plan of attack can be squandered if we are careless in our observation.

---

[3] F. J. Roethlisberger and W. J. Dickson, *Management and the Worker* (Cambridge, MA: Harvard University Press, 1939).

The Analysis of Data

The bits of information about each case that we gather during our observations are called **data,** and once we have them in hand, the end is in sight. The object at this point is to ascertain what answers we have found to our research question. This may be done in many instances by answering three questions. First, is there some association between, on the one hand, the behavior we are hoping to explain or to understand better and, on the other hand, the factors we think will help us to do so?

Suppose, for example, that we expect to find that people who differ in their level of formal education will differ systematically in the likelihood that they will vote. Our first question must be, Does this happen? Do people who differ from one another on one of these variables tend to differ consistently on the other as well? Are the more educated people consistently either more or less likely to vote than the less educated people? We might find in examining our data, for instance, that less educated people tend to vote about as often as more educated people and that knowing a person's level of education does not help us to predict or explain the difference between that person's likelihood of voting and someone else's. If this is the case, we say that one's level of education does not influence the likelihood of voting or, alternatively, that there is no association between the two variables. Our expectation is not supported by our analysis. If, on the other hand, we discover that six or seven times out of ten, knowing the level of education does allow us to predict accurately the likelihood of a person's voting, this constitutes evidence supporting our expectation that the two variables are related. It tells us that more educated people are *systematically different* from less educated people when it comes to voting and helps us understand our subjects' voting behavior. The first thing to look for in assessing a hypothesis, then, is whether the two variables are *statistically related.*

Once such a relationship has been established, we must ask an equally important second question: *How* are the two variables related? Are better educated people more likely than less educated people to vote? Alternatively, are they less likely to vote? Or is the relationship between the variables more complex still? If we have thought through our hypothesis so that we have some reasons to expect the level of education to be related to voting, we probably have one or another of these possibilities in mind.

We might argue, for example, that having more formal education increases the likelihood of one's having the skills and information needed to support an interest in politics. Accordingly, a more educated person is more likely to vote than is a less skilled or less informed person. Thus we might expect voting to be more frequent or more common among the more educated of the people we study. This type of relationship is illustrated in Figure 1.1(a), where points on the line represent corresponding values on the two variables.

We might also argue, however, that the more educated one becomes, the more one comes to believe that political activity is futile. Education, in this view, gives rise to disillusionment, which in turn reduces the inclination to vote. Here we expect voting to be more frequent among the less educated of our subjects. This type of relationship is illustrated in Figure 1.1(b).

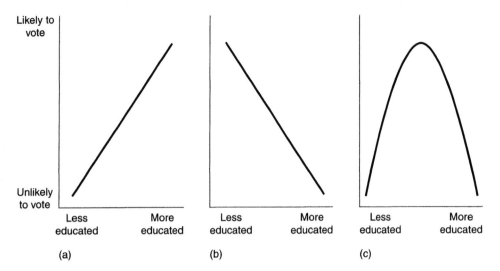

Figure 1.1
The relationship between level of education and likelihood of voting

Or we might even argue that education contributes to skills and interests to a point, but that those who are educated beyond that point (for example, those who attend college) become increasingly disillusioned and less interested in politics. Here we expect voting to be most frequent among those of moderate educational attainment, with lower levels of voting at either extreme. This more complex relationship is illustrated in Figure 1.1(c).

In each instance a relationship exists between a person's level of education and likelihood of voting, but clearly the implications of these varying relationships are vastly different. It is possible, then, to find a strong relationship between the two variables and yet fail to substantiate our hypothesis.

Finally, we must ask ourselves a third, perhaps less obvious, question. How likely is it that any relationship we have found among variables in our study of a small number of cases will also be found if we study the entire population from which those cases have been chosen? This is simply a statistical way of asking how good a job we have done in ensuring that our small sample is representative, or typical, of the larger population. If we have made the proper decisions in selecting the particular cases to be studied, then we can say with confidence that our conclusions, though based on but a few cases, may be applied to all. If we have made errors, we may be less confident. Unfortunately, as will be made clearer in subsequent chapters, when conclusions are based on a sample of the population, we can never be *totally* certain of them.

Interpretation of the Results

Finally, we reach a point where we must put all the pieces together. Have we succeeded in actually asking the research question that we set out to ask? What have we discovered? What is the substantive importance of our findings? How do these results square with our expectations? In essence, we have by this time reduced some aspect of political behavior to a set of numbers, which may or may not reveal statistical relationships. We must decide what any such relationships, as well as other things we have learned along the way, tell us about the answer to our research question. But there is more, for we must also look back with a critical eye on our research itself. Have we made some fundamental error along the way that may invalidate our findings? Have we managed to keep a close relationship between our theory and our research on the one hand and the reality of political activity on the other? Can we credit any of our apparent findings about the real world to the things we have done (or have failed to do) in our research, rather than to actual events? These are difficult questions to answer, but good researchers will always try to do so, because only when they are answered can researchers know how much confidence to place in the product of the research.

This brief overview of the six stages of the research process will give you a good idea of what scientific research into politics is like, and of what this book is about. We shall devote a good many of our pages to learning to perform and to evaluate each of these tasks. We realize, of course, that most who read those pages will never become political science researchers. But we know, too, that the same skills that go into creating good quality research for oneself may also be applied to developing more thorough and more critical skills in reading and evaluating the research done by others, and that is an ability that anyone with an interest in the study of politics will do well to possess. Social scientific research is increasingly used as a basis for both public policy and legal decisions. It is therefore increasingly important that citizens be able to judge the merits of research in order to discharge their responsibilities in a democratic society.

The body of knowledge that we call political science was not handed down on stone tablets in antiquity. It is constantly growing, changing, and being refined. Every piece of research is a potential extension of our knowledge and understanding. But that potential can be met only if the research itself can withstand critical scrutiny, only if it comes up to accepted standards. Those standards are what this book is about, and learning them, whether for research of your own or for critical reading, will provide you with a basis both for understanding the literature of political science and for making a contribution to it.

Research Exercises

1. Write a paragraph describing why you think the authors of this book have characterized operationalization as "the single most important key to conducting meaningful research."

2. Use the library to find one example each of basic research and applied research reported in a newspaper or magazine published within the past month. Write a brief summary of each.

Terms Introduced in This Chapter

empirical
normative
quantitative
qualitative
scientific research
basic research

applied research
operationalization
generalizability
reactivity
data

CHAPTER 2

THEORY BUILDING: CONCEPTS AND HYPOTHESES IN POLITICAL RESEARCH

We undertake social science research because we want to understand the complex world around us, either for the satisfaction of knowing or because we want to be able to anticipate or even control events. Scientific research, then, begins with something we want to know. This is our **research question.** It is usually very general. We might want to know, for example, why some people actively support environmental protection while others are opposed or indifferent to it. The most effective way to find an accurate (and therefore useful) answer to this question is to employ established methods of empirical research to investigate the relationships we see in the world. Before we can employ scientific procedures in an attempt to find a generally agreed-upon answer to our question, we have to reduce this highly general question to one or more highly specific ones. Unless we do this, we will not know what to observe in order to seek an answer to the question, and we cannot understand how what we observe is related to our research question.

Transforming our general research question into one or several specific ones requires developing some plausible explanations for what we observe. We might, for instance, reason that people's position on environmental protection is influenced by the nature of their job. Some occupations, for example, benefit from environmental protection measures whereas others are hurt by them (at least in the short run). We might also think that age influences people's attitude toward environmental issues, because younger people have grown up with an awareness of the problems of pollution while older people grew up before these problems were understood.

This reasoning helps us to reduce the complexity of social life and puts us in a position to begin scientific inquiry. We can apply logic and information that we already have about empirical relationships to reason out a set of things we expect to be true if our tentative explanation is valid. Now we can ask questions like these: Do younger people support environmental legislation more often than older people do? Do white-collar and professional people support environmental measures more often than blue-collar people do? We can devise ways to make observations that will allow us to answer these questions and, when we have explored enough small questions, eventually to answer our initial research question.

When we attempt to create possible explanations for events, we are **theorizing** or developing a theory. Theories are created in our effort to gain understanding. They help to direct the research we do to determine if our understanding of events is correct. This is why theory building is the first stage in the research process and why it is essential that we understand the relationship between theory and research.

An improperly developed theory can lead us to do research that is useless in answering the question that has initially sparked our interest. Without a sound theory we will not be able to tell why our research "findings" provide an answer to the research question. Suppose we begin research with only the general question posed earlier. If we ask a properly selected sample of 2,000 Americans about their position on environmental protection and a series of questions about their personal characteristics, we can use our results to *describe* the kinds of people who support and oppose environmental legislation, but we cannot tell *why* they support or oppose it.

If, on the other hand, we start with a theory that offers an explanation of why people support or oppose environmental protection policies and ask questions to check on the accuracy of the expectations that logically follow from this theory, our results will contribute to our understanding of why people take the positions they do.

To illustrate, say that we theorize that people's first concern is their economic well-being and that their position on environmental protection is determined totally by their perception of how proposed legislation will affect their income. One expectation or prediction that logically follows from this line of reasoning is that people who expect to be financially hurt by environmental protection laws will oppose them while those who expect to be helped by these laws will support them. If our theory is an adequate explanation of how people develop attitudes about environmental protection, then this prediction should be an accurate statement about real-world relationships. We can then get some idea of the usefulness of our theory by checking on the empirical accuracy of the prediction that logically follows from it. For example, we might ask people about their position on environmental protection and their perception of its effect on their income to find out whether the prediction is borne out by what we learn about actual relationships.

Regardless of the outcome, our research can then tell us something about why people feel as they do about this issue. If the research is correctly done and the prediction turns out to be supported, we are encouraged both to believe that we have developed a sound explanation for the behavior in question and to search for further evidence of its utility. If the prediction is shown to be wrong, we at least have reason to believe that this is not likely to be a useful theory for understanding people's position on this matter, and we can begin to explore other possible explanations.

Whether we start our research with a theory or without a theory, it may produce the same facts. But the facts will contribute to our understanding *only* if we can tie them together through a theory. For example, knowing that white-collar people tend to support environmental protection more often than blue-collar people do will provide an explanation of why people take the positions they do only if we can give some reason why occupation and position on ecology should be related. Otherwise, the fact could be a coincidence, and knowing it will add nothing to our ability to explain people's attitudes. Theories provide sets of reasons why facts should be connected in given ways. Therefore, *theories make facts useful by providing us with a framework for interpreting them and seeing their relationships to one another.*

This chapter is designed to help you understand how theories are developed and how they are used to guide research. In it we discuss the nature of social science theorizing, the elements of theories, and the relationship of theory to the rest of the research process. When you have finished the chapter, you should be able to begin thinking about political questions that interest you in ways that will prepare you to undertake systematic empirical research in order to find valid answers to those questions.

The Nature of Social Science Theory

We construct theories for two reasons. First, we hope they will help simplify reality so that we might understand it, in order better to control it or adapt to it. Second, once we have developed such an understanding, theories can guide us in testing its accuracy. Theories do this by providing a logical basis for expectations or predictions about the world that can be compared with reality through research. When our predictions are supported by evidence, the understanding that provides a basis for those predictions is also supported, and our confidence that we have a grasp of the way things work is increased. When our predictions are shown to be inaccurate, we begin to question our understanding of events and to look for ways to improve it.

Theories are *sets of logically related symbols that represent what we think happens in the world.* They are simply intellectual tools. Understanding this is important, because it helps us realize that theories are neither true nor false in any absolute sense, but only more or less *useful.* You cannot expect to discover a theory the way an explorer discovers a new island. Why? Because theories do not exist "out there" to be discovered. They are the products of human imagination, hard work, and sometimes good fortune.

If theories are essential to sound research but cannot be discovered by simply looking at accumulated data, how can we go about building a theory to guide our quest for an understanding of those aspects of political life that interest us? What processes are involved? The answer is not neat or simple, because theories are developed in a variety of ways. We cannot outline a set of procedures to produce a useful theory in the same way as we might describe how to build a table. We can, however, provide an explanation of the major ideas and stages commonly involved in theory construction. The first of these is the *conceptualization of the problem.*

The Logic of Theory Building

Beginning with the event or behavior we want to understand, we must first ask ourselves what we know about the phenomenon that might help us explain it. Insights might be gained from personal experience, casual observation, or creative thinking. More often we will find it useful to investigate systematically what others have found about the subject. Useful theories begin from a thorough knowledge of the events we want to explain. Without such knowledge, we might fail to understand what is to be explained or might have no clue where to begin looking for relationships that can be used to explain the events.

The massive riots that took place in many U.S. cities in the late 1960s provide an example of the importance of a knowledge of the facts in helping us to conceptualize research problems properly. When the riots first occurred, many public officials said they were the acts of a group of poor citizens without stable ties to society. If we had accepted this interpretation and sought to understand the riots, we would have defined our task as one of explaining why so many of these "riffraff" were concentrated in our cities at that time and how they were moved to riot. Many public officials turned to the alleged presence of "outside agitators" as an explanation. As social scientists conducted interviews in the riot-torn cities, however, we learned that rioting was not restricted to riffraff. In fact, as a group, rioters differed very little from the general black population of those cities.[1] This fact presents us with a very different research task from that suggested by the riffraff interpretation. We must now seek to understand how average citizens with jobs, families, and other ties to society were motivated to riot. Subsequent explanations have focused on variables such as African-Americans' reaction to white racism rather than "outside agitators."

In this case, an inadequate knowledge of the facts could have fundamentally misdirected our theory-building efforts. This is why **exploratory research,** which is designed to establish the facts in a given case, is important. It is also the reason why we must search the literature for information on the phenomena we seek to explain if we hope to develop sound theories.

But once we have as many facts we can find, how do we construct a theory to explain these observations? We generally begin by searching the facts for patterns that can account for the observed events.

For example, we might want to know what causes political protests on college campuses. Answering this question involves explaining what leads students to take part in protests. Having been or having known protesters might provide us with some insights into their motivation, but to develop an explanation of why large numbers of students participate would require information on a much larger number of people. We would be wise to seek data on the characteristics and motives of student protesters *in general* in order to frame our explanation. If we found among protesters commonalties that set them apart from nonprotesters, we might reason that these characteristics led to their participation in demonstrations. The prominence of these characteristics among college students then becomes part of our explanation of why protests occur.

The process of generalizing from what we have observed to what we have not or cannot observe is called **induction.** It forms the basis of scientific theory. Theories built through inductions from observations are said to be *empirically grounded.*

---

[1] R. M. Fogelson and R. B. Hill, "Who Riots? A Study of Participation in the 1967 Riots," in *Supplemental Studies for the National Advisory Commission on Civil Disorders* (Washington, DC: U.S. Government Printing Office, 1986).

In the process of induction, we reason from what we know to be the case in some situations to what might be the case in other, similar situations; we make a logical leap from what we have seen to a prediction about what we have not seen based on the assumption that there is some constant underlying pattern to events in the world. We all use induction in our daily life. If we observe five consecutive times that the elevator door opens after our pushing a button on the wall, we will quickly draw the conclusion that pushing the button causes the door to open. This is an inductive generalization from the few cases we have observed (pushing the button five times) to cases we have not (pushing the button more times or pushing elevator buttons in other buildings). The process of induction is diagramed in Figure 2.l(a). That diagram suggests how inductively constructed theories are grounded in facts.

There is more to theory building than induction, however, because pointing out facts does not provide an explanation unless we can show *why* those facts have led to the observed results. Let us return to the example of student protest. Suppose we find that protesters tend to be more dissatisfied with public policies than nonprotesters and that protesters also tend to have far less faith in the effectiveness of conventional politics in getting policies changed. Stating this fact constitutes an explanation of protest only if we are able to show why such attitudes should lead to protest behavior. Showing this might involve making some *assumptions* about political behavior. Specifically, it might involve assuming that people will act to change policies they strongly oppose and that they will turn to protest behavior if they feel that conventional political participation (voting, letter writing, etc.) will not alter the policies.

These **assumptions** (sometimes called *axioms* or *postulates*) then become part of our theory. They describe the conditions under which we expect the tentative explanation we have reached to be supported by evidence. They tell why we expect student protest from what we know about students on college campuses by making general statements about political behavior under certain conditions. We can now explain specific behavior (protest) by showing that it follows logically from a set of theoretical assumptions.

When we do this we are doing the reverse of what we did when we engaged in inductive reasoning. Here we are moving from abstract statements about general relationships to concrete statements about specific behaviors. This process of reasoning *from the abstract and general to the concrete and specific* is known as **deduction.** We all use deductive logic in everyday life. If we assume that elevators work on a system of wall-mounted buttons and find ourselves confronted with an elevator, we will generally deduce that the way to enter the elevator is to push the appropriate button. We have moved from a generalization to the prediction of a specific event by deduction. This process is diagramed in Figure 2.l(b).

Deduction is the process that enables us to use theories to explain real-world events. If we can show by a process of deduction that some observed event can be logically predicted from the set of assumptions that constitute our theory, then the theory provides an explanation for the observed event. The theory helps us to understand the event by giving a reason why it is as it is. The role of deduction is to provide this link between the theory and our observations.

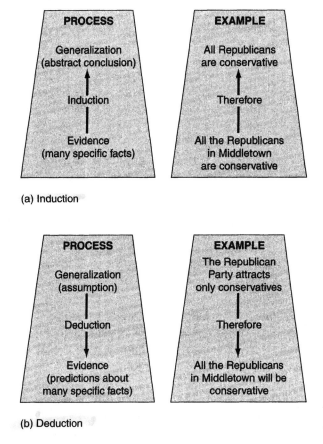

Figure 2.1
Diagrammatic representation of inductive and deductive reasoning

The process of theory construction generally involves the interaction of both inductive and deductive logic in the following stages: (1) we use induction to translate what we have observed into assumptions; (2) we employ deduction to derive predictions; (3) we test these predictions against new observations; and (4) we revise our assumptions to make them consistent with the results of our observations. Then we repeat the process in an effort to make the theory increasingly useful as a tool for understanding events.

Merely devising a theory, however, does not make it valid. We can generally come up with many theories to explain a given event. The question we must ask is, Which of these theories are most useful in helping us understand the world? Answering this question will require that we test alternative theories against reality.

Before we can discuss theory testing, however, it is important to understand two things. First, we have to know what features make a theory useful so that we can know how to go about building theories. Second, we must know how the components of a theory are related to each other and to empirical research.

For a theory to be useful in explaining observations, it must meet several standards.

1. It must be *testable*. Can we reason from the theory to expectations about reality that are concrete and specific enough for us to make observations that either support the expectations or fail to support them? Can the theory be related to the world in systematic ways, or is it only a set of abstractions?

2. It must be *logically sound*. Is the theory internally consistent? Are its assumptions compatible, and the terms it contains unambiguous?

3. It must be *communicable*. Can other, properly trained people understand the theory in ways that allow them to use it to explain events and to test hypotheses derived from it?

4. It must be *general*. Is it possible to use it to explain a variety of events in different times and places? Can we deduce predictions from it that can be tested in different circumstances, or is it tied too closely to one set of observations?

5. It must be *parsimonious*. Is it simple enough to be readily applied and understood, or is it so complex, so filled with conditions and exceptions, that it is difficult to derive explicit expectations about real-world events from it?

Theories can have each of these desirable characteristics in different degrees, and sometimes we have to choose among them in developing a particular theory. We may have to sacrifice some parsimony in order to obtain more generality or testability, for instance. We have to keep all these desirable features in mind when formulating theories if the products of our labors are to be truly useful.

Components of Social Science Theory

Theories are composed of sets of *concepts* that are related by propositions logically derived from a set of *assumptions*. This is the *logical structure* of a theory. It is this structure that allows us to use the theory to explain events, because it allows us to give reasons why we can logically expect things to be as they are.

The quest for useful theory begins with the decisions we make about the building blocks of theories: concepts. A **concept** is merely a *word or symbol that represents some idea.* There is nothing mystical about concepts. We use them every day to help us cope with the complexity of reality by categorizing the things we encounter according to some of their properties that are relevant to us. We classify the four-legged creatures we see into cows, cats, dogs, and other species, and that classification alone provides a basis for some important expectations (for example, dogs are not a good source of milk). Assigning a name to something allows us to predict certain things about it, because the name is a symbol for particular combinations of properties.

Social science concepts serve the same purpose. They point to the properties of objects (people, political systems, elections) that are relevant to a particular inquiry. One observer might be interested in a person's personality structure, another is interested in partisan identification, and a third focuses on the person's level of political alienation. The person has all of these properties (a personality, a party identification, and a degree of alienation) and many more, but only certain of the properties are relevant to any given piece of research. All three observers are dealing with the same reality; they simply choose to organize their perceptions of it differently. Concepts help us to decide which of many traits or attributes are important to our research.

The point is that concepts, like theories, do not have a life of their own. They are tools we create for specific purposes and cannot be labeled true or false, but only more or less useful. What makes a concept useful? There are three major considerations.

First, since we are involved in *empirical* inquiry the concept must refer to phenomena that are at least potentially *observable*. In medieval times, the concept of divine will played an important role in explanations of events. We cannot verify such explanations, however, because we cannot observe divine will to tell whether it is present or absent in any given case. If it is to have any scientific value, a concept must refer to something that can be measured with our ordinary senses.

This does not mean that all concepts must refer to *directly* observable things. Some of the most useful concepts in the social sciences refer to properties we cannot observe directly. For example, people simply do not have a class status in the way that they have red hair, but if we know certain things about them (their income or their occupation, for example), we can infer what their class status is. Similarly, nations do not have authoritarian or democratic political systems in the way that they have mountains or deserts, but we can *infer* the degree of democracy that exists in a nation by observing certain things about its political life (the nature of elections and provisions for civil liberties, for instance).

The question is: Can we devise a set of procedures for using our senses to gather information that will allow us to judge the presence or absence or magnitude in the real world of the thing to which the concept refers? If we can do this for a concept, it is said to have **empirical referents;** it refers to something that is directly or indirectly observable.

Second, in addition to having empirical referents, concepts must be *precise*. They must refer to one and only one set of properties of some phenomenon. We must be able to know exactly what we are talking about when we use a concept to describe an object. For instance, is the degree of inequality of distribution of wealth part of what we are referring to when we describe a nation's political system as democratic or authoritarian, or is the nature of the political system determined exclusively by other factors? Precision is important because it tells us what to observe in order to see how a concept is manifested in any given case. Only if we can determine this can we use the concept in empirically grounded explanations.

Precision also helps us identify our empirical referents and make distinctions among observed phenomena. If democracy means *only* the presence or absence of popular elections for public officials, then the former Soviet Union and the United States both were democracies. Do we want to treat these two nations as examples of the same kind of political system for purposes of our research? If not, then we need to refine the concept, to make it more precise, so that we can draw a distinction in our study between the two nations.

Finally, useful concepts have **theoretical import.** A concept has *theoretical import* when it is related to enough other concepts in the theory that it plays an essential role in the explanation of observed events.

In our hypothetical explanation of student protest, we employed two concepts. One was *intensity of policy preferences,* and the other was *perception of the effectiveness of conventional political action in changing policies.* These two concepts were tied together by the assumptions that people will act to change policies with which they strongly disagree and that they will turn to protest when they feel that other means of influence will not bring results. Given these assumptions, finding the particular combination of attitudes we have referred to will lead us to expect protest behavior. Each concept is essential to the explanation and is linked both to the theoretical assumptions and to the other concept. Each concept has theoretical import because it plays a necessary role in our explanation.

Relationships in Social Science Theory

Now we can begin to see that theory makes concepts useful by tying them together so that they can be used in formulating explanations. Theory ties concepts to one another by stating relationships between them. These statements take the form of **propositions** derived from our assumptions.

Propositions generally posit one of two major types of relationship among concepts. These are *covariation* and *causation.* **Covariational relationships** indicate that two or more concepts tend to change together: As one increases (or decreases) the other increases (or decreases). Covariational relationships tell us nothing about what causes the two concepts to change together. For instance, we might predict that level of political information and likelihood of voting covary, so that as one increases so does the other. But are people more likely to vote because they have more information, or do they gain information because they intend to vote and want to make a sound decision, or are both information level and likelihood of voting the products of some third factor, such as interest in politics or perceived civic duty? The covariational proposition does not tell us.

Causal relationships exist when changes in one or more concepts lead to or cause changes in one or more other concepts. For example, the stronger one's party identification, we might argue, the more likely one is to vote. Feeling oneself to be a member of a party can lead one to vote, but the likelihood of voting does not create one's party identification.

We are all accustomed to thinking in terms of cause and effect in our everyday life, but we generally use these concepts loosely. It is often very difficult to identify the causes or consequences of human behavior; the more important the event, the more difficult isolation of its causes can be. What brings on a war, a social movement, or the creation of a new political party?

Because of such complexities, we must be careful to postulate causal relationships only when four conditions are simultaneously met. First, the postulated cause and effect must change together, or covary. Second, the cause must precede the effect. Third, we must be able to identify a *causal linkage* between the supposed cause and effect (meaning, we must be able to identify the *process* by which changes in one factor cause changes in another). Fourth, the covariance of the cause-and-effect phenomena must not be due to their simultaneous relationship to some third factor.

This last condition cautions us about the problem of **spurious relationships.** When A and B vary together because they are both caused by C and they would not covary in the absence of C, the apparent relationship between A and B is termed *spurious.* It is essential that we carefully examine the assumptions we are making in an effort to uncover possible spuriousness in relationships before we build them into our theories as though they were the product of causal interaction. A classic instance of spuriousness is the case in which an investigator first finds that the price of imported rum and the salaries of ministers fluctuate together and then reasons that changes in the price of rum cause changes in ministers' salaries. It is more likely that both rum prices and ministers' salaries change in response to changes in general economic conditions and overall price level. The relationship between the first two variables is covariational, but it is not causal.

It is important to recognize two other features of social causation. First, one phenomenon may cause another either directly or indirectly. For example, A may cause B only in that it is the cause of C, which directly causes B. We must be alert to the role of **indirect causation** in attempting to make our theories as complete as possible. Second, we must be sensitive to the fact that human behavior generally has more than one cause. In theorizing, we should avoid oversimplifying and thus recognize the role of **multiple causation** in social life. This simply means that any one event may have several different causes, and that many events sometimes must come together to cause a given occurrence.

To cope with all of these complexities, it is generally a good idea to draw a **causal model** of the theory. This is simply a diagram that clearly specifies all the relationships posited in the theory so that it is easier to see the implications of our arguments. Figure 2.2 presents an example of such a model. Each arrow in the model represents a causal influence, and the direction in which it is pointing indicates which variable is theorized to be dependent and which independent. The theory diagrammed in Figure 2.2 asserts that a variety of factors influence a representative's decision to vote for or against welfare legislation in both direct and indirect ways. For instance, the size of the poor population in the representative's congressional district is depicted as influencing welfare voting both directly (independently) and indirectly through the electoral competitiveness of the district and the representative's seniority level.

Both covariational and causal relationships can be either *positive* or *negative.* This means that the two concepts can change either in the same direction or in

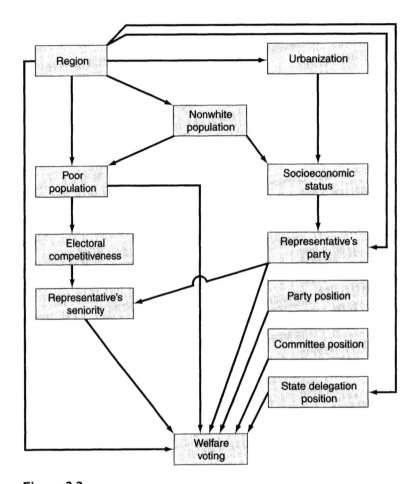

Figure 2.2
Causal model of the determinants of representatives' support for welfare legislation in the U.S. Congress
SOURCE: From Richard C. Rich, "The Representation of the Poor in the Policy Process: Changes in Congressional Support for Welfare," in Robert Eyestone, ed., *Public Policy Formation* (Greenwich. CT: JAI Press, 1984), p. 135. Reprinted with permission.

opposite directions. If they change in the same direction, the relationship is positive. A **positive relationship** is represented by the following statement: The *higher* the relative deprivation of minority groups within a society, the higher the likelihood of political violence. A **negative relationship** is posited as follows: The *higher* the degree of political alienation one feels, the *lower* the likelihood that one will take part in conventional political activities. Our theories must specify whether we expect positive or negative relationships among concepts. This information can be added to causal diagrams by placing a plus (+) or minus (−) sign on each path in order to indicate whether the relationship is thought to be positive or negative.

Theory Testing and Elaboration

Theories must never be regarded as finished products, but always as tools that occasionally need to be inspected and can often be improved. We start with a research question that asks for an explanation of observed events, we select concepts that promise to be useful in explaining those events, and we relate the concepts through propositions logically derived from a set of assumptions we choose to make in order to secure an explanation. Now our backs are against the wall. Is this lovely structure any good? It seems to explain what we want to understand, but can we check it in some way? Can we test its utility so that we can know how much confidence to place in it and persuade others of its value?

Theory testing is at the center of the research process. Because our theories are generally developed from bits of knowledge about actual relationships, the tasks of theory testing are essentially those of using the theory to formulate some expectations about other relationships we have not observed and then checking to see whether actual observations are consistent with what we expect to find. We cannot rely on relationships we have already observed, because showing that the theory leads us to expect the very relationships the theory was built to explain would be no test at all.

In our example of the elevator, after observing the elevators in one building, we will be quite confident that the elevators in that building operate in response to a system of wall-mounted buttons. We might even be willing to generalize from our observations to reach the conclusion that all elevators work this way. We can check the validity of that conclusion only by actually trying it out in other buildings. It does not help to double-check the elevators in the building we started in, because we already know that they respond to the buttons and showing that they do does not make us feel any more secure that other elevators do as well. We have to go to other buildings to see how their elevators operate.

We can never finally prove that our theory of elevator operation is correct because we can never observe all the elevators in the world. As we see more and more elevators that do work this way and we never encounter any that do not, our confidence in the validity of our generalization will increase. If we cannot find any other elevators that work by buttons, however, we will quickly conclude that we have been mistaken in generalizing from the initial observations to all other elevators.

Theory testing in the social sciences works by the same principle. We must move from what we have observed in devising the theory to what we have not observed, in order to discover whether or not the theory provides us with an accurate set of expectations about the world.

Suppose, for example, that we want to construct a theory to explain voting behavior. We review previous research on the subject and discover that, for citizens of the United States, higher education is positively related to the propensity to vote. The more years of schooling people have, the more likely they are to vote. On the basis of that observation, we include in our theory an assumption that higher educational levels lead to a greater likelihood of voting. We know that these factors are related in the United States, but what about in other nations? Could there be something unique to the educational system in the United States that creates this relationship? The only way we can find out is to observe people in other nations.

From the assumption that education increases the likelihood of voting, we might deduce the prediction that people with some college education will be more likely to vote than people with no more than a high school diploma. We can test this prediction by seeing whether it accurately reflects relationships found in data from a variety of countries. The more often we find evidence consistent with the prediction, the more confident we will feel that our theory is useful in predicting human behavior. We can never be absolutely certain that the theory is "true," because we can neither observe all cases nor be sure how the empirical relationships might change with time. But we can acquire more or less confidence in the utility of the theory by comparing the predictions derived from it with observations. If it allows us to accurately predict things we have not previously observed, then it is useful.

Theories, as sets of concepts, assumptions, and propositions, are never finally proved or disproved. Rather, our confidence in the usefulness of a theory builds as we accumulate observations that are consistent with the expectations or hypotheses derived from it. Alternatively, our confidence diminishes as we accumulate observations that are inconsistent with theoretically derived hypotheses. Therefore what we refer to as theory testing actually reduces to hypothesis testing.

Theory elaboration is based largely on a process of comparing hypothesized conditions with reality and, once we have the results, modifying our theory so that the hypotheses that can be derived from it are more and more consistent with what we observe. For this reason, it is very important that we consider how our research questions are translated into hypotheses that can guide empirical investigations and provide us with clues to the adequacy of our theoretical explanations.

The Role of Hypotheses

A **hypothesis** is essentially a statement of what we believe to be factual. It tells what we expect to find when we make properly organized observations of reality. Hypotheses are declarative sentences stating expected relationships between the phenomena to which our concepts refer. They are usually stated in the following general form:

> *The higher (lower, greater, larger, slower, etc.) the ____, the higher (lower, greater, larger, slower, etc.) the ____.*

The blanks are filled in with the names of the phenomena we expect to change together. For example, working from the theory modeled in Figure 2.2, we might hypothesize the following:

> *The larger the proportion of a district's population that is poor, the more likely that district's representative is to vote in favor of welfare legislation.*

This is a covariational hypothesis. It does not tell us how roll call voting is determined, but it does point us to something that we can observe in an effort to acquire some evidence on the fit between our theory and reality.

Acquiring that evidence through empirical observation requires that we move from the very general level of theory to a more specific level from which to organize observations. In doing this, we have to begin to think in terms of **variables.** A variable may be defined as an empirically observable characteristic of some phenomenon that can take on more than one value. Sex and nationality are two variables that can take on only a limited number of values and can be "measured" only qualitatively by designations such as "male" or "British." Age and gross national product are two variables that can take on a much wider range of values; they can be measured quantitatively by counting.

Variables allow us to translate statements containing only abstract concepts into statements with more precise empirical referents so that the empirical accuracy of the statements can be evaluated. We do not need to use different terms for concepts with clear empirical referents, such as age or sex. But more abstract concepts may require translation into variables before they can be used to guide research.

For instance, the concept of *pluralism* is important in political science, but its empirical referents are not at all clear. In order to test the empirical accuracy of any statement relating pluralism to anything else, we have to translate the concept into some variable or set of variables with clear empirical referents. We might want to use the number of organized interest groups in a nation as a variable to represent the concept of pluralism in our research. We can then reason backward from our observation of relationships among variables to evaluate the empirical validity of statements about relationships between concepts. If we are willing to assume that the variable *number of organized groups* captures the essential meaning of the concept *pluralism,* we will be willing to take evidence that this variable is related to some other variable (such as the level of government expenditures) as evidence that pluralism is also related to that other variable or the concept it represents.

Variables have a central place in the research process for two reasons. First, they help us identify what we will have to observe to test our theory by providing more precise empirical referents. Second, we can organize our observations by knowing the role variables play in hypotheses. Variables that are thought to change value in response to changes in the value of other variables are referred to as **dependent variables.** Their value depends on the value of other variables. Variables that influence the value of other variables through changes in their own values are referred to as **independent variables.**

Whether a variable is dependent or independent is determined by the relationship asserted by the hypotheses containing it. The same variable might be dependent in one study and independent in another. For example, one theorist, observing the lobbying efforts of interest groups, might reason that the larger the number of organized interest groups in a nation is, the higher the level of government expenditures will be. In this case, the number of groups is the independent variable and the level of expenditure is the dependent variable. A second theorist might reason that organized interest groups form in response to perceived opportunities for receiving benefits from government and might argue that the more the government spends, the larger the number of organized interest groups will be. Here government expenditures represent the independent variable, and the number of groups is the dependent variable. The difference between these two views of the relationships involved is diagrammed in Figure 2.3.

The differences are important because the type of research design called for is determined in part by the role assigned to different variables. If we are asserting that increases in the number of interest groups lead to increases in government expenditures, we do not observe the increase in government spending between 1980 and 1990 and then note the change in the number of organized groups between 1990 and 2000. This increase cannot logically have been responsible for a level of expenditure that has preceded it. If we are hypothesizing that increases in expenditure lead to increases in the number of groups, however, the strategy of observation just described is appropriate. Because knowledge of the dependent or independent status of our variables helps us organize our research efforts, our hypotheses must be very clear about what that status is.

A close look at Figure 2.3 alerts us to another type of variable important in social analysis. In the theory summarized by the diagram in Figure 2.3(a), lobbying activity is an intervening variable; it comes into play *between* the number of organized interest groups and the level of government spending. **Intervening variables** provide the link between independent and dependent variables. In this case, interest groups would not affect the level of government spending if they did not engage in lobbying to get funds appropriated to their cause.

In Figure 2.3(b), *perceptions of potential benefits* serve as an intervening variable. Interest group organization would not be related to the level of public spending if group members did not perceive that there was some advantage to be gained from organizing. If, for instance, almost all government spending went to defense projects and very little went to domestic programs, many citizens might not see any personal benefit to be gained from increasing government spending and might not organize even when public spending was increasing rapidly.

Intervening variables *condition* the relationships between other variables. This means that the value attained by intervening variables can affect the strength and direction of relationships between other variables. If lobbying activity is slight in Figure 2.3(a), then the relationship of interest group organization to public spend-

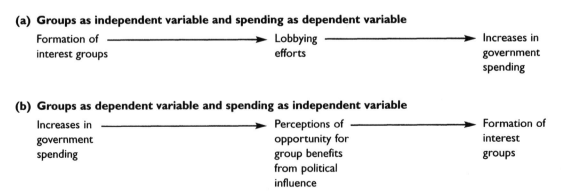

(a) Groups as independent variable and spending as dependent variable

Formation of ⟶ Lobbying ⟶ Increases in
interest groups   efforts   government
                                       spending

(b) Groups as dependent variable and spending as independent variable

Increases in ⟶ Perceptions of ⟶ Formation of
government   opportunity for   interest
spending   group benefits   groups
                 from political
                 influence

Figure 2.3
Alternative theories explaining the relationship between interest group activity and government spending levels

ing will be weak. If lobbying is extensive, the relationship between the other variables will be strong.

Because intervening variables condition relationships between other variables, our knowledge of the role they play will affect our expectations about relationships between variables. If we are theorizing that lobbying intervenes between group organization and increases in spending, then we can make the following predictions:

> *Interest group organization will be positively related to increases in government spending when lobbying activity is vigorous.*

> *Interest group organization will be related only weakly to increases in government spending when lobbying activity is highly limited.*

We will not be satisfied to predict simply that interest group organization will be related to increases in government spending, because we believe that whether the two variables are related depends on the value of the intervening variable—lobbying. For this reason, we must specify the order of relationships and the role played by each variable in our theories.

Antecedent variables constitute the final type of variable that is important in this regard. Whereas intervening variables come between independent and dependent variables, antecedent variables come into play before the independent variable does. Studies of voting behavior in the United States have shown that people who identify strongly with a political party are more likely to vote than those who do not. We might then want to theorize that party identification leads to or causes voting frequency. But what causes some people to identify strongly with a party while others do not? We might reason that the strength of their parents' party identification plays an important role in people's development of such party identification. Parents' party identification then is an *antecedent variable* in the causal chain that produces voting frequency.

Using both intervening and antecedent variables in our theories helps to clarify the *causal chains* at work in creating the phenomena we want to explain. It gives us more of a basis for deriving hypotheses through which we can test the utility of our theories, because hypotheses are essentially *statements of relationships between variables.* Hypotheses provide a basis for collecting evidence about the empirical utility of our theoretical structure. The more numerous and the more detailed the relationships we postulate, the more predictions we can make about the world and therefore the more potential tests we have of our theory.

This leads to the question of how we decide what relationships to assert in the form of hypotheses around which to build research projects.

Formulating Hypotheses

We arrive at hypotheses by either inductive or deductive reasoning. Which one we use depends on the stage we have reached in the research process. If we are still using trial and error to construct a theory, we might develop hypotheses by a process of *inductive generalization.* For example, we might observe that among the states in the United States the level of popular political participation varies directly with the extent of industrialization and might generalize that this relationship between variables is also found when we compare nations. If we find evidence to support the hypothesis, we will be more confident in including industrialization as a variable in a theory designed to explain political participation. Until we have a theory that shows *why* industrialization and participation are related, however, we cannot use the fact of their relationship as an explanation of political participation.

Hypotheses arrived at inductively can be important in *exploratory research,* which helps us construct theories, but they do not help us explain phenomena. Once we have stated a theory relating our variables in a logically coherent system, we can derive hypotheses from that theory by *deductive reasoning.* Because these hypotheses are predictions about the world that are logically implied by the theory with which we are working, finding support for them does help us explain events, because such findings reflect the validity of the theoretical system from which the hypotheses have been derived.

Deductive reasoning is a highly developed discipline, and we will not attempt to explain its rules.[2] It is important to note, however, that deductive logic is a process by which the information contained in a set of statements can be made explicit. We cannot learn anything new about relationships from deduction alone. We use it only to tease all the information we can out of what we already assume about relationships. We use deduction to *clarify the implications of our assumptions,* and it is that clarification that produces hypotheses.

The deduction contained in Figure 2.1(b) shows this. If the assumption stated there is correct, that is, if the Republican Party attracts *only* conservatives, then any subset of the members of that party will be conservative also, and since the Republicans in Middletown are members of that party, they too will be conservative. This is the kind of reasoning we refer to when we say that one conclusion "logically follows" from another. The conclusion that all Republicans in Middletown will be conservative is logically implied in the assumption that the Republican Party attracts only conservatives.

The task of hypothesis generation is logically to pull this type of conclusion from the assumptions that form our theories. It is because hypotheses are derived from theories in this way that testing hypotheses provides an indirect test of our theories. If we interview a properly drawn sample of Middletown Republicans and find that not all are conservative, we will have good reason to question the validity of our assumption. Finding liberals among Middletown Republicans shows that the party does not attract *only* conservatives. We will then want to modify our assumption so that the theory can more closely reflect reality. We may want to change it to read, "The Republican Party tends to attract more conservatives than liberals." From this assumption we can derive the hypothesis "There will be more conservatives than liberals among the members of the Middletown Republican Party."

If we find a few liberals and many conservatives among Middletown Republicans, we can say that the evidence is consistent with the hypothesis and the

[2] Wesley C. Salmon provides a highly readable introduction to this field in *Logic,* 2d ed. (Englewood Cliffs, NJ: Prentice Hall, 1963).

modified assumption from which it has been drawn. We still cannot put much faith in the validity of the assumption until we have seen it supported by evidence about the conservative or liberal character of a larger sample of the national Republican Party. After all, Middletown may be unique in some way. Perhaps, for example, there are only 10 liberals in the entire city, and the fact that only a few of the Republican Party's members are liberal is a result of this more than of the relative attractiveness of the party to liberals, and conservatives.

The important point here is that evidence about the accuracy of hypotheses represents evidence about the accuracy of a theory *only when the hypotheses are linked to the theory by deductive logic.* Only when this is the case can we safely reason backward from evidence of the validity of a hypothesis to any judgment about the parent theory. Theories are developed, expanded, and improved by this process of logically deriving hypotheses, checking them against reality, and evaluating the theory in light of the results.

One type of hypothesis that plays an especially crucial role in this process is the **alternative rival hypothesis.** There are many possible explanations for any event. Some of these explanations are fully consistent with one another; more than one may be correct. In some cases, however, the explanations are opposed to one another: if one is correct, the other cannot be. If we state our explanations as hypotheses, then those which are inconsistent with one another are termed *alternative rival hypotheses.* They are alternatives because they provide different ways of looking at or understanding the event to be explained. They are rivals because they cannot both be valid. If one is accurate, the other has to be inaccurate. We cannot test and compare all possible alternative hypotheses relating to any event, but if we are to have faith in the accuracy of any one hypothesis, we must attempt to test the major rival hypotheses to be sure that we are not being misled by our observations.

One common form of alternative rival hypothesis is that which states that the relationship between any two variables is spurious and that changes in both are in fact due to some third factor. This type of alternative rival hypothesis is especially useful in theory testing because it suggests a research finding that gives us a solid basis for judging which of the two hypotheses in question is more accurate.

Recall, for example, our illustration of inferring a causal relationship between rum prices and ministers' salaries from the finding that the two variables are in fact statistically related. One major alternative rival hypothesis is that fluctuations in both are caused by changes in general economic conditions as represented by the price level. If this hypothesis is correct, then the relationship between rum prices and ministers' salaries will disappear when we "control for" (that is, hold constant) the effect of the price level on each of these variables. Statistical procedures and research designs are available to allow us to determine whether this is the case. If we discover that the statistical relationship between rum prices and ministers' salaries vanishes when we control for general price level, we will have a basis for rejecting the original hypothesis in favor of its rival. If the relationship between rum prices and salaries remains even after our imposition of controls for general price level, we will have more confidence in the hypothesis that they are genuinely related.

Conclusion

Theories gain acceptance as useful intellectual tools as we both find evidence consistent with predictions derived from them and eliminate alternative rival hypotheses. We must keep in mind, however, that no single piece of research provides sufficient evidence for accepting or rejecting any theory or part of a theory that pertains to phenomena beyond those included in the study. There is always the possibility that some future research will produce evidence against the theory's validity. We must always be open to contrary findings and willing to return to induction to build new evidence into more useful theories.

Theory building is a process of constant interaction between conjecture and evidence and between reasoning and research. It calls for both creative ingenuity and hardheaded empiricism. We hope to provide a good dose of the latter in the chapters that follow.

Suggestions for Further Reading

The literature of social science theory is often comprehensible only to those with training in the specialized use of terms encountered in the academic discipline known as the philosophy of science. That complexity, however, should not hide the fact that some easily communicated principles underlie the process of theory building. For valuable insights we suggest the following books as readable treatments of the subject.

A broad-ranging examination of both the process of theory construction and the relationship of theory to other aspects of the research process is found in Arthur L. Stinchcombe, *Constructing Social Theories* (Chicago: University of Chicago Press, 1987). Another highly readable treatment of the role of theory in the research process is *The Elements of Social Scientific Thinking*, 6th ed., by Kenneth Hoover and Todd Donovan (New York: St. Martin's Press, 1995).

A book that moves thoughtfully and clearly through the stages of conceptualization, theory building, hypothesis generation, and hypothesis testing is *The Rebirth of Urban Democracy*, by Jeffrey M. Berry, Kent E. Portney, and Ken Thompson (Washington, DC: The Brookings Institution, 1993). Reading it gives a good picture of the links between theory and research.

Research Exercises

1. Several concepts that might be used in political research are given in the following list. List one or more variables that might be used to represent each of them. Indicate how confident you are that the variables you select to represent each concept adequately capture all that you mean when you use the concept. Do you need several variables to capture the meaning of some of the concepts?

economic development	political representation
party competition	racial discrimination
international tensions	liberalism
political equality	terrorism

2. Select any four of the concepts listed in Exercise 1 and state a hypothesis that predicts a relationship between each of those concepts and some concept *not* on the list. Formulate two of the hypotheses so that they state positive relationships and two so that they state negative relationships.

3. Select a news article about some political trend or event in which you are interested. Devise at least two explanations for the trend or event, and state them as clearly as possible. List the concepts employed in each explanation. Pair each concept with a variable counterpart for it that you could use in a research project, and indicate the status (independent, dependent, intervening, antecedent) of each variable. Diagram the causal chain implied in each of your explanations.

4. Examine the explanations you devised in Exercise 3 to determine what assumptions you are making about relationships in the world. State these assumptions as clearly as possible. Reason from the assumptions to some conclusion about events that should be valid if the assumptions are valid. State this conclusion as a hypothesis.

Terms Introduced in This Chapter

research question
theorizing
theories
exploratory research
induction
assumptions
deduction
concept
empirical referents
theoretical import
propositions
covariational relationships
causal relationships
spurious relationships

indirect causation
multiple causation
causal model
positive relationship
negative relationship
theory testing
theory elaboration
hypothesis
variables
dependent variables
independent variables
intervening variables
antecedent variables
alternative rival hypothesis

CHAPTER 3

SETTING THE FOUNDATION: TECHNIQUES OF SYSTEMATIC BIBLIOGRAPHIC SEARCH

One of the most important steps in theory building is to familiarize ourselves with the literature of political science and, more particularly, with any and all previous research or writing on our specific topic. This is true for two reasons. First, we may learn a great deal from the successes and failures, and from the ideas, of those who have already tackled similar problems. This may help us to refine our theories, to avoid pitfalls in our research, and to tighten our thinking. Second, we must realize that our own work can contribute, even if only in a small way, to the intellectual development of the discipline. By placing our work in the context of, and building directly upon, the literature, we increase the potential value of our contribution many times over. Our own work becomes, in effect, part of the literature that researchers may draw upon later.

But the literature of political science and its subfields is vast, and even in the best organized and most complete library it is scattered to three of the four winds. It is to be found in hundreds of scholarly journals and thousands of books and monographs. Some of these are available in printed form, some in electronic form, some in microfilm; some are available in virtually all libraries, some in very few. The difficulties can seem insurmountable, but they are not. What we need, quite simply, is a plan, a systematic way to identify, search out, and examine a variety of disparate sources of information related to our inquiry. In this chapter we offer such a plan by considering three questions: (1) How can we use the existing literature to help frame a research question? (2) How might we conduct a systematic search of that literature? and (3) Where should we begin our search?

Using the Existing Literature

Political science, or any academic discipline, contains a body of knowledge that has developed slowly for a long period of time through a series of relatively small intellectual advances. Even major theoretical or methodological innovations can be seen, in the longer view, to have been logical next steps that built upon the state of the art at a given time. New bits of knowledge become known, and these generate new insights. The insights themselves give rise to new research questions, which in turn give rise to still more new bits of knowledge. And so it goes on and on, the insights becoming ever more sophisticated, the bits of knowledge more complete, and the questions more pointed. It is in the context of that incremental process of developing our understanding of political reality that the importance of the careful bibliographic grounding of our research becomes clear.

Let us reduce the problem to its simplest terms to make the point. Political inquiry has been around in one form or another since the days of Socrates, Plato, and Aristotle. Empirical political science, which focuses on the systematic and objective description of political activity, has developed in large part since the 1940s, but its roots may be traced back as far as Machiavelli. Today, in the United States alone, approximately 15,000 people consider themselves political scientists of one type or another; worldwide there are many more. Given these facts, the chances are that any research question we might come up with, any set of issues we might explore, has been asked or explored, at least in part and in some form, by someone before us. That is not to say that our research can make no contribution; rather, it means that our contribution is most likely to represent an addition to an existing body of knowledge instead of the creation of a new one.

That realization can be very discouraging for someone who is just starting out in research, because at first it may seem that all the really interesting work has already been done, that the field is closed to innovation, and that no individual accomplishment can amount to much. Each of those perceptions is incorrect. For if you think about it, you should conclude that viewing the acquisition of knowledge as a cumulative and incremental process does not unduly limit or devalue the research that one might do. Such a view suggests instead that scholarship is a collective enterprise—a community, rather than an individual, activity. A new way of thinking about an issue, a fresh approach to solving a problem, or a new piece of evidence in a chain of research is no less valuable simply because someone has thought about the issue, researched the problem, or gathered other evidence beforehand. To the contrary, each new advance in concept, method, or data not only benefits from but also contributes to the significance of each earlier advance. Thus, rather than erect constraints, the research process offers opportunities. Familiarity with past political science inquiry suggests the direction for future inquiry, and the value of individual effort is enhanced by the collective context. The value of a piece of research increases as that research builds upon the existing body of political science knowledge.

In terms of everyday tasks, this means that when we begin a piece of research we must read widely, and intelligently, the existing literature on topics related to our subject. We must consider (1) what research questions have been asked (what theories have been posed), (2) how researchers have gone about answering those questions, and (3) what researchers have found. We must do so with an eye on two specific questions. First, what ideas or information has been developed in the literature that bears relatively directly on the subject we are interested in? In other words, what substantive information can we glean from the literature? Second, what useful insights have those previous researchers developed, what mistakes have they made, and what might they have overlooked in answering their research questions? Or, to put it another way, what methodological lessons can we learn from the literature?

The task, then, is to read, with a critical eye and from the perspective of our particular research interest, the relevant literature of the discipline. But how do we identify the relevant portion of that literature? How do we sort through to find the particular books and articles of interest? One approach, of course, is to head for the library, locate the political science stacks, and start reading book and article titles until we locate some of interest. The problem with this approach is that it is inefficient in two ways. First, in undertaking a blind search of this type, we waste a great deal of time. In order to find the few that might be of interest, we are forced to sift through hundreds of volumes and thousands of journal articles that have nothing whatsoever to do with the topic we are pursuing. Such a search will probably turn up some literature, but only at a great expense of time and effort. Second, because political science is so diverse a discipline (it is not at all uncommon to find political science research published in journals of sociology, psychology, communication, geography, and economics, to name only a few), because the titles of books or articles do not always offer solid guidance to their content, because library shelving systems are not geared to solving individual research problems, because not all of a library's holdings may be on the shelves at a given time (books are, on occasion, checked out), and because a blind search overlooks some of the aids to bibliographic research that can be of great assistance, a blind search simply will not turn up the greater part of the literature we need. We are likely to overlook far too much. For these reasons, the strategy of the blind search is inadequate for identifying the items we are interested in. Systematic bibliographic search provides a far better alternative.

Developing a System

Systematic bibliographic search is simply a way of preparing for, and getting the most out of, a visit to the library. It involves (1) specifying our needs, (2) planning how we will use our time at the library, (3) maximizing our use of the resources available there, and (4) maintaining a record of what we find. Let us explore each of these in turn.

The first thing we must do at this early stage of the research process is to codify our interests a bit more precisely. Just what is it that we wish to research? Under what subject headings might we locate research or other writings of interest? One very helpful exercise for answering those questions is to develop a list of **key words** or **key phrases**. Suppose, for instance, that we wish to search in the library's catalog or an online database for books dealing with the level of competition between the two major political parties in the United States. Under what words should we look in the subject index to find such references?

We might begin by considering the principal words or phrases we have used to describe our research interest. The first of these is *competition,* but a search of the catalog under that heading is more likely to locate books about athletics than about political parties. Thus, *competition* is too ambiguous or imprecise a term to be of use to us. Similarly, *United States* is too broad to be of much value. Even a more refined category, such as *United States, government and politics of,* is so inclusive that, although we may find some books of interest listed there, searching them out would be a tremendously inefficient process. That leaves only *political parties.* Looking under that heading, or a refinement such as *political parties—United States,* is likely to prove more fruitful. Not only will many of the books we find listed here pertain to our interests, but a good deal of what the library has available on our topic will also quite probably be listed here. *Political parties,* then, is a key phrase, one that is likely to lead us to a substantial part of the literature we are seeking.

Are there other, related words or phrases that, although not derived directly from the phrasing of our research problem, might nevertheless prove valuable? *Elections—United States,* perhaps further divided into local, state, and national levels, is one possibility; *voting behavior* might be another; names of particular political parties, the *two-party system,* and names of particular candidates might be still more. Making a key-word list is simply a process of compiling a list of those words or phrases we feel will be relatively efficient and effective in identifying the literature related to our subject. It is, in effect, an attempt to "outwit" the library by anticipating how the materials found there are organized.

This is not always an easy task, at least if it is to be done properly. One or two obvious choices come to mind instantly, but some hard thinking is usually required before the list can be extended much further. One of the most difficult parts of developing a key-word list is to avoid including words or phrases that, though potentially germane for the topic, are so general and so inclusive that they are likely to create more work than they save. Like so many other aspects of political science research, creating a maximally efficient key-word list is a skill that develops only with much practice.

Another problem associated with the use of key-word lists is that terminology can change over time. Just when we believe we have created the perfect key-word list for a given topic, we discover either that the authors or indexers have chosen to use different words or phrases to describe the same set of ideas, or that at some time in the past different words or phrases were used to describe the ideas. Thus a book about interest groups that was published in 1965 might be listed under *political organizations* and a similar book published in 1995 might be listed under *nongovernmental organizations.* In short, we must be sensitive to the possibility that others may use different words to describe the same concept, and we must be sufficiently flexible to accommodate them. We must not approach our search with the notion that our key-word list is carved in granite; rather, we must be willing to update and revise it as we go along.

Besides brainstorming, another way to identify key words is to consult a subject heading list, or thesaurus. When we want to search for books in the library we start with the subject heading list used in that particular library's catalog. This guarantees that we are speaking the same language as the library. Two prominent subject heading lists are the Sears List of Subject Headings, used with the Dewey Decimal Classification system, and the Library of Congress Subject Headings, used with the Library of Congress Classification system. The example in Figure 3.1 comes from

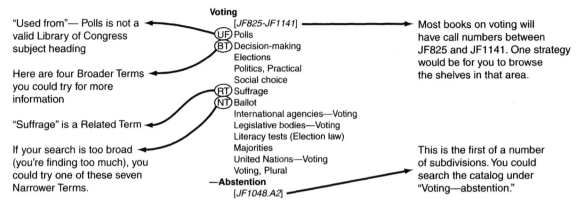

Figure 3.1
Sample listings from the Library of Congress subject headings

the Library of Congress Subject Headings. Note that this listing will not only send you to the "right" term when you have guessed "wrong" but will also suggest broader or narrower terms even when your original term is one that the listing uses.

Once we have prepared our key-word list, or at least the one we will begin from, we must next develop a plan for using our time at the library to the best advantage. This involves knowing something about the way that most libraries are organized, as well as about certain of the resources that they make available. In most libraries, books and bound volumes of journals (usually not including the most recent year) are filed by discipline according to one of two organizing schemes. One is the Dewey Decimal Classification system, used by small college and public libraries; the other is the Library of Congress Classification system, used by university and large research libraries. If the identifying marks on books in your library begin with decimal numbers of the type 327'.01'9-dc20, your library uses the Dewey Decimal system. If the identifying marks begin with a combination of letters and numbers, as, for example, JX1417.M326, your library uses the Library of Congress system. (Both identifiers, incidentally, designate the same book.) The purpose of each system is identical—to organize the library's holdings in a systematic manner according to subject matter.

Most university and research libraries today employ the Library of Congress cataloging scheme. Under that system, each book, upon publication, is assigned a unique identifying number. The numbers are assigned by topic. Each discipline or group of disciplines is assigned a letter of the alphabet. Thus *H* represents social science in general, *J* political science, *K* law, and so forth. A second letter is assigned in order to designate a subfield. Thus the *J* classification for political science is further divided as follows:

J   Official documents
JA   General works
JC   Political theory
JF   Constitutional history and administration

JK   United States
JL   British America, Latin America
JN   Europe
JQ   Asia, Africa, Australia, Pacific Islands
JS   Local government
JV   Colonies and colonization
JX   International law and international relations
JZ   International relations

The remainder of the index or identification number organizes the collection by still more specific subject headings as determined by the Library of Congress and, within each, by author. The net effect is that all books on a given topic and all books by a particular author on that topic are shelved together.

Your library catalog may be in the form of a card catalog, a computer-based catalog, or both. In card catalogs, materials are filed by author, title, and subject. The *author index* lists holdings under the name of each author and is most useful for identifying additional publications by a scholar who we already know has worked in our particular area of interest. Thus, if in our other searches we come across the titles of several works about political parties by William J. Crotty and we want to assure ourselves that we have found all of Crotty's books on the subject, we look under his name in the author index and find there a listing of each of his publications held by the library. The *title index* lists by title all of the books and journals held in the library and is useful only when we are trying to locate a specific book or journal whose title we have already noted. The *subject index* lists the library's holdings by subject heading.

Computer-based catalogs reproduce the same information found on card catalogs and are used in the same basic way the card catalog is used. We can search by author, title, and subject. Searching a computer-based catalog, however, is much faster than searching a card catalog. We can also perform more sophisticated searches. For example, many computer catalogs allow a search of key words or phrases found anywhere in the record. In other words, we can use our original key-word list and can search for books that have our key words or phrases anywhere in the book's record. This lets us be much more flexible with our search strategy. It is still important, though, to use key-word or subject heading lists so as not to miss anything.

Another advantage of computer catalogs is their capability to do what is termed *Boolean searching*. A search that requires more than a single concept or some other combination of key words can be done with **Boolean connectors** such as *and, or,* or *not.* This means we can search "political parties *and* competition," "political organizations *or* political parties" and "competition *not* athletics." The specific commands we use on a computer-based catalog depend on the type of system the library has.

The library catalog is the single best guide to the books held by a particular library, but from the perspective of the researcher it suffers from two fundamental weaknesses. First, the catalog lists mainly books, even though much, if not most, of the important research in political science or any other field is to be found not in books, but in articles in scholarly journals and in doctoral dissertations. And whereas journals themselves are listed in the catalog, their content is not. Second, most library catalogs list only the holdings of the particular library we happen to be using. Many valuable resources not found in our library may exist and can be borrowed for us from another library in a relatively short time. They are usually not listed in the catalog, however, because they are not a part of the library's own collection. Fortunately, neither of these problems is insurmountable.

Scholarly journals are indexed in a number of special publications called **periodical indexes.** Periodical indexes are available in printed or electronic format or both. In those listings, each article appearing in each issue of a great many journals is indexed by subject and by author. The listings are updated regularly.

The example in Figure 3.2 illustrates what we will find in the pages of one such publication, *Social Sciences Index.* Notice that under the subject entry "voting" is a list of suggested alternative subject terms. Then the articles on voting covered by this volume of the Index are listed. We would have to search other volumes of *Social Sciences Index,* one per year, to increase our coverage of the journal literature on voting, or we can inquire at our library about its availability in electronic format.

The first article listed—"Condorcet's Theory of Voting," by H. P. Young— appeared in volume 82 of *American Political Science Review.* We can find it beginning on page 1231 of the December 1988 issue. Of course, we still won't know whether our library subscribes to *American Political Science Review* (though the authors certainly hope so!) or what its call number will be. For that information, we would have to consult the library catalog or serials list.

Social Sciences Index is almost always the best place to start, but we will need to use more than one periodical index to find all relevant articles. A variety of more specialized indexes, described at the end of this chapter, should also be consulted. Many of these are available online as well as in print. The best person for advice on which other indexes to use is the reference librarian. Students often hesitate to ask this helpful individual for assistance, but a reference librarian can save researchers a lot of time and improve their coverage of the literature. One should try to explain one's research question as clearly as possible so that the librarian fully understands the needs.

Most libraries keep back issues of their scholarly journals in the stacks, where they are easily accessed by researchers. The journals may be located by using the Dewey or Library of Congress call number assigned to each journal. Current issue (those for the past year or so) are generally maintained in a separate area. Searching the more recent issues can be relatively tedious, because they have yet to be thoroughly indexed, but one publication, *ABC POL SCI (Advance Bibliographic Contents: Political Science and Government),* can be of assistance here. *ABC POL SCI* is a guide to current periodical literature in political science and related disciplines. Published five times a year with an annual cumulation, it reproduces the tables of contents of some 300 journals soon after they are published.

Doctoral dissertations contain a good deal of interesting information often unavailable elsewhere, but they tend to be of uneven quality and are relatively difficult to obtain. Most are summarized in *Dissertation Abstracts International* and are available either through a library's interlibrary loan service or from Universal Microfilms International (UMI) for a fee, but much lead time is often required to obtain them. Doctoral dissertations are also indexed by author and subject matter

Voting

See also

    Ballot

    Bandwagon effect

    Election law

    Elections

    Independent voting

    Legislative bodies—Voting

    Majorities and minorities

    Referendum

    Stockholders—Voting

    Voter turnout

Condorcet's theory of voting. H. P. Young. bibl
    Am Polit Sci Rev 82:1231–44 D '88

Le pouvoir dans les décisions conjointes. V. Lemieux.
    Can J Polit Sci 21:227–47 Je '88

The role of attitude importance in social evaluation:
    a study of policy preferences. presidential candi-
    date evaluations, and voting behavior. J. A.
    Krosnick. bibl *J Pers Soc Psychol* 55:196–210
    Ag '88

Rousseau's general will: a Condorcetian perspec-
    tive. B. Grofman and S. L Feld. bibl *Am Polit Sci*
    Rev 82:567–76 Je '88

Figure 3.2

Sample listing from *Social Sciences Index*

in *Comprehensive Dissertation Index* (especially useful are the volumes on law and political science and the annual supplements).

Identifying the resources held in other libraries can be a more painstaking task, but with the growth of computerized library catalogs, this process is becoming increasingly easier. The best example of a computerized multilibrary catalog is the *OCLC Online Union Catalog*, commonly referred to as WorldCat. The Online Computer Library Center database contains more than 25 million records describing materials on thousands of subjects owned by libraries around the world. It can be searched by author, title, subject, key word, document, type, year, and language, and provides location information. Not all libraries' holdings are computerized, so one may still need to use a printed catalog for a single library's collection. An example of such a catalog is the *National Union Catalog,* which lists the holdings of the Library of Congress.

There is another information resource that should not be overlooked: the bibliography. A **bibliography** is a listing of books, journal articles, and other useful sources of information on a particular subject. Bibliographies may be published as parts of books and periodicals or as separately published items. Subject-specific bibliographies are usually written by scholars or librarians, who pull together much of the significant available literature on a specific subject. These specialized bibliographies are available in many fields of political science and can be located by using the subject index of the catalog or the reference source *Bibliographic Index,* which is a general listing by subject of bibliographies. In addition, it is wise to pay close attention to the footnotes that appear in any book or article that we read. If we have been diligent in our preparation, we will already have identified most of the works cited, but occasionally we may find a new and important reference. In reading bibliographies and footnotes, we are in effect soliciting the assistance of other researchers in identifying stray sources.

Needless to say, all of this searching can become rather time-consuming, especially if the topic we are researching is a broad one or has been the subject of much attention in the literature. But there is an alternative, timesaving aid that we can use. We can employ a computer search of bibliographic databases through either of two means.

In recent years many libraries have acquired indexes and other databases on compact disc (*CD-ROM* means compact disk read-only memory). CD-ROM databases are set up on desktop computers with a disc player hooked up to a computer. Many printed library reference sources, such as encyclopedias and periodical indexes, are now available in CD-ROM format. These databases can be searched by author, title, and key words. Besides reference sources, many full-text newspapers and periodical articles are also available in CD-ROM format. The main advantages of CD-ROM databases are that libraries make them available for free for users to do their own searching and that there is usually an option to printout or download all relevant citations.

Another means of accessing electronic bibliographic and full-text information is to use online databases. Online databases are distinguished from CD-ROM databases by their being accessed from computers that connect to a larger, main computer via modem and telephone line. Online searching is often done by a librarian who assists the researcher. But unlike other library services, these computer searches can cost money.

We should always check with the library to find out if there is electronic access to any of the bibliographic resources listed in this chapter for locating books, articles, government documents, and even legal, business, and statistical information. But even in relying on a computer search, we must remember two things. First, the search is only as good as the key words we use. Second, the search is only as good as the database it covers. Either or both of these factors can significantly limit the utility of a computer-generated bibliography.

Conducting the Search

Once we have specified our interests as a series of key words or phrases and have identified those sources of bibliography that we expect to find most useful, we are ready to enter the library. The procedure is simply to employ the key-word list to peruse systematically the various sources we have listed. The best places to start this process are the subject index of the catalog (for books) and recent volumes of *Social Sciences Index* (for articles). The experience of the authors has been that in many instances one can identify perhaps 75 percent or more of all available titles on many topics by undertaking a careful search of these two sources. If undertaking a small-scale project with an early deadline, we may very well get no further. A more massive project, however, should include a more thorough search.

We should bring with us to the library a sizable stack of blank file cards (4- by 6-inch for researchers with a small handwriting, 5- by 8-inch for those with large). Each time we find listed a potentially useful source (not every title we locate will seem relevant), we should write at the top of a separate file card a complete bibliographic citation, including, as appropriate, author, title, journal (including volume number, year of publication, and pages), date and place of publication, and publisher, and, for books, the Dewey Decimal or Library of Congress call number.

It is useful to decide in advance the format we will use for reference citations in the research report and to record in that format the appropriate information about each source. Students should check with their instructor in advance to find out the preferred style for references. Generally, the library will have copies of whatever style manual is preferred. Consistency helps to prevent oversights, and including all of the information at the outset saves return trips to the catalog during subsequent visits to the stacks, as well as unnecessary trips back to the library later, when we are writing the research report. Then completed cards should be filed in two separate alphabetical listings by author: one for books, the other for journal articles. Maintaining current alphabetical files helps to avoid duplication.

Once these files have been completed, that is, once we have examined available catalogs and indexes, they should be reorganized as follows. The file of book titles should be placed in alphabetical or numerical order (depending on whether the Library of Congress or Dewey Decimal system is in use) by call number. The file of article titles should be arranged alphabetically according to name of the journal in which each article appears. Articles in the same journal should be arranged chronologically. Each journal should then be checked in the title index of the card catalog and its call number noted. The two files should then be merged into one in order of shelf code. This method facilitates the search in the stacks.

At last we are ready to begin reading the literature. Armed with our file of citations and a map of, or guide to, the library, we enter the stacks in pursuit of the collected wisdom of the ages. Much of what we find, however, will strike us as something else entirely, for many of those sources which seemed promising in the indexes, may prove upon inspection to be disappointing. The file cards for the books or articles that are of no further interest should be marked with a large X, in whatever blank area remains on the front side, as a reminder that these sources have been located but rejected. Because several trips to the library may be required for a thorough search and because the human memory seldom stores effectively information about fifty articles, each with roughly the same title, this simple practice will help us to avoid duplication of effort.

When we find items that are of interest, the file cards serve a more important purpose, though one that also arises from the frailty of memory. We use them to take notes. The notes should include all of the main points of the book or article, any especially useful tips or facts, a summary of the method used and of the findings if research is reported, and any potentially useful quotations. One minor but valuable trick in taking such notes is to make frequent page references to the specific locations of the items we record. Figure 3.3 gives an illustration of a completed bibliography

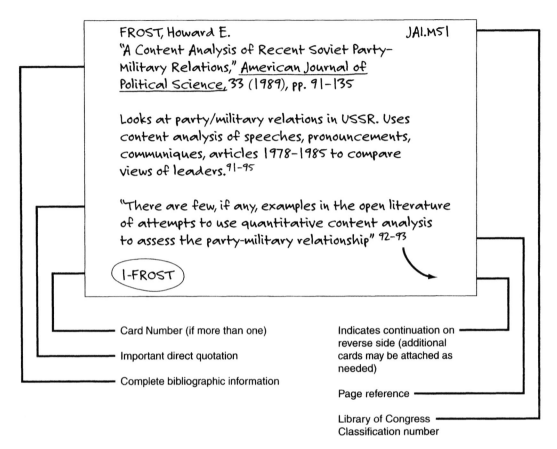

Figure 3.3
Sample bibliography card

card made with this technique. Alternatively, one might use a separate card for each piece of information, being sure to indicate the author, source, and page number on each. Individual cards require more preparation and are rather more cumbersome in a permanent bibliographic file, but they are easier to use when the time comes to actually write the research report, because each substantive point can then be moved around and organized independently of others from the same source.

If it is possible to use a laptop or notebook computer in our library, doing so will make the search much more efficient. Instead of filling out note cards, we would follow the same rules to make entries for each reference in a computer file and take notes on each source right below its bibliographic information. Having the references and notes in electronic form can save time when writing the research design or final report. For example, most word processing software allows a quick search of the entire file for key words using a "Find" function, making it easier to find all references that address a given issue. We can also lift citations and quotes from our bibliographic notes and insert them directly into the text rather than having to retype them.

A thorough job of note taking at this stage saves time in two ways. First, it lets us use, cite, and discuss any of our sources without necessitating a return to the library or a rereading of the source. Second, if for some reason we must reread a source, the page notations help to pinpoint that portion of the material that is of interest. An investment of time and careful effort now often pays great dividends

At the conclusion of this task, we shall have accomplished two major objectives. First, we shall have compiled a relatively complete listing of the literature in our area of interest. Second, we shall have sufficiently familiarized ourselves with that literature so that we may better anticipate problems and thus improve our own work, properly placing that work in the larger context of which it is a part.

Political Science Journals

Before concluding this chapter, we believe it will be helpful to include a partial listing of political science journals and some brief sense of their content. The list is not comprehensive, but it does indicate the types of materials that are available in the literature of our discipline.

Administration and Society—public and human service organizations, especially their administrative processes and their effects on society

American Journal of Political Science—primarily American government and politics, but contains articles in all subfields

American Political Science Review—articles in all areas of political science; generally regarded as the most prestigious journal in the discipline

American Politics Research—articles on American politics

British Journal of Political Science—all areas of political science

Comparative Political Studies—any aspect of comparative politics, comparative political economy

Comparative Politics—comparative analysis of political institutions and behavior

Foreign Affairs—international affairs and foreign policy

Foreign Policy—current issues in United States foreign policy

Harvard International Journal of Press/ Politics—media and politics

International Organization—international relations, international organizations, political economy, comparative foreign policy

International Political Science Review—all areas of political science

International Studies Quarterly—international politics, law and organization; comparative studies; political development; foreign policy; conflict and peace research

Journal of Conflict Resolution—research on war and peace

Journal of Politics—all areas of political science

Legislative Studies Quarterly—all aspects of parliaments and legislatures, including their relations with other political institutions, their functions in the political system, and the activities of their members

Policy Studies Journal/Policy Studies Review—policy-related research and analysis

Political Behavior—political psychology and sociology, political socialization, citizen and elite behavior, behavioral aspects of institutions, decision making symbolic politics

Political Communication—propaganda, public diplomacy, political uses of media, persuasion

Political Research Quarterly—all areas of political science

Political Science Quarterly—all areas of government, politics, and public affairs

Political Studies–all areas of political science

Political Theory—history of political thought, modern theory, American political thought

Polity—all areas of political science

Public Administration Review—management, policy issues, public budgeting and finance, personnel and labor relations

Public Opinion Quarterly—public opinion, polling, political communication, research methods (especially survey research), political attitudes

Publius—federalism, state government, local and urban government, public administration

Social Science Quarterly—articles with an interdisciplinary focus

World Politics—international relations, comparative politics, foreign policy

Nor should we overlook either journals from other disciplines or interdisciplinary journals that often contain articles of interest to political scientists. Here are examples of such journals.

American Behavioral Scientist
American Journal of Sociology
American Sociological Review
Annals of the American Academy of Political and Social Science
Communication Research
Journal of Abnormal and Social Psychology
Journal of Communication
Journal of Experimental Social Psychology
Journal of Marketing Research
Journal of Personality and Social Psychology
Journal of Voluntary Action Research
Journalism and Mass Communication Quarterly
Social Forces
Sociology and Social Research
Urban Affairs Quarterly

Bibliographic Sources

Most journals are indexed in a variety of **bibliographic sources.** Bibliographic sources are publications that list other publications in some systematic way to facilitate their location. One widely used bibliographic source in political science is *Social Sciences Index,* which lists by both author and subject all articles in a great many journals in political science and the other social sciences and which is updated quarterly with an annual cumulation. The index has undergone title changes over the years. From 1907 to March 1965, it was known as the *International Index,* and from April 1965 until March 1974, when was split into two divisions, it was called the *Social Sciences and Humanities Index. Social Sciences Index* is a very useful guide to the periodical literature of the discipline and makes for an excellent starting point for almost any bibliographic search. It is available in print, CD-ROM, and online formats.

Because the *Index* does not cover all relevant literature, another helpful index for broadening a bibliographic search is *PAIS (Public Affairs Information Service International).* Published since 1915 and now available online, *PAIS International* provides bibliographic access to books, articles, pamphlets, and government documents from publications in any of six languages (English, French, German, Italian, Portuguese, and Spanish). *PAIS* covers research in political science, public administration, international relations, law, and public policy.

A thorough search should also include an examination of *International Political Science Abstracts* because political scientists publishing elsewhere often develop ideas or research that we may find of interest even if we are not studying comparative politics or international relations per se. This bimonthly publication of the International Political Science Association abstracts articles drawn from several hundred sources. Abstracts of English-language articles are in English; all others are in French. A cumulative author and subject index is provided at the end of each year.

Another bibliographic source with international scope is *Current Contents: Social and Behavioral Sciences.* This weekly print and online publication reproduces the tables of contents of several hundred journals from all over the world shortly after new issues appear. There is no subject index, but the title word index is an alphabetic listing of the significant key words in every article title. That key-word list can easily be used with our own key-word list both to keep up on what is being written in our area of interest and to see what has been written in recent months. *Current Contents* also list the names and addresses of all first authors whose articles are listed in each week's issue so that you can make personal contact with those who are doing research on questions similar to your own.

In addition, Project Muse and JSTOR, both available online, provide full-text back issues of selected scholarly journals in the humanities, sciences, and social sciences. An extensive and especially valuable guide to other online bibliographic resources useful to political scientists can be found at *www.socsciresearch.com/ r12.html.*

The U.S. Government Printing Office is the world's largest publisher, and it would be a mistake for us to overlook access to the many hearings and special reports available from the federal government. If the library we are using is designated as a depository for federal publications, we will have access to many of these. However, they may very well not be listed in the library catalog. The *Monthly Catalog of U.S. Government Publications* identifies federal publications, covering all of them by author and subject.

Another very useful service is the *CIS (Congressional Information Service) Index,* which provides abstracts and a subject index to all congressional publications, including hearings, committee reports, and special publications. Although one should not be intimidated by government publications, this is one area where one should always enter by querying a reference or government documents librarian first.

Although not considered scholarly material, the popular press disseminates much political information. The popular press, which includes magazines, newspapers, and radio and television broadcasts, should be consulted when it is the only source for current information on political players and events; when it can be helpful in identifying the importance of political issues; and when we want to study how the media, which often shape public opinion, report an event. One standard guide to the popular press is the *Readers' Guide to Periodical Literature.* Published since 1905, it indexes popular magazines such as *Time* and *Newsweek* much as *Social Sciences Index* indexes scholarly journals. Like *Social Sciences Index,* the *Readers' Guide* is also available in electronic format. To supplement the *Readers' Guide,* one should also use *Alternative Press Index,* which indexes by subject and author more than 250 publications that advocate the alternative or radical viewpoint.

Newspapers are an excellent source for current and historical information including the texts of important speeches, commentaries on political issues, and results of public opinion polls. Newspaper indexes, available in both printed and electronic formats, identify by subject the content of individual articles. Printed and CD-ROM indexes are usually issued monthly with an annual cumulation, but like periodical indexes there is usually a four- to six-week time lag between publication date and the issuing of the index.

One of the most exciting developments in research is the advent of full-text computerized databases. These databases exist either online or in CD-ROM format. Either format offers the user full-text retrieval of newspaper or periodical articles through a free-text (key word) search of the entire contents of the file. One of the best-known full-text, online databases is the LEXIS/NEXIS service. LEXIS is the legal database that offers access to federal and state case law and legislation. NEXIS is the news database that offers access to hundreds of full-text newspapers, magazines, radio and television broadcast transcripts, executive and legislative branch documents, and much more. Another advantage of LEXIS/NEXIS is that it provides access to current information that is updated daily for newspapers, weekly for weekly magazines, and so forth. The LEXIS/NEXIS service can be very costly and is thus marketed primarily to the legal and commercial communities; however, many university libraries maintain special educational accounts, which they make available to students for free. Other full- and partial-text databases available through many university libraries include Dow Jones Interactive and Periodical Abstracts.

In identifying journals and bibliographic listings here, we have not attempted to touch all the bases. Rather, we have sought to identify those sources most likely to be of value in the greatest number of research undertakings. A comprehensive listing would be far more extensive. Still, we do believe that the sources listed here, when searched in the systematic manner outlined in this chapter, will help identify a very substantial portion of the literature pertaining to most topics of interest. Thus, even though our listing is not necessarily complete, the coverage of the political science literature in the sources we have included is substantial indeed. By using these techniques and sources, students of political science can take a major step toward developing their work to its fullest potential and placing it in the context of the discipline.

Suggestions for Further Reading

Information Sources of Political Science, 4th ed., by Frederick L. Holler (Santa Barbara, CA: ABC-CLIO, 1986), offers a comprehensive, annotated listing of the principal reference sources for political science and related disciplines. Chapter 1 offers some particularly useful tips on the research process. A similarly comprehensive and annotated listing of the principal journals and other bibliographic resources of political science, its various subfields, and related disciplines may be found in Appendix A of Barbara Leigh Smith et al., *Political Research Methods: Foundations and Techniques* (Boston: Houghton Mifflin, 1976).

For a comprehensive, descriptive listing of journals in political science, see Fenton Martin and Robert Goehlert, *Political Science Journal Information,* 3d ed. (Washington, DC: American Political Science Association, 1990). With greater breadth but less depth, Gregory G. Brunk surveys the journals across the social sciences in "Social Science Journals: A Review of Research Sources and Publishing Opportunities for Political Scientists," *PS,* 22 (1989), pp. 617–27. Michael W. Giles, Francie Mizell, and David Patterson provide a summary ranking of the perceived quality of various political science journals in "Political Scientists' Journal Evaluations Revisited," *PS,* 22 (1989), pp. 613–17.

More general guides to using libraries as a resource in your research include Robert Balay's *Guide to Reference Books* (Chicago: American Library Association, 1996), and *Walford's Guide to Reference Material* (London: Library Association Publishing, 1994).

An excellent guide to literature reviews is Harris M. Cooper's *Integrating Research* (Newbury Park, CA: Sage, 1983).

Research Exercise

1. a. Select a research question.

   b. Develop a key-word list for a search of the literature related to your research question.

   c. Outline a search strategy. What, specifically, will you do when you get to the library?

   d. Using your search strategy and at least three bibliographic sources, develop a bibliography of 10 to 15 items that appear to be of interest. Prepare a file card with all of the necessary information for each item.

   e. Locate at least three items from your bibliography in the stacks of the library. At least one should be a book and one a journal article.

   f. Read each item you have located. Take notes on what you read.

   g. Consider the relationship between what you have read and your research question. How might this item help you to better frame or pursue documents related to your question?

Terms Introduced in This Chapter

key words or key phrases	bibliography
Boolean connectors	bibliographical sources
periodical indexes	

CHAPTER 4

FROM ABSTRACT TO CONCRETE: OPERATIONALIZATION AND MEASUREMENT

Empirical research is a means of obtaining answers to questions about reality. Our questions may be primarily practical, or they may be principally of academic interest. In either case, they will probably be stated in abstract terms. Yet the answers we want are usually concrete and specific. One of the first problems in research is to devise ways of getting from the abstract level of our questions to some concrete observation that will allow us to answer them.

To take a nonpolitical example, suppose we want to resolve a debate about which of two professional quarterbacks is the greater athlete. Obviously we will need to compare the two in some way to settle the argument. But on what grounds shall we compare them? We want to determine which exhibits more of the qualities of a great athlete, but *athletic greatness* is an abstract concept. In order to evaluate each quarterback in terms of this quality, we will have to *quantify* the concept of athletic greatness. We might agree to count the passes they complete in televised games, divide that number by the number of passes they attempted, and to let the resulting quantity stand for athletic greatness. Or, more likely, we might perform several such operations on different aspects of the players' performance so that we can get a more complete picture of how well they play the quarterback position, and then combine them in some way. Once we have these numbers, we will be ready to make concrete comparisons and resolve the dispute.

What we have just described is essentially the process by which we proceed ·from abstract concept to concrete observation in social science research. It is a crucial phase in the research process, for only if it is done correctly will the information we gather represent evidence about the utility of our theories or provide answers to our questions. The process of selecting observable phenomena to represent abstract concepts is known as **operationalization,** and the specification of steps to take in making observations is called **instrumentation.** The application of an instrument to assign numerical values to cases results in a **measurement,** and it is this measurement that we finally use as evidence in making decisions and answering questions.

In this chapter we describe these processes in detail and discuss the problems that can be encountered in attempting to operationalize and measure concepts. When you complete the chapter, you should be ready to state the explanations you have devised from your search of the literature in a form that will allow you to test them through actual observations.

Operationalization: The Link between Theory and Observation

In Chapter 2 we stressed the importance of having a theory to guide observation. We described the research process principally as a matter of comparing actual observations with the expectations about reality that we derive from our theories in order to judge how much we can rely on the theories as explanations of political phenomena. These expectations are stated in the form of hypotheses, which predict relationships between variables that represent the concepts in the theory. The object of this chapter is to describe how we can devise observations that will make these comparisons possible. The question is how we can quantify our concepts in order to make precise statements about whether or not our theoretically derived expectations are supported by what we observe.

The problems encountered in doing this in the social sciences are basically the same as those encountered in the physical sciences. A simple example will help make some of the issues clear. Let us say that we want to test the hypothesis that a chemical fertilizer spread in one cornfield will stimulate more growth than the natural nutrients found in another field. Growth is an abstract concept. We cannot see it directly. We need to translate *growth* into an empirically observable variable so that we can determine when one plant has shown more of it than another.

We can let the variable *height attained* represent the concept *growth* because relative heights are empirically observable. But corn plants don't wear signs telling their height; we have to ascertain it for ourselves. But how? We can use human judgment and have observers rate plants in the two fields as tall or short. Such a procedure allows only crude comparisons between plants and is subject to all kinds of errors, because people differ in their perceptions. We need a more precise and dependable means of determining heights if we are to make meaningful comparisons.

We must translate the variable height into terms of some *measuring instrument* that can be used to yield precise, standardized indications of the extent to which the characteristic is embodied in individual corn plants. We can let height be represented by an **indicator,** such as *length in inches,* and measure the plants with a tape measure. The readings from the tape measure then become the **values** we assign to plants on the variable *height,* and these values are what we actually compare in attempting to assess the accuracy of our prediction of greater growth one field than in another.

We have moved, then, from the abstract concept *growth* to the variable *height*, and then to the indicator *length in inches*. This transformation is known as *operationalization,* because we have reduced an abstract concept to a set of values that can be obtained through specifiable operations.

We finally make the comparisons on which we will judge the accuracy of our hypothesis about relative growth by comparing the values that result from the measurement process (in this example, the readings from the tape measure). When we speak of **observation** in research, we are referring to *the process of applying a measuring instrument in order to assign values for some characteristic or property of the phenomenon in question to the cases being studied.* In other words, observation means using an instrument to measure a trait or behavior.

This is an important point to understand. It makes clear the significance of opertionalization and measurement in the research process. We can never actually compare concepts, even though our theories and our research questions will be stated in concepts. What we compare are *indicators of concepts.* We cannot compare the growth of plants in the two cornfields in our example. We can compare only the readings we get from the tape measures—the measures produced by the indicator that we have decided to let represent the concept.

This means that our *comparisons can be accurate only to the extent that the indicators selected mirror the concept we intend them to measure.* If we have improperly operationalized our concepts, the relationship between our indicators may not be an accurate reflection of the relationship between the concepts they are supposed to represent. As a result, any conclusions we draw from our observations about the concepts or the theory of which they are a part will be faulty.

Figure 4.1 illustrates this situation. Our theory posits a relationship between two abstract concepts. Our hypothesis predicts a relationship between two empirically observable variables, which we reduce to measurable indicators, and our observations reveal a relationship (or lack of relationship) between two sets of values on these indicators. Obviously we can infer something about the reality of the theoretical relationship only if the variables accurately represent the concepts *and* the indicators accurately represent the variables.

Operationalization almost inevitably involves some simplification or loss of meaning, since indicators seldom reflect all that we mean by a concept. Though we almost always have to accept some loss of meaning, we need to operationalize so as

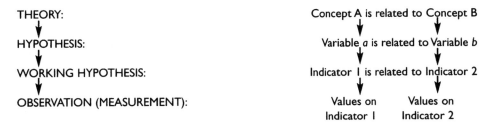

Figure 4.1
Operationalization: The relationships of concept, variable, and measure

to minimize that loss. We have to seek indicators that capture as much of the meaning of the concept as possible and that represent at least some aspects of our concepts as accurately as possible.

We can see the implications of this in our agricultural example. Once we have begun the research, we may realize that there is more to the concept *growth* than height and that the indicator *length in inches* does not fully capture what we want to measure. For instance, it may be that the amount of growth in the two fields is substantially different but all the difference is in stalk diameter, width of leaves, and weight of corn ears; the height of the plants in the two fields may not be noticeably different. In that case, if we look only at height in evaluating the effects of the fertilizer, we will be seriously misled, because the link between the concept (growth) and the variable that represents it (height) is imperfect. The variable used here does not *fully operationalize* the concept it represents. It does not capture all the meaning in the concept, and using it misleads us about the relationship that exists in the real world.

This is an especially common situation in the social sciences since most important social science concepts are **multidimensional** in that they have more than one aspect or component. Our measures of these concepts must reflect their diversity if they are to be useful indicators of the concepts. For example, if we operationalized the concept democracy only in terms of the holding of regular elections, we might classify dictatorial regimes that hold elections with only one candidate per office and do not allow freedom of expression as being just as democratic as the nations of Western Europe. To obtain an accurate measure of the degree to which nations are democratic, we obviously need indicators that reflect the various dimensions of the concept.

This example should clarify why operationalization is crucial to theory testing and the research process in general. It is not as easy to explain how to ensure proper operationalization. This is because selecting variables to represent concepts and devising indicators for the variables both involve a good deal of creativity and cannot be reduced to a set of standardized steps that will unerringly produce good measures. What we can do is to point out some of the pitfalls to be avoided in the process and to describe ways of evaluating the adequacy of operationalizations once they have been selected. We do that in the sections on measurement in this chapter.

Operational Definitions

Before moving to a discussion of social science measurement, however, we should consider what is involved in operationalizing a concept. This is done by specifying a set of procedures to be followed or operations to be performed in order to obtain an empirical indicator of the manifestation of a concept in any given case. These procedures then provide an **operational definition** of the concept and its variable counterpart. The process of operationalization essentially reduces to a matter of selecting operational definitions for concepts.

To be useful (that is, to provide valid and reliable measures of our concepts), operational definitions must tell us precisely and explicitly what to do in order to determine what quantitative value should be associated with a variable in any given case. They should specify a complete set of steps to take in the process of measurement.

We want to be precise in this for at least three reasons. First, we want to be able to tell others exactly what we have done to obtain our measures, so that they can evaluate our work and possibly repeat our study to verify its results in another setting. Second, if we have assistants actually gathering the information, we will want our instructions to them to be detailed and precise enough to ensure that each one takes the measurements in exactly the same way as the others do. If our instructions are vague and our assistants go through slightly different sets of steps in obtaining measures, their results will not be comparable and we will be unable to draw valid conclusions from them. Finally, precise and detailed statements of how to operationalize a variable will help us in evaluating the results we obtain and in eliminating rival explanations of those results that essentially claim that the "findings" have been produced by flaws in the measurement process. (We will have more to say about this in subsequent sections of this chapter.)

When devising operational definitions for variables, you should routinely write out a description of the procedures you will use to obtain measurements. Every step should be detailed. This not only provides a record of your research and ensures standardization of measuring procedures but also gives you an opportunity to think through the act of obtaining a measurement in order to discover possible errors that can damage the reliability of results.

Suppose we want to measure the degree to which members of the two main parties support their own party in a state legislature. We can operationalize the concept *party unity* as *voting together on roll call votes* and then use the percentage of the average member's votes that agree with those of the majority of his or her party as our indicator of *voting together.* Having decided to do this, however, we face a number of critical choices in actually operationalizing our variable.

We can get information on how each legislator votes from the records of the legislature, but we will then have to decide which of the many recorded votes to include in our count. Some votes are unanimous (such as a vote to issue a proclamation of praise for some national hero) and do not reflect party unity because they do not involve partisan issues. Including all votes reduces the extent to which our measure reflects our concept. We have to state criteria for selecting votes to include. In order to focus only on controversial issues, therefore, we might, for instance, choose to include only those roll calls in which at least two-thirds of the legislators vote and in which the losing position gets no less than 30 percent of the vote.

We also have to decide how to devise a procedure for determining how a majority of the party has voted in order to classify each member's votes as consistent or inconsistent with that majority position. We need to decide how to treat abstentions. Do they count as a failure to support the party, or do we exclude them from our count? In addition, we have to specify a procedure for first computing and then averaging the percentages of agreeing votes for each legislator.

With every operationalization, we face similar decisions about exact procedures to follow in obtaining measures. A complete operational definition reveals how we have decided to handle such problems and leaves no ambiguity about what we actually did in taking our measures.

Constructing an operational definition results in the development of an **instrument** for taking measurements. In the physical sciences, such instruments as scales, light meters, and micrometers are used to obtain indicators of the degree to which things exhibit some property. In the social sciences, measuring instruments take different forms. Typical social science instruments include a series of questions on a survey form, instructions on how to make and record observations of certain events (such as a debate on the floor of the United Nations), and sets of numbers to be taken from some sourcebook and the rules for combining them into a measure.

Proper instrumentation is as important in the social sciences as it is in the physical sciences. Just as we would not attempt to measure weight with a ruler, we would not want to measure *political alienation* with a series of questions that do not reveal how alienated people feel. In discussing the validity and reliability of measures in the next section, we also suggest some ways to test the instruments developed in the process of operationalization in order to increase our confidence that they measure what we want them to.

Measurement

We operationalize variables in order to have a way to quantify abstract concepts so that we can make meaningful comparisons between real-world phenomena in terms of the properties suggested by those concepts. This assigning of numerals to represent properties is known as measurement. The result of measuring is that we have a *value* to associate with some variable for a given case.[1] This means simply that we can speak with more precision about the extent to which a given unit of observation (for example, a person, a city, a nation, or an organization) exhibits the property represented by the variable being measured. Rather than say that a city has a "bad crime problem," we can speak of specific crime rates. Rather than say that a person is a "devoted Republican," we can say that one has scored a 5 on our *strength of party identification* measure.

Levels of Measurement

Measuring procedures provide a means of categorizing and ordering phenomena. Some procedures, however, produce more precise and detailed distinctions between events than do others. Because of this we speak of various **levels of measurement.** When we say a procedure produces a given level of measurement, we are classifying it according to how much information it gives us about the phenomena being measured and their relationship to one another. The levels of measurement are referred to as *nominal, ordinal,* and *interval.*

---

[1] It is crucial that we appreciate the difference between a variable and its *values*. We recognize a variable because of its capacity for taking on different values. The variable is a concept translated into empirical terms. A value is some magnitude or quality of the variable that individual cases can reflect. For example, 23 years is a value for the variable *age*; $25,000 is a value for the variable *annual income*; 12 percent is a value for the variable *percentage of population foreign-born*; and upper class is a value for the variable *socioeconomic status.*

Nominal measurement provides the least information about phenomena. It gives us only a set of discrete categories to use in distinguishing between cases. Nominal measurement is obtained by simply naming cases by some predetermined scheme of classification. Nationality is generally "measured" at the nominal level by classifying people as Swiss, Brazilian, and so on. However, that "measurement" neither tells us how *much* of the characteristic "nationality" different individuals have nor allows us to rank-order them. Using nominal measurement simply gives us a way of sorting cases into groups designated by the names used in a classificatory scheme.

To be useful, nominal measurement schemes must be based on sets of categories that are **mutually exclusive** and **collectively exhaustive.** This means (1) it must not be possible to assign any single case to more than one category and (2) the categories should be set up so that *all* cases can be assigned to some category. If we want to classify voters in the United States by use of a nominal measuring scheme, we cannot use the categories *Democrat, Republican, liberal,* and *conservative* successfully, because these categories are not mutually exclusive. Since U.S. political parties each appeal to a broad spectrum of voters, it is possible for a person to be both a Democrat and a conservative or liberal, or both a Republican and a conservative or liberal. The categories do not allow us to differentiate among voters in all cases. Similarly, if we try categorize voters by party affiliation using only two categories— *Republican* and *Democrat*—we will find that our categories are not collectively exhaustive, because some voters consider themselves independents or members of other parties.

In order to facilitate analysis, we will probably want to substitute a number for each category in a scheme of nominal measurement. It is important to recognize however, that such numbers have no real meaning in this context; they are simply symbols. Just because we choose to substitute a 5 for the *Republican* category and a 1 for the *Democrat* category, we *cannot* assume that Republicans have five times as much party affiliation as Democrats. Any number can be substituted for any category of a nominal measurement so long as each category has a unique number associated with it.

Ordinal measurement provides more information because it allows us both to categorize and to order, or rank, phenomena. Ordinal measurement allows us to associate a number with each case. That number tells us not only that the case is different from some other cases, and similar to still others, with respect to the variable being measured but also how it relates to those other cases in terms of how much of a particular property it exhibits. With ordinal measurement we can say which cases have more (or less) of the measured quality than other cases, and we can rank cases in the order of *how much* of the quality they exhibit. That ranking gives us more detailed and precise information about the cases than we would get from a nominal measurement. The concept *social class* is often measured at the ordinal level, with individuals being ranked as lower-, middle-, or upperclass.

Interval measurement provides even more information. Not only can we classify and rank-order cases when they have been measured at the interval level, but we can also tell *how much* more (or less) of the measured property they contain than other cases. Ordinal measurement is not based on any standardized unit of the variable in question and does not allow us to tell how far cases are from one another in terms of that variable. It allows us only to say that some have more or less of it than others. Interval measurement is based on the idea that *there is some standard unit of the property being measured.*

Whereas ordinal measures give us only a rough idea of the relationship between cases with respect to a variable, interval measures provide information on the "distance" between cases. The variable *income* is a clear example. Income is usually measured in units of currency (dollars in the United States). Because we can use *standard units* in our measurement, we can say that the difference in income between $10,000 and $11,000 a year is exactly the same as the difference in income between $50,000 and $51,000 a year. We cannot do that with ordinal measurement. If we measure income ordinally by dividing people into such income categories as *under $10,000* and *$10,000 to $19,999,* we can say that one person has more or less income than another, but we cannot say exactly how far apart they are in income because we cannot tell where an individual falls within the category. The income difference between a person in category 1 (under $10,000) and a person in category 2 ($10,000 to $19,999) can be as little as one dollar ($10,000 minus $9,999) or as much as $10,000 ($19,999 minus $9,999), depending on their exact incomes, but we cannot make this distinction from an ordinal measure.

In addition to giving us precise information on the absolute differences between cases, interval measurement lets us make accurate statements about the *relative* differences between concepts. We can, for instance, agree that 50,000 people is twice as large a population as 25,000 people because we can speak meaningfully of a place that has no population. There is a *zero point* in true interval measures, and it is at least conceivably possible for a case to score zero on such measures. Because there is no meaningful zero point on an ordinal scale, we cannot say, for example, that upper-class people have twice as much "class" as lower-class people, because we don't know what it means to have no class standing.

This suggests an important point about levels of measurement. Nominal-level measurement is the least useful form of measurement when we have to compare phenomena. If we use it when we can use a "higher" (more precise) level of measurement, we may be wasting potentially valuable information. If, in a study of voting behavior, we categorize people only as Republicans, Independents, and Democrats when we can ask a different set of questions and produce a rank ordering of them as strong to weak party identifiers, we may be giving up information that will help us understand the relationships we observe. Ordinal-level measurement is more useful than nominal, but it too has limitations. Interval-level measurement is the most desirable form of measurement both because of the amount of detail in the information it provides and because of the mathematical procedures it allows us to perform on our data.

The point is that we should strive for operationalizations that allow interval level measurement whenever possible and appropriate. But how do we decide which level of measurement is appropriate for the particular concepts we want to operationalize? This is a matter of both conceptualization and measurement technology.

In the theory-building stage of research, we must first ask ourselves if there is some continuum underlying the differences we see in cases. If there is, we can devise ordinal and even interval measurements for a concept that might otherwise be measured only by nominal classification. An historical example will help clarify the significance of this.

Suppose we are studying the effects of immigrants' nationality on the degree of their support for big-city political machines in the early twentieth century in the United States. If we operationalize nationality at the nominal level and categorize city voting precincts' support for the machine, we might get a picture like that presented in Figure 4.2(a). There is no apparent relationship between nationality and voting behavior, because knowing a precinct's dominant nationality does not help us rank it relative to the others.

If we examine our reasoning, however, we might decide that the reason we expect nationality to be related to support for the machine is that countries of origin differ in the opportunities they allow their citizens for political participation. When people have had little experience with democratic politics in their native land, we might reason, they will be more willing to give up to a political boss their right to self-government. If we can follow this reasoning and rank-order the nations of origin by the extent they allow their citizens political participation, we can construct a graph like that shown in Figure 4.2(b). In that graph, a relationship between

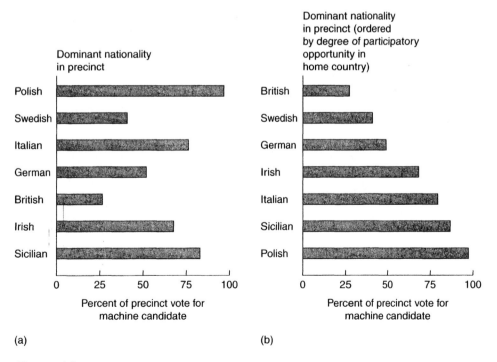

(a)

(b)

Figure 4.2
An example of how level of measurement can affect the interpretation of data

nationality and support for the machine is apparent. The ordering of categories on our independent variable helps us discover a pattern in its relationship to the dependent variable.

If we are bold enough, we may even upgrade our measurement of the independent variable to an interval level. For example, we might count the number of legal provisions for political participation in the statutes of each country in question for the years just prior to the beginning of significant immigration to the United States. We can use the resulting numbers to rank nationalities along an interval scale and make even more precise comparisons of independent and dependent variables.

Whether or not we can achieve this upgrading of variables from the nominal to the ordinal or interval level depends both on developing a theoretical rationale for doing so and on the technical possibility of applying the operational procedures that produce the higher-level measurements. Even if we can conceptualize *nationality* in interval terms in our example, we may not have access to the legal records necessary to place countries along the interval scale. In that case, *measurement technology* limits what we can do to strengthen our measures.

These situational factors make it difficult to set down rules about operationalizing concepts to achieve certain levels of measurement. We can, however, suggest that you use measures as precise as possible given the subject you are studying. This generally means upgrading measurement procedures so that they yield higher levels of measurement whenever possible. Do not settle for an operationalization that produces nominal measurement when ordinal or interval measurement is theoretically defensible and technically possible.

Having said this, we need to add a qualification to the general rule. There are cases in which too much precision in measurement is actually undesirable. W. Phillips Shively offers an example of this. Figure 4.3 is adapted from his work. In it we see the relationship between age and voting in the 1968 presidential election presented in two different ways. In Figure 4.3(a), age is measured in single years. Because there are so few people in each age group (for example, 21–22, 35–36, 50–51), the chart reveals no clear pattern in the relationship—between the two variables. In Figure 4.3(b), age is measured less precisely, in five-year groupings. With more cases in each group, we can see that there is a broad pattern to the relationship, with voting likelihood increasing to age 50 and then generally declining.

By giving up some precision in our measurement, we have gained a greater ease of analysis. This is a good trade as long as we do not go so far in the direction of less precision that we again lose sight of relationships. If we use twenty-year groupings to measure age, we will see little difference in the percentage of each age group that votes and might falsely conclude that age is unrelated to the likelihood of voting. Because we generally do not know in advance of actual data analysis how much precision will be needed to allow us to discover relationships, we should follow the rule of operationalizing our concepts as precisely as possible. We can always discard unnecessary precision by "collapsing categories" (moving to larger units of differentiation) if we find it necessary. But if we do not collect the information in the first place, we cannot draw on it later.

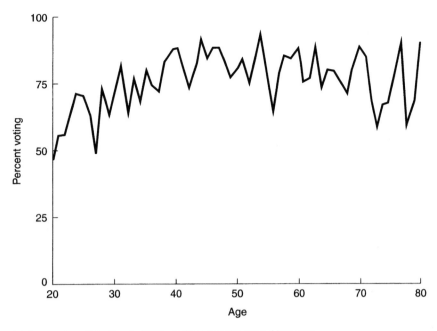

(a) Age and participation in 1968 election: age measured by years

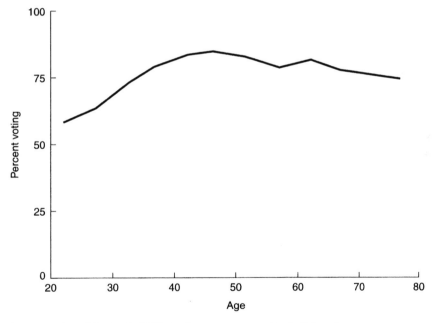

(b) Age and participation in 1968 election: age measured by half-decades

Figure 4.3
An example of the effect of grouping data on interpretation

SOURCE: W. Philips Shively, *The Craft of Political Research*, 2d ed. Englewood Cliffs, NJ: Prentice Hall, 1980, pp. 67–68. Reprinted with permission.

Working Hypotheses

Measurement assigns values to cases with respect to given variables. These values are what we use to represent concepts when we compare observations. Before we can understand the implications our observations have for our theories, we have to translate our hypotheses concerning relations between variables into working hypotheses, which state the expected relationships between measures or indicators. The next-to-last line in Figure 4.1 suggests the form that **working hypotheses** take. These hypotheses force us to state what linkages between indicators and variables we believe our operationalization has produced.

Consider an example from the study of international relations. Suppose we are interested in a theory of dominance in the international sphere. Working from the theoretical proposition *The more dominated a nation is, the more conformist its foreign policy will be,* we can hypothesize as follows: *As a nation's economic dependency increases, its support for the international policies of its patron state will increase.* We can operationalize *economic dependency* as the percentage of the nation's exports that go to the patron country. A percentage of exports becomes our indicator of the independent variable *dependency. Support* can be measured by the percentage of votes in the United Nations General Assembly in which the client nation's vote differs from that of the patron state. A percentage of votes in the United Nations becomes our indicator of the dependent variable *support for the patron state's policies.* We can now set out a working hypothesis stating the negative relationship we expect between indicators: *The higher the percentage of exports going to the patron state, the lower the percentage of votes in the United Nations that disagree with the votes of the patron state.*

This working hypothesis tells us what observations are consistent with our hypothesis and our theory. It also suggests the relationship we envision between our variables and our indicators. That relationship is diagrammed in Figure 4.4

The diagram shows how important it is that we think through the relationship between our measures and our variables. The relationship predicted by the proposition and the hypothesis is a positive one. But the relationship predicted by the working hypothesis is *negative* because the relationship between the dependent variable and its indicator is negative because of the way we have operationalized our dependent variable, a *negative* relationship between indicators will provide evidence for a hypothesis and a theoretical proposition that predict *positive* relationships between concepts and variables. We have to be aware of details like this if we are to avoid misinterpreting our data and if we are to draw accurate conclusions about the utility of our theory from our observations.

Being clear about the relationship between our indicators and the variables and concepts they represent is so important that some social scientists argue that, in addition to our theories about political phenomena, we should be able to state a **measurement theory** that sets out *why we would expect our indicators to be related to our concepts.*[2] Why should we expect economic dependency to be related to

---

[2] For example, see Hubert M. Blalock, Jr., "The Measurement Problem: A Gap between the Languages of Theory and Research," in Hubert M. Blalock, Jr., and Ann Blalock, eds., *Methodology in Social Research,* (New York: McGraw-Hill, 1968), pp. 5–27.

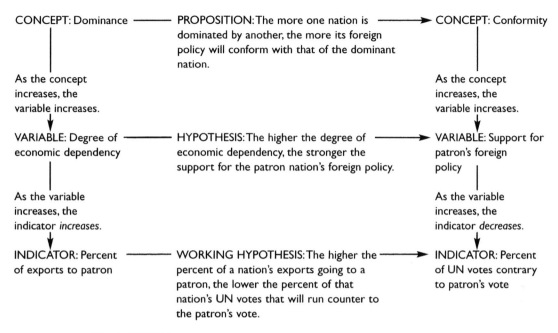

Figure 4.4
Specification of the relationships of concepts, variables, and indicators

concentration of exports? What is there about the distribution of exports that makes it a reflection of what we mean when we refer to dependency? These are the types of questions a well-developed measurement theory helps us answer. A measurement theory consists of the assumptions that explain why our indicators should change values as the degree to which cases manifest our concepts changes.

Indicators cannot be casually selected but must be chosen as a result of careful reasoning about the way things are related in the world. That reasoning is much like what we go through in constructing theories about political phenomena. The conclusions we reach may be wrong. The properties we refer to when we use a concept may in fact be unrelated to the indicators we decide to use as empirical measures for that concept.

This issue of whether or not there is any correspondence between our concept and variables on the one hand and our indicators or measures on the other is the central problem of measurement in science. The question of whether changes in our indicators are actually the result of changes in the concepts they represent gives rise to the problems of reliability and validity that we discuss in subsequent sections of this chapter. The important point here is that the idea of a measurement theory suggests the way we should approach these problems in our research.

Every operationalization of a concept is, in essence, a hypothesis. When we operationalize and say, "Let this indicator stand for that concept," we are hypothesizing that the things we mean when we use the concept are actually reflected in the indicator we select. That hypothesis may or may not be supported by observations.

We can never take the adequacy of our measures for granted but must examine our observations in order to find evidence that they represent what we mean by our concepts. The search for valid and reliable measurement procedures in the social sciences is in many ways a process of hypothesis testing. We must be ready to admit mistakes and begin again when the evidence suggests that our indicators fail to reflect our concepts. The testing of measures occurs primarily in our attempts to assess the validity and reliability of the indicators we select.

Measurement Error: The Enemy

The process of measurement results in the assignment of a variety of values to different cases on the basis of how they score on our indicators. The differences in the scores can all be attributed to two basic sources. One source is the extent to which the cases really exhibit different degrees of the property in which we are interested. Different scores occur when our measures actually pick up those differences. In this case, *real* differences in the concept are reflected in our measures. The other source of differences in the scores is the extent to which something about the measure itself or the setting in which it is applied causes different cases to get different scores. In that instance, our measures are showing differences between cases that are *not* real—in the sense that they do not reflect authentic differences in the concept we want to measure. The differences we observe when this happens result from inconsistencies in the procedure for measurement.

If our measures were perfect, they would reveal only the first kind of differences between cases. But our measures are rarely if ever flawless. Differences in the values assigned to cases inevitably reflect not only real differences in the degree to which those cases manifest the concept but also "artificial" differences created by the measurement process. Any differences in the values assigned to cases that are attributable to anything other than real differences are known as **measurement error.** They are not real differences between cases but differences that are erroneously recorded because of flaws in the measuring process.

This distinction between true variations in scores and variations due to measurement error is similar to the distinction between differences in objects apparent to the unaided eye and differences we see when we look only at their reflection in a mirror. To the extent that the mirror distorts the images, it either masks differences we would see with the naked eye or creates an impression of differences we would not otherwise perceive. In the social sciences, we can rarely see our key concepts directly and must rely on measurement procedures analogous to the mirror to reflect these concepts in any given case. Consequently, the accuracy of our impressions of the two depends on the precision with which our measures reflect reality.

What are some of the sources of distortion in the images our measures provide? We need to know the answer to this question if we are to control measurement error or recognize it when it is present in our data. We can list several of the primary sources of measurement error by identifying common sources of differences in the scores assigned to cases *other than true differences in the characteristics we want to measure.*[3]

1. *Differences in the distribution of other, relatively stable characteristics among the cases that are unintentionally revealed by our measures:* For example, the questions representing our measure of political ideology may require a given level of intelligence to interpret and answer. If this is the case, responses will reflect not only differences in people's political ideology but also differences in their intelligence. When we look at the resulting data, the effects of intelligence and political ideology will be confused, and we will be unable to distinguish differences in scores that reflect ideological difference from those that reflect differences in intelligence. Similarly, other characteristics of our units of analysis (such as the regional location of cities, the cultural traits of nations, or the sources of documents) can be inadvertently reflected in our measures and distort our perceptions of the manifestation of the target concepts. When we can identify and measure these "contaminating" influences, we should check to see whether holding their values constant wipes out, reduces, or increases differences in the scores that cases receive on our measures.

2. *Differences in the distribution of temporary characteristics among the cases that are reflected in our measures:* A person's mood or state of health can affect the way one responds to items on a questionnaire. The recent political history of cities (the revelation of corruption among public officials, for instance) can create systematic but temporary differences in the way those cities' citizens answer survey questions. A massive natural disaster can produce a drastic but temporary change in the statistics we are relying on to indicate the level of economic development. The effects of such temporary "abnormalities" are more difficult to identify and control than the effects of the stable characteristics in our cases. The only approaches for guarding against them are being alert to signs that individual cases are subject to such transient influences (for example, studying the recent political history of the cities included in our sample or advising our interviewers not to attempt to interview a person who is temporarily bedridden) and following the procedures for checking the reliability of measures described in the section of this chapter discussing reliability.

3. *Differences in subjects' interpretation of the measuring instrument:* This is a problem only when people must respond directly to questions, as opposed to when the researcher constructs measures by observing behavior. If our questions are ambiguously worded, the different interpretations our respondents place on them can produce differences in their scores on the measures composed of those questions. Suppose, for instance, we are careless enough to ask the question *Did you vote in the last election?* in a study of voting behavior. If

---

[3] A more detailed discussion of the points that follow is found in Clair Selltiz, Lawrence S. Wrightsman, and Stuart W. Cook, *Research Methods in Social Relations,* 3d ed. (New York: Holt, Rinehart and Winston, 1976), pp. 165–68. Their discussion comes from the tradition of psychology and pertains primarily to research in which the subjects are people. Many of the principles, however, are transferable to the broader range of research situations we are considering.

some of the interviewees do not know that a city election has been held the prior week, they may answer that they *have* voted, because they think the question refers to the last national election, even though they have not voted in the election to which we intend our questions to refer. We can guard against this source of unintended differences in scores by pretesting questions and testing our measures for reliability.

4. *Differences in the setting in which the measure is applied:* This is also a source of measurement error principally in research that relies on individuals' responses to questions as its measures. One well-established fact in survey research, for example, is that the race, sex, and age of interviewers can affect responses. Answers (and therefore scores on measures) can differ from interview to interview on the basis of the characteristics of the interviewer alone. Similar problems can arise outside survey research. We may, for instance, make the mistake of doing a content analysis of one country's domestic newscasts and another's newscasts intended only for foreign nations. We will then be applying the same instrument in very different settings and can expect some differences in scores from this fact alone. We can avoid this source of measurement error only by making every effort to see that the situations in which our measures are applied are standardized.

5. *Differences in the administration of the measuring instrument:* The scores assigned to cases can differ as a result of a variety of errors that occur in collecting and recording information. Interviewers may misunderstand instructions and ask questions in ways the researcher might not intend. Poor lighting may cause a respondent to mismark a questionnaire. Pencils can break and pens run out of ink at crucial moments so that observers fail to record key events in a group interaction. These kinds of variation in the administration of measuring instruments cause differences in scores independent of any differences in real values for the variable under investigation. Beyond employing only dependable assistants, the primary way to guard against such sources of measurement error is through *pretesting* our instruments. A trial run will help us discover potential "mechanical" problems with the instrument (such as insufficient space for recording typical answers on a coding form) and human factors that may affect results (such as length of time observers can work without fatigue).

6. *Differences in the processing and analysis of data:* Information has to undergo a great deal of handling before it can be analyzed. It often changes form several times. For example, interviewers may record responses by writing down every word an interviewee says in answer to a question. Those written passages may subsequently be reduced to a single number as responses get coded. The written number may be transferred to a computer file as an entry in the appropriate column of a spreadsheet. In each of these steps, data analysis has been made simpler, but with each step there is a chance of errors that can cause cases to appear to differ on a variable when they do not. The possibility of such errors makes it a good idea to always double- and triple-check each transformation of data and to keep the original form for future reference.

7. *Differences in the way individuals respond to the form of the measuring instrument:* This is especially a problem when our units of analysis are people. Measuring instruments can take such different forms as oral interviews, questionnaires to be filled out by the respondent, and observation by a trained researcher. The different forms place different demands on the people under study. An interview requires ease of speaking, and a questionnaire requires an ability to read and write, for example. If people differ in these abilities, their scores may differ even when the people are actually alike on the variable being operationalized. The best guard against this source of measurement error is the use of more than one form of measure meant to operationalize each concept. We say more about this in the next section of this chapter, which discusses validity.

All of these factors can introduce measurement error into our research. The various errors that arise from these seven sources are generally categorized as either *systematic* or *random* errors. **Systematic errors** are those that arise from a confusion of variables in the world (as discussed in item 1 in the preceding list) or from the nature of the instrument itself. They appear in each use of the instrument and are constant among cases and studies in which the same measure is used. Constant errors cause our results to be *invalid,* in that the differences (or similarities) our measures seem to reveal are not accurate reflections of the differences we think we are measuring. **Random errors** affect each application of the instrument differently. They occur as a matter of chance and are due to transient characteristics in our cases, situational variations in application of the instrument, mistakes in administration and processing, and other factors that vary from one use of the instrument to the next. They make our measures invalid in much the same way that systematic errors do. Random errors also make our measures *unreliable,* in that we cannot consistently get the same results when we use the measure if random errors are occurring.

How are we to avoid having measurement errors so distort our results as to render our research useless or misleading? To answer that question we must give careful attention to the issues of validity and reliability.

Validity

We can seldom obtain direct measures of the concepts used in social science theories. Such concepts as power, democracy, and representation cannot be quantified as simply as such concepts as length and weight. We have to use indicators that correspond only indirectly to the concepts they represent. There is always a chance then that the indicators we choose will not adequately reflect the concepts we want to measure. **Validity** is the term we use to refer to *the extent to which our measures correspond to the concepts they are intended to reflect.* To ask about a measure's validity is to ask if we are in fact measuring what we think we are measuring when we use it. Achieving validity is often viewed as the basic problem of measurement in the social sciences.

To be valid, a measure must be both *appropriate* and *complete.* If, for example, we are interested in comparing the quality of public education in different cities, we may be tempted to use the number of teachers in those cities' schools as an indicator of the quality of educational services. This measure is *inappropriate,* because the number of personnel in a school system is determined largely by the number of students and the size of the city and may have little to do with the quality of education. If we use the ratio of students to teachers as our indicator of educational services, we will have a more appropriate measure, in that differences caused by city size will be reduced or eliminated. The measure, however, will still be *incomplete.* Education involves more than teachers. It also involves school buildings, films, books, labs, and a variety of other factors. Looking at any one of these factors by itself might leave us with a false impression of the total quality of educational services. A school system may have a highly desirable student-teacher ratio but inadequate facilities and learning materials. It is a mistake to say that such a school system is equal to one with an identical student-teacher ratio *and* excellent facilities and learning materials. If we are to achieve validity, we must strive to construct measures that are both appropriate and complete.

This raises two questions: How can we create measures that are complete and appropriate, and how can we tell whether we have succeeded in doing so?

The answer to the first question begins with the operationalization process. We can define *validity* as the extent to which differences in scores on a measure reflect *only* differences in the distribution of values on the variable we intend to measure. Since we can probably never achieve complete and total validity, our goal should be to select measures that are susceptible to as few influences as possible other than differences in our target variable. This requires that we think carefully through the processes that surround our measures in search of possible causes of variations in scores. We are essentially concerned at this point with guarding against the effects of systematic error.

Consider this example. We may want a measure of the extent to which the citizens of different nations agree with the policies of their government. We decide to rely on answers to a series of survey questions as our indicator of agreement or disagreement. We hope that differences in citizens' actual opinions are the only source of differences in their responses to these questions. A moment's reflection, however, alerts us to another possible source of variation. If some of the nations included in our study have authoritarian governments that use secret police to repress dissent and that regard any criticism of their policies as acts of treason, their citizens may well be afraid to express disagreement with their government in an interview. In this case, scores on our measure may be determined at least as much by the attitude of each nation's government toward dissent as by the opinions of those being interviewed. The strong possibility of this type of measurement error makes survey questions an inappropriate operationalization.

Similarly, we must be concerned with completeness early in the research process. If we want to measure the relative influence of different interest groups in a state legislature, we may think of using newspaper reports of interest group appearances before legislative committees as our indicator. We must ask ourselves, however, whether giving testimony in public hearings is all there is to political influence. This activity is legitimately considered a *part* of the influence process, but there are so many other means of exercising influence that a measure that relies exclusively on the giving of testimony as an indicator of influence is incomplete.

Achieving appropriate and relatively complete operationalizations then depends both on knowing a good deal about the subject of our study and on conducting a careful, logical analysis of alternative operationalizations. We can check the validity of our measures in order to determine whether or not we have developed sound measures only *after* we have collected data, however. The process of evaluating the validity of our measures is referred to as **validation.**

There are four basic approaches to validation, summarized in Table 4.1. The first is often called **pragmatic validation,** because it involves assessing the validity of a measure from evidence of how well it works in allowing us to predict behaviors and events. For example, say that we devise a measure of how appealing candidates for public office are to voters. We can get some indication of the validity of this measure by applying it to all the candidates for seats in the U.S. Senate in a given election year and predicting their chances of being elected on the basis of their relative scores on our "voter appeal" measure. The more successful we are at predicting the candidates' electoral fate, the more confident we become that we have a valid measure, one that accurately reflects the intended concept. Measures that allow us to predict future events accurately are said to have **predictive validity.**

Pragmatic validation requires that there be some alternative indicator of variables that we feel fairly certain is a valid reflection of them. We check our measures against this alternative as we might check the accuracy of verbal reports of age against birth certificates. Unfortunately there are seldom any clearly valid alternative indicators for the concepts used in social science research. As a result, we generally have to rely on the second type of validation—*construct validation.*

Construct validation is achieved by *inferring* the validity of a measure from evidence of the extent to which actual relationships between scores of various measures are consistent with what we expect from the theory that has led us to use a given indicator. This involves two lines of reasoning.

Table 4.1
Types of validation

Pragmatic Validation	Construct Validation	Discriminant Validation	Face Validation
Check results obtained from use of the indicator against results obtained from use of another indicator that is known to be a valid measure of the concept, or test the *predictive validity* of the indicator by using it to predict events that reflect the concept being measured.	*Internal (convergent) validation:* Infer validity of the indicator from its relationship to other indicators of the same concept using *multiple indicators.* *External validation:* Infer validity of the indicator from its relationship to indicators of *other* concepts to which the concept being measured should *theoretically* be related.	Infer validity of the indicator from the degree to which it is *unrelated* to indicators of other concepts that are theoretically distinct from the concept being measured.	Assume validity from the self-evident character of the indicator. (Can knowledgeable persons be persuaded that this is a valid indicator of the concept?)

First we might say to ourselves, "If concept X has a positive relationship to concept Y and a negative relationship to concept Z (as our theory says it does), then it will also be true that scores on a valid measure of X will have a positive relationship to scores on a valid measure of Y and a negative relationship to scores on a valid measure of Z." We cannot validate the measure by comparing scores on it to scores on some other measure of the same variable that we know to be valid (as in the case of the birth certificate). We can, however, judge its validity by the extent to which using it as an indicator of our variable produces the kinds of relationships that our theory leads us to expect between that variable and other variables.

As an example, consider a study of international alliances. We might create a measure of the strength of an alliance based on a content analysis of newspaper articles from the countries involved. Is what the newspapers of one nation say about another nation a valid indicator of the strength of the alliance between the two countries? We might get an idea of whether it is by reasoning as follows: "Our theory tells us that the stronger an alliance between two nations is, the more often they will vote together in the United Nations and the fewer restrictions they will place on trade with each other. Therefore, scores on a valid measure of *strength of alliance* will be positively related to scores on measures of *voting together in the United Nations* and negatively related to scores on measures of *number of trade barriers*." We then proceed to do the data analysis necessary to see whether this expectation is supported by our observations. If the relationships are as expected, we will have greater confidence in the validity of our measure of *strength of alliance*. If they are not as we have expected, we will question whether we have a sound measure of this concept.

What we have just described is often referred to as **external validation**. It involves comparing scores on the measure being validated with scores on measures of *other* variables. To use this method of validation, of course, we have to include measures of the other variables in our research. This means that *we have to begin thinking about ways to validate our measures early in the research process*. Certainly by the time we are ready to develop a research design, we have to know how we will want to check the validity of our measures so that we can be certain to gather any information we will need.

Our efforts at external validation will produce convincing evidence about the validity of our measure of one variable only if we can have a high degree of confidence in the validity of the measures we use for the other variables. In the previous example, for instance, we could not conclude anything about the validity of our measure of *strength of alliance* from the relationships between scores on it and scores on the other two variables if we did not believe that our indicators of *voting together* and *trade barriers* were valid.

Because it is often difficult to find clearly valid indicators of variables to which our key variable should be related, external validation procedures must be used with caution. This is very much like testing a hypothesis. No single result guarantees the validity (or invalidity) of the measure. Rather, as instances of successful validation attempts accumulate, our confidence in the validity of our measure grows. For that reason, it is wise to seek out as many theoretically predictable relationships as possible to use in external validation. The more different tests of validity we have, the stronger our case will be.

This same logic applies to the second type of construct validation—**internal** or **convergent validation.** This type of validation involves devising several measures of the *same* variable and comparing scores on these various measures. We reason that if each of the indicators provides a valid measure of the concept in question, the scores individual cases receive on the measures should be closely related. If A, B, and C are all valid measures of X, then any individual's scores on A, B, and C should be highly similar.

For instance, suppose that we want an indicator of the quality of street lighting in residential neighborhoods as part of a study of the distribution of public services. We might want to use citizens' perceptions of the adequacy of street lighting (as revealed in survey interviews) as that indicator. We can ask a sample of citizens in a neighborhood how adequate they think the streetlights in their area are and take the average evaluation as our measure of *quality of street lighting.* In order to perform an internal validation, we may also measure street lighting quality (1) by using a light meter to get a physical measure of the brightness and distribution of lighting, (2) by having trained observers rate the lighting, and (3) by having citizens compare their street lighting with that pictured in a series of photos showing streets with different qualities of lighting and then averaging their rankings to get a measure for the neighborhood. This gives us four measures of the variable. If each is valid, all should be strongly related.

We can check this with appropriate statistics. If we find that scores on the measure based on responses to interview questions are weakly related to scores on the other three measures *and* that scores on those other measures are strongly related to one another, we will have reason to suspect that our first measure is not valid.

This is much like weighing the same object on three different scales. If each of the scales gives an accurate weight and we have no reason to assume that the object has changed weight in the course of the test, we expect the weights obtained from the three scales to be identical. If one gives a different weight, we suspect it of being out of adjustment.

Figure 4.5 suggests the differences between internal and external forms of construct validation. In Figure 4.5(a), we see that internal validation is achieved by

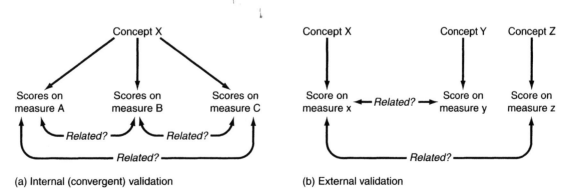

(a) Internal (convergent) validation

(b) External validation

Figure 4.5
Forms of construct validation

checking the correspondence of scores on several different measures of the *same* concept. The more closely they correspond, the more justified we feel in claiming that any of the measures is valid. In Figure 4.5(b), we see that external validation involves determining whether our measure of one variable shows it to be related to *other* variables as we expect it to be from our theory. If the expected relationships do not appear, we have reason to suspect that the indicator we have selected does not provide valid measures of the concept.

The same caution that applies to the use of external validation procedures applies to the use of internal validation. We cannot always be certain that our measures of the key concept are valid, and we should therefore always be careful about concluding that a measure is valid or invalid from any one test of validity. We can significantly increase our confidence in the results of an internal validation if we follow a simple rule: *The alternative measures of the concept should be based on as many different types of operationalization as possible.*

In the street lighting example, our measures come from four distinct types of operationalization: citizens' verbal ratings, physical measurements, observers' judgments, and citizens' selection of photographs. Each of these represents a different *mode of operationalization.* The more different modes we can use and the more independent they are of each other, the more confidence we can place in our validation. Why? The logic is as follows.

The principal source of invalidity is systematic and random measurement error. Different measures are subject to different kinds of measurement error. The more indicators we have for any variable and the more they differ from one another, the less likely it is that all the indicators will be affected by the same measurement error. If this is true, we will have a better chance of both recognizing measurement error as a source of differences in the scores on any one of our measures and getting an accurate measure of our variable if we use **multiple indicators.**

For instance, the factors that may make our physical measure of street lighting quality invalid (such as a faulty light meter) are likely to be quite unrelated to any factors that might introduce systematic errors into the measure based on citizens' evaluations (such as a tendency for people to claim out of a sense of community pride that public services in their neighborhood are as good as those in other areas). If we use only one mode of measurement, any source of measurement error may affect the scores on each measure, giving us a consistently invalid indicator and not allowing meaningful comparisons among measures. If, for example, we rely only on the physical measure of lighting but take readings in several different ways (say, on the sidewalk, on the curb, and in the street), then any flaw in the measuring instrument (the light meter, in this case) will affect all measures and none can be used to check another.

This logic suggests the great value of having multiple indicators for our variables. The availability of multiple measures not only gives us an opportunity to *test* the validity of our indicators but also *improves our chances of obtaining a valid measure* of our variables in the first place. Multiple measures can actually increase the validity of measurement by allowing us to combine the results of several different measurement procedures so as to produce a *composite score* that is more likely to be a valid reflection of the actual value of our variable than is any of the measures taken alone. This is because there is a chance that the errors that cause each measure to be invalid will cancel out when the results of several measurement procedures are combined. (In Chapter 8, the sections on scaling describe some possible methods of combining scores to produce a composite measure.)

A third approach to validation is referred to as **discriminant validation.** When we ask whether a measure exhibits *discriminant validity,* we are essentially asking whether using it as an indicator of a given concept allows us to distinguish that concept from other concepts. For example, we might want to measure the concept *trust in political officials* through a series of questions in a survey. If we also have on the questionnaire a series of questions designed to measure *trust in people* (in general), we can compare the scores on the two measures to ask whether our first set of questions actually reflects simply another way of measuring trust in people. If scores are highly similar, we say that the political trust measure does not have discriminant validity because it does not permit us to distinguish the concept of *trust in political officials* from the concept of *trust in people.*

A final approach to validation relies on the concept of **face validity.** Some measures are based on such direct observation of the behavior in question that there seems to be no reason to question their validity; such a measure seems valid "on the face of it." For example, suppose we want to measure compliance with a state law requiring each business establishment to display its operating license on its front door. Having trained observers simply note the presence or absence of such licenses seems to provide an obviously valid measure of compliance. Though we should always ask ourselves if the measures we have selected appear valid on their face, it is generally a mistake to rely on face validity alone to ensure accurate results from our research. We should attempt to ascertain the validity of our measures through established procedures, such as those already described.

Reliability

When we ask about the validity of a measure, we are asking how closely the values it yields correspond to the true values of the variable being measured. When we ask about the **reliability** of a measure, we are asking how *stable* the values it yields are. Can we get the same value for any given case when we apply the measure several different times, or does each application result in the assignment of a different value to each case? If we do not get substantially the same value for any given case from successive applications of a measure, that measure is *unreliable* as an indicator of the concept. Rulers are made of inelastic materials in order to ensure reliability. If they were made of elastic materials, they might very well show different lengths for the same object—even when the object's true length has not changed—simply because the ruler stretches and contracts.

If a measure is unreliable, it cannot be valid, because at least some of the differences in the scores assigned to cases result from measurement errors rather than from true differences between cases. Recall our example of the study of street lighting. What if the light meter we use is so sensitive that in addition to recording the light from the streetlights, it picks up light from the moon? Then the values assigned to each street on the variable *quality of street lighting* will depend both on the brightness of the street lights and on such random factors as the fullness of the moon and the density of the cloud cover. To the extent that these random factors influence our results, the measure will not be a valid reflection of actual differences in the quality of street lighting. In this case, unreliability produces invalidity.

A measure may be quite reliable and yet invalid. Recall our example of the study of the extent to which people in different nations agree with the policies of their government. We said that survey questions may give invalid measures because people in authoritarian countries are afraid to tell the truth about their opinions. Because this factor produces a systematic rather than a random error, the questions might produce very stable results. No matter how many times they are asked, people might give the same "safe" responses. This does not, however, make the measure valid.

A measure may then *be reliable without being valid, but it cannot be valid without being reliable.* Whereas validity is challenged by both systematic and random error, reliability is jeopardized only by random error. This means that if a measure has been convincingly validated in prior studies we can use it without being worried about its reliability; it has to be reliable if it is valid. But demonstrating reliability does not guarantee validity.

How do we guard against unreliability? How do we determine whether or not a given measure is reliable? Preventing unreliability depends on our being aware of the various sources of random measurement error described earlier in this chapter and doing what we can to control them. This involves thinking through the actual measurement process and pretesting our measuring instruments to discover previously unrecognized causes of random error.

It is often quite difficult to determine whether or not we have devised a reliable measure in the social sciences. This is because the true value of the variables with which we are concerned can change dramatically with time and circumstance—people change their opinions in response to experience, nations alter the way they allocate resources between social services and defense efforts in response to perceived military threats, and so on. When real values are changing, it is hard to distinguish the effects of random measurement error from genuine fluctuations in the concepts being measured. This means that tests of reliability should be conducted over as short a time span as possible.

There are essentially three broad methods of assessing the reliability of measures in the social sciences. The first is the *test-retest method.* Here the same measure is applied to the same set of cases again and again, over time. To the extent that cases get the same score each time, the measure is considered reliable. A difficulty with this technique arises when our measure involves interviewing people (as opposed to measuring inanimate objects or making concealed observations of people). If we repeat questions in a short time, interviewees may remember their first answer and, in an effort to be consistent, repeat that answer rather than respond truthfully in answering the question. If this happens, we cannot get an accurate picture of the questions' reliability as an indicator of the concept. In an effort to avoid this test effect, we might let a good deal of time pass before asking the questions a second time. If we do that, however, we will run into another problem: true values on the variable may have changed with the passage of time, and we may be unable to distinguish differences in scores caused by unreliability in the measure from actual changes in the variable.

Because of that difficulty, a second type of reliability test has been developed: the *alternative form method*. Different forms of the measure are applied to the same group of cases, or the same measure is applied to different groups *at the same time*. In this way there can be no reaction to being measured, because no case will be measured more than once, and, because no time lapses between applications of the measure, actual changes in the variables under study cannot affect the results. The success of this strategy, however, depends on the alternative forms of the measure being perfectly comparable to each other as a measure of the concept, or on the two groups being virtually equivalent with respect to the distribution of the variable being measured. If we can assume that these conditions are met, the more the scores on the two measures, or the scores of the two groups, are alike, the more confidence we have in the reliability of our measure. If we cannot come up with comparable measures or groups, however, we cannot use the method properly.

The final basic approach to testing the reliability of a measure is known as the *subsample method*. In it we draw one sample of cases and divide it into several subsamples in such a way that each is highly similar to the others in composition. We then apply the same measure to all subsamples and use the similarity or difference of responses from subsample to subsample as an indicator of the reliability of the measure. Because we use the same measure, we do not have to be concerned about comparability as in the alternative form method, and because we can rely on sampling theory to ensure the equivalence of our subsamples, we do not have to worry that the groups selected for measurement will not be sufficiently alike. Because no case is measured twice, we can discount reaction to testing as a threat to the accuracy of our reliability test, and because the measures are administered simultaneously, actual changes in the variable cannot create problems for this method, as they can for the test-retest method. However, use of the subsample method depends on our being able to draw a large enough sample that we can divide it and still have subsamples large enough for our statistical tests to be meaningful. This is not always possible and can represent a barrier to the use of the subsample method in testing reliability.

There are many variations on these methods. Which one is most appropriate for any given research project will depend both on the time and resources available to complete the research and on the nature of the study. For instance, if we want to measure street lighting by having trained observers rate the lighting on various blocks, we can easily use the test-retest method without concern about a test effect. Street lighting will not change simply because it is measured by someone, and so we can have different observers independently rate the same street on the same night. We cannot have the same confidence in this method if our measure of street lighting quality is based on citizens' responses to interview questions.

Regardless of the reliability test we choose to use, it is important to establish the reliability of our measures *before* actually beginning research. This involves pretesting the measure by collecting the data necessary for the purpose of assessing the instruments we will use in the final study. If we fail to do this, we may find only *after* the study is complete that our measures of key variables are unreliable (and therefore invalid). This means that we will not be able to place any faith in the results of the research and that our energies will have been partially or totally wasted. *Pretests of measures' validity and reliability should be part of any research project that either uses measures that have not been convincingly validated elsewhere or relies on measures that have been validated only in settings very different from those in which they will be used.*

Conclusion

At this point we have introduced all the basic elements of the research process. Figure 4.6 depicts their relationships to one another. The operationalization of our concepts through the development of measurable indicators prepares us to enter the field to make the observations on which we will base our conclusions. Before we can make

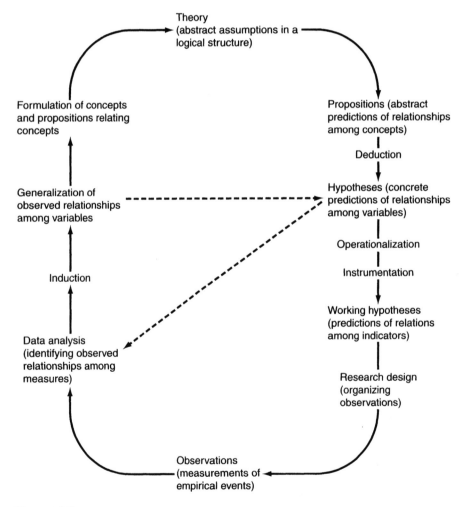

Figure 4.6
A model of the research process

those observations, however, we need a "plan of attack"—a scheme for making the observations in a way that will maximize the number of conclusions we can confidently draw from them. This plan, or *research design,* is the subject of Chapter 5.

Suggestions for Further Reading

Most explanations of measurement in the social sciences are found in literature that reports research results or develops sophisticated measurement techniques. General introductions to the subject are rare. However, one of the best introductions to measurement strategies is W. Philips Shively, *The Craft of Political Research,* 4th ed. (Englewood Cliffs, NJ: Prentice Hall, 1997). Some more advanced approaches to measurement can be found in Hubert M. Blalock, Jr., *Conceptualization and Measurement in the Social Sciences* (Beverly Hills, CA: Sage, 1982). A variety of examples of measurement strategies are found in Louise G. White, *Political Analysis* (Belmont, CA: Wadsworth, 1994).

Research Exercises

1. Using one of the political science periodicals given in Chapter 3, locate an article that reports the results of an empirical investigation. Identify at least two principal concepts from the article, and write down how each concept was operationalized. If the article uses only one operationalization for each concept, describe at least two more for each concept. If more than one operationalization is used for each concept in the article, describe at least one alternative operationalization for each. If possible, your operationalizations should rely on indicators that are in a different form from those used in the article.

2. Select another scholarly article reporting the results of empirical research. Identify at least two of the major concepts employed, and describe how they were operationalized. Then state a line of reasoning that will lead us to expect the indicator selected for each variable to change when values of the variable change. In other words, state a *measurement theory* justifying the use of that indicator.

3. Using the variables from the article selected for Exercise 2, devise at least two alternative measurement theories showing how changes in each indicator employed in the article can result from changes in some variable *other* than the one it is used to represent. In other words, identify at least two possible sources of invalidity for each indicator.

4. Using one of the articles selected for any of the above exercises, identify two key measures employed in it. Tell which of the three broad methods for testing the reliability of measures is appropriate to use in checking the reliability of each of these measures, and justify your choice. Describe how you would set up the observations necessary to implement the test of each measure. For example, you might write, "I would include at the beginning and end of each of the interviews a version of the question on which the measure is based and I would compare the answers each respondent gives to the two questions."

Terms Introduced in This Chapter

operationalization	multidimensional
instrumentation	operational definition
measurement	instrument
indicator	levels of measurement
values	nominal measurement
observation	mutually exclusive

collectively exhaustive
ordinal measurement
interval measurement
working hypotheses
measurement theory
measurement error
systematic errors
random errors
validity
validation

pragmatic validation
predictive validity
construct validation
external validation
internal (convergent) validation
multiple indicators
discriminant validation
face validity
reliability

CHAPTER 5

WORKING FROM A PLAN: CONSIDERATIONS IN RESEARCH DESIGN

Just as experienced mountaineers would not climb Mount Everest without a great deal of planning designed to ensure that they had the right equipment, took the best route, and knew what to do if certain things went wrong, social scientists would not undertake a research project without carefully planning the steps that they would take. This plan of attack is referred to as a *research design*.

"A **research design** is the scheme that guides the process of collecting, analyzing, and interpreting data. It is a logical model of proof that allows the making of valid causal inferences."[1] Without an adequate and appropriate design for research, the best of measures will be useless, since their meaning cannot be determined. Before undertaking any serious study, you should write out a research design that not only tells exactly what you intend to do in the research process and how you intend to do it but also tells *why* you are taking each step and why you are taking it in the way that you are rather than in some other way.

Research Purpose and Research Design

Up to this point we have been discussing political science research as if it were all intended to test hypotheses through the process summarized in Figure 4.6. Though hypothesis-testing studies are generally recognized as the most crucial of social science undertakings, research can have a variety of purposes, and the research design that is most appropriate for any given project depends on the project's purpose.

Some research projects consist of **exploratory research.** They are intended only to provide greater familiarity with the phenomena we want to investigate so that we can formulate more precise research questions and perhaps develop hypotheses. Such studies can be essential when we are investigating new phenomena or old phenomena that have not been studied before. Some projects involve **descriptive**

---

[1] David Nachmias, *Public Policy Evaluation* (New York: St. Martin's Press, 1979), p. 21, emphasis added.

research. They are intended to provide an accurate representation of some phenomenon so that we can better formulate research questions and hypotheses. We may, for example, need to know the frequency, geographic distribution, and sequence of events of some phenomenon or need to know what other phenomena it tends to be associated with before we can begin to theorize about what might have caused it. Finally, research can be intended to test causal hypotheses. If we can use the results of a study to argue that one thing causes another, we can begin to develop explanations of the second event. For that reason, hypothesis-testing research may be described as **explanatory research.** Such research is appropriate when we have enough knowledge about a phenomenon to begin to seek explanations for it.

The significance of this rough typology of research purposes is that research of each type requires different things of a research design. Exploratory research requires flexibility more than precision, because its purpose is to discover possible explanations rather than to test hypothetical explanations. Exploratory research designs need provide only an opportunity to observe the phenomenon in question. Descriptive research, however, requires accurate measurement of phenomena. In descriptive studies, the research design must ensure unbiased and reliable observations if the studies are to produce accurate pictures of the events of interest. Explanatory research designs must both ensure unbiased and reliable observation and provide a basis for inferring the causal influence of one or more variables on others. A research design provides a basis for causal inferences when it allows us to rule out any plausible explanations for observed results that represent alternatives to the causal hypothesis being tested.

Regardless of the specific purpose of a study, its research design should include the following *basic elements:*

1. A statement of the purpose of the research
2. A statement of the hypothesis to be tested (if any)
3. A specification of the variables to be employed
4. A statement of how each variable is to be operationalized and measured
5. A detailed statement of how observations are to be organized and conducted
6. A general discussion of how the data collected will be analyzed

Chapters 2 and 4 provide the background you need to prepare sections 1 through 4 of a research design, and Chapters 12 to 16 present an introduction to data analysis. Chapters 5 and 6 are devoted to the organization of observations. It is this aspect of research design that provides a basis for ruling out alternative rival hypotheses and that most scholars have in mind when they refer to a research design.

Coping with Alternative Rival Hypotheses Through Research Design

We can demonstrate the impact of the way we structure or organize our observations on how useful the results of research are by considering a hypothetical research project. Imagine that the justice department in your state has implemented a new program designed to reduce juvenile delinquency. The program involves taking juvenile offenders, as well as potential offenders who volunteer or are volunteered by their parents, into prisons for one-day visits during which they get a glimpse of the horrors of prison life. The program is founded on the assumption that this will discourage them from committing crimes that might result in their being sent to prison. Let us say that after the program has been in operation for some months, the state government wants to know whether it is having the desired effect, and it hires you, a skilled political scientist, to evaluate its results. How will you go about this?

Because the program, known as Operation Fright, is intended to reduce juvenile delinquency, delinquency will be your dependent variable. You might operationalize it as *being arrested for a criminal offense* and then, one year after their prison visit, simply check on the criminal records of the youths who went through Operation Fright. If they have been arrested in this time, you label them delinquent. If they have not been arrested in this time, you label them nondelinquent.[2]

Let us say that you find that 70 percent of those who have been in the program have *not* been arrested during the year following. Can you then conclude that the program has been 70 percent effective in preventing delinquency? To do so with any confidence, you need to rule out other explanations of why 70 percent of these youths have not been arrested.

Your *operating hypothesis* is that the Operation Fright experience prevents delinquent behavior. Some possible alternative rival hypotheses that may explain your findings include the following:

1. No more than 30 percent of the youths would have been arrested, even if they had not gone through Operation Fright.

2. The family background of those who were volunteered for Operation Fright is different from that of those who were not, and it is that background that has prevented their delinquency, not the state program.

3. Many of the youths have committed crimes but have not been caught.

4. Though there may be temporary effects from Operation Fright, they will wear off and the youths will revert to criminal behavior. (The program delays delinquency rather than prevents it.)

5. The youths involved in the program have been arrested more often than they would have been had they not taken part in Operation Fright, because participation labels them as potential criminals and subjects them to greater police scrutiny. (The program causes more frequent arrests regardless of its effect on behavior.)

Alternative rival hypothesis 1 essentially asserts that the program has had no impact. With a single observation you cannot demonstrate that this is or is not true. You can never know how those who have gone through the program would have

---

[2] This operationalization of delinquency treats it as a dichotomous, nominal variable. In practice, you would probably want to use an operationalization that provided more information and was more sensitive to differences between individuals. You might, for example, want to develop a "delinquency index" that combined the number of arrests in a year with some measure of the severity of the crimes for which the subjects were arrested in order to have an indicator of the *degree* of delinquency. The simple operationalization proposed here, however, is adequate to illustrate the principles of research design and helps to prevent unnecessary complexity in the example.

acted if they had not taken part in Operation Fright, but you can include in your research design a check of the criminal records of a group of youths who have *not* gone through Operation Fright but who are otherwise similar in as many respects as possible to those who have. You can then compare the delinquency rate of those who have been in the program with that of those who have not and argue that any difference in the two rates can be attributed to the program, since we can assume that those in the program would have acted essentially the same way as their peers in the absence of Operation Fright. Observing the control group (those not participating in the program) allows us to assert a causal link between the program and delinquent behavior.

Rival hypothesis 2 is a claim that any apparent relationship between program participation and delinquent behavior is spurious. It holds that family background causes both program involvement and subsequent nondelinquency. This reasoning suggests there is a selection process in which those who have the family support to help them avoid criminal behavior are also the ones most likely to have gone through the program and that this creates an *apparent* relationship between Operation Fright and nondelinquency.

A single observation will not allow you to rule out this possibility, but having a control group including youths with family backgrounds similar to those who have gone through Operation Fright does, as in the case of rival hypothesis 1, allow you to determine whether this is the case. You can check to see both whether program participants and nonparticipants do in fact tend to have different family backgrounds, and whether those with similar family backgrounds tend to have the same delinquency rate regardless of participation in Operation Fright.

Ruling out rival hypothesis 2, like dealing with hypothesis 1, requires that you make a second observation (checking the criminal records of some youths not involved in the program). In addition, however, coping with hypothesis 2 requires that you make a third observation, in which you collect data on the subjects' family backgrounds. You may be able to obtain some objective indicators of this variable (for example, presence of both parents, parents' educational level and occupation, and family income) from public records, but you may also have to conduct interviews with family members or the youths themselves. If you operationalize family background to include attitudes and the character of personal interactions, such interviews will be necessary. You will therefore not only increase the amount of data you collect but also adopt another method of data collection—the personal interview.

Rival hypothesis 3 reinforces the need for this additional data collection method. It poses the possibility that Operation Fright has made its participants more cautious and perhaps even more clever criminals rather than reducing the number of crimes they commit. It questions the adequacy of the operationalization of the dependent variable. As long as official arrest records are your only measure of delinquency, you cannot have any confidence that this is not the case.

One way to cope with rival hypothesis 3 is to operationalize delinquency so as to include reports of criminal actions from the youths themselves and to conduct interviews both before and after they go through the program. You will have to interview both participants and nonparticipants and include information on family background for each group to be sure that your results cannot be explained by hypotheses such as 1 and 2 phrased in terms of this new indicator of delinquency. With this action you have added not only another **observation point** (the preprogram interview) but also another mode of operationalization for the dependent variable.

Rival hypothesis 4 adds a time dimension to the study. If you are to discount it, you will have to interview and check on the criminal records of both program participants and the control group not only one year after the prison visit but also two and perhaps three years after as well. The reason for making subsequent observations of program participants should be clear, since hypothesis 4 contends that participants will eventually become delinquent. You will also need to observe the control group in order to ensure that changes in delinquency rates for program participants in later years are not the result of other factors, such as maturation, changes in family situation, or worsening economic conditions. Only if program participants have a subsequent delinquency rate similar to (or worse than) the delinquency rate for nonparticipants *at the same time* can you conclude that the program has been ineffective (or that it has had a negative effect).

Unlike the others, rival hypothesis 5 argues that Operation Fright has been *more* effective than your results suggest. It raises the possibility that by using arrests as the measure of delinquency, you have introduced an additional independent variable (selective treatment from authorities) whose effects cover up the actual influence of Operation Fright on delinquent behavior.

One way to cope with this possibility is to include yet another operationalization of the dependent variable. If you look at *convictions* as well as arrests for both participants and nonparticipants, you will have some evidence of whether the cases brought against program participants are any less valid than those brought against youths who have never gone through Operation Fright, and you may infer from this whether or not the police are any more likely to arrest those who volunteered for Operation Fright. If participants are arrested without ultimately being indicted or convicted significantly more often than are nonparticipants, you will have reason to believe that rival hypothesis 5 is correct.

This brief examination of a few of the possible rival hypotheses that can challenge the value of your results has provided the basis for developing a much more elaborate research design than that first suggested. If you want to be able to rule out these five alternative interpretations (and you must do so if your study is to be of any value), you will have to move from a single operationalization of the dependent variable and a single observation to a research design involving multiple modes of operationalization, multiple methods of data collection, and several observation points. The new research design might involve the following major steps:

1. Select a sample of youths who have been designated to take part in Operation Fright and a sample of youths who have the same mix of characteristics relevant to delinquency (for example, sex; age; race; education; parents' occupation, education, and income; living situation; and place of residence) but who are not to go through the program.
2. Interview those subjects designated to go through the program before they take part in Operation Fright, and at the same time interview the control group to obtain self-reports of delinquent activity and information on family background.

3. Interview members of all subjects' families to obtain information on family background.

4. One year after the subjects have visited the prison, interview both participants and nonparticipants to obtain self-reports of delinquent activity and to find out whether family circumstances have changed.

5. At the time you perform step 4, check the arrest and conviction records of both program participants and nonparticipants.

6. Two years after the subjects have taken part in Operation Fright, repeat steps 4 and 5.

7. Three years after Operation Fright, repeat steps 4 and 5.

In analyzing the data, you will want to compare the arrest rates, the conviction rates, and the differences between arrest and conviction rates for the program participants and the control group, being careful to eliminate any members of the control group who have taken part in Operation Fright after their initial selection for the study. By employing appropriate statistical procedures in the analysis of the data produced by these observations, you should be able to reach highly defensible conclusions about the value of Operation Fright as a deterrent to juvenile delinquency. Because of your ability to rule out major rival hypotheses, the state's justice department may place a good deal of confidence in your conclusions—a confidence they could not have if those conclusions are based on the first research design.

The purpose of this exercise has not been to say that complex research designs are preferable to simple ones. Sometimes a simple design is far preferable. The important consideration is the *adequacy* of the design, not its complexity. If a research design provides a logical basis for the kinds of inferences the researcher wants to make, it is adequate.

The discussion of this hypothetical study provides an example of how adequate research designs are developed. In planning a research project, you will go through the same kind of reasoning that we have just laid out. *Research design is a process of formulating alternative rival hypotheses and reasoning through the kind of observations that are needed to test those hypotheses so that they can be ruled out as explanations for potential findings.*

Alternative rival hypotheses are arrived at in the same manner as operating hypotheses. They result from logical analysis of our theories and from thorough knowledge of the facts that surround the events we are trying to explain. A true alternative rival hypothesis predicts the *same relationship* as our main hypothesis but explains it in terms of a different causal process.

It is important not to confuse true alternative rival hypotheses with what we can call *other hypotheses*. Due to the existence of multiple causation in social phenomena, it is usually possible to come up with a variety of equally valid explanations of any given event. Identifying another cause of the observed relationship produces simply another hypothesis that may in no way be a rival to the original. A hypothesis is an alternative rival hypothesis only if it is logically impossible for both that hypothesis and the original hypothesis to be true at the same time.

Identifying crucial rival hypotheses is principally a creative activity. There are no hard-and-fast rules to ensure that you will identify all the rival hypotheses that can challenge the value of your research. The process of designing a research project will differ with each study. You cannot simply select an appropriate research design from a limited set of alternatives as you might choose a pair of shoes from those that are your size in a shoe store. There are, however, several general types of research designs, each of which is suited for dealing with particular types of problems. The next section provides an overview of the major types of research design and an introduction of the logic of research design.

Experimental Research Designs

The purpose of a sound research design is to allow us to identify the effects of one variable on another with as much confidence as possible. Research designs allow us to do this by providing an element of **control** over the conditions under which variables interact. This control is the key to research design.

Consider this example. If several animals on a farm contract a disease after a new kind of feed is added to their diet, the farmer cannot feel sure that the new feed is the cause of the illness, because the animals may have been exposed to a variety of new substances (for example, insecticides in their water supply) at the same time. On the other hand, if an unusually large proportion of the test animals in a medical research laboratory contract a disease after a new substance is added to their diet, the researcher is more likely to feel sure that the substance is the cause of the disease, because here it is possible to control the environment of the test animals and ensure that they are *not* exposed to any other new substances during the observations. The setting in which the researcher works permits an element of control, whereas the farm does not.

Research designs can be classified by the degree of control they allow. The basic distinction that is of interest to political scientists is that between *experimental* and *quasi-experimental designs*.

The *experiment* is the classic model of scientific proof. It is based on an assumption that changes in the value of one variable cause changes in the value of another variable (for example, *changes in temperature result in changes in the viscosity of oil*). The experiment allows us to test this assumption by exposing those cases or **subjects** manifesting the dependent variable to the independent variable under conditions that allow us to be relatively sure that any observed change in the dependent variable is a result of changes in the independent variable.

The basic **experimental design** involves an **experimental group** composed of subjects who will be exposed to the independent variable, or **stimulus**, and a **control group** of subjects, who are like the experimental group in all relevant respects but will not be exposed to the stimulus. The value of the dependent variable in each group is measured prior to introduction of the stimulus in what is called a **pretest**, and again after the experimental group has been exposed to the stimulus in what is called a **posttest**. The impact of the stimulus (independent variable) is inferred from a comparison of the pretest and posttest scores for each group. The greater the

Table 5.1
The classic experimental design

Group	Time 1	Time 2	Time 3	Effect Formula
Experimental	Pretest	Stimulus	Posttest	Effect (of experimental variable) = $(posttest_E - pretest_E) - (posttest_C - pretest_C)$ where E refers to the experimental group and C to the control group
Control	Pretest	—	Posttest	

difference in values between pretest and posttest in each group, the greater the effect attributed to the independent variable. Table 5.1 shows the logic of the experimental research design. The advantage of this research design is that it allows us to achieve two conditions that facilitate valid causal inferences: *comparison* and *manipulation*.

The assertion that one thing has caused another is based on the concept of change. We must be able to show that some change has occurred before we can claim that causal forces have been at work, and the idea of change implies comparisons. We must be able to compare values of the dependent variable before the subjects have been exposed to the independent or causal variable with values of the dependent variable after such exposure, and if possible we should compare values of the dependent variable after exposure with some indicator of what those values might be if exposure had never occurred. The experimental design, with its pretest-posttest procedure and its test and control groups, provides an opportunity for both types of comparison.

In order to feel confident that one variable has a causal influence on another, we must be able to know which subjects have been exposed to the independent variable and which have not so that we can make the appropriate comparisons. The classic experiment provides this knowledge because it is the researcher who introduces the independent variable. The scientist manipulates the subjects' environment so that their exposure to the causal influence is not left to chance. In addition, the researcher manipulates the subjects' environment to ensure that all other possible causes of a change in the dependent variable are removed from the experiment at the time of the subjects' exposure to the independent variable.

A variety of other research designs build on the logic of the classic experiment but add modifications that are especially relevant to social scientists. Social scientists' need for more elaborate research designs is largely due to the facts that (1) the objects of their research are often affected by the very act of studying them (for example, people's behavior may change if they know they are being watched) and (2) the objects of their research are not static but ever changing (for example, people's values may change as new situations arise). Two experimental designs developed by R. L. Solomon[3] illustrate ways of dealing with these facts.

---

[3] Richard L. Solomon, "Extension of Control Group Design," *Psychological Bulletin,* 46 (January 1949), pp. 137–50.

Table 5.2

The Solomon two-control-group research design

Group	Time 1	Time 2	Time 3	Effect Formula
Experimental	Pretest	Stimulus	Posttest	Effect = $[(\text{posttest}_E - \text{pretest}_E)$
Control 1	Pretest	—	Posttest	$- (\text{posttest}_{C1} - \text{pretest}_{C1})] -$ $(\text{posttest}_E - \text{posttest}_{C2})$
Control 2	—	Stimulus	Posttest	

The first design addresses an aspect of the problem of reactivity known as the **test effect.** When experimental subjects are pretested, it is always possible that their score on the posttest will be a result of both their reaction to the stimulus *and* a reaction to the pretest itself. Any difference between pretest and posttest scores that is due solely to reactions to the pretest is known as a test effect. If we are to get an accurate picture of the impact of the stimulus on behavior, we must be able to remove this test effect from the scores. The **Solomon two-control-group research design,** illustrated in Table 5.2, allows us to do this.

The design is just like the classic experiment except that a third group is added. The third group (Control 2) receives the stimulus and posttest, but no pretest. Though changes from pretest scores to posttest scores in the experimental group can be due to both the pretest and the stimulus, changes from pretest scores to posttest scores in Control 1 can be due only to the pretest and in Control 2 only to the stimulus. If we can assume that all groups have had essentially the same value on the dependent variable initially and have reacted to the stimulus in the same way, then the difference in the posttest scores of the experimental group and Control 2 represents the test effect. The effect of the independent variable (stimulus) alone can then be gauged by subtracting this test effect from the total effect of the experiment, which is computed by the same formula used to evaluate the results of the classic experimental design. The effect formula in Table 5.2 summarizes this logic algebraically.

The two-control-group design, then, allows us to assess and, we hope, rule out the test effect as an alternative explanation of observed changes in subjects' scores. There are, however, other possible causes of change in the groups' scores on the dependent variable (DV) from pretest to posttest. One is the influence of *external factors* not under the control of the experimenter. Another is natural changes in the subjects that proceed independently of the experiment (such as aging—in long-term experiments—or mental fatigue). The impact of such erroneous factors can be judged (and therefore ruled out as a rival explanation of the experiment's results) by use of the **Solomon three-control-group research design,** depicted in Table 5.3.

This design adds a third control group, which receives neither pretest nor stimulus. Any difference in pretest and posttest scores in this group can be due only to the influence of extraneous factors. If we can subtract this change from the effect of the experiment, we can remove from our results the effects of extraneous factors and changes in the respondents, and we can hope to rule out the alternative

Table 5.3
The Solomon three-control-group research design

Group	Time 1	Time 2	Time 3	Effect Formula
Experimental	Pretest	Stimulus	Posttest	Effect = $[(\text{posttest}_E - \text{pretest}_E)$
Control 1	Pretest	—	Posttest	$- (\text{posttest}_{C1} - \text{pretest}_{C1})] -$ $[(\text{posttest}_E - \text{posttest}_{C2}) +$ $(\text{postest}_{C3} - \text{pretest}_E)]$
Control 2	—	Stimulus	Posttest	
Control 3	—	—	Posttest	

hypothesis that it is these influences rather than the independent variable that have caused the change in the experimental group's score from time 1 to time 3.

The difficulty is that Control 3 is not pretested. How can we determine how much these subjects' scores have changed from time 1 to time 3? If all of our groups are essentially alike, we can assume that their pretest scores will have been highly similar and simply assign Control 3 a pretest score equal to the average of the scores for the experimental and first two control groups. We can then subtract this score from Control 3's posttest to obtain a measure of the change due to extraneous factors and natural changes in the subjects. With this change removed, we can see more clearly the effects of the independent variable on the dependent variable.

Assigning Cases to Groups

Each of the experimental designs just described is intended to provide a sound, logical basis for conclusions about the effects of one variable on another. To be successful in this, each design is crucially dependent on the assumption that all groups in the study are essentially the same with respect to those factors that might influence their response to the experiment. If we cannot assume that the groups are essentially the same, we have no logical basis for inferring that observed differences in their scores are the result of differences in the way they have been treated in the experiment (for example, whether or not they have been pretested), and we cannot make sound arguments about the causal influence of our independent variable.

How can we ensure that members of the various groups will be essentially the same? There are three approaches to assigning members to groups. The first is by way of **precision matching.** After deciding what characteristics might influence subjects' response to the independent variable, we select a set of subjects for the experiment. For each subject selected, we locate for the control group another subject who has exactly the same combination of relevant characteristics. The result is two groups that are identical in the characteristics that might influence their response to the experiment. Ideally, their pretest scores will be highly similar, and we can use the degree of similarity we actually find when we pretest them to judge how well our matching efforts have worked.

There are several problems with this procedure. First, if we need to control for a large number of characteristics, we may find it extremely difficult to find subjects who are matched in all the characteristics, as they must be in precision matching. We might, for instance, be able to find people of the same sex, age, and race but have difficulty finding people who share those characteristics *and* have the same occupation, educational background, and length of residence in the community. In addition, if we want to use a research design calling for more than two groups, we may find it most difficult to locate three or four subjects with identical characteristics. Unless we have an extremely large pool of potential subjects or a very simple experiment, matching may be impracticable as a means of assigning subjects to experimental groups.

A second method of obtaining similar groups is **frequency distribution control**. Here we do not match each subject with another on all characteristics. Rather, we assign subjects to groups in such a way as to ensure that the groups have the same average characteristics and the same distribution of each characteristic. There may be no two subjects with the same combination of sex, age, race, and occupation, but each group will have the same proportion of males and females, the same average age, and so on. Moreover, the groups will have highly similar distributions of these characteristics among their members.

Frequency distribution control is more often practicable than precision matching, but it has two significant defects. First, it allows us to control for only one variable at a time. Frequency distribution assignment may produce, for example, two groups with equal numbers of subjects over forty years of age and equal numbers of women, but there is no guarantee that all the over-forty subjects will not be men in one group and women in the other. If it works out this way, the two groups will not be truly similar. Second, the method offers no control over any factors that influence subjects' reactions but have not been identified by the researcher. If our theory of the phenomenon under study is incomplete (and it almost *always* is), we may have failed to control the frequency distribution of some important variable. If the control and experimental groups happen to differ systematically on this uncontrolled variable, our results may be distorted.

The third method of assigning subjects to groups is more flexible than precision matching and avoids both of the problems associated with frequency distribution control. It is **randomization**. A subject selected from a list of all eligible subjects is assigned to a group by some random process, such as use of a table of random numbers. True randomization is *not* achieved by chance procedures (such as taking the first thirty people who apply for the experiment as the test group and the next thirty as the control group).

Randomization has the great advantage of allowing us to feel quite confident that all of our groups are highly similar in *all* respects, not just in terms of the variables we identify as relevant to the experiment, because random assignment ensures that differences in subjects will cancel out *when large numbers of subjects are chosen*. Randomization, then, allows us to rule out any alternative rival hypothesis that contends that some systematic difference in the groups has produced the observed results. It is *the key to successful laboratory experiments*. In Chapter 6 we discuss detailed procedures for the random selection of cases.

Field Experiments and Nonexperimental Designs

Political scientists, because of the nature of their subject matter, seldom work in laboratories. Rather, they observe events in natural settings, where they can exercise less control over the factors that might influence the results of the study. In cases when researchers can manipulate the independent variable and control subjects' exposure but cannot control other aspects of the situation, they may conduct **field experiments.**

The various "negative income tax" experiments conducted in the United States provide an example of field experiments.[4] These studies were used to gauge the effects of automatic welfare payments in the form of a negative income tax on subjects' life style and work effort. The researchers could control which subjects received negative income tax payments, but they could not control other relevant aspects of the subjects' situations. They could not, for instance, guarantee their continued good health, their marital status, or the availability of jobs in the local economy. This arrangement made it more difficult to isolate the effects of the welfare payments from other possible causes of changes in subjects' behavior, but it had the distinct advantage of giving a realistic test of how the negative income tax would work in practice. A laboratory experiment, even if it could have been arranged, would not have been as satisfactory, because we cannot be sure that the results obtained in such an artificial environment accurately represent what happens in the outside world. This is a general advantage of field experiments over laboratory studies.

In field experiments, researchers use careful selection of the subjects and random assignment of subjects to the test and control groups to gain some control over background characteristics that may influence results. They also keep a close check on subjects' circumstances throughout the experiment to rule out alternative hypotheses that attribute observed results to outside events that occur during the experiment. (For example, any subjects who became disabled and could not hold a job were dropped from the negative income tax experiment so that their unemployment could not be interpreted as a response to the welfare payments.)

In many cases, political scientists cannot even manipulate the independent variable. You can imagine the difficulty of persuading some nations to have revolutions and others to postpone them in order to conduct a field experiment on the effects of revolutions on political development! The more important the subject under investigation, the less likely it is that we can control it. Under these circumstances, researchers must attempt to approximate an experimental design, as we describe in the next section, or they resort to the use of a nonexperimental design.

In **nonexperimental studies,** the scientists can control neither the assignment of subjects to experimental groups nor the occurrence of the independent variable, and they cannot obtain pretest scores on the dependent variable. They may be forced to use what is referred to as an *after-only* design, in which a single observation is made

---

[4] The details of some of these experiments are reported in Joseph A. Perchman and P. Michael Timpane, eds., *Work Incentives and Income Guarantees* (Washington, DC: Brookings Institution, 1975), and John L. Palmer and Joseph A. Perchman, eds., *Welfare in Rural Areas* (Washington, DC: Brookings Institution, 1978).

after the occurrence of the presumed causal event. Sometimes a "control group" of similar subjects not exposed to the independent variable (IV) can be added and differences in the scores of the two groups attributed to the IV. Such designs, however, provide no basis for sound inferences about the effect of the IV, since they do not allow us to rule out even the most simple of alternative hypotheses. We cannot, for instance, even be sure that the value of the DV we observe after exposure to the IV is any different from the value of the DV before that exposure. Nonexperimental designs are suited only for descriptive or exploratory research, not for explanatory studies.

Quasi-Experimental Designs

Most of the research schemes employed by political scientists can be classified as **quasi-experimental designs.** In these studies, researchers cannot control exposure to the independent variable or the conditions under which it occurs, but they attempt to simulate an experimental design either by gathering additional data or by data analysis techniques. Properly constructed quasi-experimental designs allow us to proceed *as if* we had exercised all the control characteristic of a true experiment, and they provide a sound, logical basis for causal inferences.

Perhaps the most common type of quasi-experimental design in political science is the **ex post facto experiment.** In it researchers make a single observation and collect data about the independent and dependent variables and any other variables they feel they should control for. If we want to investigate the effects of college education on voting behavior, for instance, we may conduct a survey of randomly selected subjects. Then we analyze our data in such a way as to determine whether people who are similar in other regards (for example, race, sex, age, and region of residence) but have different educational backgrounds vote differently. There are sophisticated statistical techniques for doing this, but at the simplest level we may sort out our respondents in contingency tables so that we can examine the relationship between education and voting in different categories of other variables, looking, for example, only at women who have and have not gone to college or only at men who have and have not gone to college.

This procedure allows us to act *as if* we had set up an experiment years ago in which we had assigned people to experimental groups, had exposed some to college education (the independent variable), and were now testing them to see what impact this had had on their voting.

The members of our sample who have had less than a college education but are similar in other respects to those in our sample who have had a college education serve as a "control group." Because we have not had a pretest, we cannot be sure that it is the college education that has created any observed differences in voting, but we can use the additional data we have gathered in the survey to rule out some plausible rival hypotheses, and we can rely on random selection of the sample to cancel out the effects of variables we cannot control for in data analysis.

There are some situations in which we cannot use random sampling and cannot select comparable control groups. We will find this to be the case if our units of

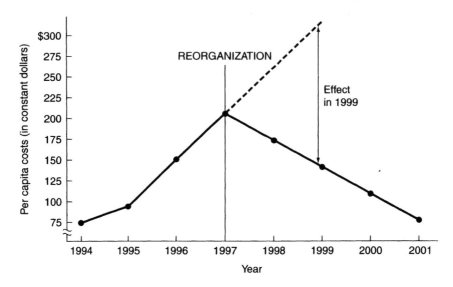

Figure 5.1
Hypothetical trend in public service costs showing that reorganization has reversed the original trend

analysis are few in number or unique in many relevant regards. An example is the situation in which a city government wants to know what effect an administrative reorganization has had on the costs of city services. To fulfill the request, political scientists might use another common research design known as a *time-series design.*

In **time-series designs,** the researcher makes several observations both before and after the introduction of some causal phenomenon and compares values on the dependent variable before and after. In our example, political scientists might use city records to compare the per capita costs of municipal services before and after the administrative reorganization. (They will have to use per capita costs and control for inflation in order to rule out the possibility that either an increasing city population or rising prices have affected the costs of public services independently of the impact of the reorganization.) Figures 5.1 through 5.3 illustrate some possible results of this study.

In a sense, time-series designs use as a control group the *same* subject or set of subjects but at an earlier time. If there is a clear trend in the values of the dependent variable prior to introduction of the independent variable, we assume that the trend would continue were it not for the independent variable, and as an indicator of the effect of the IV, we use the difference between observed values of the DV and the values that it would have if the trend were continuing.

Figure 5.1 illustrates this logic. If the data come out as presented in that figure, city officials will be delighted to learn that the reorganization not only has reduced the cost of services but also has reversed the trend toward steadily increasing costs. The effect of the reorganization in any given year can be measured *by the difference between the value predicted for that year from the original trend line and the observed value.*

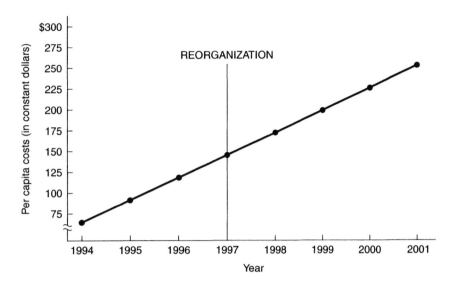

Figure 5.2
Hypothetical trend in public service costs showing no effect from reorganization

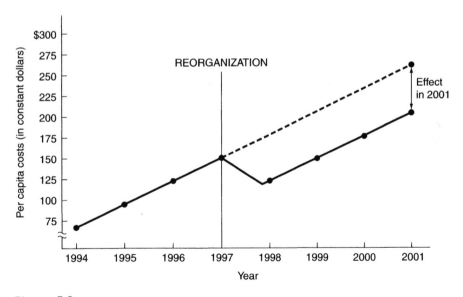

Figure 5.3
Hypothetical trend in public service costs showing that reorganization has changed the level of costs but has not interrupted the trend

If the data come out as in Figure 5.2, the predicted and observed values will be the same, and reorganization will be judged to have had no effect on costs. Figure 5.3 illustrates a case in which the reorganization has initially reduced costs but has had no effect on the trend.

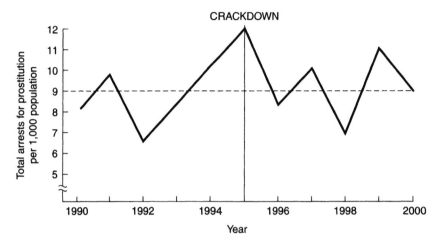

Figure 5.4
Hypothetical trend of arrests for prostitution showing no effect from the crackdown

In most instances, the trend we are dealing with is not as clear and steady as in this example. For instance, let us say that city police, alarmed by a rise in prostitution arrests, institute a crackdown on that crime and subsequently want to know how successful it has been. Figure 5.4 shows the kind of data that might be collected over a ten-year period. The values of the dependent variable (arrests for prostitution) rise and fall from year to year throughout the period. The researcher's task is to determine whether the *general* postcrackdown trend is significantly different from the general precrackdown trend. One way to do this is to compare the average annual arrests for prostitution prior to the crackdown with the average annual arrests in postcrackdown years. (Both are nine in this example.) If we assume that the original trend would continue without a crackdown, we can use any difference between the two averages as an indicator of the impact of the crackdown on the *level* of prostitution arrests. Another approach is to compare trend lines (represented by a dashed line in Figure 5.4) passed through the precrackdown and postcrackdown scattering of values for the DV to determine whether the general trend differs.

This example illustrates one of the important advantages of time-series designs. If we observe arrest rates only in 1994 and 1996, as in a typical before-after study, we may conclude that the police crackdown has reduced arrests for prostitution. The time-series data, however, allow us to see the 1994–1996 drop in arrests as *a normal fluctuation around a general trend* (represented by a dashed line), which remains unaffected by the police action.

Despite this strength, time-series designs have a weakness. In many instances, we have no control group and therefore cannot be sure what the effects of the IV are because we cannot be sure what the value of the DV would be without the IV; we can only guess that the original trend would continue. There are many reasons why this can be a mistake. One of the most important is *regression toward the*

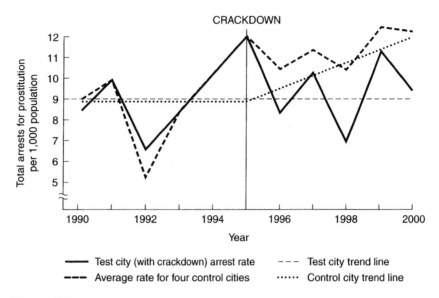

Figure 5.5
Hypothetical trend of arrests for prostitution in a test city and a group of control cities

mean. This is a phenomenon that poses a challenge to the validity of conclusions drawn from a variety of research designs.

Regression toward the mean is basically a process by which subjects who have extreme values on a dependent variable at any one time tend naturally to return to a more nearly average value on that variable in subsequent measurements *regardless of any exposure to some hypothesized independent variable.* If this regression toward the mean occurs at the time of a study, the researcher might mistake the natural regression for an effect of the IV. This can be a special problem in cases when subjects are exposed to the independent variable precisely because they have extraordinary values on the dependent variable.

In our last example, the police instituted a crackdown because of an exceptionally high number of arrests for prostitution. This was a deviation from what was normal for the city, and it might have corrected itself even if the police had done nothing.

One way to rule out regression toward the mean as an alternative explanation is to employ a *controlled time-series design.* In **controlled time-series designs,** we gather data on a case or set of cases that are as similar to our test case or group as possible in all relevant respects but are not exposed to the IV, and we use that case or group as a control in assessing the effects of the IV. In our example, we can select one or more cities very similar to the one conducting the crackdown that have not changed their policies toward prostitution and observe their arrest rates in the same years. Figure 5.5 shows some possible results.

By comparing the test (crackdown) city with a group of similar cities, we can see that while the pre-1995 trend in prostitution arrests continues unchanged in the test city, the average arrest rate rises dramatically in the control cities. This suggests that while the crackdown has failed to change the trend in the test city, it may be preventing it from being changed by the same events that are driving arrest rates up in other, similar cities. In this case, we use the difference between the test city's post-crackdown rates and those of the control cities in the same year as a measure of the effect of the IV, on the assumption that the test city would follow the trend of its companion cities were it not for the crackdown. In 2000, for example, the effect of the crackdown is assessed as three arrests per 1,000 population.

Adopting a stronger research design would prevent us, in this example, from reaching the apparently incorrect conclusion that a program that actually served as an effective deterrent had no impact.

Creating a Research Design

There are a number of both experimental and quasi-experimental designs that we have not discussed here.[5] The number of variations on these basic designs is limited only by human ingenuity, and the research design for any study will reflect its particular purpose. We do not *choose* a research design so much as we create one suited to the particular study at hand, though we generally build on one of the basic design types. The three principal considerations that guide researchers in developing research designs are the need for validity, the availability of resources, and professional ethics.

The purpose of research design in explanatory studies is to allow us to draw valid inferences about the causal relationships between variables from observed changes in our measures of those variables. Consequently, ensuring the validity of our results ought to be a central consideration in devising a research design. There are two primary types of validity associated with empirical research: internal and external.

Internal validity pertains to the degree to which the design provides a *sound, logical basis* for inferring that the independent variable does or does not cause a given change in the dependent variable. To ask about internal validity is to ask whether there is anything about the research design that will lead us to attribute a causal influence to the IV when it does not have such influence, or to fail to recognize any causal influence the IV does have. For example, if there is a strong test effect associated with the use of some particular measure, any research design that does not provide a way to control for the test effect will lack internal validity because it can lead us to misinterpret changes due to the test effect as evidence of the independent variable's causal impact.

External validity pertains to the *generalizability of our results.* Can we reasonably expect to find the same causal influences at work in other settings? Does this study tell us anything about the part of reality *not* included in it? A field experiment on the effects on the public's driving habits of adding a dollar-a-gallon surcharge to the price of gasoline, for example, has little external validity if it is conducted in a

---

[5] Some of these are described in Delbert C. Miller, *Handbook of Research Design and Social Measurement*, 5th ed. (Newbury Park, CA: Sage, 1991).

community where the average family's annual income is above $100,000, because we cannot expect middle- and low-income people to behave in the same way as these upper-class people would.

Factors That Threaten Validity

The major categories of threats to both internal and external validity include the following:[6]

Factors That Threaten Internal Validity

1. *History:* Events other than the IV that can alter posttest scores and that occur between the pretest and posttest. For example, a well-publicized statement by a political leader can alter subjects' attitudes independently of some long-term experimental treatment they are undergoing.

2. *Maturation:* Natural changes in the subjects that alter scores on the DV over time independently of the IV (for example, human fatigue, population growth in geographically defined units of analysis, aging of physical facilities).

3. *Instability:* Random changes in recorded values due to unreliable measures, inconsistent sampling of subjects, or other causes.

4. *Testing* The test effect described in this chapter.

5. *Instrumentation:* Differences in the measuring devices used that produce differences in scores independently of the effects of the IV (for example, different biases among interviewers, an improperly calibrated machine, or inconsistent precision among coders).

6. *Regression artifacts:* Changes due to regression toward the mean, discussed in this chapter.

7. *Selection:* Differences in scores resulting from differential recruitment of test and control groups (for example, when members of a test group are forced by law to be exposed to the IV, whereas members of one of the control groups volunteer to be exposed).

8. *Experimental mortality:* Different rates of loss of subjects from test and control groups. (For example, those cases that can make the control group as a whole respond to the IV in the same way as the test group may drop out of the experiment before posttest.)

9. *Selection-maturation interaction:* Biases in selection processes that lead to different rates of maturation in test and control groups. (For example, in the Operation Fright study, test subjects may be older because they have been volunteered for the program only after a series of juvenile arrests, and they may thus outgrow juvenile delinquency faster than the younger control group.)

---

[6] Adapted from Donald T. Campbell, "Reforms as Experiments," *American Psychologist,* 24 (April 1969), pp. 407–29.

Factors That Threaten External Validity

1. *Interaction effects of testing:* Posttest scores of the pretested subjects may be rendered unrepresentative of the unpretested population because of the way in which the pretest has sensitized the subjects to the IV.

2. *Interaction of selection and experimental treatment:* Biased selection processes may produce a test group that responds to the IV in ways atypical of the larger population.

3. *Reactive effects of experimental arrangements:* Conditions of the experimental setting may be unrepresentative of real-world conditions.

4. *Multiple-treatment interference:* The simultaneous application of more than one treatment may create changes that are different from what would occur if any one treatment or IV were used alone.

5. *Irrelevant responsiveness of measures:* All measures pick up multiple aspects of the environment, and some may include irrelevant components that give the appearance of change when none has occurred or that obscure actual changes.

6. *Irrelevant replicability of treatments:* When IVs are complex events (as are the visit to the prison in the Operation Fright example and college education), researchers may not be aware of what aspect of them causes the change in subjects, and they may fail to include the relevant aspect of the IV in all experimental exposures to it.

Ideally, research should employ a design that avoids as many of these threats to validity as possible. Even a perfect design, however, is useless unless we have the resources necessary to execute it. The availability of time, money, skilled personnel, facilities, and necessary data sources will always constrain the choice of research design. If researchers are not confident that the major threats to validity likely to apply to their particular study can be controlled by a design that is practical given the existing resource constraints, they should consider abandoning the project until adequate resources are available. *No research is preferable to bad research that can lead to inaccurate conclusions.*

A final, and overarching, consideration in research design is whether executing a given design will require a breach of professional ethics. Will anyone be harmed in any sense? If so, how severely? Do the benefits to society outweigh those costs? These are questions each professional must answer according to his or her values and the prevailing standards of the profession. Chapter 18 presents some examples of the types of ethical questions political scientists are likely to confront in planning a study, and Appendix B presents the recommended standards of research ethics endorsed by the leading professional associations in political science and sociology. The only general guide that we can offer for making these choices is to restate our view that science is a tool to be used in the service of humanity; it is not an end in itself.

Suggestions for Further Reading

A general introduction to social science research that contains useful discussions of research design is Earl Babbie, *The Practice of Social Research,* 9th ed. (Belmont, CA: Wadsworth,

2001). One text devoted entirely to research design issues and still widely used is Thomas D. Cook and Donald T. Campbell, *Quasi-experimentation* (Chicago: Rand McNally, 1979).

One of the most complete introductions to research design is found in William M. Trochin, *The Research Methods Knowledge Base* (Cincinnati: Atomic Dog Publishing, 1999). Excellent examples of the use of experimental designs in political science can be found in Donald R. Kinder and Thomas R. Palfrey, *Experimental Foundations of Political Science* (Ann Arbor: University of Michigan Press, 1993).

Research Exercises

1. Refer to the example of Operation Fright, used early in the chapter, and state one additional plausible alternative explanation of why so few of those going through the program are subsequently arrested. Explain in detail what modifications of the original research design described in that example would be needed to evaluate the accuracy of this hypothesized explanation.

2. You are studying the relationship between inequality in the distribution of wealth and internal political violence in the nations of the world. You have operationalized inequality as the difference in the proportion of national income that goes to the top 20 percent of income earners and the proportion that goes to the bottom 20 percent of income earners. Political violence is operationalized as the number of incidents of politically motivated violence reported by the domestic press each year in each nation. Your operating hypothesis is, *The greater the inequality in the distribution of income, the larger the number of incidents of political violence.*

   List at least three hypotheses that represent rivals to this operating hypothesis. For each alternative you suggest, list each variable you will have to control in order to be able to rule it out as a valid explanation of observed events.

3. You want to evaluate the effects of a film about race relations on the levels of racial prejudice held by the film's viewers. Assume that you can select subjects from a pool of 300 college students who have volunteered to take part in scientific experiments. Describe the research design you would use to determine the film's effects on racial prejudice if you wanted to maximize your confidence in the validity of your results.

4. Select a subject for research on which you can obtain data from several points in time (from government records or public opinion polls, for example). Select some event that may have had an impact on the phenomenon in question, and describe how you would organize a time-series or controlled time-series research design to assess that impact as accurately as possible. (For example, you might want to evaluate that impact of the impeachment of President Bill Clinton on the level of trust in government reported in public opinion polls taken before, during, and after the event.) Explain how you would establish a Logical basis for inferring that the event you select as your independent variable has caused any change you might observe in the dependent variable.

Terms Introduced in This Chapter

research design	experimental group
exploratory research	stimulas
descriptive research	control group
explanatory research	pretest
observation point	posttest
control	test effect
subjects	ex post facto experiment
experimental design	time-series designs

Solomon two-control-group research design
Solomon three-control-group research design
precision matching
frequency distribution control
randomization
field experiments

nonexperimental designs
quasi-experimental designs
regression toward the mean
controlled time-series designs
internal validity
external validity

CHAPTER 6

WHO, WHAT, WHERE, WHEN: THE PROBLEM OF SAMPLING

Once every ten years, the Bureau of Census, a part of the U.S. Department of Commerce, conducts a census in an attempt to identify, count, and measure certain characteristics of every individual living in the country at a given time. In the 2000 census, it is estimated that the federal government employed 970,000 clerks, interviewers, and others over a period of five months to obtain the information. In all, approximately 283,000,000 residents of the United States were located and studied. Over the ten-year cycle, the total cost of the 2000 count was approximately $6.5 billion.

Needless to say, few political scientists are able to marshal such vast resources in pursuing their own research interests. Yet the objects of those interests (the cases to be studied) may be, for all practical purposes, equally numerous: 100,000,000 voters, 500,000,000 residents of Western democracies, 100,000 documents—each might be the focus of political science research, yet each consists of far too many individual cases to permit a comprehensive analysis. Even the Bureau of Census, with all its thousands of workers and millions of dollars, found it impossible to ask every one of its questions of each person it located. Instead, it developed a short questionnaire for most people and a longer one for a *select few*. Like political scientists and many other researchers, the bureau found it necessary to employ a *sample*.

In this chapter, we examine the uses and the mechanics of sampling—of choosing a relatively small number of cases the study of which may tell us much about the larger population from which they have been selected. In doing so, we are concerned with **generalizability**—the ability to draw general conclusions based on an analysis of only a few cases. To this end, we must ask ourselves three questions. First, just what constitutes a *representative* sample? Second, how might one select the particular cases that would constitute such a sample? And third, how many cases must we select before a sample may be said to be representative? We consider each of these in turn.

Defining a Representative Sample

We begin, in effect, not with one question but with three: What is a sample? When is it representative? What does it represent?

A **population** is any group of people, organizations, objects, or events about which we want to draw conclusions; a *case* is any member of such a population.[1] A **sample** is any *subgroup* of a population of cases that is identified for analysis. If we want to study and reach conclusions about the decision-making behavior of state legislatures, for instance, we might do so by examining such behavior in the legislatures of Idaho, Wyoming, and Montana rather than in those of all fifty states, and from these we might *generalize* our findings to the larger population from which the three have been selected. If we wish to study the issue preferences of voters in, say, Pennsylvania, we might do so by asking questions of fifty millworkers in Pittsburgh and might generalize these results to all voters in the state. And similarly, if we wish to measure the intelligence of college students, we might test all defensive linemen enrolled at Ohio State University during a given football season and then generalize our findings to all U.S. college students. In each instance, our procedure is to identify a subgroup of a larger population; to study that subgroup, or sample, in some detail; and to generalize our results to the population as a whole. These are the basic steps involved in sampling.

It should be quite obvious, however, that each of these samples has a fundamental weakness. Although the legislatures of Idaho, Wyoming, and Montana are, for example, indeed part of the population of state legislatures, they are, for reasons of history, region, and political culture, quite likely to operate in a manner very similar to one another and very different from the legislatures of such diverse states as New York, Nebraska, and Texas. Although the fifty millworkers in Pittsburgh may indeed be Pennsylvania voters, they are, for reasons of socioeconomic status, education, and life experience, quite likely to have different views from those of many other such voters. And in like manner, although Ohio State's football players are indeed college students, they are, for a variety of reasons, likely to be different from other college students. In other words, even though each of these subgroups is, in fact, a sample, the members of each are systematically different from most other members of the population from which they are drawn. As a group, none of these is typical of the distribution of attributes (opinions, behaviors, characteristics) in the larger population with which it is associated. Accordingly, political scientists would say that none of these samples is *representative*.

A **representative sample** is one in which every major attribute of the larger population from which the sample is drawn is present in roughly the proportion or frequency with which those attributes occur in that larger population. Thus, if 50 per-

---

[1] We should emphasize here that populations may consist not only of people but of *anything* we wish to study. Thus we may speak of a population of governments, of decisions, or of court documents as readily as of a population of unemployed males living in Massachusetts. *Whenever* we refer to a population of any kind, however, *all identifying characteristics of that population must be stated, and all members of that population must share them.*

We should also note that the term *universe* is frequently used in political science research to refer to a population. Thus we might speak of a universe of governments in much the same way as we would of a population of governments. Either term is correct, and the two are interchangeable.

cent of all state legislatures meet only once every two years, roughly half the bodies in a representative sample of state legislatures should be of this variety. If 30 percent of the voters in Pennsylvania are blue-collar workers, then about 30 percent of a representative sample of those voters (as opposed to 100 percent in the previous example) should be blue-collar workers. And if 2 percent of all college students are athletes, roughly the same proportion of a representative sample of college students should be athletes.

In other words, a truly representative sample is a microcosm—a smaller, but accurate, model—of the larger population from which it is taken. To the extent that a sample is truly representative, conclusions based on a study of that sample may be safely regarded as applying to the original population. This extension of findings is what we mean by *generalizability.*

Perhaps a graphic illustration will help to make this clear. Suppose we want to study patterns of membership in political groups among adults in the United States. Figure 6.1 shows three circles, each of which has been divided into six equal segments. Figure 6.l(a) represents the population in question. Members of the population have been classified according to the number of political groups (such as parties and interest groups) they belong to. In the example, every adult is assumed to belong to at least one and not more than six groups, and these six levels of membership are equally distributed throughout the population (hence the equal segments). Suppose that we wish to study people's motivations for membership, choices of groups, and patterns of participation, but because of limited resources, we are able to examine only one of every six members of the population. Which individuals should we select for analysis?

The shaded area in Figure 6.l(b) illustrates one possible sample of the size we have specified, but one that is clearly atypical of the population. Were we to generalize from such a sample, we would conclude (1) that all American adults belong to five political groups and (2) that all group-related behavior of Americans is like that of those who belong to precisely five groups. Yet we know that the first conclusion is not accurate, and we may hold suspect the validity of the second as well. The sample illustrated in Figure 6.l(b), then, is not representative, because it does not reflect the distribution of this *population attribute* (often called a **parameter**) roughly in proportion to its actual incidence. Such a sample is said to be *biased toward* members

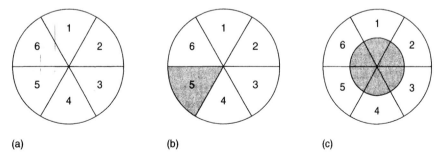

(a)   (b)   (c)

Figure 6.1
Sampling from a population with six population types

of five groups or *biased against* all other patterns of group membership. Reliance upon such a biased sample will usually lead us to draw erroneous conclusions about the larger population.

Never was this more clearly illustrated than in a public opinion polling disaster that befell a magazine called the *Literary Digest* in the 1930s. The *Literary Digest* was a periodical compilation of newspaper editorials and other opinion pieces that enjoyed a wide readership in the early years of this century. Beginning in 1920, the magazine conducted a large-scale, nationwide straw poll in which postcard ballots were sent to more than a million persons asking them to state their candidate preference in the coming presidential election. During a succession of previous election years, the *Digest* poll had proved so accurate that its release in October seemed to make the actual election in November anticlimactic. With so large a sample, how could the poll miss? Yet in 1936, it did just that in predicting a 60–40 landslide victory for Republican candidate Alf Landon. In the election, however, Landon lost to incumbent Franklin D. Roosevelt by almost precisely the margin by which he was expected to win. So great was the shock to the credibility of the *Literary Digest* that the magazine was forced to cease publication shortly afterward.

What went wrong? Quite simply, the *Digest* poll had used a biased sample. The postcards had been issued to persons whose names were drawn from two sources: telephone directories and automobile registration lists. And whereas this method of selection hadn't made much difference earlier, it did in the depression year of 1936, when less affluent voters—those most likely to support Roosevelt—could not afford telephones, let alone automobiles. In effect, then, the sample used by the *Digest* poll was biased toward those most likely to be Republicans.

How can we avoid this problem? Returning to our illustration, compare the sample in Figure 6.l(b) with that in Figure 6.l(c). In the latter, one-sixth of the population is again selected for analysis, but each of the major population types is present in the sample in the same proportion in which it is present in the entire population. Such a sample tells us that one in six American adults belongs to one political group, one in six to two, and so forth. It will also permit us to recognize other differences among members of our sample that might correspond with their varying numbers of affiliations. The sample illustrated in Figure 6.l(c), then, is a representative sample of the population in question.

This example is, of course, simplified in at least two very important ways. First, most of the populations political scientists wish to study are more diverse than that in the illustration. People, documents, governments, organizations, decisions, and the like differ from one another on many more than just one attribute. Thus a representative sample must be one that provides for *each* of the principal areas of difference to be represented in proportion to its share of the population. Second, more often than not the true distribution of the variables or attributes we wish to measure is not known in advance; it may not have been measured previously by a census of the population. Thus a representative sample must be drawn in such a way that we have confidence in its ability to reflect accurately this distribution even under circumstances when we cannot directly assess its validity. A sampling procedure must have an internal logic that assures us that if we *were* able to check the sample against a census, the sample would prove to be representative.

In order to provide both the capability to reflect accurately the complexities of a given population and some measure of confidence in their procedures for doing so, researchers draw upon certain techniques developed by statisticians. They do so in two ways. First, they follow certain rules (an internal logic) in deciding which specific cases to study, meaning, which to include in a particular sample. Second, they follow still other rules in deciding how many such cases to select. Though we do not examine these various rules in detail here, we do consider their practical implications for political science research. Let us begin by looking at strategies for selecting the cases that make up a representative sample.

Procedures for Selecting a Representative Sample

As we can see from the examples in the preceding section, not all samples are equally representative. Indeed, the *Literary Digest* fiasco, although one of the most famous, is hardly the only example of a study that relied on a badly biased sample. Straw polls, in which individuals select themselves as participants and may vote for a favored position or candidate more than once; street corner interviews, in which selection of location and lack of control over passersby may strongly influence the findings; legislators' questionnaires, the results of which depend heavily on the views of the more articulate and more politically interested few who are most likely to respond; analysis of the foreign press, of propaganda messages, or of some variety of published materials that is restricted to sources available in English, which may be systematically different from other sources of the same type; and blind sampling, in which a researcher simply leaves a stack of questionnaires at a given location with instructions for their completion and surrenders all control over the selection of respondents all provide common examples of sampling bias. In part, these difficulties may be resolved by a careful (and very strictly limited) definition of the population to which we intend to generalize. In the case of street corner interviews, for instance, we might want to generalize only to all persons passing a particular location between 10 A.M. and 11:15 A.M. On March 4. But in far larger measure, these difficulties may be resolved only by developing a systematic and relatively more sophisticated procedure for selecting the cases to be analyzed.

The guiding principle underlying such a procedure is that of *randomization*. A sample is said to be a **random sample** (sometimes referred to as *simple random* or *pure random sample*) if two conditions are met. First, the sample must be chosen in such a manner that each and every individual or case in the entire population has an equal opportunity to be selected for analysis. Second, the sample must be chosen in such a manner that each and every possible combination of n cases, where n is simply the number of cases in the sample, has an equal opportunity to be selected for analysis.

It sounds a bit complicated and is in fact a more rigorous definition of randomness than we use in everyday conversation, but it is at heart a rather simple and straightforward notion. Random selection amounts to little more than selection by lottery. If we have a population of 1,000 persons whose behavior we wish to examine by studying a representative sample of 100, we might write the names of all

10097	32533	76520
37542	04805	64894
08422	68953	19645
99019	02529	09376
12807	99970	80157

Figure 6.2
Portion of a random number table

1,000 members of the population on equal-sized pieces of paper, place them in a hopper, mix them well, and draw the names of the 100 persons in our sample. Through such a procedure, each individual has an equal chance of being selected (100 chances in 1,000, or 1 chance in 10), and every possible combination of 100 individuals has an equal chance of selection as well. It is this dual equality that makes the sample a random one.

Often, simple random samples are employed in studying populations that are too large to permit such a physical lottery procedure. Writing out the names of several hundred thousand cases, entering them in a hopper, and drawing out several thousand, after all, would be a very cumbersome process. In these instances, an alternative, but equally valid, approach is employed. Each case in the population is assigned a number. The numbers of the particular cases to be included in the sample are then identified using a *random number table*, such as Table A.1 in Appendix A, a portion of which is reproduced in Figure 6.2. The arrangement of numbers in such tables is usually created by a computer program called a *random number generator*, which, in effect, places a great many numbers in a hopper, draws them randomly, and prints them in the order in which they were drawn. In other words, the lottery process still takes place, but the computer, using numbers rather than names, conducts an all-purpose drawing. We are able to make use of this drawing simply by numbering each of our cases.

A random number table such as that illustrated in Figure 6.2 may be used in several different ways, each of which involves the combination of three decisions. First, we must decide how many digits we shall use; second, we must develop a decision rule for using them; and third, we must select a starting point and a system for proceeding through the table.

The first decision is simply a function of the number of cases in our population. If the population consists of fewer than 10 cases, we use single digits; 10 to 99 cases, double digits; 100 to 999 cases, three-digit combinations; and so forth. In each instance, we must take care to allow each of our numbered cases a chance to be selected.

Once this has been accomplished, we must devise a rule to relate the numbers in the table to the numbers of our cases. Two choices are available here. The easiest and most straightforward approach, though not necessarily the most correct, is to use only those numbers that fall within the range of our number of cases. Thus if we have a population of 250 (and are therefore using three digit numbers) and choose to begin at the top left of the table and work down each column, we will include in our sample those cases numbered, say, 100, 084, and 128, and we will ignore cases numbered, say, 375 and 990, neither of which corresponds to any of our cases. We will continue this procedure until we have identified the number of cases needed for our sample.

A more cumbersome, but technically more correct, procedure arises from the argument that *every* number of a given magnitude (for example, every three-digit number) in the table must be used to preserve the underlying randomness of the table. Following this logic, and again assuming a population of 250, we must break the range of three-digit numbers from 000 to 999 into 250 equal parts. Because there are 1,000 such numbers, we divide 1,000 by 250 and find that each equal part comprises four numbers. Thus table entries 000 to 003 correspond to case 1, 004 to 007 to case 2, and so forth. In order to identify the case number that corresponds to an entry in the table, then, we divide a three-digit table entry by 4 and round to the lower integer. When we use this method, the same portion of the table that we used earlier leads us to include in our sample cases 025 (100 ÷ 4), 093 (375 ÷ 4, rounded down), 021 (084 ÷ 4), 247 (990 ÷ 4, rounded down), and 032 (128 ÷ 4) and to ignore none of the entries in the table.

Finally, we must select a point of entry into the table and a system of use. The point of entry might be the upper left-hand corner (as in the previous example), the lower right-hand corner, the left end of the second row, or *any* other location. This decision is strictly arbitrary. Once in the table, however, we must proceed systematically. We might select the first three digits of each five-digit set, as in the previous examples; the middle three digits; the last three digits; or even the first, second, and fourth digits. (In the first five-digit set, these various procedures yield, respectively, the numbers 100, 009, 097, and 109.) We might work these procedures backward getting 790, 900, 001, and 791. We might work across rows, taking each digit in turn and ignoring the groupings of five (getting 100, 973, 253, 376, and 520 for the first row). We might work only with every third group of digits (for example, with 10097, 99019, 04805, and 99970). The possibilities are many and varied, and each is equally appropriate. Once we have decided upon a pattern of use, however, we must follow it systematically so as to maximize the randomness of the entries in the table.

Variations on Random Sampling

As you can see from even this brief discussion, the drawing of a simple random sample may be no simple matter. In addition to other problems, which we will discuss, the technique involves a great deal of clerical work, especially when it is employed on a large scale. For this reason, random sampling procedures are often modified to enhance their manageability. One common variation is called the **systematic random sample** and is used when we wish to study a relatively large population whose members are individually listed in some central location, such as a telephone book, a student directory, a list of registered voters, an index or a table of contents, an agenda, or a membership roster. The procedure is as follows.

Count (or estimate) the number of cases in the population, and divide this by the desired number of cases in the sample (we discuss sample size later in this chapter). If we label the result *k*, we are saying, in effect, that we wish to select one case out of every *k*, or to put it another way, we wish to select every *k*th case. A concrete example should help to make this clear.

Suppose that from a population of 10,000 public statements issued by the Department of Defense we wish to draw a sample of 500, and suppose further that we have at our fingertips a chronological listing that includes all 10,000 documents. To select a systematic random sample:

1. We divide the number of cases in the population by the desired sample size to determine k (in this case, $k = 10,000 \div 500 = 20$).
2. With the assistance of a random number table, we select a case number in the range 1 to k (in the example, 1 to 20) to be included in our sample.
3. We proceed through the listing of documents, selecting every kth (20th) case.

Thus if k is equal to 20 and we use the portion of the random number table illustrated in Figure 6.2, entering at the top left, seeking two-digit numbers (k here lies between 10 and 99), and using only table entries that correspond to actual case numbers (that is, only those in the range from 01 to 20), the first case selected will be 10. We then include in our sample cases 10, 30 ($10 + k$), 50 ($10 + 2k$), 70 ($10 + 3k$), and so forth, all the way up to case 9,990 ($10 + 499k$). This upper limit of the sample may be stated generally as $j + (n - 1)k$, where j is the randomly drawn first selection and n is the desired sample size. In this way, we can use the random number table in combination with a centralized list to select a sample of 500 documents for analysis.

The technique of systematic random sampling has one major advantage over simple random sampling—ease of application to large populations that meet the criterion of central listing—and it has many potential uses. Still, we must keep in mind one important caution whenever we choose this type of procedure, for systematic random sampling is less random than is a straight lottery selection, and it may therefore yield a less representative subgroup. We can see this at both the definitional and operational levels.

To begin with, recall that a random sample is one that permits every individual case *and* every possible combination of n cases an equal opportunity of selection. Systematic random sampling meets only one of these criteria. Because we begin to draw such a sample by using a random number table to select the first case, any case in the population has an equal chance of ultimately being included in the sample (though not necessarily on the first draw, because this is limited to the range 1 to k). However, because we then select only additional cases that are k numbers apart from one another, not every possible combination is allowed.

Thus in the example where $k = 20$, we may select any case from 1 to 20 to begin with, but once we select case 10, it becomes impossible for us to include, say, cases 9, 14, 237, and 5,724, simply because those cases do not differ from 10 by a multiple of k. A systematic random sample is at best, then, only an approximation of a truly random sample.

This observation becomes especially important when the list from which we are sampling contains a *systematic bias*. In alphabetical or chronological lists, this is generally not a problem, but in other kinds of lists it may be a significant one. Let us say, for example, that as part of a study of political socialization, we wish to measure the intelligence level of a sample of students at a particular school where every class consists of 20 children. The school contains 100 classes, or 2,000 students in all. In response to our request, the principal of the school provides us with a roster of all students in the school, from which we hope to draw a systematic random sample of 100. However, rather than an alphabetical listing, the roster consists of a compilation of individual class rolls listed one after another. Moreover, each class roll is arranged not alphabetically but in order of the students' class standing, with the best students listed first and the lists continuing in order of decreasing accomplishment. In such a circumstance, if we take every 20th (2,000 ÷ 100) case beginning from a randomly drawn case 1, we will have a sample of only the 100 best (and, possibly, most intelligent) students in the school. If we randomly select case 10, we will sample only the middle range of students. And if we begin from case 20, we will sample only the worst students in the school.

In other words, an underlying bias in the list upon which our sample is based will lead to the selection of an unrepresentative sample. Ultimately, this will either preclude our generalizing to the larger population or, if the problem escapes our notice, will result in our drawing potentially incorrect conclusions. Although this particular example is an extreme one developed for the purpose of illustration, similarly biased lists do exist, and the researcher who employs systematic random sampling procedures must be aware of the potential danger.

Simple random samples, then, are an ideal to which we aspire, and systematic random samples are approximations of that ideal that are often quite useful. Very often, however, a research situation does not readily lend itself to either technique. This is particularly true in the case of survey research. For one thing, centralized lists of the population to be studied are frequently nonexistent (for example, there exists no list of all U.S. voters or of all residents of a particular city), and even the number—not to mention the identity—of all the cases may not be known in advance. Thus, one of the major preconditions for simple or systematic random sampling—the existence of individual cases that can be identified in advance—may not be met. Moreover, even when this problem can be overcome, logistical difficulties and limited resources may render either of these sampling techniques impractical. This is true because random selection of individual cases requires that *specific individuals,* who may live great distances from one another or who may be very difficult to contact, *must be included in the sample.* In a strictly random process, no substitutions are permissible. These considerations can lead to massive diseconomies of time and money that might even be so great as to preclude conducting the study at all.

Fortunately, an alternative technique has been developed that preserves the quality of randomness we desire but overcomes most of the objections we have just noted. This technique, termed either **cluster sampling** or **multistage random area sampling**, has found wide application in survey research and may, by analogy, be applied elsewhere as well. The idea behind multistage random area sampling, to use the more descriptive label, is that rather than identifying members of a sample as individuals, we identify them as residents of particular housing units. The reasoning here is that people move from place to place, whereas housing units remain fixed. In addition, the location of virtually every housing unit in the country is known and has been mapped, and each is part of a variety of geographically distinct areas including, among others, blocks, census tracts, precincts, legislative districts, cities, townships, counties, congressional districts, and states.

We shall see that certain of these area types have characteristics that aid greatly in drawing a representative sample. For the moment, however, the point is that by focusing on the resident of a housing unit, a unit that is always in the same place, rather than on a particular individual, who may be more mobile, we are able to stabilize and localize our sampling procedure. In effect, we are simply redefining our population. Rather than speaking (as we might in a nationwide study) of all persons living in the United States, we speak of all residents of housing units in the United States. Because both groups are, for all practical purposes, the same, however, we may sample the latter and generalize to the former. We avail ourselves of the much simpler and, for reasons to be discussed later, much less expensive technique of sampling locations, yet we are able to generalize not to places, but to the people who inhabit them. This is the principal value of multistage random area sampling.

The procedure itself is illustrated in Figure 6.3, which is based on practices employed by the Survey Research Center (SRC) at the University of Michigan, the nation's major agency for conducting survey research in political science. For purposes of illustration, let us assume that we wish to conduct a nationwide sample survey. The same procedures that we set forth here may, of course, be modified for use on smaller-scale projects.

We begin with a map of the United States, which we divide into a large number of equally populated areas.[2] It is less work than it sounds like, because the government has already made this division (or at least approximated it) in the form of 435 congressional districts, each populated with somewhat more than half a million people. We assign a number between 1 and 435 to each such district and, using a random number table, select several congressional districts for analysis. The exact number to be selected is a function of both the ultimate size of the sample to be drawn and the available resources, but in general, the more districts we select, the better the sample.

At this point, the principal cost saving of the multistage random area technique becomes apparent, for rather than having to track down respondents all over the country, we may focus our attention (and money) on a relative few areas most of which are of manageable size. Operations may thus be centralized in a few field offices rather than scattered hither and yon.

Once the subject congressional districts have been identified, each is further divided into still smaller but equally populated areas. In many instances, these may correspond to political boundaries, such as precincts or electoral districts, while in others we may find it necessary to create our own divisions. In any event, once these areas have been identified, one or more (depending again on sample size) are randomly selected within each congressional district by the random selection procedures we have outlined. These precincts or other areas are then further divided, first into census tracts, then into blocks, and finally into dwelling units (houses and individual apartments), with the random selection process employed at each stage of

---

[2] The initial selection identifies primary sampling units, or PSUs. When equally populated areas prove an inconvenient basis for such sampling, selection probabilities can be weighted in proportion to population as an alternative. Thus if the population of area A is roughly twice that of area B, area A is given twice the chance of selection to be included in the sample that is accorded area B.

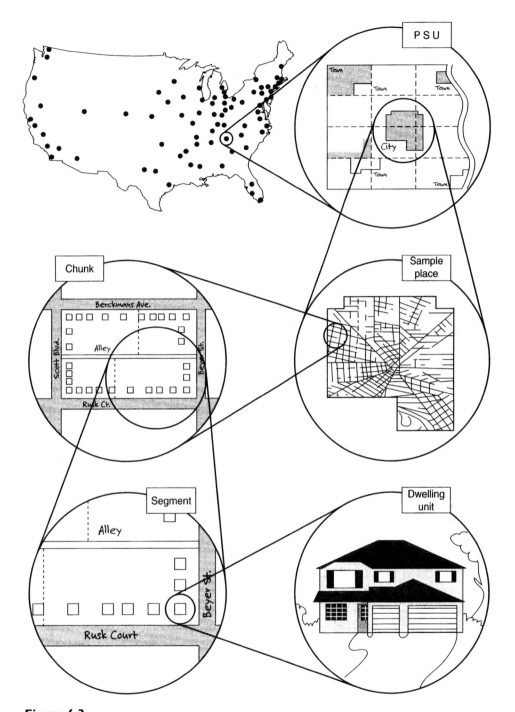

Figure 6.3
Steps in multistage random area sampling
SOURCE: *Interviewer's Manual: Survey Research Center.* Ann Arbor, MI: Institute for Social Research, University of Michigan, 1969, p. 8–2. Reprinted by permission.

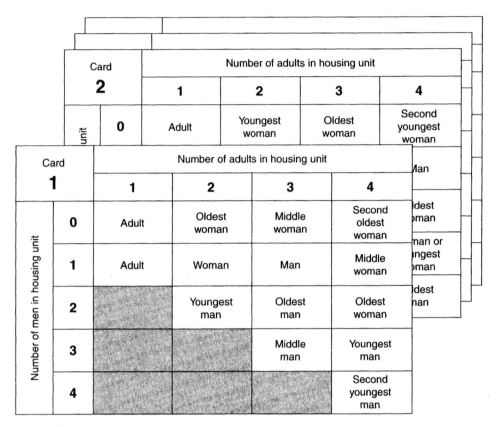

Figure 6.4
Respondent selection cards

selection. In the end, we shall have identified a number of individual dwelling units that should correspond roughly to our desired sample size. The residents of these dwelling units will become the subjects of the research.

There is, however, one additional complication. Although we generally wish for a number of reasons to interview only one person at a given address, more than one person is likely to reside in any particular dwelling unit. Which one do we interview? Most researchers who use sampling procedures of this type provide their interviewers with a series of decision rules to apply at this point, the net effect of which is to create a set of quotas based on the age, sex, and/or family standing of the respondent. In one home, the interviewer might be instructed to seek out the youngest adult male, in another the oldest adult female, and so forth. In many instances, the target respondent is determined by using cards such as those pictured in Figure 6.4. The interviewer is issued several such cards, which differ from one another in their identification of the target for a particular type of household, and is instructed to use them in succession in proceeding from one interview to the next.

We can see, then, that the term *multistage random area sampling* is truly descriptive. At each of several stages, equally populated areas (or those whose chances of selection have been weighted in proportion to their population) are selected at random until, ultimately, individual dwelling units have been identified. In each instance, the geographic location is the subject of the sampling procedure, and at each stage, several clusters of locations are identified (hence the alternative term, *cluster sampling*). Only in the final stage, that of identifying specific respondents, does the procedure diverge from the principle of randomness, but at so local a level, and with the use of such carefully constructed quotas, that the effects on the representativeness of the sample are probably minimal. In many instances, multistage random area sampling (as well as analogous procedures for sampling in other than survey research) offers a reasonable approximation of a truly random sample at a lower cost in time and resources.

We should mention one other technique, though it is less a selection procedure than a strategy. This technique is known as **stratified sampling** and is used primarily when we wish to study in detail a population subgroup that is so small that a random sample will include too few members of that subgroup to permit detailed analysis.

Suppose, for example, we wish to study the hypothesis that presidents are more open with the news media during the first two months of their administration (often termed a "honeymoon" period) than at all later times and that we wish to test the hypothesis by analyzing the content of the transcripts of presidential news conferences. Suppose further that we are able to identify 500 such transcripts for a given period, of which only 25 (or 1 in 20) are news conferences from the honeymoon period, and that we wish to sample 100 of these conferences. If we use either a simple or a systematic random sample in this instance, we might expect that sample to include approximately five honeymoon-period transcripts and approximately 95 post-honeymoon transcripts. The very small number of the former makes a meaningful comparison very difficult, because it may provide too few examples to reflect accurately the range of presidential responses to reporters' questions.

Under such circumstances, when we wish to enhance (weigh more heavily) the importance of a particular subgroup, we may choose to *stratify* our sample. In doing so, we choose, in reality, not one but *two separate samples*. The first is a simple or systematic random sample of the smaller subgroup (transcripts from the honeymoon period) and is *larger* than the expected frequency of occurrence of the subgroup in the original sample (here, perhaps 15 rather than 5 cases). The second is a simple or systematic random sample of the larger subgroup (transcripts from all subsequent periods) and is *smaller* than its expected frequency of occurrence in the original sample (here, perhaps 85 rather than 95 cases). In the example, our sample can be described as stratified according to the date of the news conference. The effect is to provide us with relatively more cases of honeymoon-period transcripts for analysis and comparison with those from later periods than we would otherwise select.

Three observations should be made at this point. First, stratification is not a substitute for simple random sampling or some other form of sampling, but an additional step to be used under particular circumstances. In effect, it is a second-order sampling procedure. In this context, stratification is frequently used, particularly by public opinion pollsters, at the late stages of a sample in order to ensure an appropriate balance of, for example, men and women. It is thus similar in purpose to the quotas that are applied in the final stage of a multistage random area sample.

Second, because it requires the drawing of separate samples, stratification may be used only when we are able to identify the relevant subpopulations *in advance.* In our example, this is not a source of difficulty, because before sampling, we can easily distinguish the honeymoon-period transcripts from those of later periods. In much survey research, however, when we may wish to stratify along less evident variables, we can encounter serious problems.

Third, because stratified sampling uses separate samples and because one can generalize from a sample only to the particular population (or subpopulation) from which it is drawn, we must exercise great care in stating our conclusions from a study based on such a sample. The reason for this is quite clear. In stratifying to increase the number of cases of a particular type in our study, we are in effect biasing our total sample in the direction of those cases. To overcome that bias, we must state our conclusions in one of only two ways. First, we may compare with one another our findings for the groups by which we have stratified (for example, we can compare our findings for honeymoon-period conferences with those for conferences from later periods). Here we are simply comparing the results of separate samples without drawing any conclusions about news conferences as a whole. Second, we may differentially weight the groups by which we have stratified in proportion to their overall share of the population and then draw general conclusions about the population. In this case, we are taking advantage of our detailed knowledge about the smaller subgroup (honeymoon-period conferences) but are reducing (or, in fact, returning to its proper proportion) its importance vis-à-vis the population of all news conferences. Under the latter procedure, a stratified sample may be used to approximate a simple random sample while providing more complete information.

On occasion, we may find it helpful to select other kinds of samples. One such is the **quota sample,** in which the members of a population are classified according to several relevant characteristics (such as sex, age, or party identification) and individuals displaying these traits are selected in proportion to their share of the population. Another is the **judgmental sample,** in which the observer simply picks out those individual cases believed for some reason to be *typical* or representative of the population from which they are drawn. This is most common in studies of small populations and when only a very small sample can be drawn from a large population. It must be remembered, however, that such samples are in general less likely to be truly representative of their corresponding populations (indeed, in contrast with random samples, their likelihood and degree of representativeness are indeterminate) and are therefore usually less desirable.

Determining Appropriate Sample Size

Having defined our terms and considered our selection procedures, we are now left with the question of how many cases to sample. In many ways, an answer to that question draws upon some sophisticated statistical concepts that lie beyond the scope of this text. For that reason, some of what we present in this section must be taken on faith, though at the end of the chapter we provide a guide to some books that do discuss these issues. We hasten to point out, however, that much of the rationale underlying the determination of an appropriate sample size is more readily understood and is worth some attention before we proceed.

Several factors help us to determine an appropriate sample size. One of the most important of these is **homogeneity**, the degree to which the members of a given population are like one another with regard to the characteristics we are interested in studying. If every individual in a population is *exactly like* every other individual, then by sampling only one individual we can obtain a truly representative sample. If, on the other hand, every individual in the population is *completely unlike* every other individual, we will be required to conduct a census of the entire population before we can claim to have a representative group. In the first instance, the population is described as completely *homogeneous*; in the second, as completely *heterogeneous*. In reality, of course, most populations lie between the two extremes.

The closer a particular population is to homogeneity—that is, the fewer the differences among its members—the smaller the sample required to represent it. Conversely, the closer a particular population is to heterogeneity—that is, the more diverse its members are—the larger the sample required to represent it. This has implications in particular for stratified sampling, because by the very act of stratification, we create subgroups that are more homogeneous than the overall population. We can thus use smaller samples within strata than we could for the overall population without a loss of representativeness.

Similarly, the more categories (variables and response options) we wish to study, the larger the sample must be. This is true because increasing the variety and sensitivity of our measures will tend to accentuate the heterogeneity of the population we are studying. In other words, the more questions we ask or the more types of answers we allow, the more likely we will be to find differences among our subjects. The more differences we examine among our subjects, the more subjects we must examine to claim a representative sample.

Another important consideration is the degree of accuracy we require. We use a sample to *estimate* the characteristics of a larger population, but any estimate is likely to include some margin of error. How much of this sampling error are we willing to tolerate? The answer is often determined by how we intend to use our results. If we are public opinion pollsters being paid to predict the outcome of a close election, we might be unwilling to accept more than the slightest margin of error. If we are political researchers attempting to spot general trends in attitudes or behaviors, we might tolerate considerably more. In general, the more accuracy we want, the larger our sample must be.

Related to this is a second question, that of just how confident we are that our estimates of the margin of sampling error are correct. The argument here may be somewhat difficult to grasp for the reader who lacks a knowledge of statistics, but it should become clear in the context of the illustration that follows. Here are the main points.

Each sample provides us with an estimate of the characteristics of a population, but because no two samples are *exactly* alike, such estimates differ somewhat from one another and from the population as a whole. The latter variation is the **sampling error**. Most samples of a given size taken from the same population are

Table 6.1
Summary of sample sizes

Percentage Sampling Error Tolerated	Level of Confidence	
	.95	.99*
±1	10,000	22,500
±2	2,500	5,625
±3	1,111	2,500
±4	625	1,406
±5	400	900
±10	100	—

*Rounded down from .997 in the source table for purposes of explanation.

very similar to one another and to the population itself, but once in a while a sample is drawn that happens, by chance, to be different. It might include, say, numbers of farmers, older persons, Republicans, college graduates, or whatever that are far out of proportion to that group's true share of the original population. Such a sample is clearly not a representative one; it will exceed the desired margin of error.

The problem is that in the real world, we do not always know the underlying population parameters our sample is intended to estimate (their discovery is frequently the very motive for our research), and we do not draw a great many samples. We draw only one. And though we may be able to check the face validity of our sample by comparing it with those used in other studies of the same or a similar population, *we cannot know for sure* that the sample we have drawn is not the odd one out—an unlikely yet possible unrepresentative sample. We know from a study of statistics, however, that we may reduce the likelihood that ours is the bad apple in the barrel by increasing the size of our sample. The more cases we include, the more likely we are to have a truly representative sample—one that does in fact fall within the error range we have specified.

We can make this discussion less abstract by considering the summary of sample sizes presented in Table 6.1. It is derived from the more extensive data found in Tables A.2 and A.3 of Appendix A. Table 6.1 lists appropriate *minimum* sample sizes for several levels of sampling error and confidence for a *simple random sample* of a relatively heterogeneous population of more than 100,000 cases. (An examination of the source tables in Appendix A shows that these numbers may be somewhat reduced for sampling smaller populations but that as the size of the population increases, the values listed here serve to limit the sample size.)

The three tables may be used in either of two ways. First, we may wish to specify the particular level of sampling error we are willing to tolerate and the confidence level at which we shall operate. Suppose that these figures are ±4 percent and .99, respectively.

The first tells us that any measurement of our sample we might make is within 4 percentage points above or below the true distribution of the same attribute in the larger population. This range is referred to as a **confidence interval.** If, for example, we find that 43 percent of our respondents in a survey report identifying with the Democratic party, we will assume that a full census of the population would show the true percentage of Democratic identifiers to be 43 percent ±4 percent, or somewhere in the range from 39 percent to 47 percent. The table tells us (if we read across at ±4 percent and down at .99) that to achieve that degree of accuracy with 99 percent confidence, we must select a sample of at least 1,406 cases. If we wish to narrow the margin of error (increase our accuracy) to, say, ±2 percent (that is, to refine our estimate to the range from 41 percent to 45 percent Democrats), we have to increase our sample size to at least 5,625 cases. At both levels of confidence, the table clearly demonstrates that increased accuracy requires an enlarged sample.

The second number that we began with refers to the likelihood that our sample is in fact representative of the larger population within the degree of accuracy we have specified and is called the **confidence level.** In this context, .95 (95 percent confidence) means that out of 100 samples of a given size that are drawn from the same population, 95 will meet this test for accuracy, and .99 (99 percent confidence) means that 99 out of 100 samples of a given size drawn from the same population will be as accurate as claimed. The chances that any particular sample will achieve the desired accuracy, then, are 95 to 5 (or 19 to 1) and 99 to 1, respectively.

As one might expect, for each level of sampling error the sample size required to attain 99 percent confidence is substantially larger than that for 95 percent confidence. Looking again at our Democrats with a margin of error of ±4 percent, for instance, we find that a sample of 625 cases allows us to say with 95 percent confidence that somewhere between 39 percent and 47 percent of the whole population are Democrats, whereas a sample of at least 1,406 cases is required before we can make the same statement with 99 percent confidence. In general, the lower the percentage of sampling error and the greater the level of confidence, the better a piece of research will be. By convention, a level of confidence of either .95 or .99 is judged to be acceptable in political science research.

We may also use this type of table in a reverse manner. If, for example, we encounter a study that employs a sample of 2,500 cases, we may consult the table to ascertain the corresponding sampling error and level of confidence. A glance at Table 6.1 shows that multiple interpretations are possible. We may interpret 2,500 cases to yield a sampling error of ±3 percent at the .99 level of confidence, or alternatively, to yield a sampling error of ±2 percent at the .95 level of confidence. Either interpretation is equally appropriate, and the two together help to make clear the tradeoff between accuracy and confidence. With the same number of cases we may be extremely confident of a relatively less precise result or somewhat less confident of a higher order of precision. We may not, however, have our research cake and eat it too.

Ideally, of course, we always prefer to operate with minimum error and maximum confidence. Unfortunately, practical considerations frequently intervene. A single personal interview in a survey project, for example, may cost as much as $50 or more in labor, transportation, and other expenses. This means that at the .99 level of confidence, the cost of reducing our margin of error from ±3 percent to ±2 percent may be more than $130,000. In many instances, the difference in the quality of the results is not worth the added expense, and in far more instances, the money is simply not available. Limits on resources thus play an important role in limiting the size of samples. Most national public opinion polls, as well as major political science survey research projects, use samples of approximately 1,200 to 1,600 respondents. Such studies yield results to within 3 to 5 percent accuracy at the .99 level of confidence and are regarded as both affordable and sufficiently precise. Projects involving content analysis or other relatively less expensive types of data-gathering techniques frequently operate closer to the upper right-hand corner of the table.

One other point should be noted before we conclude our discussion of sample size, though it is, no doubt, less obvious and less intuitively appealing than others we have raised. As an examination of Tables A.2 and A.3 in Appendix A makes clear, once it reaches a certain limiting point, the size of a population *does not* affect the size of the sample chosen to represent it. And though the proof of this assertion (which derives in part from an application of the central limit theorem in mathematics and in part from the formula for determining sample size that lies behind the figures reported in the tables) is beyond the scope of this book, its implications are not. In effect this upper limit on sample sizes means that very nearly the same size sample may be equally representative of the population of Roanoke, Virginia; of New York City; of the United States; or of the entire Western Hemisphere, so long as that sample is properly drawn. Only for relatively smaller populations is population size a significant factor in determining sample size.

In summary, then, we must take great care, when sampling, that we select not only a sufficient number of cases from a given population but also a group of cases that is likely to be truly representative of the distribution of characteristics in that population. The exercise of such due care at this point in the research process will pay substantial dividends later. Conversely, carelessness in sampling can prove a fatal flaw in any research effort.

Conclusion

One important point that is often overlooked by the beginning political researcher is that *any* time one gathers data by *any* method from *any* source, if one wishes to generalize at all beyond the particular cases examined in the research, then the data set constitutes a *sample* and its constituent cases should be selected with an eye toward the considerations we have raised. Indeed, a primary reason that we have chosen to place our discussion of sampling in a different *section* of the book from that of survey research is precisely to emphasize this point. Whether the subject of the research is elections, political advertisements, news accounts, political jurisdictions, organizations, or what have you, it is important to be aware of the significance of the selection process and its implications for the meaning and usefulness of one's research.

Suggestions for Further Reading

The statistical procedures underlying the determination of an appropriate sample size are discussed in a number of sources, which include Hubert M. Blalock, Jr., *Social Statistics,* rev. 2d ed. (New York: McGraw-Hill, 1973), ch. 9; Dennis J. Palumbo, *Statistics in Political and*

Behavioral Science, 2d ed. (New York: Columbia University Press, 1977); and, for the most thorough discussion, Taro Yamane, *Elementary Sampling Theory* (Englewood Cliffs, NJ: Prentice Hall, 1967).

A discussion of multistage random area sampling in practice may be found in *Interviewers' Manual: Survey Research Center,* rev. ed. (Ann Arbor, MI: Institute for Social Research, University of Michigan, 1976), sec. C. Other discussions and examples of sampling procedures appear regularly in the pages of *Public Opinion Quarterly.* Several variations on sampling techniques are described, and their respective strengths and weaknesses summarized, in Delbert C. Miller, *Handbook of Research Design and Social Measurement,* 5th ed. (Newbury Park, CA: Sage, 1991).

Research Exercises

1. Using Tables A.2 and A.3 in Appendix A, determine the sample size needed to meet each of the following sets of criteria:

   a. 3 percent sampling error, .95 level of confidence, population of 10,000

   b. 2 percent sampling error, .95 level of confidence, population of 50,000

   c. 1 percent sampling error, .99 level of confidence, population of 2,299,999

2. Using your local telephone book, estimate the size of the population of listed telephone subscribers (count the names in one column and multiply by the number of columns on a page and then by the number of pages in the alphabetical listing). Devise a procedure to adjust for (exclude) business listings. Draw a systematic random sample of 100 names of individuals from the directory. Can you think of any factors that would make this something less than a wholly satisfactory (representative) sample of the residents of your area?

3. Locate or construct a map of your congressional district showing all principal geographic or political subdivisions, and devise a strategy for a multistage random area sample of 1,000 persons from your congressional district. What level of confidence and sampling error will such a sample yield?

4. You are planning a study of student politics. Develop practical alternative strategies for sampling the students at your college or university, using each of the following: simple random sampling, systematic random sampling, stratified sampling (By what characteristic will you stratify? Why?); multistage area sampling; and judgmental sampling (What criteria would you apply? Why?). Summarize the advantages and disadvantages of each approach. Which would you recommend using? Why?

Terms Introduced in This Chapter

generalizibility
population
sample
representative sample
parameter
random sample
systematic random sample
cluster sampling or multistage
   random area sampling

stratified sampling
quota sample
judgmental sample
homogeneity
sampling error
confidence interval
confidence level

CHAPTER 7

SURVEY RESEARCH

Often the best (and sometimes the only) way to learn what people think or how they act is to ask them. Acceptance of this fact has made survey research one of the most fully developed and extensively used of social science methods.[1] An understanding of survey research is essential to understanding a great deal of political science since 1930. This chapter provides an overview of what this method involves, when it is appropriate, and what its principal strengths and weaknesses are.

Survey research is *a method of data collection in which information is obtained directly from individual persons who are selected so as to provide a basis for making inferences about some larger population.*[2] This information may be obtained by direct questioning through *face-to-face* or *telephone interviews* or by having the subjects complete *mailed* or *self-administered questionnaires.* All of these approaches are part of the general survey research method. Those who answer survey questions are generally referred to as **respondents.**

Surveys provide five types of information about respondents: facts, perceptions, opinions, attitudes, and behavioral reports. *Facts* include those background characteristics (age, occupation) and personal history (place of birth, first political involvement) that may be relevant to the interpretation of the other data collected. *Perceptions* are statements of what individuals know (or think they know) about the world, such as the names of public officials or the federal government's current policy toward trade with China. *Opinions* are statements of people's preferences or judgments about events and objects. Such questions as, *Do you favor legalization of marijuana?* and, *Whom do you want to win the upcoming local election?* tap opinions. *Attitudes* are relatively stable evaluations of and orientations toward events, objects, and ideas. When we want to know about people's support for civil liberties or government regulation of the economy, for example, we are asking about the attitudes on which specific opinions are often based. *Behavioral reports* are simply

---

[1] A brief history of survey research as a technique is found in Earl R. Babbie, *Survey Research Methods,* 2d ed. (Belmont, CA: Wadsworth, 1990), ch. 3.

[2] This definition excludes "surveys" not based on scientific sampling procedures. Public opinion polls and "man-in-the-street" interviews, which are based on chance samples, provide no information other than the fact that the particular individuals interviewed gave certain answers; there is no reason to believe that others would respond in similar ways.

statements of how people act (for example, how often they vote or read newspaper editorials or whether they are active in some political organization).

In survey research, concepts are operationalized through questions, and observation consists of recording respondents' answers to these questions. The method, therefore, is especially suited for studies in which individual persons are the units of analysis and the principal concepts employed pertain to individuals. If our research involves concepts such as the average daily importation of foreign oil by the United States or the number of crimes committed with handguns each year, survey research is inappropriate, because average citizens are not likely to have the information we seek (though a single interview with a representative of the Department of Energy or the Federal Bureau of Investigation might provide the necessary facts). If research focuses on the opinions, attitudes, or perceptions of individuals, a sample survey may well be the best method of data collection. It is, however, a very expensive and time-consuming method. Researchers should be aware that it may be difficult to secure adequate funding for a large project, and they should be certain that there is not some other, less expensive way of gathering the necessary data before proceeding with a sample survey.

Stages of the Survey Process

Having decided to use a sample survey as a data collection method, we must now decide what steps to go through. Survey research can be divided into fourteen basic activities.[3] In practice more than one of these may be going on at any one time, and the researcher may, on occasion, move back and forth between activities as the survey develops. Conceptually, however, the stages of survey research can be described as follows:

1. *Conceptualizing:* Specifying the purpose of the research, developing hypotheses, clarifying concepts, and operationalizing the concepts through survey items.
2. *Survey design:* Establishing the procedures to be used and deciding on the general nature of the sample to be drawn.
3. *Instrumentation:* Drafting the questions and other items that will appear on the survey instrument (the questionnaire or interview schedule) and planning the format of that instrument, as well as designing any visual aids or other devices that will be used.
4. *Planning:* Developing methods of managing the survey and anticipating the materials and personnel that will be needed.
5. *Sampling:* Selecting the persons to be interviewed according to that method among those described in Chapter 6 that best fits the purposes and resources of a given study.
6. *Training or briefing:* Preparing interviewers, coders, or other personnel to either properly contact respondents and administer the instrument to them or to process data.

---

[3]This list develops some procedures originally suggested in Charles H. Backstrom and Gerald D. Hursh, *Survey Research* (Evanston, IL: Northwestern University Press, 1963), p. 19.

7. *Pretesting:* Administering the instrument to a small sample similar to the larger sample to be contacted so as to ensure that instructions can be correctly interpreted and that items produce the desired type of response.

8. *Surveying:* Administering the instrument (by mail, phone, or personal interview) to members of the sample.

9. *Monitoring:* Ensuring that the proper persons are being contacted as respondents both by requiring records of contacts and refusals and by checking on the administration of instruments by listening in on telephone interviews.

10. *Verifying:* Using follow-up contacts to make sure that interviews have actually been performed, that mailings have reached potential respondents, and that questionnaires have been returned.

11. *Coding:* Reducing to numerical terms the data collected.

12. *Processing:* Organizing the data for analysis.

13. *Analyzing:* Working the data with statistical and other tools in order to reach conclusions about their content.

14. *Reporting:* Summarizing findings into research reports.

The remainder of this chapter highlights some of the primary points the survey researcher should take into consideration when engaged in each of these activities.

Conceptualizing

In this stage, a general research question is reduced to a far more specific set of questions that can be addressed through empirical investigation. The process should be governed by the rules discussed in Chapters 2, 3, and 4. It differs from the processes described there only in that if we want to do survey research, the operationalizations selected must be consistent with that data collection technique. We look more closely at this requirement when we discuss question wording and instrument design.

Decisions made in the conceptualizing stage have important implications for the choices that are available in sampling and survey design. For instance, in deciding to whom our theory applies, we determine what our sampling frame should be. In selecting an operationalization that requires in-person interviewing, we are dictating the level of research support needed. Even when first thinking through the theoretical aspects of the project, then, we have to be sensitive to the issues of resources and accessibility of respondents.

Survey Design

Surveys are generally either exploratory, descriptive, or explanatory in purpose. *Exploratory* surveys help us acquire information that can be helpful in formulating research questions and hypotheses more precisely when we know little about a phenomenon we consider worthy of study. *Descriptive* surveys provide precise measurement of variables that may be important in theorizing but provide no basis for making causal inferences. *Explanatory* surveys test causal hypotheses and help us understand observed patterns in terms of a theory. They must be designed so as to allow us to rule out alternative rival hypotheses. Data for each type of survey can be collected through *personal interviews, mail questionnaires, telephone interviews,* or *self-administered questionnaires.* Deciding on the objective of the survey and choosing the appropriate data-collecting method are the first steps in survey design. The purpose will be dictated largely by our level of theoretical and empirical knowledge of the subject. Which data collection technique is appropriate will be determined by the operationalizations we have chosen and by the resources that are available. Some guidelines for making this choice are offered shortly.

We must next select a way to organize the survey. The basic choice is between *cross-sectional* and *longitudinal* designs. In **cross-sectional surveys,** data are collected from respondents only once. If we have a representative sample, this design allows us to describe populations and relationships between variables in those populations at a given time, but it does not allow us to say how the characteristics or relationships have developed or will develop over time. Cross-sectional surveys offer a snapshot of a moving target. They are best suited to exploratory and descriptive studies, but together with a strong theory and proper data analysis, cross-sectional surveys can provide some basis for explanation. For example, in a study of the relationship between personality and political behavior, we may be willing to assume that a person's level of self-esteem is a relatively stable personality trait that precedes one's level of political involvement. If we find, then, that those with a high level of self-esteem tend to be more politically involved than those with low self-esteem, we might feel safe in arguing that high esteem leads to or causes high political involvement, even though we have data from only one time.

Longitudinal surveys are those in which data are collected from respondents on more than one occasion. The principal types of longitudinal survey are *trend, cohort,* and *panel* studies.

In **trend studies** samples are drawn from the same population (for example, voting-age residents of Kansas) at different times and surveyed. *Different persons* may be included in each survey, but the results will be representative of trends in the *same population,* because, as was explained in Chapter 6, each properly selected sample will be equivalent to every other sample from that population. Thus, if we find different degrees of partisan identification in two samples of the same population surveyed at different times, we may infer that there has been a change in the level of partisan identification *in the population* during the time that separates the surveys. We might also explore changes in the relationship between variables through trend studies. If we find, for instance, that the relationship between gender and political activity is weaker in the second of two surveys of samples from the same population, we might conclude that there is a trend toward the breaking down of sex roles in the political life of that population.

Whereas trend studies are representative of a *general* population (for example, American women, French voters, Algerian students) at different times, **cohort studies** focus on the same *specific* population over time. Members of the population sampled in trend studies will change with time, but cohort studies draw samples from the *same* population each time even though different members might be included in the samples. For example, we might want to draw a sample from among all of the Mexican citizens who legally immigrated to the United States *in 2000* and sample that same group again three years later to study their adaptation to life in the United States. Though there may be some loss from this population as members die or move out of the United States, no new members will be added.

Both trend and cohort studies allow us to document change in a population over time, but because different samples are drawn for each survey, we cannot identify *which* members of the population are changing. This makes it more difficult to discover causal patterns. **Panel studies,** by contrast, use the *same sample at different times.* This allows us to see which members of a population are changing and to identify the characteristics or experiences that are associated with changes. For example, we might interview the same sample of registered voters before, during, and after an election campaign in an effort to determine what aspects of a campaign are most likely to lead people to change their choice of candidates.

This important advantage of panel studies must be weighed against some disadvantages. First, panel studies are very costly, because the expense of keeping track of sample members over time must be added to the costs of conducting several interviews. Second, there can be problems of reactivity of the type discussed in Chapter 5. The very fact that people are being interviewed, perhaps repeatedly, about a subject may cause them to alter their behavior or attitudes with regard to that subject in ways they would not were they not being interviewed. This creates a kind of test effect that can distort results. At the very least it means there is a risk that the sample will become *unrepresentative of the larger population* by virtue of being included in the study. Third, *attrition* from the sample can compromise the validity of panel studies. Attrition occurs when respondents in the first wave of surveying do not respond in subsequent waves. If those who drop out of the panel share characteristics that are relevant to the study but not shared by those who do not drop out, their, withdrawal may create a highly biased sample that both distorts results and prevents generalizing to the larger population.

Despite these drawbacks, panel studies are still the strongest design for most explanatory purposes, and they often justify their expense by the additional information they yield.

A special type of longitudinal survey is the *quasi-experimental study,* in which the researcher either manipulates one or more independent variables between the first and second surveys or times the surveys to come before and after some anticipated change in an independent variable. We might, for instance, want to interview people both before and after the enactment of a new law or the election of a new president. Such studies can be used as field experiments and are especially valuable in evaluating public policies.

Instrumentation

Whatever study design is employed, the survey researcher will have to develop a set of questions to use as tools in obtaining measures. This is an extension of the operationalization process begun in the conceptualization stage and produces a *survey instrument,* which may be either a **questionnaire** (a mail questionnaire or a self-administered one), to be filled in by the respondent, or an **interview schedule,** which guides an interviewer in an in-person or telephone interview. When developing these instruments, the researcher must consider (1) the content, (2) the form, (3) the format, (4) the wording, and (5) the order of questions.

The *content* of questions determines what information can be obtained from responses to them. It is dictated by the hypothesis being tested or the question being studied. What must we know to resolve the research question, and what must we ask to obtain that information? These are the questions that should guide the choice of what to ask. It is essential to be very clear both about what information is expected from responses to each item on a survey instrument and about how that information will be used in data analysis. What will it contribute to our ability to answer the research question?

There are an infinite number of questions to be asked about almost any important subject, but survey instruments must be kept relatively short if respondents are to complete them. In-person interviews should last no longer than three-quarters of an hour under most circumstances, and telephone interviews no longer than twenty minutes. Mail questionnaires should generally be no more than four pages long. The need for brevity, however, must be weighed against the need to obtain all the information necessary to rule out the various rival hypotheses encountered in data analysis or the need to seek explanations for unanticipated results. One way to approach this problem is to follow two general rules. First, keep the number of hypotheses being tested or research questions being addressed in a survey very limited. This will restrict the number of variables on which information is needed. Second, when selecting items for inclusion, exclude any for which there is no clear and immediate role in the anticipated data analysis.

Surveys usually contain both questions that are specific to the study and general background questions that measure characteristics that past research has shown to be strongly associated with differences in the political behavior under study. The latter items are included to allow us to rule out rival hypotheses pertaining to background characteristics and to refine our understanding of relationships by seeing how they differ in different **demographic groups.** Questions that seek information on the following characteristics are often at least *considered* for inclusion on any survey instrument:

Sex	Marital status
Age	Home ownership
Race	Household composition
Income	Party identification
Religion	National origin
Education	Length of residence
Occupation	Organizational memberships

A question's *form* refers to whether it is *open-ended* or *closed-ended.* **Open-ended questions** allow respondents to answer in their own words; no options are imposed on them. For example, *What do you consider to be the most important single issue in this year's local election?* is an open-ended question. Such questions have the advantage of allowing the researcher to discover unanticipated patterns in people's answers. They also prevent the researcher's selection of response options from biasing answers or concealing information. Open-ended questions have some disadvantages, however: They make comparison of respondents' answers extremely difficult, because each person may not use the same frame of reference in answering. And they may result in irrelevant and useless answers. They encourage long answers, which are often difficult to analyze.

Closed-ended questions force the respondent to choose an answer from a limited number of options and have the advantages of making comparison of responses simple, allowing quick processing, and ensuring the relevance of responses. For example, *Do you consider yourself to be (1) a conservative, (2) a moderate, or (3) a liberal?* is a closed-ended question. The options offered in closed-ended questions should be *exhaustive* (they should include all possible responses that might be expected) and *mutually exclusive* (they should not allow more than one choice as a response to any single question). The options should also allow respondents to express differences in the *intensity* of their response when this might be relevant. A question like *Some people feel that the federal government should sponsor free abortion clinics for low-income women. Do you agree or disagree with this position?* calls for a more complex set of choices than just agree and disagree. *Strongly agree, agree, neutral, disagree, strongly disagree,* and *no opinion* would better reflect the range of opinions people are likely to hold.

Even when they are well constructed, closed-ended questions run the risk that the researcher's choice of options may influence responses. A question like *Which of the following would you say is the most important issue facing the United States today?* assumes that the researcher can list all the issues people will consider the most important. Use of this closed-ended form may prevent our discovering something we have not anticipated about public opinion. The choice between open- and closed-ended forms must be made on the basis of both the resources that will be available for data processing (open-ended requiring more) and the theoretical and empirical knowledge we have of our subject (closed-ended requiring more).

Question format refers to the technique by which the questions are presented and answered. Though the straightforward oral or written question-and-answer format is most common, a variety of other techniques are available to help respondents conceptualize choices and understand what is being asked. Many of these involve visual aids, such as charts, photographs, or cards that can be sorted into boxes. One example is the "feeling thermometer" developed at the Survey Research Center of the University of Michigan. Respondents are shown a card with a drawing like that in Figure 7.1 and asked to report how warm or cold they feel toward an object (for example, the Democratic party or their city's mayor) by choosing a temperature reading from the thermometer. This instrument facilitates the ranking of larger numbers of options (such as potential presidential candidates) than respondents could reasonably be expected to rank in an abstract mental exercise. The researcher simply asks about each choice individually and compares thermometer readings. The more complex the mental task respondents are being asked to perform, the more useful visual aids and other variations on the question-and-answer format can be.

Question *wording* is crucial to the success of a survey. Researchers can make it easier for an interviewer to do a good job by providing clear instructions and by careful question wording. Properly phrased questions can often prevent problems in the field. For example, it is easier for the interviewer to establish a good relationship

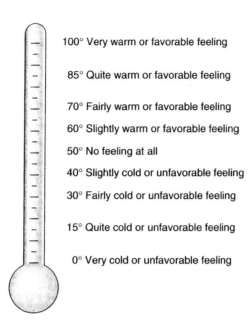

100° Very warm or favorable feeling

85° Quite warm or favorable feeling

70° Fairly warm or favorable feeling

60° Slightly warm or favorable feeling

50° No feeling at all

40° Slightly cold or unfavorable feeling

30° Fairly cold or unfavorable feeling

15° Quite cold or unfavorable feeling

0° Very cold or unfavorable feeling

Figure 7.1
The feeling thermometer as a visual aid in survey research

with the respondent and to avoid the appearance of "grilling" if questions are phrased so that respondents do not have to admit that they do not know some fact or have given no thought to the subject. A phrase such as . . . *or haven't you had a chance to read about that?* at the end of a question can considerably ease potentially tense situations.

No one can provide precise guidelines for correct wording, because the questions that have to be asked are determined by the subject under study. We can, however, describe some common errors in question wording that should be avoided. Here are some features questions should *not* have:

1. *Excessive length.* If there is a general rule about question wording, it is to use the shortest form of the question that communicates effectively. Longer questions not only consume more time but are also more likely to lose or confuse respondents. Avoid conditioning phrases and unnecessary adjectives. For example, the question *If the presidential election were to be held at this point in time, rather than in November, which of the following several candidates do you think you would vote for?* can profitably be shortened to *If the presidential election were held today, whom would you vote for?* followed by a list of candidates.

2. *Ambiguity.* The quest for brevity should not lead to incomplete or imprecise wording. To be certain that questions contain all the information necessary to elicit an informed response, ask yourself whether the respondent might have to answer the question with a question. For instance, when asked, *Do you ever complain about public services?* a respondent might answer, *Complain to whom?*

Public officials? Neighbors? Questions are often ambiguous if they are too general *(Do you feel that people think too much about politics?)* or indefinite about time, location, or point of comparison *(Did you vote in the last election? Do many Asians live here? Do you think Smith is the best candidate?).*

3. *Double-barreled questions.* These questions are often impossible to answer with a single response because they contain two distinct questions. For example, *Do you feel that we are spending too much on the military, or do you feel it is important to maintain a strong national defense?* cannot be answered with "yes" or "no" if the respondent feels that it is important to have a strong defense but also thinks that current expenditures are higher than necessary for that purpose. To avoid double-barreled questions, examine any question containing *and* or *or* to be certain it does not combine two questions that should be asked separately.

4. *Bias.* Questions can be worded so as to encourage one response rather than another. Such questions are often referred to as *loaded questions.* When asked, *You are opposed to busing innocent schoolchildren all the way across town just achieve racial balance in the schools, aren't you?* respondents will be far more inclined to agree than if asked, *Do you favor or oppose the use of busing to achieve racial balance in the public schools?* Phrases that evoke social norms (such as, *How often do you fulfill your civic duty by voting?*) clearly bias responses. Phrases that associate a position with authority figures or socially disapproved persons or groups can also distort results. For example, questions that begin with, *Do you agree with the Supreme Court that...* or *Do you share the neo-Nazi view that...* will probably produce biased results

   If there are opposing positions on an issue, it is important that questions be worded so as to make each seem legitimate. A useful approach here is to word items as follows: *Some people feel that the federal government should take control of the nation's oil companies and operate them as public utilities. Others think that would be a serious mistake. How do you feel about it? Do you think the federal government should take control of U.S. oil companies?*

5. *Response set bias.* People have a tendency to agree with statements, regardless of their own positions. Question items that fail to take this into account are said to exhibit a *response set bias.* We can see the effects of this if we measure political conservatism first by using six statements with which we expect conservatives to agree, and then again by using six statements with which we expect them to disagree. The first measure will almost always "show" that there are significantly more conservatives than will the second regardless of the actual number of conservatives in the sample. Items should be mixed so that we sometimes expect agreement to reflect a given attitude or position and sometimes expect disagreement to reflect that attitude or position.

6. *Argumentativeness.* Though it is sometimes necessary to provide background for questions, it is a mistake to argue a position. For instance, it is not wise to ask, *Since there are so many dangers associated with the operation of nuclear power plants and the disposal of waste from them, some people argue that it is foolish to invest so much in developing nuclear power when we could be*

devoting resources to the development of safe and inexhaustible energy sources such as solar or wind power. Do you agree that our nation should sharply curtail its investment in nuclear energy? In addition to being far too long, this question will probably bias responses because it omits alternatives to the position stated.

7. *Encouragement of conditioned responses.* Special problems of wording are posed when we have to ask questions that touch on sensitive subjects. Most people are reluctant to talk to strangers about such matters as their income, family life, sexual behavior, or even political preferences in some cases. For example, consider the case of questions for which society largely prescribes certain responses. Unless questions are carefully phrased, respondents will tend to give the socially acceptable answer regardless of their own opinions. Racial prejudice is a case in point. Since bigotry is generally condemned in American society, people may be reluctant to express prejudiced views.

We can suggest three tactics to use in getting genuine responses rather than conditioned or socially approved answers. The first is to indicate that socially unacceptable views are widely held or can be viewed as legitimate. For instance, ask, *Many people feel that having African-Americans in a neighborhood causes it to go downhill. Others don't think African-Americans make that much difference in a neighborhood. Do you agree or disagree with the idea that African-American residents generally cause neighborhoods to decline?* A second approach is to word questions so as to appear to assume that respondents engage in socially proscribed behavior or hold unpopular views so that they are forced to deny it if they do not. This makes it easier for them to "confess" to socially unapproved opinions. For instance, the question *How much harm do you think it would do to this neighborhood if African-Americans began to move in?* makes it easier to express prejudice than a more neutral wording such as, *Do you think it would be harmful to this neighborhood to have African-Americans move in?*

8. *Forcing a response.* Many people feel that it is socially undesirable not to have an opinion on political issues and may express opinions on matters to which they have given no thought. This can distort survey results. To avoid such responses, it is generally wise to provide a no-opinion category in response options or to word questions so as to make having no opinion seem acceptable. For instance, try opening a question with wording such as, *Some people consider the national debt to be an important political issue while others are not too concerned with it. Do you think…?*

In addition to constructing individual items, survey researchers must be concerned with the overall format and organization of the survey instrument. Sound questionnaires or interview schedules generally consist of four main parts: the explanation, some warm-up questions, the substantive questions, and the demographic questions. (With in-person interviews there is also an introduction designed to determine how the respondent fits the sample and to obtain permission to conduct the interview.)

The *explanation* informs respondents of the purpose of the study, and it should convince them that the survey is important enough to warrant their time and attention. This can often be done by associating the study with respected authority or with a worthwhile goal. If the survey has a prestigious sponsor, a line such as, *We have been commissioned by the State Employment Division...* or, *We are conducting a study for the Institute for Social Research...* can have the desired effect. In stating the purpose of a study, the researcher should not use terms beyond the everyday language of respondents. It would be unwise, for example, to say, *We are conducting a study of mass-elite linkages to determine the extent to which formal mechanisms of representation are a facade for social control by political elites,* even if this were the purpose of the study. A more effective statement would be, *We want to know what kind of contact people like you have with their elected representatives, and we hope that the results of this study will help improve the operation of our government.* Though it is never advisable to lie to respondents, the explanation should not reveal study information that would bias responses. If respondents are told that a study focuses on racial prejudice, they may give answers different from those they would give if told only that the study deals with citizens' attitudes or some other neutral term. The explanation can help interviewers establish a good rapport with respondents or encourage respondents to complete a questionnaire by assuring them that the researchers are open about what they are doing and by eliminating any fear that the study might be a front for a sales pitch.

Warm-up questions, too, can help establish a good relationship with respondents. These are impersonal, nonthreatening items used to initiate an interview or questionnaire. Asking respondents about their length of residence in their present location or what they think are the most important problems in their community or in the nation can be useful warm-ups. Any questions that are selected for this purpose, however, should be relevant to the study and have a definite role in the analysis. Otherwise, they are wasted. Warm-up questions should not be created especially for that purpose but should be selected from questions that are to be asked anyway.

Substantive questions constitute the bulk of the items on most instruments. The ordering of items within this group is determined principally by the need to achieve a logical flow in the questioning. Question ordering is not always neutral, however. For instance, researchers often want to ask the same question in different ways. When this is done, the different forms of the question should be separated so that respondents do not find the interview repetitious. Similarly, if both general and specific questions about a phenomenon are to be asked, it is usually best to ask the general questions first in order to get a response that has not been conditioned by a series of specific inquiries. It usually makes sense to place open-ended questions about a subject before closed-ended questions on that same subject in order to prevent the options offered in the closed-ended items from biasing responses to the open-ended items.

If there is reason to believe that question ordering will influence responses, the pretest will provide an opportunity to experiment with different orderings so as to determine which is best.

Demographic items seek factual information about respondents that is often regarded as personal or sensitive. They are usually placed at the end of an instrument to prevent having other parts of the interview or questionnaire affected by respondents' being ill at ease or feeling as if the researchers are snooping. Though people are generally willing to provide information on such personal matters as their income or marital status, getting adequate answers to demographic questions requires careful wording.

Placing demographic questions at the end of an instrument has the added advantage of postponing, until more interesting questions have been asked, what some people consider dull questions of the sort they frequently have to answer in filling out official forms. This can be especially important with self-administered questionnaires, because a set of routine questions at the outset can make completing the form seem like work and lead respondents to abandon the questionnaire. Asking their opinion on important issues early on, however, often excites respondents' interest in completing the instrument.

Once the principal sections of the instrument have been designed, decisions about how they will be placed on paper must be made. These decisions determine the *format* of the instrument. Earl Babbie argues:

> The format of a questionnaire can be just as important as the nature and wording of the questions asked. An improperly laid out questionnaire can lead respondents to miss questions, confuse them as to the nature of the data desired, and, in the extreme, result in respondents throwing the questionnaire away.[4]

The format of an interview schedule can be just as important. A poorly laid out schedule can confuse interviewers in ways that lead them to skip items, incorrectly record responses, and alienate respondents by appearing clumsy. We can offer some guidelines for setting up both questionnaires and interview schedules.

The first rule for both types of instruments is, *Do not crowd items*. It is difficult to overstress the harm that can be caused to a survey by crowding print on a page. To prevent errors, leave plenty of white space on each page of the instrument. With interview schedules, this facilitates the interviewer's following instructions and recording responses. In self-administered questionnaires, it helps respondents avoid misreading or mismarking and can give them the sense that the questionnaire is easy to complete. It is better to have a few questions on each of a large number of sheets in a questionnaire than to have many questions on each of a few sheets. The total number of pages matters less than the clarity of each page, but a rule of thumb is that it will take approximately 30 minutes to administer an instrument of 10 well-spaced pages, and 30 minutes is about as long as researchers can count on to hold their respondents' attention under most circumstances.

In setting up an interview schedule, researchers must balance the needs of interviewers with the needs of those who will code information from the completed form and those who will prepare that information for data entry. One of the basic questions here is whether or not to use a *precoded* instrument. The details of coding are discussed in Chapter 12. Basically it is a process of assigning numbers to represent verbal responses. A precoded instrument has these numbers already associated with the responses; one that is not precoded does not. Figure 7.2 presents an example of a portion of a precoded interview schedule. The numbers in parentheses beside the coded responses indicate the column of a computer line or entry in which the code is to be entered. Major divisions are made in the interview schedule to signal the data entry operator to move to a new line or entry.

---

[4] Babbie, p. 135.

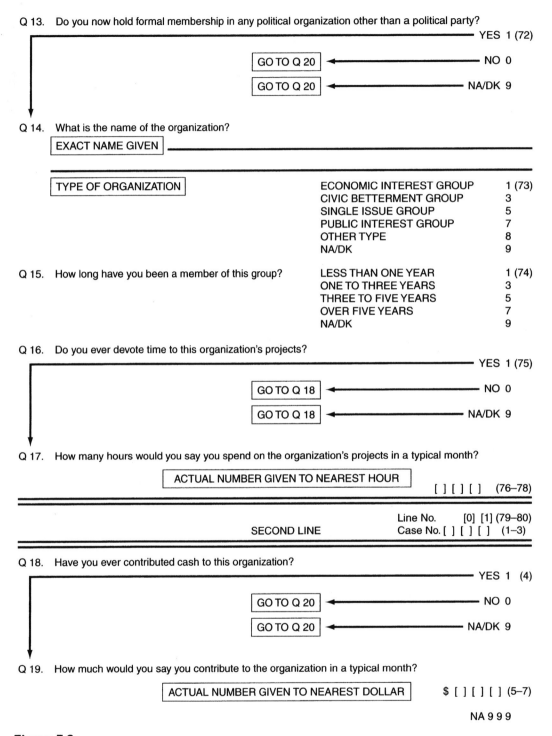

Q 13. Do you now hold formal membership in any political organization other than a political party?

YES 1 (72)

GO TO Q 20 ◄──── NO 0

GO TO Q 20 ◄──── NA/DK 9

Q 14. What is the name of the organization?

| EXACT NAME GIVEN |

TYPE OF ORGANIZATION		
	ECONOMIC INTEREST GROUP	1 (73)
	CIVIC BETTERMENT GROUP	3
	SINGLE ISSUE GROUP	5
	PUBLIC INTEREST GROUP	7
	OTHER TYPE	8
	NA/DK	9

Q 15. How long have you been a member of this group?

	LESS THAN ONE YEAR	1 (74)
	ONE TO THREE YEARS	3
	THREE TO FIVE YEARS	5
	OVER FIVE YEARS	7
	NA/DK	9

Q 16. Do you ever devote time to this organization's projects?

YES 1 (75)

GO TO Q 18 ◄──── NO 0

GO TO Q 18 ◄──── NA/DK 9

Q 17. How many hours would you say you spend on the organization's projects in a typical month?

| ACTUAL NUMBER GIVEN TO NEAREST HOUR |

[ ] [ ] [ ] (76–78)

	SECOND LINE	Line No. [0] [1] (79–80)
		Case No. [ ] [ ] [ ] [ ] (1–3)

Q 18. Have you ever contributed cash to this organization?

YES 1 (4)

GO TO Q 20 ◄──── NO 0

GO TO Q 20 ◄──── NA/DK 9

Q 19. How much would you say you contribute to the organization in a typical month?

| ACTUAL NUMBER GIVEN TO NEAREST DOLLAR |

$ [ ] [ ] [ ] (5–7)

NA 9 9 9

Figure 7.2

Excerpt from a hypothetical precoded interview schedule*

*To simplify the example, some questions have been modified from the form in which they would actually appear.

Precoding has two advantages. First, it can speed the interview process by making it easier for interviewers to record responses. In most cases, it takes less time for the interviewer to circle or write down a number to represent a response than to write out the response. This can also reduce the number of mistakes made in interpreting the completed interview schedule. Second, precoding can allow data entry operators to work directly from the completed survey instruments rather than requiring an additional step in transferring information from survey instruments to a form that can be used in data entry.

Although there are many specific techniques for setting up precoded instruments, it is important to keep all responses on the same side of the paper whenever possible. This means that neither interviewers nor data entry operators will have to move their eyes continually across the page when recording or entering data.

Items that are to appear on self-administered questionnaires can be precoded also, so that data entry operators can work directly from the returned questionnaires. The numerous parenthetical numbers can confuse respondents, however, and researchers should carefully pretest the effect of precoding before using it in a questionnaire. If precoding is to be used in this situation, its purpose should be explained simply in the introduction so that respondents are alerted to it and can better avoid being distracted by it.

One of the most important items to be built into a precoding system is a means of *identifying individual respondents* and keeping together all computer entries that contain their responses. This is done by assigning each respondent a unique number. The number must appear on each page of the interview schedule or questionnaire so that recorded data can be checked against the raw data. If there is more than one line of data per case, the last column of each can be used to denote which of the several lines assigned to one respondent that particular one is.

Providing instructions that ensure that respondents answer all appropriate questions in the proper order is one of the most difficult parts of designing survey instruments. Interviewers can be trained and given an opportunity to virtually memorize an interview schedule, but clear instructions are still needed when complex choices are involved. This need is even greater when self-administered questionnaires are used, since the respondent sees the instrument only once. Figure 7.3 illustrates some means of helping respondents follow question sequences on questionnaires. Note that a number is associated with each response. Respondents would be instructed to circle the number corresponding to their answer, and data entry operators would enter the circled number from the questionnaire. Arrows direct respondents through the proper sequence of questions.

Planning and Sampling

With the format and content of the instrument settled, the researcher is ready to move on to the next stages of the process—*planning* and *sampling*. Sampling techniques were discussed in Chapter 6 and do not require more of our attention here. The planning stage basically involves (1) deciding the kind of survey that is to be done, (2) working out the logistics of doing it, and (3) locating funding.

The type of survey required is determined by the research question being addressed, and the type *possible* is dictated by the resources available. But the basic

8. Have you ever complained to local officials about public services?   Yes 1   No 2

8a. To which type of official have you complained most often?
Mayor 1
Council member 2
City agency head 3
Other official 4

8b. How many times have you complained to local officials about poor public services in the past year?
Once or twice 1
Three or four times 2
Five to ten times 3
More than ten times 4

9. How would you say the public services in your neighborhood compare with the services found in other neighborhoods of this city?
Much better than in other neighborhoods 1
Somewhat better than in other neighborhoods 2
The same as in other neighborhoods 3
Somewhat worse than in other neighborhoods 4
Much worse than in other neighborhoods 5

10. How would you rate the quality of each of the following public services as they are delivered *in your neighborhood* today?

	Excellent	Good	Fair	Poor	Very bad
Fire protection	1	2	3	4	5
Police protection	1	2	3	4	5
Streets and sidewalks	1	2	3	4	5
Trash collection	1	2	3	4	5
Street lighting	1	2	3	4	5
Animal control	1	2	3	4	5
Recreational facilities	1	2	3	4	5

Figure 7.3
Excerpt from a hypothetical mail questionnaire

choice is always among three options: *in-person interviews, mail surveys,* or *telephone surveys.* In making that choice, the researcher should consider the following features of each type of survey.

In-person interviews are the most flexible of survey methods in that they allow the use of a variety of questioning techniques (visual aids, for example) and give interviewers a chance to pursue questions in order to ensure appropriate responses and prevent respondents' misunderstanding questions or instructions. In-person interviews also provide the largest amount of data per interview, because an interviewer can normally hold a respondent's attention longer in face-to-face interaction than over the phone or through a questionnaire. The response rate is also generally higher for in-person interviews.

They are not without disadvantages, however. In the first place, they are very expensive, and only the most important of projects can generally command the funds necessary to employ the technique. Second, in-person interviews can produce biased data because of the features of the interview process itself. Recorded responses may reflect real-world facts or attitudes less than they reflect the effects of the setting in which the interview occurs, the reactions of respondents to a given interviewer, the biases of the interviewer, the liberties the interviewer takes in asking questions, or the interview style employed. In addition, door-to-door interviews are difficult to monitor to ensure quality control. The researcher is unable to observe the interviewers in the field and must rely on a variety of post-interview techniques to ensure that interviews were properly conducted. Though such techniques as contacting respondents to see if they were actually interviewed and comparing the responses reported by different interviewers can be effective, they are not foolproof and are costly and time-consuming.

Mail surveys are an alternative with several advantages:

1. Because mail surveys cost much less to conduct, larger samples can be drawn and a wider distribution of the instrument can be achieved.

2. Many of the biases in distribution of the instrument can be avoided. Among these are biases relating to the reluctance of interviewers to work in certain types of neighborhoods and their inability to obtain interviews with certain types of individuals or members of certain types of families.

3. Response biases associated with the interviewer are avoided.

4. There is a greater chance of obtaining truthful responses both because a greater anonymity is implied by a mailed instrument and because the biasing effects of respondent-interviewer interaction are removed.

5. Respondents have more time to give thoughtful replies that may reflect their true feelings more accurately than do the hurried responses given in an interview situation.

6. Fewer personnel need be involved in the survey. This saves money and time.

Unfortunately, however, mail surveys have their limitations as well. In the first place, they require a mailing list that can be used as a sample frame and provide a representative sample. No such list exists for many of the populations to which researchers may want to generalize. Second, questionnaires have to be kept short if an adequate response rate is to be obtained. This means that less information can be secured from each contact. Third, the researcher has little control over who responds to the questionnaire. This can pose problems both because someone other than the person to whom it is addressed can complete a questionnaire and because it is difficult to obtain an adequate response rate with a mailed instrument. Fourth, mail questionnaires cannot be relied on to yield valid information about respondents' knowledge. Respondents have time to look up or otherwise learn the answers to knowledge questions (such as, *Who is your state senator?*) especially for the questionnaire.

The most significant problems associated with mail surveys are low response rates, biased response patterns, and improperly completed questionnaires. In general, a response rate of 50 percent is considered acceptable for mail surveys, and a rate of 70 percent or more is considered very good. A demonstrated lack of bias in responses is more important than a high response rate, however, because low response rates challenge the value of results chiefly by rendering the sample unrepresentative. Several techniques are available for encouraging better response rates. They include the following.

The usual procedure for mail surveys is to send a questionnaire, a letter explaining the purpose of the survey, and a return envelope all in one envelope. Research has shown that using *self-mailing questionnaires* increases response rates. Self-mailing questionnaires can be folded, sealed, and mailed without an additional envelope. That seems to make it easier for respondents to return the instrument and averts the problem of respondents' losing the return envelope. Some forms of self-mailers can incorporate the letter of introduction into a booklet, which can be mailed to respondents without an envelope and refolded for return mailing when completed.

Follow-up mailings can substantially increase return rates both by reminding respondents of the survey and by locating people who, for some reason, have not received the initial letter. Generally, three mailings (an original and two follow-ups) are best. If individual respondents can be identified from returned questionnaires, then mailing follow-ups only to nonrespondents can save money. If respondents cannot be identified, it is a good idea to do a blanket mailing to all members of the sample, thanking those who have responded and encouraging those who have not to do so. The follow-up mailing should contain both a letter reminding people to send in their completed questionnaire and a second questionnaire in case the first was lost or never arrived.

It is often wise to include in all mailings a phone number that respondents can call to get answers to questions about the survey. This can both increase the response rate and reduce the number of questionnaires returned improperly completed. Response rates can also be enhanced by carefully avoiding any marks on the questionnaires (sequence numbers, for instance) that respondents could interpret as a device for identifying their questionnaire. People are generally more likely to cooperate if they feel their responses will be anonymous.

Telephone surveys fall between in-person and mail surveys in many ways. The number of questions that can be asked is generally larger than for mail instruments but shorter than for in-person interviews. Response rates are usually lower than for in-person interviews but higher than for mail surveys. Though interviewer-related sources of bias are not totally removed, a voice over the telephone is normally less likely to create biasing effects than is a person in the respondent's living room. Finally, the personnel requirements of telephone surveys are between those of mail and in-person surveys.

The advantages of telephone surveys include the speed with which they can be completed, the control they provide over who responds, and the flexibility they offer in allowing an interviewer to ensure appropriate responses. Their chief limitation arises from the possibility that an unbiased sample cannot be obtained. Those who do not have a telephone or who have an unlisted number may also be distinctive in ways that are relevant to the study. If so, leaving them out of a sample may provide misleading results. For example, many service professionals (doctors and lawyers, for example) have an unlisted home telephone number in some communities, and very poor people often do not have a telephone. This can be crucial to a study of the relationship between income and political attitudes. Whether or not a telephone survey can provide a representative sample depends largely on the particular population about which generalizations are to be made. A sampling technique known as *random-digit dialing* has enabled survey researchers to overcome the bias associated with unlisted numbers and inaccurate listings and has significantly increased the speed with which telephone surveys can be conducted.[5]

Training and Briefing Personnel

The personal interview is simultaneously one of the worst and one of the best data collection tools available to political scientists. The most significant disadvantages of the interview stem from the fact that the interview situation is rich with opportunities for *reactivity* to affect measurement. Respondents' reactions to the appearance or behavior of the interviewer, to the wording of questions, or to the interview setting can create artificial data that contain less information about the real world than about the interview process itself.

Because respondents react not only to questions but also to the person asking the questions and the manner in which they are asked, characteristics of interviewers that should be totally unrelated to the interview can, in fact, be crucial to its success. In order to minimize error in survey research, the interviews must be standardized. This means that each question should mean the same thing to each respondent, and that each response must mean the same thing when given by different respondents. The presence of an interviewer, ideally, should not affect the respondent's perception of a question, nor the kind of answer that is given. In order to increase response rates and accuracy, interviewers should do what they can to persuade respondents to complete the interview. It is important to interview busy and less cooperative people as well as people that eagerly and/or cooperatively complete the survey. The following guidelines should help to reduce interviewer error considerably.

1. Use an informal, conversational style when asking the questions of the survey. You should be matter-of-fact and casual in your approach to questioning, as if there were absolutely no reason to expect people to refuse to answer.

2. You should be sufficiently familiar with the questions so that you sound as if you are not reading them. Do not conduct the interview in a monotonous voice, since this might make you sound disinterested in the respondents' answers. Try

---

[5]Random-digit dialing and other approaches to solving sampling problems in telephone surveys are discussed in Don A. Dillman, *Mail and Telephone Surveys* (New York: Wiley, 1978), ch. 7.

to make the respondents feel that you are listening to what they say by using affirmations such as, *I see* or *okay*.

3. Do not express your own opinions during an interview by expressing agreement or disagreement with the respondent. Remain neutral, and never suggest answers to the respondent, even if you think you "know" what the respondent thinks. Also, do not allow yourself to be drawn into conversations with the respondent about the subject of the survey, because your remarks may bias responses.

4. Let the respondents determine the speed at which you read the survey. It is, however, important to move the interview along as quickly as possible in order to avoid opportunities for the respondent to terminate the interview.

5. Do not intentionally alter the wording or the order of items. All questions should be read exactly as they are written and in the order in which they are presented. Just as survey results can be distorted when questions are reworded, they can also be distorted when questions are asked out of sequence.

6. Do not attempt to interview from memory. Always have the questionnaire before you, and refer to it for question wording and order even if you are so familiar with the instrument that it takes only a glance to remind you of the items.

7. If you are to record respondents' comments, record them in exactly the words the respondents use rather than summarizing them.

8. If respondents give indefinite answers, probe for more specific responses. Your probes should be neutral and should not suggest answers. The most effective neutral probe is repeating the original question or response categories. In well-constructed surveys, appropriate probes are indicated on the questionnaire for any question that is likely to require them.

9. Do not accept *I don't know* or *no opinion* as a response without at least one probe. Repeat the question and perhaps offer a little encouragement such as *I know some of the questions might be difficult to answer, but what is your best guess?*

10. If respondents object to question wording or the alternative answers offered, do not defend the survey instrument but merely explain that you must ask the questions as written and that you are not responsible for them.

11. Never tell respondents what others have answered in response to a given question even though respondents may ask.

12. Be prepared to answer any questions the respondent asks you about who is doing the survey and why. Each study should have a sheet prepared by the project manager that provides brief answers to these questions.

Pretesting

Pretesting a survey instrument and all the accompanying procedures of data management is as important to successful survey research as a test drive is to buying a good used car. It helps identify problems that will show up only under actual field conditions.

Pretests are conducted by administering the survey to a small sample of respondents similar to those who will be in the larger sample. The pretest sample need not be representative of the larger population. It is more important to draw the pretest sample in such a way as to ensure that members of all groups of respondents that may react differently to the instrument be included in the pretest than it is to draw a representative sample for the pretest. If, for example, less educated people are likely to have difficulties with the instrument, the researcher should take special pains to include in the pretest respondents with little education, even if they represent only a small portion of the population of interest.

Pretests can serve both to verify the utility of an instrument in which the researcher has a good deal of confidence and to help in the development of an instrument when the researcher knows less about the phenomena under study. In the former case, the instrument should be administered in the pretest in what is expected to be its final form. In the latter case, however, the researcher might want to experiment with different forms in order to learn what works best. A pretest of that type can involve:

1. Different versions of the instrument that test different question wordings or instrument formats.

2. Administering a final questionnaire through actual interviews in order to identify problems in communication.

3. Open-ended questions that help develop response categories for closed-ended questions to be used in the final version.

When these types of devices are used to refine an instrument, the researcher should pretest the instrument that is finally developed, so as to identify any remaining or newly created flaws.

When pretesting an instrument that calls for interviews, researchers often find it useful to conduct a number of the interviews themselves in order to get a feel for the dynamics set up by their instrument and a sense of whether or not it communicates effectively with typical respondents. At the very least, the researcher should meet with the interviewers as soon as they return from the field and go over the instrument and accompanying procedures in detail in order to identify any points at which instructions are unclear, specified procedures are awkward, or respondents seem confused by questions.

Often a pretest is as much a test of the sampling technique and data management procedures as it is of the survey instrument. If interviewers using the specified sampling procedure turn up an unusually small number of qualified respondents or an obviously unrepresentative sample in the pretest, the applicability of the sampling technique to that research situation should be reexamined. If personnel find it difficult to keep track of or record data using the procedures selected for the pretest, then other procedures should be developed for the full-scale survey.

Sometimes, when researchers are entering an extremely new field of study, or do not have adequate funds for a full-scale study, or are planning a very large and important study, they will carry the logic of the pretest further and conduct a **pilot study.** A pilot study is a miniature version of the anticipated final study. It is designed to test all the data-gathering, processing, and analysis techniques to be employed and to provide information on the nature of the subject under study that might not otherwise be available. A pilot study is not a pretest, however, and the instruments employed in it should be pretested in the same way as for a full-scale study.

Pretesting is costly and time-consuming, but it is an absolutely essential investment, because without it the researcher risks producing useless or misleading data. Think of it as buying insurance against finding yourself with a mountain of very expensive data that are useless because of flaws in the survey that you could have corrected if only you had been aware of them.

Surveying

After all these preparations, we are ready to conduct the actual survey. This is the heart of the study, because it is where the data are actually collected. What is done in this stage depends on what type of survey is being conducted.

Most surveys are based either on in-person interviews or on telephone interviews. Researchers generally prefer to use face-to face interviews for longer surveys or questionnaires that contain sensitive topics respondents might be reluctant to talk about on the telephone. Of course, face-to-face interviews are relatively expensive because interviews have to be conducted at the respondent's home or at a central interviewing facility to which each respondent has to be invited. In addition, surveys that rely on face-to-face interviews can be difficult to conduct in certain areas of the United States (for example in high-crime neighborhoods or extremely rural areas) and usually take much longer to complete than telephone surveys. Based on the assumption that almost all Americans can be contacted by telephone, a large number of surveys carried out in the United States are conducted by telephone.

The proliferation of computers in the past twenty years has led most survey organizations today to use computers in order to manage and conduct telephone interviews. **Computer-assisted telephone interviewing (CATI)** has mostly replaced the traditional "paper-and-pencil" method, which forced interviewers to read printed questionnaires (similar to the one displayed in Figure 7.2) to respondents and then manually record their answers.

A typical CATI system consists of twenty or more networked computers that are controlled by a server (or main computer) that functions as a central storage location for the sample and data. The server controls and displays the interview schedule on each interviewer's computer screen, selects telephone numbers and dials them automatically for the interviewer. As soon as somebody answers the telephone, CATI prompts the interviewer to take the call and then read an introduction to the study (*Hello, my name is...*). The introduction typically identifies the survey organization and the study sponsor in addition to briefly explaining the purpose of the survey. If respondents agree to participate in the survey, interviewers start to read each question directly from the computer screen and enter responses with their keyboards. While most questions require the interviewer to enter only numerical codes for each answer (for example 1 for *agree* and 2 for *disagree*), interviewers can also record longer responses by typing them into blank boxes displayed on their screens.

As soon as the interviewer has entered a response, the CATI system automatically displays the next question until the end of the survey has been reached. After completion of the interview, respondents' data are saved on the server and are available for immediate analysis.

The CATI system offers several advantages over the "paper-and-pencil" method of conducting telephone interviews: First, it increases the efficiency and accuracy of surveys by displaying questions and answer categories on the interviewer's computer screen. Since the CATI program automatically guides the interviewer through the questions and records responses as they are entered, the possibility of interviewer error is greatly reduced.

Second, CATI systems allow survey organizations to administer very complex and individualized interview schedules. Based on responses to previous questions, for example, CATI can adjust the interview schedule and skip over questions not intended for certain respondents. This so-called **question branching** would be difficult to implement if an interviewer has to flip through pages of a printed interview schedule in order to get to the next appropriate question. CATI also has the ability to take responses and automatically insert them in subsequent questions, thus allowing the interviewer to ask highly individualized questions that are appropriate to each respondent. In addition, most CATI systems allow multilingual interviews (important for surveys targeting non-English speakers), voice-capturing of open-ended question responses (eliminating the need to type them), and the playback of short audio clips (to test commercial jingles, for example).

Third, CATI systems are able to unobtrusively monitor and control interviewers during the interviews. Researchers can listen in on any interview at any time to catch and correct interviewers' mistakes. Interviewers who, for example, mispronounce names or forget to probe *don't know* answers can then be retrained or pulled entirely from the study.

Finally, because respondents' answers are directly entered into the computer during the interview, researchers can request distributions or tabulations of responses at any point during a survey project. Most CATI systems feature integrated statistical software packages that allow instant analysis of the survey data, thus eliminating the need to reformat and then export data into other statistical programs.

While the introduction of CATI systems has improved and automated the way telephone interviews are conducted today, computers have also simplified the administrative functions associated with interviewing, such as scheduling of callbacks, interviewer productivity reporting, and sample management. Moreover, integrated text editors enable researchers to write, test, and revise questionnaires easily and quickly within CATI, thus reducing the time needed between the development and implementation of new survey schedules.

Monitoring

Surveys are monitored to ensure the validity and generalizability of results. Low or unbalanced response rates can be identified and, perhaps, corrected through careful monitoring. For all types of surveys this involves keeping careful records of completed instruments as they come in.

With mail surveys, returned questionnaires should be opened, checked for proper completion, and filed. Each questionnaire should be assigned a serial identification number so that the time of its return can be determined later. The number of questionnaires that is received each day should be logged so that the researcher can keep track of the response rate. If respondents can be identified from the returned questionnaires, the researcher should record incoming questionnaires in a manner that will reveal imbalances in the return as they develop. If a certain geographic or demographic group is making an extremely low response, some extra follow-up mail effort may be called for to keep the sample from becoming unrepresentative. In addition, examination of the incoming questionnaires may reveal mistakes made by respondents, such as overlooking the last page of the instrument or misreading directions about how to mark items. If respondents are identified, a phone call or second mailing can sometimes save questionnaires that otherwise have to be discarded.

With in-person surveys, monitoring is done principally through a debriefing session as interviewers return from the field. The researcher or a trusted assistant should check the completed interview schedules to determine whether (1) the correct people in the correct households have been interviewed, (2) all completed interview schedules have been returned, (3) each instrument fully identifies the respondent and provides information on the time and date of the interview, (4) each instrument contains an identification number for the respondent and for the interviewer, and (5) all refusals are explained and any outstanding callback cards (which are used to arrange times to contact the respondents who were not available for an interview at the first visit) have been turned in. All this helps ensure proper sampling and assists in verification.

Monitoring telephone surveys that are not conducted with computer-aided hardware involves asking interviewers to turn in records of their calls at the end of each calling period and checking each completed form for the same types of information as previously given for in-person interviews. In addition, it is often possible for the researcher or field director to listen in on interviews randomly without being detected. This provides both an incentive for interviewers to be responsible and a means of detecting and subsequently correcting flaws in interviewers' administration of the instrument.

Careful monitoring can go a long way toward ensuring the validity of survey results.

Verifying

Verification is especially important with in-person surveys, when unethical interviewers have both an opportunity and an incentive to falsify interviews and when even well-meaning ones can interview the wrong people. There have been instances in which nonprofessional interviewers have sat in bars and made up interviews to avoid going outdoors on cold nights and in which baby-sitters have identified themselves as residents and completed interviews. Verification procedures allow researchers to catch this type of error and to be sure that the sampling procedure is being followed correctly.

Verification of in-person interviews usually involves contacting the intended respondent to determine (1) whether the interview has occurred and (2) whether the interviewer has asked and correctly recorded answers to all questions. To do this, ask when the interview occurred and approximately how long it took. If respondents report that the interview has been conducted, ask them to re-answer two simple questions—one from the middle and one from near the end of the questionnaire—under the pretext that the answers were not clearly recorded in the field. Then check their answers against those that were recorded.

In large surveys, verification is done on a spot-check basis, for contacting all respondents would be too costly. If spot checks reveal falsifications or significant errors in any of an interviewer's forms, all of his or her interviews should be verified.

Secondary Analysis of Survey Data

The remaining steps in a survey research project are all subjects of other chapters. Coding and data processing are covered in Chapter 12, data analysis in Chapters 14 through 17, and reporting research results in Chapter 21. We will not preview those discussions here. We do, however, want to point out some aspects of data analysis in survey research that are not covered in other chapters.

It is important to recognize that most political scientists, perhaps even most political scientists who publish books and articles based on survey data, *never conduct a survey.* They do not conduct surveys both because it is difficult to obtain the necessary funding and because it is often possible to answer the research question they want to explore by using survey data others have collected. Studying data collected by someone else is called **secondary analysis.** Such analysis is very common with survey data because they are so expensive to collect.

Secondary analysis is highly desirable for several reasons. In the first place, the results of almost any survey contain data that are never used by the original researchers because they turn out to be only marginally relevant to the particular research question under study. Another researcher may find these data perfectly suited to answering some other research question. Secondary analysis allows fuller use of data and conserves resources by saving the cost of new surveys when sufficient data already exist. Second, surveys (and any obtrusive data collection technique) run the risk of *contaminating the population.* This means that repeated studies of some subject among a population may actually cause changes in the phenomena in question or make people reluctant to cooperate with future research. By allowing research to be conducted without yet another field survey, secondary analysis minimizes the risk of contamination. Third, although there are a great many data analysis techniques available to political scientists, any one researcher is likely to use only a few in a single study. Secondary analysis allows other researchers to apply different techniques that may expand our understanding of the subject or may even produce different answers to the original research question.

The most fruitful approach to secondary analysis is to select a research question, devise hypotheses to be tested, and then seek completed studies that contain the data necessary to test those hypotheses. Working in reverse (locating a sound data set and examining it in hopes of coming up with valuable research questions it can help answer) can sometimes pay off, but it significantly constrains the range of questions that can be investigated.

The first requirement of a useful data set is that it be based on a sample of the *appropriate population*. If we want to generalize to women in the United States, a study sampling voters in Kansas will be of no use. The second requirement is that the survey instrument contain *appropriate operationalizations* of the key variables in the hypotheses to be tested. If, for example, differences between blacks and whites are central to an investigation but the data set has recorded race only as "white" and "nonwhite," it will be of little use, as racial groups other than blacks (for example, Asians and Native Americans) are included in the nonwhite category.

How do we find out if a study is usable? Good reports of research state what sample has been used and describe the operationalizations of key variables that have been employed. Consequently, books and journal articles sometimes provide enough information about a data set for us to judge its suitability, and a literature search can turn up a source of data for secondary analysis. Individual political scientists are often willing to share data sets with others when asked, so it is sometimes possible to obtain a data set through a letter to an author.

Fortunately, there is a more systematic and reliable way to locate and gain access to data for secondary analysis. There are a number of institutions that collect data sets in the same way that libraries collect books. These institutions are generally referred to as **data archives.** They classify data sets for easy location and put them in a form that facilitates the sets' use by people who were not involved in the original project in which the data were collected. The archives then make the data sets available to researchers for a fee. Some of the more important social science data archives are listed here, along with brief descriptions of their holdings.

- *Roper Public Opinion Research Center*, University of Connecticut, Storrs. One of the nations's largest archives containing data from surveys conducted in many nations and covering a wide variety of subjects (www.roper.org).

- *Inter-University Consortium for Political and Social Research (ICPSR)*, University of Michigan, Ann Arbor. A very large, general collection of surveys in the United States and abroad stressing political variables and including cross-national data sets and extensive data on political behavior in the United States (www.icpsr.umich.edu).

- *National Election Studies (NES)* produce data on voting, public opinion, and political participation that serve the research needs of social scientists, teachers, students, policy makers, and journalists concerned with the theoretical and empirical foundations of mass politics in a democratic society (www.umich.edu/~nes).

- *National Opinion Research Center (NORC)* at the University of Chicago, conducts the General Social Survey (GSS), an almost annual survey of U.S. households. The first survey took place in 1972 and since then more than 35,000 respondents have answered more than 2,500 different questions (www.icpsr.umich.edu/gss).

- *Louis Harris Data Center* at the University of North Carolina, Chapel Hill maintains a collection of surveys of the U.S. population conducted by the Louis Harris public opinion polling organization (www.irss.unc.edu).

- *International Social Survey Programme (ISSP)* is an annual program of cross-national collaboration on surveys covering topics important for social science research. It brings together preexisting social science projects and coordinates research goals, thereby adding a cross-national, cross-cultural perspective to the individual national studies (www.issp.org).

- *European Community (EC)* provides access to European public opinion including Eurobarometer, Europinion, and links to other social sciences data archives (europa.eu.int/comm/dg10/epo/org.html).

- *Data and Program Library Service (DPLS)* is the central repository of data collections used by the social science research community at the University of Wisconsin–Madison (dpls.dacc.wisc.edu).

- *Pew Research Center for the People and the Press* in Washington, D.C. is an independent opinion research group, sponsored by the Pew Charitable Trusts. The center studies public attitudes toward the press, politics, and public policy issues (www.people-press.org).

Each of these institutions publishes a list of the data sets it has that provides a general description of the data. Once a promising-sounding study has been located in a listing of archive holdings, we can determine the actual utility of the study by obtaining the **code book** for the survey. This lists all questions asked and tells how the responses have been coded, and it will allow us to judge the fit between the study's operationalizations and the hypotheses to be tested. Appropriate data can then be purchased from the archive and analyzed.

Suggestions for Further Reading

The literature on survey research is one of the largest in the social sciences. Most of it reflects the fact that the method is widely used in sociology and psychology as well as in political science and other fields. A relatively comprehensive overview of the method is provided in Floyd J. Fowler, Jr., *Survey Research Methods,* 2d ed. (Newbury Park, CA: Sage, 1993). Other excellent introductions are found in Earl Babbie, *Survey Research Methods* (Belmont, CA: Wadsworth, 1990); Herbert F. Weisberg, Jon A. Krosnick, and Bruce D. Bowen, *An Introduction to Survey Research, Polling, and Data Analysis* (Thousand Oaks, CA: Sage, 1996); Louis M. Rea and Richard A. Parker, *Designing and Conducting Survey Research: A Comprehensive Guide,* 2d ed. (San Francisco, CA: Jossey-Bass, 1997); Arlene Fink and Jacqueline Kosecoff, *How to Conduct Surveys: A Step by Step Guide,* 2d ed. (Thousand Oaks, CA: Sage, 1998). See also *The Survey Kit* (Thousand Oaks, CA: Sage, 1995).

The subjects of question wording and questionnaire design in general are addressed in Abraham N. Oppenheim, *Questionnaire Design and Attitude Measurement* (New York: St. Martin's, 1992); William H. Foddy, *Constructing Questions for Interviews and Questionnaires: Theory and Practice in Social Research* (New York: Cambridge University Press, 1993); Floyd J. Fowler, *Improving Survey Questions: Design and Evaluation* (Thousand Oaks, CA: Sage, 1995); Douglas R. Berdie, John F. Anderson, and Marsha A. Niebuhr, *Questionnaires: Design and Use,* 2d ed. (Metuchen, NJ: Scarecrow Press, 1986).

Interviewer skills are covered in Jack D. Douglas, *Creative Interviewing* (Beverly Hills, CA: Sage, 1985) and in Floyd J. Fowler, Jr. and Thomas W. Mangione, *Standardized Survey Interviewing: Minimizing Interviewer-Related Error* (Newbury Park, CA: Sage, 1990).

A very detailed discussion of how to conduct surveys by mail rather than through in-person interviews is found in Paul L. Erdos, *Professional Mail Surveys* (Malabar, FL: Krieger, 1983) and in Thomas W. Mangione, *Mail Surveys: Improving the Quality* (Thousand Oaks, CA: Sage, 1995). Telephone survey methods are covered in James H. Frey, *Survey Research by Telephone*, 2d ed. (Newbury Park, CA: Sage, 1989) and in Paul J. Lavrakas, *Telephone Survey Methods: Sampling, Selection, and Supervision*, 2d ed. (Newbury Park, CA: Sage, 1993). One of the most widely referenced books on these techniques is Don A. Dillman, *Mail and Internet Surveys*, 2d ed. (New York: Wiley, 2000).

Political scientists who are not conducting their own surveys but are planning to use data collected by others might want to turn to Herbert H. Hyman, *Secondary Analysis of Sample Surveys* (Middletown, CT: Wesleyan University Press, 1987).

Research Exercises

1. Break the following question into several questions using a contingency question convention. Write down the new questions in an appropriate format for a questionnaire.

   Have you ever belonged to a political organization, and if so which one, and are you still a member, and if not then and why did you leave the organization?

2. Write a series of three to five statements with which you might ask respondents to agree or disagree in order to get a measure of each of the following concepts:

   support for the Democratic party
   opposition to gun control legislation
   political liberalism

3. Using any sources you can find in the library, locate two survey research items that researchers have used to operationalize any two of the following concepts:

   political efficacy
   political activism (participation)
   authoritarianism
   political conservatism

   Write down the items used in the operationalization along with a full citation of the study in which they were reported.

4. Select a politically relevant topic of interest to you and identify a dependent variable and three independent variables you might want to use in a study of the subject. Devise an interview schedule designed to provide measures of these four variables, and write it out in a form that can be used in interviewing. Include a system of precoding for answers.

5. Devise a simple theory (one involving only a few independent variables) to explain why people differ on *one* of the following variables:

   party identification
   political alienation
   regularity of voting
   membership in voluntary associations

   Write out the theory as a set of testable hypotheses, carefully identifying the variables involved.

   Now locate an existing survey research data set that you can use in a secondary analysis to test these hypotheses. Your best bet for doing this is to locate literature from the

ICPSR, which lists and describes available data sets. Find some promising-sounding studies, get a copy of the code book for each so that you can see exactly what questions were asked, and make your selection on that basis.

Terms Introduced in This Chapter

survey research
respondents
cross-sectional surveys
longitudinal surveys
trend studies
cohort studies
panel studies
questionnaire
interview schedule
demographic groups
open-ended questions
closed-ended questions

question format
in-person interviews
mail surveys
telephone surveys
pretests
pilot study
computer-assisted telephone
    interviewing (CATI)
question branching
secondary analysis
data archives
code book

CHAPTER 8

SCALING TECHNIQUES

One of the most common problems we encounter in designing survey or other instruments arises when we must find a way to assign a single representative value or score to a complex attitude or behavior. As an example, consider how one might go about measuring the degree of people's prejudice toward college students. Such prejudice can take a number of forms, depending on which attributes of college students a particular individual might focus upon. That is, some people might judge college students by students' dress, others by their mannerisms, and still others by their behavior, their social or economic status, or even their personal hygiene. Some people might hold stereotypic views based on one or two encounters, either pleasant or unpleasant, with specific students, and others may barely differentiate between college students and other members of the community. These elements of judgment may vary quite widely in substance, direction, and degree, but each is, at least potentially, a component of the larger concept *prejudice.*

As researchers hoping to tap these factors, we must design an instrument that is at once sufficiently broad to detect and measure as many of these component elements as possible and sufficiently concise to allow us to summarize in some meaningful way the extent to which the more general concept in question is present. Put another way, we need a device that captures or represents a notion such as prejudice in all its complexity *and* tells us how much of it each respondent (or case) has. One important means by which we can accomplish this is through *scaling.*

Scaling is a procedure in which we combine a number of relatively narrow indicators (in the example, survey questions about specific perceived traits of college students) into a single, summary measure that we take to represent the broader, underlying concept of which each is a part (prejudice). Thus we might measure a respondent's attitudes about various behaviors of college students (that they drink too much or have too many loud parties, for example) or about their mannerisms (that they are snobbish or self-important or inconsiderate), but we would not take any one of these items *alone* to stand for so broad a concept as prejudice. Rather, we must pull together *several* of these narrow measures in some way that allows us to draw conclusions about the more general point of view to which each may contribute or that each may reflect. And more than that, we must accomplish the task in such a way that we can compare the amount of prejudice (or whatever it is we are measuring) that characterizes one respondent with the amount that characterizes another, in effect making a judgment (in the example) about which is *more* prejudiced. The unifying measure that represents a given underlying concept is called a **scale**. The individualized assessment of the degree to which any given case manifests that underlying concept is called a **scale score**. Scaling, or scale construction, is simply the procedure by which we build scales and assign individual scale scores.

Scale Construction: Two Basic Concerns

Scaling, then, seems to be a fairly straightforward process. The task of the researcher is simply to identify several components of the underlying concept, to develop indicators to measure each, to combine those indicators into a summary score by reciting a few magic words or statistical incantations, and—presto—it's done. Unfortunately, this apparent simplicity is deceptive, for there are some potential dangers to which we must be especially sensitive in selecting and interpreting scale components. Most important among these are two with which we are already familiar—the concerns posed by the notions of validity and reliability.

Validity, you will recall, is concerned with the question, Are we in fact measuring what we think we are measuring? In the present context, this question asks, in effect, whether there is reason to believe that each of the individual components (specific questions) in a given scale is actually related directly to the underlying concept and whether, collectively, those components capture the full essence of it. Putting that another way, we must ask ourselves whether it really makes sense to combine a particular set of indicators *and,* once we have done so, whether it really makes sense to attach to this set of indicators the particular label we have chosen. Thus, in our example, we must ask ourselves first whether persons' attitudes toward student behavior really have anything in common with their attitudes toward student mannerisms or styles of dress, and second whether all these attitudes together can really be considered to reflect the degree of those persons' prejudice toward students.

Reliability, on the other hand, is concerned with the question, Regardless of what we are measuring, are we measuring it consistently? Here this question translates into a concern with whether the various component indicators of a scale are in fact related to one another in a consistent and meaningful manner. In effect, we are asking not whether a particular set of questions or indicators differentiates between apples and oranges, but rather whether, once the apples have been identified, it provides us with consistent standards for sorting them by size, color, and variety. If so, then combining the measures will tell us more about apples than will any single measure. But if our standards are inconsistent or ambiguous, then our observations based upon them may prove misleading.

Perhaps a different example will help to make these points clear. Consider a scale in which each respondent is instructed to express either agreement or disagreement with each of the following statements:

1. The Cubans are evil and cannot be trusted.
2. The French are evil and cannot be trusted.

3. The Japanese are evil and cannot be trusted.

4. The Chinese are evil and cannot be trusted.

Let us suppose that this scale is intended to measure *xenophobia*—the fear and distrust of foreigners. Presumably, the more statements with which particular respondents agree, the more xenophobic we may take them to be. But is that really the case? A person who believes only the Cubans and the Chinese are evil and not to be trusted may, in effect, be expressing anticommunism rather than xenophobia. A person who believes only the Japanese and the Chinese are evil and not to be trusted may, in effect, be expressing racism rather than xenophobia. Even a respondent who regards all four groups as evil and untrustworthy may, upon closer inspection, be expressing not xenophobia but a feeling that *all* people or *all* governments, even the respondent's own, are evil and not to be trusted. Because we cannot say with any assuredness that this scale measures xenophobia per se, the scale lacks validity. And what of reliability? Even if the scale were measuring xenophobia, could we claim that its components measured consistently? Fear and distrust of the Chinese, for example, may be an indicator of at least two very different characteristics–one ideological and the other racial—and two respondents might give the same answer for very different reasons. Is our anticommunist respondent in some meaningful sense *equally* xenophobic with our racist one? Probably not. To combine these particular items into a single measure by simply adding them together, then, is at best an exercise in futility and at worst a source of erroneous conclusions.

Problems of this type cannot always be overcome easily, and as a result, scaling must be used with great care in some instances and must be forgone in others. Yet the overriding advantages inherent in the ability to develop a single number or score to represent a complex attitude or behavior provide a substantial incentive to employ scaling techniques in a great many instances. In the remainder of this chapter we discuss four different approaches to the development of meaningful scales. Each of these should be viewed not only in terms of its procedures but also in terms of its strengths and weaknesses in overcoming the problems of validity and reliability.

Likert Scaling

The first such technique, and probably the least satisfactory in these terms, is **Likert scaling**—a simple technique by which each respondent is presented with a series of statements requiring a value judgment. Figure 8.1 illustrates a typical series of such items, which might constitute a measure of prejudice toward college students.[1] In each instance, respondents are asked whether they agree strongly, agree, disagree, or disagree strongly with the statement. Each such respondent is assigned a numerical score, with 5 representing the strongest agreement and 1 representing

---

[1] In this figure statements have been worded in only one direction (that is, all agreements with the items reflect the presence of prejudice) for purposes of illustration. In practice, some items would be reworded so that the negative responses evidence prejudice, and the score values would be reversed accordingly. The goal of such a procedure is to minimize *response set bias*—the tendency of some respondents to give the same answer to every question.

Please indicate whether you *agree strongly, agree, disagree,* or *disagree strongly* with each of the following statements:

1. There may be a few exceptions, but in general college students are pretty much alike.
2. The trouble with letting college students into a nice neighborhood is that they gradually give it a typical student atmosphere.
3. To end prejudice against college students, the first step is for the students to try sincerely to get rid of their harmful and irritating faults.
4. There is something different and strange about college students; it is hard to tell what they are thinking and planning, and what makes them tick.
5. Most college students would become overbearing and disagreeable if not kept in their place.
6. College students prove that when people of their type have too much money and freedom, they just take advantage and cause trouble.

Figure 8.1
Typical Likert scale items
SOURCE: Adapted from the E (Ethnocentrism)Scale used by Theodore Adorno et al. in *The Authoritarian Personality* (New York: Harper& Row,1950).

the strongest disagreement. A middle or neutral response is assigned the value 3. To obtain the summary measure of prejudice for a particular individual, one adds all the individual scores and divides by the number of statements. Thus a respondent who has answered questions 1 through 6 as follows

Item 1: Agree(4)

Item 2: Strongly agree (5)

Item 3: Neutral(3)

Item 4: Agree (4)

Item 5: Disagree(2)

Item 6: Agree (4)

is assigned the summary score 3.67 ([4 + 5 + 3 + 4 + 2 + 4]/6), which might be rounded to 4.

In general, the higher a person's scale score, the more of the measured characteristic (in this case, prejudice toward college students) he or she is presumed to have.

The problems here are precisely those already noted in our xenophobia scale, which was, in fact, an oversimplified Likert-type scale. For one thing, we know nothing about the relationships among the component items. Each may in fact measure different aspects of the same underlying trait, and on its face each appears to do so, but we cannot be sure.

The items that compose a good (or reliable) scale should have high internal consistency—that is, they should be highly correlated with each other. Different statistical models exist for measuring internal consistency. One approach, called the *split-half method,* divides the scale items into two parts and correlates one half with the other. For example, the even-numbered question items in Figure 8.1 might form one-half and the odd-numbered items the other half. The prejudice scale in our example (item 1 through item 6) would be internally consistent if the total score of the first half of the test (item 1 + item 3 + item 5) correlates highly with the score on the second half of the test (item 2 + item 4 + item 6).

Probably the most commonly used reliability coefficient for items that have three or more answer categories is *alpha* (also called *Cronbach's alpha*), which is based on the average inter-item correlation. For items with two answer categories (true/false or agree/disagree, for example), the related *Kuder-Richardson 20 (KR20)* coefficient usually is used.

One point that should be clear even now, however, has to do with the way in which the summary (average) score is determined: one simply adds the individual item scores and divides by the number of items. But if we look more closely at the response categories (that is, *strongly agree, agree,* etc.), we find that they represent measurement at the ordinal level. That is, they distinguish between mutually exclusive categories and rank each relative to the others (they tell how strongly one agrees or disagrees with a statement). They do not, however, establish known and equal intervals (the difference between *strongly agree* and *agree* is not always the same, either from item to item or from one respondent to the next). Accordingly, it is meaningless and misleading to add these numbers together, let alone to average them. A more appropriate procedure, but not a commonly used one, is to calculate a different kind of average, called a *median,* for each respondent's answers and to assign this as the scale score. Determination of the median is discussed in Chapter 14.

Guttman Scaling

Many of the problems associated with Likert scaling can be overcome in certain circumstances by using a more sophisticated technique known as *Guttman scaling.* **Guttman scaling** begins from the assumption that certain attitudes (and behaviors) are related to one another in such a way that holding (or engaging in) one is more difficult or requires more effort than holding (or engaging in) another. Perhaps the best analogy here is to a person standing on a ladder. A person standing on the fifth rung quite likely has climbed there by stepping on the first, second, third, fourth, and fifth rungs. It is possible but less likely that the person skipped one or more of the lower rungs on the way up. It is most unlikely that someone would step directly from the ground to the fifth rung of the ladder, at least without enduring some pain. In effect, then, our climber has reached the fifth rung by engaging in a series of progressively higher-order behaviors and can reasonably be *assumed* to have traversed the lower positions to reach the highest one.

Similarly, even if we know that a particular person has voted in a presidential election—an act we know from many studies to be one of the most common and least demanding in politics—we cannot assume with any degree of assurance that the same person has also participated actively in some political organization—a far more demanding and much less common action—or has run for public office—one of the most demanding and least common political acts of all. Yet if, on the other hand, we know that an individual has been active in a political organization, we *may* assume with some degree of confidence that that person has also engaged in such lesser political acts as voting, though not that the person has taken the further

Please indicate whether you *agree* or *disagree* with each of the following statements:

1. Given a choice, I would like to see college students kept out of my community.
2. It is okay for college students to visit my community.
3. If a college student wanted to live in my community, that would be okay with me.
4. I would not want to see a college student living in my neighborhood.
5. I would have no objection to someone in my family bringing home a college student as a guest for dinner.
6. I would be displeased if someone in my family were to marry a college student.

Figure 8.2
Typical Guttman scale items
SOURCE: Adapted from the Social Distance Scale developed by E. Bogardus in *Social Distance* (Yellow Springs, OH: Antioch Press, 1959).

step of running for office. And by extension, if an individual has been a candidate for office, we have reason to assume that the person has also voted and engaged in organizational activity. These assumptions will not always prove correct, but they will be supported far more often than not.

Certain attitudes may be seen to relate to one another in much the same way. We can see this illustrated in Figure 8.2, which represents an alternative approach to measuring a person's degree of prejudice against students.[2] In a procedure similar to that for Likert scaling, respondents are asked whether they agree or disagree with each item in a series of statements. The response that most reflects the trait being measured (for example, prejudice) is scored with a +, and alternative responses are scored with a −. Thus agreement with item 1 would be scored + as reflecting prejudice, and agreement with item 2 would be assigned a −, reflecting its absence. The statements themselves may be seen to bear a relationship with one another such that the various responses reflect the degree of one's prejudice or freedom from it. In effect, the closer a perceived threat comes to one's own family or self, the more difficult it presumably is for one to remain free of prejudice. What this means is that there is, at least potentially, a logical, ordinal relationship among the items in the scale—a factor that is missing under the Likert procedure.

Moreover, Guttman scaling provides appropriate procedures not only for summarizing the degree of a characteristic possessed by a given respondent but also for assessing the degree to which a particular set of components meets the assumption of ordinality in the first place. These procedures are illustrated in Table 8.1, which reports the responses of 170 hypothetical persons to the statements presented in Figure 8.2.

Several points in the table are worthy of note. To begin with, the items are ordered on the left-hand side of the table in ascending order according to their number of supportive responses (+). This number is ascertained by summing the number of cases (*n*) for which a + has been recorded for a particular item. (In Table 8.1 these numbers have been assigned arbitrarily and may be found at the bottom of each corresponding column.) The assumption here is that the number of agreeing

---

[2] In this figure, the statements have been arranged in order of their degree of difficulty for purposes of illustration. In practice, their order should be mixed to obscure any implicit ranking.

Table 8.1

Hypothetical distribution of Gutman scale responses[*]

Item 1	Item 2	Item 3	Item 4	Item 5	Item 6	n	Error (e)	n(e)	Scale Score
+	+	+	+	+	+	10			7
−	+	+	+	+	+	20			6
−	−	+	+	+	+	30			5
−	−	−	+	+	+	30			4
−	−	−	−	+	+	10			3
−	−	−	−	−	+	10			2
−	−	−	−	−	−	5			1
+	−	+	+	+	+	30	1	30	(7) or (5)
+	+	+	+	−	−	5	2	10	(7)
−	+	−	+	+	+	20	1	20	(6) or (4)
45	**55**	**95**	**145**	**150**	**160**	**170**		**60**	

Marginals (used for ordering items)   **Totals**

*+ Indicates a response reflecting prejudice.

responses will decrease as the difficulty of holding (or the extremeness of) a particular attitude increases. In the example, this ranking happens to correspond with our expectations in that the observed ranking is in the same order as our initial ranking, but this is not always the case.

Each line in the table represents a group of individuals who have given a particular combination of responses to the six items. Thus the first line represents those 10 people ($n = 10$) who have responded to each of the six questions in a manner reflecting prejudice toward students. The second line represents those 20 respondents whose answers indicate prejudice on items 2 through 6, but not on the more extreme item 1, and so forth. The first seven lines in the table represent those combinations of responses that are wholly consistent with the assumption that the six items are ordinally related with one another. Persons displaying any one of these combinations of responses are termed *perfect scale types.*

In Guttman scaling, there will always be one more perfect scale type than there are items in the scale, because the total absence of the characteristic being measured (*no* prejudice, as in line 7) is regarded as a perfect score. Each perfect score is assigned a number from 1 to $i + 1$, where i is the number of items, with 1 identifying those respondents possessing the lowest level of the trait in question and $i + 1$ those possessing the highest. The appropriate score is then recorded for each respondent. Thus, in the example, each of the 10 persons in line 1, whose responses reflect the highest degree of prejudice, are assigned the score 7 ($i + 1 = 6 + 1 = 7$), each person in line 2 the score 6, each in line 3 the score 5, and so on, until the five respondents in line 7 are each scored 1. These scores rank each respondent vis-à-vis every other respondent according to his or her degree of prejudice.

We have yet to account, however, for the 55 respondents represented by lines 8, 9, and 10 in the table. One or more of the responses of these individuals do not fit the pattern predicted by our ordering of the items. These are, in effect, people who skipped one or more steps while climbing the ladder. Accordingly, these sets of responses are said to contain one or more *errors*. The term *error* here refers not to a mistake by the respondent but to a failure of the assumptions of Guttman scaling to apply to these cases. When such errors occur, and they are quite common, we proceed on a line-by-line basis as follows. First, we count the *minimum* number of changes in the line that, if made, would result in a perfect scale score. In line 8, for instance, we can change the + in column 1 to a − to obtain a response of 5, or alternatively, we can change the − in column 2 to a + to obtain a response of 7. In either event, we are changing only one item, and so we say line 8 contains one error. This is indicated in the column labeled "error (*e*)." We then multiply the number of errors (1) by the number of cases in which the error occurs (30) and enter our result in the next column. Finally, we assign to each case the scale score it would receive if the error did not occur. Though we have only one error in line 8, we have a choice of two possible corrections, one of which yields a score of 5 and the other a score of 7. Unless there is some compelling reason to choose one of these scores over the other, the standard practice is to assign each of the 30 cases randomly to one or the other scale category.

We move next to line 9 and repeat the procedure. Here we are required to make a minimum of two changes, for we must convert both − scores to +. Again, we note the number of errors, multiply by the number of cases, and assign a scale score. Here, however, only one score is possible, since we have no options when making our corrections. The procedure is then repeated for line 10, as it is for any additional nonscalar combinations.

In proceeding through liens 8, 9, and 10, we have, of course, assigned scores to each case as if it fitted our scale perfectly, though we know for a fact that it does not. This means that to the extent that we rely upon our scale scores to describe those 55 cases, we risk reaching an improper conclusion. The question thus arises of just how serious a risk this is. Fortunately, Guttman scaling procedures suggest an answer.

Recall that we have kept track of the total number of errors in the scale. In effect, an assessment of risk requires us to ask whether this total error is relatively small and therefore unimportant or whether it is so large as to invalidate the scale itself. We may answer this question by calculating a statistic called the *Guttman coefficient of reproducibility* (C_R), the formula for which is as follows:

$$C_R = 1 - \frac{\sum n(e)}{i(N)}$$

where n = the number of cases in lines in which errors occur

e = the number of errors in each line

i = the number of response items

N = the total number of cases

For the example, the coefficient of reproducibility is determined by substituting the appropriate values:

$$C_R = 1 - \frac{30 + 10 + 20}{6(170)} = 1 - \frac{60}{1,020}$$

$$= 1 - 0.06 = .94$$

In this formula, the quantity $\sum n(e)$ represents the total number of "mistakes" in the scale, and the quantity $i(N)$ represents the total number of possible mistakes if *no* items or respondents fit the scale. The fraction

$$\frac{\sum n(e)}{i(N)}$$

thus tells us what proportion of all possible mistakes have in fact been made. By subtracting this proportion of error from one, we ascertain the proportion of scale entries that are error free. As a matter of convention, any Guttman scale with a C_R of .90 or higher is accepted as sound, and any scale with a lower C_R is considered suspect and is generally not used for purposes of analysis.[3]

We can see, then, that for items that meet the criterion of inherent ordering by degree of difficulty, Guttman scaling is a potent technique by which we may bring together a number of indicators into a single summary value that meaningfully represents a more general characteristic of a respondent.

Thurstone Scaling

Yet another technique for creating summary measures, though one intended to solve a rather different problem, is the *Thurstone equal-appearing interval scale.* You will recall from our earlier discussion that in phrasing questions to measure such variables as social class, the researcher may choose to measure respondents' characteristics according to some externally imposed criterion, such as income or occupational prestige, or may alternatively permit respondents to apply their own standards of judgment, as by asking them what social class they *identify* with. The first approach enhances the comparability of data from case to case; the second may yield less comparable but more meaningful data. **Thurstone scaling** is a procedure for pursuing the second strategy (but with improved comparability) by letting a few members of the population to be studied actually participate in designing the scales that will be used to measure the characteristics of the population itself. By providing for the internal definition of the meanings of indicators, the Thurstone technique enhances the validity of a scale. By eliminating from consideration all but the most

---

[3] Two points should be noted here, though their exploration is beyond the scope of this book. First, Guttman scaling procedures can be used to eliminate or reorder response items through a procedure similar to the calculation of C_R in which errors are assigned to individual questions with minimum criteria established for question acceptance. Second, C_R has been demonstrated to have certain weaknesses, including a tendency to inflate the value of a particular scale. Some have suggested that these problems can be overcome by using a variety of more sophisticated statistical techniques, including factor analytic tests of undimensionality. Certain of these procedures, however, may exceed the support capability of the underlying ordinal data, and they should be used only with care.

widely agreed upon scale items, we enhance the reliability of the scale as well. The technique is rather complicated, but once we have these goals clearly in mind, it is not difficult to understand.

In constructing a Thurstone scale, the researcher first gathers a large number of statements, perhaps as many as 100, that reflect a variety of attitudes about some object. A number of "judges" are then selected at random from the population to be studied. These are simply individuals on whom the list of statements will be tried out. The judges usually number at least 50, and they may include as many as several hundred persons when resources permit. Each judge is presented with an 11-point scale—ranging from *favorable* (11) to *neutral* (6) to *unfavorable* (1)—and with a stack of cards—on each of which is printed one of the statements. The judge is asked to examine each statement as it relates to the object in question and to place each card in one of 11 piles corresponding to his or her evaluation. Thus those statements a judge regards as most favorable toward some object, such as college students, may be placed in pile 11, those slightly less favorable in pile 10, and so forth. In this manner, the researcher obtains every judge's understanding of the evaluative meaning of each statement.

At this point, each statement is assigned a scale score indicating its relative position on the favorable-unfavorable continuum, with higher scores going to those statements that are seen as more favorable. Many researchers assign these scores by calculating a mean, that is, by summing all of the individual scores for each item and dividing by the number of judges.[4] A more appropriate procedure is to find the median value assigned to each statement (see Chapter 14) and to treat this as the scale score. Those items that are assigned widely divergent scores by different judges (for example, those that are spread over five or six categories) are eliminated at this point. From the remaining list, some 15 to 20 final items are selected for inclusion in the questionnaire. The items should be those on which the judges most closely agree, and they should collectively cover the full spectrum of evaluations. Figure 8.3 illustrates a few typical statements that might be included in a Thurstone scale of attitudes toward college students.[5]

When these final items reach the interview stage, respondents in the study sample are asked either which of the statements they agree with or, alternatively, which two or three statements are closest to their own view of the object in question, in this case, college students. The median[6] value of the items so designated by each individual is then determined and is assigned as that respondent's scale score, the summary of his or her views toward the object. When the responses of a given individual are scattered widely over several noncontiguous items, the researcher generally concludes either that the individual has no attitude toward the object in question or that his or her attitude is organized differently from the structure assumed by the scale. In such cases, no scale score is assigned. But when, as is much more

---

[4] Proponents of this procedure argue that with as many as 11 categories, the ordinal character of the scale is converted to quasi-interval status, and on this basis they justify the use of interval-level statistics (hence the term *equal-appearing interval scale*). The authors, however, reject this argument.
[5] These statements have been ordered from most favorable through neutral to most unfavorable for purposes of illustration. In practice, their order should be assigned randomly to obscure any systematic relationships. Scale values should not be shown on the questionnaire.
[6] Some would argue for the mean.

Please consider each of the following statements and indicate which ones you *agree* with:

1. It may not be widely known, but far more college students have volunteered for the military services than one would expect on the basis of their percentage in the population as a whole.
2. Some college students are definitely much superior in intelligence to other people in this community.
3. Whatever their faults, college students contribute a great deal to the quality of life in this community.
4. There is little truth in the image of college students in this community as being less ambitious or hard-working on the average than many other groups.
5. Some college students are clean and some are dirty, but the average college student does not differ in any way in his personal habits from the average person.
6. When you come right down to it, college students are just like anybody else in this community; they have their good points and they have their bad points.
7. While there are no doubt a few exceptions, in general college students tend to be especially clannish and to stick together.
8. While every group has a right to get ahead, college students are a little apt to disregard the rights and possesions of other people.
9. College students sometimes try to enter stores, hotels, and restaurants where they are just not welcome.
10. Many people in this community would accept college students more easily if there were less drunkenness, self-righteousness, and public demonstrations of sexual looseness and immorality among them.
11. It is a fairly well-established fact that college students have a less pleasant body odor than other people in this community.

Figure 8.3
Typical Thurstone scale items
Source: Adapted from a scale reported by H. Schuman and J. Harding in "Prejudice and the Norm of Rationality," *Sociometry*, 27 (1964), pp. 353–71.

often the case, the responses do cluster tightly in one portion of the continuum, the researcher can have reasonable confidence in the validity and reliability of the measure. This is due in no small part to the role of the judges in designing the research instrument.

The Semantic Differential

The fourth and final scaling procedure we shall discuss is termed the *semantic differential*. This procedure, which is quite different in structure and purpose from those already discussed, relies on a series of adjective pairs to bring out the meaning a given individual attaches to a particular concept. A typical series of these adjective pairs is illustrated in Figure 8.4. Respondents are presented with such a list, usually on a separate card, and are asked to rate a particular object, again in the illustration using college students, on a 7-point scale from one adjective to the other. Measurement of this type allows for variation in both the intensity and the direction of the attitude being measured, with neutrality being represented by the midpoint on the scale. The ordering of adjectives in each pair is determined randomly to prevent response set bias.

Although some researchers do break such scales into various underlying dimensions and sum the responses within each, most agree that semantic differential scales

Listed below are several pairs of words that could be used to describe college students. Between the words in each pair are several blanks. Please put an X on the blank for each pair that best describes how you feel about college students.

In general, college students are:

1.	Boring	— — — — — — —	Interesting
2.	Clean	— — — — — — —	Dirty
3.	Emotional	— — — — — — —	Rational
4.	Gentle	— — — — — — —	Violent
5.	Good	— — — — — — —	Bad
6.	Dishonest	— — — — — — —	Honest
7.	Serious	— — — — — — —	Humorous
8.	Idealistic	— — — — — — —	Realistic
9.	Noisy	— — — — — — —	Quiet
10.	Pleasant	— — — — — — —	Unpleasant
11.	Rich	— — — — — — —	Poor
12.	Pleasing	— — — — — — —	Annoying
13.	Sincere	— — — — — — —	Insincere
14.	Superficial	— — — — — — —	Profound
15.	Valuable	— — — — — — —	Worthless

Figure 8.4
Typical semantic differential items

do not readily yield scale scores in the same way as the other techniques we have discussed. Rather, semantic differential scales are useful primarily either for purposes of comparison from object to object (Are ostensibly similar objects viewed by respondents in similar terms?) or for the development of scales measuring more general concepts (for example, What types of actions or views are regarded as either liberal or conservative?). In effect, then, the semantic differential serves a somewhat different and more fundamental purpose in the research process—that of helping to construct and evaluate definitions—than do the Likert, Guttman, and Thurstone techniques.

There are, we should note, several other scaling techniques that one might employ in survey research. Those we have discussed, however, are the most common and within the limits noted, among the most useful. Together they should suggest the types of options available, and the criteria one must consider, when it becomes necessary to develop multiple but narrow measures of broad, underlying concepts.

Suggestions for Further Reading

Gary M. Maranell has brought together many of the seminal works in the literature on scaling in *Scaling: A Sourcebook for Behavioral Scientists* (Chicago: Aldine, 1974). Lee F. Anderson et al., in Chapter 6 of *Legislative Roll-Call Analysis* (Evanston, IL: Northwestern University Press, 1966), provide an especially useful summary of Guttman scaling techniques. John P. McIver and Edward G. Carmines provide succinct overviews of Likert, Guttman, and Thurstone scaling at a slightly more sophisticated level than that presented here in "Undimensional Scaling" in *Quantitative Applications in the Social Sciences* (Beverly Hills,

CA: Sage, 1981). An application-oriented introduction to scaling is Robert F. DeVellis, *Scale Development* (Newbury Park, CA: Sage, 1991).

For a comprehensive survey and discussion of many specific scales found in the literature of social science, see John P. Robinson, Phillip R. Shaver, Lawrence S. Wrightsman, eds., *Measures of Personality and Social Psychological Attitudes*(San Diego, CA: Academic Press, 1991) and John P. Robinson et al., *Measures of Political Attitudes* (San Diego, CA: Academic Press, 1999). For an example of scale construction, see Ada Finifter, "Dimensions of Political Alienation," *American Political Science Review,* 64 (1970), pp. 389–410.

Research Exercises

1. Select a multifaceted concept (for example, *political alienation*) and identify twenty survey items that might be considered indicators of the concept. Construct both a Thurstone scale and a Likert scale from these items. Administer the survey items to ten friends or classmates and assign each a score on both the Thurstone and the Likert scales. Compare the results.

2. When carrying out Exercise 1, also ask respondents for information on their actual behavior that can be used to check the validity of the scale scores you obtain as indicators of the concept. (For example, do people who score high on political alienation act as we would expect alienated people to behave, whereas those who score low on alienation report what we would regard as nonalienated behavior?) Now compare the scale scores with the behavioral reports and write up your findings by comparing the Thurstone and Likert scales for validity.

3. Develop six indicators of individual political participation (for example, registering to vote) that you believe will meet the requirements of Guttman scaling (that is, they are related to one another such that each successive behavior is more difficult or demanding than the last). Prepare an instrument like that in Figure 8.2, and administer it to all of your classmates (for this project, relatively large *n*'s are important). Include a measure of the sex of each respondent.

   a. Prepare a summary of responses like that in Figure 8.1, and calculate the coefficient of reproducibility. Discuss your findings.

   b. Assign individual scale scores to each classmate based on his or her responses to your questions. Summarize these scores and compare them across sexes. Discuss your findings.

   c. Experiment a bit by eliminating first one then another item from your scale or by reordering the items in the summary table. Recalculate the coefficient of reproducibility each time. How do you account for the differences? What does this suggest to you?

4. Select a series of adjective pairs to construct a semantic differential scale measuring perceptions of the heads of state of five countries. Prepare an instrument like that in Figure 8.4 and administer it to a sample of your classmates. Compute a summary score for each descriptor pair and each head of state. What have you learned about your classmates? What have you learned about their perceptions of each head of state and of heads of state generally? Which adjective pairs were most useful in drawing meaningful distinctions and conclusions? Why were these most useful?

Terms Introduced in This Chapter

scaling	Likert scaling
scale	Guttman scaling
scale score	Thurstone scaling

CHAPTER 9

CONTENT ANALYSIS

Very often, a political scientist may learn a great deal about individuals, groups institutions, or even nations through a careful examination of the communication patterns associated with them. Do campaign advertising and election year news reports provide much information about candidates' preferences and abilities? Do the internal memoranda of a large corporation reveal a systematic plan on the part of management to bribe representatives of foreign governments they wish to deal with? What does the *Congressional Record* tell us about the relative influence or importance of each U.S. senator? Do diplomatic communiqués between the United States and Russia reflect the public perception of a reduction in the level of conflict between these two nations?

These questions and others like them may best be answered by a direct examination of various items of communication. In general, these items fall into one of three classes: (1) those that are internally generated by the individual, organization, or government we are studying and internally directed (such communications as corporate memoranda, which represent or reflect the decision-making process itself), (2) those that are internally generated and externally directed (such publications as the *Congressional Record,* which are purposefully molded to create a particular image for the source among outsiders and which may reflect or obscure the process and outcome of decision making), and (3) those that are externally generated and internally directed (things like campaign propaganda, which, when viewed from the perspective of the recipient, provide potential source material for decision making). Each class of communication may be different in purpose or effect, as well as in accessibility and usefulness for research, but each provides potential opportunities to further our understanding of political behavior.

In each instance, the most appropriate technique for pursuing these opportunities is **content analysis**—the systematic counting, assessing, and interpreting of the form and substance of communication. Content analysis provides us with a method—really a set of methods—by which we may summarize fairly rigorously certain direct physical evidence of the behaviors of, and the relationships between, various types of political actors. In this chapter we shall discuss when it is appropriate to use content analysis, how the technique is applied, and how the results of content analysis should be interpreted, as well as certain limits of content analytic procedures.

Preparing to Use Content Analysis

Content analysis may be used to answer research questions whenever there is a physical record of communications by, to, within, or among the political actors we are interested in, as long as the researcher has access to that record. Examples of such a record include books, pamphlets, magazines, newspapers, phonograph records or CDs, audiotape and videotape recordings, photographs, Web pages, transcripts of meetings or proceedings, government documents, memoranda, films, diplomatic communiqués and instructions, political posters and cartoons, political advertising, speeches, and even letters and diaries. Some of these records may be extremely detailed and precise (as is a verbatim transcript of a congressional hearing), while others are much less so (for example, the agenda for the same hearing). Many will have been created independently of the research process (as are newspaper articles by or about the person or group we wish to study), while others must be created by the researchers themselves (as, for example, videotapes of television news programs). But all sources of data for content analysis will have in common one principal characteristic: the existence of a physical record of communication. Whenever such a record exists or can be created, content analysis may serve as an appropriate research method.

The first step in preparing to undertake a content analysis is to define the population of communications we want to study. Here we have a number of options. Which is the best will be determined by our particular research question. For example, if we are interested in studying the development of political themes in twentieth-century American novels, we might define our population as all novels (the type of communication) written by Americans (the type of communicator) and published in the United States (the location of communication) between January 1, 1900, and December 31, 1999 (the time period of communication). If we wish to study newspaper coverage of a political campaign, we might define our population as all campaign-related newspaper articles (the type of communication) of two column-inches or more in length (the size of the communication) published in daily newspapers (the frequency of communication) that are home delivered (the distribution of the communication) in the sixth, seventh, and eighth congressional districts of Ohio (the location of the communication) during the period September 1 to November 5 of the election year (the time period of communication). Or, similarly, if we want to study the level of tension between the leaders of the United States and those of Serbia, we might define our population as all diplomatic messages (the type of communication) passed between the governments of the United States and Serbia (the parties to the communication) during a given time period.

In each instance, we define the population of messages to be studied by establishing sets of criteria to be met by each item. In the examples, these criteria include the type of communication (novels, newspaper articles, or diplomatic notes), the type of communicator, the parties to the communication (the sender or the receiver or both), and the location, frequency, minimum size or length, distribution, and time period of the communication. Although other criteria may be used on occasion, some or all of those listed here will be found in most studies that employ content analysis. The first task in preparing for a content analysis is to choose those criteria that relate most directly to the research question at hand.

Once we have defined our population, we are faced with the problem of deciding which particular cases we shall examine in detail. Because the cases to be analyzed are often limited in number and relatively accessible and because content analysis is generally less expensive per case than other methods (most notably survey research), we are sometimes able to examine every case in a given population—to conduct, in effect, a census. Indeed, the opportunities it offers for the examination of large numbers of cases is one of the major attractions of content analysis as a research technique. More often than not, however, even content analysis must be based on a more limited sample drawn from the larger population. Since documents, newspaper articles, and the like are frequently indexed or otherwise listed in some central location and since such indexes or lists may easily be created by the researcher, the most common sampling procedures used in content analytic studies are the simple random and systematic random techniques. Even when sampling is required, however, the accessibility and relatively low cost of researching messages of various types come into play, and the sample sizes drawn for content analysis may be substantially larger than those employed in other types of research. The result, of course, is a reduction in sampling error and an increased level of confidence in generalizing from our results.

Finally, in preparing to undertake a content analysis, we must decide on our unit of measure, or, as it is more commonly termed, our *unit of analysis.* The **unit of analysis** for content analysis is simply the particular element or characteristic of a given communication that we shall examine, count, or assess. The most basic element of a communication, for example, is the *word,* and it may be employed in a fairly straightforward manner. As reflected in each one's public statements, was Bill Clinton, George Bush, Ronald Reagan, Jimmy Carter, Gerald Ford, or Richard Nixon most directly concerned with world peace? We might simply sample the statements of each and count the number of times the word *peace* (and, perhaps, some other related words as well) occurs in the text. In speeches before the United Nations during the period 1975 to 2000, which country was most conciliatory on questions of eliminating conflict in the Middle East: Israel, Egypt, Syria, or Saudi Arabia? Again, we might examine the record of all such speeches and count references to such words as *peace, brotherhood,* and *compromise.* In each instance, we identify certain important words and count the frequency with which they appear.

Even in so simple a procedure, however, we must take care to avoid at least two pitfalls. First, we must remember that nonstandardized measures can lead to biased results. If over the years in question, the Israelis have uttered a total of 100,000 words, including 50 salient references (to the words we wish to count), and the Egyptians have uttered some 200,000 words, including 100 salient references, we might reach either of two conclusions from a study of these speeches depending on whether or not we have chosen to standardize our indicator. If we simply count salient references, we will conclude that the Egyptians have been twice as concerned as the Israelis with procuring a settlement. If, however, we standardize our measure to obtain the *proportion of* all words that are in fact salient (for example, salient references *per 1,000 words*), we will conclude that both sides have shared an equal concern about settling their differences. Which approach is better? This is a fundamental problem in operationalizing variables, and the answer is best determined by looking closely at how we have conceptualized the research question initially. The point here is that the use of even such a seemingly concrete indicator as *number of salient words spoken* can entail some ambiguity. The researcher must recognize and deal with that ambiguity, because the decisions made (or overlooked) can have a substantial impact upon the conclusions one draws.

A second potential pitfall in the reliance upon raw word counts arises because the same word may be used in many different ways: "We seek peace, *but* . . ."; "The Arab brotherhood *can never allow*. . ."; "There will be *no* compromise." In the absence of any sort of control, references such as these to peace, brotherhood, and compromise will be included as positive references and will, at the very least, inflate our assessment of the interest on the part of one or both sides in reaching an accommodation. If such usages are sufficiently common, they may well mislead us altogether. For this reason, if we choose to count words, we should in most instances choose to count them in context.

At least two alternatives exist for doing so. First, we may use *judges* or **coders**—people who are part of the research team or are employed by it—to read each salient reference *in context* and to judge that context as positive, neutral, or negative. Usually more than one coder should read each reference, and a relatively high level of agreement among coders should be required before a final determination is reached. (We say more on this point later in this chapter.) This contextual judgment can then be used to enrich our data by allowing us to count and interrelate not only all references to the words we are focusing on but also the proportions of positive and negative references.

Another possible response to the problem of interpreting individual words in context, though it is at best only a partial solution, is to move to, or add, a second unit of analysis—the *theme*. A theme is a particular combination of words or ideas, such as a phrase, a sentence, or even a paragraph. In effect, when we count themes, we search for recurring subjects in a text, as, for example, the expressions *cold war, refugee problem, national health insurance,* or *faith-based politics.* The procedure is similar to that for counting words and represents an improvement to the extent that themes incorporate the modifiers (adverbs, adjectives) and explanatory text that both accompany usage of a particular word and help to establish its meaning.

The problem with analysis at the thematic level, however, is that, although it does make clear the context in which individual words are used, it does so at the cost of much added complexity. This is true in that the same theme may be referenced in very different ways and by very different sets of words. Sometimes these references may be very subtle, displaying few or none of the overt characteristics we are looking for. References to immigration issues, for example, may be veiled in conciliatory words about political asylum, whereas those applied to religion in politics may be cloaked in nationalistic rhetoric. Do such words and rhetoric constitute salient references? Is the theme present, or is it not? These questions do not have simple answers. To the contrary, they generally require us to arrive at some clearly stated but potentially limiting definitions and to develop a series of highly formalized decision-making rules (for example, allowing only overt references that contain one or more words or phrases from a given list to be counted), which may make our findings more reliable but at the same time less meaningful.

A third unit of analysis commonly used in content analysis research is the *item*—the communication itself taken as a whole. What proportion of *books* published in the United States in 1935 advocated socialism? Which presidential candidate in 2000 was the subject of the greatest number of favorable newspaper *editorials*? How did *letters* written by Richard Nixon after his resignation from office differ from those written earlier? In each instance, we treat the item of communication as a unit and we examine its *overall* characteristics. Does it or does it not deal with a particular issue? Does it or does it not reflect a certain set of values or preferences? Such questions lose some of the subtlety of judgment required by lesser units of analysis, and they necessitate the making of summary evaluations, but for precisely these reasons, their analysis is generally more manageable than is that of words or themes, in a sense making fewer demands of the researcher. This is true because variables may be operationalized at a less specific level, one on which events (that is, occurrences of a salient reference) are often more apparent and on which measurement is often more reliable.

Item-based studies of the use of words and themes have become in recent years much easier to perform due to the development of computer databases like LEXIS/NEXIS, which was discussed in Chapter 3. Suppose, for example, we wanted to know how often George Bush referred to Saddam Hussein as Hitler-like during the months leading up to the 1991 Persian Gulf War. Using NEXIS, we could request both a full-text search to count all of the articles in the *New York Times* (or any of a large number of other newspapers, magazines, or broadcast transcripts) in which the words "George Bush," "Saddam Hussein" and "Hitler" appeared for each given month of the period under review. Once in the relevant file, and depending on the software one used for access, the instruction might look something like this:

((George Bush) OR (President Bush)) AND ((Saddam Hussein) w/10 Hitler) AND (Date = September 1990)

This string of terms would identify any article published during September 1990 in which Mr. Bush's named appeared *and* in which Mr. Hussein's name also appeared *within 10 words in either direction* from the word "Hitler." Similar searches would allow us to test (1) whether Mr. Bush was referred to more often by title rather than by first name as the crisis moved more clearly toward a military resolution (as might be the case, for instance, if the media were subtly enhancing his stature as the nation neared a war), (2) whether Mr. Bush led or lagged behind other political leaders in his use of the Hitler analogy, or (3) numerous other hypotheses related to the framing of public perceptions of the conflict.

The results of item analysis may be at least as meaningful as those of component analysis in many instances. Is it more important that the Egyptians have made, say, seven conciliatory references in a given speech at the United Nations, or simply that they have made a conciliatory speech? Is it more important that the United

States has sent to Iraq a note with four overt references to military intervention, three veiled references to the failure to disarm, and two sharply critical references to military expansion, or that the United States has issued a note that can be characterized as contentious in tone? In content analysis, sometimes, though by no means always, we risk losing sight of the forest for the trees or, by analogy, of the overall significance of a communication for its component parts. For this reason, we must be very careful to select a unit of analysis that will allow us the particular perspective on our research question that will prove most advantageous.

Undertaking a Substantive Content Analysis

Once we have settled upon a population, a suitable sample, and an appropriate unit of analysis, we are ready to get under way. **Substantive content analysis** is based on a study of words, themes, and items that focuses on the *substantive content* of a given communication. Thus, in preparing to analyze these elements, we must anticipate their substance and we must define each possible observation in accordance with our expectations.

What this means, in effect, is that as the first step in undertaking a content analysis of this type, we must create a sort of dictionary in which we define each and every observation we might make according to the particular category it fits. Suppose, for example, we are interested in studying all of the sixth-grade schoolbooks used in Havana, Cuba, last year and in identifying in them all references to Americans and the United States? Before we can proceed with such an analysis, we must define just what constitutes a salient reference. Do we look only for the words *American* and the *United States*? If we do so, we may miss a great many salient references using such derogatory terms as *Yankee aggressors, northern imperialists, gringos, invading forces at Guantanamo,* and *the outlaw regime in Washington.*

A parallel but more difficult problem arises when the *absence* of a word or phrase has substantive meaning and must be captured. For example, maps in a sixth-grade civics text published in 2000 for use in Palestinian schools pictured a long green shape separating the West Bank from the Gaza Strip, but it did not label that strip, which, of course, was Israel. Nor did the Israeli capital of Tel Aviv appear on these maps. These omissions are meaningful and significant, and a content analysis scheme for studying such books must capture them. Incidentally, as with our hypothetical Cuban texts, these very real books characterized Israel in such indirect terms as "the occupier."[1]

The point is that we must anticipate not only the references we are likely to encounter but also the contextual elements of their use, and we must devise a thorough and systematic set of decision rules for judging each usage as it occurs. This problem is usually resolved by a combination of pretesting the population of communications to be analyzed (that is, reading through a selection of items to identify

---

[1] Lee Hockstader, "Israel Not on Map in Palestinian Textbooks," *Washington Post,* September 3, 2000, p. A1.

Best of a bad lot
Best available
Better than the opponent
Our first choice
Finest candidate in a crowded field
Everything the people of this state could ask for
An outstanding leader
Promising
One of the nation's best
Lesser of two evils
Best the selection process could produce
Our perennial favorite
Woman (Man) of the hour
Acceptable
Most acceptable
Recommend with reservations
Recommend without reservations
Wholeheartedly endorse
Warmly recommend
Offer our support
Enthusiastically commend to your attention
Urge you to vote for

Figure 9.1
Sample phrases in newspaper editorials endorsing a candidate (random order)

the types of salient references most likely to be encountered in a subsequent and more thorough analysis) and developing informed judgments about the contexts and uses of terms. Here, as in the later formal analysis, the observations of several researchers are preferred over those of one.

A more difficult problem arises when we must assign *evaluations* to salient references—when we must decide whether a particular reference is good or bad, favorable or unfavorable, pro or anti, and so forth—and when a series of such references must be ranked according to their intensity (which is most favorable, which is next most favorable, and so forth). Here we are concerned with developing and applying indicators that are sufficiently refined to tell us not only how the political actor feels but also how strongly the actor feels that way. A situation of this type is illustrated in Figure 9.1. The figure summarizes a number of ways in which a newspaper might endorse a candidate. If our goal is to determine which of several newspapers most strongly supports that candidate, then our immediate task is to decide how to rank these statements according to the intensity of support each reflects.

Several techniques are available to assist us in making these decisions. Two of the most prominent of these ranking techniques are the *Q-sort* method and *pair-comparison scaling*. Like the Thurstone scaling technique described in Chapter 8, each relies upon the decision of a group of judges about the meaning or intensity of a term, though here the judges may be drawn from the issuers of the communication, the receivers of the communication, a group of scholars familiar with the general subject area under study, the general population, or the researchers themselves. The techniques differ from one another and from the Thurstone method, however, in the tasks they assign to these judges.

In this regard, the Q-sort is closest to the Thurstone procedure. The **Q-sort** uses a forced distribution scale of 9 points in which 1 represents the lowest degree of intensity of the attribute we wish to measure (for example, the least favorable) and the highest degree of intensity (for example, the most favorable). In contrast to the way it is done in the Thurstone procedure, no provision is made for neutrality or antithetic judgments. The purpose here is merely to rank in one evaluative direction. Moreover, judges are far more constrained in their use of the scale than in the Thurstone procedure. Each judge is given what amounts to a quota for each of the categories in the scale—an expected number of words or phrases to be assigned thereto—and is instructed to distribute a given set of terms so as to meet those quotas. The quotas are based on the assumption (not necessarily valid) that the intensity of words and phrases will follow a *normal distribution* (with cases clustered toward the middle of the scale and symmetrically decreasing in number toward the extremes). The judges are thus forced to make *relative* judgments about specific words and phrases and to decide where on the scale each one fits.[2] The procedure is illustrated in Table 9.1.

The table consists of three lines. The first represents the value assigned to each category of the scale and ranges from 1 to 9. The second represents the percentage distribution of all cases throughout the nine categories. These numbers are the quotas assigned to each judge. Thus each is required to assign 5 percent of all cases to category 1, 8 percent of all cases to category 2, 12 percent of all cases to category 3, and so forth. The third line of the table represents the specific number of cases these percentages determine for a given research problem. In the table, we have assumed each judge will be asked to rank 50 words or themes. The numbers in this line thus represent the percentages from line 2 applied to a total *n* of 50, and they tell each judge how many of the statements must be assigned to each category.[3] In undertaking a Q-sort, lines 1 and 2 in the table *will always be the same,* and line 3 will be adjusted according to the number of statements or items to be ranked.

Once this ranking has been completed by a number of judges, we calculate the mean (average) category score for each statement and rank each accordingly. (The rationale for doing so is similar to that underlying the use of interval level statistics for analyzing data derived from Thurstone scales.) We then use these intensity rankings in assigning codes to the texts we are analyzing as the words or themes we have scored appear. In this way we substitute the collective wisdom of a number of judges for the arbitrary judgment of one researcher in deciding the meaning of communication content.

---

[2] For a broad discussion of Q-sort methods, see Bruce McKeown and Dan Thomas, *Q Methodology* (Newbury Park, CA: Sage, 1988).

[3] Since this would result in either fractional entries or an asymmetry in the distribution, cases have been slightly redistributed toward the center of the table in order to preserve normality.

Table 9.1
Distribution of items in the Q-sort method

Category (value)	1	2	3	4	5	6	7	8	9
Distribution (percentage)	5	8	12	16	18	16	12	8	5
Distribution (number of cases)	2	4	6	8	10	8	6	4	2

The goal of **pair-comparison scaling** is the same, but the procedure itself is rather different. Each item to be evaluated by the judges is paired with *every* other item, in a series of comparisons, and each judge is asked to decide which word or phrase in each pair is the stronger or more intense. Thus if we have five statements for comparison, each judge compares item 1 against items 2, 3, 4, and 5; item 2 against items 3, 4, and 5; and so forth—in each instance designating one or the other as more intense. By counting the number of times each statement is so designated by each judge, by totaling these numbers for each item for all judges, and by dividing by the number of judges (that is, by calculating the average score the judges as a group have assigned to a particular statement), we are able to arrive at a quantitative ranking of the intensity of each item. The higher its mean score, the stronger the judges consider a statement.

At least two problems are associated with both the Q-sort and pair-comparison procedures. First, both techniques rely entirely on the decisions of judges whose criteria for judgment may or may not be appropriate or consistent. The standards for expertise in such undertakings are not always clear, or at least are not always clearly stated, and as a consequence, the judgments themselves are open to question. Indeed, it is not uncommon for a single judge to assign different scores to the same statement in a series of identical tests. Because we are sampling content and not humans here, there is neither a clear reference population, as there is in Thurstone scaling, nor a set of underlying parameters to be approximated. The selection of judges, in other words, is extremely arbitrary. Thus the reliability of results derived by depending upon such judges may be minimal. In addition, judgmental methods can become tedious and cumbersome. A Q-sort of, say, 100 or 200 items that requires repeated determinations of minute shades of difference or a pair comparison of, say, 50 items that requires an examination of 1,225 different pairs ($n[n-1]/2$, where n is the number of items) can try the patience of even the best judge. As a result, such procedures must be approached with a good deal of caution.

Undertaking a Structural Content Analysis

In addition to, or in lieu of, words, themes, or other elements that denote the substantive content of a communication, several units of analysis are available that allow **structural content analysis.** Here we are less concerned with *what* is said than with *how* it is said, and while we must retain a concern with the subject matter, we measure something else.

We may be concerned, for example, with the amount of space or time devoted to a given subject in a particular source. How many words or column inches of newspaper coverage have been accorded each candidate in a particular election campaign?

ID Number			Article type	Publication Date	Candidate	Newspaper	Preference	Prominence	Graphics	Headline	Content	Total	Column	Inches	Candidate	Column	Inches

Figure 9.2
Typical coding sheet for structural content analysis

How many articles or pages in political science journals published in the United States are devoted each year to an analysis of governments and politics in Africa? Has the number changed, or has it remained constant over the past three decades?

Alternatively, we might be concerned with other, and perhaps more subtle, aspects of the communication format. Is a particular news item accompanied by a photograph or illustration of some sort? Those that are have been found to attract more attention from readers than those that are not. How large a headline accompanies a news item? Does coverage of a particular subject receive front-page prominence, or is it buried among the truss ads? In answering questions like these, we are less concerned with subtleties of meaning than with styles of presentation. We watch for the presence or absence, the prominence, and the extent of treatment of general themes rather than for substantive nuance. The result in many cases is an analysis whose measurements are much more reliable than those employed in a more substance-oriented study (since there is less ambiguity built into the indicators), but one whose lessons may, as a direct consequence, be less rich.

Figure 9.2 illustrates a typical coding sheet for recording data from a structural analysis of content. It is drawn from a study of newspaper coverage of congressional elections.[4] The unit of analysis for this particular study was the *candidate insertion,* which was defined as any newspaper item that mentioned by name or implication any candidate for Congress in the district in which the newspaper was distributed. Thus each row on the coding sheet summarizes the characteristics of a single candidate insertion.

While we shall wait until Chapter 12 to discuss the assignment of particular numbers to each column on such a sheet, it is worth pointing out here the type of information that is recorded. After each item was assigned a unique identification number, it was classified according to type (news story, feature article, editorial, letter to the editor), the date of publication, the candidate it referred to, the newspa-

---

[4] Jarol B. Manheim, "Urbanization and Differential Press Coverage of the Congressional Campaign," *Journalism Quarterly,* 51 (1974), pp. 649-53, 669.

per in which it appeared, the general preferences expressed in the item (if any), its prominence of placement (front page, inside page), the presence or absence of accompanying photographs or drawings, reference to the candidate in the headline of the item, the primary content of the item (news of a campaign event, content of a speech, endorsement), the overall size of the insertion, and the proportion of the insertion actually relating to the candidate in question. The point to note here is that measurements of this kind require only a general concern with the actual substance of each insertion rather than the highly detailed and specific focus necessary in the substantive approach discussed earlier. As a result, structural content analysis is usually easier to design and carry out, and therefore less expensive and often more reliable, than is substantive content analysis. And though its results may be less satisfying in that they provide us with what amounts to a sketch of a communication rather than a finished portrait, those results often prove entirely adequate in answering a particular research question.

Special Problems in the Use of Content Analysis

Although content analysis is a relatively inexpensive technique that draws on a relatively accessible database and although there are few special ethical dilemmas that we are likely to encounter in undertaking it (unless we are analyzing confidential or classified communications), we must still be careful to avoid several potential difficulties when we use this method.

For one thing, we must be aware that communications are issued, and may be specifically designed, for a purpose, whether it be description, persuasion, exhortation, direction, self-protection, or even obfuscation. In analyzing such communications, therefore, we must attempt to interpret their content in the context of their apparent purpose. For example, it is common to find in the Chinese press statements of the type, "*All of the Chinese people believe* that membership in the World Trade Organization is a major step forward in the progress toward social revolution." Taken at face value, such statements are demonstrably false, since not every one of many millions of people would be aware of, let alone agree upon the value of, any single policy. From this perspective, we might be inclined to view these statements as the most blatant form of propaganda. We have learned from studying the Chinese press, however, that statements of this type are not printed for purposes of external propaganda at all, but rather are intended to suggest to the Chinese people themselves the beliefs that their government wishes them to hold. In other words, the purpose of such statements of consensus is not descriptive, but directive. Knowing this, we may interpret them as useful indicators of the policy interests of the Chinese leaders rather than as meaningless items of propaganda, and we may employ them to some advantage. The purpose of a communication, then, can provide an important context for understanding its content, and we must attempt, when possible, to ferret out this information.

Similarly, the distribution that is accorded a particular item of communication can have significant implications for its meaning. A pamphlet that circulates only among Chinese dissidents, a solicitory letter from a candidate or special interest group that reaches only those people on a particular mailing list, a document that circulates only among a small group of persons—each is an example of a communication with a limited or specialized distribution. Even a newspaper that is generally available may have a limited or specialized clientele. The *New York Times,* for example, has a readership that is generally more affluent and better educated than that of the *New York Daily News,* yet both are readily available to all of the city's newspaper readers. The *Wall Street Journal* has nationwide distribution, but its readership does not extend equally to all socioeconomic classes. Very often, if we are to assess properly the significance of a communication, we must know whom it reaches. Whether by judgment (rendered, for example, by knowledgeable experts, as might be the case in studying communication among Chinese dissidents), by inquiry (as when we ask a candidate or group which mailing lists were used), by self-evidence (which we have when a document is accompanied by a routing slip listing, and perhaps initialed by, all who have read it, or when a Web page includes a counter showing the number of visitors), or by reliance on an audience survey (such as the kind usually taken by newspapers to document their circulation claims), we must attempt to measure or to estimate how widely a message has been disseminated and to whom. Having this information enables us to judge the value or the importance of the material we analyze.

Third, we must try to gauge the degree of our own access to the items at issue. Have we been provided with free choice over the materials we shall analyze? Are those materials available in an unbiased manner (that is, do we have access to *all* of them), or has some external control been imposed by someone other than the researcher? Do we, for instance, have access only to documents that have been declassified, only to Chinese newspapers that are published for and distributed primarily to foreigners, only to records of *formal* meetings of a government commission? The issue here is one of generalizability, and the question is whether the research population itself, not to mention the sample, is truly representative. If it is not, the researcher may, if not exercising care, at the very least be misled and at the worst be manipulated.

The problem in each of these instances is that the information we require to make informed judgments may simply be unavailable. We may not know, and may be unable to ascertain, the purpose of a communication, its distribution, or the degree of access to it that we have been accorded. The dangers here are manifold, and the content analyst must be sensitive to them. We must not allow appearances to cloud our judgment but must maintain a healthy skepticism regarding our data as long as these questions remain unanswered. That is not necessarily to say that we should not undertake content analysis under conditions of uncertainty, but merely that we should not lose sight of the uncertainty itself once the analysis is under way.

Finally, we should say a few words about *intercoder reliability.* With the exception of raw word counts and other content analysis procedures that have been thoroughly computerized (several programs embodying concept dictionaries and search or count procedures have been developed), all content analysis depends on human judgments about communication content. Messages, after all, do not analyze themselves. They are poked and prodded, counted and classified by *Homo sapiens* in the form of the researcher. Therefore individual researchers may differ from one another in their understanding of the content of a given communication. Indeed, only when some degree of consensus can be reached about that meaning can we have real confidence in our measurements. **Intercoder reliability** is the term political scientists use to describe the degree of that consensus. The higher it is, the better. In general, intercoder reliability may be promoted by taking three basic steps:

1. Operationalize all variables carefully and thoroughly. Make sure that all meanings have been clearly stated and as many ambiguities as possible have been eliminated. In effect, this will create *common standards of judgment* that can be used consistently in classifying and measuring content.

2. Use as many observers (coders) as possible. The larger the number of subscribers to the consensus, the more confidence we can have in it. This may, of course, mean more work and considerable duplication of effort (and, if proper training is not provided, it carries a risk of increased measurement error), but the payoff can be substantial. The limiting factor here is usually cost.

3. Maximize the interaction among the observers. Hold common practice sessions and argue out all differences of interpretation so that ultimately the consensus extends not only to the data but also to the real meanings of the operational definitions themselves.

The success of this process can be measured in either of two ways, both of which draw upon statistical concepts that we develop more fully in Chapter 15. One approach, used primarily in substantive content analysis, is to have all observers who are working on a given project analyze and code independently (assign their own numerical values to) the same communication, then to calculate a statistic called a correlation coefficient (Pearson's *r*) among the codes recorded by each pair of observers. This coefficient (discussed in detail in Chapter 15) measures the degree of correspondence in the judgments of the reseachers on whether and how often a particular word or theme is present. The coefficient ranges from –1 to +1, and readings of +.90 or better are usually interpreted as indicating a high degree of intercoder reliability.[5]

An alternative measure may be more useful for structural content analysis, in which we are less concerned with the treatment of themes than with their presence or absence and in which duplicated measurement is less necessary. Here we treat the differences between observers as a variable in their own right, and we ask whether that variable is associated with systematic differences in any other variable we have measured. In other words, we are concerned with the possibility that one or more observers have recorded results consistently differently from the others. If it can be assumed that all cases have been distributed to the observers in an unbiased manner (some effort is generally made to distribute them *randomly*), any systematic differences we observe are more likely to be the result of differences between coders than of underlying differences in the cases that happen to have been assigned to the aberrant observer. The coefficient of intercoder reliability here takes the form $(1 - \eta^2)$, where η^2 is a measure of the variance in each subject variable that is accounted for

---

[5] More complex variants of this procedure with applications to the measurement of intensity may be found in Robert C. North et al., *Content Analysis: A Handbook with Applications for the Study of International Crisis* (Evanston, IL: Northwestern University Press, 1963), chs. 4 and 5.

by differences between coders.[6] By subtracting this "observer error" from 1, we obtain the proportion of error-free observations. The coefficient is calculated separately for each variable and should exceed +.90 if we are to have confidence in the reliability of our measures.

In sum, content analysis is a widely applicable technique with advantages in cost, sample size, and, often, access to data. Perhaps more than any other technique, however, it demands careful operationalization of all variables and constant monitoring of the process of observation. Its results may be highly informative, but they must be understood in a context that it is often beyond the scope of the content analysis technique itself to describe. For this reason, content analysis is often used to best effect in combination with other data-gathering methods (surveys, direct observation) in what are termed *multimethod designs*.

Suggestions for Further Reading

The three most useful texts dealing with the techniques of content analysis and their application to political science research are Robert C. North et al., *Content Analysis: A Handbook with Applications for the Study of International Crisis* (Evanston, IL: Northwestern University Press, 1963), which focuses primarily on methods of scaling intensity and measuring reliability; Philip J. Stone, ed., *The General Inquirer* (Cambridge, MA: MIT Press, 1966), which discusses and gives examples of the application of a widely used computerized procedure for content analysis based on sentence structure; and Klaus Krippendorff, *Content Analysis: An Introduction to Its Methodology* (Beverly Hills, CA: Sage, 1980), which is a broad overview of content analytic techniques.

A quick overview can be obtained from Robert Philip Weber, *Basic Content Analysis,* 2d ed. (Beverly Hills, CA: Sage, 1990).

Some of the more interesting examples of content analysis at work are Richard L. Merritt, *Symbols of American Community, 1735–1775* (New Haven, CT: Yale University Press, 1966), which examines the development of the American national identity in the Colonial press; Jib Fowles, *Mass Advertising as Social Forecast: A Method for Futures Research* (Westport, CT: Greenwood Press, 1976), which uses advertising content as a basis for predicting social trends; and George Gerbner and Larry Gross, "Living with Television: The Violence Profile," *Journal of Communication*, 26 (1976), pp. 173-99, which discusses the measurement of violent content in daily television fare. Doris A. Graber, *Processing the News: How People Tame the Information Tide,* 2d ed. (White Plains, NY: Longman, 1988), describes the application of content analysis to the coding of diaries, elite interviews, and media and exemplifies both the techniques and the genuine conceptual advantages of an integrated multimethod design. Examples of content analysis in use, together with discussions of related methodological issues, appear regularly in the pages of *Journalism and Mass Communication Quarterly, Journal of Communication,* and *Political Communication.*

Research Exercises

1. List three hypotheses that can be tested using content analysis.
2. List as many words or phrases as you can that might constitute references to human rights abuses in news stories about China, Indonesia, Mexico, and the United States.

---

[6] The formula and computational procedure for this statistic, which is a measure of association between one nominal and one interval variable, may be found in Linton C. Freeman, *Elementary Applied Statistics: For Students of Behavioral Science* (New York: Wiley, 1965), pp. 120–29.

Using first a Q-sort and then a pair-comparison procedure, rank these terms in order of intensity. Compare the two rankings.

3. Design a study using *structural* content analysis to answer this question: Is the *New York Times* biased in its coverage of the Middle East? What are the principal variables to be measured in such a study? Next, design a *substantive* content analysis to answer the same question. Will the principal variables in this second study differ from those in the first? In what ways? If you had to choose, which method would you pick as most appropriate to answer the research question? Why?

4. Write a research design to determine which of the following publications—*Newsweek, The Economist, Time,* or *U.S. News and World Report*—devotes more attention to international affairs. Be sure to examine each publication carefully before developing your design.

5. The journal *Political Communication* publishes many research articles that employ content analysis. Locate and read one such article, then summarize and evaluate the content analysis procedures employed by the author(s).

6. If you have access to the Lexis-Nexis database, design a search strategy that will allow you to ascertain whether editorials in the *Denver Post* were more favorable to Bill Clinton, George Bush, or Ronald Reagan during the first six months of their respective administrations, and to compare the result with a similar assessment of editorials in the *Boston Globe*. Conduct the research using your search strategy. Finally, decide what changes you might make in your original strategy to improve the research.

Terms Introduced in This Chapter

content analysis
unit of analysis
coders
substantive content analysis

Q-sort
pair-comparison scaling
structural content analysis
intercoder reliability

CHAPTER 10

SOURCES AND APPLICATIONS OF AGGREGATE DATA

Political scientists (as scientists) are interested in individual persons only to the extent that those individuals are part of some group of people about whom they want to learn. For example, we may study the behavior of a particular governor, not because we want to know about Governor So-and-So, but because we think we can better understand or predict the behavior of governors in the United States from what we observe about Governor So-and-So. Political scientists are usually interested in the study of groups or collections of persons, such as American voters, Indian peasants, or Russian bureaucrats.

Sometimes, in order to study these groups we have to gather information on the individual members of the groups (or a representative sample of them) and combine or *aggregate* that information to secure information about the group *as a group*. Often, however, there already exists aggregated information about the group. Data on the characteristics of an entire group or aggregate of individuals are referred to as **aggregate data.**

There are two general categories of aggregate data. The first category—**summative indicators**—includes large sets of measures of group characteristics that are created by combining the behavior of all members of the group. For example, the population of a nation is an aggregate datum derived by adding inhabitants as units. Birth, death, literacy, suicide, and crime *rates* are aggregate data created by adding up the number of particular events (births, deaths, crimes, etc.) in a group and expressing it in a standardized unit such as *per thousand persons in the population.* In each case, the aggregate datum quantifies some *group* characteristic that individual members of the group cannot possess. Individuals may be born or learn to read and write but cannot have a birth or literacy *rate* in the same sense that a nation does. These data are measures of aggregate characteristics.

A second general category of aggregate data consists of those measures that quantify group characteristics that are derived not from any combination of individual members' characteristics but from qualities of the group *when acting as a group*. They are often referred to as **syntality indicators.** For example, *form of government* is a system-level variable, and a given nation may have a democratic or a nondemocratic form of government regardless of whether its individual citizens hold democratic or nondemocratic values and attitudes.

Data from each category are available on many different kinds of groups from a variety of sources. Such groups may be broadly classified into **areal groups** (those defined by residence within a geographic area, such as a nation, city, or census tract) and **demographic groups** (those defined by personal characteristics, such as age, race, or occupation).

In this chapter you will learn that proper use of aggregate data involves solving some challenging methodological problems. The advantages of using such data, however, often far outweigh the costs. Political scientists may find the use of aggregate data necessary or desirable because individual-level data are either unobtainable or too expensive to obtain.

As examples of studies for which individual data might be impossible to obtain, consider the following cases: If we want to do a historical study, at least some of the groups on which we need data (for example, the population of Chicago in 1880) may be dead. Members of some politically important groups such as international terrorist organizations may absolutely refuse to be identified or interviewed. More often, political scientists find themselves in situations in which it is theoretically possible to collect individual level data, but such collection is prohibitively expensive. This is especially likely to be the case when we are interested in comparing nations, because the cost and logistical problems of multinational survey research are enormous.

If you are interested in research questions for which individual-level data are unavailable, you may find it worthwhile to search for aggregate data that contain the basic information needed. In this chapter we introduce you to the types of aggregate data that are available, suggest some sources of these data, discuss some of the methodological problems encountered in using aggregate data, and, finally, offer some guidelines for collecting aggregate data. You will soon recognize that the proper use of aggregate data requires the mastery of data collection, processing, and analysis techniques. As a student and as a professional political scientist, however, you are probably more likely to work with aggregate data than with data collected through any of the methods described in preceding chapters, because aggregate data are so readily available.

Types of Aggregate Data

Most of the aggregate data available to political scientists are gathered by non-social scientists for reasons other than research. Therefore, they often seem to bear only a tangential relationship to our research. In fact, one of the most challenging aspects of aggregate data analysis is often that of finding some way to use existing data as indicators of concepts of immediate theoretical interest to the researcher. For example, at first glance there is little reason to believe that a political scientist will be concerned with the number of radios or newspaper subscriptions purchased in some nation. We are not, after all, marketing agents for the press. But these figures may be useful as partial indicators of the amount of political communication that goes on within a nation or of its level of economic development, and these clearly are appropriate concerns for political scientists. Similarly, the number of hospital beds per thousand persons in the population takes on political significance when it is viewed as an indicator of, say, the distribution of health care facilities among groups within a city or state.

The point is that aggregate data are often of no intrinsic interest and have to be transformed in some way to be of use. Do not look only for ready-made indicators of concepts, but be alert to the possibility of combining seemingly unrelated measures into useful indicators.

We can identify six types of aggregate data.[1] They are explained here in roughly *descending* order of the extent to which they are likely to be valid and reliable.

1. *Census data.* Many of the world's nations attempt to survey their entire population (or at least all households) periodically in order to gather information to be used for such purposes as levying taxes and planning public policy. The information commonly collected includes such things as number of people in the family, sex of the head of the household, length of residence, educational levels, family income, and condition of housing, among others. Though census data are collected from individuals, by the time they become available to researchers as part of the public record, they usually appear as summary figures (the total number of persons who own an auto in a given geographic area, for instance).

Census data have several desirable characteristics, which make them extremely valuable in aggregate data analysis. First, although errors can occur, census data are generally quite reliable. Second, because the variables measured are normally straightforward, census data are usually regarded as highly valid. Third, some nations have been collecting relatively standardized data for many years. Thus census data provide an opportunity to trace historical trends or to test hypotheses about change over time. Fourth, because census data are generally standardized (that is, they contain responses to the same questions and classify responses in the same categories) within nations and are often comparable between nations, they are useful in comparing different cities, regions, or nations. In addition, census data are easily available. Many nations publish reports of both major census projects (generally undertaken once every 10 years) and any of a wide variety of specialized surveys undertaken in between. The United Nations (www.un.org) publishes the annual *Demographic Yearbook,* describing the census data available from various countries. In the United States, the Bureau of the Census (www.census.gov) maintains a large User Services Division, which can assist social scientists in gaining access to and working with the wide variety of data available from the bureau.

2. *Organizational statistics.* In every nation, the various levels of government, businesses, and organized groups such as labor unions and professional associations gather data related to their own operations. If these statistics happen to fit the requirements of a particular social scientist's research project, they can be of great value.

Some organizations collect their own data, as does a multinational corporation keeping a record of its capital investments, a hospital recording information on

---

[1] The typology offered here is adapted from that presented by Richard L. Merritt, *Systematic Approaches to Comparative Politics* (Skokie, IL: Rand McNally, 1970), pp. 27–36.

patients, or a city government recording property assessments for tax purposes. Others use data generated by other agencies, such as the United States Department of Commerce (www.doc.gov), to create data in the form of various indices of, for example, economic performance or population shifts.

With either type of official statistics, there can be problems. The first, and perhaps greatest, problem is that of gaining access to the data. Data compiled by government agencies are generally part of the public record and readily available, but data collected by nongovernmental organizations are private property. Some organizations, especially businesses, consider their data sensitive and are *most* reluctant to share them. Often the problem is less gaining access to the data than simply learning of their existence. There are no central listings of the statistics collected by the thousands of public and private organizations engaged in such record keeping. Researchers may, therefore, miss major opportunities because of a lack of information about the existence or content of particular statistics.

A second problem is that the content and quality of the data may vary greatly, making comparisons and generalizations difficult. If teachers' unions in Indiana and Ohio do not collect comparable data on their members, we cannot use their statistics to make meaningful comparisons between them. In addition, if we do not know how data have been collected, we may not know how much confidence to place in the figures.

Finally, data may not be in a usable form. A local government's vital statistics (records of births, deaths, marriages, deeds) may be available only in unaggregated form and only in a central location, so that a researcher has to sit for countless hours in a government office tediously hand recording the data so that they can be converted to a machine-readable form and totaled. This can require an unjustifiable investment of time and money.

These problems are not found in all official statistics, and even when they are encountered, the potential payoff in economical research is generally worth the effort required to solve them.

3. *Sample surveys.* Survey research is designed to gather individual-level data. When surveys are based on samples that are representative of a population in which we are interested, it is often possible to use their results as aggregate data. Suppose, for example, we want to compare the political information level of two nations' citizenry. If each nation has a public opinion polling organization that regularly surveys a national sample (as Gallup and Roper do in the United States) and that asks questions about such behavioral matters as frequency of watching TV news reports or subscriptions to news magazines, we might use the results to construct aggregate measures of our variable. Similar use can sometimes be made of individual surveys conducted for academic purposes. Survey data, if properly collected, have the advantage of being quite reliable, and they can be as valid as the researcher is wise in constructing indicators. They are also generally available (at least for a price) from the agencies or scholars who have collected them, and they are often in a readily usable form.

4. *Publications' content.* In a construction of aggregate data, content analysis can be applied to publications sponsored by or distributed among particular groups. For example, if we are examining political socialization processes in Great Britain,

we might content analyze the textbooks used in civics courses to determine the extent to which they stress democratic values, and we might then use the combined results as one indicator of the nation's democratic orientation. Similarly, we might rely on content analysis of the major newspapers of developing nations to derive an indicator of those nations' relative attention to international and domestic events or of their support for the United Nations. In each case, the product of the content analysis is an indicator of a group characteristic.

This type of aggregate data is generated by the researcher specifically for the purpose of a given research project instead of being collected from a primary source, such as a census report. As a result, access to such data depends on the availability of the publications or databases (such as LEXIS-NEXIS) needed for a content analysis and on the researcher's having the resources necessary to perform the content analysis. The reliability and validity of the data depend in turn on the skill with which the researcher applies the rules discussed in Chapter 9. Aggregate data collected through content analysis of publications have the advantage of being adaptable to an individual study but generally provide only highly imperfect indicators of underlying concepts. Ask yourself, for instance, how confident you would feel in making statements about the kind of political values British schoolchildren learn from an analysis of their civics texts.

5. Event data. Often, political scientists are interested in the occurrence of discrete events that are not recorded in census reports or organizational data because they are too infrequent or fall outside the responsibility of any one agency. Riots, revolutions, assassinations, the breaking of diplomatic ties, protest demonstrations, indictments of public officials for crimes in office, coups d'etat, and the creation of new political parties are all examples. Information on these events can be useful in the construction of indicators of group properties. For instance, we might want to measure a nation's political stability by counting the number of acts of political violence occurring there in a given time period or want to compare the level of political corruption in several cities by counting the number of indictments of public officials for bribery.

Event data are gathered by a process very similar to content analysis. After deciding what events are important to our study and carefully operationalizing them (for example, deciding what actions constitute a riot), we systematically survey sources such as newspapers, yearbooks, and radio broadcast transcripts that are likely to contain reports of them, and we take a tally (being careful to avoid double-counting the same event when it is reported in more than one source). In addition, we can use content analysis techniques to produce more detailed data about these events. We can, for example, classify riots according to their duration, their level of violence, or the number of people involved in order to produce a measure of severity.

Event data can be made relatively reliable by careful training and supervision of those who read the source materials. However, it is extremely difficult to make event data *valid*. The major problem is comprehensiveness in reporting. Even when all known sources or reports of some type of event have been reviewed, the researcher cannot be sure that some such events have occurred but have not been reported. In some nations the government carefully controls reports of political events in order to present the preferred image to the world, so that many important happenings (such as the use of troops to break a strike) may not be reported and no valid measure of the events can be constructed. A second and related problem grows from the potential inaccuracy of reports. Even when events are recorded, the details of their occurrence can be distorted intentionally or unintentionally. Such problems are not insurmountable, but researchers must be aware of them in designing their studies around event data, and they must realistically assess their chances of acquiring valid measures by this means.

6. *Judgmental data.* Occasionally there simply are no data available to use for construction of measures of particular aggregate properties. In these cases, researchers can sometimes use as data the opinions of experts or persons with special knowledge.

Consider the example of a study of the lobbying efforts by several interest groups for and against environmental protection legislation. There may be no public record on the subject, but researchers can ask key legislators about their judgment of whether and how strongly each group supports or opposes such legislation in its lobbying efforts. Similarly, if researchers are unable to gather data on the force governments employ to stay in power in various nations, they can ask other scholars who have studied those nations' political systems for their judgment about the coerciveness of the governments.

Obviously, judgmental data suffer from some limitations. In the first place, their accuracy is subject to the biases and limited experiences of the judges. Using many judges and checking their estimates against one another represent one way to avoid relying on false or partial judgments. It is often difficult, however, to find several qualified judges who differ in their background and their experience with the subject matter, so that even using multiple judges is no guarantee against inaccurate data. Second, even when judges provide perfectly accurate information, judgmental data are generally imprecise. We are, after all, asking for opinions and impressions of complex phenomena, not counts of discrete events. These limitations need not be debilitating, however. It is important only that researchers recognize them in designing studies and in analyzing judgmental data. It would be an error to treat judgmental data as more reliable and precise than such data are.

Problems in the Use of Aggregate Data

From the foregoing discussion you can see that the specific types of problems encountered in aggregate data analysis vary with the types and sources of data being used. There are, however, some general problems that may be confronted in any use of aggregate data analysis. We discuss two. Our purpose is not to provide solutions but to alert you to the need to be on the lookout for these problems in your research and the research of others.

It is important to consider first the general problem referred to as the **ecological fallacy,** because knowledge of it should guide the design of research and the specification and operationalization of variables, as well as the very decision to use aggregate data to address a specific research question.

Researchers run the risk of committing one of several types of ecological fallacy anytime they attempt to generalize to one level of analysis from data collected at another. For example, if we collect data on the racial characteristics of individual welfare recipients in each *state* in the United States and find a strong positive relationship between being nonwhite and receiving public assistance, we may be tempted to generalize "up" to the national level, claiming that this relationship holds for the nation as a whole, or to generalize "down" by assuming that the relationship found in any given state will also be found in each of its counties. If, however, we actually do aggregate our data at the national or county level, we may find that the relationship is significantly different from that found when data are aggregated at the state level. Empirical studies of the ecological problem have shown that relationships may not only be weaker or stronger at different levels but may even change directions.[2] When researchers generalize from one level of analysis to another, they run the risk of seriously misinterpreting their data and reaching conclusions that are simply wrong.

Does this mean that we must use only data that are aggregated at the level of whatever units of analysis we choose for our studies and can never generalize up or down in research? No. There are techniques of data analysis that, under some conditions, can at least minimize the risks involved in making inferences between levels of analysis.[3] If researchers find that they must use data aggregated at a level other than that with which they are concerned, they should plan to employ one or more of these data analysis techniques and should take care that their data meet the requirements of this type of analysis before investing time and resources in gathering them.

Perhaps even more important, awareness of the risks of ecological inference should make researchers extremely cautious when planning a study and operationalizing concepts. Whenever possible, they should avoid selecting indicators that require inferences between levels of analysis. For example, suppose we are studying the relationship between union membership and support for the Democratic party in the United States and we discover aggregate data for congressional districts that give the percentage of each district's labor force holding union memberships and the percentage of each district's voters that have voted Democratic in recent elections. We will be able to use these data if congressional districts are our unit of analysis and our goal is to be able to make statements such as, *Those districts with proportionately more union members tend to elect Democratic candidates.* However, if individual voters are our units of analysis, we will want to be able to make statements such as, *Labor union members tend to support Democratic candidates.* In this case we *cannot* use with any confidence the aggregate data from congressional districts, and we will be wise to seek data on *individuals'* union membership and voting behavior.

A second, and related, set of problems often encountered in aggregate data analysis relates to the difficulties of creating valid indicators from aggregate data. It is rare to find aggregate figures that can be used directly as a measure of some concept of interest to political scientists. Most frequently, we find numbers representing variables that can be viewed as part of the larger phenomena to which our concepts

---

[2] See Hubert M. Blalock, Jr., *Causal Inferences in Nonexperimental Research* (Chapel Hill, NC: University of North Carolina Press, 1972), pp. 102–4, and William S. Robinson, "Ecological Correlations and the Behavior of Individuals," *American Sociological Review,* 15 (June 1950), pp. 351–57.
[3] Several of these are explained in W. Phillips Shively, "Ecological Inference: The Use of Aggregate Data to Study Individuals," *American Political Science Review,* 63 (December 1969), pp. 1183–96, and in Laura Invin Langbein and Allan J. Lichtman, *Ecological Inference* (Beverly Hills, CA: Sage, 1978).

refer. In studying the political impact of modernization, for instance, researchers may not be able to find aggregate data directly reporting the level of modernization of various nations. They might, however, be able to find information on the proportion of each nation's population that lives in communities of more than 25,000, is engaged in nonagricultural employment, or is literate, all of which can be considered components of modernization. Such figures are often referred to as **raw data;** they are of no intrinsic interest in themselves but can be used to create indicators of concepts that are of interest.

The problem that aggregate data analysts face is one of finding theoretically and methodologically justifiable ways of converting raw data into useful measures. Two basic approaches to this are the creation of indices and the transformation of data.

Index construction is a means of reducing complex data to a single indicator that more fully captures the meaning of a concept than does any of its components. Three commonly used types of index are additive, multiplicative, and weighted. An **additive index** is appropriate when available data represent different measures of the *same* underlying variable. For example, we might want simply to add together reported numbers of exported bushels of wheat, corn, and soybeans in order to obtain an indicator of the concept *agricultural exports.*

Often, however, aggregate data represent measures of *different* aspects of a phenomenon and cannot be added. There is, for instance, no mathematical logic by which we can add the number of people involved in a riot to the number of hours it lasts in order to create an index of riot severity. Number of participants and length of duration are nonadditive elements of the phenomenon we call *riots.* We can, however, argue that those two elements interact with one another to determine how severe a riot is. By this logic we might *multiply* the number of participants by the number of hours of duration to create an indicator of the severity of the riot by measuring the "demonstrator hours" devoted to it. Such an indicator is called a **multiplicative index.** Indices of this type are called for anytime we have measures of different aspects of a concept.

In some circumstances raw data have to be weighted by some standard to become a useful indicator of concepts. For example, the *number* of persons attending antigovernment rallies is a useful indicator of the legitimacy accorded a government only when it is expressed as a percentage of the population. When we do this we are weighting one variable (the number attending antigovernment rallies) by a second (the population) to create a **weighted index.** Similarly, we might want to weight the number of antigovernment demonstrations by the variable *time* to create an index of demonstrations per year on the assumption that ten demonstrations in one year indicates more political unrest than ten demonstrations spread over ten years. This particular type of weighting is known as *standardization.*

Weighting is technically simple to do, but it is often conceptually difficult to determine whether a measure should be weighted and by what it should be weighted. For instance, it is not clear whether arms races are triggered by the absolute level of armaments held by nations or by the ratio of one nation's armaments to another's. Should a nation's armament level be weighted by its opponents' armament level before the figure can be used as an indicator in a study of arms races? Answers to such questions are often to be found in an empirical examination of how the use of weighted and unweighted indicators affects the results of statistical analysis.

Often, in the use of aggregate data, measures are encountered that cannot be made useful simply by combining them with others, but that must be individually modified. Sometimes even indices can be made more useful if they are modified. Such modifications are referred to as **data transformations.** Data are transformed principally in order to meet the requirements of certain statistical procedures that researchers want to employ in data analysis. In general, the justification for transforming data is to avoid having the results of statistical analyses distorted by features of the distribution of the raw data.

There are many techniques of data transformation, and each is designed to correct different flaws in raw data. However, the *logarithmic transformation* can serve as an example of how transformations work. Some of the most useful statistical procedures can legitimately be applied only to data that are normally distributed. (We discuss normal distributions in Chapter 15.) Application of these procedures to data that are not normally distributed can result in serious underestimates of the strength of relationships between variables, as well as other misleading results. Yet raw aggregate data are often not normally distributed. Logarithmic transformations are designed to make data more nearly approximate a normal distribution. The basic procedure is to add a constant to the score for each case on the raw data and then substitute the appropriate logarithm for the original score by using a log table. The effects of such a transformation on data are suggested in Figure 10.1, which shows the results of transforming hypothetical data on the number of people taking part in "gay rights" demonstrations in fifty-seven U.S. cities. The distribution of the transformed data (Figure 10.1(b) does not form a normal, or bell-shaped, curve, but it is much more nearly normal than the distribution of the raw data (Figure 10.1(a).

You should not interpret anything we have just said as meaning that having multiple measures of some concept is a problem that must be solved. To the contrary, it is highly desirable to have *multiple indicators* of concepts, and though it is

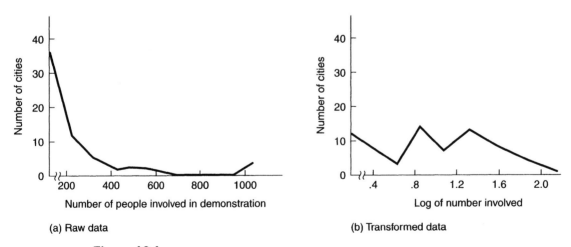

(a) Raw data   (b) Transformed data

Figure 10.1
Effects of logarithmic transformation on hypothetical data on gay rights demonstrations in 57 U.S. cities

often useful to combine measures into indices, it is usually wise also to record the individual measures and examine them separately at some stage of the data analysis. The reason is that multiple indicators can be used to check the validity of our operationalization of concepts.

For example, suppose we want to measure the concept *gender discrimination in employment* among the American states. We might be able to find aggregate data on the following variables:

The ratio of the average salary paid to women to the average salary paid to men

The proportion of all professionals in the state who are female

The ratio of the unemployment rate for women to the unemployment rate for men

We can use all three indicators by scoring each state on each variable and comparing the results. If those states that appear to have the most discrimination by one measure also rank high on discrimination by the other measures, we will feel more confident that each measure is a valid indicator of the underlying concept *gender discrimination in employment.* If, on the other hand, we find that those states that rank high on discrimination as measured by two of the indicators rank low on discrimination as measured by the third, we will be reluctant to use the deviant measure as an indicator of our concept.

The more independent indicators we can locate for each concept, the better, for with more indicators we can provide more convincing tests of the validity of each. For instance, in the preceding example, with only three measures, we might not be altogether sure that the deviant measure is not, in fact, the valid one and the other two invalid. It may be its very validity as an indicator of our concept that makes it stand apart from the others in the way it ranks states. If, however, we have five or ten measures that produce consistent rankings of states and one that stands apart, we can feel quite confident that it is the deviant measure that is invalid. A variety of techniques are available for using multiple measures to test and enhance the validity of our indicators.[4]

There is one additional very important issue of which anyone using aggregate data should be aware. This potential problem stems from the fact that aggregate data are often available in a form that does not allow valid comparisons across units. For example, if we are interested in the degree to which different states in the United States exhibit a commitment to public education, we might find data on how much each state spends on education each year. It would be inappropriate, however, to compare the total number of dollars Texas spends on education to the total number of dollars Rhode Island spends because the two states differ so radically in size and wealth. Rhode Island may spend only a fraction of the amount Texas does and yet exhibit a stronger commitment to education because it is spending far more *per school-age child* or a far greater *portion* of its total state budget on schooling.

---

[4] A general discussion of the multimeasurement approach and its role in research is found in David C. Leege and Wayne L. Francis, *Political Research* (New York: Basic Books, 1974). Some sophisticated techniques for using multimeasures are presented in Part II of Hubert M. Blalock, Jr., ed., *Measurement in the Social Sciences* (Chicago: Aldine, 1974).

To make a valid comparison among the states, it would be necessary to restate the amount they spend on education in some way that controls for differences in population and wealth. Unless we do this, we will not have a valid indicator of our concept, and our conclusions will be determined by the relative size and wealth of states rather than by their relative commitment to education.

Situations like this require that we *standardize* our measures in some way. A **standardized measure** is one that is stated in a way that, in order to allow valid comparisons, takes into account the differences that might exist among cases on variables other than the one it represents. It is very often necessary to standardize aggregate data prior to making comparisons among units of analysis. This may involve collecting data on variables that are of no direct relevance to the project. For example, in a study of commitment to education, we might need to collect data on the populations and total governmental expenditures of the states in order to standardize their educational expenditures by stating them as dollars per school-age child or a percentage of total state expenditures. Similarly, if we wanted to measure the concept *militarization* by observing the amount of money nations spend on the military, we would need to standardize the measure by stating it as a percentage of a nation's gross national product (the total value of all goods and services produced in the country) before making comparisons. Unless we did this, a wealthy nation might look more militaristic than a poor nation even though it devoted only a tenth as much of its total wealth to the military as a poor nation did.

Whenever you anticipate making comparisons among groups (nations, cities, organizations, etc.), you must be alert to the need to standardize your measures and must plan to collect the additional data necessary for this standardization. Standardization is generally achieved by stating measures either as a percentage or proportion of some other variable or as so many units per unit of some other variable. This often results in the computation of a *rate* such as a crime rate (crimes per 10,000 persons), literacy rate (literate persons per 1,000 population), or infant mortality rate (infant deaths per 1,000 live births). The additional work of collecting data on the variables on which your key variable must be standardized is *absolutely necessary* for valid comparisons among cases that differ significantly in theoretically relevant ways.

The point of this section has been that aggregate data analysts should not only be cautious about using raw data as indicators of concepts but should also be alert to possibilities of improving indicators by combining, standardizing, or transforming measures and to the potential uses of multiple indicators.

Sources of Aggregate Data

The amount of aggregate data available in the world is so great that one is inclined to believe it possible to find indicators for almost any empirically useful concept. In fact the very abundance of the available data sometimes poses problems as researchers find themselves having to search scores of sources to find all available indicators. Yet, even with this reservoir of data, researchers are sometimes unable to locate exact indicators of the concept they want to measure, for exactly the right time period, and aggregated at exactly the right level.

We cannot begin to list *all* the sources of aggregate data here. We can, however, list those sources of general data that are most likely to be of use to political scientists. Whereas some data sources contain data on a variety of subjects and cannot be neatly characterized as a source of one particular type of data, we have classified the sources listed here by the major type of data they are likely to yield. Most college and university libraries have the publications listed here or are able to help you locate them.

The key to successful use of any of the documents or data archives described here is knowing precisely what type of measures you are seeking. The hypotheses you are testing, the theory you are working from, or a precise statement of your research question can tell you what type of data (such as a measure of nations' economic productivity or of the size of their military forces) are needed to operationalize the concepts utilized in your research. If you simply go to the library with the idea of poking around in available data sources until you run across some indicators that look useful, you will almost certainly meet with the dismal failure you so richly deserve. If, on the other hand, you go with a clearly conceptualized research strategy in mind, you will at least be able to tell the reference or social science librarian what you need.

1. *Demographic and related data on the United States.* All statistics released by agencies of the federal government are indexed in the *American Statistical Index,* which can be used to locate sources for specific measures. In addition, statistics on economic and population trends, foreign trade, energy use, and other issues collected for more than 100 federal agencies can be accessed through the Internet at FedStats (www.fedstats.gov). The publications of the Bureau of the Census are indexed in the *Catalog of United States Census Publications,* which describes the data available from the censuses of housing, population, governments, and agriculture, among others. Many of these data are summarized each year in the publication *Statistical Abstract of the United States,* which presents selected statistical profiles of the United States and its subdivisions and contains an extensive guide to public and private data sources. Each of the various censuses of the United States is summarized in *Subject and U.S. Area Reports.* The *Bureau of the Census Catalog* describes all census bureau materials, published and unpublished. It is indexed by subject and state and local area and is published quarterly.

Some frequently used sources of specialized data about the United States are the *Congressional District Data Book,* which provides demographic and economic information and voting records for United States congressional districts, and the *County and City Data Book,* which contains demographic and economic data for states, counties, cities, unincorporated places of more than 25,000 in population, and urbanized areas in the United States on an annual basis. Similar data are presented in the *State and Metropolitan Area Data Book* from the census bureau. Voting data are summarized in the *Guide to U.S. Elections,* which gives returns for presidential, Senate, House, and gubernatorial races since 1824, and in *America Votes,* which covers national elections and primaries since 1952.

2. *Demographic and related data on other nations.* Recognizing the difficulties in locating comparable measures of any given variable for different countries, a variety of sourcebooks contain data collected by different nations and international bodies. Researchers who use these must be especially sensitive to the need to ensure the comparability of reported figures before basing comparisons on them.

The United Nations Statistics Division (www.un.org/depts/unsd) publishes three especially useful documents: The *Statistical Yearbook* summarizes data on population characteristics, economic activity, education, communications, and other matters for the world's nations each year, the *Yearbook of National Accounts Statistics* reports detailed information on economic activity, and the *Demographic Yearbook* gives historical data on population characteristics and annually examines a special subject, such as population distributions, mortality rates, or ethnic compositions. In addition, the United Nations Educational, Scientific, and Cultural Organization (UNESCO) publishes the *Statistical Yearbook* (www.unescostat.unesco.org), which summarizes data on education, communication, science, and technology in more than 200 countries.

The *Statesman's Yearbook* provides detailed information about nations that has been compiled from a variety of national and international sources. The European Union publishes the *Eurostat Yearbook,* which provides demographic, social, political, and economic data for EU member states and candidate countries for leading EU economic partners (www.europa.eu.int/eurostat.html). Further summary figures on national characteristics can be found in the *World Almanac* and *Worldmark Encyclopedia of Nations* in well-indexed form. A good deal of economic data can be found in the *Yearbook of International Trade Statistics.*

3. *Data on governments in the United States.* U.S. federal, state, and local governments turn out thousands of publications reporting figures on their own operations and on the social conditions that either call forth or result from public policies. The federal government is by far the most prolific producer of data. Its many publications are listed in the *Monthly Catalog of U.S. Government Publications* (MOCAT). An Internet version of MOCAT can be accessed through the Government Printing Office at www.gpo.gov. If you know what agency or branch of the government is likely to produce the data you are seeking, you can locate its publications in the *Monthly Catalog.* Correspondingly, if you know what you are looking for, the index of the *Monthly Checklists of State Publications* can be used to direct you to specific state publications. The *County Yearbook* and the *Municipal Year- book* provide data on political, economic, and demographic variables at local levels.

4. *Event data.* By their nature, event data are not reported in regular, summary form. They have to be discovered in running records of daily events that are not necessarily compiled with the social scientist in mind. Two of the most comprehensive reference sources for events reported in newspapers are the indexes for the *Times of London* and the *New York Times. Facts-on-File* is a weekly digest of current events classified by subject and compiled into the annual *News Dictionary,* which stresses events in and related to the United States. Perhaps the most extensive general news digest is *Keesing's Contemporary Archives: Weekly Diary of World Events,* which contains transcripts of important speeches, some election and statistical data, and news summaries and is indexed by subject and proper name.

5. *Survey data.* All of the sources named thus far present data in printed form. Using them for large studies requires recording the data and transferring them to machine-readable form. The most useful sources of survey data, by contrast, are actual data sets-machine—readable records of raw data. These are available from a variety of data archives. Several of these were identified in Chapter 7.

In addition to these sources, it is important to recognize the rich variety of private sources of data. Which of these are appropriate to any given study will be suggested by the subject of the study. For a study of the investment patterns of West European firms, for example, useful data may be held by individual banks or by national and international associations of banks.

Collecting Aggregate Data

Once the sources of data needed for a study have been identified, unless the data are already available on computer files, researchers face the task of transferring the data from a source to their records in a machine-readable form. The basic challenge is one of systematically coding and recording data.

Though this takes only a fraction of the time required to collect the same data through field research, it can be a very time-consuming task. It is important, then, to do it as efficiently as possible. The way to begin is by carefully thinking through in advance the research design and the data analysis you intend to perform so that you can specify exactly both which cases you want data on and what measures you want to record for each. Failure to do this can lead to your wasting time by recording data for which you ultimately have no use. Moreover, if you have carefully planned the study, you can list all cases and variables in some order of importance so that if you run short of time or funds in the data collection stage, you can make a rational choice to leave out certain cases or variables in order to terminate data collection in the least harmful manner. Keeping this option open means that you must proceed sequentially, either collecting all data on each case one at a time (if you want to be able to drop cases but need all variables) or collecting data for all cases on each variable one at a time (if you need all cases but want to be able to leave out some variables).

In either event, you need two basic tools for data collection: a set of *data specifications* and a *recording form*. **Data specifications** are simply detailed descriptions of the data that are to be recorded for each case and variable, including any coding instructions. Sometimes a single phrase will serve as a data specification for census data or organizational statistics—for example, *total number of municipal employees in 1990* or *adult population in 1990*. However, apparently simple pieces of data can require extensive qualifications. For instance, if we want a figure on total state expenditures for public welfare programs in a given year, we have to identify those programs that qualify as welfare for purposes of the study; if we want a measure of the number of persons in nations' armed forces, we have to include instructions for excluding domestic police from the count for countries in which the police are formally part of the military. Being able to provide these details in data specifications requires prior study of the subject and the reporting systems of your units of analysis. Even then, unexpected difficulties can arise. You may, for example, discover that budgeted and actual welfare expenditures differ considerably or that corrections for inflation have to be added in time-series studies. The adjustments you make in response to these problems must be both technically correct and consistent with the meaning of the concept operationalized by the measure.

When collecting event data, you will require quite detailed data specifications in order to ensure that essential distinctions are made. You will want, for instance, to be able to distinguish between riots and peaceful demonstrations or between pro-government and antigovernment demonstrations. The most dependable way of doing this is by incorporating in a coding manual to be used in completing a recording form the details of those characteristics that distinguish from other events the events in which you are interested. (We say more about the use of coding in Chapter 12.)

The **recording form** is essential to smooth aggregate data collection. It is similar to an interview schedule in survey research in that it is a means of systematizing and coding observations. If data are to be placed in computer files, the columns to be used for each piece of information can be indicated on the recording form in order to speed data entry. Ted Robert Gurr provides an example of how recording forms for event data should be constructed. Figures 10.2 and 10.3 reproduce his illustrations. Clearly, those using the form must be carefully instructed in how to record events on it.

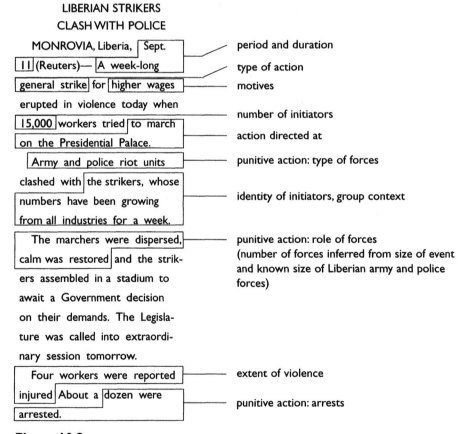

Figure 10.2
Coding of an article for aggregate data analysis
Source: Ted Robert Gurr, *Politimetrics*, Englewood Cliffs, NJ: Prentice Hall, 1972, p. 93. Reprinted by permission

CIVIL STRIFE CODING SHEET (rev. 6/66)　　　　　　Polity __Liberia__

Coder __Tg__　　　　　　　　　　　　Month and Year of Coding __7/66__

Source(s) __N.Y. Times__

Issue and Pages __9/13/61__　　__p.21__

Summary __Clashes with police in general strike__

col. num.	contents of columns	col. num.	contents of columns
1–3	Polity I.D. Number _0_ _6_ _0_	(18)	8 some, undifferentiable 9 other _____
4–7	Polity Population (100,000's) _0_ _0_ _1_ _0_	19	Regie Classes ⓪ none or insignificant 1 military/police 2 public employees 3 political elite 4 military/police, employees 5 political elite, employees 6 military/police, elite 7 all three 8 some, undifferentiable 9 other _____
8	Character of Report 1 single report, current period, continuing event 2 single report, all of continuing event, to date ③ single report, concluded event 6 cumulative report, current period, continuing event 7 cumulative report, continuing event, to date 8 cumulative report, concluded event		
9–10	_6_ _1_ (Year Event Began)	20	Domestic Initiators, Summary 0 none or insignificant ① lower classes only 2 middle classes only 3 regime classes only 4 lower and middle classes 5 lower and regime classes 6 middle and regime classes 7 all domestic classes
11–16	Period Covered by Report from (_9/5/61_) to _6_ _1_ _0_ _9_ _1_ _1_ Year　　Month　　Day		
	I.　IDENTITY OF INITIATORS	21	Resident Alien Initiators ⓪ none or insignificant 1 pastoral migrants 2 foreign workers 3 foreign students 4 refugees 5 political exiles 6 foreign clandestine group 7 several of the above (ck.) 8 other _____
17–21	bbbbb no basis for judging		
17	Lower Classes 0 none or insignificant 1 farmers/peasants 2 rural wage laborers ③ urban wage laborers 4 unemployed 5 farmers, wage laborers 6 wage laborers, unemployed 7 farmers, laborers, unemployed 8 some, undifferentiable 9 other _____	22–26	Number of Initiators, Proximate 00000　(go to next heading) bbbb1　　1 to　　40 bbbb3　　41 to　　80 bbbb8　　81 to　　240 bbb16　241 to　　400 bbb32　401 to　　900 bbb64　901 to　1,700 bb128　1,701 to　3,500 bb250　3,501 to　6,500 bb500　6,501 to　14,000 ⓑ1000 14,001 to　27,000 b2000　27,001 to　55,000 b4000　55,001 to　110,000 bbbbb no basis for judging
18	Higher Classes ⓪ none or insignificant 1 students 2 petite bourgeoisie 3 professionals 4 students, bourgeoisie 5 students, professionals 6 bourgeoisie, professionals 7 all three		

Figure 10.3

Example of a recording form for aggregate data

SOURCE: Ted Robert Gurr, *Politimetrics*, Englewood Cliffs, NJ: Prentice Hall, 1972, pp. 94–97. Reprinted by permission.

(continued on next page)

col. num.	contents of columns	col. num.	contents of columns
27–30	Number of Initiators, Estimate (0000) (previous heading coded) bbb4 less than 100 bb40 101–1,000, "hundreds," "many" b400 1,001–10,000, "thousands" 4000 10,001–100,000 bbbb no basis for judging other _____	37	Conspiracy Events 0 none 1 plot 2 purge 3 assassination 4 bombing 5 small-scale terrorism 6 small-scale guerrilla war 7 coup/putsch 8 mutiny
	II. GROUP AND SOCIAL CONTEXT		
31–32	Initiators Acting as Members of b0 unstructured crowd b1 territorial group b2 ethnic/linguistic group b4 religious group b5 apolitical student group b6 political group (b7) economic group b8 governing hierarchy b9 clandestine group _____ _____ clash between two of above; specify categories other _____ bb no basis for judging	38	Internal War Events 0 none 1 large-scale terrorism 2 large-scale guerrilla war 3 civil war (secessionist) 4 private war 5 large-scale revolt 6 turmoil/conspiracy event is part of internal war
33–35	Social Area bb1 rural village or county bb3 several villages, counties or a small town bb5 a large town b10 several towns, or a city, or a small state b20 large state, or part of the capital city (b40) several large states or several cities, or entire capital city b60 several states or cities and the capital city b80 almost the entire polity 100 the entire polity other _____ bbb no basis for judging	39	Summary of Form of Event 1 turmoil 2 conspiracy 3 internal war 4 turmoil and internal war 5 conspiracy and internal war 6 other _____
		40	Number of Actions 1 single occurrence 2 two, "several" 3 three, "some" 4 4–6 5 7–11 No. Reported 6 12–20 7 21–35 1 8 36–60 9 61+
	III. TYPOLOGY OF ACTION	41	Incidence of Action 1 single occurrence 2 multiple sporadic 3 multiple simultaneous
36	Turmoil Events 0 none 1 demonstration 2 political strike 3 riot 4 localized rebellion 5 banditry/raiding 6 political clash 7 nonpolitical clash	42–45	Duration of Action bbbb no basis for judging bbb1 1/2 day or less bbb3 1/2 to 1 day bbb5 1 to 2 days bb10 2 to 4 days (bb20) 4 days to 1 week bb40 1 to 2 weeks bb80 2 weeks to 1 month b160 1 to 2 months b320 2 to 4 months b640 4 to 9 months 1217 9 to 15 months 2000 15 months to 2 years 4000 2 to 4 1/2 years other _____

Figure 10.3
(continued)

col. num.	contents of columns	col. num.	contents of columns
	IV. ACTION DIRECTED ACT	50	Economic Motives 0 none or minor 1 retaliation 2 seize economic goods ③ change distribution patterns 4 oppose economic actor 5 several of the above (ck.) 6 diffuse economic motives 7 other _____
46–48	bbb no basis for judging		
46	Property Targets ⓪ none or negligible 1 foreign public 2 foreign private 3 all foreign 4 domestic public 5 domestic private 6 all domestic 7 foreign and domestic		

		51	Social Motives
			⓪ none or minor
			1 retaliation
			2 promote/oppose belief
			     system
			3 promote/oppose community
			4 increase social goods
			     (status, education, etc.)
			5 several of the above (ck.)
			6 diffuse social motives
			7 other _____

47	Political Actor(s) 0 none or negligible ① major domestic 2 minor domestic 3 military/police, domestic 4 private political group 5 several of the above (ck.) 6 undifferentiable domestic 7 foreign public 8 foreign military 9 domestic, foreign actors (ck.)		
			VI. PUNITIVE ACTION
		52	Role of Punitive Forces 0 not committed or committed after end of action 1 victims 2 present but passive 3 defensive action ④ moderate suppressive action 5 extreme suppressive action 6 provoked action b no basis for judging
48	Nonpolitical Actor(s) ⓪ none or negligible 1 random actors 2 ethnic actors 3 religious actors 4 communal actors 5 economic actors 6 several of the above (ck.) 7 undifferentiable 8 foreign nonpolitical actors 9 other _____		
		53	Type of Punitive Forces 0 none 1 police 2 domestic military units ③ police and domestic mili- tary 4 foreign military units 5 domestic and foreign b no basis for judging
	V. STATED OR APPARENT MOTIVES		
49–51	bbb no basis for judging		

49	Political Motives
	0 none or minor
	1 retaliation
	2 seize political power
	3 increase pol. participation
	4 injure/suppress competing
	     political group
	⑤ promote/oppose specific
	     domestic policy
	6 promote/oppose specific
	     domestic political actor
	7 oppose foreign nation's
	     policy or actors
	8 several of the above (ck.)
	9 diffuse political motives
	     other _____
		54	Number of Punitive Forces
			0 none
			1 1 to 10
			2 11 to 100
			③ 101 to 1,000
			4 1,001 to 10,000
			5 10,001 to 100,000
			6 100,001 to 1,000,000
			b no basis for judging

		55	Arrests and Detentions 0 none 1 1 to 10 No. Reported ② 11 to 100 _a dozen_ 3 101 to 1,000 4 1,001 to 10,000 5 no basis for judging

Figure 10.3
(continued)

col. num.	contents of columns	col. num.	contents of columns
56	**Executions** ⓪ none 1 1 to 10 No. Reported 2 11 to 100 3 101 to 1,000 _____ 4 1,001 to 10,000 b no basis for judging	69–72	**Number of Injuries** bbb0 none, none likely (bbb4) 10 or less, "few" bb40 11 to 100, "scores, many" b400 101 to 1,000, "hundreds" 4000 1,001 to 10,000 bbbb no basis for judging No. Reported _____ Other _____

col. num.	contents of columns	col. num.	contents of columns
	VII. EXTENT OF VIOLENCE		VIII. EXTERNAL SUPPORT
57–58	**Damage in Affected Area** (00) none or presumed neglig- able 01 slight 03 moderate 07 extensive 10 massive bb no basis for judging	73–76	bbbb no basis for judging (0000) none apparent
59	**Who are Casualties?** 0 none, none likely ① initiators 2 victims 3 punitive forces 4 initiators, victims 5 initiators, punitive forces 6 victims, punitive forces 7 all three 8 some, unspecified b no basis for judging	73	**Degree of Support for Initiators** 0 none apparent 1 arms and supplies 2 provision of refuge 3 provision of facilities, training 4 military advisors, mer- cenaries 5 military units
		74	**Degree of Support for Regime** 0 none apparent 1 nonmilitary aid 2 military material 4 personnel, facilities 5 military units
60–64	**Number of Deaths, Proximate** 00000 (go to next heading) (bbbb0) zero, none likely bbbb1 1 to 2 bbbb3 3 to 6 bbbb8 7 to 16 bbb16 17 to 32 bbb32 33 to 64 bbb64 65 to 130 bb128 131 to 250 bb256 251 to 500 bb500 501 to 1,000 b1000 1,001 to 2,000 b2000 2,001 to 4,000 b4000 4,001 to 8,000 b8000 8,001 to 16,000 other _____ bbbbb no basis for judging No. Reported _____	75	**Number of Nations Supporting** **Initiators** (identify) ____ (USA; China; USSR; UK; No. ____; ____; ____; ____.
		76	**Number of Nations Supporting** **Regime** (identify) ____ (Metro. power; France; No. USA; UK; ____; ____; ____.
65–68	**Number of Deaths, Estimate** (0000) (previous heading coded) bbb4 10 or less, "few" bb40 11 to 100, "scores, many" b400 101 to 1,000, "hundreds" 4000 1,001 to 10,000 bbbb no basis for judging No. Reported _____	77	**Reliability of Report** ⓪ unclassified 1 unknown 2 questionable
		78–80	Event Identification <u>G</u> <u>F</u> <u>T</u>
			COMMENTS, OTHER INFORMATION

Figure 10.3
(continued)

Conclusion

As a closing remark, we want simply to encourage beginning researchers not to overlook the potential of aggregate data as a *supplement* to other forms of data. There are countless studies that can be based exclusively on aggregate data, but it is also often the case that aggregate data can be used to check the accuracy of results obtained from other forms of data. For example, students of voting behavior are sometimes faced with the problem that is created when people who are eager to associate themselves with a winner falsely report in interviews conducted after the election that they have voted for the successful candidate. In this case, aggregate voting data can be used to estimate the "liar effect" present in a sample. If responses from a sample show that 75 percent of a district has voted for the winner of a recent presidential election but voting statistics show that only 25 percent of that district actually voted for the winner, we have to consider that district's survey responses to be at least potentially an invalid indicator of support for the winner in that district.

In addition to this use, aggregate data can often be relied on to provide additional indicators of concepts so that the multiple indicator approaches to validity discussed earlier can be employed. For instance, in a study of neighborhood stability, we might ask residents about their commitments to stay in the neighborhood and, as an additional indicator, seek aggregate data on the frequency of turnover in home ownership in the neighborhood in recent years. When the findings of a study are confirmed by data collected by such diverse methods, confidence in those findings is greatly enhanced.

Suggestions for Further Reading

There are no textbooks devoted exclusively to aggregate data analysis. Most of the material is scattered among the literature reporting studies that have employed the various techniques of aggregate data analysis. The best general discussions of how to use aggregate data for beginning political scientists are probably Ted Robert Gurr, *Politimetrics* (Englewood Cliffs, NJ: Prentice Hall, 1972), and Richard L. Merritt, *Systematic Approaches to Comparative Politics,* ch. 2 (Skokie, IL: Rand McNally, 1970). David W. Stewart and Michael A. Kamins, *Secondary Research,* 2d ed. (Newbury Park, CA: Sage, 1993), offers some practical tips and an excellent review of the issues surrounding use of aggregate data. More advanced discussions of the problems and techniques of using aggregate data and some examples of its use are found in Charles L. Taylor, ed., *Aggregate Data Analysis* (Paris: Mouton, 1968). Additional examples of studies based on aggregate data are collected in Edward R. Tufte, ed., *The Quantitative Analysis of Social Problems,* ch. 3 (Reading, MA: Addison-Wesley, 1970).

A particularly imaginative use of content analysis of publications as aggregate data is found in Philip L. Steward et al., "Political Mobility and the Soviet Political Process: A Partial Test of Two Models," *American Political Science Review,* 66 (December 1972), pp. 1269–90. Richard F. Hamilton, *Class and Politics in the United States* (New York: Wiley, 1972), provides an example of the use of survey results as aggregate data on groups within a nation (social classes in this case). A major example of the use of judgmental data is Arthur S. Banks and Robert B. Textor, *A Cross-Polity Survey* (Cambridge, MA: MIT Press, 1963). An instructive example of the use of demographic data and organizational statistics is Michael S. Lewis-Beck, "The Relative Importance of Socioeconomic and Political Variables for Public Policy," *American Political Science Review,* 71 (June 1977), pp. 559-66.

A useful discussion of index construction is found in Tapani Valkonen, "Individual and Structural Effects in Ecological Research," in Matti Dogan and Stein Rokkan, eds., *Social Ecology* (Cambridge, MA: MIT Press, 1968), pp. 53–68, and some valuable hints on data transformations (and on the collection and use of aggregate data generally) are offered in Eugene J. Webb et al., *Unobtrusive Measures*, rev. ed. (Thousand Oaks, CA: Sage 2000).

Research Exercises

1. The *Municipal Yearbook* provides data on the number of business establishments devoted to manufacturing, retailing, and services in each U.S. city. Use the data reported on this variable in a recent issue of the *Yearbook* to determine the proportion of firms devoted to manufacturing in the cities of Detroit, Houston, Pittsburgh, and Seattle. Write down the proportions for each city. Which of these cities would you say is the most industrialized according to this measure?

2. Using measures from the *Congressional District Data Book,* devise indices to represent (a) the level of party competition in and (b) the socioeconomic status of congressional districts. Then use the data reported in the *Data Book* to assign scores on each of these indicators to every district in the state of Indiana.

3. Select a research question and state a hypothesis relating to it that you can test using aggregate data. List the variables involved in the hypothesis and identify the units of analysis to which the hypothesis applies. Then use library resources to locate sources for at least three indicators for each variable in the hypothesis. Write a description of each measure, indicating the source in which it is found and the variable it is to represent.

4. Devise a definition for the concept *act of political terrorism* that can be used to identify terrorist acts from newspaper stories. Use the index to the *New York Times* to obtain a count of the number of acts of political terrorism taking place in Turkey, Germany, and Israel for any single year between 1983 and 1993. Which nation suffered the most terrorist acts? Can you devise a means of classifying terrorist acts by their level of violence? By this classification, were the acts in any one nation typically more violent than those in the others?

Terms Introduced in This Chapter

aggregate data	additive index
summative indicators	multiplicative index
syntality indicators	weighted index
areal groups	data transformations
demographic groups	standardized measure
ecological fallacy	data specifications
raw data	recording form
index construction	

CHAPTER 11

CROSSING BORDERS: THE PRACTICE OF COMPARATIVE RESEARCH

DONNA L. BAHRY

All of the research strategies we have dealt with thus far could easily be carried out without ever setting foot—either literally or figuratively—outside our country. On most questions we can obtain more than enough data from our own nation's experience to help us explain political life. But an exclusive focus on one nation has some limitations. If we want to improve our ability to explain and predict political events, then one way is to take a comparative approach. This offers a broader range of information about the issues we want to study and in fact allows us to pose some kinds of questions that data from a single country might not answer. Thus whether the question is about the causes of political violence, the reasons people become alienated from government, the effects of different kinds of political organization on public policy, or something else, comparative research can increase the chances of our reaching valid conclusions.

Why should there be any limitations in studying only one country? First, our results are likely to be *culture bound*. That is, each nation has certain unique traits that can bias the findings. Suppose, for example, we want to explore the connection between socioeconomic class and voting choice. If we look only at data from the United States, we are likely both to conclude that class and voting are only modestly related and to question the notion that political preferences are shaped by the socioeconomic conditions in which voters must live and work. If, on the other hand, we expand our sample to include other Western countries—say, Britain, France, or Germany—we are likely to find a far stronger link, partly because of differences in the historical development of social classes in those countries. Thus the United States might not be a representative example.[1]

---

[1] Note, though, that class differences in partisan support (as measured by votes cast) have changed over time in Western Europe as well as the United States. See Paul Nieuwbeerta and Wout Ultee, "Class Voting in Western Industrialized Countries, 1945–1990: Systematizing and Testing Explanations," *European Journal of Political Research*, 35 (1999), pp. 123–60; Geoffrey Evans, "The Continued Significance of Class Voting," *Annual Review of Political Science*, 3 (2000) pp. 401–17.

To take another case, suppose that we focus on voter turnout in national elections. For the United States, we will find that close to half of all eligible voters simply stay home on election day. We may explain this by arguing that democratic elections, especially at the national level, tend to discourage voter participation, because the large number of voters makes any individual ballot almost meaningless. But that conclusion, too, will be quite different if our sample includes other nations. Electoral turnout averaged 82 percent of eligible voters in Norway during the 1970s, and more than 90 percent in Italy during the same period, even though the large numbers of voters still dwarf the effect of any single ballot.[2] Thus there must be other reasons for the lower rate of participation within the United States, and these come into sharper focus when we add data from other nations. A comparative analysis shows that electoral competitiveness, and institutional features such as electoral laws and the existence of a two-party or multiparty system go a long way toward explaining different rates of voter turnout.[3] These examples suggest that there are specific features in the U.S. system—or in any system—that can distort our conclusions about political relationships.

Focusing on only one country also limits us in another way: It prevents our drawing conclusions about *system-level* traits. In other words, there are some variables, such as type of political system or type of territorial organization, that describe whole countries, and their effects can be studied only by comparing two or more nations. Consider, for example, the impact of federalism. We might argue that federal arrangements—in which power is shared between two or more levels of government—make for an inequitable distribution of public funds among localities. When regions or localities have power independent of the national government, they are likely to have different views about how much public money to spend and how to spend it.

In order to test this, we need to study at least one unitary system (in which regions and localities have no formal power independent of the national government) as a standard of comparison. Only if we found significant differences between nations with federal systems and those with unitary systems could we conclude that federalism was an important variable influencing the distribution of public funds. Similarly, we might make a case that economic growth in newly industrializing countries hinges on a government's ability to coerce and control the labor force. Our test of this proposition requires a sample that includes countries with varying degrees of control over labor.[4] Of necessity, then, any concern with system-level attributes implies a cross-national study.

Cross-national research can also be a valuable tool for those committed to political reform. Studying other nations can offer insight into the advantages and disadvantages of alternative political "rules of the game." It thus helps to pinpoint the

---

[2] G. Bingham Powell, Jr., "American Voter Turnout in Comparative Perspective," *American Political Science Review,* 80 (March 1986), pp. 17–43.
[3] Robert W. Jackman, "Political Institutions and Voter Turnout in the Industrial Democracies," *American Political Science Review,* 81 (June 1987), pp. 405–24. Andre Blais and Agnieszka Dobrzynska, "Turnout in Electoral Democracies," *European Journal of Political Research,* 33 (1998), pp. 239–61.
[4] This example is from Barbara Geddes, "How the Cases You Choose Affect the Answers You Get: Selection Bias in Comparative Politics," *Political Analysis,* 2 (1990), pp. 131–50.

potential costs and benefits of political reform at home. Some analysts in the United States, for example, advocated reforms in the 1950s along the lines of the British system in order to encourage more unity within each major political party and a clearer choice between parties for the average voter. Others have been intrigued by proportional representation (as in France), giving out legislative seats to each party in proportion to the number of votes it receives, so that many different parties and groups have a legislative voice equal to their electoral support. In each case, the experience of other countries speaks volumes about both the benefits and the problems that flow from such political arrangements.

Comparative analysis is thus an important part of political research, because it allows us to generalize beyond the sometimes narrow confines of a single culture and because it permits us to test for the effects of system-wide characteristics. Needless to say, it should meet all the standards for good research that we have discussed in other chapters. But cross-national studies also require sensitivity to some additional issues. The first lies in conceptualizing what we want to address: *We need to ensure that the questions we pose actually permit cross-national study.* The second lies in operationalization: *Each variable we use must be an equivalent measure of the same concept for every culture in our sample.* The choice of a sample raises a third issue: *Countries should be chosen to minimize cultural biases that can affect our conclusions.* Finally, the sample must also satisfy another rule: *Observations must be independent from one country to another.*

The following sections explain each of these requirements in turn, describing how they can influence the results we obtain and offering examples of questions that invite comparative analysis.

Finding Questions that "Travel"

The first requirement in cross-cultural research is to pose questions that *apply* from one culture to another. Stated so baldly, this might seem too obvious to require comment. But its simplicity can be deceptive, because many of the questions we raise in political science are applicable only to a very select group of countries.[5] Take, for example, the case of explaining electoral behavior—one of the mainstays of political science research. Our long-standing interest in the reasons why people cast a ballot and in the factors that influence their choices has produced a rich body of theory and a set of sophisticated methods that should be applicable in any setting, domestic or otherwise.

Yet questions about why and how people vote do not "travel" well, because they restrict us to studying countries that have regular, competitive, free, and fair elections—a qualification that automatically eliminates many of the world's nations. We would, for example, be likely to exclude consideration of single-candidate or single-party elections, since there would be little variation in electoral behavior and

---

[5] The idea that concepts should be able to travel is suggested by Giovanni Sartori "Concept Misformation in Comparative Politics," *American Political Science Review,* 54 (December 1970), pp. 1033–53.

basically no choice other than to abstain. Without variation, there is not much to explain. The factors that lead people to cast a ballot in a certain way in a country with competitive voting appear to make no difference in a noncompetitive election.

Thus, by choosing to analyze elections, we have set up a research question in terms that are specific to certain countries. This in itself might not seem too big a drawback, because we still have a large number of countries in our potential sample. But there is a second problem, one that relates to our ability to draw more general conclusions from voting data. If we assume, as many researchers do, that ballots reflect support for, or alienation from, the political system or reflect a preference for a certain candidate, party, or policy, then we have, in effect, equated elections with political expression. We are treating votes as measures of the more general concept of political participation. Almost by definition, this excludes the possibility that countries without regular and competitive elections provide their populations with a way to express satisfaction with, alienation from, or preferences for the government.

Do they? Or are we unnecessarily limiting ourselves by framing our research around competitive electoral behavior? Will we come to different conclusions if we redefine what we want to study? If, for example, we start by asking about the more general topic of how people express satisfaction, alienation, or choices among leaders or policy options, we will find that average citizens in countries without competitive elections may have alternative means of participation and can transmit their preferences to the government in ways that we normally associate with the casting of a ballot in more democratic countries.[6]

For example, voting may be a formality, but citizens might view other forms of participation in a much more favorable light. Thus many people who took an active role in Soviet public organizations (such as housing commissions or trade union committees) in the Brezhnev era felt themselves to be influential in the organization and in Soviet society at large, even though the single-candidate elections of the time were largely a political ritual.[7] And many activists in public life felt that their participation made a difference, though they were not necessarily satisfied with the system as a whole.[8]

In addition, even though elections traditionally offered very restricted choices to citizens in communist nations, voters still used them, in a sense, to express demands for government action. In the USSR, for instance, voters had some ways of catching the ear of local authorities through the ballot box, even when elections featured a single candidate. The Communist party typically expected Soviet local government officials to ensure that their citizenry turned out to vote, and this, according to a former election official, gave individual voters leverage to demand improvements in

---

[6] In fact, voting has typically been found to be a low-intensity form of participation, even in competitive electoral systems. People invest more energy and attention in, and attach more value to, other forms of political involvement. See, for example, Sidney Verba, Norman H. Nie, and Jae-On Kim, *Participation and Political Equality: A Seven-Nation Study* (Chicago: University of Chicago Press, 1987; first published in 1978), p. 53.

[7] Donna Bahry and Brian D. Silver, "Soviet Citizen Participation on the Eve of Democratization," *American Political Science Review,* 85 (December 1991).

[8] Theodore Friedgut, *Political Participation in the USSR* (Princeton, NJ: Princeton University Press, 1979).

local public services. Voters reportedly threatened to abstain unless the local government responded to their demands to correct problems they had with public housing, sanitation, roads, and other local public services.[9]

Moreover, though voters in such a noncompetitive election might not decide who would govern, they still had several ways of transmitting opinions and preferences to the government itself. One way was to question or complain: Official newspapers typically published daily questions and comments from readers about the performance of public agencies and about public policy, touching on issues from the quantity and quality of consumer goods to the protection of the environment and the wisdom of reliance on nuclear energy. Individuals could also contact government agencies directly for help with a specific problem such as housing space or pensions.[10] The range of permissible issues was clearly limited; "political" complaints about top political leaders or the role of the party, for example, could bring serious reprisals. Yet on bread-and-butter issues, many citizens reported that they received some satisfaction from public agencies. Some Soviet citizens also had yet another channel for transmitting opinions: Public agencies often consulted with relevant professional groups about policy questions, offering the people most interested in a particular issue a way of influencing public decisions.[11]

Obviously, the system of citizen participation changed dramatically with Mikhail Gorbachev's campaign for more open elections, increased citizen participation, and broader civil liberties and the emergence of fifteen new countries in the former Soviet Union. Still, there are some striking continuities in citizen politics from the pre-perestroika days. Citizens continued to contact public authorities, predominantly on bread-and-butter issues such as housing, and many people active in new, informal political organizations were the activists engaged in "old" public organizations of earlier years. Had we focused strictly on voting as a measure of participation, these continuities in the transition to more democratic rule would have been overlooked. The important point here is that each country may offer its citizens *different* modes for expressing preferences or complaints about what the government does, and this is something we overlook if we design our research to deal only with behavior in competitive electoral systems.

To take another example, we might want to explore the patterns of court cases among different countries as a means to test for the connections between democratic political institutions, the frequency of litigation, and the outcomes of court decisions. Here, too, the question of courts and litigation might not travel well, because societies can have very different modes of resolving disputes. In some countries, the emphasis may be on mediating conflicts through local notables rather than bringing them before a formal court, and such countries would be omitted from our analysis

[9] This description of the Soviet electoral process comes from Victor Zaslavsky and Robert Brym, "The Function of Elections in the USSR," *Soviet Studies,* 30 (July 1978), pp. 362–71.

[10] See the data on contacting presented in Donna Bahry and Brian D. Silver, "Public Perceptions and the Dilemmas of Party Reform in the USSR," *Comparative Political Studies,* 25 (July 1991), pp. 171–209.

[11] See, for example, H. Gordon Skilling's review of interest group case studies in "Interest Groups and Communist Politics Revisited," *World Politics,* 36 (October 1983), pp. 1–27.

of formal court activities.[12] If, like most political scientists, we are interested in drawing valid conclusions that are not culture bound, then our initial research question must be phrased to allow us to generalize beyond one or a few countries.

Our initial question must also be appropriate to the countries included in the study. Suppose for example, that we are studying the development of women's rights. One approach might be to explore how workplace grievances are resolved, since questions about pay equity and working conditions are a central concern for many women's groups. Yet, if we focus on jobs alone, we overlook a critical issue. In some countries, especially those with strong traditions of social democracy, campaigns for women's rights may focus much more on social policies—parental leave, child care, or other benefits—rather than on individuals at work. Thus the more appropriate question for us to pose is, *What kinds of women's rights issues are on each nation's political agenda?* Our original question needs to be recast in terms that are appropriate to the countries we study.

In this brief discussion, we have not touched on all the possible biases that might color our initial research questions. We have, for example, dealt only with cases involving advanced industrial societies, in which government is embodied in the work of large, highly specialized bureaucracies. Clearly, the modes of political expression, and the provision of public goods and services, take quite different forms in societies without such institutions (such as many of the developing countries), and these are things we need to consider when we form the questions that will guide our research. Whatever the issue, and whatever the countries we study, we need to be sure that our research is constructed in a way that permits us to generalize about our conclusions and in a way that fits the context of the countries we want to explore. In effect, our design should be able to travel and to focus on questions appropriate to the sample we ultimately choose.

Using Equivalent Measures

Once we have settled on a question that allows cross-national study, we will need **equivalent measures** in each country we observe. In other words, comparative research should measure the same concept from one culture to another. There are two ways we can do this: first, by using the same variable everywhere, and second, by choosing variables that are specific to each country. At first glance, this might appear to be a lopsided choice, for nothing should ensure equivalence between countries better than using the same variable in each one. But this is true only if our "identical" variable means the same thing in every country we study.

To understand why this might be a problem, suppose that we want to compare levels of tolerance for minority rights across nations. We might adopt one of two approaches. In one, we might compare the degree to which people in each nation are willing to grant political rights to particular groups such as a religious sect. Based on this measure, we are likely to conclude that citizens of some nations are

---

[12] For comparative studies that highlight such differences, see Martin Shapiro, *Courts: A Comparative and Political Analysis* (Chicago: University of Chicago Press, 1981), and Laura Nader and Harry F. Todd, Jr., eds., *The Disputing Process: Law in Ten Societies* (New York: Columbia University Press, 1978).

more tolerant than others. But if people in the nations under study are more or less hostile to the specific group in question, this measure may be revealing how the group under study is perceived by people in different nations and *not* how tolerant those people are of minority rights. This means that our "identical" measure of tolerance does not have the same meaning in each nation.

Alternatively, we might ask people about their willingness to grant political rights to the groups *they most dislike*. This would allow us to control for differences in the acceptance of different groups across nations. This raises another question, however. In some nations, the most disliked groups are larger and more powerful than in other nations, where they may be tiny minorities with little power. If so, the degree to which people are willing to grant political rights to a group may reflect the degree of threat the group poses to the majority. In that case, our measure may reflect fear of a given group rather than citizens' general level of political tolerance. Thus, for comparisons to be valid, *we need measures that tap the same underlying concept* whatever the countries we include in our sample.

Similar problems may arise no matter what question we take up or what countries we study. Suppose, for example, we want to compare the relative commitment to social welfare between nations at different levels of development. We might predict that the more developed a country, the more resources it will commit to social programs. Our measure of commitment to welfare should be relatively easy to define: we can look at expenditures on social welfare programs (such as pensions and aid to the disabled and poor) as a share of a country's total government spending or a share of all the goods and services it produces (as measured by its gross national product). With this measure, we are likely to discover that our prediction holds true: more developed countries devote a greater share of resources to welfare.

Yet here, too, our measure may not be equivalent for all the countries we might want to study. By defining it in terms of formal programs such as government pensions and aid to the disabled and poor, we may be underestimating the degree of noninstitutional, local effort that aids the most needy in countries where formal government programs either do not exist or are limited in scope. If farmers and local villagers in less developed countries organize to contribute food, shelter, and other kinds of assistance to their indigent relatives and neighbors, then they are, in effect, redistributing community resources in the same basic sense that welfare programs do in more developed systems. Thus different communities may rely on different methods of providing for the needy, so that a measure based only on formal programs may well exclude informal but significant redistribution. If this is the case, then our measure of welfare provision is more a reflection of a society's degree of institutalization than of its commitment to aiding the indigent.

Both examples illustrate how the use of identical measures in all countries can lead to serious problems when our variables take on different meanings from one country to another. As an alternative, we may decide on measures that are *country specific;* that is, we may use a different variable for each nation we study, with the choice depending on the local culture. In this case, we need to be sure that every indicator reflects the same underlying concept. As with the selection of identical or common indicators, this can create a problem, since there is no guarantee that our choices will in fact be equivalent. As evidence of this, consider the issue of political protest. Clearly, if each political system has somewhat different rules governing political life, then protest against the system may take different forms from one country to another. While one government may permit open dissent or demonstrations, another may impose severe penalties for the same behavior, forcing people to vent their dissatisfaction by other means. Thus, where open dissent is costly, we may anticipate that people protest through indirect methods, such as evasion of government demands and regulations.[13] The discontented may avoid overt ways of expressing antisystem attitudes and may turn instead to beating the system by misappropriating funds, evading taxes, or bending bureaucratic rules. Thus in order to compare the extent of antisystem activity between countries, we may look at open dissent in one place and noncompliance or evasion (assuming that we can measure it) in another.

We can thus make a plausible case that the two are equivalent measures of protest, but we cannot prove it conclusively. Another researcher may argue that the two activities really reflect different things: Open dissent may actually be a good barometer of our underlying concept, whereas white-collar crime is not. People may misappropriate funds, evade taxes, or bend bureaucratic rules for any number of reasons, none of them directly related to protest against, or dissatisfaction with, the political system. If this is the case, then our two measures are not equivalent, and we are not really tapping the same thing in each country. In other words, white-collar crime may not be a valid indicator here, because it may not reflect what we want to measure. Our use of country-specific variables, then, is not necessarily a guarantee that we have comparable data for all the nations we include in our sample.

This suggests that both of our options for choosing variables—the use of identical or country-specific indicators—have their limitations. Neither guarantees equivalence. But we can offer some ways to minimize the problem. First, we clearly need a good, basic knowledge of the culture of each country we study, so that we can determine when a given measure is appropriate. Second, we need multiple measures or indicators. If we can define several different ways of measuring protest, for example, and if those ways tend to produce the same conclusions, then we can have some confidence that we are in fact tapping the right dimension. Using these strategies can help to give us equivalent or comparable data for all the countries we study.

Choosing Cases to Study

Given an appropriate question and a sensitivity to the problem of equivalence, we need to be sensitive as well to the problems involved in selecting a sample. Ideally, we should not have to choose among countries: the best way to keep our results from being culture bound is to include data from every possible nation. But in practice, our range of options is much narrower, because the data available to us are limited. If, for instance, we rely on data provided by each individual country, we are limited by the fact that many nations publish little or no information about the issues we want to study. In some countries, accurate and timely publication of polit-

---

[13] James C. Scott makes this argument with respect to peasants in *Weapons of the Weak: Everyday Forms of Peasant Rebellion* (New Haven, CT: Yale University Press, 1985).

ical, economic, and social data remains a luxury. And even where resources are available, some topics may be considered too sensitive (such as data on political unrest) or not salient (such as statistics on domestic violence) to warrant publication. Countries that do provide information often use different ways of defining and reporting data, so that published information may not really be useful for comparison. If, on the other hand, we want to collect our own data—as, for example, in the case of survey research—the costs of research abroad can be prohibitive and the amount of data collected will be limited.

These constraints mean that for most questions we study, we have to work with a sample of a few select countries, chosen expressly to minimize bias. Our choice thus has to be made with some care because, as we have seen in Chapter 6, it can have a significant effect on what we find. We might follow one of two strategies common in comparative research. The first, called a **most-similar-systems design,** focuses on countries that are very similar, on the grounds that the characteristics they share can thus be held constant. Then, if the countries differ in some other trait, we can eliminate the shared characteristics as explanations for the variation.[14]

To visualize how this might work, imagine that we have decided to explore differences between countries in the scope of government activity. Why do governments play a much larger role in the economic and social life of some nations than of others? There are several possible explanations, ranging from differences in levels of economic development to differences in cultural norms about politics. Cultural norms, though, are sometimes difficult to measure precisely. Accordingly, we might control for their effects by looking at variations in the scope of government action among countries with similar cultures, such as the United States and Britain. Then, whatever differences we find in the reach of political institutions cannot be attributed to cultural factors, because such factors are, in effect, roughly constant across our sample. To put this another way, focusing on countries that have similar traits means that we can safely rule out these specific factors in explaining the differences we find.

Alternatively, we might adopt the opposite strategy: choosing countries that are different in as many ways as possible. This is referred to as a **most-different-systems design.** In this case, if we find a common characteristic across our sample, we can rule out the differences between countries as explanations. As an example, consider our earlier question about social welfare. We might choose a set of countries at different levels of economic development and with different types of political systems but, using an equivalent measure for each, discover that they devote roughly the same share of resources to welfare. If so, then the differences between them must not affect what each country spends to help needy citizens. Or consider the connection between social stratification, working conditions, and individual values. Research in the United States has shown that people with a higher status job (with a higher level of education and higher pay) tend to value work that offers a challenge, avoids the routine, and imposes a minimum of close supervision. One

---

[14] See, for example, Arend Lijphart, "The Comparable Cases Strategy in Comparative Research," *Comparative Political Studies,* 8 (July 1975), pp. 158–77.

logical interpretation for this would focus on America's culture of individualism. A country that emphasizes individual rights and self-direction would, we could argue, place a premium on autonomy in the workplace. And autonomy would be especially prevalent at higher levels in the occupational hierarchy. Yet cross-national evidence challenges this cultural explanation, because the same link between social stratification, working conditions, and individual values also appears in countries as diverse as Poland and Japan.[15] Thus the impact of social structure and job characteristics holds independently of the country being studied. Choosing countries that differ on several characteristics lets us eliminate these characteristics while explaining some shared trait.

Which of the two options should we choose? The answer depends in part on how well we have developed the theory that guides our research. For example, the most-similar-systems approach is appropriate when we can identify all of the important factors that might influence what we find and can locate a set of countries that share them. But because few countries are likely to be so well matched, it is normally much easier to find a sample that differs on the important dimensions. In that case the most-different-systems design is likely to be more suitable. This design also makes it less likely that we will find a common pattern between widely different countries. It thus gives more credibility to the results when we do find a common pattern. In effect, then, a most-different-systems approach offers us somewhat better control over the factors that might influence or bias what we find, as well as more assurance that our results are valid.

Finding Independent Observations

In choosing a sample, we are usually guided by the notion that the more countries we can include, the more confidence we can have in our results. A large sample increases the chance that we have included a representative range of values for key variables and lends more weight to whatever statistical procedures we might employ. This is true, though, only when each observation is *independent*. The advantages of a large sample hold only when data from one country are not influenced by events in another. If the two are not independent, then we really do not have two separate pieces of information backing up our results.

Consider a historical example from the Soviet bloc. When the Soviet party leader Joseph Stalin died in 1953, both the USSR and its East European satellites experienced major changes: Leadership changed hands in most countries, and policy priorities imposed by Stalin were revised. The main priority in each country up until 1953 had been almost exclusively to develop heavy industry, even if it meant taking resources away from building houses or making consumer products. In the wake of Stalin's death, most Soviet bloc countries began to place more emphasis on improving the lot of the average consumer. We could argue that these changes in leadership and in policy were part of a natural progression or trend in communist

[15] Melvin L. Kohn, "Cross-National Research as an Analytic Strategy," *American Sociological Review,* 52 (December 1987), pp.713–31.

political development and that communist countries experience such changes when they reach a certain stage of development; the evidence from the different countries seems to bear this out.

Yet the observations in our sample are not independent, because both leadership and policy changes in the bloc were set in motion—if not controlled outright—by the USSR. Thus our conclusion that a developmental trend caused the changes in Eastern Europe would be incorrect, for the changes were actually initiated by events in only one country—the Soviet Union. A similar logic applies for post-communist countries on the fast track to membership in the European Union. Common patterns of deregulation, welfare reform, and social policy have been influenced substantially by the desire to join the E.U.

The process whereby events in one country affect the life of another is referred to as *diffusion,* and testing for its effects on cross-national research is referred to as **Galton's problem** after the author who first described it. It suggests that we may see a strong causal connection between two variables—such as a country's reaching a certain stage of development and its experiencing shifts in policies—where none really exists, all because several countries in our sample are jointly influenced by another country. If so, then having a large sample is of no real value, because all the extra observations really add no new information.

Actually, we would be hard-pressed to find a sample in which all of the data are completely independent. It is almost inevitable that some degree of diffusion influences virtually everything we study in cross-national research. If this is true, then we need strategies that can minimize diffusion's effects. One, of course, is to look for explicit signs that one country in our sample has been influenced by another and to exclude it from our analysis. Another is to adopt a most-different-systems design, choosing countries that are as divergent as possible and choosing observations from different time periods. If it can be assumed that diffusion effects wane with distance and time, then this strategy can help to increase the chance that each piece of data in our sample is independent of the others.

Finding Data

Each issue that we have discussed corresponds to a stage in comparative research, from developing the appropriate question to deciding how best to choose measures and select a sample. In theory, at least, the last stage is to locate the actual data (though sometimes the whole sequence is reversed). If our goal is to find consistent and comparable information, we will need to take several issues into account.

For aggregate data, these include substantial variations in the scope and quality of information from one country to another, and even more variations in the availability of data on different topics. Not surprisingly, more developed countries generally have better infrastructure and resources for assembling and publishing national data. They are also likely to face more domestic demand for such information. Thus comparable aggregate data are far easier to find on the United States, Western Europe, and other developed states than on poorer countries. One comprehensive source, for example—the CIA's *World Factbook*—offers country-by-country overviews of political structure and economic conditions such as GDP per capita and percentage of the population living in poverty.[16] But the data are much more complete for wealthier states than for poor ones. Even for wealthier countries, however, we are likely to encounter differences in definitions and coverage of ostensibly identical data. To take our earlier example of public spending on social welfare programs, each country may include different types of expenses or programs in its national statistics; and some may include state and local spending, while others may not.[17]

Data availability also differs by topic. Summary data on political structures (such as national electoral systems or the shape of the national legislature) have become increasingly easy to locate,[18] as have data on election results.[19] Other types of information can be more difficult to collect. As one example, consider the question of whether democratization breeds greater income equality. To anser it, we would need data on the timing of democratization and on the distribution of incomes during and after the shift from authoritarian rule. For measures of democratization, we might tap data from Polity IV,[20] a data set housed at the University of Maryland with country-by-country evidence on regime changes extending back to the 1800s, or Freedom House's annual ratings of civil liberties and political rights.[21] But comparable measures of income inequality are far harder to locate. Even if the data exist, they may be issued sporadically, making it difficult to determine how inequities respond to changes in the political system.

Similar limitations arise in using survey data on individuals. Such data are generally far easier to find for wealthier countries, where resources, logistics, and political stability facilitate individual interviews. Many major cross-national survey projects have thus focused predominantly on more developed states.[22] And, as with aggregate data, coverage varies by topic. It can be much easier to find cross-national surveys on elections and partisan choice, or on core attitudes and values than on individual political behavior, or on interethnic relations. Thus we are generally limited to the topic and questions defined by other researchers.

The alternative, collecting new survey data, does give us control over the choice of sample and variables employed. But as with aggregate data, the more countries and time periods we include, the more difficult it becomes to guarantee that we are measuring the same thing in each one. In fact, collecting data on individuals in other cultures can be an extremely complicated task. Assuming that we have the resources to carry out a cross-national study—say, a survey of political alienation or of participation—and that we have the cooperation of the government in each of our sample countries (which should not be taken for granted), we need to consider several issues.

---

[16] Online at www.odci.gov/cia/publications/factbook.

[17] Arnold J. Heidenheimer outlines the problems in "Throwing Money and Heaving Bodies: Heuristic Calisthenics for Comparative Policy Buffs," in Louis Imbeau and Robert McKinlay, eds., *Comparing Government Activity* (New York: St. Martin's, 1996), pp. 13–25.

[18] See, for example, Arthur S. Banks, *Political Handbook of the World*, (New York: McGraw-Hill, annual).

[19] One broad-ranging source is the Website of the International Foundation for Electoral Systems (www.ifes.org).

[20] The most recent version is online at http://k-gleditsch.socsci.gla.ac.uk/polity.html.

[21] See Freedom House's Website at http://freedomhouse.org.

[22] Note, though, that in recent years, coverage in major cross-national surveys has expanded well beyond the United States and Western Europe. For example, see the World Values Survey (http://wvs.isr.umich.edu) and the International Social Survey Programme (www.issp.org).

The first concerns how to ensure that our survey is *linguistically equivalent*—that is, how to be sure that the questions we use in one language are translated accurately into others. This clearly requires fluency (or translators who are fluent) in the language of each individual we interview, as well as back-translations to ensure that the questions are indeed equivalent. Even the most fluent researcher, though, may still have some difficulty in expressing some concepts. Certain ideas or terms derived form one culture may simply have no counterpart in another. Take, for example, the notion of an interest group (that is, a collection of like-minded individuals who attempt to influence government policy) and the notion of pluralism (a political order in which different groups compete and cooperate to influence the government's actions). Because the two notions are products of Western democratic theory, both may have equivalents in Western democratic systems. But in other cultures, neither idea may even exist, because each derives from the experience of highly institutionalized political systems that give rise to formally organized groups. When such differences occur, our survey questions will have to be rewritten in terms that allow equivalent translations between cultures.

In addition to the possibility of differences in concepts and language from one country to another, there is the possibility that cultural traits may influence the way people respond. Thus, for example, respondents in some countries may view the survey as a game in which their role is simply to string along an interviewer, whether their answers are accurate or not. Others may place a high value on cooperation or deference to authority and thus may be inclined to give the responses they think the interviewer wants to hear.[23] Finally, some may not acknowledge having certain reactions or values, because they go against what local society prescribes (for example, racial or ethnic stereotyping). In each case, culture produces a bias that influences the responses we obtain.

As with other aspects of the equivalence problem, part of the solution lies in in-depth research on each country to help identify factors that might influence the way people answer. Another lies in the use of multiple measures of what we want to study. If other types of evidence support our survey results, then we have more reason to believe that our findings are valid.

This very short overview identifies neither all of the data sources available for cross-national research nor all of the problems we might encounter in using them. But it does suggest that each source has different strengths and weaknesses, and these are things that we need to recognize in any comparative study.

Conclusion

We began this chapter with the argument that comparative analysis is a necessity if we want to develop generalizations that apply beyond national borders and if we want to study system-level traits. Yet cross-national research must be designed in accordance with several considerations, including the framing of truly comparative

---

[23] Debra Javeline addresses this issue in "Response Effects in Polite Cultures," *Public Opinion Quarterly,* 63 (spring 1999), pp. 1–28.

questions, use of equivalent measures, choice of an appropriate sample, and inclusion of observations that are independent from one country to another. Why stress these? Because they clearly help to determine what we—or other researchers—find, and they can thus shape our conclusions about political relationships. Given the state of our theories about politics and our access to information, we obviously do not have perfect solutions for each of the problems that comparative research might raise. Yet we still need to take each one into account when we design a study and interpret its results. The more clearly we recognize and control for possible biases, the more confidence we can have that our conclusions—about substantive issues—are right.

Suggestions for Further Reading

Several authors present a more detailed discussion of issues and problems in comparative research, and many more take up some aspect of the various examples we have discussed in the text. For a general discussion of comparative methods, consult Adam Przeworski and Henry Teune, *The Logic of Comparative Social Inquiry* (New York: Wiley-Interscience, 1970); David Collier, "The Comparative Method: Two Decades of Change," in Dankwart A. Rustow and Kenneth Erickson, eds., *Comparative Political Dynamics: Global Research Perspectives* (New York: HarperCollins, 1991), pp. 7–31; B. Guy Peters, *Comparative Politics: Theory and Methods* (New York: New York University Press, 1998); and Todd Landman, *Issues and Methods in Comparative Politics: An Introduction* (London: Routledge, 2000). For an excellent general overview of the choices to be made in comparative research design, see Gary King, Robert O. Keohane and Sidney Verba, *Designing Social Inquiry: Scientific Inference in Qualitative Research* (Princeton, NJ: Princeton University Press, 1994).

For more details on specific methodological questions, read David Collier and James E. Mahon, Jr., "Conceptual 'Stretching' Revisited: Adapting Categories in Comparative Analysis," *American Political Science Review,* 87 (December 1993), pp. 845–55, on choosing the appropriate research question and using categories that travel; William Chandler and Marsha Chandler, "The Problem of Indicator Formation in Comparative Research," *Comparative Political Studies,* 7 (April 1974), pp. 26–46, on equivalent indicators; and Marc Ross and Elizabeth Homer, "'Galton's Problem' in Cross-National Research," *World Politics,* 27 (October 1976), pp. 1–28. On the choice of cases to compare and the implications of selection bias, see Theodore Meckstroth, "'Most Different Systems' and 'Most Similar Systems': A Study in the Logic of Comparative Inquiry," *Comparative Political Studies,* 8 (July 1975), pp. 132-57; Barbara Geddes, "How the Cases You Choose Affect the Answers You Get: Selection Bias in Comparative Politics," *Political Analysis,* 2 (1990) pp. 131–150; and David Collier and James Mahoney, "Insights and Pitfalls: Selection Bias in Qualitative Research," *World Politics,* 49 (October 1996) pp. 56–91.

Research Exercises

1. Choose four countries to include in a *most-similar-systems design* to study each of the issues listed below and explain why you would choose each. Choose four countries to include in a *most-different-systems design* for each issue, and explain your choices.

   a. The relationship between poverty and extent of protest against the government

   b. The effect of economic development on political democratization

2. To get a sense of the types of information that different countries make available, you might examine a United Nations publication such as the *Statistical Yearbook*. Do all countries provide data in all categories listed in the yearbook? Answer the following questions:

   a. How does the level of economic development or the type of political system influence the amount of information that some countries report?

   b. Does each country's definition of a category match others, say, for the percentage of the population living in urban areas or the percentage unemployed? What effect might differences in definitions have on comparative analysis?

3. Imagine that you are about to set up a study to explain why the scope of government varies from one country to another. Select three possible indicators you might use to measure the extent of government activity. Would these necessarily be equivalent measures in a study that includes countries at different levels of development and with different types of political systems?

4. Of the various examples of political phenomena we have presented in this chapter, some are more or less likely to be influenced by diffusion than others are. Select three examples from the chapter, tell how likely each is to be affected by diffusion, and explain why it is likely to be affected.

Terms Introduced in This Chapter

equivalent measures

most-similar-systems design

most-different-systems design

Galton's problem

Chapter 12

Data Preparation and Data Processing

We have reached the stage of the research process when we have our data in hand and we must decide upon the most efficient and effective strategy for analyzing them. It is at this stage that we begin to create a finished record of our effort—in the form of charts and graphs, statistics, and other elements of our final research report; these are the products of our research that will be seen and read by others. Yet there remains one far less visible set of operations with which we must come to terms before we can draw from our data the fullest sense of their significance: the preparation and processing of data, which serve as the focus of this chapter.

How do we assign numerical values to the information we have gathered so that it may be analyzed thoroughly? How can we use these numbers to communicate in some meaningful way with computers, without which our masses of data would often prove unmanageable? What, for that matter, can computers tell us about our data? These and related questions must be resolved before we can proceed to the analysis of data and the reaching and presentation of conclusions.

Coding: What Do All Those Numbers Mean?

The process of assigning numerical values to our observations is termed **coding.** Coding is to measurement what the alphabet is to speech: a mechanism for making a precise and lasting record of information. Just as each letter or combination of letters in the alphabet represents a certain sound, each number or combination of numbers in a code represents a particular characteristic or behavior of a research subject. And just as letters allow those who know the alphabet to communicate complex ideas with each other without speech, numbers allow those who know the codes to communicate complex ideas to one another in much abbreviated form. But numerical **codes** allow the researcher to go one step further, for coded information, precisely because it is in numerical form, can be transformed and manipulated according to the rules of mathematics so that the findings may yield meaningful conclusions that might remain obscure were there no resort to numerical representations. Coding, in other words, allows us to learn more from our research than might otherwise be the case.

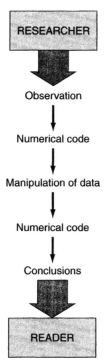

Figure 12.1
Coding in research

In research, particular numbers are assigned to represent each value on a given variable. Thus, if we measure the educational achievement of members of a given population in which each respondent is scored either as not having completed high school, as having completed high school but not college, or as a college graduate, we might assign the numbers 1, 2, and 3, respectively, to represent the three levels of achievement. Alternatively, if we wish to score each respondent on the number of years of schooling completed, we might assign to each a numerical code equivalent to that number (for example, the code 7 might represent seven years of schooling). Both coding schemes accurately summarize the findings of our study, though each conveys a meaning different from the other. Once we have assigned one or another set of such numbers, we may process and analyze the data to our heart's content before reconverting our codes into verbal expressions as we prepare our research report. This process of translation from concept to number and back may be summarized as shown in Figure 12.1.

The most important thing to keep in mind as we develop codes for our data is that our numerical representations must always be consistent with the measurement characteristics of the variables we are researching. That is, nominal-level variables should have nominal codes, ordinal-level variables should have ordinal codes, and interval-level variables should have interval codes. The numbers may *look* very much the same in each instance, but their meanings will differ substantially. Once we convert from words or concepts to numbers, we may be overwhelmingly tempted to analyze or manipulate our data in ways that simply cannot be supported by their underlying level of measurement (this problem becomes more apparent in later chapters, when we focus more directly on techniques of analysis). Such temptations must be resisted if we are to preserve the usefulness of our research, for, as we learned in Chapter 4, not all numbers are created equal.

The mechanics of encoding (or decoding) data are really quite simple. We begin from the values (categories) on each variable in our study. In the case of *nominal* variables, when our numbers need distinguish only between mutually exclusive categories without respect to rank, we merely assign scores in whatever manner is convenient. If, to choose a relatively typical example, our subjects' religious affiliation is to be classified as Protestant, Catholic, or Jewish, we might assign codes according to any of the following schemes:

1	Protestant	1	Catholic	1	Jewish	43	Protestant
2	Catholic	5	Jewish	2	Protestant	17	Catholic
3	Jewish	8	Protestant	3	Catholic	27	Jewish

In each instance, a unique numerical value is used to represent one value or category of the variable. Since religious affiliation is a nominal characteristic, the order and magnitude of the codes have no significance whatsoever. We can use 1-, 3-, or even 10-digit numbers in our codes if we so desire. It is, of course, best to keep the codes as simple and manageable as possible, and we will generally opt for the lowest numbers and the fewest digits we can, but this is a function of our concern for **parsimony** rather than of any mathematical requirement.

It is possible to use slightly more sophisticated nominal coding schemes in order to convey more complete information. Suppose, for instance, that we wish to further categorize our Jewish and Protestant subjects by their specific denominations. Here we might use a two-digit code that builds on our earlier classification. The first digit would be selected as above (for example, 1 representing Protestants; 2, Catholics; and 3, Jews). The second would add the new information. Consider the following scheme:

10	Protestant	20	Catholic
11	Baptist	30	Jewish
12	Methodist	31	Orthodox
13	Presbyterian	32	Conservative
14	Lutheran	33	Reform

Here our codes preserve (in the first column) the gross differences between the categories but allow as well (in the second column) for some fine-tuning. The result is a more complete record of our subjects' characteristics, which still preserves the essence of the less precise variable with which we began.

Were we to list all of the Protestant denominations, of course, the "10" codes (those from 10 through 19)would soon be exhausted and we would be forced to modify our scheme. Either of the following alternatives can easily meet this challenge, though the desirability of choosing one or the other may vary depending on one's analytical requirements.

10	Protestant	100
11	Baptist	101
12	Methodist	102
13	Presbyterian	103
14	Lutheran	104
15	Episcopalian	105
16	Church of Christ	106
17	Latter-day Saints	107
18	Church of God	108
19	Christian Science	109
20	Wesleyan	110
21	Assembly of God	111
30	Catholic	200
40	Jewish	300
41	Orthodox	310 (or 301)
42	Conservative	320 (or 302)
43	Reform	330 (or 303)

In the first instance we simply expand the number of decades (sets of 10 codes) assigned to the Protestants; in the second we add a digit. Again, since the variable in question is nominal, neither the specific numbers nor the number of digits has any significance. As long as our coding system is parsimonious, and as long as the coding categories are mutually exclusive, any numbers will suffice.

When we code *ordinal* variables, we are a bit more constrained. Because ordinal measurement does not include equal, or even known, intervals between values, we remain free to employ numbers of any magnitude. But because ordinal measurement requires that we preserve in our codes the relative positions (rankings) of these values, we must, at the very least, take care that our numbers are properly ordered. Thus for the variable *level of political development* or any variable entailing differences of level, degree, or likelihood, any of the following coding schemes might be equally correct (and equally meaningful):

1	Lowest	1	Lowest
2	Low	6	Low
3	High	7	High
4	Highest	9	Highest

Each preserves the order inherent in the variable. None is in any way more precise than the others, because precision is a function not of the numbers themselves but of the underlying ordinal measurement. As was true earlier, our concern with parsimony might well lead us to select the first of the two schemes, but beyond that, our choice is strictly arbitrary.

In contrast, neither of the following schemes is appropriate:

1	Lowest	1	Highest
9	Low	2	High
6	High	3	Low
7	Highest	4	Lowest

Though the relative magnitude, or ordering, of numerical codes (and therefore the direction of their ordering) has no significance for nominal measurement, it is very important when we work with ordinal data. In the first of the two examples just given, the ranking of the numbers has been mixed; in the second, it has been reversed. As a result, neither coding scheme satisfactorily preserves the relative position and magnitude of the values on the variable. Thus the codes are an inaccurate translation of our observations. Either they deprive us of the opportunity to rank our cases one against another, or they mislead us about the nature of any ranking we develop. Accordingly, such schemes are to be avoided with ordinal data.

Developing codes for interval measures may prove the easiest. Here numbers take on more precise meanings, and our options in assigning them are substantially reduced. A dollar is a dollar, a year is a year, and the difference between 47 percent and 43 percent is the same as that between 73 percent and 69 percent. In interval measurement, not only are values mutually exclusive and indicative of rank, but also the distances between any two sets of adjacent categories are constant and equal. The coding of interval variables must preserve these characteristics.

In order to code scores on an interval variable, we must find a set of numbers such that each is mutually exclusive of the others, each corresponds to a value of the variable, each is equally distant from its nearest neighbors, and the distance between any two adjacent values is known. Finding such numbers is generally an easy task, for unlike most nominal or ordinal scales, for which the researcher must, in effect, invent numerical equivalents for observations, many interval codes are naturally occurring. That is, interval codes are far more likely than those at lesser levels of measurement to derive *directly* from the operational definitions of variables. If we define a person's income as the number of dollars earned in a given period, then each specific quantity of dollars earned constitutes not only a value of the variable income but a code for that value as well. As a result, the emphasis in the coding of interval data is generally less on *creating* meaningful codes than on recognizing and preserving them.

As we pointed out in Chapter 4, situations occur in which the researcher may, in order to enhance the manipulability or the explanatory power of a data set, wish to collapse internal data into ordinal categories. It may, for example, be both easier and more meaningful for us to compare respondents according to their general level of income than to focus on each dollar of difference. In such instances, it may be that the initial coding of the data will preserve their interval character and that these categories will subsequently be reaggregated according to the needs of the researcher (for example, we might record the actual number of dollars earned by respondents and then later group these earnings into larger categories), or the design may be to collapse the data at the time of acquisition (as when we simply classify respondents into general income categories (e.g., $20,000–$49,999) and make no record of their specific earnings). Each method entails both advantages and disadvantages, which should be weighed in the context of the research question at hand. Whichever is selected, however, researchers should be sure that their ultimate coding scheme meets the measurement requirements of the indicator in question.

As should be evident by now, the assignment of appropriate codes to data is inseparable from the process of operationalizing variables. Indeed, *codes are nothing more than numerical manifestations of our operational definitions.* For that reason, it is somewhat misleading to have placed our discussion of coding so late in this book. Decisions about what codes to associate with values on a variable must be made early in the research process. Such decisions are merely one more important part of proper planning. Yet the real usefulness of codes does not become apparent until later in the research process, for it is when we begin to analyze our data that codes come to bear most directly on our enterprise. It is here that coding provides for the transition first from observation to data processing and then from data processing to interpretation. To understand how this transition takes place, let us now consider the structures and uses of several code-related mechanisms.

The Codebook and the Coding Sheet

The first such device we must examine is the codebook. A **codebook** is simply a listing of each variable to be employed in a study, of each value the variable might take on, and of the numerical scores—the codes—associated with each of these values.

Suppose, for example, that on July 1, 1995, the governments of Iran, Nicaragua, and Vietnam hired public relations firms to improve their images in the U.S. press and that we wish to design a study to determine the effect these efforts have had on news and editorial content. In such a study we might compare the periods immediately before and immediately after the starting date of these campaigns to see whether, after the contracts took effect, (1) the amount of coverage of each nation increased or decreased significantly and (2) the various nations were presented more or less favorably than they had been in the earlier period. (In reality, we would also have to control for such additional factors as regular seasonal variation in coverage, as in the case of countries that get more press attention during the tourist season or the occurrence of newsworthy events such as political upheavals or natural disasters, but for purposes of illustration let us assume these are not problems.)

To assess the effects of these image-enhancing efforts, we can turn to any of a number of print or electronic indexes of news coverage and either analyze the index entries, which will be in the form of either titles or abstracts of various news articles and may, in fact, convey a good deal of information, or use them to identify the actual articles themselves. For purposes of illustration, let us design a project using index entries in the *Readers' Guide to Periodical Literature* (which indexes the contents of a large number of popular magazines and is available in both print and online versions) under the headings "Iran," "Nicaragua," and "Vietnam." Our independent variable is the introduction of professional public relations activities or, more correctly, their absence (before July 1, 1995) or presence (after that date).

Following on the two questions identified, we will have two sets of dependent variables. The first set will measure the *quantity* of news coverage and might include the number of index entries each month in the pretest and posttest periods and the proportion of such entries (as evidenced by their titles or index classifications) that refer to the political, economic, or social system, respectively, of each country. We might further classify these as focusing on domestic or international concerns. The second set of variables will measure the *quality* of news coverage through judgments on such matters as whether the article (again, as evidenced by its title) suggests progress or decline in the nation's fortunes. Finally, in any such study we should include codes identifying each individual article, the country to which it refers, the date of publication, its length, and the specific publication or type of publication in which it appears.

An abbreviated codebook for this hypothetical study is illustrated in Table 12.1. As you can see, the codebook summarizes the indicators to be used in the study and their associated values. It is, in fact, little more than a formal statement of the operational definitions with which any piece of research begins. Here, however, these definitions are set out in complete detail, including instructions for their interpretation, and are organized not with respect to our hypotheses per se but with an eye toward facilitating the actual gathering of information. The codebook provides step-by-step guidance to what we are looking for and how we can recognize it when we find it.

The codebook identifies the computer columns in which data will be stored and provides a description of the information to be found in each location. It also tells what codes were used to represent nonnumeric data. For example, the codebook depicted in Table 12.1 indicates that a number 1 found in computer column 16 signifies that the type of magazine in which the article in question was found is a news weekly (like *Time* or *Newsweek*). Having this information in a central location helps researchers record data correctly and accurately interpret the results of data analysis when it is completed. It also makes it possible for others who may use the data set to see how data are organized and to interpret the results of data analysis without relying exclusively on the original researcher.

Once the codebook has been prepared, it is a quick and easy step to the next stage of data preparation—the development of a coding sheet. A **coding sheet** is a data recording device whose structure is based on the codebook and whose form will aid in computerizing our information once it has been gathered. The survey questionnaire and the recording form for structured observation described in earlier chapters, for instance, are both examples of coding sheets, as is the form presented in Figure12.2 for our study of coverage of foreign nations in the American press.

In Figure 12.2 the column labels correspond to the indicators developed in the codebook. A column is reserved on the coding sheet for *each digit* in a given code; thus a two-digit code (such as that for month of publication) requires two columns on the coding sheet. Similarly, each row represents one case, and each numerical entry a value on the indicator in question for that particular case. Thus we see that case number 0001 is an article about Iran that appeared in a news weekly in January

Table 12.1
Abbreviated codebook for a hypothetical study of public relations of foreign nations

Column	Variable	Values	Code
1–4	Article (case) ID number		—
5	Nation referenced	Iran	1
		Nicaragua	2
		Vietnam	3
6–7	Month of publication	July 1995	01
		August 1995	02
		January 1996	07
		May 1997	23
		June 1997	24
8	Reference to political system in title (including references to government, political leaders or events, political parties, public policies)	No reference	0
		Reference present	1
9	Reference to economic system in title (including references to industry, the currency, the workforce, production, markets, trade, economic opportunity, etc.)	No reference	0
		Reference present	1
10	Reference to social system in title (including references to cultural, religious or social institutions, social events or actors, social structure, etc.)	No reference	0
		Reference present	1
11	Reference to domestic or international context	Exclusively domestic	1
		Both domestic and international	2
		Exclusively international	3
		Does not apply, NA	9
12	Reference to progress or decline	Reference exclusively to progress	1
		Reference to both progress and decline	2
		Reference exclusively to decline	3
		Does not apply	9
13–15	Number of pages in article		—
16	Type of magazine	News weekly (*Newsweek, U.S. News & World Report,* or *Time* only)	1
		Other, primarily political (including opinion magazines and featuring primarily political news and analysis)	2
		Other, primarily nonpolitical (including general audience magazines and those with specialized but primarily nonpolitical coverage)	3

Identification number	Country	Month of publication	Reference to political system	Reference to economic system	Reference to social system	Domestic/international context	Progress/decline	Number of pages	Type of magazine
0 0 0 1	1	0 7	1	0	0	1	3	0 0 3	1

Coding sheet number ________________

Date coded ________________

Coded by ________________

Figure 12.2
Coding sheet for studying effects of public relations of foreign nations

1996, focused exclusively on the political system, and made reference to the nation's declining fortunes and to certain weaknesses in its domestic situation. Such scores might derive, for example, from an article in *Time* entitled "Iran in Chaos: Leaders Unable to Halt Executions, Stability Threatened." In this manner, relevant characteristics of each article title we encounter can be recorded on the coding sheet, with each case taking up one row or line. Thus if we study, or *code,* 821 cases, we can expect to end up with 821 rows of data. In each instance, corresponding data about the various cases will appear in the same column(s) on the coding sheet.

Finally, all coding sheets should be numbered (to ensure that none has been lost), dated (dates are often useful, for example, if we are forced to alter a definition or add a variable in midstream and must recode or add codes to all previous cases), and signed or initialed by the coder (as a basis for measuring intercoder reliability, as discussed in Chapter 9). If more than one coding sheet is required for each case, as when the number of indicators to be measured is quite large, all sheets for the same group of cases should be both stapled together and numbered identically. This minimizes the chances of their being separated and mixed up during processing.

Data Entry and Data Processing

Once the recording of data has been completed, we turn our attention to processing or manipulating our numbers to arrive at our findings. You can well imagine that in a study with large numbers of indicators and cases, the jumble of numbers can be absolutely overwhelming. To deal with this problem and to increase the ease, accuracy, and sophistication of our analysis, we rely on the computer.

Some analyses—especially those employing large data sets or very elaborate statistical procedures—are performed on mainframe computers, but most political science research can be accommodated by the speed and capacity of the latest personal computers. Today, a wide variety of software packages are available for performing statistical analysis on computers. One of the most established programs found at many universities and research companies is Statistical Package for the Social Sciences (SPSS), which provides a fairly intuitive click-and-drag interface for analyzing and graphically displaying data. Other common statistical programs are, for example, SAS, Statistica, Genstat, or Minitab. Software packages with full statistical programming languages like S-Plus, STATA, or SHAZAM can provide more flexibility for creating graphics and using new statistical methods. In the end, choosing a program will depend on the analyses you want to do as well as your statistical background and your programming skills.

While the choice of statistical programs can be bewildering, most of them allow the user to enter data into a spreadsheet or data-editing screen. When using such a spreadsheet to enter data, you should first define and label one column for each variable of interest. Then, you enter the data line by line, with each line representing a different case or observation. If, for example, you would like to analyze ten characteristics (your variables) of 200 newspaper stories (your cases), you would use one line of data for each of the 200 newspaper stories. In this example, each line of data would use ten columns, one for each of the ten variables. In addition to the columns that represent the variables in your analysis, you should also add one column for a case identification number in order to keep track of your data. All of that should sound familiar, for it is directly analogous to the coding sheet described above.

While manual data entry has become easier due to the introduction of spreadsheet-like data entry systems, other methods of data entry are available. Optical scan sheets, with which most students probably are familiar ("fill the bubbles with a number two pencil…"), are becoming more popular due to the increased availability of optical scanners and new software that allows the creation and scanning of questionnaires to produce data files. Optical scan sheets are especially useful for recording large amounts of data that have been recorded on predesigned, standardized forms, thus avoiding the arduous task of entering this data manually. There are, however, a few disadvantages of using optical scan sheets for data entry. First, scan sheets only allow data to be entered in a predetermined way. Notes in the margins of the scan sheet, for example, will not be recognized by the scanner and therefore will not appear in the final data file. Second, optical scanners often do not recognize markings on scan sheets that do not conform with the predesigned option. Thus, scan sheet bubbles that are not completely filled, or are smudged or wrongly marked will probably not be recognized correctly by the scanner. Finally, some people might find it difficult to record data on scan sheets because of their often generic layout or the difficulty in identifying the appropriate space for marking the data on the sheet.

Once the data have been entered into the computer, the next step is to carefully check them for errors, a process that is also called "data cleaning." Manual data entry can easily lead to errors because of typos, incorrect reading of the codes, or simply a tired person entering the data. The easiest way to check data for erroneous entries is to print out the distribution for each of the variables in your data set and then look for inappropriate codes. For example, you might have decided to code the variable *party identification* as 1 for Republicans, 2 for Democrats, and 3 for Independents. If you see in the printed distribution that one of the cases has been coded as 5, it is obvious that an error has been made during the data entry. After identifying the errors, all you have to do is go back to the original questionnaires and check for the correct codes.

Conclusion

Before we conclude, three final points are in order. First, it is not unusual for those without prior computing experience to be both bewildered and intimidated by computers. Such feelings are understandable, but they should not be allowed to stand in the way of learning. With all of the programs, manuals, and online help functions now available, using the computer is much simpler than it used to be. In fact, once you overcome your self-doubt you will probably find that you are hooked on the computer and that you greatly enjoy using it.

Second, don't be ashamed if you make mistakes. Careful data entry and proof-reading eliminate many errors, but as with any new skill you will invent ways to make more. This is a common pattern and should not trouble you. When you think about it, making and correcting mistakes represent two of the most important ways that we learn. Track down your own errors when you can, get help when you must, and keep trying.

Finally, don't get carried away. Computers are inherently stupid; they process information and they follow instructions precisely, but they do not think. By using the software packages we have described here, you can easily get a computer to perform the most elaborate statistical analyses imaginable even on data of such low quality that the results, though impressive looking, are meaningless. Accordingly, it is quite important that you think through and understand the statistical and analytical procedures that you call upon the computer to perform and that you select only those that fit your needs and your data. Those procedures are the subjects of the next several chapters.

Suggestions for Further Reading

For a more detailed discussion of coding procedures, see Kenneth Janda, *Data Processing: Applications to Political Research*, 2d ed. (Evanston, IL: Northwestern University Press, 1969).

Useful examples of codebooks and other related devices may be found in the appendixes to Morris Janowitz, *The Community Press in an Urban Setting: The Social Elements of Urbanism*, 2d ed. (Chicago: University of Chicago Press, 1967), and David A. Leuthold, *Electioneering in a Democracy: Campaigns for Congress* (New York: Wiley, 1968).

Two excellent and easy-to-understand books for new and advanced users of SPSS are Marija J. Norusis, *SPSS 10.0 Guide to Data Analysis* (Upper Saddle River, NJ: Prentice Hall, 2000) and Earl R. Babbie, Fred Halley, Jeanne Zaino, *Adventures in Social Research: Data Analysis Using SPSS 9.0 and 10.0 for Windows* (Thousand Oaks, CA: Pine Forge Press, 2000).

Research Exercises

1. a. Prepare a codebook for a hypothetical study using survey research or content analysis.

    b. Develop a coding sheet to correspond to your codebook.

    c. Either gather data on 25 cases or make up imaginary data on 25 hypothetical cases. Enter these data on your coding sheet.

    d. Find out what software packages are available at your computer laboratory. Obtain and peruse the manual for at least one of these packages.

    e. Enter your data into the computer, using the rules stated in the manual. Be sure to proofread and correct any errors.

    f. Experiment with writing a set of instructions to analyze the data you have entered.

2. Find the Website of the Inter-university Consortium for Political and Social Research (ICPSR) at the University of Michigan (www.icpsr.umich.edu) and access their archive for computerized social science data. Chose one of the listed topics and examine the available abstract and codebook. (*Note*: the codebook is listed together with the dataset.)

Terms Introduced in This Chapter

coding
codes
parsimony

codebook
coding sheet

CHAPTER 13

DESCRIBING THE DATA: THE CONSTRUCTION OF TABLES, CHARTS, AND DIAGRAMS

The problem we face at this point in the research process is how best to share with others the results of our work. We must seek a style of presentation that is clear, concise, precise, and, above all, true to our data. Yet at the same time, we must help others to understand the meaning or significance of what we have found. That is, we must present our results in such a way that they may be readily interpreted. In part, the successful presentation of data involves statistical analyses, whose discussion we shall postpone to the next chapter. But in large measure, the effective communication and interpretation of research data depend on the quality of tabular and graphic presentation; on the tables, charts, and diagrams that one chooses; and on the appropriateness and clarity of their construction.

The variety of types of tabular and graphic presentations is vast, especially given the ever-expanding graphics capabilities of software packages for the analysis and presentation of data. Common programs such as Microsoft Word, Excel, or Powerpoint, for example, all have interactive tools and templates to create a wide range of presentation-quality tables and charts. Similarly, statistical programs such as SPSS make it very easy to display data in the form of bar or pie charts, histograms, or scatterplots, to name but a few options. In most of these programs you must first enter the data for the chart into a separate "worksheet" (or spreadsheet) and then choose the graph type through a graphical user interface. Once the chart is created, modifications can be made interactively by changing the data or the graph itself. For example, you can insert or delete graphical elements, change colors and textures, rotate three-dimensional graphs, and adjust lines and surfaces.

Another nice feature of interactive charts is that they allow you to visually explore data by changing the order of the variables or the way the data are displayed. The fact that data can now be examined so easily by reorganizing the layout of a graph or viewing different levels of detail has added a new dimension to the art of data analysis that should not be underestimated. While graphs might be useful to display complex information in a simple and easy-to-understand way, the introduction of interactive graphs has created an entirely new technique for exploratory data analysis.

Unfortunately, we are unable here to describe all or even the most common software packages that allow the tabular or graphical presentation of data. Rather, by examining a few typical examples, we suggest the kinds of concerns you need take into account when either reading or preparing tables and graphs and the like. In the process, we deal with such questions as, When should you employ a graphic representation? Which is better—a table or a chart? What should tables, charts, and diagrams look like (what is their structure)? How can tabular and graphic presentations help you to better understand your findings?

The Enumerative Table

We begin our discussion of these issues by looking at a device with which you are probably already familiar—the enumerative table. An **enumerative table** is simply a tabular presentation of research data in what is essentially the form of a list. Table 13.1, for example, summarizes the Democratic presidential vote and its racial components for the period 1960 to 1976. Each column in the table represents a different variable (there are four variables in all). The fact that the table is ordered by the variable year, which appears in the first column, provides a cue for the interpretation of the data. It suggests that the table has been constructed to answer the question, How has the Democratic presidential vote varied from year to year?

A close examination of Table 13.1 reveals a number of points about the proper format for tabular presentation. As in the example, all tables should be numbered consecutively. In a lengthy paper with several numbered sections (or in a thesis or book with several chapters), these numbers may take the form Table 3.1, Table 3.2, and so forth, or Table III:1, Table III:2, and so forth. In a shorter or more simply structured paper, single-numbered listings (Table 1, Table 2) are quite sufficient. When tables appear in the same work with charts, graphs, or other illustrations,

Table 13.1
Size and racial composition of the Democratic vote, 1960–1976[*]

Year	Democratic Vote (%)	White Democratic Vote (%)	Black Democratic Vote (%)
1960	50	49	68
1964	61	59	94
1968	43	38	85
1972	40	34	89
1976	51	48	83

SOURCE: Data reported in this table are drawn from the quadrennial surveys of the Hypothetical Survey Research Company.
[*]Data on Asian and other nonwhite voters other than blacks, though present in the data sets from which this table is drawn, have been excluded from the present analysis.

they are usually numbered separately. Graphic presentations are generally referred to as, for example, Figure 1 or Figure 3.1.

Each table should have a title that accurately summarizes the nature of the data it reports. This title should give the reader enough information to decide whether to examine the table in detail, but it should not go so far as to save the reader the trouble of doing so. Thus a title for Table 13.1 such as *Data Showing That Democrats Polled More Than Half of the Votes Three Times in 1960-1976 and Did Better Among Blacks Than Whites* would be inappropriate. In general, a title should simply indicate the major variables for which data are reported in a given table. When, as in Table 13.1, these data cover a particular time period, the period in question should be incorporated into the title as well. When a table is drawn in whole or in part from another source, the reference should be placed immediately below the table. Explanatory references pertaining to the table as a whole (the first footnote in the example) should be indicated with superior lowercase letters or other symbols following the title. Those pertaining to parts of the table (the second footnote in the example) should be placed appropriately within the table. The footnotes themselves should be located immediately below the table and should follow a source identification when one is present.

Other points to keep in mind when preparing tables:

1. The table number and title should be separated from both the preceding text and the table itself by open space. When you type a table, it is usually best to leave three spaces above the title, two between the title and the table, and three below the table. An alternative style is to place each table on a separate page. At the point in the text where the table is discussed, skip a line, type "INSERT TABLE 1 HERE" in capital letters in the center of the page, skip another line, and continue the text. In either instance, external boundaries of the table should be double-lined and internal boundaries single-lined.

2. If possible, it is best to avoid drawing vertical lines to separate cells within the table. Make sure you take advantage of the table funciton available in most graphics, word-processing, or database programs. Microsoft Word, for example, allows you to quickly create tables and automatically format them with a variety of borders, fonts, and shading. This feature is especially useful for "hiding" vertical lines in tables and giving all tables in your paper a consistent look.

3. Labels and data within the table should be double-spaced to facilitate reading, except that titles and category labels that will not fit on one line should be single-spaced. Category labels should describe as briefly as possible the variables or values in question, but they should always be sufficiently complete to make clear the meaning of the data.

As a rule of thumb, no table should be included in a research report unless it can generate at least a page of discussion. That discussion should not merely repeat the contents of the table. The table is, after all, there for the reader to see. Nor should one overload the discussion with percentages or other quantitative terms, though these can be used sparingly. Rather, the discussion of a table should make clear any relationships demonstrated in the table and should focus the reader's attention on any highlights or particularly noteworthy findings. The discussion may also be used to report the results of any statistical tests one has performed on the data in the table (see Chapters 14-16). In the present example, a thorough discussion would probably touch on the overall level of and changes in the Democratic vote during the period in question and on the relative contributions of white and black voters to that vote. It might treat as well the possible reasons for any similarities or differences noted. Specific points to be discussed might include the range of variation and the consistency (if any) in the pattern of variation for the variables, any notable inconsistencies in the data, and even the reliability of the source from which the data have been obtained.

The Line Diagram

Sometimes we may wish to augment or replace tabular presentations with visually simpler graphics. This may be done either to clarify the presentation (consider the difficulty of interpreting Table 13.1 if it covered the period of 1876 to 1992) or to illustrate some particular aspect of the data. Many different design techniques are available for doing so, one of the simplest of which is the line diagram of the type illustrated in Figure 13.1. A **line diagram** connects with a continuous line all the data points for a given indicator and provides for a comparison of data points across indicators by representing each in a separate corresponding line, often in a contrasting style. Line diagrams are especially useful for representing trends.

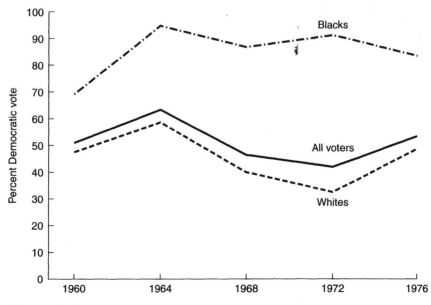

Figure 13.1
Line diagram: Size and racial composition of the Democratic vote, 1960–1976

The diagram in Figure 13.1 reports the same data as does Table 13.1, but in graphic form. In contrast to the table, which requires a thorough reading, a quick glance at Figure 13.1 is sufficient to tell us that between 1960 and 1976 Democrats polled, in general, between 40 and about 60 percent of the vote in presidential elections; that they did better in 1960, 1964, and 1976 than in 1968 or 1972; that the pattern of white voters' support for the party followed very much the same path as its overall fortunes (whites deserted the party in 1968 and 1972, but returned in 1976); that support for the party among black voters was consistently higher than among whites; and that black support sustained its high levels regardless of the party's success or failure. The fine detail available in Table 13.1 is less evident in Figure 13.1 (for instance, it is difficult to distinguish between 50 percent support in 1960 and 51 percent in 1976), but the overall lessons of the data emerge much more readily.

In general, graphics of this type should have a format similar to that used for tables. Each figure should be numbered separately and titled appropriately. Both the vertical and horizontal axes, when present, should be labeled, and great care should be exercised to ensure that each is properly and consistently scaled.[1] Vertical-scale labeling should be placed above the vertical scale numbers. Horizontal-scale labels should be placed below the diagram. If the horizontal-scale numerals are years (as in the example), further labeling is optional. In the case of a complex line drawing, a **key** (an itemized explanation) to the lines should be placed below the diagram. When necessary, additional explanatory labels may be placed on the diagram proper.

The Pie Diagram and the Bar Chart

Both the enumerative table and the line diagram are useful primarily for describing and summarizing the information in question. With some slight transformation of the data, however, it is possible to use graphic techniques to analyze or interpret these numbers as well. Suppose, for example, we are interested in highlighting the relative importance of black and white voters to the fortunes of Democratic presidential candidates. In particular, we might be interested in such questions as whether blacks' or whites' support is more crucial to Democratic victories and whether (as was widely argued at the time) black voters put Jimmy Carter in the White House in 1976. And let us suppose further, to keep our argument simple, that in each of the five election years we are considering, 90 percent of all voters were white and 10 percent black. (In reality, blacks indeed account for roughly 10 percent of voters, but turnout rates vary from one election to the next, and other groups, most notably Asians and Hispanics, also account for small proportions of the electorate.) Combining this pattern of turnout with the data presented in Table 13.1, we can identify the components of the Democratic vote in each election in terms of their proportional support.

---

[1] Improperly or inconsistently scaled axes can confuse the reader, or even the researcher, by either overstating or understating orders of magnitude or degrees of change. Indeed, truncated graphs (those whose lower values are not included) or stretched graphs (those on which the scale is smaller for one range of values and larger for another) may be deliberately employed to misinform a careless reader. Fortunately, use of these devices is more common in advertisements or commentaries reporting research than in the research literature itself.

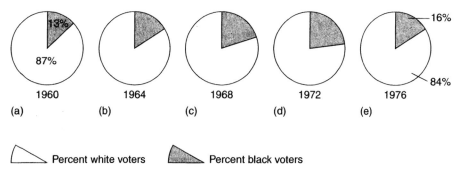

Percent white voters   Percent black voters

Figure 13.2
Pie diagram: Racial components of the Democratic coalition, 1960–1976

With regard to 1976, for example, we know that 48 percent of white voters supported the Democrats and that 90 percent of all voters were white. Taking 48 percent of 90 percent, we find that 43.2 percent of all voters were whites who voted Democratic. Similarly, we know that 83 percent of black voters supported the Democrats and that 10 percent of all voters were black. Taking 83 percent of 10 percent, we find that 8.3 percent of all voters were blacks who voted Democratic. Together these figures account for the 51.5 percent of all voters who went Democratic in 1976.[2]

But let us carry this calculation a step further. We know that these white and black voters constituted some 51.5 percent of the popular vote in 1976. What proportion of its support did each contribute to the Democratic party? To ascertain this we simply divide each individual figure by 51.5 percent (43.2 ÷ 51.5 and 8.3 ÷ 51.5) to find that in 1976 some 84 percent of Democratic votes came from whites and some 16 percent from blacks. Similar calculations for each of the four preceding elections show blacks to have contributed 13 percent, 15 percent, 20 percent, and 23 percent of all Democratic votes in 1960, 1964, 1968, and 1972, respectively; whites contributed 87 percent, 85 percent, 80 percent, and 77 percent. These figures may be illustrated graphically by a pie diagram, such as that illustrated in Figure 13.2.

A **pie diagram** is a figure in which a circle (or in this case, a series of circles) representing a given population has been segmented to show the distribution of particular attributes. In Figure 13.2, each circle represents 100 percent of the *Democratic* presidential vote in a given year. The shaded area represents the proportion of that vote provided by black voters. Note that the title and key to the figure are similar in style and placement to those in Figure 13.1 and that each circle, or pie, is labeled individually at the bottom of the figure. Percentages of the pie taken up by each segment may be labeled either within the diagram as in Figure 13.2(a) or outside it as

---

[2] The numbers are fractionally different from those in the table in part because of rounding and in part because the actual turnout rates that underlie the data reported in Table 13.1 only approximated the 90 percent and 10 percent figures used here. Were we to use the actual turnout rates as well as fractional percentages in the table, the sum of its parts would indeed match the whole of Democratic support. Our estimations are especially likely to be at variance with the values in the table in 1960 and 1964, when blacks were still actively excluded from voting in some areas and when their turnout rate was relatively lower.

in Figure 13.2(e), whichever is clearer. Alphabetic labels (a, b, c, and so on) for separate elements within the diagram often make it easier for the researcher to discuss the diagram in the text and for the reader to follow the discussion.

Looking at Figure 13.2, one may be struck by the steady increase in the proportion of Democratic votes contributed by blacks between 1960 (when they accounted for 13 percent of the Democratic vote) and 1972 (when they accounted for 23 percent, or nearly twice as much) and by the reduced Democratic dependence on the black vote in 1976. Using this figure (and assuming the accuracy of the underlying data), one might thus be tempted to argue in answer to one of the questions posed earlier that in fact Jimmy Carter was not put into office by black votes. On the contrary, he depended less on support from blacks than had previous candidates from his party. Indeed, substantiation for this argument is apparent from even the most cursory inspection of the pie diagrams. Unfortunately, in the present instance, the pie diagrams, although quite accurate, offer evidence that is incomplete and that consequently may prove misleading. This is true because the size of the Democratic vote varied from election to election (50 percent one year, 61 percent the next) while the size of the circles in the diagram, representing 100 percent of that vote regardless of size, remains constant. Thus in order to be not only accurate but also complete, the pies themselves have to vary in size to account for variations in the overall Democratic vote.

The visual interpretation of sectored circles of differing sizes, however, is difficult at best. People are simply not good at it. Accordingly, such diagrams can defeat the goal of effective communication of our research results. Some alternative must be found, but before we find it, we want to emphasize that our point here is not that pie diagrams are always misleading and should never be used. On the contrary, pie diagrams are quite useful and are often the most effective graphic device for putting across an argument. Rather, the point is that *any* form of chart or diagram must be used with care. We must understand the data that underlie a graphic presentation, and we must be sure that the graphic is appropriate for the data *in the context in which they will be used.* (In the context of some research questions, for example, such as that of whether the proportion of black votes in the Democratic coalition has been steadily rising, the diagrams in Figure 13.2 are perfectly appropriate, because they do provide the relevant information.) Only in this way can graphics make a positive contribution to the interpretation of our data and the presentation of our research.

Returning to the problem at hand, we must find an alternative graphic device that can illustrate the proportion of black votes for the Democrats in a given year while at the same time making clear the fluctuations in the overall level of Democratic votes. One such device is the bar chart or in this instance, a segmented bar chart like that illustrated in Figure 13.3. A **bar chart** is a graphic representation in which the height, and occasionally the width, of a series of bars illustrate a set of observations on one or more variables. In a **segmented bar chart,** each individual bar is subdivided to illustrate an additional set of observations relating to the distribution of attributes among the population represented by the bar itself. Note once again that the format is similar to those of Figures 13.1 and 13.2 except that in a bar chart, the key is typically found *above* rather than below the chart itself.

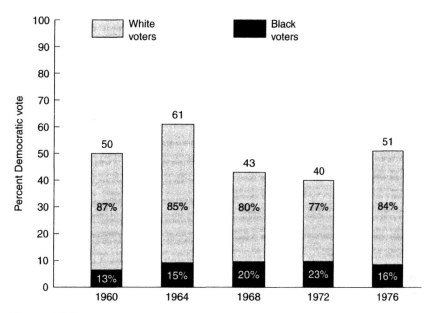

Figure 13.3
Bar chart: Racial components of the Democratic vote, 1960–1976

(Occasionally, bar charts are drawn horizontally beginning at the left margin rather than vertically as in Figure 13.3. In such instances, the key should be placed either below the chart or to the right.)

In Figure 13.3, the black vote is again represented by the shaded area of the diagram. The bars, however, vary in size according to the overall percentage of the Democratic vote. This percentage is evident both in the scale along the left-hand margin of the chart and in the labels atop each individual bar. As a result, the impression one gets from the figure is rather different from that suggested by the pie diagrams, for here we see that though the black Democratic vote did shift up and down a bit, it did so within a relatively narrow range. Instead, it was the white vote that proved most volatile, expanding and contracting in concert with the party's fortunes. Returning to our research question of whether black or white support is more crucial to the Democrats, we are now able to answer that both are important but in different ways. Blacks provide a relatively small but consistently strong base of support, which can constitute the margin of victory in close elections. The white vote is far less consistent and reliable but is so overwhelming numerically that it is more important in determining at least the closeness of, and often the margin of victory or defeat in, a given election. Whites, in other words, have both helped and hurt the Democratic candidates, often decisively. Blacks have primarily helped the party, but not always decisively. The data used to arrive at this conclusion are essentially the same as those reported in Figure 13.2, but they are more complete. As a result, the conclusions we may draw from them are both more sophisticated and more satisfying.

The Bilateral Bar Chart

Another type of chart commonly found in the research literature of political science is the **bilateral bar chart**—a two-directional figure that is used to illustrate variation above or below some norm as represented by a center line. Two typical bilateral bar charts are illustrated in Figure 13.4. In Figure 13.4(a), the center line represents the average (mean) percentage of whites who voted Democratic in presidential elections from 1960 to 1976 (46 percent). The bars represent variations around that average in each of the five elections, with bars to the right of the line signifying above-average support among white voters for the Democrats and those to the left signifying below-average support. The length of the bars represents the degree of variation from the average, and the numerals indicate the precise degree of difference. For example, the average of 46 percent plus the variation of 3 percent in 1960 yields the 49 percent support noted in that year in Table 13.1. Figure 13.4(b) presents a similar analysis of the black vote based on an average level of Democratic support of 84 percent.

These figures add yet another dimension to our analysis of the data reported in Table 13.1, for taken together they suggest that blacks opposed the party in 1960 in numbers unequaled later in the period, that both whites and blacks gave unusually high support to the Democrats in 1964, that whites deserted the party in 1968 and 1972 while blacks voted slightly more heavily Democratic than average, and that voting among both groups in 1976 was roughly in line with their average behavior throughout the period in question. When we combine this new information with our earlier findings, we get a rather thorough picture of the role of black and white voters in the Democratic party during these years. And more generally, we can see that the type of information available from a bilateral bar chart complements and supplements that which can be developed by using other graphic devices.

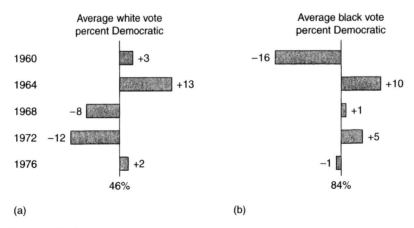

(a) (b)

Figure 13.4
Bilateral bar chart: Variations in presidential voting by race, 1960–1976

The Contingency Table

One other form of tabular presentation deserves attention before we move on to a discussion of statistics. Indeed, it is perhaps the single most common form of table used in contemporary political science research and provides the basis for a number of the statistical calculations we examine in the next chapter. This form of presentation is known as the **contingency table** and is illustrated in Tables 13.2 and 13.3.

In format and structure, the contingency table resembles the enumerative table presented earlier, but its substance is different. Contingency tables are based more directly upon hypotheses and are so structured as to facilitate an examination of the relationships between variables. Table 13.2, for example, summarizes the relationship between race and presidential vote for 1964; Table 13.3 summarizes the comparable data for 1972. In each instance, the data are drawn from hypothetical surveys of 1,500 voters. These tables are organized so as to permit us to examine the hypothesis that blacks, for one reason or another, are more likely than whites to vote Democratic in any given year.

Each entry (exclusive of totals) in each table is termed a *cell*. The tables may be described by the number of rows and columns that they contain, where each row represents a particular value on one variable and each column a particular value on the other. Thus Tables 13.2 and 13.3 are each referred to as a 2×2 (two-by-two) table, since each table has two rows of cells and two columns of cells, excluding totals.

Contingency tables are always arranged so that the data sum on the independent or explanatory variable. In the present instance, that variable is race. This

Table 13.2
Racial differences in presidential voting, 1964

	Presidential Vote			
Race	**Democratic (%)**	**Republican (%)**	**Total (%)**	**Number of Cases**
White	59	41	100	1,350
Black	94	6	100	150
All voters	61	39	100	1,500

Table 13.3
Racial differences in presidential voting, 1972

	Race		
Presidential Vote	**White**	**Black**	**All Voters**
Percent—Democratic	34	89	40
Percent—Republican	66	11	60
Total percent	100	100	100
Number of cases	1,350	150	1,500

means that if the table contains percentages, they will both be based upon and sum to 100 percent along the independent variable. Thus Table 13.2 tells us that in 1964, 59 percent of whites voted Democratic but not that 59 percent of all Democrats were white. It would be possible to calculate our percentages in the other direction, but in the present instance this would tell us nothing of explanatory value, because one's party preference *invariably* is acquired later than one's race. The sum of all of the percentages in line 1 of the table accounts for all (100 percent of) white voters, in line 2 for all black voters, and in line 3 for all voters. The column labeled "number of cases" reports the number of respondents to our hypothetical survey who were classified as members of each group. These numbers constitute a *frequency distribution* (discussed in the next chapter) and because of their position in the table, are often referred to as the *marginals*.

The independent variable in a contingency table may be either the *row* variable, as in Table 13.2, or the *column variable,* as in Table 13.3. Both forms are common in the research literature. However, once we have selected one form or the other, it is important that we use that form consistently throughout a particular research report so as not to confuse our readers.

In examining tables such as these, it is often possible to tell in general terms whether or not one's hypothesis is supported by one's data. In both Table 13.2 and Table 13.3, for instance, it is evident that blacks did vote consistently more Democratic than whites. In 1972, blacks went heavily for the Democrats, whereas whites voted heavily Republican, and even in 1964, when both groups voted heavily Democratic, blacks constituted a stronger bloc than whites. Still, such eyeball measures are rough at best, and when tables are more complex than these, as is often the case, they are generally unreliable. In the next chapter we consider some statistics that enable us to state more precisely the degree of harmony between hypothesis and data.

Some Words of Caution

In conclusion, let us restate for emphasis three important points about the use of tabular and graphic presentations.

First, these devices should be used both imaginatively and constructively. As part of the research process itself, they can be extremely helpful in developing our concepts to the fullest and in bringing us to a firm understanding of what our data tell us. Flexibility and an openness to new forms of analysis can contribute greatly to expanding our knowledge of political phenomena, and even techniques as simple as these can help us to give shape to our discoveries.

Second, tabular and graphic devices should be used appropriately. As may be evident from even this brief treatment, it is possible to present research results deceptively through the subtle abuse of these techniques, and it is equally possible to fool oneself by their careless misuse. Researchers have both an ethical obligation to others to report their findings not only accurately but fairly and an intellectual obligation to themselves to examine them rigorously. Together these obligations are the cornerstones of research. We must be sensitive to them.

Finally, in the presentation of research, tables and graphics should be used - parsimoniously. Too many such materials in a research report clutter the text and detract from its readability. The author's decision to include a table or diagram is taken by the reader as an indication of the importance the author attaches to the particular information contained therein. The author has an obligation to make those choices, and not simply to offer the reader a smorgasbord of information. Not only does such discretion enhance authors' reports; it forces them to think more clearly and decide what is important, thus directly contributing to the research effort.

Suggestions for Further Reading

Probably the best discussion of the use of tables and diagrams in political science research is to be found in Oliver Benson, *Political Science Laboratory* (Columbus, OH: Merrill, 1969), chs. 2 and 3. Useful texts on the practical aspects of graphic presentations include William S. Cleveland, *Visualizing Data* (Summit, NJ: Hobart, 1993) and *The Elements of Graphing* (Summit, NJ: Hobart, 1994) by the same author. Another good introduction to the graphical display of statistical data is Gary T. Henry, ed., *Creating Effective Graphs: Solutions for a Variety of Evaluation Data* (San Francisco, CA: Jossey-Bass, 1997).

More theoretical discussions of the use of graphics can be found in William G. Jacoby, *Statistical Graphics for Univariate and Bivariate Data* (Thousand Oaks, CA: Sage, 1997); William G. Jacoby, *Statistical Graphics for Visualizing Multivariate Data* (Thousand Oaks, CA: Sage, 1997); and Gary T. Henry, *Graphing Data: Techniques for Display and Analysis* (Thousand Oaks, CA: Sage, 1995). Edward R. Tufte offers both a discussion of the conceptual approaches to graphic representation and a collection of examples covering some three centuries in *The Visual Display of Quantitative Information* (Cheshire, CT: Graphics Press, 1997). In a companion volume, *Envisioning Information* (Cheshire, CT: Graphics Press, 1995), Tufte provides many examples of the use of graphics to summarize data. Tufte's latest book, *Visual Explanations: Images and Quantities, Evidence and Narrative* (Cheshire, CT: Graphics Press, 1997), examines the logic of depicting quantitative information and explores how visual evidence influences design strategies. For insights into the subtleties and potential abuse of graphic presentation, see Gerald E. Jones, *How to Lie with Charts* (San Francisco, CA: Sybex, 1995). One of the best examples of the use of graphic techniques for the presentation and analysis of political science data is Sidney Verba and Norman Nie, *Participation in America: Political Democracy and Social Equality* (Chicago, IL: University of Chicago Press, 1987).

Research Exercises

1. Using the list of political science journals presented in Chapter 3, find three examples of graphic presentations from three separate articles. Reproduce each and write a brief summary of the information it conveys.

2. Using the list of political science journals presented in Chapter 3, find three examples of contingency tables from three separate articles. Reproduce each and write a brief summary of the information it conveys.

3. Consult the most recent editions of the *State and Metropolitan Area Data Book* (published by the census bureau), and the *UNESCO Statistical Yearbook*. Examine and compare the structures of the tables in these sources. Are these enumerative or contingency tables?

Table 13.4
Contingency table

	I	II	III	IV
I				
II				
III				

4. Using data from the *State and Metropolitan Area Data Book,* arrange the 50 states of the United States into three groups according to their population ranking in the 2000 census. Prepare a contingency table comparing the three groups of states according to their respective per capita income levels in the same year. This will require that you develop ordinal categories of per capita income, determine which is your independent variable, count the number of cases in each cell of the resulting table, and calculate the appropriate percentages. In doing so, you may wish to use as a worksheet a grid similar to the one in Table 13.4.

5. Using your population categories for the states from Exercise 4, develop diagrams or charts to summarize data about the 50 states on three additional variables. Use a different type of presentation for each of these variables.

6. The examples in this chapter employed data from presidential elections in 1960 through 1976. Use the resources of your library to find the proportions of black and white support for the Democratic party in the elections since 1976. Then use the various types of graphs presented here to bring the analysis forward. What do you find? Which graphic format best helps to communicate this? Why?

Terms Introduced in This Chapter

enumerative table
line diagram
key
pie diagram

bar chart
segmented bar chart
bilateral bar chart
contingency table

CHAPTER 14

STATISTICS I: SUMMARIZING DISTRIBUTIONS ON ONE VARIABLE

Often in political science research, tables and charts alone do not tell us enough about our data to permit a satisfactory answer to our research question. In part this is a problem of complexity (our variables may have either too many values or too many cases—or there may even be too many variables involved—to lend themselves to ready analysis) and in part a question of precision (degrees of difference or subtle variations among variables may be important, and they are often difficult to assess accurately by simply eyeballing a table or chart). In instances such as these, as well as others that call for highly sophisticated analysis, political scientists employ *statistics*.

In this context, **statistics** are numbers that summarize either the distributions of values on or the relationships between variables. They are a form of mathematical shorthand capable of telling us at a glance and with great precision what our data show (or, in many cases, what they do not show). What is the political philosophy of the typical college student? Do Hispanic voters differ systematically in their party preferences from blacks? What kinds of actions or situations in the world community are most likely to give rise to armed conflict? If the proper data are applied for analysis, statistics can answer these questions and many more.

Statistics can be extremely complex. It is equally true, however, that many of the primary concepts and techniques of statistical analysis are extremely simple, can be learned in a short time, and can get you a good deal further into the subject than you might imagine. In fact, if you passed high school algebra, you already know just about all the mathematics you will need, and you may be surprised at how intuitively obvious many statistical concepts really are.

We should make clear that this chapter and the two that follow will not teach you all there is to know about statistics, nor even all there is to know about the particular statistical measures we shall discuss. Still, by the time you complete these chapters, you should have a good sense of what statistics are and of how you can use them (or why you might want to), you should have some understanding of the concepts that lie behind the numbers and the calculations, and you should have a reasonable facility in the use of several specific statistics. Together, these skills will enable you both to employ statistical analysis in your own research and to comprehend more fully and more critically what you read in the scholarly journals and in other reports of political science research.

In this chapter we examine statistics that answer the following types of questions about a given set of data: How are the cases distributed among the values of each of our variables? What does the typical case look like? How typical is it?

In each instance, we examine a different statistic for each level of measurement: nominal, ordinal, and interval. You will recall from Chapter 4 that these levels differ from one another in that the first merely differentiates categories, the second ranks them, and the third assumes constant degrees of difference between them. In effect, then, nominal, ordinal, and interval numbers are different kinds of numbers with different qualities. In a sense, nominal numbers are soft numbers; they don't tell us very much. Because they merely separate objects into groups and serve as no more than labels for those groups, they cannot even be added or subtracted. Accordingly, we cannot use very sophisticated statistical methods in analyzing nominal data. On the other hand, interval numbers are much harder, or more rigorous, in that they convey a great deal more information about the data they represent. They can be added, subtracted, squared, and variously transformed. As a result, they offer much more flexibility and an opportunity for far more sophisticated analysis. It is for this reason that different techniques are applied to different levels of measurement. For the same reason, of course, one must take care to use each technique appropriately.

Measures of Central Tendency and Dispersion

Two types of statistics are used to describe the distribution of cases over the values of a single variable. The first—the measure of **central tendency**—helps us to identify the most typical value: the one value or score that best represents the entire set of cases on that variable. Suppose we were told that the so-called average American male is a blue-collar worker, is a high school graduate, and, together with his wife, has 1.7 children. Clearly not every American male fits these categories, but when we look at all American males in some summary manner, this set of characteristics might well come closest to a general description of what we find. It is this same notion of an average, or typical, case that we employ in calculating a measure of central tendency. Indeed, it was precisely such measures that identified these particular traits of American males in the first place.

As we have noted, however, not every member of the male population fits this description. Many are white-collar or professional workers or perhaps even unemployed, some have finished only grade school while others hold advanced degrees, and some may have 10 or 20 children while others remain unmarried and childless. In other words, the "typical" American male may well represent the *tendencies* within the population, but he does not accurately reflect each individual case. For this reason, once we have identified such a typical case, we must ask a follow-up question: How typical is it? How good a job does this average score do of summarizing the distribution of scores for all the cases on a given variable? We answer this question by using a second type of statistic—the measure of dispersion. The measure of **dispersion** tells us whether the variation around the average value we have identified is limited, in which case we can have confidence that our average is a meaningful one, or whether that variation is so great that the most typical case is not really very representative of the population after all.

This raises an important point, which should be explained before we proceed any further. Statistics are powerful tools of analysis; they can tell us a great deal about our data that we could not otherwise ascertain. But statistics, on their own, are mindless. One can calculate and report *any* statistic on *any* set of numbers and in the process appear to be wringing the last drop of knowledge from one's data. For two reasons, however, many of these "results" may be meaningless. The first reason is one we have discussed already and whose logic should become more evident as we go on. Put most simply, the level of sophistication of our statistics may exceed the level of sophistication of our data. If our statistic requires us to add two numbers but our data are based on nominal-level measures for which the whole concept of addition is inappropriate, we could in fact go through the mechanical process of combining the coded values, but the result would be worthless. Thus if the score 1 represented blue-collar workers; 2, white-collar workers; and 3, professional workers, we could add 1 and 2 and get 3, but would we really want to argue that one blue-collar worker plus one white-collar worker *equals* one professional? Certainly not.

The second reason that statistical results may be less than meaningful is that one statistic, by itself, often cannot tell the whole story. If the single *most* typical level of education of American males is completion of high school but only 25 percent of the population have both reached that level and stopped there, how much does this average really tell us? Not much. And how many people do you know who actually have 1.7 children? Thus while we can calculate and report these figures accurately, they should not be allowed to stand alone. Each measure of central tendency should be qualified or evaluated with an accompanying measure of dispersion. And similarly, as we shall argue later, whenever we are dealing with a sample, each measure of association between two variables should be accompanied by a measure of statistical significance, which is an indication of how likely that finding is to represent a substantive relationship between the variables in question. Thus statistics must be not only appropriate to the level of measurement of the data but substantively meaningful as well if they are to prove of much value.

All measures of central tendency and dispersion are based on a summary of values and cases termed a *frequency distribution*. A **frequency distribution** is simply an ordered count of the number of cases that take on each value of a variable. For example, suppose we ask 100 people to tell us their present occupation and then we classify their responses according to type. For the variable *type of occupation*, we might arrive at the frequency distribution shown in Table 14.1. The frequency distribution simply lists each value on the variable and reports the number of cases that take on that value. The same information may be communicated by a bar graph, which, when used for this particular purpose, is often called a **histogram**, as illustrated in Figure 14.1. Using this information, we may identify the most typical case and determine its descriptiveness.

Table 14.1
Frequency distribution: Type of occupation of respondents

Code	Value	Number of Cases
1	Blue-collar	25
2	White-collar	23
3	Professional	22
4	Farm	20
5	Unemployed	10

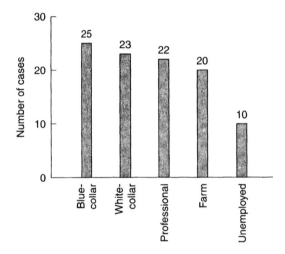

Figure 14.1
Histogram: Type of occupation of respondents

Measures for Nominal Variables

As we suggested earlier, different measures of central tendency and dispersion are appropriate for different levels of measurement. Since *type of occupation* is a nominal variable, let us begin to examine these calculations by focusing on statistics appropriate for nominal-level measures. At this level, where numbers represent merely category labels, without regard to order, the only available measure of central tendency is the mode. The **mode** is simply *the most frequently occurring value—* that which is taken on by the greatest number of cases. In the example, this is category 1, or the value *blue-collar.* We refer to this as either the mode or the modal category. (A distribution in which two categories tie for the greatest number of cases is said to have two modes, or to be *bimodal,* and it is possible to have a tie between even more than two categories.) Blue-collar employment, then, is the single most typical type of occupation among our sample of 100 persons.

But clearly, most people in this sample (in fact, fully 75 percent) are not blue-collar workers, so even though we can identify the most typical value in this distribution, that information may not be very meaningful. We can be more precise in judging just how meaningful it is by calculating the appropriate nominal-level measure of dispersion—the **variation ratio**—the formula for which is as follows:

$$v = \frac{\sum f_{\text{nonmodal}}}{N}$$

$$or \; v = 1 - \frac{f_{\text{modal}}}{N}$$

where $\sum f_{\text{nonmodal}}$ = the sum of all cases *not* falling into the modal category

f_{modal} = the number of cases in the modal category

N = the total number of cases.

In effect, this statistic tells us the *percentage of all cases that do not fit into the modal category.* In the example,

$$v = \frac{23 + 22 + 20 + 10}{100} = .75$$

or in the simplified form,

$$v = 1 - \frac{25}{100} = .75$$

The variation ratio ranges between 0 (when all cases take on the same value) and $1 - 1/N$ (when each case takes on a different value). In general, the lower the variation ratio, the more typical or more meaningful the mode. In the case of bimodal or multimodal distributions, one modal value is arbitrarily selected for purposes of calculation, and v is determined precisely as above.

Measures for Ordinal Variables

When dealing with ordinal-level data, we have a bit more information, since our codes represent not only categorization but relative position or ranking as well. Our selection of measures of central tendency and dispersion should both reflect and take advantage of this fact. The appropriate measure of central tendency for ordinal data—the median—does precisely this. The **median** is simply *the value of the middle case in a distribution*—the case above and below which an equal number of other cases lie. Obtaining the median, then, requires only that we count from either end of the distribution toward the center until we find the middle case and then ascertain the value associated with that case. When we have an odd number of cases, we will be able to locate one middle case (for example, for 99 cases, the 50th case from either end of the frequency distribution will have 49 cases both above and below it). The value of this case is the median. When N (the number of cases) is an even number, two middle cases will emerge (for example, for 100 cases, the 50th

Table 14.2
Educational achievement in three samples

Code	Value	Sample 1 (N)	Sample 2 (N)	Sample 3 (N)
1	Grade school	25	25	10
2	Some high school	23	23	40
3	High School graduate	22	22	35
4	College Graduate	20	20	10
5	Advanced degree	9	10	5
Total N		99	100	100

and 51st cases from either end together constitute the midpoint of the distribution). If both of these cases take on the same value, that value is the median. If they take on different values, the median is said to be the midpoint between those two values. An example may help to make this clear. Let us consider the distribution of educational achievement in three samples (Table 14.2).

In the first, we identify the middle case (the 50th from either end), note its value, and determine the median level of education to be 3, or *high school graduate*. In the second, we identify two middle cases (the 50th and 51st from either end), note that each takes on the same value, and determine the median once again to be a score of 3. In the third sample, however, the middle cases split between the *some high school* and *high school graduate* categories. Here the median is the midpoint between the two values in question, or $(2 + 3)/2 = 2.5$. Because fractional values have no meaning in ordinal measurement, this figure merely tells us that the midpoint of the distribution lies somewhere between 2 and 3.

Any of several measures of dispersion for ordinal variables, termed **quantile ranges,** tell us how tightly the various cases cluster around the median or, again, how typical or representative the median is of the whole distribution. A **quantile** is a measure of position within a distribution. For example, a percentile divides a distribution into 100 equal parts such that the first percentile is the point or value in that distribution (counting from the lowest score up) below which 1 percent of all the cases lie, the second percentile that point or value below which 2 percent of all the cases lie, and so forth. Or, to use what may be a more familiar example, the prospective college student who scores in the 85th percentile on the SAT has achieved a test score that is higher than the scores of 85 percent of all who took the test. Similarly, a decile divides the distribution into tenths (for example, the third decile would be the point below which 30 percent of all the cases lie), a quintile into fifths, a quartile into fourths. Any of these can be used to indicate dispersion around the median, though the decile and quintile ranges are most commonly found in the literature.

Let us use the quintile range to illustrate the procedure. The quintile range (q) is defined as follows:

$$q = q_4 - q_1$$

where q_4 = the fourth quintile (the value below which 4/5, or 80 percent, of
    the cases lie)

q_1 = the first quintile (the value below which 1/5, or 20 percent, of the
    cases lie).

The narrower the range of values separating these two points in the distribution, the more tightly clustered the cases are about the median and the more truly
representative of the distribution the median will be. In sample 2 in Table 14.2, for
instance, where $N = 100$, we calculate q by locating the 81st case (below which 80
percent of the cases lie) and the 21st case (below which 20 percent of the cases lie),
starting our count within the frequency distribution from the lowest scores. We then
subtract the value associated with the 21st case from that associated with the 81st
($q = q_4 - q_1 = 4 - 1 = 3$) to obtain the quintile range. In sample 3, the equivalent
computation yields a quintile range of 1 ($q = 3 - 2 = 1$), suggesting by comparison
that this distribution is better typified by its median of 2.5 than is sample 2 by its
median of 3. An examination of the two frequency distributions will confirm the
validity of this conclusion.

One difficulty in interpreting quantile ranges is that they are extremely sensitive
to variation in the number of categories on a given variable. The more categories
there are, the greater the range is likely to be. For this reason, quantile ranges can
prove difficult to interpret for comparison between variables that differ in their
number of categories. For similarly coded variables, for longitudinal or cross-sectional comparisons of the values of any single variable, or for some absolute indication of variability around the median, however, they are generally quite adequate.

Measures for Interval Variables

Interval data, of course, provide us with the most complete information of all,
including categorization, rank, and distance. Interval values can be subjected to any
arithmetic manipulation. Consequently, our measures of central tendency and dispersion for internal data can and should take this added information and capability into account.

The measure of central tendency for interval data is the **mean**—a measure that
locates *the central point of a distribution* in terms of both the number of cases on
either side of that point and their distance from it. The mean of a distribution is the
statistic many people commonly associate with the term *average*.

Let us visualize the nature of the mean by using Figure 14.2. If all the cases in
a distribution are represented by equal weights and if they are arranged on a board
at fixed intervals so that those with the most extreme values are farthest from the
center in one or the other direction and those with equal values are placed at the
same point on the board, the mean value of the distribution will be the fulcrum
point—the value at which the combined weights and distances to one side precisely
balance those to the other. As illustrated in the figure, both weight (number of cases)
and distance (extremity of the scores) are important in ascertaining the mean.

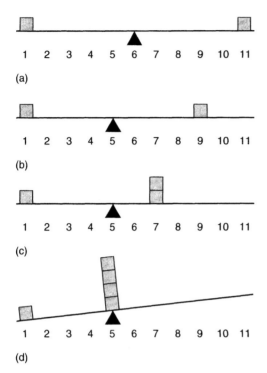

Figure 14.2
The mean as a point of balance

The mean of a distribution, designated $\overline{X}$, is calculated by taking the sum of the values of the individual cases and dividing by the number of cases. This procedure is summarized in the following equation:

$$\overline{X} = \frac{\sum_{i=1}^{N} X_i}{N}$$

where X_i = the value of each individual case

N = the number of cases

$\sum_{i=1}^{N}$ = an instruction to take the sum of all the individual values of cases 1 to N.

Note, too, however, as illustrated in Figure 14.2(d), that precisely because it is sensitive to distance, the mean is subject to distortion in a distribution that has one or a few very extreme cases. That is, a small number of cases with very extreme scores can cause the mean to be less than a truly typical value. Let us see how this might occur.

Consider a group of 11 persons, 10 of whom earn $10,000 a year and 1 of whom earns $1 million. The mean income for this group equals $100,000,

$$\frac{(10 \times \$10{,}000) + \$1{,}000{,}000}{11}$$

but 10 of the 11 members of the group actually earn one-tenth of that amount. Thus the mean, while correctly calculated, is not as representative as, say, the median, which in this case is $10,000.

The most commonly used measure of dispersion for interval data—the **standard deviation**—is probably one of the least intuitively obvious statistics we use, yet in a sense it is one of the cleverest. It would seem at first glance that to determine how typical of a distribution a given mean is, all we need do is measure the distances of all cases from that point (taking account of direction), add these together, and divide by N (the number of cases). In effect, we would calculate the mean of the distances around the mean as in the formula

$$\text{Dispersion} = \frac{\sum\limits_{i=1}^{N} (X_i - \overline{X})}{N}$$

The greater the dispersion for a given distribution, then, the *less* typical the mean; and the less the dispersion, the *more* typical the mean.

But when we try this with, for example, the three cases illustrated in Figure 14.2(c), a problem emerges. Applying the formula to the example, we find

$$\text{Dispersion} = \frac{(1 - 5) + (7 - 5) + (7 - 5)}{3}$$

$$= \frac{-4 + 2 + 2}{3} = 0$$

Even in a distribution with such clear divergence as our income example, we find

$$\text{Dispersion} = \frac{10(10{,}000 - 100{,}000) + (1{,}000{,}000 - 100{,}000)}{11}$$

$$= \frac{-900{,}000 + 900{,}000}{11} = 0$$

Indeed, for *any* mean in any distribution the result is the same. The reason is a simple one. We have, in effect, *defined* the mean as precisely that point where these weights and distances cancel out, or the point or value about which all variations are balanced. Therefore once we have calculated the mean, we should hardly be surprised to find exactly the effect we have intended. Yet the notion that we ought to be able to measure dispersion by comparing the closeness of cases to, or their remoteness from, the mean retains its appeal. Enter the standard deviation.

The standard deviation (s) employs a mathematical device to accomplish our purpose. In effect, it is a procedure that eliminates the tendency of opposing distances to cancel one another out by the simple expedient of squaring those distances (thereby eliminating all negative signs), averaging the *squares* of the distances around the mean, then taking the square root of the result so as to return to the original units of distance. The formula by which all of this is accomplished resembles the rejected formula except for the use of the squared distances and the square root of the result. That formula is

$$s = \sqrt{\frac{\sum_{i=1}^{N} (X_i - \overline{X})^2}{N}}$$

where X_i = the value of each individual case

$\overline{X}$ = the mean

N = the number of cases

$\sum_{i=1}^{N}$ = an instruction to take the sum of the individual values for cases 1 to N.

Thus in the example from Figure 14.2c,

$$s = \sqrt{\frac{(1-5)^2 + (7-5)^2 + (7-5)^2}{3}}$$

$$= \sqrt{\frac{16 + 4 + 4}{3}} = \sqrt{\frac{24}{3}} = \sqrt{8} = 2.8$$

It is expressed in the same units as the original data.

When two variables are measured by the same or comparable scales, the standard deviation provides a basis for comparing the representativeness of the means: the greater the standard deviation, the less representative the mean. But when scales differ substantially or when a single variable is being analyzed, the interpretation of the standard deviation is rather less clear.

One exception to this applies to variables whose values closely approximate a **normal distribution**, or one in which there is *a single mode in the very center of the distribution and in which the frequencies decline symmetrically as the values become more extreme in each direction.* (The bell-shaped curve with which you may be familiar is simply a graphic representation of a normal distribution.) In these cases, we know (through procedures that lie beyond the scope of the present discussion) that 68.3 percent of all cases will lie within +1 and −1 standard deviation from the mean, 95.5 percent will lie within +2 and −2 standard deviations from the mean, and 99.7 percent will lie $+3$ and -3 standard deviations from the mean. In fact, for such distributions, we can locate the exact number of standard deviation units any particular value lies above or below the mean, then use this information for comparing the relative position of two cases on the same variable or, alternatively, the relative scores on two variables for the same case. The measure that allows us to do this is called the **standard score** (or z-score), and it is calculated by simply subtracting the mean ($\overline{X}$) from the score (X) and then dividing by the standard deviation (s):

$$z = \frac{(X_i - \overline{X})}{s}$$

What makes the standard scores so useful is the fact that they allow us to compare scores that are based on very different units of measurements (for example, age measured in number of years, and height measured in inches). Since z-scores all have a mean of 0 and a standard deviation of 1, each score simply tells us how many standard deviation units a variable (age, height, etc.) is above or below the mean.[1]

Suppose, for example, that we have data showing the per capita spending by each state for education, the number of teachers per 1,000 students each employs, and the number of high school degrees per 100,000 population awarded by each in a given year and that values on these variables are distributed among the states in a manner approximating the normal curve. Suppose further that we wish to use these data to examine educational policy in, say, Arizona and Virginia. We first calculate the mean ($\overline{X}$) and standard deviation (s) for each variable for all 50 states and then determine the respective standard scores (z) on each variable for the two states in which we are interested. The result will be two sets of scores in standard units (no longer dollars, teachers, and certificates but the number of standard deviations about the mean) that can be used to construct indices of educational policy, determine an average position for Arizona or Virginia among the states, or provide for standardized comparisons across substantively different measures. As the basis for the standard score, then, the standard deviation may be an especially useful statistic.

Conclusion

In this chapter we have focused on statistics that summarize the distribution of scores on one variable. Because these statistics describe the characteristics of individual variables, they are often called **univariate statistics**. We have seen that different univariate statistics are appropriate for variables with different levels of measurement: nominal, ordinal, and interval. In the next chapter we examine what are termed **bivariate statistics**—those that summarize the relationship between *two* variables.

---

[1] Table A.6 in Appendix A summarizes the area between the mean and z, as well as the area beyond z in the distribution, for standard scores between 0 and 4, which is to say, for all values between the mean and a distance of four standard deviations in either direction around it. The values in the table can be used to locate for purposes of comparison any number of cases relative to the means on different variables.

Suggestions for Further Reading

At the end of Chapter 16 we suggest several books you might read to begin learning about statistics in more detail. For the present, it might be more useful to start with books that can put you at ease about using statistics and at the same time help you grasp some important basic concepts. For this purpose, we suggest Darrell Huff and Irving Geis, *How to Lie with Statistics* (New York: Norton, 1993), a classic and lighthearted examination of the uses and abuses of statistics, or what the authors term "statisticulation," and Jerald G. Shutte's rather complete *Everything You Always Wanted to Know About Elementary Statistics (But Were Afraid to Ask)* (Englewood Cliffs, NJ: Prentice Hall, 1977). Another humorous and very readable book that looks at the use of statistics with examples from everyday life is Jefferson Hane Weaver, *Conquering Statistics: Numbers Without the Crunch* (New York: Plenum Trade, 1997). For those who prefer to absorb their statistics through the medium of cartoon drawings, we recommend Larry Gonick and Woollcott Smith, *The Cartoon Guide to Statistics* (New York: HarperPerennial, 1993).

Research Exercises

1. For each of the following frequency distributions, determine the mode and variation ratio, the median and quintile range, and the mean and standard deviation. Think about your results.

Value	Sample 1	Sample 2	Sample 3
1	0	50	14
2	0	0	14
3	0	0	14
4	100	0	16
5	0	0	14
6	0	0	14
7	0	50 ,	14

2. Both of the following frequency distributions approximate the normal (bell-shaped) curve. For each one, calculate the mode, median, and mean.

Value	Sample 1	Sample 2
1	5	0
2	10	5
3	20	20
4	30	50
5	20	20
6	10	5
7	5	0

3. Consider again the frequency distributions in Exercise 2. Both have the same mean, and both approximate a normal curve.

   a. Draw a bar graph summarizing each of these distributions. Which would you expect to have the smaller standard deviation! Why?

   b. Calculate the standard deviation for each of these distributions. Did you find what you expected?

Terms Introduced in This Chapter

statistics
central tendency
dispersion
frequency distribution
histogram
mode
variation ratio
median

quantile ranges
quantile
mean
standard deviation (s)
normal distribution
standard score (z)
univariate statistics
bivariate statistics

CHAPTER 15

STATISTICS II: EXAMINING RELATIONSHIPS BETWEEN TWO VARIABLES

In most political science research, we are less concerned with describing distributions on single variables than we are with determining whether, how, and to what extent two or more variables may be related to one another. It is these bivariate (two-variable) and multivariate (more-than-two-variable) relationships that usually cast light on the more interesting research questions.

In general, when examining the relationship between two variables, one asks three important questions: The first is whether and to what extent changes or differences in the values of one variable—generally the independent variable—are associated with changes or differences in the values of the second, or dependent, variable. The second examines the direction and form of any association that might exist. The third considers the likelihood that any association observed among cases sampled from a larger population is in fact a characteristic of that population and not merely an artifact of the smaller and potentially unrepresentative sample. In this chapter we introduce some of the statistics that are most commonly used to answer these questions, and we explain when it is appropriate to use them and what they tell us about relationships.

Measures of Association and Statistical Significance

An **association** is said to exist between two variables when knowing the value of one for a given case improves the odds of our guessing correctly the corresponding value of the second. If, for example, we examine the relationship between the size of a country's population and the proportion of its adults who are college-educated we might find (1) that larger countries generally have a greater proportion of college-educated adults than smaller ones, (2) that smaller countries generally have a greater proportion of college-educated adults than larger ones, or (3) that there is no systematic difference between the two—that some countries from each group have relatively high proportions of such people but that some from each group have low proportions as well. If our research shows that either case 1 or case 2 holds, we can use our knowledge of values on the independent variable, *size of population*, to guess or predict values on the dependent variable, *proportion of adults who are college-educated*, for any given country. In the first instance, for any heavily populated country, we predict a relatively high proportion of college-educated adults, and for a less populous nation, we predict a lower proportion. In the second, our prediction is precisely reversed. In either event, although we may not guess every case correctly, we will be right fairly often because of the underlying *association* between the two variables. Indeed, the stronger the association between the two variables (the more the individual countries tend to align on each in precisely the same order), the more likely we are to guess correctly in any particular instance. If there is total correspondence in the alignments on the two variables, high scores with high scores or, alternatively, high scores on one with low on the other, we can predict one from the other with perfect accuracy. This contrasts sharply with the third possibility, which permits no improved prediction of values on the education variable based on our knowledge of populations. In such instances, when cases are, in effect, randomly distributed on the two variables, there is said to be no association.

To get a mental picture of what a strong association might "look like," consider the two maps presented in Figure 15.1, which relate to the murder rate in Washington, D.C., in 1988. Figure 15.1(a) shows the location of known drug markets in the nation's capital; Figure 15.1(b) shows the location of homicides. Both are based on information provided by the city's police department. The apparent similarity in the locations of clusters of drug dealing and murders suggests an *association* between the two phenomena.

Clearly there can be more or less association between any two variables. The question in each instance then becomes, Just how much association is there? The answer is provided by a set of statistics known as coefficients of association. A **coefficient of association** is a number that summarizes the amount of improvement in guessing values on one variable for any case based on knowledge of the values of a second. In the example, for instance, such a measure would tell us *how much* our knowledge of a country's population size helps us in guessing its proportion of college-educated adults. The higher the coefficient, the stronger the association and, by extension, the better our predictive or explanatory ability. In general, coefficients of association range from 0 to 1 or -1 to 1, with the values closest to unity indicating a relatively strong association and those closest to 0 a relatively weak one.

In addition to the magnitude of association, it is useful as well to know the direction or form of the relationship between two variables. Take another look at the earlier example about level of education of a nation's adults, and most particularly at options 1 and 2. We have already suggested that the closer we get to either case, the higher will be our coefficient of association and the better our chances of guessing a particular country's proportion of college-educated adults based on our knowledge of its population size. It should be obvious, however, that our predictions in the cases are precisely opposite. In the first instance, higher values of one variable tend to be associated with higher values of the other, and in the latter

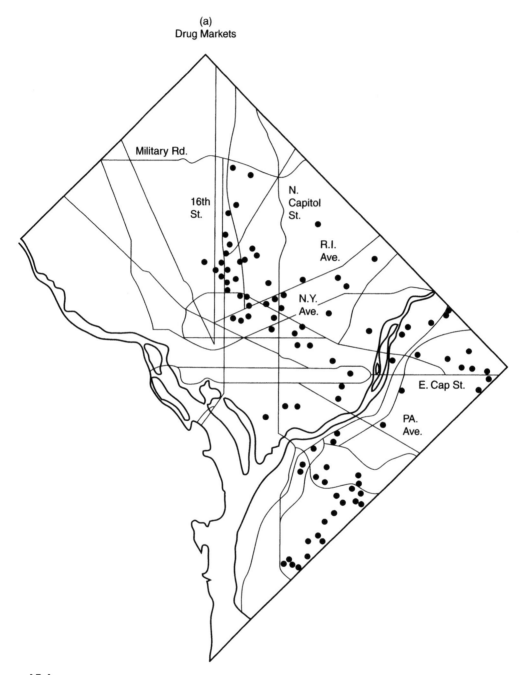

Figure 15.1
Drug markets and homicide locations, Washington, D.C., 1988
SOURCE: Reprinted from the *Washington Post*, January 13, 1989, p. E1, with permission of the publisher.

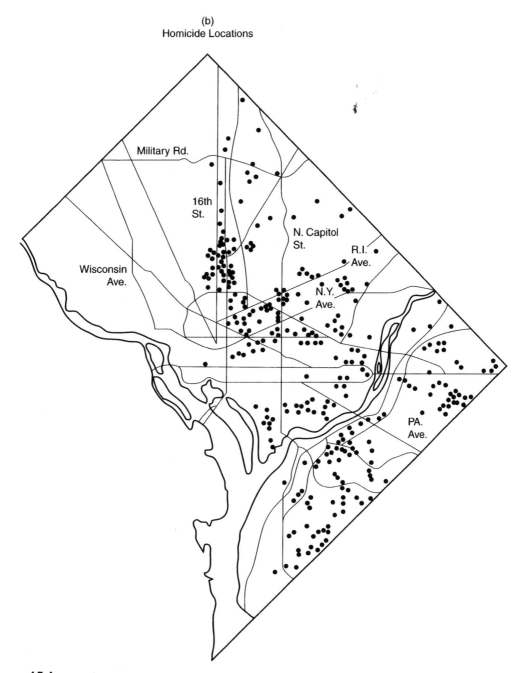

(b)
Homicide Locations

Military Rd.

16th
St.

N. Capitol
St.

R.I.
Ave.

Wisconsin
Ave.

N.Y.
Ave.

PA.
Ave.

Figure 15.1
Drug markets and homicide locations, Washington, D.C., 1988
(continued)

instance, higher values of one tend to be associated with *lower* values of the other. Such relationships are said to display differences in *direction.* Those like the first, in which both variables rise and fall together, are termed *direct,* or *positive,* associations. Those like the second, in which scores move systematically in opposing directions, are termed *inverse,* or *negative,* associations. This additional bit of information, which is represented by a plus or a minus sign accompanying the coefficient of association, makes our guessing even more effective. Thus a coefficient of −.87 (negative and relatively close to 1) might describe a relatively strong relationship in which the values on the two variables in question are inversely related (moving in opposite directions), whereas a coefficient of .20 (positive—the plus sign is usually omitted—and rather close to zero) might describe a weak direct association.

Finally, we should say a word about tests of *statistical significance,* though our discussion of the topic will be purposely limited.[1] You will recall from our discussion of levels of confidence and sampling error in Chapter 6 that when we draw a presumably representative sample and use that sample to develop conclusions about the larger population from which it is drawn, we run some risk of coming to incorrect conclusions. This is true because there is a chance that the sample is not in fact representative and that the actual error in our measurement exceeds that specified for a given sample size (Tables A.2 and A.3 in Appendix A). The *chance* of such improper generalizing is known, but we cannot tell whether or not it has occurred in any particular instance. For a level of confidence of .95, that chance is .05, or 1 − .95. For a level of confidence of .99, it is .01. These values represent the likelihood that any generalization from our sample to the larger population, even allowing for the estimated range of sampling error, is simply wrong.

Tests of **statistical significance** perform the same function in evaluating measures of association. They tell us just how likely it is that the association we have measured between two variables in a sample might or might not exist in the whole population. Let us see if we can clarify this point.

Suppose, to continue our example, we have a population of 200 nations for which we *know for a fact* that the coefficient of association between population size and the proportion of adults with a college education is 0. There is, in reality, no relationship between the two variables. But suppose further that we take a sample of only 30 of these countries and calculate the association between these two variables. It might come out as 0, but this is actually unlikely, because the strength of association is now based not on all the countries but on only 30 and will probably reflect their particular idiosyncrasies. In other words, the coefficient itself is determined by *which* 30 countries we pick. If, by chance, we pick 30 countries that are truly representative of all 200, we will in fact find no association. But chance might also lead us to pick 30 countries for which the association between population size and education level is unusually high, say, .60. In that case, our coefficient of association measures a characteristic of the particular sample in question, but if we generalize to the larger population, our conclusions will be incor-

---

[1] A full explanation of statistical significance requires a much more extended treatment than we are able to provide here. The reader is encouraged to consult one of the statistics texts listed in the suggestions for further reading at the end of Chapter 16.

rect. Knowing this, of course, we reject our measure of association based on this particular sample.

The problem is that in the real world we seldom know the underlying population parameter, which is the true degree of association in the whole population. Indeed, the reason we draw samples in the first place is exactly because we often simply *cannot* study whole populations. It follows, then, that more often than not the *only* tests of association we will have will be those based on our sampling. Moreover, these calculations will usually be based on only *one* sample. The question thus becomes one of how confident we can be that a test of association based on a single subgroup of a population accurately reflects an underlying population characteristic. The job of the test of statistical significance is to pin a number on that confidence—that is, to measure the probability or likelihood that we are making an appropriate, or, conversely, an inappropriate, generalization.

To see how this works, let us continue our example. Suppose that we draw not one sample of 30 nations from our population of 200, but 1,000 separate and independent samples of the same size and that for each we calculate the coefficient of association. Because the true coefficient for the entire population is in fact 0, most of the coefficients for our 1,000 samples will also be at or relatively near 0. Some particular combinations of 30 countries may yield relatively higher values (that is, we might by chance happen to pick only countries scoring either high-high or low-low on the two variables), but the majority will be nearer to the population parameter. Indeed, the closer one gets to the true value, the more samples one finds represented. These distributions, in fact, often resemble the normal curve we mentioned earlier. This is illustrated in Figure 15.2, where the height of the curve at any given point represents the number of samples for which the coefficient of association noted along the baseline has been calculated. As you can see, most of the sample coefficients cluster around the true population parameter.

What, then, is the likelihood that any particular coefficient is simply a chance variation around a true parameter of 0? Or in other words, if we take a sample from some population and find in that sample a strong association, what are the chances that we will be wrong in generalizing so strong a relationship from the sample to the population? The normal curve has certain properties which enable us to answer this question with considerable precision.

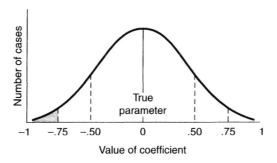

Figure 15.2

Normal distribution of coefficients of association for samples of 30 cases

Suppose, for example, we draw from our 200 nations a sample of 30 for which the coefficient of association is $-.75$. How likely is it that the corresponding coefficient for the population as a whole is 0? From Figure 15.2, the answer must be a resounding *Not very!* The area under the curve represents all 1,000 (actually any number of) sample coefficients when the true parameter is 0. The much smaller shaded area at and to the left of $-.75$ represents the proportion of such coefficients that are negative in direction and .75 or stronger in magnitude. Such cases constitute a very small proportion of the many sample coefficients. For this reason, the odds of drawing such a sample in any given try are quite slim. If 5 percent of all samples lie in this area, for instance, then only one time in 20 will we be likely to encounter a sample from a population with a true coefficient of 0 for which we find a coefficient in our sample of $-.75$. Yet that is precisely what we have found in this instance.

In other words, we have just drawn a sample with a characteristic that has a 5 percent likelihood of being an erroneous representation of a population in which the two variables in question are not associated with each other. Thus if we claim on the basis of our sample that the two variables are in fact associated in the larger population (that is, if we generalize our results from the sample), we can expect to be wrong 5 percent of the time. That means, of course, that we will be right 95 percent of the time, and those are not bad odds. Indeed, levels of statistical significance of .05 (a 5 percent chance of erroneous generalization), .01 (a 1 percent chance of such error), and .001 (a 1/10 of 1 percent chance of such error) are commonly accepted standards in social science research.

If we look again at Figure 15.2, it should be apparent that more extreme values such as $-.75$ are less likely to give rise to this kind of error in generalization than are those closer to the center (for example, a greater proportion of samples from such a population will, by chance, show coefficients of $-.50$ or stronger, and so forth). It seems, then, that we can never be very confident of the trustworthiness of weaker associations, since we can never eliminate the heavy odds that they are simply chance occurrences in a population with a true coefficient of 0. We can solve this problem, however, simply by increasing our sample size. If instead of 30 cases per sample we draw 100 or 150, each will be more likely to cluster around 0. In effect, the normal curve will be progressively squeezed toward the middle, as illustrated in Figure 15.3, until ultimately there is only one possible outcome—the true parameter. In the process, with a set of sufficiently large samples, even a coefficient of association of .10 or .01 can be shown to have acceptable levels of statistical significance. We can conclude, then, that some combination of sufficiently extreme scores and sufficiently large samples allows us to reduce to tolerable levels the likelihood of incorrectly generalizing from our data.

In the balance of this chapter we present a brief discussion of the most common measures of association and significance for each of the three levels of measurement. Although the procedures employed in calculating each of these measures differ, the purpose in each case, as well as the interpretation of the result, will remain relatively consistent, for each coefficient of association is designed to tell us to what extent our guessing of values on one variable is improved by knowledge of the corresponding values on another. Each test of significance tells us *the probability that any*

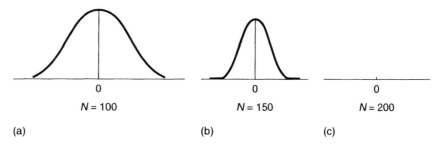

Figure 15.3
Sampling distribution for differing numbers of cases in a population of 200

observed relationships in a sample result from bias in the sample rather than from an underlying relationship in the base population.

The examples we use to illustrate these statistics involve comparisons of variables that are operationalized at the same level of measurement. However, researchers often want to look for relationships between variables that are at *different* levels of measurement (as in the case of an ordinal-level independent variable such as socioeconomic status and a nominal-level dependent variable such as party identification). To select the correct statistic in these situations, you need to be aware of a simple rule: you can use a statistic designed for a lower level of measurement with data at a higher level of measurement, but you may *not* do the reverse (because doing so would produce statistically meaningless results). It would, for example, be legitimate to use a statistic designed for the nominal level with ordinal-level data, but illegitimate to use an ordinal-level statistic with nominal-level data. This means that when comparing variables that are measured at different levels of measurement, *you must choose a statistic suitable to the lower of the two levels.*

Measures of Association and Significance for Nominal Variables

A widely used coefficient of association for two nominal variables where one is treated as independent and the other dependent is λ (lambda).[2] **Lambda** measures the *percentage of improvement* in guessing values on the dependent variable on the basis of knowledge of values on the independent variable when both variables consist of categories with neither rank, distance, nor direction.

Suppose, for example, we measure the party identifications of 100 respondents and uncover the following frequency distribution:

Democrats   50
Republicans   30
Independents   20

---

[2] Actually, the statistic we shall describe here is λ_a, or lambda asymmetrical, a measure that tests association in only one direction (from the independent to the dependent variable). A test of mutual association, the true λ, is also available.

Suppose further that we want to guess the party identification of each individual respondent, that we must make the same guess for all individuals, and that we want to make as few mistakes as possible. The obvious strategy is simply to guess the mode (the most populous category), or Democratic, every time. We will be correct 50 times (for the 50 Democrats) and incorrect 50 times (for the 30 Republicans and 20 Independents), not an especially noteworthy record but still the best we can do. For if we guess Republican each time, we will be wrong 70 times, and a guess of Independent will lead to 80 incorrect predictions. The mode, then, provides the best guess based on the available information.

But suppose we have a second piece of information—the party identification of each respondent's father—with the following frequency distribution:

Democrats	60
Republicans	30
Independents	10

If these two variables are related to each other—that is, if one is likely to have the same party identification as one's father—then knowing the party preference of each respondent's father should help us to improve our guessing of that respondent's own preference. This will be the case if, by guessing for each respondent not the mode of the overall distribution, as we did before, but simply that person's father's party preference, we can reduce our incorrect predictions to fewer than the 50 cases we originally guessed wrongly.

To test this, let us construct a contingency table summarizing the distribution of cases on these two variables. In Table 15.1, the independent, or predictor, variable (father's party identification) is the row variable, and its overall distribution is summarized to the right of the table. The dependent variable (respondent's party identification) is the column variable, and its overall distribution is summarized below the table. The numbers in the cells have been assigned arbitrarily, though in the real world they would, of course, be determined by the research itself.

With this table we can use parental preference to predict respondent's preference. To do this, we use the mode just as before, but we apply it *within each cate-*

Table 15.1
Paternal basis for party identification (1)

Father's Party Identification	Respondent's Party Identification			
	Dem.	Rep.	Ind.	Totals
Democratic	45	5	10	60
Republican	2	23	5	30
Independent	3	2	5	10
Total	50	30	20	100

gory on the independent variable rather than to the whole set of cases. Thus for those respondents whose father is identified as a Democrat, we guess a preference for the same party. We are correct 45 times and incorrect 15 (for the 5 Republicans and 10 Independents). For those whose father is identified as a Republican, we guess Republican. We are correct 23 times and incorrect 7. And for those whose father is identified as an Independent, we guess a similar preference and are correct 5 out of 10 times. Combining these results, we find that we are now able to guess correctly 73 times and are still wrong 27 times. Thus knowledge of the second variable has clearly improved our guessing. To ascertain the precise percentage of that improvement, we use *the general formula for a coefficient of association:*

$$\text{Association} = \frac{\text{Reduction in error in guessing}}{\text{Amount of original error}}$$

$$= \frac{\begin{array}{c}\text{Amount of} \quad \text{Amount of} \\ \text{original error} - \text{remaining error}\end{array}}{\text{Amount of original error}}$$

In the present instance, this is

$$\text{Association} = \frac{50 - (15 + 7 + 5)}{50}$$

$$= \frac{23}{50} = .46$$

By using father's party identification as a predictor of respondent's party identification, we are able to improve (reduce the error in) our guessing by some 46 percent.

The formula for calculating λ, which will bring us to the same result though by a slightly different route, is

$$\lambda = \frac{\sum f_i - F_d}{N - F_d}$$

where f_i = the maximum frequency *within each subclass or category* of the *independent* variable

F_d = the maximum frequency in the *totals* of the *dependent* variable

N = the number of cases.

Lambda ranges from 0 to 1, with higher values (those closer to 1) indicating a stronger association. Because nominal variables have no direction, λ will always be positive.

Our next step is to decide whether the relationship summarized by λ arises from a true population parameter or from mere chance. That is, we must decide whether the relationship is statistically significant.

The test of statistical significance for nominal variables is χ^2 (**chi-square**). This coefficient tells us whether a nominal-level association between two variables, such

Table 15.2
Paternal basis for party identification (2)

Father's Party Identification	Respondent's Party Identification			
	Dem.	Rep.	Ind.	Totals
Democratic				60
Republican				30
Independent				10
Total	50	30	20	100

as the one we have just observed, is likely to result from chance. It does so by comparing the results we actually observe with those that would be expected if no real relationship existed. Calculating χ^2, too, begins from a contingency table. Consider Table 15.2, which resembles Table 15.1 in that the marginals for each variable are the same as those of Table 15.1, but Table 15.2 does not include any distribution of cases within the cells.

To begin the determination of χ^2, we ask ourselves what value we *expect* in each cell, given these overall totals, if there is *no association* between the two variables. Of the 60 cases whose father was a Democrat, for instance, we might expect half (50/100) to be Democrats, almost a third (30/100) to be Republicans, and one in five (20/100) to be Independents, or, in other words, 30 Democrats, 18 Republicans, and 12 Independents. Similarly, we might arrive at expected values for those with a Republican or Independent father. These expected values are summarized in Table 15.3.

The question then becomes, Are the values we have actually observed in Table 15.1 so different (so extreme) from those that Table 15.3 would lead us to expect if there were, in reality, no relationship between the two variables that we can be rea-

Table 15.3
Paternal basis for party identification (3)

Father's Party Identification	Respondent's Party Identification			
	Dem.	Rep.	Ind.	Totals
Democratic	30	18	12	60
Republican	15	9	6	30
Independent	5	3	2	10
Total	50	30	20	100

sonably confident of the validity of our result? Chi-square is a device for comparing the two tables to find an answer to this question. The equation for χ^2 is

$$\chi^2 = \sum \frac{(f_o - f_e)^2}{f_e}$$

where f_o = the frequency *observed* in each cell (Table 15.1)

f_e = the frequency *expected* in each cell (Table 15.3)

We calculate χ^2 by filling in the values in Table 15.4 for each cell in a given table. The ordering of the cells in the table is of no importance, but f_o from Table 15.1 and f_e from Table 15.3 for any particular line must refer to the same cell. The rationale for first squaring the differences between f_o and f_e and then dividing by f_e is essentially the same as that for the treatment of variations around the mean in determining the standard deviation. Chi-square is determined by adding together all the numbers in the last column. In the example, this yields a value of 56.07.

Before we can interpret this number, we must make one further calculation, that of the so-called degrees of freedom. The **degrees of freedom** (*df*) in a table consist of simply the number of cells of that table that can be filled with numbers before the entries in all remaining cells are fixed and unchangeable. The formula for determining the degrees of freedom in any particular table is

$$df = (r - 1)(c - 1)$$

where r = the number of categories of the row variable

c = the number of categories of the column variable.

In the example, $df = (3 - 1)(3 - 1) = 4$.

We are now ready to evaluate the statistical significance of our data. Table A.4 in Appendix A summarizes the significant values of χ^2 for different degrees of freedom at the .001, .01, and .05 levels. If the value of χ^2 we have calculated (56.07) exceeds

Table 15.4
Values used in deriving χ^2

f_o	f_e	$f_o - f_e$	$(f_o - f_e)^2$	$\dfrac{(f_o - f_e)^2}{f_e}$
45	30	15	225	7.50
5	18	-13	169	9.39
10	12	-2	4	.33
2	15	-13	169	11.27
23	9	14	196	21.78
5	6	-1	1	.17
3	5	-2	4	.80
2	3	-1	1	.33
5	2	3	9	4.50

that listed in the table at any of these levels for a table with the specified degrees of freedom (4), the relationship we have observed is said to be statistically significant at that level. In the present instance, for example, in order to be significant at the .001 level (that is, if when we accept the observed association as representative of the larger population we run a risk of being wrong one time in 1,000), our observed χ^2 must exceed 18.467. Since it does so, we may be quite confident in our result.

Measures of Association and Significance for Ordinal Variables

A widely used coefficient of association for ordinal variables is G, or **gamma**, which works according to the same principle of error reduction as λ but focuses on predicting the ranking or relative position of cases rather than simply their membership in a particular class or category. The question treated by G is that of the degree to which the ranking of a case on one ordinal variable may be predicted if we know its ranking on a second ordinal variable.

When we examine two such variables, there are two possible conditions of perfect predictability. The first, in which individual cases are ranked in exactly the same order on both variables (high scores with high scores, low scores with low), is termed *perfect agreement*. The second, in which cases are ranked in precisely the opposite order (highest scores on one variable with lowest on the other and the reverse), is termed *perfect inversion*. Predictability, then is a function of how close the rankings on these variables come to either perfect agreement (in which case G is positive and approaches 1) or perfect inversion (where G is negative and approaches −1). A value of G equal to 0 indicates the absence of association. The formula for calculating G is

$$G = \frac{f_a - f_i}{f_a + f_i}$$

where f_a = the frequency of agreements in the rankings of the two variables

f_i = the frequency of inversions in the rankings of the two variables.

G is based on the relative positions of a set of cases on two variables. The cases are first arranged in ascending order on the independent variable. Their rankings on the dependent variable are then compared. Those for which the original ordering is preserved are said to be in agreement, and those for which the original order is altered are said to be in inversion. Limitations of space do not permit us to consider this procedure in detail or to discuss the calculations of G when the number of cases is relatively small and/or no ties are present in the rankings. Rather, we shall focus on the procedures for calculating G under the more common circumstances, when ties (more than one case with the same rank) are present and the number of cases is large.[3] Here, as before, we work from a contingency table, such as that depicted in Table 15.5.

---

[3]In such applications, G may be unreliable, but it is included here to facilitate the discussion of association as a concept. A related statistic, Kendall's *tau*, may be more reliable, but its determination is less intuitively obvious for the beginning statistician.

Table 15.5
Centralized contingency table

Independent Variable	Dependent Variable		
	Low	**Medium**	**High**
Low	a	b	c
Medium	d	e	f
High	g	h	i

To measure the association between these two variables, we determine the number of agreements and inversions relative to each cell in the table. An agreement occurs in any cell *below* (higher in its score on the independent variable) and to the *right* (higher in its score on the dependent variable) of the particular cell in question. Thus agreements with those cases in cell *a* include all cases in cells *e*, *f*, *h*, and *i*, since these cases rank higher than those in cell *a* on *both* variables. An inversion occurs in any cell *below* (higher in its score on the independent variable) and to the *left* (lower in its score on the dependent variable) of the particular cell in question. Thus inversions with those cases in cell *c* include all cases in cells *d*, *e*, *g*, and *h*, since these cases rank higher on one variable than those in cell *c*, but lower on the other. The frequency of agreements (f_a in the equation), then, is the sum for each cell of the number of cases in that cell multiplied by the number of cases in all cells below and to the right ($a[e + f + h + i] + b[f + i] + d[h + i] + e[i]$). The frequency of inversions (f_i in the equation) is the sum for each cell of the number of cases in that cell multiplied by the number of cases in all cells below and to the left ($b[d + g] + c[d + e + g + h] + e[g] + f[g + h]$). The resulting totals are simply substituted in the equation.

If, for example, the variables in Table 15.1 were ordinal, we could calculate *G* as follows:

$$f_a = 45(23 + 5 + 2 + 5) + 5(5 + 5) + 2(2 + 5) + 23(5)$$
$$= 1,575 + 50 + 14 + 115 = 1,754$$

$$f_i = 5(2 + 3) + 10(2 + 23 + 3 + 2) + 23(3) + 5(3 + 2)$$
$$= 25 + 300 + 69 + 25 = 419$$

$$G = \frac{f_a - f_i}{f_a + f_i} = \frac{1754 - 419}{1754 + 419} = \frac{1335}{2173} = .61$$

This tells us that there is 61 percent more agreement than disagreement in the rankings of the cases on the two variables. If f_i exceeded f_a, the sign of *G* would be negative, in order to indicate the existence of an inverse relationship.

The test of the statistical significance of *G* is based on the fact that the sampling distribution of *G* is approximately normal for a population with no true association, as was the sampling distribution of the hypothetical coefficient of association we discussed earlier. Since this is so, we can determine the probability that any particular value of G has occurred by chance by calculating its standard score (z), locating its position under the normal curve, and assessing the probabilities. The actual calculation of z_G (**standard score of gamma**) will not be presented here, because the formula is complex and its understanding requires a more detailed knowledge of statistics than we have provided. Suffice it to say that when z_G exceeds ±1.645 (when G lies at least 1.645 standard deviation units above or below the mean), G is sufficiently extreme to merit a significance level of .05, and that when z_G exceeds ±2.326 (when G lies at least 2.326 standard deviation units above or below the mean), G achieves significance at the .01 level. The interpretation of these results is precisely the same as that in the earlier and more general example.

Measures of Association and Significance for Interval Variables

The measure of association between two interval variables is the Pearson product-moment correlation (r), also known as the **correlation coefficient.** This coefficient summarizes the strength and direction of a relationship using the same notion we have already presented—about proportionate reduction in error in guessing values on one variable on the basis of known values of another—though the procedure, like the data for which it is designed, is more sophisticated than others we have discussed to this point. Here, rather than using the mean of the dependent variable (usually designated Y) to predict the values of individual cases, we use its geometric relationship with the independent variable (usually designated X) for this purpose. More particularly, we focus on the degree to which the equation of a particular straight line can help us to predict values of Y based on knowledge of corresponding values of X.

The determination of r begins with the examination of a **scatter diagram,** which is a graphic summary of the distribution of cases on two variables, in which the base line, or X axis, is denoted in units of the independent variable; the vertical line, or Y axis, is denoted in units of the dependent variable; and each dot represents observations of one case on both variables. Such a diagram is presented in Figure 15.4, in which the independent variable is age, the dependent variable is years of schooling completed, and the number of cases is 25. The circled dot thus represents one case—a person 30 years old with 10 years of schooling. The values in the figure have been arbitrarily assigned but would in reality be ascertained by the research itself.

The next step is to draw a straight line, called a **regression line,** through this field of dots so that no other line comes closer to touching all of the dots. This *line of best fit* for the relationship between two variables is analogous to the mean in univariate descriptive statistics. Just as the mean represents a most typical case in a frequency distribution, the regression line represents a most typical association between two variables. Just as we might use the mean to guess values on a variable in the absence of additional information, we can use the regression line to guess values on one variable on the basis of our knowledge of the values of another. If, for example, we know the value of X for a given case, we can project a vertical line from that point on the X axis to the regression line, then a horizontal line from there to the Y axis. The point of contact on the Y axis gives us a predicted value of Y.

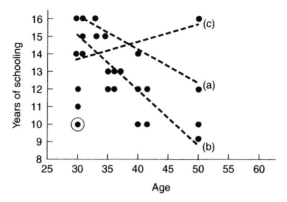

Figure 15.4
Scatter diagram showing relationship between age and years of schooling

But just as a mean may be the single most typical value yet not be a good summary of a particular distribution, a regression line may be the best possible summary of a relationship between two variables and yet not be a very useful summary. Accordingly, just as we use the standard deviation (*s*) as a measure of dispersion or goodness of fit around the mean, we use the correlation coefficient (*r*), or, more correctly, for purposes of interpretation, the square of that coefficient (*r*²), as a measure of the *goodness of fit* of the various data points around the regression line. It is, in effect, a measure of how typical that line is of the *joint* distribution of values on the two variables.

Where all points actually fall directly on the line, as in Figure 15.5(a) and (e), the line provides a perfect description of the relationship between the two variables. Where the points are generally organized in the direction indicated by the line but do not all fall upon it, as in Figure 15.5(b) and (d), the line provides an approximation of the relationship between the two variables. And where, as in Figure 15.5(c), no one line is closer to the data points than any other, no association exists between the two variables. The problem then, is twofold: First, what does this line of best fit look like? Second, how good a fit to the data does it in fact provide?

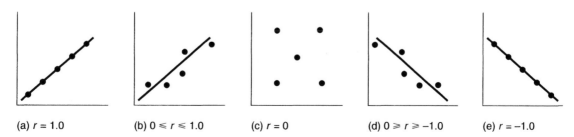

(a) *r* = 1.0   (b) 0 ⩽ *r* ⩽ 1.0   (c) *r* = 0   (d) 0 ⩾ *r* ⩾ −1.0   (e) *r* = −1.0

Figure 15.5
Summary of regression lines and values of r

You may recall from your study of algebra that any straight line takes the form

$$Y_i = a + bX_i$$

where a = the value of Y when X = 0

b = the slope of the line

X_i = the value of a given case on the independent variable.

The regression line is simply the one set of guessed values of this form that provides for the most accurate prediction of values of Y based on knowledge of values of X.

For reasons we shall not explore here, the slope b of that line will always take the form

$$b = \frac{\sum_{i=1}^{N}(X_i - \overline{X})(Y_i - \overline{Y})}{\sum_{i=1}^{N}(X_i - \overline{X})^2}$$

where X_i and Y_i are the corresponding values of the independent and dependent variables for case i, and $\overline{X}$ and $\overline{Y}$ are the respective means. Applying this formula and using a chart similar to the one we used in computing χ^2, we are able to ascertain the slope of any particular relationship between two interval variables. This process is illustrated in Table 15.6 for the data reported in Figure 15.4. For these data, $\overline{X} = 37.08$ and $\overline{Y} = 12.88$. Substituting these values in the equation, we find

$$b = \frac{-136.79}{1,151.93} = -.12$$

In a **linear relationship**—one described or summarized by a straight line—a particular change in the value of the independent variable X is always accompanied by a particular change in the value of the dependent variable Y. Moreover, in such a relationship the rate of change is constant; that is, no matter what the particular values of X and Y, each change of one unit in X will be accompanied by a change in Y of some fixed size determined by the slope of the regression line. Relationships in which slight changes in X are accompanied by relatively large changes in Y are summarized by lines that have a relatively steep slope ($b > 1$). Relationships in which large changes in X are accompanied by smaller changes in Y are summarized by lines that have a relatively flat slope ($b < 1$). Relationships in which one unit of change in X is accompanied by one unit of change in Y are summarized by lines for which b is equal to 1. Lines that slope upward from left to right, such as those in Figure 15.5(a) and (b), have a positive slope and represent relationships in which increases in X are accompanied by increases in Y. Those sloping downward from left to right, such as the lines in Figure 15.5(d) and (e), have a negative slope and represent relationships in which increases in X are accompanied by *decreases* in Y. Indeed, the slope of the line is simply the rate of change in Y for each unit of change in X. In our example, then, where b is equal to $-.12$, we know that the regression

Table 15.6
Values used in deriving the equation of the regression line

X_i	$(X_i - \overline{X})$	$(X_i - \overline{X})^2$	Y_i	$(Y_i - \overline{Y})$	$(X_i - \overline{X})(Y_i - \overline{Y})$
30	−7.08	50.13	10	−2.88	20.39
30	−7.08	50.13	11	−1.88	13.31
30	−7.08	50.13	12	−.88	6.23
30	−7.08	50.13	14	1.22	−7.93
30	−7.08	50.13	16	3.12	−22.09
31	−6.08	36.97	14	1.12	−6.81
31	−6.08	36.97	15	2.12	−12.89
31	−6.08	36.97	16	3.12	−18.99
33	−4.08	16.15	15	2.12	−8.65
33	−4.08	16.15	16	3.12	−12.73
35	−2.08	4.33	12	−.88	1.83
35	−2.08	4.33	13	.12	−.25
35	−2.08	4.33	15	2.12	−4.41
36	−1.08	1.17	12	−.88	.95
36	−1.08	1.17	13	.12	−.13
37	−.08	.01	13	.12	−.01
40	−2.92	8.53	10	−2.88	−8.41
40	−2.92	8.53	12	−.88	−2.57
40	−2.92	8.53	14	1.12	3.27
42	−4.92	24.21	10	−2.88	−14.17
42	−4.92	24.21	12	−.88	−4.33
50	−12.92	166.93	9	−3.88	−50.13
50	−12.92	166.93	10	−2.88	−37.12
50	−12.92	166.93	12	−.88	−11.37
50	−12.92	166.93	16	3.12	40.31
Totals	0	1,151.93		0	−136.79

line will slope downward from left to right and will, if the two variables are drawn to the same scale, be relatively flat.

To arrive at the formula we used to compute the slope of the regression line, we had to assume that the line passes through the intersection of $\overline{X}$ and $\overline{Y}$—the means of the respective variables. This is a reasonable assumption, because the means represent the central tendencies of these variables and because we are, in effect, seeking a joint or combined central tendency. Because we know both means and have now determined the value of b, we can easily find the value of a (the point at which the regression line intercepts the Y axis) and solve the equation. The general equation of the regression line is

$$Y' = a + bX_i$$

and at the point where the line passes through the intersection of the two means

$$\overline{Y} = a + b\overline{X}$$

It must then follow that

$$a = \overline{Y} + b\overline{X}$$

Because all these values are now known, we can determine that

$$a = 12.88 - (-.12)(37.08)$$
$$= 12.88 + 4.45 = 17.33$$

Thus the equation of the regression line—the single best-fitting line—for the data reported in Figure 15.4 would be

$$Y' = 17.33 - .12X$$

Using this equation, we can predict the value of Y for any given value of X.

Once this equation has been determined, we may use the correlation coefficient (r) to assess the utility of the regression line. The formula for r_{XY} (the coefficient of correlation between X and Y) is

$$r_{XY} = \frac{N\sum XY - \sum X \sum Y}{\sqrt{[N\sum X^2 - (\sum X)^2][N\sum Y^2 - (\sum Y)^2]}}$$

where

X = each value of the independent variable (the subscript i has been omitted here to simplify the presentation)

Y = each value of the dependent variable

N = the number of cases

Although the assertion is certainly not obvious and although its algebraic proof lies beyond our present discussion, this working formula is derived from a comparison of the original error in guessing values of Y by using $\overline{Y}$ (the mean of the frequency distribution) with the error remaining when one guesses values of Y using Y' (the equation of the regression line). Thus the procedure for computing r is analogous to that for computing both λ and G. It may best be accomplished by setting up a chart of the type with which we are now familiar in which the columns include X, Y, XY, X^2, and Y^2. The sums required by the equation are then provided by the column totals. Thus, for the data represented in Figure 15.4, whose regression line we have already determined, the chart is completed as in Table 15.7.

We substitute these totals in the equation

$$r = \frac{25(11,803) - (927)(322)}{\sqrt{[25(35,525) - (927)^2][25(4,260) - (322)^2]}}$$

$$= \frac{295,075 - 298,494}{\sqrt{(888,125 - 859,329)(106,500 - 103,684)}}$$

$$= \frac{-3,419}{\sqrt{(28,796)(2,816)}}$$

Table 15.7
Values used in deriving the correlation coefficient (r)

X	Y	XY	X²	Y²
30	10	300	900	100
30	11	330	900	121
30	12	360	900	144
30	14	420	900	196
30	16	480	900	256
31	14	434	961	196
31	15	465	961	225
31	16	496	961	256
33	15	495	1,089	225
33	16	528	1,089	256
35	12	420	1,225	144
35	13	455	1,225	169
35	15	525	1,225	225
36	12	432	1,296	144
36	13	468	1,296	169
37	13	481	1,369	169
40	10	400	1,600	100
40	12	480	1,600	144
40	14	560	1,600	196
42	10	420	1,764	100
42	12	504	1,764	144
50	9	450	2,500	81
50	10	500	2,500	100
50	12	600	2,500	144
50	16	800	2,500	256
Totals 927	322	11,803	32,525	4,260

$$= \frac{-3,419}{\sqrt{81,089,536}}$$

$$= \frac{-3,419}{9,005}$$

$$= -.38$$

This tells us that the slope of the regression line is negative and that the points cluster weakly to moderately around it (because r ranges from $+1$ to -1, with the weakest association at 0).

Unfortunately, r itself is not easily interpreted. However, r^2 may be interpreted as *the proportion of reduction in the variance of Y attributable to our knowledge of X*, which is to say, it is the proportion of variation in Y that is predictable (or explainable) on the basis of X. The quantity r^2 is often referred to as the percentage of *explained variance,* and the quantity $1 - r^2$ is often termed the percentage of *unexplained variance.* Thus in our example, the *r* of $-.38$ means that differences on the independent variable *age* account for some 14 percent, or $(-.38)^2$, of the variance in the dependent variable *years of schooling* for the cases under analysis.

For reasons that lie beyond the scope of the present discussion, we are able to specify the statistical significance of *r* only when *both* the independent *and* dependent variables are normally distributed. This is accomplished by using Table A.5 in Appendix A, for which purpose two pieces of information are needed. The first is *r* itself, which, of course, is known. The second, analogous to the χ^2 test, is the number of degrees of freedom of the regression line because any two points always determine a line (in this case, the intersection of $\overline{X}$ and $\overline{Y}$ was the first and the intercept with the *Y* axis the second), all other data points may fall freely, so *df* will always equal $(N - 2)$, where *N* is the number of cases. To use the table, then, we locate the appropriate degrees of freedom (in the example, $N - 2 = 25 - 2 = 23$) and the desired level of significance (for example, .05), just as we did for χ^2; identify the threshold value of *r* necessary to achieve that level of significance; and evaluate our actual observation. In the present instance, this requires that we interpolate values in the table between $df = 20$ and $df = 25$. For $df = 23$, these values would be .3379, .3976, .5069, and .6194, respectively.) Thus our *r* of $-.38$ is statistically significant at the .10 level (it exceeds .3379) but not at the .05 level (it does not exceed .3976). The interpretation of this result is the same as those for other measures of statistical significance.

Conclusion

In this chapter we have introduced some of the more common statistics that are used to summarize the relationship between two variables. As in Chapter 14, we found that differing measures of association and statistical significance were appropriate depending on the level of measurement that characterized the data being analyzed. Together with the techniques presented earlier, these various coefficients provide the researcher with some very useful basic tools with which to summarize research results. In the next chapter we outline some more sophisticated statistical techniques, which can further enrich our ability to analyze and understand what we have discovered.

Suggestions for Further Reading

A bibliography on statistics and related topics is found at the end of Chapter 16.

Research Exercises

1. Find a recent report of a Gallup poll or some other public opinion poll (try your local newspaper or the *New York Times*) in which a bivariate relationship is presented. What statistics might the pollsters have used to evaluate their findings? If sufficient information is present, construct a contingency table for the two variables in question, and then calculate and interpret the appropriate coefficient of association.

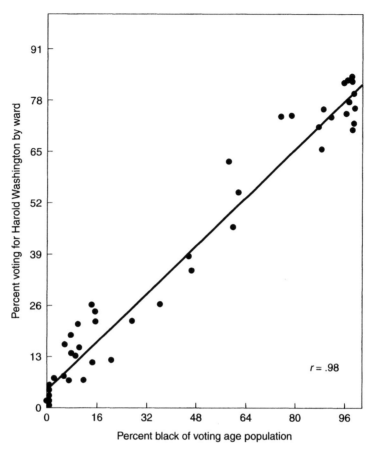

Figure 15.6
1983 Democratic mayoral primary in Chicago
SOURCE: Reprinted from Kenneth Janda, "A Preliminary Analysis of the 1983 Chicago Mayoral Election," *Vox Pop*, Winter 1983, p. 7, by permission of the author.

2. Figure 15.6 reports the level of voting support—by ward (section of the city) in the 1983 Chicago Democratic primary—for Harold Washington, a black candidate who was eventually elected mayor.

   a. What does the figure tell us about the relationship between the racial composition of Chicago wards and their voting patterns?

   b. What does the figure tell us about housing patterns in Chicago?

   c. The correlation coefficient (r) for the data reported in Figure 15.6 is .98. What proportion of the variance in voting behavior from ward to ward is explained by the racial composition of the respective wards?

3. Recalculate r and r^2 for the data in Figure 15.4, eliminating the data points at $X = 30$, $Y = 10$; $X = 30$, $Y = 11$; $X = 30$, $Y = 12$; and $X = 50$, $Y = 16$. How do you account for the difference in explained variance between this and our earlier result? Is the new value of r statistically significant?

Table 15.8

	Interest in Politics				
Level of Education	**Very Low**	**Low**	**Medium**	**High**	**Very High**
College	16	21	34	40	36
High School	37	32	43	26	14
Grade School	41	37	25	12	3

4. For the data presented in Table 15.8, determine the mode and the median for each variable and compute G. Write a substantive interpretation of the result.

Terms Introduced in This Chapter

association
coefficient of association
statistical significance
lambda
chi-square (χ^2)
degrees of freedom (df)

gamma (G)
standard score of gamma (Z_G)
correlation coefficient (r)
scatter diagram
regression line
linear relationship

CHAPTER 16

STATISTICS III: EXAMINING RELATIONSHIPS AMONG SEVERAL VARIABLES

The univariate and bivariate statistics described in the preceding chapters are often important to our understanding of the subjects we are researching. However, univariate and bivariate analyses almost never provide convincing tests of hypotheses or the theories from which they were derived. To test a hypothesis convincingly, we must be able to rule out major alternative rival hypotheses. Though a sound research design can sometimes allow us to dismiss alternative rival hypotheses, social scientists commonly find that they must rely on data analysis rather than research design to examine the validity of rival hypotheses. This requires the use of **multivariate analysis,** which is analysis of the simultaneous relationship among three or more variables.

Tabular Analysis

Many of the statistical tools we have already discussed can be employed in multivariate analysis. To illustrate, we can use a highly simplified example to suggest the way in which contingency tables and bivariate statistics can be adapted in order to conduct a multivariate analysis. Suppose we want to explore the relationship between political ideology and attending college. If we reason that going to college gives people a stake in maintaining the status quo by preparing them to do relatively well within the existing socioeconomic system, we might begin with the hypothesis that those who have completed college will be more conservative than those who have not. To test this hypothesis, we might interview a sample of 50 people who have completed college and 50 people who have not completed college.

Imagine that we got the results shown in Table 16.1. The diagonal "loading" of cases in this table indicates that those who have attended college are more likely to be classified as conservative than those who have not attended college. By calculating a chi-square for this table, we find that the relationship between college and

Table 16.1

Hypothetical relationship between college education and political ideology

| | Ideology | | | |
Education	Liberal		Conservative	Totals
College	40%	(20)	60% (30)	(50)
No college	60%	(30)	40% (20)	(50)
Totals	100%	(50)	100% (50)	(100)

political ideology is statistically significant at the .01 level. All this is consistent with our original hypothesis.

Before we rush to submit this finding to *American Political Science Review,* however, we need to test some alternative rival hypotheses to be sure that our result is valid. One approach to doing this is to extend our bivariate analysis into a multivariate analysis that will allow us to "control for" the effects of other variables on the relationship between college and ideology. For example, one alternative rival hypothesis that merits examination derives from the observation that men are more likely to be conservative than women. If, by chance, more of the people in our sample who went to college were male than female, the results shown in Table 16.1 may reflect gender differences rather than an actual effect of college attendance on political opinions.

To explore this possibility, we could examine the relationship between college and ideology separately for men and for women by constructing two contingency tables such as Tables 16.2 and 16.3. If the alternative rival hypothesis is valid, the statistical relationship between college and ideology shown in Table 16.1 will *not* show up in these new tables, because the effect of gender on that relationship will be eliminated. This process of holding constant the influence of a third variable on the relationship between two other variables is referred to as **controlling** and is a major step in all forms of multivariate data analysis.

In this case, Tables 16.2 and 16.3 actually show that the relationship between college and ideology is essentially the same for men and women. Although the women in our sample are, as predicted, less likely than the men are to be classified as conservative, the "loadings" in these two tables are highly similar to each other, and calculation of the chi-square for each table shows that the relationships they represent are statistically significant. In such a situation, researchers say that the original relationship has "survived control" and that an alternative rival hypothesis can be "ruled out" as an explanation of the original findings. If a relationship survives enough such controls, it will be accepted as valid.

We have thus conducted a very simple multivariate analysis using techniques designed for bivariate analysis. We could extend this logic to evaluate more alternative rival hypotheses by controlling for two or more additional variables *at the same time*. To illustrate, one of our alternative rival hypotheses might contend that racial differences between whites and nonwhites in terms of both political values and the likelihood of attending college created the apparent relationship between college and ideology shown in Table 16.1. To hold constant the effects of both race and gender on the relationship between college and ideology, we would have to set

Table 16.2
Hypothetical relationship between college education and political ideology for males

Education	Ideology		Totals
	Liberal	*Conservative*	
College	33% (5)	57% (20)	(25)
No college	67% (10)	43% (15)	(25)
Totals	100% (15)	100% (35)	(50)

Table 16.3
Hypothetical relationship between college education and political ideology for females

Education	Ideology		Totals
	Liberal	*Conservative*	
College	43% (15)	67% (10)	(25)
No college	57% (20)	33% (5)	(25)
Totals	100% (35)	100% (15)	(50)

up four contingency tables showing the relationship between college and ideology: one for white males, one for white females, one for nonwhite males, and one for nonwhite females.

Under the right circumstances, this approach to multivariate analysis can be a great help in evaluating hypotheses. However, it has significant limitations. First, it becomes very cumbersome to use and its results become difficult to interpret if the variables involved have many possible values. This makes it impractical for analysis of interval-level data and difficult to use with many nominal and ordinal variables. For instance, to compare an independent and dependent variable each having 5 values while controlling for a third variable with 10 values would require analysis of 10 tables with 25 cells each. In that situation, unless we have an exceptionally large and diverse sample, many of the cells in the tables will have no cases in them, which can make it impossible to calculate some measures of association and significance. We might try to avoid this by collapsing certain categories of the variables in order to create fewer values and hold down the number of tables and cells needed (as when we reduce the measure "years of education" to a dichotomy of "less than 12 years" and "12 years or more"). However, it would mean giving up potentially important information contained in our original measures and may produce misleading results. Moreover, the same problem will appear, even after collapsing categories, if we tried to apply several control variables at once in order to examine the *combined effects* of different variables. Second, even if we can complete such an analysis, its results may be difficult to report because the patterns are likely to be complex and there are no overall statistics with which to summarize the results.

Fortunately, there are a variety of statistical procedures that are designed specifically for multivariate analyses, that can be used in a wide range of situations, and that provide easily interpretable results. The procedures are important because of their value in hypothesis testing (allowing us to examine the relationship between two variables while holding the effects of other variables on each constant), but their greatest value may come from the ways in which they help us understand the complex and subtle networks of relationships within which social phenomena are usually embedded. In this chapter we introduce you to two of the most commonly used multivariate techniques so that you can know when and how to apply them in your research and can judge the skill with which others have applied them when you are reading research reports. We selected these techniques from among the many that are available because (1) they are very widely applicable, (2) they illustrate many basic principles of multivariate analysis, and (3) they are based on the same basic mathematical techniques and can therefore be explained more quickly than techniques that rest on different mathematical foundations.

Multiple Regression

The bivariate correlation and regression procedures described in Chapter 15 can be extended to cases in which you want to explore the relationship between one dependent variable (DV) and several independent variables (IVs). The purpose of **multiple regression** is to provide (1) an estimate of the *independent* effect of a change in the value of each IV on the value of the DV and (2) an empirical basis for predicting values of the DV from knowledge of the joint values of the IVs.

Analysis begins with your statement of an equation that you feel accurately describes the causal influences you are investigating. Because this equation can be viewed as a **model** of the process in which you are interested, this step is referred to as **model specification**. It involves translating your verbal theory of the phenomenon into a mathematical equation. The general form for a **multiple regression equation** is

$$Y' = a_0 + b_1X_1 + b_2X_2 + b_3X_3 \ldots + b_nX_n + e$$

which you should recognize as an extension of the bivariate regression equation explained in Chapter 15. Understanding of this equation is simplified by the introduction of a concrete example.

Let us say that we are interested in assessing the validity of the argument that election to the U.S. Senate can be "bought" by heavy spending on a media campaign. We might do this by attempting to explain the percentage of the vote that candidates get as a function of (1) the amount they spend on media advertising and (2) the percentage of the electorate in their state that has the same party identification as the candidate. We might begin with the following simple model of the electoral process:

$$Y' = a_0 + b_1X_1 + b_2X_2 + e$$

where Y' = the predicted percent of the vote received by the candidate

a_0 = the average value of Y when each IV equals 0

b_1 = the average change in Y associated with a unit change in X_1 (the amount spent on advertising), *when the effects of other variables are held constant*

X_1 = the amount the candidate spends on advertising (in units of $1,000)

b_2 = the average change in Y' associated with a unit change in X_2 (the percentage of the electorate that shared the candidate's party identification), *when the effects of other variables are held constant*

X_2 = the percentage of the electorate that shares the candidate's party identification

e = an "error term" representing any variance in Y that is not accounted for by variance in the IVs in the model.

We might test the accuracy of this model by collecting appropriate data on 100 races for U.S. Senate seats. Successful application of multiple regression techniques to this or any other task, however, requires that our model and the data with which we hope to test it conform to five assumptions that underlie the regression procedure:

1. The model is *accurately specified* (it accurately describes the actual relationships in question). This includes the assumptions that (a) the relationship among variables is linear, (b) no important IVs have been excluded, and (c) no irrelevant IVs have been included.

2. There is *no error in measurement* of the variables.

3. Variables are measured at the *interval level.*

4. The following are true of the error term, *e:*

   a. Its mean (the expected value for any given observation) is 0.

   b. The error terms for each observation are *un*correlated.

   c. The IVs are *un*correlated with the error term.

   d. The variance for the error term is constant for all values of the IVs.

   e. The error term has a *normal distribution.*

5. None of the IVs is perfectly correlated with any of the other IVs or with any linear combination of other IVs. If this is true, there is *no perfect multicollinearity.*[1]

If our study comes *close enough* to meeting these assumptions,[2] we can substitute actual values from our research for Y', X_1, and X_2 and solve the regression equation representing our theory for the unknown terms a, b_1, and b_2 using the logic of least squares estimation. One hypothetical result of such a solution could be

$$Y' = 10 + .1X_1 + 1X_2$$

---

[1] For an explanation of these assumptions and an extended discussion of multiple regression generally, see Elazar J. Pedhazur, *Multiple Regression in Behavioral Research: Explanation and Prediction,* 3d ed. (Fort Worth, TX: Harcourt Brace, 1997).

[2] Studies seldom meet these requirements fully, and it is often impossible to know in advance of analysis whether or not they are met in a given data set. In this context, "close enough" means that the effect of any violation of assumptions can be corrected for or at least estimated and taken into account in drawing conclusions. See Pedhazur, op. cit.

Interpreting Multiple Regressions Results

The *least squares procedure* for multiple regression works in a manner similar to bivariate regression in that it passes a line through a plotting of the values of cases on several variables in such a way as to minimize the sum of the squared distance of each point from that line. The difference is that the "line" in the case of multiple regression is a set of mathematically estimated points on a plane that cannot be represented in a two-dimensional scatterplot. The *a* or intercept term is generally of little practical interest, because the values of the IVs are rarely 0. However, the substantive interpretation of an *a* of 10 in the equation is that even if the candidate spent no money on advertising and 0 percent of the voters in the state shared the candidate's party identification, the candidate would receive 10 percent of the vote just by being on the ballot.

It is far more important to understand the b_i terms. They are referred to as **partial regression coefficients** and describe the unique contribution of each IV to the determination of the IV. In our electoral example, a b_1 of .1 would be substantively interpreted as meaning that every additional $1,000 spent on advertising increases the candidate's portion of the vote by one-tenth of a percentage point, and a b_2 of 1 would indicate that for every 1 percent increase in the percentage of voters that share the candidate's party identification there is a corresponding 1 percent increase in the share of the vote that goes to that candidate. In calculating these coefficients, regression statistically holds constant the effect of any variables that influence both the individual IV and the DV through use of the formula

$$b_i = \frac{\sum(X_n - X'_n)(Y - Y')}{\sum(X_n - X'_n)^2}$$

This statistical control simulates the control we might have obtained in an experimental setting and is thus valuable in two important respects. First, as we will explore shortly, it allows us to assess the *relative* importance of different IVs in determining the value of the DV. Second, it allows us to rule out the alternative hypothesis that the relationship between the DV and any given IV is spurious. If we are willing to assume that we have included all important causes of change in the DV in our model and we find that the partial regression coefficient for any given IV is significantly different from 0, we can conclude that the relationship between that IV and the DV is *not* spurious. If, however, the *b* is near 0 or statistically insignificant, we must conclude that there is no independent relationship between that IV and the DV. In that case, we would drop the IV from our model in order to make it conform more closely to observed reality. Clearly, then, multiple regression can be a valuable tool in refining and improving our theories of political phenomena.

We can assess the completeness of our theory by calculating a **coefficient of determination**, or R^2 (sometimes referred to as the *multiple R*), using the formula

$$R^2 = \frac{\sum(Y' - \overline{Y})^2}{\sum(Y - \overline{Y})^2} = \frac{\text{Regression sum of squares}}{\text{Total sum of squares}}$$

This coefficient tells us how close all the data plots came to touching the "line" projected by our model and is commonly interpreted as the *proportion of the variation in the DV that is "explained"* (accounted for) *by variation in all of the IVs.* For example, an R^2 of .57 would be interpreted as showing that the IVs in the model from which it was calculated explain 57 percent of the variance in the DV. R^2 can range between 0 and 1; the closer it is to 1, the more complete the model is. The size of R^2 can almost always be increased by adding additional IVs to the model, but the researcher must ask if additional variables make the model too complex or add anything of value to our understanding of the phenomenon in question. In the case of our electoral example, for instance, we could probably increase the R^2 by adding the number of letters in the candidate's last name to the equation, but to do so would be to forget that research is a quest for more complete and useful understanding of the world and not a competition to see who can produce the most impressive statistics.

Solving Common Problems in Multiple Regression

Neither data nor reality always conforms to the conceptual model underlying multiple regression analysis. Relationships are not always linear, measurement error is almost always present, and so on. Fortunately, statisticians have devised ways for us to adapt multiple regression in order to compensate for some of these problems. In this section we discuss adaptations to three of the most commonly encountered problems so that you can (1) learn how to cope with these issues in your applications of multiple regression and (2) get a sense of the flexibility of multiple regression as an analytic technique.

Noninterval Data In the social sciences, important variables often are not (and sometimes cannot be) measured at the interval level, thus violating the assumption of interval-level measurement. Noninterval data can, however, be used in multiple regression under two conditions.

First, if the measure is (or can be converted into) a *dichotomy,* it can be entered directly into the regression by simply coding the value of the dichotomy as 1 and the other as 0. For example, in a study of international trade, goods might be classified as "foreign" or "domestic," with a code of 1 being assigned to the value "foreign" and a code of 0 assigned to the value "domestic." Regression would treat this scheme as if it were interval, because dichotomies have special mathematical properties. As a result, we can interpret the partial regression coefficient computed for any variable coded as a dichotomy just as we would if it were measured at the interval level.

Second, noninterval variables that have multiple categories can be incorporated into multiple regression by use of a system of *dummy variables.* For example, consider the case in which occupational status is measured only as "high," "medium," or "low" in a study that seeks to predict the number of political organizations to which a person belongs as a function of education (number of years of schooling) and occupational status. We can use the ordinal data on status in multiple regression if we create two dichotomous dummy variables to represent the variable occupational status. The equation would be

$$Y' = a + b_1X_1 + b_2X_2 + b_3X_3 + e$$

where Y' = the number of organizational memberships

X_1 = the number of years of schooling

X_2 = a dummy variable scored 1 if occupational status = "low" and 0 otherwise

X_3 = a dummy variable scored 1 if occupational status = "medium" and 0 otherwise.

Why use only two dummy variables to represent a noninterval variable with three categories? Because the value of the third dummy variable would be an exact linear function of the values of the other two, thus violating the assumption of no perfect multicollinearity and making it impossible to obtain a unique estimate of the various coefficients.

Whenever we use dummy variables, we should follow the rule of creating *one fewer dummy variables than there are categories in the noninterval variable* being represented. In practice, it is usually advisable to leave out the category in which you expect the fewest cases. In our example, the "high" category was not represented by a dummy variable because there are relatively few high-status jobs.

Interaction Effects   Conventional least squares regression assumes that the effects of different IVs on the DV are independent of one another and can be added together to determine the total effect of a set of variables. In practice, the effects of many variables reinforce or amplify the effects of some other variable. Whenever the impact of one IV depends on the value of another IV, an *interaction effect* exists. To return to the electoral example used earlier in this chapter, we might argue that the effect of advertising expenditures is different for incumbents (who tend to be well-known) and challengers (who need to make voters aware of their qualifications).

Multiple regression can be adapted to this situation by including the interaction between advertising and incumbent status as a separate variable. If we let incumbent status be represented by a dummy variable (X_3) coded 1 for challengers and 0 for incumbents, the new regression model would be:

$$Y' = a + b_1X_1 + b_2X_2 + b_3(X_1X_3) + e$$

where X_1X_3 is an interaction variable created by multiplying X_1 by X_3. This procedure allows us to interpret b_1 as the unique contribution of advertising expenditures to vote percentage by breaking off the *joint* effects of advertising and incumbency into b_3, and it can yield more accurate predictions of Y.

Multicollinearity   Regression analysis requires that no IV be perfectly correlated with any other IV or any linear combination of other IVs. It is usually easy to meet this strict requirement because few social science variables can be perfectly predicted from knowledge of any other variable or set of variables. However, many important variables are highly correlated with each other. (Consider urbanization and industrialization, education and income, or party and ideology in Western Europe.) This condition is referred to as **multicollinearity**. If the correlations among IVs in a regression model are high enough, estimations of the coefficients become inaccurate and we cannot place any confidence in the results of the regression analysis. Significant multicollinearity can cause such large variances in the estimation of partial regression coefficients that it becomes impossible to compare the relative effects of different IVs on the DV. In addition, coefficients may fail to attain statistical significance even where there is a substantial relationship, leading us to falsely identify bivariate relationships as spurious.

It is therefore essential that researchers make a serious effort to determine if multicollinearity is present and to make the adjustments necessary to correct for it. Multicollinearity is usually indicated by one or more of the following symptoms:

1. A high R^2 for the equation but statistically insignificant regression coefficients (b's).

2. Dramatic changes in regression coefficients (b's) for given variables when other IVs are dropped from or added to the equation.

3. Regression coefficients that are *far* larger or smaller (either in absolute terms or in relation to the coefficients for other IVs) than theory and knowledge of other research results would lead us to expect.

4. Regression coefficients that have the wrong sign—that are negative when we have good reason to expect them to be positive or positive when we have good reason to expect them to be negative.

When any of these symptoms is noted in a regression analysis, it is important to test for multicollinearity. This is done by *regressing each IV on all other IVs*. We would, for example, test the equation

$$Y' = a + b_1X_1 + b_2X_2 + b_3(X_3) + e$$

by running the following equations:

$$X_1 = a + b_2X_2 + b_3X_3$$
$$X_2 = a + b_1X_1 + b_3X_3$$
$$X_3 = a + b_1X_1 + b_2X_2$$

If the R^2 for any of these equations were higher than, say, .8, we could conclude that significant multicollinearity existed.

There are several possible approaches to correcting for multicollinearity. If we have the option of adding cases to our sample (as when we are collecting data from published records and can simply go back and resample), then increasing the sample size will sometimes eliminate multicollinearity. A second strategy would be to determine *which* of the IVs are highly related to each other and then combine them into a single indicator. If, for example, we had originally measured expenditures on radio, television, and newspaper advertising separately in our study of senatorial elections and found these three indicators to be highly correlated, we could combine the three into a single measure called *media expenditures* in order to eliminate the destabilizing effects of multicollinearity. Clearly, any such combining of variables works only when it is theoretically justified. We could not, for instance, solve a problem of multicollinearity by combining the incumbent status of the candidate with the regional location of the state since these are theoretically distinct concepts. Finally, we can attempt to cope with multicollinearity by discarding one or more of the highly intercorrelated variables. This can produce specification error, but by dropping first one and then the other correlated IV and comparing the results of different regressions, we can at least get a firm estimate of the damage done by both multicollinearity and misspecification.

Comparing IVs　It is often important to know which of several IVs exerts the most influence on a DV. If we wanted to encourage people to wear seat belts, for instance, we might want to know which of several factors that could lead to this behavior actually has the most impact on the decision to buckle up so that we can invest our resources in the most efficient way. Multiple regression analysis is well suited for this purpose since it provides estimates of the unique contribution of each IV to variance in the DV in the form of its partial regression coefficients. Unfortunately, determining the relative effects of different IVs is not a simple matter of comparing the size of their regression coefficients.

When IVs are measured in different units (number of dollars versus percentage of voters, for instance), regression coefficients do not reflect the relative influence of IVs on the DV. One way to cope with this is to *standardize* the variables—so that they are measured in the same units—and obtain new estimates of the regression coefficients. Standardization of a case's score is achieved by converting the raw score into units of standard deviation from the mean value of the variable using the formula

$$X^* = \frac{X - \overline{X}}{s_X}$$

where the * indicates that the variable is standardized, X is the score for a given case, $\overline{X}$ is the mean score on that variable for all cases, and s is the standard deviation of the distribution of values on variable X (see Chapter 14).

When standardized scores are substituted for raw scores in the regression equation, the a term drops out because standardization forces it to 0, and the equation takes the general form

$$Y'^* = \beta_1 X_1^* + \beta_2 X_2^* \ldots \beta_n X_n + e$$

where β represents a *standardized partial regression coefficient*, referred to as a **beta weight** or **beta coefficient**. A beta weight corrects the unstandardized partial regression coefficient by the ratio of the standard deviation of the IV to the standard deviation of the DV and can be calculated by the formula

$$\beta_i = b_i \frac{s_{Xi}}{s_Y}$$

A beta weight can be interpreted as representing *the average standard deviation change in Y associated with a standard deviation change in X* when the effects of other IVs are held constant. Thus a β of .5 would indicate that one standard deviation change in the value of an IV would be associated with a change of one-half standard deviation in the DV.

Standardizing thus allows us to compare the influence of different IVs *within a single sample.* However, when we are seeking to compare the influence of variables *across samples,* it can be misleading. If we wanted to compare the effects of campaign spending on the electoral success of candidates in the United States and Mexico, for example, we would find that there were substantial differences in the variance (and thus the standard deviation) of key variables because media campaigns cost more in the United States and election outcomes are usually significantly closer in one nation than in the other. Since the size of β is a function of variance (the larger the variance, the larger the β, other things being equal), we could be misled into thinking that spending had much more effect in one nation than in the other simply because of mathematically determined differences in β. To avoid this error, it is important to use the *un*standardized partial regression slopes (b's) for a variable whenever we are seeking to compare the effects of an IV in different samples if *the variance for that variable differs considerably from sample to sample.*

Path Analysis

Regression analysis can be quite useful in testing specific hypotheses and assessing the relative impacts of different IVs. Regression, however, assumes a model of causation that does not always reflect the complexities of the real world. If we wanted to investigate the determinants of racial segregation in public school systems, for instance, we could hypothesize that school segregation was caused by segregation in housing (since most schools draw on a given geographic area), which was in turn caused by racial differences in income. A causal diagram or model of these relationships developed according to the advice given in Chapter 2 is shown in Model 1.

Model 1

(X_1 = *racial differences in income,* X_2 = *housing segregation,* and
X_3 = *school segregation*)

This simple diagram is typical of the causal model assumed by conventional regression analysis because it indicates that the IVs exert their influence on the DV independently. In real social situations, however, IVs often influence *each other* as well as the DV. To return to our example, the least bit of knowledge about our subject would suggest that income differentials affect housing segregation as well as school segregation, because more and less expensive houses each tend to be geographically clustered. Taking this into account would require that we revise our model. We might propose a developmental sequence in which one IV exercises its influence on the DV exclusively by causing changes in another IV. This would be diagramed as in Model 2.

$$X_1 \quad \longrightarrow \quad X_2 \quad \longrightarrow \quad X_3$$

Model 2

A more sophisticated understanding of our subject might lead us to realize that racial differentials in income affect school segregation directly as well as through housing segregation because more affluent people can place their children in private schools. This information would be incorporated into the model by creating an arrow directly from X_1 to X_2 as in Model 3.

Model 3

Path analysis is a statistical technique by which we can evaluate the accuracy of such models by empirically testing the direct *and indirect* effects of one variable on another. It has been widely used in the social sciences because it is applicable to a great many research questions and has the advantage of allowing us to test large pieces of a theory at once rather than one hypothesis at a time. Our objective in this section is to introduce you to the basic procedures of path analysis and to teach you to read the path diagrams you are likely to encounter in the literature. We do not attempt to address the many issues involved in more sophisticated applications of the technique, so you would be wise to do additional reading before attempting to apply path analysis to complicated research questions.

Recursive and Nonrecursive Models   Path analysis begins with a conceptual model that specifies the causal relationships the researcher thinks are at work in the world. For purposes of path analysis, Model 3 would be redrawn as Model 4, where the R's represent the variance in the variable with which they are associated that is *un*explained by variance in other variables in the model.

$$R_u \quad \longrightarrow \quad X_1 \quad \longrightarrow \quad X_2 \quad \longleftarrow \quad R_v$$
$$\searrow \qquad \downarrow$$
$$X_3 \quad \longleftarrow \quad R_w$$

Model 4

The model is then stated as mathematical equations. However, any model in which the IVs are not independent of each other (as they are in Model 1) cannot be represented in a single equation but must be described by a set of *structural equations*. Model 4 would be represented by the following set of equations:

$$X_1 = p_{1u}R_u$$
$$X_2 = p_{21}X_1 + p_{2v}R_v$$
$$X_3 = p_{32}X_2 + p_{31}X_1 + p_{3w}R_w$$

The p's in these equations represent *path coefficients* that summarize the amount of influence one variable has on another when the effects of all other variables are held constant. The standard way of writing path coefficients is as p_{ij}, which indicates the path *to* variable *i from* variable *j*. The set of equations just given, then, tells us that X_1 is caused entirely by factors outside the model, X_2 is caused by X_1 and factors outside the model, and X_3 is caused by X_1, X_2, and factors outside the model. Variables like X_2 and X_3 that are determined at least partially by other variables in the model are referred to as *endogenous,* and variables that are determined entirely by factors that are left out of the model are called *exogenous.*

Models are classified as *recursive* or *nonrecursive*. A model is **recursive** if all of its variables can be ordered so that the first one is determined only by factors outside the model, the second is determined only by factors outside the model and the first variable, the third is determined only by factors outside the model and the first and second variables, and so on. In essence, this means that *all causal influence must flow in one direction,* with no "feedback." Model 4 is an example of a *recursive model.*

If there is feedback (reciprocal causation) among any of the variables in the model, it is referred to as **nonrecursive**. For example, we might add the variable "occupation" (X_4) to our model of school segregation and argue that segregated schooling leads to racial differences in occupational attainment that in turn cause income differentials, so that the model would look like Model 5. The model no longer contains any variable that is determined entirely by factors outside the model and is now nonrecursive. Such models require special analysis techniques that are beyond the scope of this book. Recursive models, however, can be successfully examined by using the ordinary least squares regression techniques described earlier in this chapter. When variables are stated in standardized form, the path coefficients can be estimated as the *standardized regression coefficients* produced by regression.

$$R_u \longrightarrow X_1 \longrightarrow X_2 \longleftarrow R_v$$
$$\downarrow$$
$$X_3 \longleftarrow R_w$$
$$\downarrow$$
$$X_4 \longleftarrow R_x$$

Model 5

Using Path Analysis   We can test the empirical accuracy of the predictions implied in a model by running a series of regressions in which each endogenous variable is regressed on all variables that are theorized to influence it. To take a purely hypothetical example, we might work with the five-variable recursive model in Model 6 (eliminating the residual terms for simplicity of presentation). To test this model, we would regress X_5 on X_1 through X_4; X_4 on X_1 through X_3; and X_2 on X_1. X_1 and X_3 are considered exogenous. If any of the path coefficients (standardized regression coefficients) produced by this process approaches a value of 0 or is statistically insignificant, we know that we have misspecified the model by anticipating a relationship that is not actually found in the data.

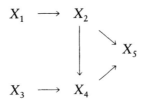

Model 6

In addition, we would test the validity of our assumptions about the *absence* of effects by regressing endogenous variables on others to which they are *not* supposed to be related. For example, in testing Model 6, we would regress both X_3 and X_4 on X_1 to see if the arrows we omitted should have been drawn in. If the resulting path coefficients are substantially different from 0 ($\geq .2$, for instance) and statistically significant, we would conclude that the model (and our theory about the events it represents) should be modified by adding a path.

One of the major advantages of path analysis is that it facilitates *theory elaboration* by bringing theory and data analysis into a fruitful interaction in which each informs the other. A path analysis of this type will tell us not only whether or not the variables in our model are related in the way we hypothesize but also *what relative influence each variable has on other variables in the model*. The *total effects* of one variable on another are equal to the value of the direct path between the two plus the indirect paths by which they are linked. An indirect path is equal to the products of the direct paths of which it is composed. For example, in Model 6, the total effect of X_2 on X_5 is equal to

$$p_{52} + (p_{42} \cdot p_{54})$$

and the total effect of X_1 on X_5 would be

$$(p_{21} \cdot p_{52}) + (p_{21} \cdot p_{42} \cdot p_{54})$$

As long as we are using *standardized* regression coefficients, we can use this procedure to compare the total effects of different variables in the system. Such knowledge can be of great practical significance because it can help citizens and policy makers to focus their energies where they will be most effective. For instance, if we were trying to encourage students to resist drugs, we could find out if one of several factors that contribute to that decision has a disproportionate impact and invest our resources in changing that variable.

Path analysis can also be used to compare the effects of variables in different settings. To return to the school segregation example, we might gather data on, say, Atlanta, Los Angeles, and Detroit and test the accuracy of Model 4 in each city. If we do not standardize our data and we use *unstandardized regression coefficients,* we can compare the effects of, say, housing segregation on school segregation in each of these cities to see if the causal processes we are interested in differ from city to city. It is necessary to use the unstandardized coefficients because standardizing makes the size of the path coefficient dependent on the variance of the variable in the sample. If, for example, there is a great deal more school segregation in one city than another, the relative size of the standardized regression coefficients will reflect that difference in variance rather than reflect any real difference in the relative strength of the influence of variables in the different cities.

The general rule is to use *standardized* coefficients when comparing the effects of different variables in the same sample and to use *unstandardized* coefficients when comparing the effects of the same variable in different samples. It is the unstandardized coefficients that are viewed as representing the "causal laws" that drive social processes.

Conclusion

We end this chapter with two notes of caution. First, it is important to recognize that we have discussed only a fraction of the many multivariate statistics that are available for the analysis of both interval and noninterval data. Each of these techniques is applicable to different analytical tasks. Among the most important commonly used techniques that we have *not* discussed here are *discriminant analysis,* which seeks statistically significant differences in dichotomous groups and is therefore especially applicable to experimental and quasi-experimental designs; *analysis of variance,* which is used to test hypotheses about differences of means in various groups and can be especially valuable in identifying the effects of some "treatment" or intervention on the degree to which cases manifest a concept; and *factor analysis,* which is used to identify common factors that reflect the relatedness of apparently independent indicators. Explanations of when and how to use these and other techniques can be found in the readings suggested at the end of this chapter.

With such a wide variety of statistical techniques to choose from, the task of selecting the statistical procedure that is most appropriate to your data and research question can be quite challenging. An excellent aid in this task is Frank M. Andrews, Laura Klem, Terrence N. Davidson, Patrick M. O'Malley, and William L. Rogers, *A Guide for Selecting Statistical Techniques for Analyzing Social Science Data* (Ann Arbor, MI: Institute for Social Research, 1981). This publication helps researchers select the correct statistical procedure from among almost 150 options by asking a series of questions about the data and the answers being sought. It is also very useful as a way of learning about the properties of the most commonly used statistics in the social sciences.

The second caution is that this text has not prepared you to actually execute more sophisticated data analysis techniques. Fortunately, you need not be a statistician to use most of the important methods because statistical analysis programs such as SPSS or SAS will carry out the calculation for you if you know how to set up the analysis correctly. Most of these programs have "help" functions that will enable you to learn both the statistics and the programming necessary.[3] Therefore, a distaste for math or statistics need not be an insurmountable barrier to relatively sophisticated data analysis and empirically grounded research on important political issues.

Suggestions for Further Reading

Some of the many texts that provide a general introduction to statistics appropriate to the social sciences are David S. Moore, *Statistics,* 3d ed. (New York: Freeman, 1991); James V. Couch, *Fundamentals of Statistics for the Behavioral Sciences,* 2d ed. (St. Paul, MN: West, 1987); George W. Bohrnstedt and David Knoke, *Statistics for Social Data Analysis,* 3d ed. (Itasca, IL: F. E. Peacock, 1994); and Barbara G. Tabachnick and Linda S. Fidell, *Using Multivariate Statistics* (New York: Harper & Row, 1983). Somewhat more detailed introductions to the types of statistics most often used in hypothesis testing include Sam Kash Kachigan, *Multivariate Statistical Analysis,* 2d ed. (New York: Radius Press, 1991), and Richard Lindeman, Peter F. Merenda, and Ruth Z. Gold, *Introduction to Bivariate and Multivariate Analysis* (Dallas, TX: Scott, Foresman, 1980).

Procedures for analyzing noninterval data are covered in detail in Jean Dickinson Gibbons, *Nonparametric Methods in Quantitative Analysis,* 3d ed. (Columbus, OH: American Sciences Press, 1997). David R. Heise, *Causal Analyses* (New York: Wiley, 1975), provides a highly readable introduction to path analysis. Detailed and generally quite readable explanations of many specific analysis techniques can be obtained from the monographs in Sage Publications' series *Quantitative Applications in the Social Sciences.* Most of these monographs provide empirical examples of applications of the techniques they describe. Additional examples of the application of various statistical techniques to analyses of a wide range of research questions are Hubert M. Blalock, Jr., ed., *Causal Models in the Social Sciences,* 2d ed. (New York: Aldine, 1985), which focuses on path analysis, and Terrel L. Rhodes, Theodore S. Arrington, and Robert J. Mundt, *Applied Political Inquiry* (New York: University Press of America, 1983).

Research Exercises

1. Does spending more on public education reduce the amount of poverty? Select a sample of 30 of the states in the United States and use *Statistical Abstracts of the United States* to gather data on three variables for each state: (1) whether it is above or below the national average on the amount it spends on public education per student, (2) whether it is above or below the national average on the percentage of its population that is below the poverty line, and (3) the political party that controls its legislature. Set up a contingency table to show the relationship between variables 1 and 2. Set up contingency

---

[3] One general introduction to statistics that illustrates the use of a popular software package is Nelson C. Dometrius, *Social Statistics Using SPSS* (New York: HarperCollins, 1992).

table to show the same relationship *controlling for variable 3*. Use the formulas given in Chapter 15 to compute lambda and chi-square for each of the tables. Write an interpretation of your findings.

2. Devise a theory to explain differences in the rate of growth in the gross national product of Third World nations that includes four IVs. Write a single multiple regression equation that summarizes this theory, and explain what each term in the equation represents.

3. Draw a path diagram illustrating the theory you developed for Exercise 2, being sure that at least two of the IVs are endogenous. Then write the structural equations necessary to represent this model in a path analysis, explaining what each term in the equations represents.

4. Examine the path model in Model 7, and write the formula by which to compute the *total effects* of X_1 on X_5 and of X_2 on X_5.

$$X_1 \longrightarrow X_2 \longrightarrow X_4$$
$$\downarrow \qquad\qquad \downarrow$$
$$X_3 \longrightarrow X_5$$

Model 7

Terms Introduced in This Chapter

multivariate analysis
controlling
multiple regression
model
model specification
multiple regression equation
partial regression coefficients

coefficient of determination (R^2)
multicollinearity
beta weight or beta coefficient
path analysis
recursive
nonrecursive

CHAPTER 17

MATHEMATICAL MODELING

PHILIP A. SCHRODT

[Human and physical events are] equally susceptible to being calculated and all that is necessary to reduce the whole of nature to laws similar to those which Newton discovered with the aid of calculus is to have a sufficient number of observations and mathematics that is complex enough.

Marquis de Condorcet (ca. 1790)

The difference between international politics as it actually is and a rational theory derived from it is like the difference between a photograph and a painted portrait. The photograph shows everything that can be seen by the naked eye; the painted portrait does not show everything that can be seen by the naked eye, but it shows, or at least seems to show, one thing that the naked eye cannot see: the human essence of the person portrayed.

Hans J. Morgenthau, *Politics Among Nations*

A **mathematical model** is a simplified version of the world that is used to study key characteristics of that world. Charles Lave and James March describe a model as follows:

> A model is a simplified picture of the real world. It has some of the characteristics of the real world, but not all of them. It is a set of interrelated guesses about the world. Like all pictures, a model is simpler than the phenomena it is supposed to represent or explain.[1]

During the past century, numbers and mathematics have come into wide use in the social sciences and are now found in virtually all fields of political science, from the awarding of contracts for urban garbage collection to the avoidance of a war.

---

[1] Charles Lave and James G. March, *An Introduction to Models in the Social Sciences* (New York: Harper & Row, 1978), p. 3. Copyright © 1995 by Longman Publishers USA.

A mathematical model is in many ways comparable to an engineer's scale model of an airplane or an architect's cardboard model of a building. The model airplane and model building lack many of the characteristics of the full-scale item: they are smaller, many details are only approximated, and many of the mechanisms inside the real item are missing from the model. But the model is still useful in portraying the fundamental characteristics of the full-scale object. An airplane model may be used in wind-tunnel tests; a cardboard building shows the structure in three dimensions before it is constructed. Models of social processes perform a similar task by capturing for study and experimentation the key characteristics of those processes.

Economics was the first of the social sciences to become heavily involved with mathematical models. Complex mathematical models of economic behavior were first developed near the end of the nineteenth century, using mathematical modeling techniques that had been developed earlier to study physical phenomena. In economics, the transition from verbal theory to mathematical theory was simplified by the fact that the major topic of interest in economics—money—is usually expressed numerically; thus the transition from numerical accounting to mathematical economic theory was made with little difficulty. At about the same time, some psychologists adopted techniques from biology, which in turn had adapted some of its methodology from mathematical physics and chemistry.

Political science trailed these two other disciplines but gradually became more quantitatively oriented during the 1950s and 1960s. Today, judging from introductory mathematical modeling textbooks, it is second only to economics in the widespread use of models of social behavior. Though this may seem surprising, political processes do have a number of characteristics that lend themselves to mathematical study.

To begin with, many political decisions have a large economics component, and hence models developed in economics often play a role in political policymaking. Both economics and political processes involve extensive "rational" (goal-directed) decision making under conditions of constraints, uncertainty, and, often, competition. Although, to date, political science has borrowed more from economics than economics has borrowed from political science, economics modelers are increasingly realizing the necessity of incorporating political components into their models. Interestingly, three of the Nobel prizes awarded in economics have gone to individuals (Kenneth Arrow, James Buchanan, and Herbert Simon) who have made major contributions in political science.

Money is not the only variable of interest to political scientists that can be studied mathematically: votes are numerical. Military preparations have come to be expressed largely in numerical terms (number of missiles, number of tanks, etc.). Survey research expresses political opinions in terms of percentages of individuals who agree with certain statements. More generally, the use of statistics in political science rests on a foundation of mathematics. In these areas, the step from a numerical study to a mathematical model is a small one.

Finally, mathematical modeling is not confined to dealing with *quantities*; it can also deal with the *qualitative* characteristics of a political process. Some political processes, such as electoral decision making and reapportionment rules, can be defined in completely mathematical terms. Mathematical models are a means of exploring the logical implications of these rules, which have frequently proven to be far more subtle than anyone had expected.

With mathematical models, political scientists are able to explore the characteristics of political processes with greater ease than would otherwise be possible. Often, mathematical models can express in a few equations what would otherwise take numerous pages of text to describe, and in many cases, processes can be simulated with computers. By using mathematical tools, political scientists are able to tap into a large set of techniques developed in mathematics, logic, statistics, physics, economics, and other fields and apply these to the study of political behavior. Finally, mathematical models are very clear and explicit and leave no doubt as to the relationships being proposed.

The Process of Modeling

Mathematical modeling involves a research strategy somewhat different from the dominant forms of political science research described elsewhere in this book, because modeling is both inductive and deductive. This section will discuss the general processes of constructing a model, which are summarized in Figure 17.1.

The first step in constructing a model is inductive: selecting the observations about the process one wants to model. This is roughly analogous to choosing the variables and the population in a hypothesis-testing design, though it is usually done

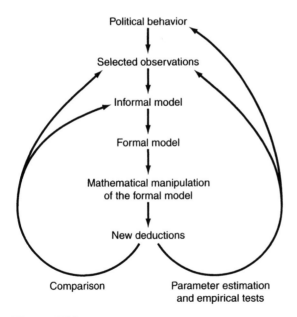

Figure 17.1
Modeling process

more informally than it would be in hypothesis testing. One way of thinking about this initial step is in terms of "problem definition"—deciding what to look at and what to ignore. This step is important to the subsequent modeling efforts, because if a process is too complex for the methods one has available or if one looks at the incorrect variables, the modeling effort will probably not get very far. Finding a problem that is interesting, nontrivial, unexplored, and still solvable takes a combination of luck, intuition, and experience and is similar to the problem of finding an interesting theory, as discussed in Chapter 2. Models usually involve a smaller number of variables than hypothesis-testing approaches: hypothesis-testing approaches use a simple set of processes (for example, linear regression) on a large number of variables, whereas models use a complex set of processes on a small number of variables.

The second step is to go from defining the problem to actually constructing an informal model. An **informal model** is a set of possible mechanisms that might explain the selected observations but does not state the mechanisms or check their logical consistency with great precision. For example, in constructing a model of an arms race (Example 1 on page 299), the informal model might state, *Nations want to increase their arms level because they fear the weapons of other nations, but these increases are constrained by the cost of buying weapons.* This gives some of the mechanisms driving an arms race but does not have the specificity of the final model.

At this stage, most modelers look at a variety of sets of informal assumptions that might explain the same data. That is, they look at several potential models and try to decide which will provide the best representation of the problem they are studying. In short, modelers try to find different ways of stating the *logical correspondence* between their model and the world. If the informal model of the observations is incorrect, it is unlikely that the formal model will accurately represent the behavior.

As one becomes experienced at modeling, informal modeling is often replaced by a search among existing formal models for an appropriate process that can apply to the observations. A **formal model** differs from an informal model in that the assumptions are stated in mathematical form. These existing models are in effect a set of tools. Since these models have already been studied, some of the deductions possible from the assumptions of the model are known, giving the modeler some direction in developing new models.

Rather than choosing an arbitrary set of informal assumptions, an experienced modeler will think in terms of "zero-sum game," "prisoners' dilemma game," "linear difference equation," "Downs's model," and other models whose general behavior is known. The experienced modeler uses this "toolbox" to go from thinking, "The solution of this problem requires a number of small, chisellike metal objects aligned on a plane and capable of disrupting the cellular structure of wood when moved in a reciprocal fashion," to thinking, "I need a saw."

The third step is *translation* of the informal model to a mathematical model. Translation involves taking the textual description of the informal model and finding the appropriate mathematical structure to represent the same ideas and processes. This is probably the most difficult step of the entire process and presents an opportunity for innumerable mistakes and ambiguities, since in any process of translation, content will be both lost and added.

The translation stage can involve a couple of pitfalls. First, informal models tend to be ambiguous, and there is usually more than one way to translate an informal model into a mathematical model, yet these alternative mathematical models may have very different implications. Indeed, this is one of the reasons for using mathematical models to begin with: mathematics is a language that is more precise and unambiguous than natural language, and it allows one to explore implications of subtle differences in formulation that would be very difficult to explore using natural language.

A second possible problem is the addition to the informal model of implicit assumptions that come with the mathematical methods being used. This is particularly important when calculus and statistical techniques are involved. The grand structures of differential and integral calculus and of probability theory were built on the basis of a few simple assumptions that have tremendous mathematical utility but may or may not correspond to the conditions in the political and social world. By and large, the assumptions of calculus correspond to what we observe in the physical world—and hence calculus has been extremely useful in modeling that world—but those assumptions may not be equally applicable to the realm of social behavior. Even if a given model were designed initially for social situations, one still must be aware of its implicit assumptions and deal with them cautiously.

The translation of the informal model into mathematical language is another point where experience and good judgment play important roles. In some instances, one can save time and effort by making certain assumptions that allow the model to be dealt with easily once one gets to the stage of manipulating the model mathematically; in other instances, those same assumptions might cause the model to depart significantly from the original informal theory. In the actual process of modeling, one adjusts both sides of the translation. Attributes of the mathematical model may lead one to adjust some of the assumptions of the informal theory; if the informal theory appears to make sense but the mathematical model does not, one may try another mathematical version of the model.

For example, if we assume that the reason people vote is to affect the outcome of the election by breaking a possible tie and a mathematical analysis shows that the probability of a tie is so small that most people would not vote in most elections, the fact that people do vote means that we may have forgotten some other reasons for voting, such as civic responsibility or expressing political opinions. Alternatively, perhaps our mathematical definition of a tie was too literal. For example, if people vote when they think an election will be close, with the candidates separated by, say, less than a percentage point in the vote totals, then this probability might be sufficiently high to explain why people vote.

The next stage, *mathematical manipulation of the formal model,* is the crux of mathematical modeling. It is at this stage that one uses the methodology of mathematics—logic, algebra, geometry, calculus, probability theory, computer simulation—to derive new deductions formally from the assumptions of the model. At the mathematical manipulation stage, one is usually dealing with pure abstractions, whatever the original source of the problem, and the mathematical tools used are the same whether one is dealing with arms races or bouncing springs. Here is *the deductive core of the modeling enterprise,* where the modeler seeks to find novel and unexpected implications from plausible assumptions.

Finally, these new deductions go through another translation process, this time from mathematical language back into natural language. The cautions referred to in the translation into the original formal model apply here as well: the translation necessarily involves losing and adding some information and assumptions. This final translation can be a very difficult stage of the modeling process: One is often left facing a series of equations and graphs asking oneself, What does it all mean?

While in general the modeler is looking for a particular result with a particular real-world meaning, this is often accompanied by unexpected results that are potentially more interesting than the results one was initially expecting. The modeling literature is filled with examples of individuals taking a model developed elsewhere and getting from it interesting implications that the originator of the model had not seen. For example, the phenomenon of "cyclical voting"—situations in which three or more proposals are being decided by majority vote and none of the proposals can defeat all of the others in pairwise contests—has been known as a mathematical curiosity since the eighteenth century. Only in the 1950s did the full significance of cyclical voting become apparent, when it was used in Kenneth Arrow's "impossibility theorem," which demonstrates some fundamental inconsistencies in all democratic voting systems.

The modeler now loops back to the initial stages to refine the model: Did the deductions of the model correspond with what was originally expected? Do these deductions make sense in light of empirical observations? If so, can the model be refined to produce still other interesting deductions? Can it be made more general? Can it produce the same deductions with a simpler set of assumptions? If the model does not make sense, was the formal model wrong, or was the initial conceptualization wrong? Were some of the implicit mathematical assumptions not translated well from the informal theory? These questions must be constantly monitored throughout the modeling process. One may loop through the informal comparison and refinement of the model numerous times before actually doing an empirical test.

Ultimately, most models require this kind of empirical testing to establish their validity. This is not always the case: In some situations the assumptions totally describe the process (for example, the rules of an election procedure), and the deductions do not need testing. But usually the assumptions include factors that are not fully specified in the theoretical development of the model and must be estimated from the actual data. Since virtually all models of social processes assume an element of randomness, empirical tests also indicate how accurate the predictions of the model will be. The testing of models involves the same stages of operationalization, measurement, and statistical analysis discussed elsewhere in this book, though mathematical models frequently require some adaptation of standard statistical techniques before the model can be tested.

Why Model?

As noted, there are a variety of reasons why political scientists use mathematical models. However, the method has disadvantages as well as advantages. Modeling is a process of simplification and deduction. Simplification involves loss of information about a situation. Mathematical deduction frequently involves complex mathematical manipulations, and models that use these are, at least initially, more difficult to deal with than natural-language arguments. Therefore, the first question one might reasonably ask about modeling is, Why bother?

The first reason for modeling political behavior is that it formalizes what we all do anyway. Quite simply, there is sufficient regularity in political events, so that simplified, informal models of political life are useful. Most things that happen politically are not very surprising; in fact, the very existence of surprise indicates that we have certain preconceptions that things will work out in a certain way and recognize something unexpected when it occurs. This indicates that we have *mental models of how political systems operate,* even if we never formulate those models explicitly. Mathematical models make those informal models explicit.

As an example of a mental model, suppose that in the next U.S. presidential election, one candidate won 95 percent of the popular vote. There is nothing in the Constitution or in our voting methods that prevents this from happening. On the other hand, we regard it as very unlikely, for a number of reasons. First, we assume that a sufficiently large number of people from each party will vote so as to make any purely random fluctuations in the vote total relatively small. Second, we assume that neither party will choose a candidate who is so unpopular as to get only 5 percent of the vote. Third, we assume that most of the votes are counted honestly. This list could continue—we all have a number of assumptions about the U.S. political system that would justify surprise at a 95 to 5 percent split of the vote in a presidential election.

All of these assumptions are simplifications of the real world. We don't know the exact number of people who will vote; nor do we need to—we just know that it will be large. We don't know the exact characteristics that make a candidate acceptable to some voters and not to others, but we assume that highly unpopular candidates will not be nominated. In any election, relatively few people have sufficient direct experience with the electoral procedures so as to ascertain whether or not the counting is fair, but people assume that counting is fair if the results of previous elections seemed to correspond to voter preferences.[2] Since these assumptions do not lead to incorrect predictions very often, we use this model of the political system in informally predicting the future. In fact, whenever a candidate wins with 95 percent of the vote, people get very suspicious of the election procedures and may demand an investigation, so our model partially determines our attitudes and behaviors as well.

A second reason for mathematical modeling is to formulate explicit mechanisms that explain the informal predictions we make. Though all individuals have expectations for the behavior of a political system, they frequently do not know precisely *why* they expect these things or precisely *what* is expected. A formal model goes beyond the loosely stated assumptions of an informal model and makes precise predictions that can often be tested.

The voting example just given is a deduction from the Downsian model, which we examine later in the chapter. Downs's formal model proposes a mechanism that

---

[2] The opposite is also true, which is why a large number of international election observers are used when a nation without a record of fair elections is attempting to elect a new government.

predicts that parties will choose candidates and platforms to appeal to as many vot-ers as possible, given the choice of the other party. This and some additional assumptions lead to the deduction that parties tend to split the vote almost equally, which is what is frequently observed in U.S. elections. Thus this particular formal model has gone from predicting not only that 95 to 5 percent is an unexpected out-come but also that 50 percent to 50 percent is expected and has given some reasons why this is so.

At times mathematical models seem to be merely confirming the obvious. This is a necessary characteristic of models, since they are, by and large, expected to repro-duce what is occurring in everyday political life. However, human beings tend to be very vague about what is "obvious." Examination of an assortment of contradicto-ry aphorisms ("birds of a feather flock together" and "opposites attract"; "absence makes the heart grow fonder" and "out of sight, out of mind") indicates that com-mon sense is often right, because it is so vague that it is impossible for it to be wrong.

The precision of formal models, in contrast, means that they can be wrong, so models seem at times to have a worse track record than the more ambiguous com-mon sense. Far from being a weakness, this is a *virtue* in modeling: The assumptions and predictions are sufficiently precise that one can test them and see whether and how they are going wrong. A model that survives a number of attempts to falsify it is likely—though not certain—to provide accurate predictions in the future. A model that has consistently failed to provide accurate predictions can probably be eliminated from consideration.

A third advantage to formal models is that they can systematically handle a higher level of complexity than can unaided intuition or even a carefully reasoned argument in natural language. Natural languages, such as English, evolved as tools of communication, not as tools of logical deduction. Mathematics, in contrast, is designed primarily for logical deduction and for systematically manipulating con-cepts. Mathematics has proved, through experience, to be a very useful language in that regard. For their part, political scientists are only beginning to see what further understanding of political behavior can be obtained through modeling, and in sev-eral cases new areas of mathematics have had to be developed (most notably game theory) before social scientists could see the commonalties in disparate social behav-iors. Mathematical modeling of social behavior has been going on for only a few decades, and there is little indication that we are reaching the limits of its usefulness at this point.

A final advantage to mathematical modeling is that it allows for the sharing of tools and techniques across academic disciplines. Examples of this are many: the models used in political science not only utilize the basic tools of mathematics but also borrow extensively from mathematical economics, sociology, and the biologi-cal sciences. Survey research—which is a complex mathematical model of the dis-tribution of opinion in a population—is a widely shared technique used by most of the social sciences. The borrowing works in reverse as well: systems engineers work-ing on large computer models of global population and development turned to polit-ical science models to refine the political aspects of their simulations. Similarly, game theory was originally developed by economists and political scientists to ana-lyze competition and has since become a field of research in pure mathematics.

But beyond the sharing of techniques and insights across disciplines, mathematical models are also useful in demonstrating that situations that at first appear to have nothing in common are in fact the same. The following example, though trivial in itself, illustrates this type of commonality.

Suppose we are playing a simple game consisting of two players, who alternate turns picking up tiles numbered from 1 to 9:

1   2   3   4   5   6   7   8   9

The object of the game is to be the first person to pick up tiles totaling exactly 15. When playing this game, you will doubtless discover that there are some strategies—in particular, you can use the defensive strategy of picking up tiles the other player needs to complete the total of 15—but an overall strategy is probably not obvious.

To generalize the game, rewrite the numbers in the following form:

4	9	2
3	5	7
8	1	6

Notice that in this formulation, each row, column, and diagonal adds up to 15, the desired total. Playing the game involves choosing three numbers in a row. This version of the game now looks very familiar: It is tic-tac-toe, and the appropriate strategy can be learned from any five-year-old. By a recasting of the game in a systematic fashion, something that initially appeared unfamiliar now seems very familiar, and a solution we used in the past can now be used in a new context.

This exercise, though with more complicated techniques and on more important subjects, is characteristic of finding commonalities by using mathematical models. In a wide variety of cases, a mathematical model first developed for one problem will prove equally applicable to another. For example, the Richardson arms races (Example 1 below) works not only in an application to international arms races but also to model the increasing campaign expenditures of two political parties or the bidding by two firms for a prime piece of real estate. The prisoners' dilemma game applies not only in the trench warfare example we shall discuss but also in the competition between two gas stations engaged in a price war or when two nations are deciding whether to develop a new weapons system. A variation on the prisoners' dilemma, called "chicken," was originally based on a game played by youthful malcontents on isolated roads in the California desert; it can be applied to the stability of nuclear deterrence in the face of a potential thermonuclear war. This list could go on indefinitely, but the key point is that most good mathematical models have applications far beyond the problems for which they were originally developed.

In summary, mathematical models have four potential advantages over natural-language models: (1) they systematize the mental models we use already; (2) they are precise and unambiguous; (3) they can handle a deeper level of deductive complexity than can natural language; and (4) they allow one to find shared solutions to problems that may at first seem to have little in common.

Examples of Mathematical Models of Political Behavior

The examples that follow were chosen to give some illustration of the scope of mathematical models of political behavior, as well as to introduce some of the most widely used models. In each of the examples, only a fraction of the deductions possible with the model are discussed, for each of these models has been the subject of literally hundreds of studies. The suggestions for further reading at the end of the chapter provide further information on each model.

Example 1: The Richardson Arms Race Model

In 1918, British meteorologist Lewis F. Richardson returned from ambulance service in World War I shocked by the violence and destruction he had seen. He was determined to apply his substantial mathematical skills and modern scientific techniques to the understanding of war. Because World War I had been preceded by an arms race, Richardson turned his attention to that phenomenon. From his work in physics, he was well acquainted with differential equations, which are used to model variables that change over time. The accumulation of weapons in an arms race, he reasoned, was such a process and could be approximated with a mathematical model.

After experimenting with dozens of detailed mathematical formulations, Richardson finally settled on a relatively simple model involving only three factors: threat, expense, and grievances. First, nation X feels *threatened* by the arms of its opponent, nation Y. The more arms Y has, the more arms X will want to acquire in response to this perceived threat. At the same time, however, nation X must meet basic social needs and cannot devote its entire economy to producing weapons. Hence the more arms X has, the fewer additional arms it will be able to acquire due to the burden of *expense*. Finally, Richardson reasoned, there are past *grievances* that affect overall arms levels, which are unaffected by the current levels. The same logic that applies to nation X also applies to nation Y, which has a similar equation. Mathematically, this argument reduces to

$$X_{t+1} = kY_t - aX_t + g$$
$$Y_{t+1} = mX_t - bY_t + h$$

The terms X_t and Y_t are the values of the arms levels at time t, and X_{t+1} and Y_{t+1} are those values for time $t+1$. The coefficients k, m, a, and b are all positive; g and h are either positive or negative, depending on whether nations X and Y are basically hostile or basically friendly toward each other. The threat is modeled by the terms kY_t and mX_t because these terms increase as the arms level of the opposite side increases. The terms $-aX_t$ and $-bY_t$ provide a model for the constraint of expense, because they decrease as the one's own arms level increases, and this reduces the level of arms in the next year. Finally, the constants g and h model grievance, which is considered fixed in the model.

The beauty of the Richardson model is that it is *self-contained:* If you know the values of the coefficients and of the arms levels X and Y for one year, you can predict the arms levels for all future years. This gives the model the potential, in theory, of predicting the future, and Richardson hoped that if politicians could predict oncoming wars, they could learn to avoid them.

Richardson's strikingly original work was ignored for decades. He continued his efforts in the field of mathematical international relations throughout his career and into his retirement but achieved no recognition for it in scholarly or political circles. Richardson died in 1953, famed for his work in mathematical meteorology but unknown in the field of political science.

In the late 1950s, a group of mathematical social scientists at the Universities of Chicago and Michigan rediscovered Richardson's work and began to publicize it. The *Journal of Conflict Resolution* devoted an entire issue to Richardson. Publication of Richardson's two microfilmed manuscripts—*Statistics of Deadly Quarrels* and *Arms and Insecurity*—was arranged, and his work became a keystone in the new field of mathematical international relations. By the 1970s, the model had been tested on dozens of different arms races in hundreds of variations.

It worked. Not perfectly, by any means: Arms races occur for a complex set of reasons, and no single simple model captures all of these. But the model generally works well for short-term predictions, and more important, no other self-contained model works better. From the European confrontation between NATO and the Warsaw Pact, to the massive arms races of the Middle East conflicts, to the tragic 30-year war in Southeast Asia, the Richardson arms race model captures the basic characteristics of the arms race. And in doing so, another empirical application of the model was discovered.

One important characteristic of the Richardson model is called *stability*. In the simplest form, stability determines whether the arms race is increasing at an increasing rate or increasing at a decreasing rate.[3] Figure 17.2 shows two examples of arms races: the stable NATO–Warsaw Treaty Organization race and the unstable Iran-Iraq race; both figures give the military expenditures reported in the Stockholm International Peace Research Institute (SIPRI) yearbooks. In an unstable race, once arms levels start increasing, they continue increasing indefinitely. In the model, they go to infinity; in actual arms races, war usually intervenes first.

The avoidance of war was, of course, Richardson's impetus for developing the model in the beginning. It turns out that the model is a fairly good predictor of war, because almost all modern wars have been preceded by unstable arms races. Richardson postulated this in his original work, and it has been verified in more systematic studies.

In the late 1970s, Michael Wallace found that arms race instability correlated strongly with war. Using a somewhat more complicated definition of an arms race than Richardson did, Wallace found that in 28 serious international disputes that involved an arms race during the period from 1816 to 1965, fully 23 resulted in war. In 71 disputes in which no arms race was involved, only three resulted in war.[4]

---

[3] Stability also describes what happens to the arms race if it has settled down to a mutually agreeable level of arms, called an *equilibrium point,* and something happens to change the arms levels from that value. A stable arms race will return to the equilibrium; an unstable race will go further away from it.

[4] Michael Wallace, "Arms Races and Escalation: Some New Evidence," *Journal of Conflict Resolution,* 23 (1979), pp. 3—16.

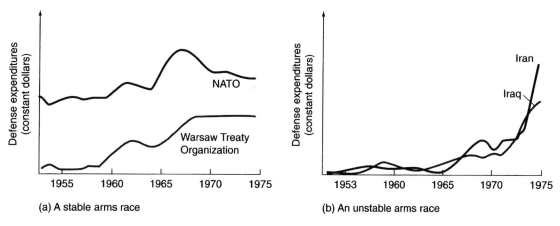

Figure 17.2
Examples of arms races

Another example will further illustrate this point. In 1976, W. Ladd Hollist studied four arms races using the Richardson model and SIPRI military expenditure data.[5] The arms races were between the United States and the USSR, India and Pakistan, Iran and Iraq, and Israel and Egypt for the period 1948 to 1973. Of the four, all but the U.S.–USSR race were unstable, which presented something of a problem. India-Pakistan and Israel-Egypt were unstable and had resulted in war, as the Richardson model predicted. U.S.–USSR was stable and had not resulted in war, also as predicted. But Iran and Iraq were engaged in an unstable arms race with no resulting war. This discrepancy was resolved in 1980, four years after Hollist's article, when the long-simmering dispute between Iran and Iraq finally erupted into war. The Iran-Iraq arms race had been stable until the late 1960s and became unstable only in the 1970s, further narrowing the prediction of when war might occur.

The Richardson model is only one of a very large class of **dynamic models**—those modeling the development of a process *over time*. Many of these models are implemented using differential equations, and many borrow techniques that are used to model population growth and other biological processes. Even more complex are dynamic **computer simulations,** which model complex processes by using large sets of equations too complicated to be solved algebraically. Computer simulations frequently deal with entire nations or global political and economic systems, and they are increasingly used to deal with what-if scenarios in national and international public policy.

Until recently, most of the dynamic models studied in political science produced fairly regular behavior. In the past decade, considerable work has been done on **chaotic models,** which are slightly more complicated than the Richardson model and have no random component but over time generate behavior that appears to be

---

[5] W. Ladd Hollist, "Alternative Explanation of Competitive Arms Processes: Tests on Four Pairs of Nation," *American Journal of Political Science*, 21 (1977), pp. 313–40.

random. Dynamic chaos may explain how a regular political process can sometimes generate highly irregular behavior, such as civil war or parliamentary instability.

Example 2: The Prisoners' Dilemma Game

One of the most extensively developed fields in the mathematical modeling of social behavior is called **game theory.** "Games" in this theory are situations in which two (or more) individuals are making choices about actions, and the rewards to each individual are dependent on their joint choices. Traditional games such as chess, poker, and football are examples of this type of situation, because the outcome of the game depends on the actions of the players, hence the name of the theory. The games studied in game theory are usually more formalized than traditional games, and the payoffs are usually more complex than simply winning or losing, but the principle of competition is the same.

Game theory originally developed around a type of competition called a **zero-sum game,** meaning that whatever one player won, the other lost. Most conventional games are of this category, as are some "games" encountered in politics, such as elections. But most political situations are non–zero-sum or cooperative, since it is possible in some situations for both players to be better off (that is, the fact that one player wins does not mean that the other loses an identical amount). The most widely studied cooperative game is called the **prisoners' dilemma game,** an example of which is given below.

Consider the situation of trench warfare in World War I. The British and German armies face each other across no-man's-land, huddled in trenches, with snipers standing in parapets waiting to slay the unwary soldier who stands in an unprotected location for even a moment. In the initial phases of this stalemate, the casualties from sniper attacks are high, and both sides remain tightly, and uncomfortably, confined to their trenches. But as time passes and the same units face each other week after week, the rate of sniper attacks drops off, and eventually the only casualties happen by accident. Visitors to the front are surprised to see both sides wandering about fully unprotected, with neither attempting to kill the other. This is not the way wars in the movies are fought, but cooperation becomes the rule, and inexperienced officers on either side who try to force the troops to violate this norm have a nasty tendency to die in accidents. This informal truce occurs without any overt communication between the two sides.

This is not a pacifist fantasy but instead describes an actual situation. Robert Axelrod quotes the memoirs of a British officer in World War I:

> I was having tea with A Company when we heard a lot of shouting and went out to investigate. We found our men and the Germans standing on their respective parapets. Suddenly a salvo arrived but did no damage. Naturally both sides got down and our men started swearing at the Germans, when all at once a brave German got onto his parapet and shouted out, "We are very sorry about that; we hope no one was hurt. It is not our fault, it is that damned Prussian artillery."[6]

---

[6] Robert Axelrod, *The Evolution of Cooperation* (New York: Basic Books, 1984), p. 84.

Table 17.1
Payoff matrix for trench welfare

British	Germans			
	Cooperate		Double-cross	
Cooperate	Cell 1	−1, −1	Cell 2	−10, 0
Double-cross	Cell 3	0, −10	Cell 4	−3, −3

This phenomenon is explained by the very broadly applicable prisoners' dilemma game. In the prisoners' dilemma, two sides have the alternative of cooperating or double-crossing each other. In the example we have given, the payoff matrix, given in terms of the number of individuals killed per day, might look like that in Table 17.1. In this matrix, the payoffs are given in the order (British, German) and refer to the average number of soldiers killed per day. The cooperate strategy means not to deliberately try to kill soldiers on the other side; the double-cross strategy means to try to kill. If both sides cooperate (Cell 1), we assume that the deaths will be accidental, and one person will die per day on each side. If both sides are deliberately sniping (Cell 4), there will be more deaths, but not greatly more, because both sides will be stuck in their trenches and not present many targets. Finally, if one side starts sniping while the other side is cooperating (Cells 2 and 3), the side that was trying to cooperate will sustain a large number of casualties, and we presume that the other side will be prepared and not sustain any casualties that day.

The interesting thing about the prisoners' dilemma is that if each side assumes the worst of the other, both will use the double-cross strategy. If a side chooses to cooperate, the worst outcome is that the other side will double-cross, resulting in 10 deaths. If the side chooses to double-cross, the worst outcome is that the other side will also double-cross, but this results in only 3 deaths. Therefore the way to make the best of the worst outcome—which is called the *minimax solution*—is to double-cross. Yet if both sides cooperated, they would both be better off than they would by double-crossing, each losing only one soldier per day. Therein lies the dilemma of the prisoners' dilemma game.

The example given here is only one of a very large number of situations to which the prisoners' dilemma game is applicable.[7] Some other standard examples include the mutual observance of arms control agreements, the observance of business contracts, the control of food prices through underproduction by farmers, the maintenance of cartel agreements, the decision to start a conventional war, and even the decision of students not to study for an exam that will be graded on a curve!

The intriguing aspect of the prisoners' dilemma is that in the real world, players frequently choose to cooperate despite the pressure to double-cross. The question for the game theorist is *why* such cooperation occurs. The question seemed

[7] For one unusual example, see Richard C. Rich, "A Cooperative Approach to the Logic of Collective Action: Voluntary Organizations and the Prisoners' Dilemma," *Journal of Voluntary Action Research*, 17 (July–December, 1988), pp. 5–18.

especially puzzling because studies of zero-sum games indicated that the minimax solution—which predicts a mutual double-cross—had some desirable properties. Therefore, the mechanism for cooperation in the prisoners' dilemma was unclear.

The key to that cooperation seems to be that the game is *iterated*—played a number of times—which allows each side to punish the other side for a double-cross. In a very ingenious set of experiments done in the early 1980s, Robert Axelrod showed that the simple strategy of tit for tat—doing to the other side whatever it did during the previous play of the game—is highly favored in a situation in which a large number of players are engaged in prisoners' dilemma games.[8] In particular, if two players are both using the tit-for-tat strategy, once they start playing cooperatively, they will continue to do so. If a tit-for-tat player encounters another player who is inclined to double-cross, both will end up destroying each other. Consequently, in a world characterized by prisoners' dilemma situations, the players likely to be most successful are those who are willing to cooperate in a tit-for-tat fashion. In a situation in which individuals who do not cooperate are less likely to survive—as in the trench warfare situation described or a situation of businesses obeying contracts—the typical survivor will be a tit-for-tat player with whom it is safe to cooperate. This goes a long way to explain why cooperation can exist even in a world where there is no enforcement of contracts, there is no communication between players, and a reward exists for double-crossing an opponent who is trying to cooperate.

The example given here provides only the basic outlines of the rich literature on the prisoners' dilemma game and Axelrod's and others' solutions to that game. By making minor changes in the prisoners' dilemma game, one can also explore issues such as the use of threats, the advantage a player might gain by cutting off options (the burning-one's-bridges strategy), the importance of bluffs and feints, the possible value of random behavior, and a number of other characteristics of competitive situations. The suggestions for further reading at the end of this chapter provide a guide to getting started in this large literature.

Example 3: Downs's Model

For five weeks following the 2000 presidential election in the United States, the outcome of the contest was uncertain. While the Democratic candidate, Al Gore, had won the national popular vote by a small margin—around 500,000 votes out of about 105 million cast (0.5 percent)—the choice of the next president depended not on the popular vote but rather on the electoral vote which was decided on a state-by-state basis. The electoral vote tally was nearly tied, and the pivotal state that would decide the election was Florida. Here Gore trailed his Republican opponent, George W. Bush, by fewer than 1,000 votes out of more than 5.8 million votes cast. If Bush could maintain this lead, he would win the presidency.

---

[8] Robert Axelrod, "Effective Choice in the Prisoners' Dilemma," *Journal of Conflict Resolution* 24 (1980), pp. 3–25; and "More Effective Choice in the Prisoner's Dilemma," *Journal of Conflict Resolution* 24 (1980), pp. 379–403.

Thirty-six days of legal wrangling over the Florida results witnessed recounts started and stopped, lawsuits filed at every level from Florida county courthouses to the U.S. Supreme Court, and the public introduced to a new esoteric vocabulary for assessing punched-card ballots, including "hanging chads," "dimpled chads," and even "pregnant chads." The Florida election returns were eventually certified with Bush having a lead of 537 votes, a difference of only 0.009 percent. On that difference, Bush became the forty-third president of the United States.

While the close election in Florida captured most of the attention in 2000, it was far from the only close race in that year. In the presidential race, the major party candidates were separated by only 366 votes out of about 573,000 cast in New Mexico (0.06 percent), and 6,460 out of more than 1.4 million in Oregon (0.04 percent). In the Senate race in the state of Washington, Democrat Maria Cantwell defeated Republican Slade Gordon by 2,229 votes out of almost 2.4 million cast (0.09 percent). In the Eighth Congressional District of Michigan, Republican Michael J. Rogers defeated Democrat Dianne Yvonne Byrum by 152 votes out of 290,000 cast (0.05 percent).

As noted earlier, we accept that close elections are a normal part of the political process. To put this into perspective, however, consider the probability that 100 million individuals, given the choice of putting a green bead or a red bead into a very large jar, would make their choices so that the final mix of colors in the jar comes within 0.01 percent of a perfect 50–50 split. Even under the most optimistic assumption—that people are equally likely to put a red or green bead in the jar—this probability is only 0.00016 or 1 in 6,250. But a result this close occurred in Florida, and results almost as close occurred in a number of other races.

To a mathematical modeler, this presents a puzzle: Why are so many elections far closer than would be expected by chance? In one of the earliest works on formal modeling in political science, Anthony Downs proposed a simple mechanism to explain this phenomenon.

Downs adapted a model originally proposed by Harold Hotelling in 1929 to explain why two grocery stores in a small town might choose to locate next to each other.[9] For example, assume that the town is an isolated mining community, with the next nearest store 50 miles away. Two competing store managers come into town to open stores. From their experience in mining camps, they know exactly what supplies to stock, and hence the miners will be indifferent as to which store they patronize. The only thing that distinguishes the two stores is location, and miners will go to the nearer store. In such a case, there is a uniquely ideal place for both stores—the point that minimizes the average distance that each miner must travel. If both store owners recognize this fact, they will locate their stores in the same place, despite the fact that this means that the stores are right next to each other and, one might add, despite the fact that locating the stores some distance apart would reduce the travel time for the customers and still allow the store

---

[9] Anthony Downs, *An Economic Theory of Democracy* (New York: Harper and Row, 1957); and Harold Hotelling, "Stability in Competition," *Economic Journal*, 39 (1929), pp. 41–57.

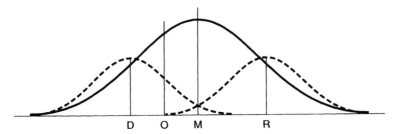

Figure 17.3
Vote distributions

owners to split the business equally (this latter point illustrates another instance of the prisoners' dilemma).

Downs applied the logic of the Hotelling model to candidates in an election. In the simplest Downsian model, assume that voters are arrayed across an ideological spectrum from liberal to conservative, as illustrated in Figure 17.3. Voters are assumed to vote for the candidate who is closest to them in ideology. In such a situation, candidates will want to be as ideologically close to the middle of the voters—the point labeled *M*—as possible. If one candidate takes a position at *M* and the other candidate takes a position different from *M*, say at the position marked *O*, the latter will lose the election: The candidate at *M* gets the 50 percent of the votes to the right of *M*, then splits the votes between points *M* and *O* and so wins the election. This mechanism is self-reinforcing: A candidate may ignore it, but only at the expense of losing the election. We would therefore expect that experienced politicians—those who have won several elections—would have the ability to figure out where this political middle is located.

This model explains the basic observation that many elections are very close because experienced candidates try to be as close to the center of the vote as possible. But the Downs model predicts that candidates will have almost identical positions, which is not necessarily the case. Candidates in U.S. elections are, for the most part, fairly close ideologically, but rarely are they as close as this model suggests. Therefore, we need to see if the model requires some additional assumptions.

There are several ways around this problem, but the most straightforward involves the observation that a candidate in most districts must survive two election challenges: one in a primary election and one in the general election. In the primary election, the distribution of ideology is skewed away from the center. The dotted lines in Figure 17.3 show a hypothetical distribution for the separate Republican and Democratic primaries: the Republican primary voters are usually farther to the right, the Democratic primary voters are farther to the left, and many of the independent voters in the center do not vote in primaries. Applying the Downs-Hotelling model to the primary race, we see that in order to win the primary, each candidate will try to take an ideological stance at the middle of the party votes—marked *D* and *R* on the figure—which then places the candidates away from the center, *M*.

If voters placed no value on consistency, then the logical strategy for each candidate would be to take a party-centered position in the primary, then immediately shift to the electorate-centered position M after the primary. Voters are not so forgetful, however, and candidates must instead try to move toward the center while not appearing inconsistent with their earlier position. Furthermore, if the party-centered position was a substantial distance from the electorate-centered position, the candidate elected in the primary may find it impossible to take a winnable position in the general election and may lose by a large percentage (as happened, for example, to Barry Goldwater in 1964 and George McGovern in 1972). As long as *both* candidates stay away from the center point, they can still almost perfectly split the vote by choosing appropriately symmetrical positions on either side of M while not being identical in position. As the frequency of improbably close elections indicates, U.S. politicians seem to be very good at choosing precisely these positions.

The model presented here is only the simplest version of the Downsian approach, and both Downs and other researchers have explored more complex versions than this. In actual elections, voters are not neatly arrayed in a bell-shaped curve on a single ideological dimension but instead take positions on a variety of dimensions and hold strongly divergent positions on some issues. But even this simple model provides a mechanism to explain why some but not all elections split almost 50-50, why candidates do not take identical positions in the general election, and why candidates frequently shift their ideological position between the primary and general elections.

Other Types of Models

The examples given in this chapter only scratch the surface of the variety of mathematical models of political behavior. Some additional categories of models should at least be mentioned; these can be explored more thoroughly by consulting the suggestions for further reading at the end of this chapter.

There is a large literature involving **expected utility** decision making, which is a means of modeling decision situations involving risk or uncertainty. These models are used extensively in public policy analysis. Typical expected utility problems would involve deciding, say, whether to build a nuclear power plant in an area subject to earthquakes, how much sand and salt a highway department should stockpile before winter, or whether to spend $1 million straightening a potentially hazardous stretch of highway. These models are widely used in *prescriptive modeling* (deciding what action to take) in the policy arena; they are less useful in *descriptive modeling* (predicting what individuals will actually do), because most individuals do not follow this model in their own decision making.

Related to the expected utility models are **optimization models,** most of which have been borrowed from economics and engineering. Most rational (goal-directed) behavior involves some sort of maximizing or minimizing, and a variety of complex mathematical techniques are available for determining such optimal behaviors. These are useful both in "games against nature," in which the "opponent" is an unpredictable future; in competitive situations against a small number of other actors; and in market situations in which the environment is determined by a very large number of other factors. Because these models are fairly general and have been extensively developed, they are potentially powerful tools in the study of some problems in political behavior.

A new field of mathematical modeling deals with **computational models,** which are related to the more general field of computerized artificial intelligence. Whereas most of the existing models are based in classical mathematics—usually logic, geometry, algebra, and calculus—computational models are based in computer science and involve *algorithms* (precisely stated sequences of instructions) rather than equations.

The most common form of computational model is the *expert system,* which uses a large number of "if . . . then" rules. Expert systems have been shown to be able to duplicate human performance in a variety of fields and are particularly attractive in modeling political behavior because bureaucracies and legal systems are explicitly rule-following. Computer modeling is also central to the study of **complex systems,** a relatively new field. In these models not only do the values of variables change over time, but also the underlying mathematical processes change, usually in an evolutionary fashion or through learning.

Problems with Modeling

Under the guidance of Niven's dictum—"There is no cause so noble that idiots will not adhere to it"—we should close with a few cautions about the use, and misuse, of mathematical models.

The first and most general caution is the classical "garbage in, garbage out" proviso: Models are no better than the assumptions that go into them. More specifically, an argument that makes no sense in natural language is not rendered any more sensible by being translated into mathematical form. It is always important to keep in mind that mathematics is useful solely as a means of deriving logical conclusions from your assumptions, and hence the validity of a model rests on those assumptions, not on the techniques.

There are times when it may be useful to accept some simplification of assumptions in order to use certain powerful techniques that could not otherwise be used, but even these simplifications must pass the muster of empirical validity and common sense. If the assumptions of a model are false, it does not mean that the conclusions of the model will be false, but it does mean that the validity of those conclusions does not rest in any way on the assumptions.[10]

The most common problem encountered in models consists of *oversimplified assumptions*: in words attributed to Einstein, "Models should be as simple as possible . . . and no simpler." It is the purpose of mathematical models to simplify, but those simplifications are valid only insofar as the model as a whole continues to reflect the basic processes that are the subject of the model. In almost all cases, there

---

[10] This premise, obvious as it may seem, is not universally accepted in mathematical modeling circles. Adherents to the "positive economics" tenets of Milton Friedman argue (vociferously) that the strength of a model rests on the validity of its conclusions and that unreasonable sets of assumptions may be used to generate those conclusions if necessary. Though arguments can be made for this approach, the average consumer of the mathematical modeling literature is far better off applying the strict criterion of *caveat emptor* to the empirical validity of the assumptions of a model.

will be situations in which the simplifications of the model break down. For example, the Richardson arms race model fails to work very well in situations involving nuclear weapons, because nuclear weapons effectively give virtually unlimited "threat" at very little economic expense. In such cases, it is important for the modeler to indicate the limits within which the model can be expected to hold. These limitations, it should be noted, are no different from those encountered in the physical sciences: for example, various chemical reactions will occur predictably only if a large number of conditions, such as temperature, pressure, and humidity, are held within a certain range of values.

Models must be tested before they are believed, unless the model has been completely specified by the assumptions. In most cases, models involve parameters that must be estimated externally or that involve assumptions about the world that must be verified. This is another way of testing the validity of the assumptions: If the results of the model are false and the model itself is logically correct, it follows that the assumptions must be false.

Finally, the results of the model must be properly translated back into natural language. A common problem in modeling is that individuals will take a fairly straightforward model, do some plausible things with it, and then overstate the generality of the conclusions. It is a common human tendency to become infatuated with one's creation and claim for it more than one has actually shown it to do—in modeling circles this is known as the *Pygmalion syndrome*. Periodically, the popular media become intrigued with a modeling technique and attribute all sorts of miraculous properties to it. In reality, mathematical models generally improve gradually through years of hard work and experimentation. The cautious consumer of mathematical modeling is advised to check that the results claimed for a theory can actually be deduced from the assumptions of that theory without any additional assumptions, leaps of faith, and granting the benefit of the doubt to the model.

Conclusion

In summary, mathematical models can take one considerably further in deriving complex conclusions from sets of assumptions than can natural language. Furthermore, the political world appears to be sufficiently regular that the deductions based on many mathematical models prove to be valid when subjected to empirical tests. The field is only a few decades old but has made tremendous strides during that time, with few limits in sight.

The modeling of political and social phenomena is complex—usually considerably more complex than many problems in the physical sciences, because humans are more complicated and unpredictable than atoms. This complexity has two implications for models of political behavior.

First, modeling will start with the simpler and more regularly observed behaviors first and only later build up to more complicated behavior. As a consequence, some of the phenomena being modeled may appear trivial, and "big questions" cannot be addressed from the beginning. In contrast, the intuitive, informal approach to political analysis can address any question at any time, and big questions are often dealt with in such a fashion. The answers provided, however, are often wrong—a skimming of the history of wars, massacres, human misery, and stupid mistakes will indicate that intuitive models are scarcely flawless. Since we will always have those intuitive models to fall back on, we can only improve on our record of political analysis by using formal models.

Second, the mathematics necessary to deal with political problems is probably going to be different and likely more complex than the mathematics that dealt with the problems of classical physics. It is not clear what those differences are going to be, but there are going to be differences. In particular, models of social processes will probably involve a larger amount of information, a larger number of variables, and a larger amount of randomness than models of physical systems do. At the same time, the advent of computer technology has made it possible to deal with formal systems that are far more complex than could be dealt with in the past, and the computer may enable modelers to go considerably further in the future.

Suggestions for Further Reading

A useful survey of the literature on mathematical modeling of political processes can be found in the following works.

Kenneth A. Shepsle and Mark S. Boncheck, *Analyzing Politics: Rationality, Behavior and Institutions* (New York: Norton, 1997) is the best current introduction to models of domestic politics; Peter Ordeshook, *A Political Theory Primer* (New York: Routledge, 1992) covers the game theory and social choice literature at a more advanced mathematical level; William Riker and Peter Ordeshook, *An Introduction to Positive Political Theory* (Englewood Cliffs, NJ: Prentice Hall, 1973), is somewhat older but was the standard reference for a number of years. Rebecca B. Morton, *Methods and Models, A Guide to the Empirical Analysis of Formal Models in Political Science*(Cambridge, England: Cambridge University Press, 1999), is a book-length discussion of the process and methodology of mathematical modeling.

In the field of international relations, Michael Nichelson, *Formal Theories in International Relations* (Cambridge, England: Cambridge University Press, 1989), provides a good overall disucssion. At the basic introductory level, Anatol Rapoport, *Fights, Games, and Debates* (Ann Arbor: University of Michigan Press, 1974), is still a classic, and several books by Steven Brams, such as *Paradoxes in Politics* (New York: Free Press, 1976) and *Superpower Games* (New Haven, CT: Yale University Press, 1985), provide text-level introductions. A general review of the current literature can be found in Paul Johnson and Philip Schrodt, "Analytic Theory and Methodology," in William Crotty, ed., *Political Science: Looking to the Future* (Evanston, IL: Northwestern University Press, 1992).

Robert Huckfeldt, Carol Kohfeld, and Thomas Likens, *Dynamic Models: An Introduction* (Beverly Hills, CA: Sage, 1982), provides an introduction to dynamic models of political behavior, and Samuel Goldberg, *Introduction to Difference Equations* (New York: Wiley, 1958), is a good introduction to basic techniques. Diana Richards, *Political Complexity: Nonlinear Models of Politics* (Ann Arbor: University of Michigan Press, 1996) and L. Douglas Kiel and Euel Elliot, *Chaos Theory in the Social Sciences* (Ann Arbor: University of Michigan Press, 1996) are good surveys of chaos models and other nonlinear methods. Surveys of the use of large-scale computer simulations in the modeling of international behavior can be found in Michael Don Ward, *Theories, Models and Simulations in International Relations* (Boulder, CO: Westview, 1985) and Barry B. Hughes, *International Futures*(Boulder, CO: Westview, 1993).

Game theory has an extensive literature: Morton Davis, *Game Theory: A Nontechnical Introduction* (New York: Basic Books, 1983); Martin Shubik, *Game Theory in the Social Sciences* (Cambridge, MA: MIT Press, 1985); Roger Myerson, *Game Theory* (Cambridge, MA: Harvard University Press, 1991);), James D. Morrow, *Game Theory for Political*

Scientists (Princeton, NJ: Princeton University Press, 1994); Herbert Gintis, *Game Theory Evolving: A Problem-Centered Introduction to Modeling Strategic Interaction* (Princeton, NJ: Princeton University Press, 2000); and Ken Binmore, *Fun and Games. A Text on Game Theory* (Lexington, MA: Heath, 1992), are several examples of introductory texts in the field. Other books on game theory include the classic by R. D. Luce and Howard Raiffa, *Games and Decisions* (New York: Wiley, 1957), and the very readable J. Williams, *The Compleat Strategyst* (New York: McGraw-Hill, 1954). Peter Ordeshook, *Models of Strategic Choice in Politics* (Ann Arbor: University of Michigan Press, 1989), and Scott Gates and Brian D. Humes, *Games, Information, and Politics: Applying Game Theoretic Models to Political Science* (Ann Arbor: University of Michigan Press, 1997), focus explicitly on political applications.

The field of cooperative games has a somewhat less technical literature, and notable in this field are the works of Thomas Schelling: *The Strategy of Conflict* (Oxford, England: Oxford University Press, 1960), and *Micromotives and Macrobehavior* (New York: Norton, 1978). Peter Ordeshook, *Game Theory and Political Theory* (Cambridge, England: Cambridge University Press, 1986), and Mark Irving Lichbach, *The Cooperaters' Dilemma* (Ann Arbor: University of Michigan Press, 1996), are two more works that deal extensively with applications of game theory. Robert Axelrod, *The Evolution of Cooperation* (New York: Basic Books, 1984), is an excellent introduction to the prisoners' dilemma game and an important work in its own right.

The extensive literature on elections and collective decision making is covered in the Shepsle and Boncheck, the Ordeshook, and the Riker and Ordeshook texts cited, as well as in Norman Frohlich and Joe A. Oppenheimer, *Modern Political Economy* (Englewood Cliffs, NJ: Prentice Hall, 1978). Richard Niemi and William Riker, "The Choice of Voting Systems," *Scientific American*, 234 (1976), pp. 21-27, is a good short introduction to the basic models. James M. Enelow and Melvin J. Hinich, *The Spatial Theory of Voting* (Cambridge, England: Cambridge University Press, 1984), offers a good introduction to the spatial voting literature.

Two more books dealing with the formal interlinkages between political and economic behavior are Joe B. Stevens, *The Economics of Collective Choice* (Boulder, CO: Westview, 1993), and Patrick Dunleavy, *Democracy, Bureaucracy and Public Choice* (New York: Prentice Hall, 1991). Donald P. Green and Ian Shapiro, *Pathologies of Rational Choice Theory: A Critique of Applications in Political Science* (New Haven, CT: Yale University Press, 1994), is a widely read critique of the rational choice approach.

In the area of computational modeling approaches, Valerie Hudson, ed., *Artificial Intelligence and International Politics* (Boulder, CO: Westview, 1991), discusses a variety of techniques for modeling foreign policy behavior; Robert A. Benfer, Edward E. Brent Jr., and Louanna Furbee, *Expert Systems* (Newbury Park, CA: Sage, 1991), discusses expert systems in the context of social sciences models; and Philip A. Anderson, Kenneth J. Arrow, and David Pines, eds., *The Economy as an Evolving Complex System* (Reading, MA: Addison-Wesley, 1988), provides an introduction to many of the contemporary techniques for modeling complex systems.

Research Exercises

1. Find a social, political, or economic situation other than those discussed in the text that could be modeled by an iterated (repeated) prisoners' dilemma game. Explain your rationale for the payoffs in each cell, and discuss whether the cooperation predicted for the iterated prisoners' dilemma occurs in real-world instances of the game. If it does occur, how do the players communicate and enforce that cooperation? If it does not occur, where is the model inaccurate?

2. For some political system and level of analysis (local, state, national, international, etc.), find a case of empirical regularity in political behavior and construct an informal model to explain it. Back up your model with some empirical evidence of the regularity, and try to find some deductions from the assumptions of the model.

3. Suppose a third candidate enters an election being contested by two candidates using a Downsian strategy of taking positions equally distant from (but not at) the center of voter preferences. What is the best position for the third candidate? What is the best response strategy on the part of the other two candidates? Is this situation typical of actual elections in the United States, or do third-party candidates behave differently from what the model would predict? If there is a difference, can you see a way to modify the model to account for this?

Terms Introduced in This Chapter

mathematical model
informal model
formal model
dynamic models
computer simulations
chaotic models
game theory

zero-sum game
prisoners' dilemma game
expected utility
optimization models
computational models
complex systems

INTRODUCTION TO QUALITATIVE METHODS

We are providing an introduction to this section of the book because its chapters represent a significant departure from the material presented in prior sections. We feel that you can better understand the ideas covered in this section if we offer some general background to qualitative research before describing specific methods.

From the time scholars began using scientific methods to study social phenomena, some academics (and some public officials and political activists) have seen limitations in quantitative methods. These critics often raise three types of concerns.

First, some believe that research methods developed in the physical sciences, with their stress on treating all cases alike and reducing complex concepts to numeric representations, can never fully capture important dimensions of human thought and interaction. To these critics, even the most carefully executed quantitative research does not provide a meaningful understanding of the actions of humans who are each unique in many ways and may see very different meanings in the same phenomena.

Second, some argue that quantitative research methods require that we remove subjects from their natural setting and pay attention only to limited aspects of who or what they are. People, they argue, may not behave in real contexts in the same way as they behave in, for example, the artificial setting of a survey interview. Moreover, they contend that actions can only be fully understood by understanding the context in which they occur, for it is that context that gives them meaning.

Finally, some view quantitative methods as so inherently politically biased that they are inappropriate for the study of some subjects and populations. For example, these critics argue that applying the methods of the physical sciences can never capture crucial aspects of the lives and thinking of marginalized groups—people who, because of some personal characteristic, are excluded from political, social, and economic power. They often argue that quantitative methods are a cultural artifact of the same processes that created the currently dominant social and political culture. Accordingly, they believe that we cannot employ quantitative research to gain a valid understanding of the deep cultural roots of contemporary political or social behavior.

Scholars who share these concerns have sought alternative means of gaining an understanding of the empirical world through the development of a very diverse set of research approaches described collectively as **qualitative methods**. To their advocates, these means of inquiry provide a more complete, meaningful, and useful understanding of social phenomena by studying them *in their entirety*, *in the context in which they occur*, while *considering the meanings those being studied give to* *their actions and to the actions of others.* Catherine Marshall and Gretchen Rossman capture the distinct features of this approach when they write that qualitative research "entails immersion [of the researcher] in the everyday life of the setting chosen for study, values and seeks to discover participants' perspectives on their worlds, views inquiry as an interactive process between the researcher and the participants, is both descriptive and analytic, and relies on people's words and observable behavior as the primary data."[1]

This indicates there can be some fundamental differences between qualitative research and the type of inquiry we have described so far. There are, however, substantial similarities between the way many qualitative and quantitative researchers approach their studies. In the chapters in this section we will focus only on those aspects of qualitative research that share a good deal with quantitative methods.

Our decision to do this does not reflect any lack of appreciation for the more fundamentally distinctive qualitative approaches. Rather we choose to describe only qualitative approaches that require the least additional explanation simply to limit the scope and length of our text. In addition, we have selected qualitative methods that are most self-evidently *empirical*, even though not quantitative, in order to highlight the fact that *empirical research can be either quantitative or qualitative* so long as its purpose is to characterize real-world phenomena rather than interpret them in some normative context.

At the end of this section introduction, we provide some suggestions for readings through which you can explore other types of qualitative research if you want.

Comparing Qualitative and Quantitative Methods

You will find it useful to understand some of the most basic distinctions between these two approaches in terms of the major steps in the research process. In making these comparisons, we will speak of qualitative and quantitative researchers as if they were two different groups. Please remember that the same individual scholar can (and often will) employ both types of methods—sometimes even within the same study. In addition, it is important to recognize that the distinctions discussed are generally more matters of degree than absolutes. The two types of methods often require only different *forms* of work, and not entirely different work.

Empirical Focus of Research Questions   Both qualitative and quantitative research begins with a research question. While scholars using each of the approaches tend to pursue rather different research questions, both approaches are designed to produce knowledge of the empirical world. Both rely on concepts that are, at least in principle, observable with the ordinary human senses. Thus qualitative researchers are just as obligated to represent accurately the reality that they observe as are those using strictly quantitative methods.

---

[1] Catherine Marshall and Gretchen B. Rossman, *Designing Qualitative Research*, 3d ed. (Thousand Oaks, CA: Sage, 1999), p. 7.

Theorizing   Qualitative researchers are less likely than those using quantitative methods to be interested in testing pre-formed theories and more likely to seek to gain insight into some phenomenon which they can translate into a conceptual understanding or theory. Qualitative researchers seek to be "taught by the world" to a far greater extent than quantitative researchers. They often form their theories as they make their observations.

This, they argue, makes their theories more firmly grounded in reality. By contrast, their critics worry that this practice opens the door to unintentionally shaping theories to fit observations so that the theories cannot be tested or challenged. They also contend that such "theories" apply only to the cases actually observed and, as a result, are of limited usefulness.

Research Design   It is important for those using qualitative methods—just as it is for those using quantitative methods—to be clear about their research question and to know what they are seeking to learn from their study. However, qualitative researchers are far less likely to base their research design on the logic of the experiment than quantitative researchers. They are usually unconcerned with control groups, pretests, or any of the other elements of experimental and quasi-experimental designs that allow researchers to "hold constant" some factors in order to make causal inferences.

A qualitative research design will generally focus on who or what is to be observed, in what settings they are to be observed, how observations are to be conducted, what methods will be used to secure the information needed, and how data will be recorded. There will be far less concern with being able to establish cause and effect relationships and more concern with viewing the people or events in question as they "naturally" occur. Only in this way, qualitative researchers argue, can they fully and accurately describe and understand behavior, beliefs, values, social interactions, and the like.

Sampling   Qualitative researchers also differ from their quantitatively oriented colleagues in that they are less concerned with generalizing conclusions to large populations and more concerned with gaining insights into specific cases from which they can construct an understanding (rather than a statistical explanation) of broad phenomena. As a result, they use very different sampling methods than we have described in earlier chapters.

Sampling for quantitative research is often based on the logic of probability and designed to produce statistical representativeness. It is usually done in advance of data collection. The sample for a qualitative study, by contrast, will often "emerge" as the study progresses. That is, researchers will select an initial case to observe and then let what they learn from those observations determine who or what they observe next. This strategy reflects their belief that we can determine where to look for the answers we seek only after having gained a partial understanding of the subject by direct experience with it.

Qualitative researchers are also often far less concerned with observing "representative" cases than they are with observing cases that will yield the insights they seek. To illustrate, a qualitatively oriented scholar might try to understand the fundamental assumptions that constitute a "political culture," not by surveying a representative sample of "ordinary" citizens, but by conducting in-depth interviews with a few people who do not share these assumptions and reject the dominant political culture. By understanding the political thought of these "outsiders," the researcher would hope to see how accepting the assumptions of the prevailing political culture influences the majority's thinking about politics.

As a result of both a lack of concern with statistical representativeness and the highly time-consuming nature of their methods, qualitative studies are usually based on far fewer cases than are quantitative studies.

Data Collection   Some of the most dramatic differences between qualitative and quantitative methods appear in the data collection stage. At a superficial level, there is the fact that data in qualitative research usually consist of words (or sounds and images translated into words) rather than numbers. This calls for the use of different procedures and instruments for data collection. There is a more fundamental difference, however.

For qualitative research, data collection usually involves extended observation of (or even participation in) the phenomenon under study. Rather than standing apart from the people or events to be studied, the researcher often is intimately engaged with them. Only in this way can researchers probe for the information they need to understand, for example, why people act as they do, how complex processes unfold, or what impact some specific event had on those who experienced it.

While some qualitative research attempts to avoid the problem of reactivity by concealing the observer or the purpose of the research from the subjects (as we explain in Chapter 19), much qualitative research takes a very different approach to reactivity. Since researchers have to interact with those they are studying, they depend, not on deception or concealment, but on trust (and their own perceptiveness) to avoid artificial reactions.

The argument here is that over time the researcher can build a strong enough relationship with those being observed that they will reveal their true feelings or reasoning and will act "naturally" because they are sure the researcher will not judge or harm them. At a minimum, the researcher will learn enough about the subjects and their context to know when they are not being truthful or are modifying their behavior because of the study. Effective use of this approach to control reactivity obviously requires a great deal of effort and skill.

Data Analysis   The distinction between data collection and data analysis is far less clear for qualitative studies than for quantitative ones. In quantitative studies, data analysis is usually planned in advance so that data can be obtained in the necessary form, and it is then carried out after all the data are gathered. In studies using qualitative methods, data collection and analysis generally proceed together.

Since data collection in qualitative research consists primarily of observing and recording those observations, the very act of deciding what to pay attention to and how to record it involves some analysis. To illustrate, consider a researcher who seeks to understand the political power structure in a voluntary organization by observing its meetings.

This person will see, hear, and feel a great deal at each meeting—for example, the temperature in the room, noises from outside, whether or not people bring small children to the meeting—but will regard most of it as irrelevant to the research. However, some seemingly irrelevant things may be important in understanding the power structure. Deciding whether to record and how to describe such things as what clothes different people wear to the meeting, the order in which they arrive, or the tone of voice they use in asking questions involves deciding what each of these things mean in the context of the study. That requires analysis both on the spot and when writing up the notes later.

Failing to recognize the significance of an event when it is observed or transcribed can lead to a failure to understand accurately the subject under study. Thus, some level of analysis must begin immediately. As a result, qualitative researchers often modify their data collection techniques in the course of the project as a result of new insights they gain from this early analysis.

Another distinction between qualitative and quantitative research is in the use of computers in data analysis. Computers have become central to most quantitative analysis. Qualitative researchers are far less likely to make much or any use of them because the form of data they have (narratives) does not lend itself to computerized manipulation. A number of computer programs have been developed to assist in the analysis of qualitative data, so this distinction is not as stark as it once was.[2] However, it is highly unlikely that computerized analyses will ever be as extensively used in the interpretation of qualitative data as they are in quantitative research.

Standards of Evidence Quantitative researchers are usually able to employ some well-established rules of analysis in deciding what is valid evidence for or against their theory. These include such tools as measures of statistical significance and statistical tests of validity, as well as formal logic. Qualitative researchers generally lack this type of commonly agreed to and "objective" tool.

Rather, they must rely on their ability to present a clear description, offer a convincing analysis, and make a strong argument for their interpretation to establish the value of their conclusions. Advocates of qualitative methods argue that this is an inevitable result of seeking to deal with the richness of complex realities rather than abstracting artificially constructed pieces of those realities for quantitative analysis. Critics of their approach contend that the vagueness and situational nature of their standards of evidence make it difficult (if not impossible) to achieve scientific consensus and, therefore, to make progress through cumulative knowledge.

Reporting the Results Reports of quantitative research usually rely heavily on presentations of numerical data to provide an accurate image of the subject and to make the case for the interpretations offered. Reports of qualitative research, in contrast, usually consist entirely of narratives describing and interpreting what was observed.

More substantively, reports of qualitative projects often include long quotations from the people being studied, or present the "stories" they told the researcher

---

[2] Eben A. Weitzman and Matthew M. Miles, *Computer Programs for Qualitative Data Analysis: A Software Sourcebook* (London: Sage, 1995).

about their "lived experience." This is necessary not only to capture the full complexity of the subject matter, but also to give readers a way to judge the validity of the researcher's interpretations (as explained in the discussion of rules of evidence above). Accordingly, the process of writing the report is even more crucial to qualitative projects than to quantitative ones. Qualitative researchers must be highly concerned with avoiding even unconscious bias in deciding what evidence (quotations, observations, etc.) to include in the report if they are to give other scholars a chance to critically evaluate their conclusions.

Research Ethics   Qualitative and quantitative research projects must meet highly similar ethical standards. However, because qualitative methods generally require far more extensive interaction between researchers and subjects, the use of qualitative methods generally raises more ethical questions and often raises them in more extreme forms. We will explore this challenge to qualitative methods in the chapters that describe specific approaches.

Irreconcilable Differences?

There are disagreements about many aspects or applications of all types of research methods. In most cases these disagreements arise from a sincere desire to make research as accurate and valuable as possible. Such debates usually have the positive effect of making all researchers examine their methods and conclusions very carefully, and thus produce better science.

The differences scholars have over qualitative versus quantitative methods are generally more extensive and profound than differences within either of the research traditions. This calls for a brief examination of these differences in this section introduction.

Most empirical researchers work primarily with either qualitative or quantitative methods but can see value in the other approach. The differences between the two traditions can often be resolved by using the insights provided by both to gain a more complete understanding of a subject, or by using results obtained with one type of method to generate questions to be explored using the other. In some cases, the two types of methods can even be used as complements to each other in a single study, with the results from each approach providing a form of validation for findings generated from the other. Scholars who take this position do not feel that qualitative and quantitative methods are fundamentally at odds.

However, there are researchers who view the differences between the two traditions as so profound that they can not accept the validity of research based on the tradition they reject. Some quantitatively oriented scholars regard at least some qualitative work as so dependent on the perceptions of the individual researcher and so focused on specific cases as to be unverifiable and essentially useless. In contrast, some qualitatively oriented scholars judge quantitative methods to be so incomplete in their representation of reality as to be empirically misleading and politically biased in favor of existing power arrangements.

Scholars on both sides of this divide sometime see themselves as defending "scientific truth" against misguided ideas. As a result, their criticism of the other approach can be quite strident. The sharpest conflicts, however, usually occur when research touches most directly on normative issues. If the distinction between empirical and normative inquiry is not recognized (or respected), intense debates from the world of politics can be introduced into scholarly research. Since some qualitative research is intended to be at the boundary between normative and empirical inquiry, it can evoke strong disagreements.

You will have to gain a great deal more experience with both social science research and politics in general before you are in a position to fully understand or take a position on this debate. However, we do want to alert you to the depth of the differences here so you are not surprised to read or hear strongly worded criticisms of certain research from some scholars. You may also find cases in which research results are challenged as strongly on the basis of methodology and political values as they are on substantive grounds. We hope this quick review of the divisions among qualitative and quantitative researchers can help you put these cases into context if you encounter them.

Suggestions for Further Reading

One entry-level text that provides a broad overview of qualitative methods is Uwe Flick, *An Introduction to Qualitative Research* (Thousand Oaks, CA: Sage, 1998). Norman K. Denzin and Yvonna S. Lincoln, eds., *Handbook of Qualitative Research*, 2d ed. (Thousand Oaks, CA: Sage, 2000) provides a collection of readings that illustrate the various paradigms for doing qualitative work, the strategies developed for studying people in their natural setting, and a variety of techniques for collecting, analyzing, interpreting, and reporting qualitative findings.

The conceptual foundations of qualitative research are explored in Anselm L. Strauss and Juliet M. Corbin, *Basics of Qualitative Research: Techniques and Procedures for Developing Grounded Theory* (Thousand Oaks, CA: Sage, 1998). Some treatments of specific methodologies include, Irving E. Seidman, *Interviewing as Qualitative Research: A Guide for Researchers in Education and the Social Sciences*, 2d ed. (New York: Teachers College Press, 1998), and Danny L. Jorgensen, *Participant Observation: A Methodology for Human Studies* (London: Sage, 1989). The analysis stage of qualitative research and the challenges of linking qualitative and quantitative methods are covered in Matthew B. Miles and A. Michael Huberman, *Qualitative Data Analysis: An Expanded Sourcebook* (Newbury Park, CA: Sage, 1994).

CHAPTER 18

ELITE AND SPECIALIZED INTERVIEWING

We begin our overview of selected qualitative methodologies with a discussion of in-depth (or intensive) interviewing techniques because they have a good deal in common with survey interviewing which we covered as one of the major quantitative techniques. This makes discussion of this technique a good transition to the different frame of reference called for by qualitative research. As you read this chapter you will see that this qualitative technique, like most others, can be designed to yield more or fewer quantitative results depending on the objectives of the project and prior knowledge of the researcher. Its greatest value, however, is not likely to be as a way to obtain precise measures of concepts, but as a means of gaining in-depth understanding of a phenomenon and discovering aspects of that phenomenon that you did not anticipate.

As you read about elite and specialized interviewing, be alert to the ways in which effective use of this technique requires attention to a different set of concerns than survey interviewing or any other quantitative data collection method. Pay special attention to the distinct "mind-set" required for qualitative inquiry. You will find that you must be less concerned with carrying out a precisely planned research design and measuring process than you are in quantitative research, and more concerned with being open to learning what your subjects can uniquely teach you about the subject.

Elite Interviewing

Many important research questions in political science can be answered only if we can learn how certain individuals or types of individuals think and act. For example, whereas we can always speculate about reasons for the passage of a specific piece of legislation, we can learn the actual reasons only by finding out what the legislators thought. Answering these types of questions requires **elite interviewing** rather than surveys of the general population.

In this context, people are referred to as *elite* if they have knowledge that, for the purposes of a given research project, requires that they be given individualized treatment in an interview. Their elite status depends not on their role in society but on their access to information that can help answer a given research question. While people who get elite treatment in research *are* often persons of political, social, or economic importance, they need not be.

A central difference between sample survey interviewing and elite interviewing is the degree to which the interview is *standardized*. In sample surveys, each respondent is treated as much like every other respondent as possible. This is because the purpose of the interview is to obtain specific information that can be used to make quantitative comparisons between respondents in an effort to generalize to some larger population. In elite interviewing, each respondent is treated differently to the extent that obtaining the information that that individual alone possesses requires unique treatment. The purpose of elite interviewing is generally not the collection of prespecified data but the gathering of information to assist in reconstructing some event or discerning a pattern in specific behaviors.

A second major difference between elite interviewing and survey interviewing is that whereas survey interviews are generally highly **scheduled interviews,** elite interviews are largely **unscheduled interviews.** An interview is highly *scheduled* if the questions to be asked and the order of their appearance are predetermined and inflexible. In a totally *unscheduled* interview, the interviewer is guided only by a general objective (for example, to find out how a given decision was made in a particular state agency) and has no predetermined set of questions to ask.

Highly scheduled interviews produce standardized data because they require that all respondents answer the same questions and select from the same options in answering. This has the advantage of allowing comparisons between respondents and facilitates data processing. Strict scheduling, however, has the disadvantage of restricting the information gained from interviews to that which the researcher has already decided is necessary for understanding the phenomena under study. Scheduling restricts the researcher's opportunities to learn what respondents consider relevant or important and to gain new theoretical insights.

Unscheduled interviews, by contrast, produce data that are difficult to condense and summarize and that may not allow precise comparisons among respondents. The asset accompanying this liability is a greater opportunity to learn from respondents and to acquire unexpected information that can lead to truly new ways of understanding the events being studied. Unscheduled interviews are especially suited to elite interviewing, because in elite interviewing, the researcher is interested in learning what the respondent perceives as important and relevant to the research and lets the respondent's observations suggest what questions should be asked in order to gain useful information. The interviewer is concerned with discovering facts and patterns rather than with measuring preselected phenomena.

Elite interviews can provide crucial information about political events that is otherwise unavailable. Elite interviewing involves some very real scientific risks, however. It generally means asking people who are deeply involved in a political process to shape the researcher's definition of the process. This may threaten the scientific validity of the information obtained if respondents (1) have so narrow a view of the events in question that they do not understand which aspects are important in explaining them; (2) have inaccurate information (either because they misperceived events in the first place or because they have forgotten important elements); (3) have convinced themselves, in order to rationalize their own actions, that things are one way when in fact they are another; or (4) intentionally lie in order to protect themselves or others. For example, interviews with ranking members of Richard Nixon's administration about the events referred to as Watergate might produce instances of invalid information for each of these reasons.

Though researchers cannot control what respondents say, they can guard against drawing invalid conclusions from elite interviews by following some general guidelines. First, never treat what interviewees say as factual data, but rather *treat the fact that they said it as data.* For an understanding of political behavior, it is often as important to know what people believe or claim to be true as it is to know what is true. For example, if you want to know why residents of a given community have organized to demand the closing of a nearby chemical plant, finding out how much of a safety hazard the plant actually poses may be less useful than finding out how much of a safety hazard residents *believe* the plant poses.

Second, never rely on a single respondent for information about any event, but obtain information about each event from as many respondents as possible before drawing conclusions.

Third, always seek ways of verifying information from elite interviews by comparing it with information from outside sources. If we interview party leaders to learn why a given candidate has been selected as the party's nominee in an election and respondents refer to "the obvious public support for the candidate" as their reason for supporting him or her, we will want to look for public opinion polls that supply evidence of the degree to which the public has supported the candidate.

Fourth, learn enough about the subject to be able to recognize incorrect statements or to perceptively analyze responses for possible sources of invalidity. We should be able to answer questions such as the following before engaging in elite interviewing: Is there any reason why respondents might want to believe something other than the truth or want to have others believe something other than the truth? Do they stand to gain economically or politically from given statements? What answers are plausible given the facts we know about the subject from other, reliable sources?

So serious are the threats to validity in elite interviewing that Lewis Dexter, a leading authority on the method, wrote:

> no one should plan or *finance* an entire study in advance with the expectation of relying chiefly on interviews for data *unless the interviewers have enough relevant background to be sure that they can make sense out of interview conversations or unless there is a reasonable hope of being able to hang around or in some way observe so as to learn what is meaningful and significant to ask.... Any planning for a study assuming a heavy reliance upon elite interviews should have a contingency plan ... so that if elite interviews prove basically uninformative some other technique can be substituted.*[1]

---

[1] Lewis Anthony Dexter, *Elite and Specialized Interviewing* (Evanston, IL: Northwestern University Press, 1970), p. 17; Dexter's italics.

Despite these drawbacks, elite interviewing has tremendous potential for shedding light on important political phenomena and can often be a valuable supplement to studies relying principally on other data collection techniques, as well as provide the sole basis for important conclusions. It is crucial to remember that information from people with inside knowledge is no substitute for a sound theoretical understanding of the subject. In order to reach scientifically valuable conclusions, political scientists must always impose their own analytic categories and conceptual schemes on the information gathered from elites.

Techniques of Elite Interviewing

One of the first questions faced in elite interviewing is whom to interview. In survey interviewing, all of the respondents are treated as equally able to contribute information that can be used in answering the research question, and sampling methods are available to help determine whom to interview. Elite interviewers have to assume that potential respondents differ in how much they can contribute to the study and that each respondent has something unique to offer. Often, background research will identify the entire population of those likely to have relevant information. If we are studying the decisions of a presidential commission, for instance, a little research will identify the members of the commission and their staff personnel, as well as any experts they may have relied on. However, if we are doing a "community power study" to determine who controls public policy in a certain city, we will not find any official list of people who exercise political influence in the city. Finding out whom to interview in this case is one of the objectives of the interviews themselves.

Once a group of potential interviewees has been identified, the question of what order to see them in arises. It is tempting to see first those people who should be most willing to talk and most sympathetic, or to want to see first the person believed to have the most information. Two things should be kept in mind, however.

First, elite interviewing is a process of discovery. We seldom come to the interviews knowing everything important to ask. Early interviews may teach us things that help us get the most useful information from subsequent interviews. Often it is best to interview the most central figures late in the study.

Second, in elite interviewing, we are generally not dealing with isolated and uninvolved persons, as we are in surveys. Each respondent is likely to have a unique (perhaps self-interested) view of the situation under study and may intentionally or unintentionally give inaccurate advice about who should be interviewed. Under no circumstances should the researcher let early interviewees' suggestions *determine* the choice or order of subsequent interviews, although those suggestions can provide partial data on which to base such decisions. Sometimes the fact that early interviewees have suggested certain other persons is evidence in itself, as it may reveal alliances or communication patterns.

In addition, because elite respondents are likely to know each other and be involved with the subject matter, the researcher must be cautious that early interviews do not jeopardize the study by identifying it with a particular group among the potential respondents. If possible, it is best to avoid interviewing first the mavericks, opposition leaders, persons thought to have extreme views, or leaders of any dominant coalition, because word of this may be passed to other interviewees and make them hostile or defensive.

Considering all this, researchers may find that the best initial interviews may be with people who are somewhat marginal to the situation but who are viewed as neutral or "mainstream" by most participants. In a study of politics in a state legislature, for example, it may be best to interview members of the legislative council (a general service agency used by all members of the legislature) first, rather than starting with key legislators. It is also wise to explain to the first respondents that the interview is preliminary and exploratory and that you may want to see them again because you may learn what other questions to ask or how to interpret answers only after subsequent conversations.

Actually arranging interviews with elite respondents can be quite difficult, because such individuals are often busy people and such interviews generally demand large amounts of their time (an hour or more is common). The following tips will generally help in securing interviews, *though it will sometimes be impossible or inadvisable to follow them in particular situations.*

1. Always call or write in advance to arrange for the interview rather than simply showing up, as in survey interviewing.

2. Be sure to request the interview by speaking with the person to be interviewed rather than a secretary or aide. You want to be certain the respondent understands the purpose of the meeting so he or she will not feel you are being deceitful.

3. Avoid highly detailed explanations of the purpose of the interview, because these can bias responses or cause potential respondents to refer you to a staff person who has "expert" knowledge.

4. Always try to determine the reasons for refusals, and try to see whether you can remove the cause. For example, if scheduling is a problem, you may offer to interview after work hours; if confidence is a problem, you may be able to secure references from people the potential respondent trusts.

5. Always have on hand materials that identify you and the sponsor of the research, in case questions arise. If possible, give contact information for someone who can verify the purpose and legitimacy of your study.

Once an interview has been arranged, it should *not* proceed by the rules given for survey interviewing. Dexter says that "the most nearly universal rule for elite and specialized interviewing is that *the best way to interview in a concrete situation depends upon the situation* (including the skills and personalities of the interviewers)."[2] Elite interviewers have to be more flexible and have a wider range of interviewing styles than survey interviewers, but there are some general guidelines that will fit most situations:

---

[2] Dexter, p. 23; Dexter's italics.

1. Always introduce yourself and restate the broad purpose of your study at the beginning of each interview rather than assuming that the respondent remembers these facts from a letter of introduction, phone call, or even a prior interview session with you.

2. The setting of an interview can be crucial. It is generally best to arrange a private interview away from potential distractions. Interviews over meals in restaurants or in the presence of the respondent's children usually do not go well. Occasionally, however, it is useful to have an interview in an unorthodox place (a park, the Lincoln Memorial, a bus) if it serves to put respondents at ease or jog their memory of past events.

3. Though group interviews can sometimes help produce a consensus on facts or reveal personal relationships, it is normally best to interview only one person at a time.

4. The tone of the interview should be reflective and conversational. Avoid firing questions in rapid succession. Do not be afraid of pauses as you or the respondent processes information and collects thoughts.

5. Plan initial questions carefully. Though the bulk of the interview will be unscheduled, the first few questions can be so important in focusing respondents' attention, stimulating their memory, and clarifying their perception of what you want that they should be planned in advance. Initial questions should be (a) clearly related to the stated purpose of the study, (b) likely to be answered with ease so that no ego threat arises, (c) phrased to show the respondent that the interviewer has knowledge about the subject of the study, and (d) conducive to the kind of free-flowing answers that the researcher hopes to receive in the interview rather than to flat, factual answers (if you need background information on the respondent, it can be obtained later in the interview). Questions that stress the respondent's feelings about or definition of a situation can be especially useful opening questions.

6. In contrast to survey research, questions should often be subject to multiple interpretations. Remember that the objective is to learn how *respondents* see the situation and what they feel is relevant.

7. Comments, as well as questions, can be used to evoke a response. A remark like, *That is not the way it is usually done,* for example, can lead to revelations about how respondents believe things do work.

8. Always maintain eye contact when possible (unless interviewees seem uncomfortable with this), and make it clear that you are listening intently and sympathetically. Phrases like *I see* or *Of course* or simply a thoughtful *Yes* can serve to encourage respondents and keep them talking.

9. Remember that one of the chief rewards respondents get from granting in-depth interviews is the chance to "teach" someone who is knowledgeable about and genuinely interested in a subject of great importance to them. It can be important to let them realize that they are, in fact, helping and informing you.

10. It is generally best to appear to accept whatever comments respondents make. Do not appear to reject their opinions or challenge their statements of fact.

11. An exception to rule 10 occurs when respondents are reluctant to reveal information you feel sure they have. In that situation, it may be necessary to employ what is often referred to as the *Nadel technique*.[3] Here you play the role of critic or antagonist, questioning and challenging respondents' remarks in hopes of forcing them to reveal information in order to defend their views or prove a point.

12. Respondents who are reluctant to divulge information because they fear the way it may be used can sometimes be reassured by a reminder that the information will be kept confidential or that the researcher is really not in any position to affect the situation in any way.

13. Note taking can be used as a tool to improve interviews. In elite interviewing (in contrast to survey interviewing, in which note taking should be kept inconspicuous), respondents can often be encouraged to give more information or stay on a given subject by the way an interviewer takes notes. Intense recording can serve as a cue that you find comments useful, and putting the pencil down altogether can signal that the respondent has ventured off the central topic. Because you have to take such extensive notes that it is probably impossible to be inconspicuous, you may as well use note taking for all it is worth.

14. Always be sensitive to the interviewee's personality and personal style, and adapt your tactics to it. Some people are highly formal and others very casual. Some deal in ideas almost exclusively, and others tend to personalize everything. Some people are accustomed to interacting mainly with superiors, and others mainly with subordinates. You may be able to get more information by adopting one of these roles. Never enter an interview with a fixed idea of the style you will use, but decide what is necessary as you talk with the respondent.

15. Always review your interview notes as soon as possible after the interview to elaborate at points where you could get only an outline and to make comments about your interpretation of the interview. This may mean sitting in a cold parking lot or buying an unwanted cup of coffee in order to have a place to write, but it is important to trust to memory as little as possible.

16. Type up handwritten notes as soon as possible. Make several hard or electronic copies and store them in separate places to insure against loss.

Tape recorders are controversial tools in interviewing. Obviously they can help you avoid mistakes about what is actually said, and they can capture subtle facts about the *way* in which things are said. They can also help interviewers learn how they sound to respondents. This is useful because the way in which a question is asked can be important to consider in interpreting a response. A drawback is that respondents are often inhibited by a tape recorder, because it denies them the chance of claiming that they have not made some remark if it later proves embarrassing. Sometimes they fear that technicians can edit the tape to make it appear as if they had said things they have not. Moreover, the mechanics of working the recorder can distract from the interview.

---

[3] This approach was first popularized in S. F. Nadel, "The Interview Technique in Social Anthropology," in F. C. Bartlett et al., eds., *The Study of Society* (London: Kegan Paul, Trench, Trubner & Co., 1939), pp.317–27.

Researchers must decide about the use of recorders on the basis of the type of question they are investigating, the nature of the interviews they expect, and the character of the respondents. If the subject matter is highly sensitive or respondents are likely to be inhibited by recorders, the costs of using them probably outweigh the advantages. If lengthy, detailed, and technical interviews are necessary and specific facts are crucial to the study, recorders may be necessary.

If a recorder is used, the researcher should ask permission to use it and should place the device in full view of the respondent. Pretest the recorder to ensure that it is suitable for the kind of interview anticipated (sufficiently sensitive, simple to operate, able to play long enough tapes). *Never depend exclusively on a recorder.* It can malfunction and cause the loss of an irreplaceable interview. Always take written notes as well.

A final issue in elite interviewing is confidentiality. This can be more important with elite interviews than with surveys, because elites are often asked for information that, if revealed or misused, may have considerable public impact. If confidentiality is promised, and it generally must be, *researchers should make every reasonable effort to safeguard information.* This is often easier than in survey research, because large numbers of personnel are not generally required in elite studies, but interviewers can buy a little insurance by storing records in secure places and keeping the purpose of the study from becoming general knowledge, if possible. The most common threat to confidentiality occurs when a typist is used to record handwritten notes or taped interviews. If researchers absolutely cannot do this work themselves, they should both employ only dependable people to do it and conceal from the typist the identity of respondents when possible. Never make interview records available to people not involved in the project.

Specialized Interviewing

In some studies, political scientists do not want to obtain information from specific individuals, as in the case of elite interviewing, or from respondents who are representative of the general population, as in surveys, but need information from persons who are representative or typical of some particular group within the population. This often calls for **specialized interviewing.**

A specialized interview is any interview in which the characteristics of respondents demand procedures different from those employed in standardized survey interviewing. Interviews with children, illiterate adults, prison inmates, homeless persons, non–English-speaking migrant workers, mental patients, and members of a religious cult are all examples.

Such interviews differ from survey interviewing in several ways. One is that researchers cannot assume that they and their respondents share a *common vocabulary.* Words that researchers use frequently may not be understood by respondents. Similarly, respondents may use terms or slang with which the researcher is not familiar or may use conventional words in special ways the researcher does not understand. A second distinctive feature of specialized interviews is that interviewers often cannot assume that respondents can read or have the ability to reason or follow a line of argument that would be expected of an average person in the culture. In addition, specialized interview situations often involve distinctive relationships between respondents and interviewers. Whereas ordinary respondents regard interviewers largely as equals who can be trusted to a degree and treated cordially, specialized subjects may view interviewers as authority figures or "outsiders" and may be hostile and suspicious. In these circumstances, communication can be difficult and the validity of responses can suffer.

All of these features of specialized interviews combine to create settings in which researchers cannot take communication for granted. Rather, interviewers have to carefully establish a basis for communication and then check to be sure that communication is occurring.

Consider this example. If we want to know the degree to which children consider the U.S. political system legitimate, we first need to define the concept of legitimacy and be sure that our young respondents know what we mean when we speak of the political system. Once we have verified their grasp of these concepts and have asked our central questions, we need to ask additional questions to determine whether the children's answers mean to them what we would expect the same answers to mean if they came from typical adults. One way to do this is first to give our respondents examples of children acting in ways that suggest they accord either a high or a low level of legitimacy to some institution, then to ask our respondents to interpret the actions described as showing either high or low legitimation, and then to tell us whether or not they would be likely to take these same actions. If children frequently misinterpret the fictitious actions or say they would take actions that are inconsistent with the level of legitimacy they have told us they accord the political system, we will not feel safe in assuming that they understand their answers in the same way we do.

Interviews can be an enormously rich source of data for social scientists. But they require the development of almost artistic skills to be effectively used. No amount of reading about in-depth interviews can substitute for experience with them.

Suggestions for Further Reading

Two texts that explain in-depth interviewing in detail are Steinar Kvale, *Interviews: An Introduction to Qualitative Research Interviewing* (Thousand Oaks, CA: Sage, 1996) and Herbert J. Rubin and Riene S. Rubin, *Qualitative Interviewing: The Art of Hearing Data* (Thousand Oaks, CA: Sage, 1995). For an examination of the role of interviewing in the larger context of qualitative methodologies, see John Lofland and Lyn H. Lofland, *Analyzing Social Settings: A Guide to Qualitative Observation and Analysis,* 3d ed. (Belmont, CA: Wadsworth, 1995). Carl V. Patton and David S. Sawicki, *Basic Methods of Policy Analysis and Planning* (Englewood Cliffs, NJ: Prentice Hall, 1993), pp. 97–105, offers a description of the use of in-depth interviewing in public policy research.

Research Exercises

1. State a research question that can be answered through elite interviewing. List the types of information you would need in order to answer the question, and identify either by name or by official position (for example, all federal district court judges in the eleven Southern states), the people you would expect to interview in gathering that information.

Tell what steps you would take to ensure the validity of your conclusions. How would you check the accuracy of what respondents tell you?

2. (*Do not undertake this exercise without permission from your instructor.*)

   a. State a research question dealing with the local government of your community or with decision making in your college that can be studied through elite interviewing. List the types of information you will be seeking and the specific persons you will have to interview.

   b. After the project has been approved by your instructor, arrange and conduct interviews with three of the persons you need to interview. (*Remember:* You need to tell these people that this is part of a class assignment, so do not set your sights too high. You may well be unable to see the mayor of a large city or the president of a large university. Also, to avoid embarrassing yourself and creating a poor opinion of students at your school, you should do enough background research to ask intelligent questions on the subject you have selected.)

   Type up the notes from the interviews along with all of your observations about the significance and interpretation of different remarks. Explain what you have learned about the subject from these interviews, state what else you need to know, and tell how you would proceed if you were going to carry the research further. Also identify any steps you feel could be used to verify the information gained in the three interviews.

Terms Introduced in This Chapter

elite interviewing
scheduled interviews

unscheduled interviews
specialized interviewing

CHAPTER 19

DIRECT OBSERVATION

In the other data collection techniques we have discussed in this text, researchers must rely to some degree on others' experience with the political events they are seeking to understand. When we use aggregate data, we usually rely on information collected by public or private agencies to represent the events we are studying—we do not actually observe coups, agricultural production, the distribution of income, or any of the other phenomena represented by the figures with which we work. Even when we conduct surveys, we are relying on respondents' memories of their experiences or perceptions of their surroundings—we do not actually observe their actions or the setting in which those actions occurred. Although there is a great deal to be learned through these data collection methods, there are times when researchers need to see and hear events for themselves in order to gain a full understanding of them.

One circumstance in which this may be the case occurs when a new phenomenon develops and demands study for the first time. For example, the alternative political parties that developed in the authoritarian states of Eastern Europe in the 1990s were a new phenomenon—political parties seeking to gain power through elections in previously non-democratic Soviet bloc nations. To understand their functioning, we could try to apply theories of political party behavior that have been developed by observation of parties in democratic nations of the West. However, there are good reasons to suspect that these new parties will operate according to very different rules because they exist in a dramatically different context from, say, Canadian or French political parties. To formulate theories about their operation, we may need to observe them firsthand.

A second situation calling for direct contact with the subject of research is one in which we cannot be confident of the usefulness of others' reports of some ongoing behavior. In some cases, even though we could interview participants in the events we are interested in, we may feel they will be unable to give us the understanding we need, because they do not share our conceptual framework. We might, for instance, be looking for the effects of institutionalized ideology on the decisions of U.S. embassy personnel in handling requests for political asylum. If we ask the officials how they made decisions, they will quite sincerely cite the written rules they followed. But if we saw for ourselves the procedures followed, we might be able to identify unofficial ideological criteria at work.

Another situation in which we might not be willing to rely on others' accounts of events is one in which those who can supply the information might have a personal or professional interest in misleading us. Real estate agents, for example, would have good reasons for giving the impression that they always comply with federal equal housing opportunity laws even if they knew that their practices often did not satisfy the requirements of that legislation.

In these and other circumstances, researchers may need to turn to **direct observation.** When we collect data by direct contact with the events we are studying *as they happen,* we are employing direct observation.

Scientific Method and Direct Observation

Despite its rich potential for providing insight, direct observation is not used very often by political scientists. One reason for this is that many of the subjects political scientists study are too large in scale to allow direct observation. Elections, for example, happen all over a nation simultaneously and therefore cannot be physically observed directly as complete events. Individual researchers must rely on indirect observation.

A second reason for the infrequent use of direct observation in political science is that we often do not have access to events that could fruitfully be studied by this method. Spontaneous popular uprisings such as those that unseated the Milosevic government in Serbia in 2000, for example, occur too rapidly to allow us to plan a research project. Similarly, even ongoing phenomena may be inaccessible to us. We would be unlikely to get permission to observe the White House staff making national security decisions, for instance.

A third set of reasons that we do not see more use of direct observation relate to the nature of the method. First, it is usually a very time-consuming technique that may take months or years to produce results and can be quite expensive to carry out. Second, it often demands a great deal of the researcher, who may have to become immersed in the study to the exclusion of other activities, and it can seldom be carried out by assistants.

Political scientists, however, often choose not to use direct observation, even when it is appropriate and possible, because they question its scientific validity. This is usually a result of either or both of two concerns. First, there is often a perception that direct observation produces highly *subjective data* dependent on the unique insights and, perhaps, biases of the observer. Second, some direct observation, as we explain later, generally produces only *qualitative* data. Because some researchers think that only quantitative data can be scientific, there is a tendency to view data collected through direct observation as "soft" (subjective and subject to challenge). Neither of these concerns is totally without foundation. Improperly done direct observation *can* produce highly subjective results that are influenced by the researcher's preconceptions. Even well-executed observations depend a great deal on the skill, energy, and insight of the observer and may be difficult to reproduce. In addition, much of the data that come from direct observation *are* qualitative in nature and do not lend themselves to standard data analysis techniques.

These facts, however, for at least five reasons, should not deter social scientists from using direct observation.

1. Research has different purposes at different stages of the study of a topic, and as discussed in Chapters 1 and 5, the requirements for scientific precision differ with the purpose of research. Direct observation is especially well suited to the exploratory and descriptive stages of research, when we are seeking to *develop* theories rather than to test them. Descriptive research can be crucial to the scientific process in that it can provide an accurate picture of how a social or political process unfolds. A description of the process can serve as a foundation for using inductive logic to devise testable theories that provide a scientific understanding of the phenomenon in question. When used at the proper stage of the research process, direct observation is not only adequate to the task but often far superior to other methods of data collection.

2. Many of the fears about subjectivity in reporting results can be overcome by proper execution of direct observation. If researchers follow correct procedures in making and recording observations, it is possible for others to verify their conclusions or at least judge the degree of confidence that should be placed in them.

3. Even qualitative data can be analyzed in rigorous and objective ways if the analyst employs the right techniques. The fact that direct observation may produce primarily qualitative data, therefore, need not be taken as a major limitation on its applicability.

4. Under the right conditions, and with the right approach, direct observation can even be used to *test* theories and should not be ruled out as a potential data-gathering technique in explanatory research.

5. Against any of the limitations associated with the method, we must weigh the fact that direct observation has the distinct advantage of providing a very high level of *external validity* for our research. Because we observe *actual behavior* (not oral reports, written accounts, or simulations of it) and observe it *in the context in which it naturally occurs,* we can obtain a realistic view of the events of concern to us and can get highly valid measures of our concepts. Moreover, in some types of direct observation, *reactivity may be less than with more obvious data-gathering techniques.*

In the rest of this chapter, we explore the potential of direct observation and suggest some methods for using it to its full potential.

Approaches to Direct Observation

Direct observation can take several forms. First, we can distinguish between *obtrusive* and *unobtrusive* approaches. **Obtrusive research** occurs anytime the persons being studied are aware of being observed. It always carries some risk of provoking reactivity and, thus, producing at least partially invalid results. **Unobtrusive research** occurs anytime subjects are unaware of being observed and, therefore, unlikely to alter their natural behaviors in response to the research itself. This has the advantage of increasing the chances of obtaining valid data.

Direct observation can be either obtrusive or unobtrusive. In *obtrusive* observation, the researcher or trained assistants request permission to observe subjects and are identified as observers at the time of the data collection. An example of this approach is the case in which an investigator attends meetings of a committee of the state legislature and observes its decision-making processes. Committee members are aware of the observer and know the general purpose of the study.

In *unobtrusive* observation, the researcher is either concealed from those being studied or is visible, but the purpose of the observation is unknown to the subjects of the study. In the first type of study, the observer might be concealed from view or might use a hidden camera. An example would be a project in which the researcher is given permission to study the behavior of public personnel by observing the interaction of welfare clients and welfare agency caseworkers from behind a two-way mirror when neither the caseworkers nor the clients know they are being observed. In the second type, the observer may be in full view, but the purpose of the study is concealed. There are two versions of unobtrusive observation.

The first is exemplified by a case in which a researcher attends all public meetings of a city council and openly sits with other citizens in the audience but carefully watches the debate to analyze patterns of influence on the council *without the knowledge of the council members*. A second form of unobtrusive observation is known as *participant observation*. When researchers actually become part of the events under study, they are engaging in **participant observation**. The researcher studying a given political organization who joined that group as any other citizen might, attended its meetings, served on its committees, took part in its fund-raising efforts, voted on its policies, and otherwise acted as a member *without the other members of the organization knowing that they were being observed as part of a study* would be using unobtrusive participant observation.

The obvious advantage of unobtrusive observation is that it virtually eliminates the possibility that subjects will alter their behavior in reaction to being studied and can yield highly valid information. However, unobtrusive observations can be very difficult to arrange and conduct and, as we discuss later in this chapter, often pose serious ethical questions for the scholar.

A second division of approaches to direct observation is made between *structured* and *unstructured studies*. This distinction is made on the basis of the degree to which the researcher organizes or *structures* the process of observation by imposing a preconceived set of concepts and categories. In a **structured observation**, we use our understanding of the events under scrutiny to construct a *protocol* to guide the observer. The protocol tells the observer what to look for, the order in which to make observations, and the way to record the results. This approach is especially suited for gaining accurate descriptions of events.

As an illustration, we might want to study the ways in which members of the U.S. Congress use debate on the floor of the House of Representatives to gain support from interest groups and constituents. If we have a strong enough theory of how this is done, we could develop a checksheet listing the techniques that we expect to be used. We could then observe floor debates and use the checksheet to record whether or not each representative used given devices to send messages to potential supporters. The protocol would restrict our attention to a limited range of what was happening when representatives made public statements but would provide more objective data than a survey and would facilitate comparisons of the behavior of different House members.

By contrast, if we were in an earlier stage of our study of this subject, we might be unwilling to restrict our observations to a list of items on a protocol. Such a situation would call for use of **unstructured observation,** in which we attempt to pay attention to all that goes on in a debate, to take careful notes, and to analyze the notes in an effort to discover patterns that can provide a basis for theorizing about how representatives use floor debate to influence potential supporters.

Structured and unstructured observation can be combined in a single research project. In fact, it is quite common for researchers using direct observation to mix the two approaches and is usually highly beneficial. A study may start with unstructured observation to gain a broad understanding of an event and formulate concepts with which to analyze it. The researcher may then use these insights to structure subsequent observations of the same phenomenon in order to test the utility of the conceptualizations. Alternatively, the two approaches may be combined by structuring portions of the observational task while leaving other parts unstructured.

It is important to recognize that the distinction between structured and unstructured observations is *not* a true dichotomy, with "pure" types of observation on either side. It is a continuum ranging from the least structured to the most structured methods of observation. Even the least formally structured observation involves an element of structure in that the researcher approaches the task with a set of questions about the event under study and with perceptions of how it might work that direct attention to certain aspects of the event more than to others. Similarly, even in a highly structured observation, an alert researcher often notices unexpected qualities of the phenomena under study and may learn more than what is anticipated by the observation protocol. In this sense, the two approaches to observation are almost always blended to some degree.

We can offer some guidelines for the effective use of structured and unstructured techniques in both obtrusive and unobtrusive research.

Techniques of Unstructured Observation

Unstructured observation is used to develop a full understanding of the behaviors and relationships under study. It requires that investigators be open to discovering new dimensions to the behavior and willing to devise new ways of thinking about the topic. Observers are seeking to be taught by the world and want to get as close to the reality of the events as possible without being so constrained by preconceived notions of how things work that they overlook some important patterns.

The procedure for unstructured observation begins with identifying the set of behaviors that have to be observed in order to acquire a full understanding of the events in question. Refining the research question so that it provides a better guide to observation may require doing some background reading, talking with others who have had contact with the subject, and engaging in some very preliminary theorizing about what processes might be at work.

Next, the researcher needs to gain access to the subjects for purposes of observation. How this is done depends on whether he or she is using obtrusive or unobtrusive methods, and varies with the details of the project. It can be one of the most challenging portions of the work. Clearly, some subjects will be less willing to be observed than others, and most subjects will find some objectives in the study to be more acceptable than others. For example, revolutionaries conducting a guerrilla war will not be open to outsiders under almost any circumstances. By contrast, bureaucrats who may be willing to cooperate with research described as "a study of chains of command in public agencies" may be quite unwilling to participate in "a study of corruption in the management of public agencies."

This early step in the research process may very well present an ethical dilemma: Do you tell people they are being observed and, if so, do you tell them the real purpose of the study even if doing so risks losing their cooperation or at least creating a serious problem of reactivity? We address this and other ethical issues of direct observation later in this chapter. For now, assume that the ethical questions are resolved in favor of taking an obtrusive approach and that we can move to the third stage in the process.

The primary activity here is to observe and take careful notes on all that is seen and heard. The *written record of observations* is referred to as **field notes**. Though field notes are not as structured as interview notes, there are definite general rules for proper taking of field notes.

First, you should *clearly define the objectives of the research* so that you know what you want to learn about the events under observation. From that you can develop a list of the types of things you are looking for, so as to focus your attention on those features of the events that are most important to observe. Having such a list is not inconsistent with keeping an open mind and being willing to change your focus as you gain a better understanding of the behaviors in question. It merely simplifies the task of reducing all that you will observe to a manageable number of entries for your notes.

This list will be nothing more than a set of broad categories of information you hope to obtain about the events you are observing. For example, if you were observing meetings of opposing teams of negotiators who represented two sides of a civil war, you might want to note such things as (1) how often each side initiates proposals, (2) how eager each side seems to be to continue the talks as opposed to breaking them off, (3) how willing each side is to make concessions, and (4) whether each negotiating team is united or seems divided into factions. As you learn more about the process, you will want to refine these broad, overlapping categories into a more focused list of things to look for, with each observation building on what you learned in the prior one.

Second, you should *never take notes in the presence of those who are being observed*. The primary reason for this is that open note taking can make your subjects even more aware of your presence and cause them to alter their normal behavior. Your objective is to put the subjects so at ease that they act exactly as they would if you were not present. This requires that you develop the skill of making *mental notes* of all that you see that is relevant to the study so that you can write up detailed notes later. This is a difficult task, so in advance of going to the field, it is wise to practice mental note taking by observing some group or individual engaged in activities similar to those you are to study and then trying to re-create the events on paper later. If the practice subjects agree and you have the necessary equipment and setting, you can check on your accuracy by recording or filming the events observed and comparing with the recorded record of the events the impression conveyed by your field notes.

Though you should not take detailed notes in the presence of subjects, it is sometimes possible to keep a small notebook concealed so you can inconspicuously jot down key words or phrases that will later serve to jog your memory of events when writing up field notes.

Third, *always write up field notes as soon as possible after actual observation* so that your memory of the events is clear. This is often difficult, because you may be tired at the end of several hours of observations and there may not be a convenient place to sit to write up your notes. However, it is *essential* that you find a way to get the observations on paper as soon as possible so that you have a detailed and accurate record. Some investigators expedite this process by using a tape recorder or dictaphone to record their field notes verbally and then have them transcribed later. If you choose this approach, it is crucial to immediately check the tape to ensure that it worked properly; in that way, you will avoid discovering several days later, when you may find it difficult to re-create them from memory, that notes from an observation session have been lost.

It may take up to half as much time to make notes on observations as it took to actually make the observations, but this is time well spent because *field notes are the foundation of a direct observation project.*

Fourth, *make field notes as complete and detailed as possible.* Especially in the early stages of a project, it is important to put in almost everything that was observed. Facts that at first seemed unimportant may turn out to be crucial as you acquire a fuller understanding of the topic.

Fifth, *always distinguish clearly in your notes between descriptions of actual behavior and your speculation about the meaning or importance of that behavior.* It should be clear to you, even after your memory of the events has faded, what was actually said and done by the subjects and what you *inferred* about their behavior at the time.

Because the content of field notes is dictated by the objectives of an individual project, it is difficult to state rules for what to include. In general, however, it is better to include too much than to risk leaving out useful information. Excessive detail in field notes may complicate the task of analyzing them, but this problem can be dealt with. There is no way to remedy the problem of not having information if you failed to put it in at the time. Remember that one of the major objectives of direct observation is the creation of a complete and accurate description of a political phenomenon. More detail, therefore, is usually preferable to less.

Figure 19.1 provides an example of the kind of information that is recorded in field notes. It presents observations from a hypothetical study of several communi-

Figure 19.1
Example of transcribed field notes from
hypothetical study of community organizations

October 24, 2000. Observation of a demonstration by members of the Waterside Neighborhood Improvement Assoclation to protest the announcement by the city government of plans to open a landfill on some abandoned property in the Waterside neighborhood.

Background: The Waterside community is composed of large old homes that were left behind as members of the upper class abandoned the city for the suburbs in the 1950s and 1960s. Today it is a fairly poor area with few remaining local businesses and inhabited almost exclusively by Hispanics. The neighborhood organization was formed in 1985 to combat problems of crime, unemployment, and poor public services in the area.

Observations: The demonstration was held on the steps of city hall during the noon hour, when a large number of people were entering and leaving the building. The organization had obtained a permit from the police department, and all members remained on a grassy area beside the main entrance so that they did not block pedestrian traffic. Thirty-three members of the Waterside Association took part in the demonstration. In addition, there were two officials of the Catholic church, the president of a statewide Hispanic political organization, and a member of the city council, who represents the neighborhood. The event was covered by two reporters from the local paper, a camera crew and reporter from each of the two local TV stations, and a reporter from National Public Radio.

The demonstration began promptly at noon and consisted of the following activities: (1) Throughout the demonstration, 12 of the participants waved handmade signs with slogans condemning the landfill. They were careful to face the TV cameras at all times. (2) The association president, the city councilman, and the state political leader (in that order) each stood on an old oil drum the demonstrators had brought to the site to make speeches lasting about 10 minutes each. (3) Between each speech, a very energetic member of the group used a megaphone to lead chants about the injustice of the landfill decision. The chants were defiant in tone (e.g., "We won't take your trash!"), and one accused the mayor of "selling out." All members of the association who attended the demonstration were very active during the action, shouting, cheering, clapping, calling out to passersby, and shaking their fists in the cameras. The demonstration ended with a short speech and prayer by one of the priests. The signs and chants were in English, but the speeches were primarily in Spanish. Each speaker referred at least once to the fact that Waterside was a Hispanic community. Each asked at least once why the landfill was not put in Carlton (an affluent predominantly white neighborhood at the edge of the city, which had been recommended by a consultant's study as the most logical site).

When she was not speaking, the president of the Waterside association was moving among the demonstrators, encouraging them to wave their signs, shout, and otherwise show their feelings. She pulled reporters into the middle of the group on three occasions and coached the camera crews on what to shoot. Comments made by the other speakers revealed she had personally invited them to attend and speak. While the group was returning to the neighborhood on a church bus borrowed for the occasion, the president made a statement about how she was sure that the event had made a difference and how important it was for Hispanics to stand up for their rights. She then went down the aisle and personally thanked everyone on the bus for taking part in the demonstration, using a lot of handshaking, backslapping, and hugs. Everyone else had carried out the tasks assigned to them, but no one seemed to share responsibility for making the demonstration work.

Comments: This group has a well-organized. highly disciplined core of active members and a good deal of support from other community institutions. The president, however, appears to be the main moving force. She seems to come up with most of the ideas and to mobllize others with her energy. The members seem to be motivated by a combination of ethnic pride and social solidarity. Much of what they do is predicated on their minority status, but they also seem to have developed a sense of comradeship in which each one carries on partly because they do not want to let the others down. The president apparently encourages both of these tendencies—perhaps because she knows that she can't promise the members much In the way of material rewards. I can't help but wonder how the organization would survive if she stepped down. She takes on so much responsibility that no one else seems to be getting any leadership training. Her strength may be the organization's weakness.

ty organizations in which the investigator is seeking to understand how leaders of these organizations persuade residents of a neighborhood to join and remain in the group. Note the detail in which events are recorded. Notice also how notes on actual events are set off from interpretations or analysis of those events.

The next stage in the direct observation project is to analyze the field notes. With other methods there is a clear distinction between data collection and data analysis. This is not true of direct observation, because the process of making field notes blends both data collection (writing down descriptions of what happened) and analysis (noting your impressions about the reasons for or importance of what happened). *Data analysis begins with the making of field notes.* Moreover, in direct observation, the researcher must not wait until all the data are in to begin analysis. It is vital that investigators review field notes from time to time *during* the period in which they are making observations. The purpose of this is to begin to look for patterns in what has been observed so as to be alert to the most important aspects of events in the next observation session.

Once all observation has been completed, you will formally shift to data analysis. With direct observation data, this means *using inductive reasoning to discover patterns among the many discrete facts recorded in the field notes.* The first step is usually to review the notes in order to find some meaningful categories to use in distinguishing among the events observed.

As an example, consider a hypothetical study of legislative committees designed to investigate the degree to which they are subject to influence by organized interest groups. You might observe the meetings of several committees and then ask: Are there any systematic differences in the way these groups function? After examining your notes, you may decide that the groups differ along two important dimensions: the degree to which power is centralized in the formal leaders versus being widely shared among the members, and the degree to which the groups are businesslike and rule driven in transacting their business versus being more collegial and relying on personal interaction. If we break these two dimensions in the middle and juxtapose them, we get the typology of committee operating styles presented in Figure 19.2, and we have a way of classifying committees for analysis.

The next step in analysis would be to examine the field notes for evidence of differences *between* and *within* categories or types. In the example of a study of congressional committees, we would ask if committees of different types responded differently to interest groups and if the same type of committee treated different types of interest groups differently. We might ask if it seems to be easier for interest groups to gain access to some types of committees than to others or if the ease of access

Style of Operation	Power Configuration	
	Decentralized	Centralized
Collegial	Populist	Machine
Rule driven	Democratic	Authoritarian

Figure 19.2
Hypothetical typology of congressional committees

depends more on the characteristics of the interest group (such as how well financed it is, how professional its lobbying staff is, or how politically active it is in the representatives' home districts).

The major challenge in both taking and analyzing field notes is to avoid the natural tendency to see only that which we anticipate in the processes we observe. If we are to gain a truly accurate understanding of these events, it is crucial that we be open to the possibility that things do not work as we expected and *avoid imposing patterns* that are not there. An excellent example of this need for an open mind in field research is found in Michael K. Brown, *Working the Street* (New York: Russell Sage Foundation, 1981), which is based on a direct-observation study of police officers' exercise of discretion in enforcing laws. Brown reports that he began the study with the assumption that all officers used a common set of unwritten rules to guide their exercise of discretion and that his task was to discover what those common rules were. As he observed, he realized that each officer operated differently in this respect, so he shifted the focus of his research to understanding these individual differences. The result was a far more sophisticated understanding of the functioning of "street-level bureaucrats."

One technique for keeping an open mind about your subject and ensuring that you are not overlooking important relationships is to occasionally ask trusted colleagues who are *not* involved with your research project to read over portions of your field notes and share their impressions of what is going on with you. They may be able to see patterns that your preconceived theory of the events has hidden from you.

Techniques of Structured Observation

If unstructured observation is used to gain a more refined and accurate understanding of political behavior so that we can develop theories of it, structured observation is used to verify the utility of our understandings and to test hypotheses derived from our theories. Conducting a structured observation requires that we have a clear idea of what we expect to see when we observe and what specific behaviors we are looking for. We are interested primarily in *recording specific behaviors,* not in finding the meaning our subjects attach to their behaviors or the patterns that unite those behaviors. It is similar to carrying out a survey or a content analysis in that we are guided by an instrument that makes our observation very systematic and facilitates recording what we see in ways that make comparing cases easier. In direct observation, this instrument is known as an *observation schedule.*

An **observation schedule** is a detailed list of specific things to be observed and a system for recording them. The content and design of observation schedules depend on the nature of the research project and can vary *widely* so that it is difficult to provide firm guidelines for their construction. Our objective here is merely to suggest some very general rules to follow and techniques to use in designing useful observation schedules.

Before we turn to a discussion of those rules, it is important to mention three features of structured observation that set the context for development of an observation schedule. First, structured observation can be either obtrusive or unobtrusive. However, because the observer must pay attention to a great many details and is most concerned with precision in recording events, *it is essential that observations be recorded as they are made.* As a result, structured observations run a greater risk of creating reactivity than unstructured ones do when they are done obtrusively. Subjects who see an observer busily taking notes on their actions are very likely to be keenly aware that they are being studied and may alter their behavior as a result. Structured techniques, then, are probably most effective when used unobtrusively.

An additional implication of the need in structured observation to record events as they happen is that *it is almost never possible to use structured techniques in a participant observation.* It would be virtually impossible to keep detailed records of behaviors while acting as a participant in most groups and would almost certainly give away your purpose in being there.

The second contextual feature of structured methods to consider before discussing the construction of observation schedules is that structured observations are often made by someone *other than the principal investigator.* Because the observations are more routine and often more numerous than those involved in unstructured methods, researchers commonly hire assistants to carry out the observations. This means that the observation schedule must be detailed and informative enough that it (1) can be used by an assistant *as the researcher intends it to be used* and (2) leaves very little discretion to the observer, so that the observations recorded by different assistants can legitimately be compared.

Finally, it is important to recognize the basic design of a structured observation in order to understand what is needed in an observation schedule. This design involves first identifying a *unit of analysis* for the study. In direct observation, units of analysis usually consist of recurring events. Examples are a compromise at a negotiating session, a debate on a motion before the U.N. Security Council, and an argument between members of opposing groups at a demonstration in front of an abortion clinic.

After identification of a unit of analysis, the next step is to *designate the aspects of that event to be observed.* Here is where the observation schedule comes in. An observation schedule is far more than a simple checklist in several ways: (1) It often provides more than simple yes or no options for recording behaviors. Observers are usually asked to record events in degrees or frequencies. (2) It usually contains instructions on *how* to conduct the observations by telling the observer what procedures to follow. (3) It generally includes some fairly detailed definitions of the behaviors to be observed so that observers know what to look for.

That last feature is vitally important. An observation schedule *is always based on operational definitions of the behaviors in question.* If it is to be useful, it must reduce a set of potentially complex events to basic elements so that the observer can be sure when the event has been observed and can distinguish it from other, similar behaviors or events. To do this, an observation schedule breaks events into discrete variables, gives the observer an operational definition of each, and provides a scheme for recording observations of it.

To illustrate, let us return to the example of the study of the operating styles of congressional committees. One unit of analysis for such a study might be a public disagreement among members of the committee. The researcher would need to define what constitutes a disagreement and then identify the features of the event (the variables) to be observed—that is, the dimensions along which to classify each disagreement. These dimensions can be highly specific or quite broad. In the committee study, we might want to know something as specific as how often the parties to the disagreement interrupted each other, whether or not certain words were used by either side, and who spoke last. Alternatively, the dimensions may be as broad as whether the tone of the argument was hostile or cordial, whether or not it seemed to be conducted within mutually accepted norms, or what role the committee chair played in mediating the argument.

Which approach is better depends on the specific research project. However, *the broader the dimensions to be observed, the greater the discretion the observer has in classifying events.* More narrow dimensions may seem to trivialize the subject, but they have the advantage of limiting observers' discretion and, thereby, producing data that are more standardized and more comparable from observation to observation. Researchers are usually well-advised to be as specific as possible in constructing an observation schedule.

A major reason for this is that one of the most important rules for designing an observation schedule is that *the categories used to classify events must be exhaustive and mutually exclusive.* It must be possible to place all observed events in some category. However, it must not be logically possible to place any single observation in more than one category, because if it is, the classification is totally up to the observer and the meaning of any record of the event is lost. The best way to achieve this mutual exclusivity of categories is to be very specific—to break larger variables down into smaller ones. For example, rather than asking the general question about whether or not a disagreement seemed to be governed by mutually accepted norms, we might ask if the parties to the argument interrupted one another, raised their voices, or yielded the floor promptly when asked to do so by the chair.

Figure 19.3 is a segment of a hypothetical study of community organizations in which the meeting is the unit of analysis. Note that some items require only that the observer record objectively verifiable information about the meeting (when it started, how many people were in attendance, etc.), whereas other items require a judgment on the part of the observer (whether the members paid attention to the chair when the chair spoke, if the members were cordial and friendly to each other before the opening of the meeting, etc.). This mix is almost inevitable, but the investigator should provide observers with clear instructions on how to make a judgment about those matters that require judgment. It is wise to check their understanding of these instructions by having the assistant record observations of an event that the researcher also observes and then comparing the assistant's classification of events with those of the investigator.

Those who use structured observation to gather data have to be just as concerned with the validity and reliability of their measurements as those who use other data collection techniques. It is therefore important to build into the data-collection effort ways to check on this. Since data from an observation schedule are quantitative, they can be analyzed with standard statistical techniques and are subject to the same tests of validity and reliability discussed in Chapter 4.

However, the observation schedule almost always gives observers some degree of discretion about how to record events. Therefore, if more than one observer is

```
┌─────────────────────────────────────────────────────────────────────────┐
│                COMMUNITY ORGANIZATION OBSERVATION SCHEDULE                │
│                                                                           │
│   1.  a. Name of organization _____    │
│       b. Date and time of meeting _____      │
│       c. Location of meeting _____      │
│       d. Nature of meeting:   (1) regular business                        │
│                               (2) annual meeting                          │
│                               (3) special or emergency                    │
│                               (8) other _____       │
│       e. Purpose of meeting:  (1) routine business                        │
│                               (2) to elect officers                       │
│                               (3) to discuss a problem                    │
│                               (4) social gathering                        │
│                               (5) to recognize members/accomplishments    │
│                               (8) other _____       │
│                                                                           │
│   2.  Premeeting socializing: (1) less than half participated             │
│                               (2) about half participated                 │
│                               (3) most members participated               │
│                                                                           │
│   3.  a. Was there a written agenda for the meeting?   YES   NO           │
│       b. If yes, was it distributed to the members?   YES   NO            │
│       c. If yes, when was it distributed?   (1) before the day of the     │
│                                                  meeting                   │
│                                             (2) just prior to the meeting │
│                                             (3) after the meeting         │
│                                                                           │
│   4.  How many people attended the meeting? _____                     │
│                                                                           │
│   5.  a. Was the meeting open to the public?  YES   NO                    │
│       b. How many persons who were apparently not members attended? ___   │
│       c. Were any nonmembers on the formal program?  YES   NO             │
│       d. If yes, who (city council member, police officer, etc.)? _____  │
│                                                                           │
│   6.  Who presided at the meeting (by office)? _____    │
│                                                                           │
│   7.  What other persons had a formal role in the meeting (made a         │
│       presentation, gave a report, etc.)? _____                         │
│       _____    │
│       _____    │
│                                                                           │
│   8.  Did the presiding officer say that members were encouraged to       │
│       speak during the meeting? YES      NO                               │
│                                                                           │
│   9.  How many members made comments or asked questions during the        │
│       meeting? [Use tic marks to keep track.]                             │
│       _____    │
│                                                                           │
│  10.  How closely were parliamentary procedures followed in managing      │
│       the meeting?                                                        │
│          _____    (1) not at all                                         │
│          _____    (2) loosely                                            │
│          _____    (3) fairly closely                                     │
│          _____    (4) strictly                                           │
└─────────────────────────────────────────────────────────────────────────┘
```

Figure 19.3
Partial observation schedule for a hypothetical study of community organizations
(continued on next page)

11. What are the main topics discussed during the program?

a. _____

b. _____

c. _____

d. _____

e. _____

12. a. How many formal votes were taken? [Use tic marks to keep track.]

b. How was voting done?   *(1) show of hands*

(2) voice vote

(3) paper ballot

(8) other _____

c. What was the issue and outcome on each vote taken?

ISSUE	OUTCOME
Vote 1:	
Vote 2:	
Vote 3:	
Vote 4:	
Vote 5:	

(CONTINUE ON BACK IF NEEDED)

Figure 19.3
Partial observation schedule for a hypothetical study of community organizations
(continued)

used, it is also especially important to pay attention to **interobserver reliability**—the degree to which different observers classify similar events in the same way on the observation schedule. This is essentially the same as the problem of intercoder reliability in content analysis and can be verified by procedures similar to those discussed in Chapter 9. It is crucial, however, that investigators build into the instrument and data-collection procedure the means of collecting the information they will need to verify the validity and reliability of their measures.

It is also a good idea to *pretest the observation schedule and procedure* before beginning actual field work. A pretest involves using the schedule to record an event like the one you are studying to be sure that the categories are exhaustive and mutually exclusive, that the instructions on the form are easy to follow, and that the explanations of how to classify are clear enough that different observers can agree on the coding for the same or highly similar behaviors and events.

Sampling Procedures in Direct Observation

After identifying a set of behaviors to treat as a unit of analysis, we must decide which of these units to study. Because we cannot observe all instances of the behaviors that serve as our units of analysis, we are forced to select a sample of them. The objective of this sampling—which is the same objective followed in survey research or other methods of data collection—is *to examine a representative group of cases*.

We want to understand how the events in question *usually* happen and do not want to be misled by observing atypical episodes. However, what we are sampling is not people or nations or publications, but events and behaviors. The important point about this is that we can seldom predict in advance when (and sometimes where) these events will take place. As a result, it is often impossible to apply standard random sampling procedures to the type of events that are most often studied through direct observation.

The sampling procedure that *is* used depends on the nature of the study. If the events reoccur on a regular basis and occur frequently enough, it may be possible to take a random sample of these events to study. For instance, if we were studying the way a large administrative agency processes citizens' complaints and we knew that formal complaints were accepted every workday between the hours of 2 and 5 P.M. and that the agency heard an average of four complaints a day, we could set up rules for drawing a random sample of the anticipated complaints. In the room where complaints were reviewed, we could station observers on random days with instructions to record the details of the handling of one complaint each day until some minimum number had been observed. We could have a good deal of confidence in the representativeness of this sample because of the number and regularity of the events.

However, if there are far fewer instances of our units of analysis or if we cannot predict when or where they will occur, then standard sampling procedures cannot be relied on to yield a good sample. To illustrate this, let us change the above example to say that the agency scheduled the hearing of complaints *only once a month* at a regular time but still heard an average of only four complaints at each session. We could sample by way of the procedure just described but would have to observe the organization over *many* months before our random procedure had produced a representative sample (because random procedures are not dependable with small numbers of cases). We may not be able to stretch our research out over such a long period.

To modify the example again, assume that the agency accepted complaints at a window in its offices *at any time of any workday*. Because we cannot predict when citizens will show up with complaints, it is impossible to apply standard sampling procedures to select complaints. However, if we had reason to believe that complaints were fairly evenly spaced throughout the day and the week, we could divide the workweek into hours and sample certain *time periods*. Observers could watch the window at preselected hours of specified days of the week and record all complaints filed at those times. With a sufficiently large number of complaints, this could provide a representative sample. However, if the number of complaints is small (only one or two each day, for instance), most observation periods would not include a complaint, and it would again take a very long time to observe enough complaints to have confidence in our sample. This would be both time-consuming and expensive, because few observers work for free.

When we turn from events that occur with some regularity to more sporadic events, sampling problems become even greater. To stay with our administrative example, say that we are concerned with complaints made only by certain types of citizens (elderly persons, minority-group members, etc.) or only with a certain type of complaint (like those that involve allegations of nonenforcement of a given rule, willful misconduct by an agency employee, or gender discrimination in service delivery). We have no way of knowing when and if such complaints will arise and cannot effectively sample them using some variant of random sampling.

When our subject is a behavior that is relatively infrequent and random, we almost always have to rely on a *judgmental sample* as described in Chapter 6. We use what we know about the nature of the event to select a set of occurrences that will be *typical* of the behavior of interest if not representative in a strictly statistical sense.

To illustrate, say that our study of complaint handling was focused entirely on complaints about nonenforcement of agency rules and that we knew from agency records or prior research that complaints of this type came almost exclusively from low-income communities. We might choose to observe only complaints filed at those agency offices serving low-income neighborhoods in the hope of locating enough complaints of the desired type. If background research makes it possible to build a statistical profile of the events we want to study (when and where they happen most often, what types of people participate, what amounts of money are involved, how long they last, etc.), this information can assist in the judgmental selection of typical cases.

The task in judgmental sampling is to select for observation events that informed readers of the research can be persuaded are likely to be representative. At a minimum, this means avoiding choosing cases that are obviously exceptional in some way. If we wanted to study the internal dynamics of U.S. political interest groups, for instance, we would *not* choose the Arian Nation because it is likely to operate in a very different way from other organizations due to its unique ideological orientation.

Coping with Method Effects in Direct Observation

In Chapter 5 we pointed out that researchers must always be alert to the possibility that their data collection efforts have, in some way, influenced the data that are obtained and have produced an inaccurate picture of the reality they hope to understand. (For example, because people tend to give what they feel are socially acceptable answers to survey questions regardless of their true feelings, one effect of using the personal interview to gather data is a tendency to *understate* the occurrence of behaviors and attitudes that are contrary to dominant social norms.) This impact is referred to as a **method effect**. The possibility of a method effect is especially high in direct observation for at least two reasons. First, in most direct observations, researchers are in closer and more extended contact with the subjects than with other methods, so there are more opportunities for the observer's actions or presence to influence subjects' behavior. We call this effect *reactivity*. Second, because observers exercise so much discretion in determining what to record and how to record it, direct-observation data are heavily influenced by observers' values and expectations. We call this effect *bias*. If we fail to minimize these method effects, we lose the main advantage of direct observation—the high degree of external validity it provides our research.

Which strategies are appropriate for minimizing method effects depends on the character of the specific project. We can, however, offer some general guidelines. The most effective means of coping with reactivity is to employ *unobtrusive observation*, because subjects who are not aware they are being observed do not react to being studied. Investigators should always consider the possibility of arranging an unobtrusive observation. However, as we explained earlier, it is often impossible to use unobtrusive methods (especially in structured observation), and, as we soon will discuss, it may sometimes be judged unethical to do so.

Moreover, one particular technique of unobtrusive study—participant observation—may not get around reactivity problems even when it is possible. Even if the observer's identity and purpose are concealed from members of the group, the observer's actions *as a member of the group* can cause other members to act differently from ways they otherwise would. If a researcher posing as a member of a political organization takes part in the group's debate about what action to take in response to some new threat to its interest, for example, that participation may sway the decision. Similarly, the researcher's work on one of the organization's projects may lead to its success when it otherwise would have failed or to its failure when it otherwise would have succeeded.

This sort of effect is difficult to avoid if the investigator is to retain credibility as a devoted member of the organization, but observers have to be very sensitive to it and attempt to strike the delicate balance between losing credibility and actually shaping the events they are trying to study. It is also important to attempt to judge the degree to which researcher participation influenced outcomes so that this effect can be discounted in attempting to form an accurate picture of the processes under investigation.

When obtrusive methods are the only possibility, researchers can still take steps to minimize reactivity. The key to success in this lies in investigators' ability to *control their relationship to the subjects and the subjects' perception of the researcher.* Researchers must consciously manipulate subjects' perception of their character, values, and purpose in order to put the subjects so at ease that they behave as they normally would. Subjects must come either to ignore the observer as harmless, or to trust the observer enough to reveal their true feelings and behavior patterns. To accomplish the first end, observers must *blend in*; to accomplish the second, they must *fit in*.

To *blend in*, observers can use several tactics. (1) They can physically stay in the background or at the margins of any action they are observing so that subjects easily forget their presence when focusing on the activity. (This practice often has the added advantage of placing observers in a position that provides a good vantage point from which to survey the entire scene at once.) (2) Observers can adopt a passive manner, which makes it easy for others to overlook them or to consider them unthreatening. In this mode, they will certainly want to avoid commenting on what they see or confronting subjects in any way. (3) Observers can exercise patience and perseverance by showing up again and again so that they become commonplace and subjects begin to relax in their presence. The objective is to make the process of observation seem normal to the subjects—part of everyday life. This can take a great deal of time to accomplish. (4) Observers can blend into the group physically by grooming themselves and dressing in a manner that is inconspicuous under the circumstances. Wear what the subjects wear, but be careful to avoid violating any dress codes that may exist in the group by, for instance, wearing something recognized as a symbol of rank in the group or something reserved for persons with special status in the group. (5) Researchers can blend in socially by learning to converse comfortably with the subjects. This involves talking about things that are common topics of conversation among the subjects, using a personal style that is appropriate to the norms or the group (loud and outgoing or reserved and introspective, openly sharing feelings or putting up a front, frequently touching or keeping your hands to yourself, etc.), and respecting any clear role definitions within the group such as a norm that says that women don't talk about politics or that younger members don't volunteer information about themselves unless asked by an elder. It is important not to carry this too far by trying to imitate subjects' accents, mannerisms, or dress if it seems unnatural for the observer to act that way. An observer with a strong New England accent probably should *not* dress like the Marlboro man in an effort to study the political culture of western bars. Unnatural behavior will only attract attention and may be seen as an insult to the group.

Observers can *fit in* by using some of these same tactics. However, fitting in demands much more interaction between observer and subjects than blending in. It is a much greater concern in participant observation than in nonparticipant observation. Fitting in requires that the researcher consciously project an image as one of the group. This is done primarily by expressing values consistent with those of the subjects (perhaps a disregard for authority, prejudice toward some other group, or acceptance of a given political ideology). Behaving like one of the subject group may be necessary to build trust, but it has its dangers.

First, there is sometimes a risk that adopting the identity of a group member will make observers lose their objectivity about the study. Coming to see the world as subjects see it is known as **going native**. Investigators must be alert to this prospect because going native can prevent researchers from gaining scientifically useful insight into the behaviors under study. To avoid losing perspective, observers should strive to escape the group setting frequently if possible and should discuss with trusted people outside the group what it is they are observing to get those people's views of what the observer is seeing.

This is not a simple matter, because there is a fine line between going native and "getting inside" subjects to understand their motivations, values, and the like. Successful researchers can get close to subjects without losing sight of their objectives and interpretive framework. Observers who seek to fit in also face ethical problems if they find that they must deceive subjects. They are very likely to have to lie about how they feel, what they have done, how they live, their background, and so on. We address this problem in the last section of this chapter.

A second method effect associated with direct observation is the bias that can result when observers' values or expectations influence their perception and interpretation of what they see. Direct observation is especially subject to this danger because, with this method, *the observer is the primary instrument of measurement.* Bias can result from a researcher's rigid adherence to preconceptions about the phenomena under study or from a researcher's uncritically accepting the perspective and interpretations of the subjects (going native). Avoiding bias requires being both open-minded about and detached from the subject of our studies. Several strategies can help achieve this end.

First, in obtrusive research when observer and subjects can interact, observers can avoid letting their preconceptions lead them to wrong conclusions by periodically *checking their interpretations of what they see with the subjects.* Rather than simply assuming we know what motivated subjects to take a particular action, we can ask subjects why they did what they did. Their understandings of the situation or their values may be so different from the researcher's that their motivations are just the opposite of what the researcher had thought. Someone from an industrialized nation might think the harsh punishment of a Third World child by its parents is motivated by spite and the desire to inflict pain. In fact, the parents may act as they do because they love the child and want to make it strong enough to survive the hardships of life in a harsh environment. Similarly, researchers may assign meaning to events that subjects do not. An example would be the case in which an observer interprets as a danger signal a group of teenagers "hanging out" on a block, but a local resident knows the youths and views them as protecting the block from intruders by their presence.

It is wise to ask subjects how they interpret events before making assumptions. However, it is important to be subtle in asking these questions, phrasing them in terms familiar to the subjects, and presenting them as concerned inquiries, not demands for explanations. After observing a heated verbal exchange, for example, an observer should not ask, "Why were you so hostile toward her?" but may ask, "Do you think she will be mad about this?" to find out if the actor saw the exchange in the same terms as the observer. This does *not* mean that observers should let subjects determine their analysis of events, but only that they should check to see if subjects are thinking what the observers believe they are thinking.

Second, observers can avoid the mistake of seeing events too much as subjects see them by (1) periodically discussing with someone outside the study what they have seen and how they interpret it and (2) soliciting the views of persons who are marginal to the group, such as the lone environmentalist on a planning commission generally unconcerned about environmental issues, or people who have recently moved back into a community after living elsewhere. Such persons can be a valuable resource for researchers, because they have the insight born of close association with the events in question but can still take a critical perspective on those events.

Third, it is often useful to blend direct observation with some other form of data collection so the other data can be used to verify impressions formed from direct observation. A direct-observation study of the effect of crime on citizens' behaviors might be augmented by a survey in which the same people who had been observed are asked direct questions about how fearful they are and how their behavior has changed as a result of their fear. The survey would not provide as much detailed data as the direct observation and may have less external validity. It could, however, be used to verify impressions gained from direct observation by asking such questions as, "Do respondents see the actions that observers attributed to fear (e.g., staying off the streets at night) as being motivated by fear of crime, or do they have other explanations for this?" A wide variety of data sources (content analysis, public records, etc.) can serve this verification function.

These and other means of *cross-validating* the conclusions drawn from observation can reduce the degree of subjectivity involved in the method and add significantly to the degree to which results are accepted as valid.

The Ethics of Direct Observation

Any research project can raise questions of what is ethically right or fair. The unique features of direct observation make it even more likely to put researchers in situations when they must confront questions of ethics. The two areas in which ethical issues are most likely to arise concern *the relationship of the researcher to the subjects* and *the reactions of the researcher to what is observed*.

Problems can arise in the relationship of observer to the observed, because there is often a fundamental tension between being honest and obtaining scientifically valid information. If subjects know they are being studied or know why they are being studied, they may refuse to cooperate or may alter their behavior in ways that make it impossible to secure a valid answer to a research question. Yet, getting around these problems by using unobtrusive observation or by concealing the true purpose of the study from subjects involves some degree of deception. Investigators are most likely to face choices about whether or not to use deception with regard to (1) *the grounds on which they gain access to opportunities to observe* and (2) *the development of trust between themselves and their subjects*. We can examine these issues in turn.

If it is possible to observe subjects without their knowledge, observers first face the question of whether or not to tell subjects they are being studied. The issue here is whether the researcher has a right to watch and possibly report people's actions when they have not given their consent and cannot control what the observer sees or reports. Researchers confront a similar situation when they tell subjects they are being studied but deceive them as to the purpose of the study. Are such actions an invasion of privacy and a denial of the fundamental human right to control of our lives?

This is not always a simple issue. It is often possible to argue in *favor* of deception in a given project for any of several reasons: (1) Subjects will not be harmed in any way by being observed given the purposes of the study. (2) Researchers will keep subjects' identity secret in any reports from the study, so no one will be hurt. (3) Subjects would agree to the study if they were given the opportunity to do so but cannot be asked in advance without risking reactivity. (4) The good that will come from the findings of the study outweighs any harm that may be done to subjects through the deception. Researchers, funding agencies, sponsoring agencies, and critics must decide whether these are valid arguments in any given case by careful examination of the facts of the situation.

Ethical questions can arise with respect to the issue of trust between observer and observed. First, in order to gain subjects' trust, observers may have to lie about who they are, why they are there, how they feel about events, and so forth.

Moreover, once trust is established, do researchers have the right to use what is told them in confidence to advance the purposes of the research or to report such information in a write-up of the project? Can deception be justified in the name of science when we abhor it when used for personal, political, financial, or social gain? Deception at this stage can sometimes be justified by the same kind of arguments previously cited.

The next arena in which ethical issues may arise deals with the observer's reactions to what is observed. Those who investigate behaviors that are potentially illegal or morally repugnant to society put themselves in situations in which they may witness actions that outrage or disgust them. Some actions may impose a moral obligation to report the events to some authority. At other times, observers may witness actions their own moral code demands that they intervene to stop.

Consider the example of a researcher engaged in participant observation of the politics of Nazi skinheads. What if the skinheads shout insults at and spit on minority children? What if they vandalize a synagogue? What if they beat up an old Jewish man? Researchers who react as their value system dictates would "blow their cover" and put an end to the project. (To keep the case as simple as possible, assume that such reactions would not endanger the researcher.) What are the researcher's obligations in this situation? Can the need to understand what motivates people to join such groups and how the groups function outweigh the obligation to express personal moral outrage? Can it negate the obligation to report violations of the law? Can it possibly justify allowing someone to be physically harmed? How do we balance long-term objectives against the short-term need for justice? How do we balance benefits to society (in this case, added knowledge about how to control a problem) against the welfare of individuals who may be harmed if we do not act?

These questions have to be answered in the context of a specific research project and situation. The value of some projects will justify actions that could not be justified by others. On rare occasions it is possible to come up with creative arrangements that allow researchers to minimize ethical dilemmas. For instance, it may be possible to observe without informing subjects but to tell them later, show them how the observations of their behavior will be used, and give them the right to veto use of the data. In most cases, however, investigators must confront ethical questions head-on and make hard choices between unattractive alternatives.

The important point is that it is vital that those who plan to use direct observation consider *in advance* the ethical implications of their decision. Before putting themselves in situations that pose ethical dilemmas, researchers should think through the problems that are likely to arise, and they should weigh the relative value of the good of the project against the rights of subjects or social and moral obligations. Most important, they must *be very clear about their own values and, if at all possible, decide in advance where they will draw the line in cases of ethical conflict.*

Our position is that scientific knowledge can be of such great value to society that acquiring it sometimes justifies exceptions to normal rules of conduct. However, it is very clear that science must always be viewed as a means to the end of improving the human condition, not as an end in itself. Some values are so basic that they should never be sacrificed even in pursuit of knowledge.

Suggestions for Further Reading

Principles of direct observation are addressed in Raymond M. Lee, *Unobtrusive Methods in Social Research* (Philadelphia: PA: Open University Press, 2000). Participant-observation techniques are discussed in Patricia A. Adler and Peter Adler, *Membership Roles in Field Research* (Newbury Park, CA: Sage, 1987). Perhaps the most comprehensive examination of the ethical issues associated with direct observation is provided by Maurice Punch, *The Politics and Ethics of Fieldwork* (Newbury Park, CA: Sage, 1986), who goes beyond alerting us to the questions to trying to provide some pragmatic guidelines for working out answers. Issues of data analysis are addressed by David Silverman, *Interpreting Qualitative Data* (Thousand Oaks, CA: Sage, 1993).

Research Exercises

1. Develop a research question that can be answered through direct observation about one of the politically oriented student groups on your campus—groups like Progressive Student Alliance and College Republicans. (For example, you might ask if the role of female members is different in liberal and conservative groups or what common values members share beyond their political ideals.) Write out a list of the things you would have to observe in the group to answer this question.

2. Attend a meeting of the student group and observe it according to the list you developed for the previous exercise. Keep mental notes and write up formal field notes immediately afterward. Then write a short essay on what you learned that you had not expected to. How did what you saw and heard differ from the way you thought things would work? How would you modify your list of things to look for in light of what you actually observed?

   As an extension of this exercise, have another student in your class observe the same meeting and write up a set of field notes independently. Then compare your notes with the other students' and write a description of the ways in which they differ and the points on which they agree.

3. Devise a simple hypothesis about the operation of your city council. (For example, "Economic issues will produce more serious disagreements than social issues.") Develop an observational schedule that fully operationalizes the concepts involved in the hypothesis and any strong rival hypotheses you feel you would have to be able to rule out before having confidence in the original hypothesis. Observe at least two meetings of the council, and use the observation schedule to record what you see. Write an essay both on what you concluded about your hypothesis and on how you would change the observation schedule after having had some experience with it. What shortcomings did you find?

Terms Introduced in This Chapter

direct observation
obtrusive research
unobtrusive research
participant observation
structured observation
unstructured observation

field notes
observation schedule
interobserver reliability
method effect
going native

CHAPTER 20

FOCUS GROUP METHODOLOGIES

Researchers frequently want to study questions that few if any others have investigated, or they may want to gain a fresh perspective in an area where past research has failed to resolve major questions. In such cases, they will be unable to rely on prior theories or empirical studies to guide their efforts. If the phenomenon in question is new (or at least new to the researchers), there may not even be first-hand knowledge of the events in question. In these situations, scholars may need to gather information through the use of focus groups.

At the most basic level, **focus group** methods involve bringing together small groups of carefully selected individuals for an in-depth discussion of some topic, guided by a **moderator,** in order to learn how people think about that topic. Focus groups can be used for different purposes at different stages of the research process. They can help formulate hypotheses for future studies, develop indicators to be used in data collection, improve the interpretation of data collected by other means, or produce data that are directly useful in answering a research question.

This chapter explains why and when researchers might use focus group methods either as their primary methodology or in support of other data-collection methods. It then describes some of the basic rules for conducting focus groups and using the information they produce.

Why Use Focus Groups?

Focus group methods were developed in the 1940s by researchers who wanted to get as realistic a view of people's thinking as possible. In fact, most of the focus group techniques used today were first described in some of the earliest works in this field.[1]

Government agencies, political advisors, and social scientists have been making more use of focus groups in recent years, but the approach has been used most extensively in *market research* to help businesses explore aspects of consumer behavior as part of their effort to develop and sell products. Businesses often use

---

[1] See Robert K. Merton and Patricia L. Kendall, "The Focused Interview," *American Journal of Sociology,* 51 (1946): pp. 541–57, or Robert K. Merton, Marjorie Fiske, and Patricia L. Kendall, *The Focused Interview* (Glencoe, IL: The Free Press, 1956).

focus groups to gain insights into such questions as how consumers will react to a new product, how effective a proposed advertising campaign might be, and why consumers prefer one product over another.[2] Survey research or individual interviews can often be used for these purposes, but early researchers recognized at least five limitations to survey-based methods.

First, respondents can give us only the information we know to ask for, and many problems may have aspects that researchers will not think to ask about. For example, in a survey, we might ask voters to rate two opposing candidates on each of five dimensions that we feel will determine how voters vote. We might then be surprised to find that the candidate who earned the higher rating did not win the election because voters used a different set of criteria in making their actual choice. Voters had answered our questions honestly, but we had asked the wrong questions. Second, even if we use open-ended questions, respondents may be influenced by the style in which questions are asked or by subtle aspects of their interaction with the interviewer. Third, surveys are very expensive and time-consuming. If we don't have a clear understanding of what we want to know and how to ask questions in order to get that information from respondents, we run the risk of making a large investment to obtain useless data. Fourth, survey results are not always "self-explanatory" because there are always possibilities that respondents interpreted questions differently from the interpretations the researchers intended and that respondents' answers meant something different to respondents from what the answers meant to the researchers who were trying to interpret the results. Finally, people do not make decisions in isolation but are influenced by others' opinions and reactions. A survey interview, however, asks people to act in isolation from their social context in expressing opinions or making judgments. As a result, the data produced by a survey or interview may not accurately reflect social reality.

To avoid these limitations of interview-based data collection, researchers could turn to direct observation. However, whereas that approach may be very valuable for certain research questions, it may be inappropriate for others. Scholars who are interested in a fairly narrow subject may face four problems with direct observation. To illustrate, let us use the subject of how heterosexuals perceive the goals of the gay rights movement.

First, it may be difficult to find a site at which to observe interaction on this topic. Where can researchers go to be sure they will hear a discussion of the gay rights movement by nongays? Second, in a natural setting, it may be necessary to observe *many* hours of discussion of other topics in order to hear a few minutes of conversation about gay rights. Third, even if the subject comes up, the discussion may not address the aspects of the issue that are of interest to researchers; with direct observation, researchers have no way to guide the discussion. Finally, even in natural settings, discussion may be artificially constrained. For example, people who work together may avoid expressing political disagreement for fear that they will damage relationships in the workplace. Properly designed and executed focus groups can help overcome all of these problems.

---

[2] For a discussion of the use of focus groups in marketing, see Jane F. Templeton, *Focus Groups: A Guide for Marketing and Advertising Professionals* (Chicago: Probus, 1987).

The central feature of focus group methods is that they *rely on interaction among the participants to generate insights into the subject under study.* As you will see when we describe the technique, focus groups enable their members to interact with very little direction from the researcher. As a result, participants have a chance to express their true feelings on the topic under study and can bring up any aspect of that topic that they feel is important. The group process may also allow them to come to understandings about the topic that no one of them could have achieved alone.

This means that focus groups have three substantive advantages: they *may* provide more accurate insights into what people actually think than do other techniques that involve more influence from the researcher; they can produce results that reflect social realities more accurately than methods that ask people to act in isolation; and they give us the ability to study *group dynamics* in ways that other techniques do not. In addition, focus groups offer some practical advantages: First, though they are *not* inexpensive, focus groups typically cost far less than a large survey and take far less time than direct observation. Second, because focus groups do not require elaborate measuring instruments and procedures, they can usually be conducted with far less preparation than interview-based research or even direct observation. This saves time and money.

Limitations of Focus Groups

For all these strengths, focus groups, like other methods, have their limitations. We will describe four common limitations and suggest ways to cope with them. Each of the limitations may affect any given focus group session, but they do not all affect every focus group project equally. This is because there are many different ways to structure focus groups and because focus groups are held for many different purposes. If recognized and properly addressed, the limitations of focus groups need not damage the usefulness of the method.

1. *Subjective interpretation:* The primary product of a focus group is a *transcript* of what was said. To contribute to our understanding, that transcript must be interpreted by someone. Since the transcript does not consist of hard data that can be subjected to statistical tests, its interpretation inevitably involves more objectivity than do the analyses associated with other methods. As a result of differences in their own background or values, different observers may reach different conclusions about what "lessons" are to be learned from the focus group.

Remember that the interpretation of quantitative data can also be subject to debate. We are saying only that focus groups are more prone to the interpretation problem than some other methods are, and *not* that focus groups have this problem when other approaches do not.

Since subjectivity is inherent in the interpretation of focus group sessions, the only protection against being misled by it is some combination of the following steps. Researchers must be honest with themselves about their biases and try to be as objective as possible. They can bring in disinterested but qualified persons to do independent interpretations of the focus group results. They can also share their work with other scholars who can judge the validity of their interpretation and suggest alternatives before they consider their conclusions final. In addition, when writing up the study, researchers can faithfully describe enough of what was said to allow others to draw their own conclusions.

2. *Limited representativeness:* The small numbers of people that can be involved in focus groups can never be statistically representative of any large population. As a result, we cannot generalize to the larger population with the same precision or confidence that we can when larger samples are used. There is always the chance that even carefully selected groups may be atypical of the population and thereby lead us to incorrect conclusions. Moreover, even if the focus groups are quite typical of the larger population, we have no objective measures to tell us so in advance (as we do with probability sampling) and must either hope we are not misled or wait until we can verify focus group results through some other method.

The appropriate responses to this problem consist of the researcher's awareness of the potentially unrepresentative nature of the results of focus groups and the researcher's avoidance of making unwarranted generalizations. Clearly it would be unwise to attempt very precise predictions of popular behavior on the basis of focus group results. One could not on the basis of focus group results justifiably claim, for example, that "68.6 percent of citizens will vote against higher taxes to be used to retrain defense workers for civilian jobs." Scholars might, however, by observing focus groups, be able to reach conclusions like, "the participants tend to see the retraining of defense workers as a personal rather than a public responsibility."

3. *Artificial setting:* The major purpose of focus groups is to get people to express themselves freely and reveal their true thinking without the restrictions imposed by a survey or interview. They often do this very well. However, we must recognize that the focus group is *not* a natural setting. Even if the moderator succeeds in creating a "permissive environment" that encourages self-expression, responses may be sincere but still unlike what they would have been in a different setting. As a result, we may not be able to generalize from the results of the focus group to the way people will behave in other settings.

For example, the composition of the group may be unlike that of any group with which the participants are likely to interact in their daily life. If we have intentionally selected participants of mixed socioeconomic backgrounds but who seldom cross socioeconomic lines in their social life, the group dynamic that develops may not be typical of any that would occur in the real world. Similarly, the permissive environment of the focus group may allow people to express ideas they would never otherwise verbalize in naturally occurring groups that have more restrictive norms. As a result, a consensus may emerge that is unlike any that would be produced by a real-world interaction.

In addition, each focus group develops its own dynamic as a result of some chance factors such as who happens to express an opinion first or the direction or tone of the first set of comments. The same members might behave differently on another evening or if paired with another group. As a consequence, the results of any given focus group may be unrepresentative both of real-world outcomes and of the thinking of the group participants as individuals.

In short, even a carefully designed and well-run focus group may create false impressions because it is not itself a natural setting. There are two main avenues to coping with these issues. First, researchers can run a number of groups and form conclusions based on *patterns* rather than isolated results. Second, they must be sensitive to both the ways in which focus groups may differ from natural settings and the effects these differences may have on the outcome of the sessions, and they must incorporate that awareness into their analysis of the focus group observations.

4. *Possible method effects:* Most observational methods carry the risk of influencing subjects' responses in some way. (Recall, for example, our discussion in Chapter 7 of biased question wording and resulting survey responses.) Focus groups are no exception. *Method effects* can arise from biases introduced by the behavior of the moderator, who may have preconceived notions about what the focus group will or "should" reveal and who may unconsciously steer the discussion in that direction. Moderators who conduct several focus groups on the same subject may have had early experiences that cause them to lead discussions in subsequent groups in the direction of being consistent with the early groups. Similarly, unintentional cues given to participants before the group session (through a description of the purpose of the group or simply the naming of its sponsor, for example) may shape the outcome.

When Are Focus Groups Useful?

Researchers must weigh the strengths and weaknesses of focus groups in the context of specific research situations and tasks. Focus groups can be of great value under some conditions and of little use under others. There are five general situations in which focus groups often represent an appropriate method.

1. *Exploratory research:* When researchers venture into an area that is so completely unexplored that they do not even know how to go about studying it or when they want a fresh perspective on an old but unresolved subject, focus groups can help them formulate ideas about both what questions to ask and what methods to use. An example of this can be found in study of the transformation of East European nations from authoritarian to democratic political systems after the fall of communism after 1989. Researchers might want to know how citizens who have been denied any opportunity for meaningful participation in politics approach the tasks of democratic citizenship when they are given the chance. Because the transition from communism to democracy has never happened before, we have no prior theories or studies to guide us. Moreover, Western scholars have generally been unable to conduct surveys in those nations for decades and have little knowledge of how citizens there thought about politics before the transition. In this case, focus groups consisting of citizens of the changing nations could help researchers discover what is to be explained and develop hypotheses to guide research.

2. *Refining data collection instruments:* Even when researchers know enough about an area to formulate hypotheses, they may be unsure about the best way to operationalize concepts. For example, standard question wording on a survey may not communicate effectively with unusual respondents. In the case of the East

European nations, we cannot even be sure that their citizens think about politics in the same terms as citizens of Western nations do. A series of focus groups could provide information that would assist in the development of appropriate wording for survey questions to be used with this population. Alternatively, researchers who plan to use direct observation to study political participation in East European nations could use focus groups to learn the meaning of different expressions or actions so that they would know what significance the people being observed attached to their own words and deeds.

3. *Interpreting quantitative findings:* When researchers have used other methods to collect data that show clear patterns, they may still be unsure about how those patterns developed or what the patterns mean to the people who exhibit them. Again, focus groups can often provide answers. For example, many studies of environmental politics have found that women are far more likely than men to express concern about environmental hazards and to regard technologies as risky. Focus groups in which men and women discuss environmental issues may help researchers understand differences in the way the sexes tend to judge environmental hazards: what standards they use, how they process information, whom they trust as an authority, and so on. Scholars could then make more sense of the statistical relationships observed in their data.

4. *Study of group processes:* Whether they are legislative committees, juries, military units, law enforcement task forces, workplace teams, street gangs, or any of dozens of other collections of people, small groups make many of the decisions in our society. Understanding the processes by which groups influence their members' perceptions and reach decisions can, therefore, help us understand social phenomena or formulate public policies. Social scientists have long recognized that one behaves differently in a group from the ways one behaves alone and that the only way to understand *group* behavior is to study *group dynamics*. If our interest is in some aspect of group dynamics, then focus group methods offer an excellent way to observe efficiently and without raising some of the ethical issues involved in direct observation.

5. *Designing and evaluating public policy:* Focus groups can often help public officials and policy analysts to gain an understanding of how citizens see problems, evaluate services, and are likely to react to new programs. Such insight can then be used to create new policies that address problems or to evaluate how well existing policies are working. To illustrate, public housing officials could conduct focus groups to help them anticipate how residents of a public housing development would react to a system of tenant management that gave the residents a voice in running the housing project. Based on what they learn, they could try to build into the tenant management program a realistic set of incentives for participation rather than guess at what might motivate residents to take part.

An even more practice-oriented use of focus groups is to design and evaluate specific communication materials and strategies. To illustrate, imagine that public health officials wanted to convey to an immigrant community that had its own distinctive subculture certain information on a serious health hazard. The officials might use focus groups composed of members of the immigrant population to determine such things as what channels of communication would be most effective in reaching those residents and whether or not a given message would successfully capture residents' attention and be properly interpreted.

This use of social science methods to achieve very practical ends is commonly referred to as *applied research,* and focus groups constitute one of the most commonly used methods in "applied" settings.[3] Such groups have, for example, proven especially valuable in designing election campaigns because they help campaign managers identify voters' most powerful concerns, thus enabling managers to get a feel for the ways that different appeals will be interpreted by voters.

Planning and Conducting Focus Groups

Once researchers have decided that focus groups are an appropriate method to use in a given study, they will confront several basic choices in planning and conducting the focus group sessions. We can explore these choices as responses to a series of questions.

What Are the Goals of the Focus Groups?

The first step is to determine exactly what is to be learned from the focus groups. Objectives can range from the very general to the very specific. A relatively general goal might be "to gain insight into the impact of a localized environmental hazard on the lives of residents in order to formulate hypotheses about what determines how residents respond to the hazard." A more specific goal might be "to find out which of five possible sources of information about the hazard citizens are most likely to trust in order to devise a plan for conveying believable information to the public."

It is only once you are clear about what you hope to learn that you will know what to listen for in the focus group discussions. From a practical standpoint, however, there are at least three reasons to identify goals as clearly as possible.

1. The goals will affect *the selection of participants and composition of groups.* If, for instance, you wanted to find out how the controversies surrounding the hazard had affected social relations within the community, you would want to be sure to include in the groups people on both sides of any issues. The statement of goals should help researchers identify important characteristics to be considered in recruiting participants and assigning them to groups.

2. The goals will influence *the degree of moderator involvement.* Some goals will require that members of the focus group perform a task while others do not. You may, for example, want the group to reach a formal consensus, solve a hypothetical problem, or make a recommendation about how to address some issue.

---

[3] See Jarol B. Manheim, *Strategic Public Diplomacy and American Foreign Policy* (New York: Oxford, 1994) for an account of the use of focus groups to design the Bush administration's presentation to the American public of its rationale for U.S. involvement in the Gulf War.

If so, you will need to have the moderator be more active in guiding the discussion to be sure that the task is completed. If the goals are very general, moderator involvement can be minimized. Selecting goals is therefore the first step in the planning of focus group sessions and the instructing of the moderator.

3. The goals will direct *the development of a "guide" for the moderator.* Even in largely unstructured focus groups, researchers will want the moderator to have a **guide** which sets forth some rules for the discussion and provides a very general outline of how the session should proceed in order to be sure that all of the important points are raised and addressed. A focus group guide is not as detailed as an interview schedule in survey research or even an observational schedule in direct observation. Each guide will be different and will reflect the objectives of the study. Most will cue the moderator to step in at appropriate times to move the discussion along or bring it back to the main issue if it strays too far. Most guides list the main points to be addressed in some appropriate order, suggest phrases to use in making the transition from one subtopic to another, and may even set time limits for the discussion of subtopics or lay out procedures to be used in performing tasks (for example, "Have the group break into three equal subgroups . . . ").

How Many Focus Group Sessions Should Be Held?

It is almost always necessary to conduct more than one focus group session to rule out the possibility that there was something atypical about the participants or the group dynamic that developed in any one group. If similar patterns appear in more than one group, we can have more confidence that those patterns accurately reflect reality. Since two groups may give exactly opposite impressions or reach opposing conclusions, many practitioners consider *three* to be the minimum number of group sessions that should be held. Two other considerations, however, will weigh heavily in the choice of the number of sessions.

On the substantive side, your research objectives may dictate that you hold separate sessions for different subgroups within a general population or in different geographic locations. In the environmental contamination example, you may want to have separate sessions for citizens who choose to move away and those who will stay in the contaminated community, or you may want to hold groups in various towns facing different types of environmental hazards so you can compare the groups' reactions. You would need to hold several sessions *for each subgroup* to have confidence in the results. These design considerations may dictate a larger minimum number of sessions.

From a practical standpoint, focus groups are expensive and time-consuming to plan, arrange, conduct, and analyze. The amount of time and money and the number of personnel available for the project may impose a limit on the number of sessions that can be held. The costs of *each* focus group session generally vary from $1,500 to $4,000 depending on such variables as whether a professional firm is hired to conduct the sessions, how much money participants must be paid, how transcription is done, and transportation costs.

How Many Participants Attend Each Session?

Experience has shown that focus groups rarely work well with fewer than six or more than ten participants. With smaller numbers of participants, especially strong personalities tend to exert too much influence on the outcomes, and individuals may feel too much pressure to carry a share of the conversation. With larger numbers, it is both difficult to give all members enough time to express their thoughts and hard to keep the discussion focused.

Again, the time and money available for the project will play some role in determining how many participants to include given the decision to hold a certain number of sessions. One reason this is true is that it is frequently necessary to pay participants. The appropriate fee varies with the prevailing wage scale in a given area and with the characteristics of the participants. A group of, say, physicians or business executives may require far higher compensation than those who earn less. Occasionally, people can be persuaded to volunteer their time if the purpose of the research is one they value or if the sponsor of the research is one that commands respect and support. Local public health officials, for example, may be willing to take part in a study sponsored by their professional association and conducted for the purpose of improving public health services in the community.

How Are Participants Selected?

Once the number of participants has been determined, the task of recruiting them begins. The first issue here is what kind of people you want to attract. The key answer is that you want people who are typical of the population group under study. Depending on the focus of the study, you may be able to work from a telephone book if any of the residents of a given community will do, or you may need more specialized lists of people such as welfare recipients, public school teachers, or members of local civic organizations. Once you have a list to work from, it is common to conduct a **screening interview** to determine whether specific individuals are suited for the study and are willing to take part. This is usually done by phone and followed with a written invitation and a follow-up call to confirm prospective participants' acceptance.

In the recruiting process, researchers must be alert to several additional issues. First, there is a tendency for people with unusually strong feelings about a subject to be more willing to participate than those with less emotional involvement in the issue. To keep this from distorting results, researchers should make a conscious effort to recruit some people with little initial interest in the subject. Second, unless friendship ties, work relationships, or family roles are a specific part of the research focus, it is usually better to recruit people who do not know each other. Strangers are usually less inhibited in their responses. Finally, researchers need to consider the effects of placing in the same focus group people who have different *social roles*. If the topic to be discussed relates to the expectations and interests associated with different social roles, participants in "mixed" groups may change their behavior as a result. Generally, it is unwise to put into the same focus group people with significantly different but interacting roles (like managers and workers or regulatory agency officials and members of the regulated industry) if those roles are relevant to the topic of the discussion. Unless interaction between people in different social roles is specifically part of the research objectives, it is better to select *relatively homogeneous groups* in order to have a sufficient basis for communication among the participants.

What Physical Arrangements Are Necessary?

Since the main product of a focus group session is a transcript of what was said, it is important to arrange to make a high-quality audio recording of the event for later transcription. Audio equipment should be tested in advance to be sure it picks up comments from all positions in the room, and the moderator should have a backup system on hand in case the primary recording equipment fails. Well-funded projects use professional technicians for the recording of the session. In some cases, it may also be desirable to videotape the sessions in order to capture the nonverbal communication that may occur. This advantage has to be weighed against the possibility that video cameras may make respondents self-conscious and that hidden cameras can seldom be positioned properly so as to pick up all the action.

In any case, it is important both to tell participants they are being recorded and to get their permission. Professional ethics require that such recordings and any transcripts made from them be kept strictly confidential by the project staff and not be used for any purpose beyond the research.

Focus groups are best conducted in a room large enough to allow participants to sit around a single table (or at least in a circle) but small enough to feel intimate. The room should be furnished and decorated in a manner that puts people at ease. Sometimes researchers want to observe the sessions in person and need a place to sit to the side. Other times they may not want to be seen and thus need a room with a one-way mirror so they can observe without affecting the dynamics of the group. Actual discussions usually last about one and a half hours, but it is wise to allow two hours per session in case participants are late arriving, technical problems arise, or the discussion simply runs longer than anticipated.

What Role Does the Moderator Play?

No single factor is more important to the success of a focus group than the competence of the moderator. The moderator is responsible for putting participants at ease, ensuring that all relevant topics are covered in the discussion, keeping more aggressive speakers from dominating the conversation, and helping to characterize the results of the session in a set of field notes for the researchers. Accordingly, it is important to hire an experienced and skilled moderator if the budget allows and to invest substantial time in training someone to serve as moderator if an experienced one cannot be hired. It is generally unwise for a researcher to serve as the moderator because a researcher may unintentionally bias the results.

Moderators should usually share enough characteristics with focus group participants to help participants feel free to talk and to understand well enough what they *mean* by their remarks so as to respond properly. This is especially true with distinctive groups (for example, farmers, unemployed industrial workers, or female state legislators) and when the topic is one that touches on tensions between social groups.

An *assistant moderator* is almost always necessary. The assistant sits to the side and takes more detailed notes on the session than the moderator can take while interacting with the participants. The assistant may handle mechanical tasks such as greeting participants when they first arrive or distributing any written materials to be used in the session. Assistants can also serve as a backup since they often are familiar enough with the focus group process to step in if for some reason the moderator cannot attend a session. The assistant's most important function, however, may be to serve as a check on the moderator's perception of the sessions. The assistant works with the moderator in writing up an accurate set of field notes after the session. If the two disagree on an event, both opinions should be included in the notes for the researcher to consider.

Once moderators are hired or trained, they must be instructed. As explained earlier, much of the moderator's role is dictated by the objectives of the project and outlined in the focus group guide. Even in those cases when moderators are expected to take a fairly active role in moving the discussion along, it is vital that they not influence the outcome. Doing this requires that they strike the proper balance between empathy and detachment, being accepting of all opinions expressed but not rewarding any particular type of statement. The emphasis must be on *having the participants express their opinions*.

At the end of the session, the moderator should write up a set of field notes summarizing themes or conclusions that emerged from the discussion, pointing out any facts about the session that might influence the researcher's interpretation of the transcript. The moderator might note such issues as a high level of tension in the group, the exceptional influence of one or more participants over the group, or an apparent reluctance of some subset of participants to express opinions. Moderators might also compare the results of different sessions they have conducted.

This raises the issue of whether to use *one or more than one main moderator*. Using the same moderator for all sessions offers more consistency in the way the sessions are run and provides a better basis for comparing sessions. It also allows a moderator to develop some insight into the topic and may help a moderator to anticipate problems and do a better job of running sessions subsequent to the first one or two.

However, researchers may want to use more than one moderator in several circumstances. One is the situation in which very different social groups are represented in different sessions and it is necessary to use different moderators to match participants' characteristics. For instance, if race relations is the topic and groups are racially homogeneous, it would be wise to select a moderator of the same race as the participants in each session. A second situation that calls for more than one moderator is one in which researchers want the results of each session or group of sessions to be totally independent of each other and there is some fear that a moderator might influence the outcomes on the basis of expectations developed in early sessions. Finally, logistical considerations such as geographically separated research sites or the need to conduct several sessions at once in order to meet a deadline or avoid "contamination" of the groups by news reports appearing between sessions might dictate the need for multiple moderators.

How Are Sessions Run?

Focus group meetings usually open with the moderator's explaining the general purpose and the ground rules for the discussion. Commonly this is followed by an opening statement by each participant. Such statements usually tell a few basic facts about the individual. Having each person speak helps participants feel as if they have been introduced and makes the discussion more relaxed. It also encourages less outgoing individuals to speak up later in the session. The key objective of the opening moments of a session is to make it clear that the moderator wants to hear each member's story in each member's own words and that the purpose of the exercise is for the moderator and the session's sponsors to learn from the participants. Thereafter, the moderator should ask general questions like, "How do you feel about X?" "Has anyone had any experience with Y?" and "Does anyone want to respond to that?" This keeps things focused and moving. Most of the discussion will involve the participants' reacting to one another.

One variation on this procedure is to ask participants to fill out a questionnaire before and/or after the session. Such questionnaires can be used to gather background information on the participants that might not be evident from the discussion but that influences interpretation of participants' comments; to show how participants' views changed as a result of the focus group discussion if the same questions are asked both before and after the session; and to get from participants their assessments of the focus group process in order to improve the running of subsequent sessions. Presession questionnaires must be very carefully constructed so as not to influence the direction of the session by asking questions that suggest positions on issues or set up expectations about how the session will go. As a result, presession questionnaires should be used only if the benefits outweigh any threat of distorting the results of the sessions.

Analyzing Focus Group Results

As a qualitative method, focus groups do not produce numerical data that can be analyzed using statistics to identify patterns and relationships. Focus groups produce a very large volume of verbal data in the form of transcripts, recordings of sessions, and moderators' field notes. The tasks of reducing all of this information to a readable summary and of drawing some justifiable conclusions from it can be daunting. We can provide no step-by-step guide for focus group analysis both because there is so much variation in project objectives and focus group procedures and because qualitative analysis relies heavily on insight and creativity. We can, however, suggest some general guidelines that will help you recognize good analysis.

The first principle of focus group analysis is that researchers should always begin with a clear picture of what they hope to learn from the data. This step should have been taken in the identification of the purpose for the study as the first step in designing the project. Returning to that objective helps identify relevant information from the sessions and eliminate marginal information. It gives a benchmark as to how detailed the analysis must be. For example, if the purpose were largely descriptive (such as finding out what terms ordinary people use to discuss some political issue), only a summary may be needed. If the purpose were more analytical (such as determining why people were opposed to nuclear power), the analysis would have to be much more complex, and certain subtle features of the discussions might take on importance.

Once the objective has been established, researchers face the task of organizing the data for analysis. One approach is to read through the transcripts and literally cut out sections addressing specific topics. Researchers can then physically reassemble the sections so that all the comments relevant to a given subtopic are together. If the transcript is on an electronic medium, a word processor can speed the process. This approach can help reveal themes more clearly and can reduce the volume of data to be considered at any one time. It may, however, take comments out of their context and can conceal *meaning*.

In analytical studies, it is especially important to listen to the recordings of the sessions in order to be sure that the context of members' comments is taken into account and their *meaning* understood. Transcripts can be produced so as to reflect some of the subtle texture of oral communication by means of certain conventions such as typing in all capitals those words that speakers stressed or putting interpretive comments in parentheses. For example: "Oh, I *never* believe what *my* mayor says" (*laughing*). However, even these practices may conceal subtle differences in meaning that only listening to the tape can reveal. Taken in context, for instance, the comment about the mayor may have been sarcastic, indicating that the speaker *does* believe the mayor. Researchers therefore rely on moderators to report significant *nonverbal communication* (body language) that went on in the group and that may influence the interpretation of verbal comments.

Researchers may be tempted to try to reduce the vast amount of data coming from focus groups by "quantifying" it through such strategies as determining the percentage of participants who spoke in favor of some proposal. Sometimes such a strategy can help clarify a certain aspect of the discussions. It might help determine, for example, whether or not a majority of participants favored some proposal when the sessions began or whether men or women were more likely to favor the proposal.

It is *very* important, however, to use any such quantification only as a supplement to the main analysis and, even then, to apply great caution. In the first place, because participants are not statistically representative of some larger population, we cannot use quantitative data from the focus groups to generalize about the population. The use of such quantification is, therefore, very limited. More important, however, is the fact that qualitative analysis is about *gaining understanding and insight* rather than measuring relationships. Any use of numbers should not deflect researchers from this central objective.

One potentially productive application of a more quantitative approach to focus group data is the use of content analysis to help identify themes in the discussions. For example, if focus group participants were asked their reasons for opposing a hazardous waste incinerator, they would probably offer many different answers. A sophisticated content analysis of the transcripts might help by grouping those answers into a smaller set of related arguments that identified themes in the responses and indicated which occurred most often.

In all this, the researcher's job is to form an impression of how the participants felt about the topic and to produce a summary statement of their expressions. The object is not to explain why participants feel as they do in the scientific sense of explanation discussed in Chapters 2 and 5. Analysts might, however, draw on existing theories or their knowledge of the subject in order to offer interpretations of what participants meant by various comments, why participants said what they did in the manner in which they said it, or even how they developed these attitudes. Often the most useful insights derived from analyses of focus group results come from linking what was observed to larger theories or processes in order to highlight the *larger significance* of what was said in the focus groups. For instance, if focus groups reveal that residents of racially divided communities are denying the problem, a researcher may turn to theories of social psychology to interpret those residents' remarks as examples of coping mechanisms.

Reporting Focus Group Results

Reporting focus groups results can be as challenging as analyzing them. Whereas quantitative data can be reduced to measures of association and presented in tables, it is difficult to reproduce the richness of qualitative data for simple presentation. It is worth putting a good deal of time into meeting this challenge because the report is very important to the success of a project.

Richard Krueger suggests that reports perform three primary functions.[4] First, and most obvious, a report communicates to a given audience information about the results of a study. Only if it is easy for the intended audience to understand, and clear in its message, will it actually have an impact on how that audience sees the topic of the study and thereby influence scholarship or public policy. Second, the act of writing a report assists researchers in developing their own personal understanding of a project and the subject it was designed to address. Third, a report provides a usable historical record of the results of a project. Because focus group data are so complex, it is especially important to have a compact summary if the results are ever to be used as background for future studies.

Researchers usually choose among three basic approaches for reporting focus group results: (1) They can *present enough carefully selected quotations* from the participants to convey an accurate picture of the discussions. This amounts to providing a representative sampling of what was said so readers can draw their own conclusions. (2) They can *summarize statements* by participants to point out major themes, using quotes only for illustrative purposes. This is a descriptive approach in which researchers assume responsibility for deciding what is important enough to report but also in which they offer little analysis. (3) They can *interpret what was said* so as to provide understanding, using description and quotes only to support their conclusions or illustrate points. Which strategy is appropriate depends on the purpose of the focus group project and the nature of the intended audience for the report.

To know what kind of report is called for, researchers must ask who will receive it and what use will be made of it. To understand the significance of this, recall the list of conditions under which focus groups are useful that was presented earlier in

[4] Richard A. Krueger, *Focus Groups* (Newbury Park, CA: Sage, 1988), p. 125.

this chapter. If the focus groups were used to supplement another data collection technique, then the primary users of the report will be the researchers themselves, who will use understandings gained from the focus groups to formulate hypotheses, develop indicators, or assess their interpretation of data gathered by other means. Others may never see any more about the focus groups than a brief statement in a subsequent report to the effect that focus groups were used to frame the research question, design the project, or verify interpretations. In those cases, the report on the focus group results may be closer to the representative sampling of quotes just described, because the intended audience has the capability to draw informed conclusions from raw data.

If the focus groups were used to evaluate some aspect of public policy or assist in policy development, the audience for the report is likely to be persons who are less interested in the details of the sessions and more interested in the lessons to be learned from them. Such persons are, however, still also likely to want a strong sense of the thrust of the sessions. In this case, the report will probably rely heavily on summarized statements and a description of the key themes. Finally, if focus groups were used as a primary source of data collection (as in a study of small-group dynamics) and the results will appear in an academic publication, the report will have to be briefer and will have to stress interpretation of the sessions.

In conclusion, we want to highlight the point we made at the outset of this chapter. Focus groups can make a contribution at several stages of the research process. Not only can they serve as the primary data collection method for more qualitative studies, but they can also be integrated with quantitative methods. In the early stages of research, they can help clarify research questions or suggest new approaches to old problems. Once under way, they can help design measuring instruments to be used in interviews or direct observation. In the analysis stage, focus groups can improve our interpretation of quantitative data by shedding light on the meanings people attach to responses or actions.

Suggestions for Further Reading

A relatively brief general introduction to focus group methods is David W. Stewart and Prem N. Shamdasani, *Focus Groups: Theory and Practice* (Newbury Park, CA: Sage, 1990). William A. Gamson's *Talking Politics* (New York: Cambridge University Press, 1992) illustrates the use of focus groups in political science. A book that offers practical advice on how to conduct focus groups and that examines the kinds of problems that might be encountered is David L. Morgan, ed., *Successful Focus Groups* (Newbury Park, CA: Sage, 1993). For a more extensive treatment of the methodology, see David L. Morgan, *Focus Groups as Qualitative Research*, 2d ed. (Newbury Park, CA: Sage, 1997). Also see Thomas L. Greenbaum, *The Handbook for Focus Group Research*, 2d ed. (Newbury Park, CA: Sage, 1998).

Research Exercises

1. (This is an exercise that is best done by a team of students and can involve an entire class.) Conduct a focus group or, if possible, a set of focus groups to learn how college students perceive and are affected by the issue called "political correctness." Much attention has recently been focused on the idea that the words we use to discuss people and

events reflect our attitudes about the subjects of those discussions and help determine the status of those people and events in society. By that reasoning, means of expression are political and can be judged as more or less consistent with some set of values and, therefore, as "correct" or "incorrect."

Some commentators are worried that political correctness is being so strongly enforced that it threatens to stifle meaningful discussion of ideas, especially on college campuses. Others argue that there is no such danger and that advocates of "politically correct" language are simply calling attention to the biases inherent in much of what has come to be accepted as everyday speech. Who is right?

Write a statement of objective for a focus group, stating what you hope to learn about political correctness from the group. Develop a "guide" to the focused discussion, in which you identify some questions about political correctness that you want explored in a focus group composed of college students. You may want to know, for example, whether students are even aware of the issues raised by the idea of political correctness, whether they are receptive or hostile to the idea of politically correct language, whether they feel pressured to be politically correct, or how political correctness might be enforced (if at all) in their social circles. Then devise a set of standards by which you would select participants for such a focus group. You will want to consider whether the group should be heterogeneous—in terms of race, gender and social status—or should be homogeneous. Your choice will be affected by the purposes you devised for the group and by the number of groups you plan to hold.

Recruit 6 to 10 students who are not in your research methods class to take part in the group. Conduct the group using one of your team as the moderator and having the other members observe and take notes. Tape-record the session if possible. After the group leaves, go over the notes as a team, come to agreement about what was observed, and write a summary of the session. Analyze the discussion and ask yourself if it offered answers to the questions around which you designed the focus group.

Ideally, you can divide your entire class into several teams, have all the teams conduct focus groups with different students, and then compare results at the end to see how input from several groups may change the conclusions drawn from one group alone.

2. This exercise shows how focus groups can be used to enrich the information gathered through other means. It is also best done by a team.

Part A: Draw on what you learned from Exercise 1 above and from Chapter 7 on survey research to devise a brief questionnaire designed to measure people's opinions about *political correctness*. Write up an explanation of the ways in which the things you learned in Exercise 1 influenced the questions you choose and the expressions you use to phrase those questions.

Part B: Administer the questionnaire to 10 students from diverse backgrounds. Total the responses and look for simple patterns (for example, different answers from men and women or from people with different majors). Shortly after that, get as many of those students as possible to participate in a focus group that will review their reactions to the questionnaire. Try to find out what they thought was being asked with each question, how they chose their answer, what other issues they felt each question was related to, and how responding to the questionnaire made them feel. Review the notes from this focus group and make a list of all the things that surprised you—things that were revealed by the focus group that you had not thought of when you devised the questionnaire or that might affect your interpretation of the responses you received.

Terms Introduced in This Chapter

focus group	guide
moderator	screening interview

CHAPTER 21

WRITING (OR READING) THE RESEARCH REPORT

If the purpose of science is to discover or to understand the world we live in, then the purpose of scientific writing must be to communicate our discoveries or understandings to others in as effective a manner as possible. Just as science, or social science, itself must be explicit, systematic, and controlled, the descriptions and assessments of scientific findings must be clear, complete, and—most especially—well organized. Because it often constitutes the first statement of discovery, and because it provides a primary means for developing a shared understanding, the research report is one of the most important, and potentially most effective, instruments of scientific communication.

But good research reports do not simply emerge, unassisted, from good research. Rather, the writing of a solid report requires every bit as much craftsmanship, and every bit as much practice, as any other stage of the research process. It requires the same planning, careful organization, clarity of thought and expression, and attention to detail that have been exercised all along the way. And while it is true that good research eases the writing of a good research report, it is equally true that a poorly written report can obscure the value of even the best research effort. After all, the research report is the *only* means we have to tell others of our work, and, conversely, it is the *only* means by which those others can learn what we have accomplished. If we fail to communicate fully and effectively, the value of our research itself is greatly lessened.

In general, considerations of style, organization, proper grammar and usage, and other elements of effective writing lie well beyond the scope of this book. There are, however, a number of practical concerns that have a particular bearing on the writing of the research report and that do deserve some comment. In the present chapter we examine several of these very briefly and present an annotated example of research reporting to help illustrate applications. Although the chapter itself is oriented toward writing a research report, the points we present provide as well a basis for the *critical reading* of research reports prepared by others.

The Plan

Planning a research report should begin at the earliest stages of the research process. The selection of a topic, the systematic examination of related literature, the formulation of hypotheses, the determination of what type of evidence is required and how it is to be obtained, the decision about how the resulting data are to be analyzed—each of these actions contributes in an important way to the writing of the research report, and each should be undertaken with that fact in mind. Indeed, one of the greatest dangers the beginning researcher can confront is the tendency to compartmentalize the work, to treat each stage in the research process as if it were virtually independent of every other stage. In point of fact, the reverse is true. No stage of research, from problem formulation to the reporting of results, stands alone. Not only is each stage dependent on every other stage, but each must also be carried out with the others in mind. We may speak of six stages of the research process, but we speak of only one unified *process*.

Nowhere is this interdependence of parts clearer than in the writing of a research report, for it is in that report that we must join the pieces of our work together. We must state precisely our concepts and definitions; demonstrate the linkage between concept and research; describe, summarize, and evaluate our procedures and results; and assess our findings as they relate back to our concepts. In reality, then, the planning of a research report is inseparable from the planning of the research itself, and the writing of a report is inseparable from the conduct of our inquiry.

The Structure

Because different subjects and different approaches to research can give rise to many different forms of research report, it is neither possible nor desirable to set forth hard-and-fast rules for the structure of these communications. We can, however, suggest the basic elements that should be present in any such report and point out the most commonly accepted way of organizing them. Those elements are (1) the introduction, (2) the statement of research methods, (3) the statement of findings, and (4) the conclusion.

The introduction to a research report should state clearly the theme or purpose of the research, the principal hypotheses (work that is primarily descriptive may not include hypotheses), and the rationale underlying both the conduct of the research and the writing of the report. Whenever possible, these elements should be integrated by a review of the relevant literature that brings to bear both the research and the theories of those who have worked on related problems in the past. The author may challenge or discount that literature but should be sure to cite it when appropriate and to state clearly the reasons for making certain judgments. In general, the purpose of the introduction is to set forth the *goals* of the work, to defend them, and to put them into what the author regards as the proper perspective.

It is at this point, too, that we alert readers to what we see as the major significance (the main contribution) of the research being reported. Only if the purpose of the work is stated clearly at the outset can readers judge the relevance to the central point of each argument or piece of data analysis presented. Surprise endings may be appropriate for short stories, but in a research report they only create extra work for readers.

The introduction is usually followed by a discussion of the method used in the study. What was the source of data for the research? How were data gathered? Was there a sample? How was it selected? How many cases were included? How were the principal variables operationalized? Did the study encounter any special problems or develop any special instruments (for example, a new scale for measuring a particular attitude or behavior) worthy of note? The object here is to make a complete and precise statement of the steps taken in performing the research. As we pointed out in the introductory chapters, one important benefit of science as a way of knowing is that the findings of science are replicable, that the scientific method provides a way for sharing and evaluating both knowledge and the way to knowledge. Only if we state explicitly what we have done during the undertaking of our research can the results of our work be judged fully and critically by others. *The statement of the method of our study is the component of the research report that contributes most directly to such sharing.* For that reason, it must be written with honesty, thoroughness, care, and precision.

The third major element of a research report is the presentation of findings. It is at this point that we include, for example, tables, graphs, or charts that may help to summarize the results of our work, together with statistical or other analysis that may prove germane. Many researchers have a tendency at this point in their writing to include every shred of evidence and every table or chart that they examined when analyzing their data. The result is often a presentation that overwhelms the reader with unedited facts, some of which may be only marginally useful. It amounts to something of a *laissez-faire* approach to writing: here are the facts—you decipher them however you wish. Yet no one is better placed to identify and assess the meaning of a set of research results than is the researcher. Indeed, it is an obligation of the researcher to present in as clear a manner as possible only those results that speak most pointedly to the issues at hand.

Two suggestions, one general and one more specific, may offer some guidance here. First, the presentation of findings should be organized so as to illustrate the principal variables, hypotheses, or arguments set forth in the introduction to the report. Results not relating directly and importantly to these foci should not be included. By keeping this in mind, the researcher not only can eliminate a great deal of trivia from the report but also can present in a logical and, from the perspective of the reader, a meaningful manner those findings that are included. Second, it is a general rule of thumb that any table, chart, or graph included in a research report should be accompanied by at least a page of text in which the points illustrated and their significance are discussed. If the researcher cannot generate enough points of discussion to fill a page, it is quite likely that the particular table, chart, or graph in question is not sufficiently important to warrant inclusion in the report.

We also should note at this point that the researcher should not be reluctant to report either unexpected results or "nonfindings." The fact that a hypothesis is not supported by one's data may be just as important and scientifically interesting as the fact that it is. Thus the criterion for including or excluding a piece of evidence in writing a research report is not whether or not it shows anything or whether or not what a piece of evidence shows is what was predicted, but, rather, whether what it shows is of any importance or interest.

Finally, a research report generally concludes with a summary of findings, a discussion of the relationships between those findings and the theory in which the research was grounded, and, in some cases, an evaluation of the method of the study. Have we found anything of significance? If so, why is it significant, and what does it tell us? If not, why not? Were our hypotheses simply incorrect, or did we make some error or encounter some problem in designing or carrying out our research that prevented us from finding supporting evidence? Where do we go from here? This section of the report is, in effect, retrospective toward both the research paper and the research process. It presents the researcher with an opportunity to place the work in proper perspective between past and future scientific effort.

The placement of these several elements can vary somewhat depending on the development of a particular research report, but all or most will usually be present. In fact, these components can serve as an outline or organizing basis for most research reports, and the beginning researcher should take some care to see that each component is represented where appropriate and also that the relationship among them in the body of the report is both straightforward and logical.

The Style

Research reports are not—nor should they be—written like best-selling novels. Unlike novelists, scientists often must communicate very complex technical information to a specialized audience in a relatively small space. But it does not follow that scientific writing must be stodgy and heavy-handed, nor so overburdened with jargon as to be virtually incomprehensible to all but a select few. A more appropriate mode is one in which readability is coequal with precision, and clarity with thoroughness. The following guidelines may help you to achieve these goals.[1]

1. Work from an *outline.* Be sure the logic of your writing is clear to the reader.
2. Use words and phrases with which you are comfortable. Do not use big words just because they sound impressive. At the same time, use the word that most precisely defines your terms.
3. Reread, revise, and rewrite. Reading your work aloud to see if it sounds right can help to identify and smooth out obvious rough spots. First drafts are *never* final drafts.
4. Seek others' opinions when possible. Often researchers are so close to their subject that they cannot clearly see what is necessary to convey the information they want to communicate. Asking friends or colleagues who are likely to be familiar with your basic research method to read a draft of the report can alert you to errors that countless readings on your own will not reveal.

---

[1] For a more extensive disucssion of these and related points, consult William Strunk, Jr., with E. B. White, *The Elements of Style,* 4th ed. (Boston: Allyn and Bacon, 2000).

5. Do not overstate a point. For example, you will find very few exclamation points in scientific writing. Rhetoric and research should remain separate.

6. Be sure to differentiate between observations and opinion.

One additional element of style—the proper footnoting and documentation of source materials—deserves mention. Footnoting and documentation are not petty harassments or empty formalisms dreamed up by professors as a means of torturing students. They are essential to the academic enterprise. Documentation keeps us intellectually honest by preventing the fabrication of convenient evidence. More important, it provides a basis on which others can judge the validity of our arguments. If we draw evidence from dependable sources or rely on the opinions of informed authorities in reaching our own conclusions, the persuasiveness of our argument is increased. Without proper documentation, readers cannot evaluate the merit of our conclusions except to the extent that they derive from abstract logic or from our own data.

If we use the ideas of others or cite facts they report, we must document this either with a bibliographic entry that includes a full description of the source and a footnote that ties specific material in our paper to particular pages in the source document or, alternatively, with a more complete footnote that combines both types of information. Footnotes should be used *whenever* we borrow facts or ideas from another author. Not only direct quotations, but *any* data or ideas we draw from the work of others must be accompanied by footnotes. Information on the form and placement of footnotes and a bibliography is best obtained from a style manual, three of which are listed at the end of this chapter. Alternatively, we might adopt the footnote style of a major journal, such as the *American Political Science Review* or the *Journal of Politics*. Consistent form and complete information are the keys to documenting a research report correctly.

The Title and Abstract

The title of a research report should be descriptive and complete, but it should not be overly detailed. It should give readers a good idea of what the report discusses, but not so good an idea that one need not read the paper. Compare, for example, the following alternative titles for the same research:

1. *Politics on the Day That Hell Freezes Over*

2. *Control over the Distribution of Scarce Resources at Such Time as the Temperature of Certain Regions Remains below 0° Celsius throughout the Month of July, as Measured on a Mercury Thermometer and through the Use of Pretested Survey Instruments, Including Guttman Scales, on a Small Population of Residents of Minot, North Dakota: An Experiment*

3. *The Effects of Climate on the Distribution of Political Resources*

Title 1 is short and to the point but not sufficiently descriptive to give the reader much idea of the article's content. Title 2 is so comprehensive as to be unwieldy. Only title 3 conveys the content of the report without undue attention to detail. The point is that the title should tell the reader the general topic of the report, but should not itself substitute for the sections of the report that deal with methods and findings.

Often, we find it useful to follow the title page of a report with an **abstract,** a brief statement, usually not more than 150 words and often no more than one or two sentences, in which we briefly summarize the contents of our report. The summary usually includes in barest outline a statement of what we have found, how we found it, and why it is important. Consider the following example:

> *ABSTRACT: The Effects of Climate on the Distribution of Political Resources*
> Using both temperature and survey data from a study of Minot, North Dakota, the author concludes that resource allocations vary systematically with changes in the weather. More particularly, the data suggest that the poor are more adequately cared for and the downtrodden raised higher on the proverbial cold day in July than at other times. This finding offers considerable support for the hypotheses of Marx, Weber, and others.

By giving readers a concise summary of the accompanying report, the abstract tells one whether the material is likely to be of sufficient interest to warrant a close reading and thereby obviates the need for an extended title.

Conclusion

One final question that often arises pertaining to research reports is that of length. How long should a report be? There is no simple answer to this question. Most journals in political science prefer manuscripts of some 25 to 30 pages typed double-spaced. A master's thesis may run to 100 or 200 pages, and a doctoral dissertation may take several hundred. Student research reports may run anywhere from 10 to 50 pages, though 25 to 30 is probably more common. In general, it is probably best to let the material itself determine the length of the report. The argument should be adequately developed and the appropriate literature adequately reviewed. The method of the study should be fully expounded, and the results fully but judiciously reported. The conclusions should be both well developed and properly supported. Yet the length of each portion will vary from one report to the next. How long, then, should a research report be? As long as it must, but no longer.

A Case in Point

The remainder of this chapter is devoted to an annotated example of a research report. The example illustrates most of the elements we have described, and it should suggest to you the ways in which these components can be combined to produce an informative research report. The source of this report is Jarol B. Manheim and Robert B. Albritton, "Changing National Images: International Public Relations and Media Agenda Setting," *American Political Science Review,* 78 (1984), pp. 641-57; reprinted by permission of the publisher.

Changing National Images:
International Public Relations
and Media Agenda Setting

Jarol B. Manheim

Robert B. Albritton

Research within the agenda-setting framework has generally ignored the potential influence of purposive efforts by external actors (those outside the political system) to manipulate media coverage related to their interests. The present study uses interrupted time-series analysis to examine one such set of manipulative efforts, those undertaken by professional public relations consultants to influence the images of foreign nations as portrayed in the United States press. Data represent New York Times *coverage of six nations that signed public relations contracts with American firms during the period from 1974 to 1978, and one nation that expressly rejected such a contract. The analysis identifies consistent patterns of improvement along two primary dimensions of national image, visibility and valence, which are associated in time with the public relations contracts.*

None of the regular ways you report in the United States apply. You can't run to people on the streets and stick a camera in their faces. You don't speak their language, and if they don't like you, then they shoot you. It's very, very frustrating to work in places like that [Lebanon]....The normal ways in which you pursue stories just go totally out the window.

It is difficult to go beyond the information that is chewed up and dispensed to you every day. It's maddening when you have to rely on the [official] spokesmen, and you strongly suspect that they're not playing it down the middle....For most of us, we're constantly going to be thrown into situations under enormous time pressure, under enormous pressure to produce....Those are problems I really don't see a solution to. (Josh Mankiewicz, ABC News foreign correspondent, cited in Weisman, 1983)

Even for senior officials, reading dispatches from newspaper correspondents abroad can provide a useful corrective to the intelligence reports and diplomatic cables that cross their desks every day; indeed, a good many of those reports and cables are themselves based on analysis of stories in the foreign press. For lesser officials and for legislators not privy to the full flow of internal documents, the press is often the main source of up-to-date information on goings-on in other capitals.

If officials in one government rely on foreign correspondence as a source of information, then officials in another government have some incentives to use the news to transmit information to them. (Leon V. Sigal, 1973)

Everybody [uses reports from the newspapers to measure the decline of political violence in El Salvador]. That's basically the general source. (Thomas Enders, at the time Assistant Secretary of State for Inter-American Affairs, on *The MacNeil-Lehrer Report,* January 21, 1983)

Introduction

One of the most interesting trends in political image-making in recent years has been the growing use of professional public relations consultants by national governments.[1] This trend has been especially pronounced in the United States, where such assistance is readily available and where, the assumption seems to be, an improved national image can be translated into more concrete gains.

Although a few such efforts had been undertaken earlier, the 1970s saw a veritable explosion of lobbying and public information campaigns on behalf of foreign governments. Foreign agent registration records of the Department of Justice show, for example, that between 1974 and 1978 alone some 25 nations contracted with American public relations firms for assistance. Although the goals of these campaigns vary, one of the most common is to improve the client nation's image in the American press.[2] In the present analysis we shall examine the impact that such public relations efforts have had on news coverage of the contracting nations in one of the most influential newspapers in the United States, the *New York Times*.

The Agenda-Setting Framework: An Overview

Review of literature

Discussion of graphic presentation

Social scientists have long recognized the importance of images and symbols in public information campaigns. Most recently this recognition has centered on the notion of agenda setting and its implications for the exercise of political control. As indicated in Figure 1, this conceptualization has emphasized the structuring and interactions among three distinct agendas, those of the mass media, the public, and policymakers. In general, the policy agenda (often referred to as the "formal" agenda) has been described as specific, decision-oriented, detailed, and based primarily on direct or experiential information that is relatively independent of the relationships illustrated in Figure 1 (Cobb & Elder, 1972, especially pp. 82–93). The public agenda has been seen as more general, more ambiguous or symbolic in character, and more likely to be based on indirect (mediated) information for most issues (Cobb & Elder, 1972; Miller, Goldenberg, & Erbring, 1979; Robinson & Hefner, 1968; cf. Kelman & Ezekiel, 1970). The media agenda has been pictured as actively interpretive, market oriented, and based on a mixture of direct (reporter as observer) and indirect (reporter as conduit) information (Bennett, 1983; Epstein, 1973; Sigal, 1973).

Source citation

Agenda setting, then, is the process by which items enter upon or pass between these respective agendas, and its study emphasizes the ways in which each interacts with the others and with their mutual external environment. Indeed, the most recent work within this framework has been the most generic in this regard. Graber (1984), for example, has demonstrated the psychological processes by which members of a news audience select and internalize information from the media. Page and Shapiro (1983) have demonstrated

Explanatory footnote

---

[1] Although the present analysis focuses on use of public relations by governments to influence their images in another country, similar practices are emerging even within countries. The British government, for example, recently contracted with an American public relations firm to generate support among its own citizens for the deployment of intermediate-range nuclear missiles ("U.K. Plans ads to support deployment of missiles," 1983).

[2] Each of five firms responding to our request for information about the services they provide for such clients reported that these informational efforts were central to their activities.

Graphic presentation

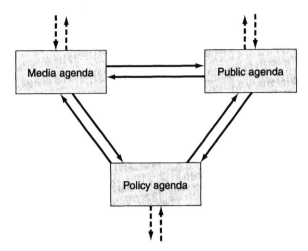

Figure 1   *The Agenda-Setting System*

leading effects of the public agenda on the policy agenda for both foreign and domestic issues, and Iyengar, Peters, and Kinder (1982) have shown that media coverage of issues influences their presence and importance on the public agenda. Cook et al. (1983) have provided preliminary evidence that the mass media exercise direct influence on policymakers and others influential in the policy process. In addition, Cook (1982) has examined the ways in which issues disappear from the agenda, an aspect of the process that had previously been overlooked.

Much of the research on agenda setting, and especially that exploring linkages between the media and public agendas, has focused on political campaigning (Patterson & McClure, 1976; Shaw & McCombs, 1977), and indeed, the important, early work on media agenda setting (McCombs & Shaw, 1972) was undertaken in this context. Because the campaign represents an empirically distinguishable set of communications which are overtly persuasive in intent, are bounded by identifiable time points, and have an audience (potential voters) that has been presensitized to both their availability and their significance, campaign messages represent a target of opportunity for political communication researchers. We believe, however, that for precisely these same reasons campaign communication is atypical not only of political communication generally, but of communication with a persuasive intent in particular. Rather, we believe that most such communication is more subtle in style, more diffused through time, less readily recognizable to its audience, and less clearly tied to judgmental or behavioral expectations. Such communication often takes the form less of generating a set of messages than of directing, facilitating, inhibiting, and generally controlling the overall flow of information.

The balance of research into agenda setting, that which examines non-campaign communication, is often characterized by a similarly limiting assumption, namely that the external environment in which the process operates is benign, or at least neutral. Public officials and reporters may try to manipulate one another (Sigal, 1973), the media may attune their coverage and editorial criteria to their audience (Bennett, 1983) or their corporate well-being (Epstein, 1973), and symbolic outputs may substitute for substantive policymaking (Elder & Cobb, 1983), but all of these are viewed merely as regular transactions within and among the media, the public, and the policymakers. The generation of information from outside, that which the various actors gather independently of one another, is regarded, if the absence of scholarly attention is an indicator, as a controlled exercise. The information is there for the taking, and those who supply it are passive sources. Here, too, we believe that the present conceptualization of agenda setting falls short in that it directs our attention away from forces that may well be shaping the flow of information.

Statement of how the literature applies to the problem at hand; the statement of purpose

It is in this context that we have undertaken the present research, which focuses on systematic attempts by external actors to manipulate the media agenda, and through it the public and policy agendas. These efforts are illustrated in Figure 2. In particular, we shall examine the effectiveness of structured attempts by foreign nations to manipulate the ways in which they are portrayed in the United States press. (The broken line in Figure 2 represents direct lobbying efforts which are often associated with, but for our purposes will remain analytically distinct from, the attempt to control the flow of information to and through the media.)

Rationale underlying approach to the research

Such efforts to manipulate media coverage of foreign actors, events and policy issues are relatively likely to succeed for several reasons. To begin with, foreign affairs are generally unobtrusive, i.e, the public is unlikely to have any direct experience with them (Eyal, 1981). In the absence of direct personal contact, individuals' images of the actors and events on the international scene will be heavily, and unavoidably, media dependent. (This is a logical extension of the argument raised by Palmgreen and Clarke, 1977.) Second, because they are limited in their ability and inclination to devote staff and resources to foreign affairs (and because audience interest in such matters is relatively low in any event), American media may be especially vulnerable to manipulation of their international coverage (Becker, 1977). Third, information gathering about such issues is difficult even for public officials (Cohen, 1963; Sigal, 1973), and as a consequence policymakers themselves may be forced to rely in some measure on media reports for information about events or settings. Indeed, even the direct reports on which foreign policymakers most rely are often based to some extent on local or international media coverage and interpretations. The protagonists in these manipulative efforts, for-

Graphic presentation

Figure 2 *Public Relations and Agenda Setting*

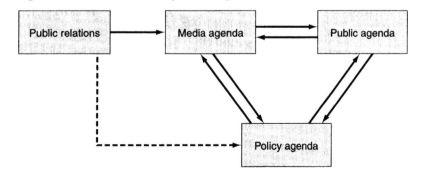

eign governments, clearly lie outside the system of agenda exchanges, but their interest in its operation is nevertheless keen. Media coverage has long been used by such external actors both to reach interested publics in the United States and to provide an informal communication channel to United States policymakers themselves (Davison, 1974; Sigal, 1973).

This combination of motive and opportunity places foreign governments in a potentially very favorable position vis-à-vis the dynamics of agenda setting. For one thing, they are precisely situated to catch the system with its figurative guard down, in effect to sneak past the gatekeepers by entering the agenda-setting process at a point where the independent information-gathering powers of all three primary actors are most limited. Yet at the same time, they can take full advantage of the operating propensities of that system. As Page and Shapiro (1983), Graber (1983) and others have demonstrated, the internal forces of agenda setting function in foreign affairs much as they do in the domestic arena. The process works in those instances where it is vulnerable to such external intervention just as it does elsewhere. Thus with its emphasis on public relations interventions in behalf of foreign governments, the present research examines a situation in which the internal operations of the agenda system are likely to be functioning in a normal fashion, but in which the external environment may be, in a sense, relatively more proactive (and more effectively so) than is generally recognized.

Agenda Manipulation and Image Change

Definition of the research question

For the present, we shall confine our attention to the first stage of these attempts at agenda manipulation, the influencing to a nation's advantage of its coverage in the United States press. In general, long-term patterns of foreign news coverage have been found to vary in association with the levels of trade and telecommunications traffic between the United States and the nation in question, that nation's overall status or importance in the world, the population of the country, the apparent national interest of the United States, the occurrence of crises, and the problems posed by foreign censors (Charles, Shore, & Todd, 1979; Lent, 1977; Peterson, 1981). With the possible exception of crises, we see these factors as establishing a baseline for the overall level and type of coverage any given nation is likely to receive. This baseline is then subjected to trends in the long term as these factors undergo secular change, and to disturbances in the short term as events of varying character and duration occur. All of the nations we have studied were, at the times in question, experiencing political difficulties that undoubtedly contributed to the decision of each government to attempt to manipulate the media agenda. It is important to note, however, that by and large these difficulties continued unabated throughout the entire period of our analysis in each case, and that there was no apparent, consistent structural or temporal pattern of issue or event maturation associated in time with the respective decisions of these various countries to undertake manipulative behaviors.

Identification of the independent variable

The particular behavior we examine is the signing by various governments of contracts with American public relations firms for the sole or partial purpose of influencing the flow of information about that country to or within the United States. Mendelsohn (1973) has demonstrated that when used with some sophistication, information campaigns can have an impact on public perceptions, and, more recently, Merritt (1980) has suggested that governments are becoming sophisticated communicators by learning to structure informational settings to facilitate persuasion rather than by relying on more heavy-handed propaganda techniques. Marcum (1963) has documented such an instance in which Portugal, at the time fighting to maintain control of Angola, successfully employed an American public relations firm to guide American attitudes into opposing the struggle for national liberation. And Davis (1977) has provided a comprehensive longitudinal case study of the use of public relations in behalf of Nigeria and its various regional and economic interests that focuses directly on the terms and conditions of the contracts themselves.

As one might expect, the preparation of press kits, direct mailings, newsletters, and brochures is prominent among the services provided under public relations contracts. More important, however, public relations firms also routinely counsel their international clients' embassy personnel on how to talk about such problems as terrorism or human rights, schedule and conduct field trips for the press, organize visits with editors and lunches with business groups, conduct financial seminars dealing with opportunities offered by the countries, use their own contacts to help representatives of the client states develop personal relationships with officials of the United States government, and provide a variety of advice about specific policies or approaches to policy that a client government might adopt to improve its image. Perhaps one of the most important services such firms offer is to provide easier access to officials of the government in question for American reporters (Cooney, 1979; Davis, 1977).

Definition of key concept

Nimmo and Savage (1976, p. 8) have defined an image as "a human construct imposed on an array of perceived attributes projected by an object, event, or person" which is subject to influence by messages issued by some external actor. This definition provides a useful starting point for the present analysis because it allows us to distinguish between the perceived image (which Nimmo and Savage emphasize and which will provide the ultimate measure of public relations impacts on the public agenda) and the projected image, the messages through which imagemakers attempt to generate or change public perceptions. In this article we shall focus on the latter.

Identification of the dependent variables

Two aspects of national images as portrayed in the United States press are of particular importance. The first, visibility, refers to the amount of media coverage that the country receives. The second, valence, refers to the degree to which the content that is available reflects either favorably or unfavorably on the country. The relationship between these primary components of national image is illustrated in Figure 3.

Discussion of graphic presentation

Quadrant 1 in Figure 3 represents countries with negative images that receive relatively heavy media attention. This type of coverage is likely to be accompanied by substantial public awareness of the country in question and of its projected image (Benton & Frazier, 1976). In such circumstances, overt efforts to portray a country in a positive light are likely to be rejected, either by the media or the public, as propaganda in the most pejorative sense (Merritt, 1980; Wolfsfeld, 1383). Hence effective public relations on behalf of such

Development of conceptual model

countries should probably take the form of reducing visibility, perhaps by controlling access to events and information or, alternatively, by altering or reducing the amount of government-generated information. But whatever the tactic, constructive image change here should be centered on the visibility dimension.

Graphic presentation

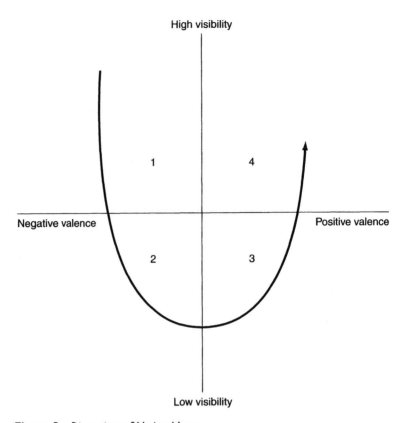

Figure 3   *Dimensions of National Image*

Quadrant 2 represents countries whose images may be quite negative, but whose visibility is sufficiently low that the public is unlikely to know or to think much about them. This is similar to what Krugman (1965) has described as a condition conducive to low-involvement learning in which an audience is particularly susceptible to certain types of persuasive communication that it might otherwise find unpalatable, and also corresponds to the type of setting that Wolfsfeld (1983) sees as the most conducive to successful persuasion through international propaganda. Thus for countries in quadrant 2, and especially for those whose visibility in the media is the lowest, effective public relations should emphasize more substantive forms of image enhancement rather than mere withdrawal from the agenda. Put another way, the lower a country's initial visibility, the more the target of any efforts at constructive image change should move from the visibility to the valence dimension. Although not concerned directly with the valence of policy images, Eyal (1981) has suggested that most foreign policy issues would have relatively low visibility and low levels of associated public awareness, and in fact the images of all but one of the countries we have analyzed lay within quadrant 2 and could be so characterized.

Passing between quadrants 2 and 3, one crosses the boundary between what Cohen (1973) has termed reactive manipulation (putting out fires) and active manipulation (positive image development). And indeed quadrants 3 and 4 are to an extent mirror images of their negatively valenced counterparts.

Because countries in both quadrants start from a more favored position, the focus of their public relations is more likely to be on increasing visibility and further enhancing valence in order to reinforce a desired image. McGuire (1964) has suggested for such purposes a strategy of inoculation against negative slippage which uses such persuasive themes and devices as the forging of links between the image in question and various valued goals of the public or, alternatively, encouraging public expressions of acceptance of the image. None of the nations in this study could be characterized as having had a positive image either at the time the contract was signed or during the preceding year. This should not be surprising, because countries with more positive images are less likely to perceive a need for public relations counseling. Accordingly, our analysis will focus on countries in the first two quadrants.

Use of conceptual model to predict influence of independent variable on dependent variables

Taken together, the situation-specific strategies we have described above suggest that an informed approach to public relations activity on behalf of foreign nations is likely to vary systematically depending upon the initial position of the client state on the two dimensions of the informational setting represented in Figure 3. The goals and associated tactics of such efforts are summarized by movement along the path indicated in the figure. The question at hand is whether actual public relations campaigns produce effects that are consistent with the pattern suggested here. Evidence of such a pattern may well indicate the effective exercise of agenda manipulation.

Analysis of News Coverage

Selection of samples

Our analysis centers on coverage of six nations—the Republic of Korea, the Philippines, Yugoslavia, Argentina, Indonesia, and Rhodesia—in the *New York Times,* each during a two-year period associated with a professional public relations effort, and of a seventh nation, Mexico, which in December 1975 expressly declined to contract for such services.[3] The contracting

Sampling criteria

nations were selected to reflect a variety of factors including differences in population, location, and historical and political circumstance, as well as constellations of differing visibility and valence characteristics that are useful for examining the questions we have raised. Mexico, which faced image problems quite similar to those of the other nations, represents the only specific control we have been able to identify during the period in question in that it is the only country for which we have been able to document a specific decision at a specific point in time *not* to seek professional public relations counseling

Selection criteria for source of data on dependent variables

from an American firm. The *New York Times* was selected because it is the most widely read newspaper among elites both within and outside of government (Weiss, 1974) and among the most widely cited by policymakers (Grau, 1976), it has been shown to have a strong agenda-setting effect on public opinion (Winter & Eyal, 1981), it carries a higher volume of foreign news than other major U.S. newspapers (Semmel, 1976), and it is often used as a source of events data by researchers (Topple, 1982). In addition, precisely because it is atypical of the U.S. press in that it devotes more of its own space and resources to foreign news coverage and is therefore among the most

Footnote specifying cases and time periods

[3] Analysis periods were as follows: Republic of Korea, April 1977 through March 1979; Philippines, February 1977 through January 1979; Yugoslavia, December 1976 through November 1978; Argentina, June 1975 through May 1977; Indonesia, July 1976 through June 1978; Rhodesia, December 1975 through November 1977; and Mexico, January 1975 through December 1976.

independent of U.S. newspapers in its information gathering, the *New York Times* represents not only a primary target for public relations efforts, but an acid test of their effectiveness as well.

**Selection of cases and
time period**

From the mandatory foreign agent registration records of the Justice Department, we first identified those countries that had hired American public relations consultants during the period from 1974 to 1978 and the month in which each contract was signed.[4] For purposes of analysis, we defined the first day of the following month to be the point of intervention in each instance. For Mexico, the same treatment was applied to the date of the decision to forgo a contract. We then determined for each country a unique 24-month period including the 12 months immediately before and after the intervention, and gathered serial data on several qualitative and quantitative indicators of the news coverage of that country in the *New York Times*. Our data were drawn from the summaries of all articles provided in the *New York Times Index*.[5]

Unit of analysis

Coding procedure

Treating each insertion in the index as a unit of analysis and the aggregates for each month as a single observation, we coded news coverage of each country on several variables including (but not limited to) the number of articles pertaining to the country and the number of such articles which could be judged as portraying either a positive or a negative image. Negative references included any mention of decline, weakness, poverty, liabilities, lack of progress, instability, or unreliability on the part of a given country. Positive references included such points of discussion as a country's progress, advances, resources, assets, strengths, continuity, stability, reliability, or dependability.[6]

**Discussion of
independent variable**

The actual public relations advice, of course, was provided in private meetings to which we were not privy, and although we have been able to obtain some materials developed by public relations firms for their international clients, we can do little more than guess at the specifics of what suggestions were made, which were accepted, and how they were implemented. In effect, although the intervention is a matter of public record, its precise nature is, for the present, something of a black box. What we can observe, however, is any change in the behavior or news coverage of a given client state associated in time with the contract to determine the effects of the public relations effort and to support speculation about its elements. Thus our primary concern here is less with the components of the intervention than with its effects.

**Discussion of context of
the research**

At the anecdotal level, several patterns of behavior can be noted among the countries under review which are associated in time with, and seem to reflect, the public relations effort. These include such devices as visits of the

---

**Footnote discussing
selection of cases**

**Footnote discussing
validity of index-based
content analysis**

**Footnote reporting
reliability of measures**

[4] The initial population of 25 contracting countries was reduced to 15 by eliminating those for which the overall amount of *New York Times* coverage was too limited to permit meaningful statistical analysis. To the best of our knowledge, none of the contracts analyzed here represented an extension of an earlier agreement.

[5] Previous research has shown that index entries even substantially more abbreviated than those in the *New York Times Index* provide a useful indication of the content of the items in question (Ptacek et al., 1975), and others have used the *New York Times Index* itself (e.g., Azar et al., 1972). Graber (1983) has found in a study of domestic campaign coverage that coding the index as opposed to the full *New York Times* text tends to understate the amount of coverage of foreign affairs issues, but since we are dealing here primarily with identifying objects and general characteristics of coverage rather than specific assertions, and since, in any event, Graber's data suggest no reason to suspect systematic differences in coverage between periods, we do not believe the variations she has observed will materially bear on the present data except to warn that we may actually be understating public relations effects by using relatively insensitive measures.

[6] The coefficients of intercoder reliability (in this case Pearson's *r* measuring the correlation between two coders' scoring of the same text) for number of articles and number of negative and positive references were 1.0, .90, and .84.

head of state to the United States or the issuance of an invitation for the American president or vice-president to visit a given country, ending of political arrests followed by one or more releases or reductions in the sentences of either leading dissidents or masses of political prisoners, government-organized field trips for journalists to locations which call attention to the government's own agenda or point of view, cosmetic redistributions of power within the country, initiation of or recommitment to extended international negotiations, the scheduling of elections, establishment of overseas information offices, and the dissemination of particular stories or symbols that are clearly designed to appeal to certain constituencies in the United States or elsewhere. A brief review of the circumstances and events in each of our countries will help to illustrate the point.

Republic of Korea. The analysis period includes the two years beginning in April 1977. During this period, the United States gave prolonged consideration to a reduction of its forces stationed in the country, the government engaged in a series of disagreements with the Roman Catholic church, the United States was accused of spying on South Korean leaders, Korean bribery of U.S. congressmen was under investigation, and opposition leader Kim Dae Jong was placed under arrest after disappearing from Japan. Among the anecdotal evidence of public relations activity during the post-intervention period were a visit by Soviet leader Leonid Brezhnev (a reminder of the potential dangers of an American military withdrawal), resumption of on-again-off-again negotiations with North Korea over reunification, a meeting between Presidents Park and Carter, continuation of an earlier pattern of prisoner releases, a U.S. Senate study tour of the country, and the development of a newly discovered North Korean infiltration tunnel into a publicized tourist attraction. In addition, the *New York Times* reported some two months after the intervention that the Korean government had become noticeably more sensitive to its image abroad.

The Philippines. The analysis period began in February 1977. Events during this period included a continuing Moslem rebellion in the south, imposition of martial law, detention of journalists, discussion of continuing leases for U.S. military bases, and a series of incidents of political violence. Post-intervention events in this instance included a visit by Vice President Mondale, formation of a new pro-Marcos political party and holding of elections by President Marcos, a promise that increased power would be granted to the legislature, the reluctant freeing of a leading dissident and a series of pardons, amnesties and releases of political prisoners, signals of improving relations with China (again a reminder of the country's strategic importance) including a Chinese visit to Manila, and the highly publicized discovery of a primitive tribe in a remote area (despite some indications that the tribe had actually been discovered earlier). The public relations contract itself briefly surfaced as an issue when, in a rare opportunity to appear on television during the election campaign, President Marcos's opponent charged that the government had hired an American public relations firm with CIA connections.

Yugoslavia. Here the analysis period began in 1976. During the two years in question, Yugoslav agents and activities overseas were subjected to several attacks by Croatian dissidents, President Tito traveled extensively (France, Portugal, Algeria, China, the Soviet Union, North Korea, and, after the intervention, the United States) and was visited by heads of state and by Vice President Mondale, the government negotiated a series of international loans and trade arrangements, and the nation prepared for the transition of power after Tito's death. Anecdotal evidence relating to the public relations campaign here is more difficult to identify, but may include a series of articles on the stabilizing role to be played by the military during the transition.

Argentina. The analysis here covers the period beginning in June 1975. During the two years under review, inflation, strikes, and government deficits plagued the Argentine economy, terrorists and guerrillas threatened the stability of the Perón regime and the President herself took a leave of absence to avert a military coup, an investigation was launched into charges of government corruption, Perón announced that she would not seek re-election and later withstood an attempt at impeachment, cabinet changes were regular events, Perón was arrested in a military takeover (month 10) and Videla was elected president, Videla narrowly escaped two assassination attempts, and the government was repeatedly criticized for its human rights policies. Post-intervention activities of the military government included the release of political prisoners, reopening of a leading university, imposition of a ban on anti-Semitic and pro-Nazi literature, frequent announcements that foreign debt and other economic problems were being resolved, replacement of several generals in the government with moderate civilians, and calls by President Videla for a rapid return to democracy.

Indonesia. Here the review period commenced in July 1976. Major events included bribery scandals involving international oil companies and the Indonesian military, a foiled coup attempt, the banning of *Newsweek*, charges of human rights violations, an electoral victory by President Suharto, reductions in U.S. military assistance, a kidnapping incident in the Netherlands involving an Indonesian ethnic group (South Moluccans), and a crackdown on the press. During the postintervention period the government granted amnesty to and released political dissidents, opened talks with the United States on its human rights policies, hosted a visit by Walter Mondale, reopened the nation's newspapers (the ban, too, came after the intervention), and began talks on a new constitution.

Rhodesia. The analysis period, commencing in December 1975, opened with the start of constitutional talks aimed at shifting from white minority to black majority rule, a process of negotiation that continued with greater or lesser intensity throughout until, in the final month of observation, the Smith government accepted majority rule in principle. During this time the country was wracked by guerrilla warfare, engaged in a series of border clashes with the socalled frontline black nations, and was regularly maligned by a variety of foreign leaders. Two months before the intervention there occurred what seemed to be a breakthrough in the negotiations, but at least in the public record this proved to be short-lived and of no apparent significance to the question at hand. In the postintervention period Prime Minister Smith purged his party of opponents to majority rule and conducted an election to demonstrate his mandate to arrive at a settlement. Evidence of public relations activities after the contract date included frequent meetings between Smith and various western diplomats with maximum publicity, a guided tour for journalists to a village that had just suffered a guerrilla attack, attention to the "kidnapping" of children by Botswana-based guerrillas and to guerrilla attacks on Roman Catholic missions, an easing of the government's own conflict with the Roman Catholic church, a series of government reforms to enhance the apparent power of blacks, establishment of "protected villages" for blacks, establishment of a Rhodesian information office in Washington, and a report that white women throughout the country were contemplating suicide at the very thought of majority rule. Six months after the intervention, an article in the *New York Times* reviewed the government's public relations campaign, pointing out that it was effective in keeping the guerrillas' version of the war out of the press and in equating the black liberation movement with a communist insurrection (Windrich, 1977).

Mexico. The analysis period began in January 1975. By December of that year, Mexico was in many ways a classic example of a country with an image problem in the U.S. Press. News coverage and commentary were focused on guerrilla attacks and subversion, repressive measures taken by the government, economic instability and dependence, political infighting, policy failures (particularly in land reform), tourist boycotts, and a general feeling of anti-Americanism. But unlike the other governments under review here, that of Mexico opted not to retain a public relations firm. The government did demonstrate concern over its image, particularly in an advertising campaign expressly intended to convince U.S. tourists and businesses that the country was not in fact anti-American, a tactic that runs directly contrary to the appropriate strategy indicated in Figure 3 for a country in Mexico's situation, but as a matter of choice it did not undertake a professionally orchestrated campaign of image polishing. During the year following this decision, coverage of social, political, and economic problems continued to dominate the news of Mexico. In fact, such news proliferated.

Discussion of need for quantitative analysis

Because of the inherently selective and speculative nature of such evidence, however, and because some of these events undoubtedly took place for other, less image-related reasons as well, we do not find such anecdotal arguments in themselves to be meaningful indicators of public relations effects. Rather, we find them suggestive of behavioral tendencies on the part of both national actors and journalists which we believe to be associated with the public relations intervention. Only in combination with quantitative support for the impressions such data create can we accept with confidence their implications for the manipulation of information about, and ultimately images of, foreign nations in the United States press. It is in pursuit of such supporting evidence that we have undertaken the more systematic analysis of the effects of these various public relations efforts to which we now turn.

Quantitative Effects of the Public Relations Intervention

Selection of research design

The most appropriate design for testing the effects of such interventions is what Campbell (1969), Cook and Campbell (1979) and others describe as an interrupted time series design. The question is whether a government policy or intervention (in this case, the public relations contract) changes the level or direction of a series of observations of theoretical or practical interest (such as coverage in the *New York Times*) subsequent to the intervention in sufficient degree to falsify the null hypothesis that such changes arise from chance. Where the magnitude of change makes chance factors a highly unlikely explanation, the analyst infers that it is attributable instead to the policy of intervention.

Method of the study

In applying an interrupted time series design to the present analysis, we regress a particular series of indicators for a given country (e.g., total references, negative references) on a binomially coded variable (0 or 1) indicating the absence or presence of effects of the intervention, then examine the result.

Assessment of strengths and weaknesses of the design

The regression coefficient and its sign represent the size and direction of change in the dependent variable (a particular aspect of news coverage) attributable to the intervention. A t-test allows inferences about whether or not this change is substantially different from zero.[7] The coefficient of determination (r^2) indicates the explanatory power of the intervention for determining the entire series. Finally, a Durbin-Watson test for autocorrelation of residuals indicates whether the estimates are biased by serial correlation.

This latter test is important in this case because there are special problems inherent in time series analysis. Many time series are characterized by the trends associated with growth or development over time. These and other autoregressive components that determine the series violate several assumptions of regression analysis, particularly one that requires that residuals must be substantially uncorrelated. Here residuals may be highly correlated unless certain trends and autoregressive components are removed. Positive serial correlation inflates the t-test so that a researcher might reject the null hypothesis when it is in fact true. This could become a problem for the present analysis if, for example, a series of events before a contract was signed produced month-to-month increases in reporting. These effects can be estimated and controlled by a variety of methods. The most precise of these requires considerably more time points than we have included in our analysis. On the other hand, longer time periods would maximize noise and influence from extraneous sources. For relatively short series such as these, the most satisfactory method is application of a form of generalized least squares (GLS), the Cochrane-Orcutt iterative process. Essentially, this technique estimates the amount of damage from serial correlation and controls for its effects (Johnston, 1972). For purposes of the analysis, this technique will be applied whenever ordinary least squares (OLS) proves vulnerable to bias from autoregressive components of the series.

Discussion of plausibility of alternative rival hypotheses

As in any quasi-experimental design, analysis of this type is vulnerable to rival hypotheses as explanations of the observed effect. The effects of such reasonable alternatives should be handled either by logically ruling out their plausibility or by controlling for their effects. In this analysis, the independent variables for each country (the signing of the contract) are independent of one another. There is little logic or evidence that connects the signing of a public relations contract by the Republic of Korea, for example, with similar action by any other nation, apart from a general trend toward greater awareness of the importance of national images among many nations of the world. We noted no evidence of any comprehensive historical event that systematically affected reporting on all of the countries at the disparate times when their respective contracts were signed. Moreover, given that our analysis is based on several countries of differing size, location, and circumstance, the likelihood that localized, idiosyncratic random effects rather than the respective interventions account for our observations seems quite low. And the likelihood that five of the six governments in question hired a public relations con-

Most-different-systems type design

Footnote explaining unusual statistical procedure

---

[7] The t-test, usually an inferential statistic, is used here in a somewhat unorthodox manner. Some scholars argue that since a time series includes a series of observations, no inferential statistic is appropriate. We hold that the t-test can be used as a descriptive statistic to indicate significant fluctuations about a trend. Essentially, it measures whether the posttest series changes by an amount in excess of two standard errors (if the statistical criterion is .95). By definition, then, a change in excess of two standard errors is one that is significantly different from zero.

sultant precisely three months before their images changed (and the sixth at the very moment of image change), and that the subsequent image change of each country was consistently in the direction predicted by our conceptualization irrespective of those public relations contracts, seems equally low.

Discussion of strategies to assure the validity of the research

Three separate strategies would seem to offer potential controls for the experimental effect. These include comparing coverage in the *New York Times* with corresponding coverage of the same nations and time periods in non-U.S. newspapers, comparing the experimental series against a random selection of series for various countries and time periods, or matching the experimental series with others that differ only with respect to the intervention itself. Let us examine each of these alternatives in turn.

The comparison of *New York Times* coverage of these nations with that in the foreign press would provide a check on the validity of the present research if and only if the effects of the public relations efforts by American firms are reasonably expected to be demonstrated only in U.S. media. This would be the case, for example, if the public relations counselors limited their activities to such visible devices as issuing press kits and press releases to U.S. news outlets. In reality, however, public relations activities are both more subtle and more pervasive, for they include the provision of training and advice that can change more fundamentally the policy behaviors of government, the packaging of those behaviors, or at the very least, the actions of a government to facilitate or to restrict the flow of information generally. Indeed, our conceptual framework suggests quite clearly that a campaign that defined public relations as simply the generating of more publicity would be counterproductive in many circumstances. Thus the immunity of the foreign press to these efforts cannot be safely assumed; its degree is an empirical question, and for that reason, reports in the foreign press cannot provide an unambiguous control for the present analysis. Their correspondence (or lack of correspondence) with U.S. news coverage represents less a test of the validity of our findings than a potential corollary hypothesis.

At first glance, the comparison of the experimental series against a random selection of series capturing coverage of various nations in various time periods appears more promising, but this promise is deceptive because once time series dependencies have been eliminated through procedures like those used here to initialize the data, every such series is stochastically generated in principle except for the intervention. Thus, even if we took one of our experimental series and started it at a different time (e.g., three months before the intervention rather than 12), it, too, might well appear to be stochastic. The likelihood of randomly selecting as a control a series where stochastic processes generate a pattern mimicking the experimental effect at the matching timepoint, which is to say, the likelihood of encountering a serious challenge to the validity of our findings, is extremely low. Accordingly, although such an approach would undoubtedly establish the apparent validity of our findings, we believe this result would be spurious.

A more genuine test of validity in the present circumstance is to identify a set of control series based on coverage of countries that are matched as closely as possible to the experimental cases but for which an appropriate time period for comparison can be specified. In effect, what one needs here is a set of countries that at some point in time made a specific decision *not* to contract with an American public relations firm. Such a decision would constitute, in essence, a nonexperimental, time-specific event and would allow the analyst to identify a particular time series for comparison. This is by far the most rigorous test of validity for the present work, and it is the most appropriate, but because it requires the documentation of a specific nonevent at a specific time, its conditions are very difficult to satisfy. Nevertheless, it is this third approach to assessing validity that we have adopted here.

Use of a control

In actuality, we have been able to document only one appropriate control series, that for Mexico. As we have suggested above, events in Mexico and news coverage of them during the first half of the series resembled in key respects those in the experimental countries. In these regards, Mexico constitutes an acceptable match to a general profile of contracting countries. Where Mexico differs, again as noted earlier, is in its decision not to hire an American public relations counselor. This decision, taken in December 1975, defines the appropriate time series for comparison with the experimental cases and permits a genuine test of the experimental effect, which is to say, the impact of the public relations intervention. Although confidence in our results would surely be strengthened by the inclusion of more control series, we regard the identification of even one such case as most fortuitous given the evident constraints. This limitation notwithstanding, however, a comparison of this type is the most meaningful and least ambiguous test of validity available to us. And to the extent that the results of the Mexican nonexperiment differ from those of our other cases, our confidence in the validity of the observed effects of the public relations contracts is enhanced.

Discussion of time lags in the research design

In the analysis that follows, regression parameters are estimated with a variety of assumptions about lag effects of the public relations contract. A guiding assumption is that changes in the time series might not be observed in the month in which the contract was signed, although in many instances virtually immediate consequences are detectable in the indicators. By minimizing the sum of squared residuals over all possible lags, however, we have found the best-fit equations to suggest a lag of three months before the impact of the intervention typically reaches its zenith. This compares with a typical lag variously estimated at six weeks to six months between changes in the media agenda and corresponding changes in the public agenda(Eyal, 1981; Stone & McCombs, 1981), and a similar lag of roughly one year between changes in the public agenda and corresponding changes in the policy agenda (Page & Shapiro, 1983). In the present instance, the observed lag conforms to what might reasonably be expected to constitute a start-up period for the public relations effort. Consequently, except where noted, the equations reported below are estimated with a three-month lag assumption, the full force of the intervention beginning in the fourth month.

Presentation of the results

All of the nations selected for the present study had negative pre-intervention images, but the degrees and components of those images did differ. Table 1 presents seven indicators that suggest the image problems faced by these countries with regard to their coverage in the U.S. press. Two of these are especially noteworthy.

Discussion of table

The first, percent negative reporting, represents the proportion of all articles about a country that can be characterized as negative. According to this indicator, Argentina clearly had the most negative press image. Fairly close behind came the Philippines, Republic of Korea, Mexico, Rhodesia, and Indonesia. In contrast, Yugoslavia had a much less negative image in the press, with about 24% negative references. But this ranking on negative image, which might be considered a major target of public relations efforts, can be misleading if viewed in isolation. For as our earlier discussion made clear, a high proportion of negative references may well be partially offset by low scores on a second factor, visibility. Thus Rhodesia, which ranks only fifth among the countries under review in its proportion of negative mentions, but which received roughly two to three times the press attention of any other country and had the greatest absolute imbalance of negative over positive references (over 17 per month in the pre-intervention period), probably faced the most difficult public relations challenge of all the countries under review.

Discussion of table

Table 2 indicates the changes in image associated with a public relations contract related to each country's initial position on summary indicators of visibility and valence. As the table shows, the Republic of Korea and Argentina, which ranked initially among the top three countries in visibility and possessed the two most negatively valenced images (Table 1), each experienced decreases in visibility of approximately 11 articles per month and a corresponding doubling of the positive valence, both associated in time with the signing of the public relations contract and both wholly consistent with our expectations. The Philippines and Yugoslavia, whose relatively low initial visibility would seem to position them especially well to make positive changes in the valence of their respective images, show a slightly different pattern. Here movement centered on a reduction in visibility; valence was essentially unchanged. This observation may reflect either a partially successful effort at manipulation along both dimensions, the employment of an alternative unidimensional strategy designed to curtail negative reporting by the simple expedient of reducing all reporting, or the operation of a regression effect in which the low initial visibility of these countries means that even with substantial proportionate reductions on this indicator it is very difficult to achieve correspondingly significant increases in positive valence. Whichever explanation holds, the net effect of the public relations contract in both cases was an improvement in image centered on changes in visibility.

Despite substantial movement in the predicted direction, the data on Rhodesia show no statistically significant changes in either of the indicators. In general both visibility and valence in this case appear to be functions of reporting on violence in the guerrilla war between the Smith regime and insurgent black nationalists. As we have shown elsewhere (Albritton & Manheim, 1983), significant reductions in reporting of violence are associated with the public relations contract. In fact, a detailed examination of this reporting adds considerable support to the notion that news coverage is responsive to public relations activities and even offers some insights into the differential effects that such public relations campaigns may have on particular classes of information and reporting.

Indonesia's very low visibility before it signed a public relations contract permits us to test our expectation that such conditions provide an opportunity to effect important changes in the valence component of national image. Table 2 demonstrates significant movement in precisely the direction we had anticipated. One very important difference between this case and the others is that there is no significant change in visibility associated with the public relations contract. Instead, there is a significant positive shift in valence of approximately 14%. Moreover, again in contrast with the other contracting nations, this positive shift in the valence component is not a result of reduced negative reporting. To the contrary, the only other significant change associated with the intervention (not shown) is a more than doubling in the

Facing page: tables (note format and use of explanatory notes)

Table 1. Average Monthly Scores of Seven Nations on Selected Indicators of Image Visibility and Valence during the Pre-Contract Period

	Republic of Korea	Argentina	Philippines	Yugoslavia	Rhodesia	Indonesia	Mexico
Total articles (N)	18.3	21.6	10.3	10.2	54.3	5.1	3.7
Articles with negative valence (N)	9.8	16.1	7.2	2.6	26.6	1.3	1.9
Articles with positive valence (N)	2.8	1.9	2.7	1.7	9.2	0.7	1.1
Articles with negative valence as % of total	56.1	75.0	68.2	23.7	48.5	46.4	49.5
Articles with positive valences as % of total	14.8	8.0	30.2	17.9	23.0	33.1	38.3
% of positive-negative articles (N)	23.0	10.0	29.9	49.8	30.7	34.2	44.5
Net of positive-negative articles (N)	-7.0	-14.1	-4.5	-0.8	-17.4	-0.6	-0.7

Table 2. Estimation of Change in Visibility and Valence Associated with a Public Relations Contract

	Republic of Korea	Argentina	Philippines	Yugoslavia[a]	Rhodesia	Indonesia	Mexico[b]
Visibility (total number of articles)							
Equation (type of estimation)	OLS	OLS	GLS	OLS	GLS	OLS	OLS
Coefficient of regression (b)	-11.37	-10.71	-8.92	-5.17	-17.61	0.09	6.11
t-test	3.93[c]	3.95[c]	3.22[c]	2.67[c]	1.19	0.03	3.92[c]
Coefficient of determination (r^2)	.40	.42	.71	.25	.20	.00	.41
Durbin Watson coefficient	1.38	2.16	1.88	2.23	2.05	1.39	1.66
Postcontract mean	7.6	10.9	4.0	5.1	43.2	5.2	9.8
Valence (percent positive of all valenced articles)							
Equation (type of estimation)	OLS	OLS	OLS	OLS	OLS	GLS	OLS
Coefficient of regression (b)	23.80	11.76	1.22	-3.33	3.96	12.95	-3.87
t-test	2.75[c]	2.78[c]	0.11	0.23	0.62	2.31[c]	0.29
Coefficient of determination (r^2)	.25	.26	.00	.00	.02	.52	.00
Durbin Watson coefficient	1.91	1.59	2.24	1.96	1.40	2.21	1.63
Postcontract mean	54.6	22.0	29.6	46.4	32.6	46.7	40.7

[a]Estimated with no lag.

[b]Estimated with no lag. However, similar estimates with a three-month lag show no significant differences from the results reported here.

[c]Change exceeds two standard errors.

frequency of positive reporting. Thus in the one contracting nation where conditions posited by our conceptualization for making significant positive changes in the valence component of image are especially favorable, we find the only instance in which significant increases in positive reporting (rather than reduction of negative mentions) are associated with introduction of the public relations contract, and the only instance in which positive image change is centered wholly on the valence dimension.

Discussion of control case

In this light, Mexico offers an especially interesting contrast. At the time it rejected a contract, Mexico was in one of the most advantageous positions of any nation we examined. Its visibility was even lower than Indonesia's, providing an opportunity to duplicate that nation's success, and its valence (44.5% positive) was exceeded only slightly by Yugoslavia's and, although still generally negative, was substantially less so than that of any other nation considered here. Yet the pattern of image development following rejection of a contract is strikingly different from our other observations. Not only do the data reflect an absence of progress in enhancing positive valence, but there is actually a decline to 40.7% positive mentions. In addition, visibility increases dramatically, more than doubling during the postrejection period The net result is virtually the opposite of that found in nations operating with public relations assistance. Instead of using its initially favorable position to enhance its valence, Mexico appears to move in precisely the wrong direction, gaining visibility while its valence slips.

Discussion of graphic presentation and tabular data

To reconcile our observations regarding the public relations efforts undertaken (or not undertaken) in behalf of these seven nations with the analytical framework that we developed earlier, we have imposed specific parameters on the graphic representation of dimensions of national image first presented in Figure 3 and have located each of our countries in the appropriate positions for the pre- and postintervention periods on the two indicators reported in Table 2.[8] The result is illustrated in Figure 4.

Within this framework, we can see that Rhodesia begins as rather clearly a quadrant 1 country, whereas the others are initially distributed at various points within quadrant 2; that is, Rhodesia scores high on visibility and low on positive valence, whereas the others score low on both visibility and positive valence. A glance at the data in Table 1 and a review of the above discussion should make clear not only that these categorizations are correct, but that the categories themselves are substantively meaningful.

Assessment of correspondence between predictions based on theory and actual observations

The strategy of influence specified in Figure 3 suggests that, as a result of contracting with an American public relations firm, a nation's image will shift on both visibility and valence in the form of a parabolic arc. A key question is whether the empirical data summarized in Figure 4 fit this specification. The fact that both the pre- and postcontract locations represent coordinates rather than unidimensional values poses problems for conventional methods of curve-fitting. Still, the theory stipulates that when a contract is in effect, the shift from the precontract to the postcontract locations is a function of both coordinates in the precontract period. One way to test the theory under this

---

Footnote explaining scaling in graphic presentation

[8] We have arbitrarily set the maximum value of visibility at 60 articles per month for purposes of illustration. Our theory deals with the relative positions of national images more than with absolute distances, and the most salient point here is that Rhodesia's image is clearly and substantially more visible than that of any other nation under review.

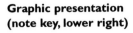

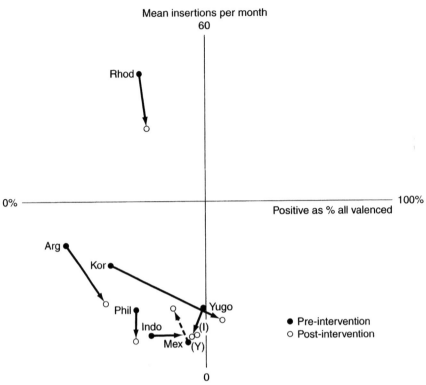

Figure 4   *Directions of Image Change*

specification is to determine how well visibility and valence in the postcontract period separately can be predicted from the values on both dimensions before the contract is signed. Since we are here assessing only how well the observations fit the theory, the appropriate tests are simply those that measure goodness of fit, i.e., the correlation coefficient and the distribution of residuals.

Table 3 shows a strong relationship between the theory and the data. The visibility dimension in the postcontract period is almost wholly determined by the model. The inference is that movement on this dimension associated with the public relations contract is uniformly in the expected direction. Movement on the valence dimension is not as strongly associated with the contract, but the theory does account for some 38% of the variance on this dimension as well.

Perhaps the most important implications of the data reported in Table 3 derive from the comparison of goodness-of-fit criteria for zero-order polynomial and parabolic arc specifications respectively. Although changes in the R^2 indicate only a moderate relative advantage for the parabolic model, examination of the sums of squared residuals shows that a parabolic specification represents a significant improvement over at least one important alternative in fitting the data. Thus the movement of the data from the precontract to the postcontract period in the form of a parabola, although inconclusive because of the small number of cases, does offer substantial support for the theoretical specification in Figure 3.

Discussion of statistical analysis

Table

Table 3. *A Comparison of Goodness of Fit Criteria to Zero-Order Polynomial and Parabola Specifications for Changes in Visibility and Valence of National Images as a Result of Contractual Relationship with American Public Relations Firms (N = 6, Mexico Excluded)*

	Zero-Order Polynomial	**Parabola**
Visibility		
R^2	.9726	.9970
Sum of squared residuals	31.55	3.39
Valence		
R^2	.3005	.3841
Sum of squared residuals	542.08	477.33

Discussion

Conclusions

Taken together, these results suggest two conclusions. First, there exists a clear temporal correspondence between the signing of a public relations contract by a given nation and shifts in the image of that nation as portrayed in the *New York Times*. We have observed this correspondence across six nations of varying size, location, and circumstance, and found it absent only in a seventh, noncontracting nation whose pretest image was comparable to those of the others. Second, those image changes that did occur in association with the public relations contracts were consistent with the pattern suggested by the literature we have cited and with the predictions of our own conceptual framework. Put another way, our findings are precisely those we would expect if the public relations consultants in question were pursuing a set of strategies predicated on the same arguments we have raised, and if they were doing so effectively.

That such persuasive efforts might take this form should come as no surprise. The literature on attitude stability and change has long recognized the importance to persuasion of controlling the flow of information and the degree of discrepancy between new messages and existing cognitions (summarized in Kiesler, Collins, & Miller, 1969); that on the diffusion of innovation has almost literally been built on the role of awareness in the movement of behavior-related information (summarized in Savage, 1981); and that on propaganda, although using rather different terminology, has applied many of the same lessons (summarized in Kecskemeti, 1973). Wolfsfeld's (1983) recent work, with its synthesis of the attitude change and propaganda literatures, provides a conceptual bridge between microlevel psychological processes and macrolevel communication strategies that makes clear the interdependence of image content, awareness, and persuasibility.

Discussion and interpretation of results

What is surprising, however, is the lack of recognition of the first and more fundamental point, that external actors not only try systematically to influence the media-public-policy agenda system, but that they succeed. For our data clearly demonstrate that public relations efforts in behalf of foreign countries do give rise to changes in the media portrayal of those countries. In case after case, significant improvements in projected images follow upon the signing of the public relations contract. Clearly, then, efforts to analyze the interactions that occur within the agenda system must take into account external environmental factors that may well influence such exchanges.

We do not contend that (projected) image improvements of the type we have observed translate immediately into public (perceived) image or public policy bonanzas for the various client states, or even that they will be associated with particular, identifiable behaviors on the part of either voters, members of issue publics, or policymakers. To the contrary, we have specifically distinguished between these efforts at persuasive communication and others, such as political campaigns, that are directed at inducing particular behaviors. What these more subtle activities may well accomplish, however, as Merritt (1980) recognized, is a change in the general informational context within which a country is perceived, and a secular shift in the propensity of either mass or elite political actors to behave supportively toward it when such behavioral opportunities present themselves. (For an example, see Smith, 1970.) Given the flow of information and the behavioral connections among the three agendas that are becoming increasingly evident in the literature on agenda setting, these propensities may well translate over time into policy outputs of real value to the countries in question.

The literature on agenda setting has established a series of linkages that tie projected images in the media to perceived images among the public, and, in turn, perceived images among the public to the policy agenda and its products. Although various details of these interconnections remain to be documented, the notion of linkage and the workings of its basic mechanisms are widely recognized. The role of mass media in generating and disseminating images of reality that channel political debate assumes special importance in this conceptualization. The media are seen as gathering information from the public, policymakers, and the external environment, then packaging that information for consumption. The product of this activity becomes a primary source of both public opinion and policy action. The present research suggests that actors external to this process are not necessarily passive or benign, that to the extent of their dependence on such actors as sources of information the media are vulnerable to manipulation, and, by extension, that such manipulation of projected images of reality has the potential to influence public opinion and the policy process.

References

Albritton, R. B., & Manheim, J. B. News of Rhodesia: the impact of a public relations campaign. *Journalism Quarterly,* 1983, *60,* 622-628.

Azar, E. A., et al. The problem of source coverage in the use of international events data. *International Studies Quarterly,* 1972, *16,* 373-388.

Becker, L. B. Foreign policy and press performance. *Journalism Quarterly,* 1977, *54,* 364-368.

Bennet, W. L. *News: the politics of illusion.* New York: Longman, 1983.

Benton, M., & Frazier, P. J. The agenda-setting function of mass media at three levels of "information holding." *Communication Research,* 1976, *3,* 261-274.

Campbell, D. T. Reforms as experiments. *American Psychologist,* 1969, *24,* 409-429.

Charles, J., Shore, L., & Todd, R. *The New York Times* coverage of equatorial and lower Africa. *Journal of Communication,* 1979, *29,* 148-155.

Cobb, R., & Elder, C. *Participation in American politics: the dynamics of agenda-building.* Boston: Allyn and Bacon, 1972.

Cohen, B. *The press and foreign policy.* Princeton, N.J.: Princeton University Press, 1963.

Cohen, B. *The public's impact on foreign policy.* Boston: Little, Brown, 1973.

Cook, F. L. Toward a theory of issue decline on policy agendas. Presented at the symposium on new directions in the empirical and normative study of public policy, Evanston, Illinois, September 23, 1982.

Cook, F. L., Tyler, T. R., Goetz, E. G., Gordon, M. T., Protess, B., Leff, D. R., & Molotch, H. L. Media and agenda setting: effects on the public interest group leaders, policy makers and policy. *Public Opinion Quarterly,* 1983, *47,* 16-35.

Cook, T. D., & Campbell, D. T. *Quasi-experimentation: design and analysis of time series experiments.* Boulder, CO: Colorado Associate University Press, 1979.

Cooney, J. E. Public relations firms draw fire for adding repressing countries. *Wall Street Journal,* January 3, 1979, *1,* 30.

David, M. *Interpreters for Nigeria: the third world and international public relations.* Urbana: University of Illinois Press, 1977.

Davison, W. P. News media and international negotiation. *Public Opinion Quarterly,* 1974, *38,* 174-193.

Elder, C., & Cobb, R. *The political uses of symbols.* New York: Longman, 1983.

Epstein, E. J. *News from nowhere: television in the news.* New York: Vintage, 1973.

Eyal, C. *Time frame in agenda-setting research: a study of the conceptual and methodological factors affecting the time frame context of the agenda-setting process.* Unpublished doctoral dissertation, Syracuse University, as cited in McCombs, M. E. The agenda-setting approach. In D. D. Nimmo & K. R. Sanders (Eds.), *Handbook of political communication.* Beverly Hills, Calif.: Sage, 1981.

Graber, D. A. *Hoopla and horse-race in 1980 campaign coverage: a closer look.* In W. Schulz and K. Schoenback (Eds.), *Mass media and elections: international research perspectives.* München: Olschlager, 1983.

Graber, D. *Processing the news: how people tame the information tide.* New York: Longman, 1984.

Grau, C. H. What publications are most frequently quoted in the *Congressional Record, Journalism Quarterly,* 1976, *53,* 716-719.

Hopple, G. W. International news coverage in two elite newspapers. *Journal of Communication,* 1982, *32,* 61-74.

Iyengar, S., Peters, M. D., & Kinder, D. R. Experimental demonstrations of the "not-so-minimal" consequences of television news programs. *American Political Science Review,* 1982, *76,* 848-858.

Johnston, J. P. *Econometric methods* (2nd ed.), New York: McGraw-Hill, 1972.

Kecskemeti, P. Propaganda. In I. de S. Pool et al. (Eds.), *Handbook of communication.* Chicago: Rand-McNally, 1973.

Kelman, H. D., & Ezekiel, R. S. *Cross-national encounters: the personal impact of an exchange program for broadcasters.* San Francisco: Jossey-Bass, 1970.

Kiesler, C. A., Collins, B. E., & Miller, N. *Attitude change: a critical analysis of theoretical approaches.* New York: John Wiley, 1969.

Krugman, H. E. The impact of television advertising: learning without involvement. *Public Opinion Quarterly,* 1965, *29,* 349-356.

Lent, J. A. Foreign news in American media. *Journal of Communication,* 1977, *27,* 46-51.

Marcum, J. *The Angolan revolution* (vol. 1). Cambridge, Mass.: MIT Press, 1969.

McCombs, M. E., & Shaw, D. L. The agenda-setting function of mass media. *Public Opinion Quarterly,* 1972, *36,* 176-187.

McGuire, W. J. Inducing resistance to persuasion: some contemporary approaches. *Advances in Experimental Social Psychology,* 1964, *1,* 192-202.

Mendelsohn, H. Some reasons why information campaigns can succeed. *Public Opinion Quarterly,* 1973, *37,* 50-61.

Merritt, R. L. Transforming international communications strategies. *Political Communication and Persuasion,* 1980, *1,* 5-42.

Miller, A. H., Goldenberg, E. N., & Ebring, L. Typeset politics: impact of newspapers on public confidence. *American Political Science Review,* 1979, *73,* 67-84.

Nimmo, D., & Savage, R. L. *Candidates and their images: concepts, methods and findings.* Pacific Palisades: Goodyear, 1976.

Page, B. I., & Shapiro, R. Y. Effects of public opinion on policy. *American Political Science Review,* 1983, *77,* 175-190.

Palmgreen, P., & Clarke, P. Agenda-setting with local and national issues. *Communication Research,* 1977, *4,* 435-452.

Patterson, T. E., & McClure, R. D. *The unseeing eye: the myth of TV power in national elections.* New York: G. P. Putnam's Sons, 1976.

Peterson, S. International news selection by the elite press. *Public Opinion Quarterly,* 1981, *45,* 143-163.

Ptacek, P., Kricos, P. B., Black, J. W., & Hyman, M. Titles as measures of trends in research and training. *General Semantics,* 1975, *42,* 198-201.

Robinson, J. P., & Hefner, R. Perceptual maps of the world. *Public Opinion Quarterly,* 1968, *32,* 271-280.

Savage, R. L. The diffusion of information approach. In D. D. Nimmo & K. R. Sanders (Eds.), *Handbook of political communication.* Beverly Hills, Calif.: Sage, 1981.

Semmel, A. K. Foreign news in four U.S. elite dailies: some comparisons. *Journalism Quarterly* 1976, *53,* 732-736.

Shaw, D. L., & McCombs, M. E. *The emergence of American political issues: the agenda-setting function of the press.* St. Paul: West, 1977.

Sigal, L. V. *Reporters and officials: the organization and politics of newsmaking.* Lexington, Mass.: D.C. Heath, 1973.

Smith, D. D. Some effects of Radio Moscow's North American broadcasts. *Public Opinion Quarterly,* 1970, *34,* 539-551.

Stone, G. C., & McCombs, M. E. Tracing the time-lag in agenda setting. *Journalism Quarterly,* 1981, *58,* 51-55.

U.K. Plans ads to support deployment of missiles. *Wall Street Journal,* January 31, 1983, p. 33.

Weiss, C. H. What America's leaders read. *Public Opinion Quarterly,* 1974, *38,* 1-22.

Windrich, E. Rhodesian "information." *New York Times,* May 13, 1977, p. 27.

Winter, J. P., & Eyal, C. E. Agenda setting for the civil rights issue. *Public Opinion Quarterly,* 1981, *45,* 376-383.

Wolfsfeld, G. International awareness, information processing, and attitude change: a cross-cultural experimental study. *Political Communication and Persuasion,* 1983, *2,* 127-146.

Suggestions for Further Reading

A book that addresses the writing of political analyses is Diane E. Schmidt, *Expository Writing in Political Science* (New York: HarperCollins, 1993). For excellent suggestions on ways to improve your writing style, see William Strunk, Jr., with E. B. White, *The Elements of Style,* 4th ed. (Boston: Allyn and Bacon, 2000). *Bartlett's Roget's Thesaurus* (Boston: Little Brown, 1996), can contribute much to the clarity and variety of your presentation and can, on occasion, offer direction for reducing your reliance on jargon. For guidance on the proper form and placement of footnotes and bibliography, consult *The Style Manual for Political Science,* rev. ed. (Washington, DC: American Political Science Association, 1993; Kate L. Turabian, *A Manual for Writers of Term Papers, Theses, and Dissertations,* 6th ed. (Chicago: University of Chicago: Press, 1996); or Joseph Gibaldi and Walter S. Achtert, *MLA Handbook for Writers of Research Papers,* 5th ed. (New York: Modern Language Association, 1999). James D. Lester offers many helpful suggestions for report writing in *Writing Research Papers: A Complete Guide,* 9th ed. (Glenview, IL: Longman, 1999), and Joyce S. Stewart and Marjorie Smelstor provide, and analyze, numerous examples of available styles in *Writing in the Social Sciences* (Glenview, IL: Scott, Foresman, 1984).

The best place to find sample research reports is in the journals of political science and related disciplines described in Chapter 3. Excerpts from articles that illustrate many of the principles of research discussed in this text are found in Marcus E. Ethridge, *The Political Research Experience,* 2d ed. (Guilford, CT: Dushkin, 1994).

Research Exercises

1. Read and *outline* three research articles in political science journals. Decide whether all the necessary elements of a research report are present in each case.

2. Read and *evaluate* the writing of three research articles in political science journals. Pay attention both to the method of the study and to the structure of the research report.

3. Read and *abstract* three research articles in political science journals. Where possible, compare your abstract with that prepared by the author of the article (which you should not read until you have finished your abstract).

Term Introduced in This Chapter

abstract

CHAPTER 22

OVERVIEW

We have now presented the basic information you need to plan and execute a complete research project. In Figure 4.6 in Chapter 4 we provided an overview of the research process. We have explored the components of that process at length in the remainder of the text. In this closing chapter we will review the research process as an integrated whole. We will stress the ways in which the steps you have seen separated by chapter boundaries are, in practice, interwoven and interdependent. Our purpose is to facilitate your attacking research questions with a full understanding of the research process rather than a disjointed focus on each stage as it is reached. The value of an integrated understanding, of course, is that *many research problems can be avoided if the researcher is aware of the implications of decisions made at one stage of a project for subsequent stages.*

Developing Hypotheses, Measures, and a Research Design

Research begins with a research question that asks why things are as we observe them to be. We are generally seeking an explanation for observed events. The place to start looking for this explanation is in the social science literature pertaining to our general subject. If we are fortunate, a literature search will turn up a ready-made explanation in the form of a theory that others have developed to explain events like the one that interests us. More often, however, we have to use the literature more creatively to *devise* the best explanation we can, given existing information about the subject. The remainder of the research process is then devoted to testing this explanation to see how much it adds to our understanding of the events in question.

The first step in this testing is to state some hypotheses that logic tells us must be accurate if our proposed answer to the research question is valid. These hypotheses serve several key functions. In the first place, they identify the units of analysis that must be observed if we are to assess our explanation. Second, they isolate the variables for which we must devise indicators. Finally, hypotheses suggest ways in which our observations must be organized in order to provide useful evidence of the validity of our explanation. In stating hypotheses we must always ask whether we can actually observe the stated relationship. Can we locate the necessary data, or do we have the resources required to collect them for ourselves? It is essential that researchers select hypotheses that can be adequately tested with the time, skills, and resources available to them. To do otherwise is to ensure failure.

Next, the variables identified in the hypotheses must be operationalized so that we can obtain measures to compare in reaching a conclusion about the accuracy of our predictions. In selecting operationalizations or measurement procedures, we must be acutely sensitive to the resources required to apply them. If we don't have the necessary time, money, or cooperation of subjects, we cannot use the measuring procedure. In addition, we have to ask whether we are altering the meaning of any of the concepts included in our explanation when we let the results of any given measuring procedure represent them in our research. Though validity can often be assessed in data analysis, the question of validity must be faced well in advance of data collection, for no amount of clever data analysis can make an invalid measure useful.

When creating measures, we must already be thinking ahead to the data analysis stage of the research. Researchers should examine their hypotheses to determine exactly what mathematical and statistical comparisons will be necessary to test their accuracy. They must then be sure that the measuring procedures they have selected will yield data suitable for those procedures. A central consideration here is the fit between the level of measurement obtained from a given operationalization and the level of measurement required by the statistical procedures that will be used to test the hypotheses. Those who plan to use a measure of association that requires ordinal-level measurement must be certain that their measuring process yields at least ordinal data. A second consideration here is the similarity between the distribution of the values obtained with a measurement procedure and the distribution assumed by the statistical procedures that will be applied. Those who plan to use a test of statistical significance requiring a normal distribution to be valid should be certain their measuring procedure does not preclude obtaining a near normal distribution.

The next step is the development of a research design to guide the application of our measuring procedures. The central purpose of research design is to ensure that we can feel confident that any relationships we observe are the result of the processes described in our explanation and not of some other set of processes. Research designs provide this confidence by allowing us to rule out alternative rival hypotheses. A good research design, then, begins with a review of the literature. That review (along with logical analysis of situations) can suggest the major alternative rival hypotheses that must be ruled out before we can place confidence in our central explanation of observed events.

Research designs are developed by (1) identifying the comparisons that must be made in order to test a hypothesis, (2) deciding what observations must be made (of whom or what, in what order, by what means, under what conditions) before those comparisons can be made, (3) anticipating all results that might be obtained from making the comparisons (no relationship, a positive relationship, a negative relationship, and so forth), (4) identifying the major alternative rival hypotheses that can explain each possible result, and (5) organizing a set of observations that will allow the additional comparisons necessary to test the validity of the most important of these alternative rival hypotheses as explanations of whatever results are observed.

It is essential that we know what statistical analyses we want to perform when we develop a research design, for it is the design that determines what data will be available for analysis. For example, if we anticipate controlling for many variables in the data analysis stage, we must be certain that our research design will yield enough cases to allow for such a complex breakdown of the sample. If we want to hold party affiliation constant by examining measures of association between two key variables for members of each party separately, we must include enough members of each party for computation of valid measures of association and must plan to obtain information on subjects' party affiliation. If we plan to use time-series analysis in a study employing aggregate data, we must be sure that data on values of our independent variable come from a period prior to the time at which data on the dependent variable are collected if we have theoretical reasons to believe that there is a lag in the impact of the IV on the DV.

In the design of research, as in the selection of hypotheses and the devising of measures, it is essential that we ask whether we are setting ourselves too ambitious a task. The best research design in the world is useless if the researcher lacks the resources to execute it. One has to give careful consideration to the costs and logistics of data collection in designing research projects.

Data Collection and Analysis

As we have presented the research process, data collection and analysis are carried out in order to test hypotheses. We have discussed the primary rules to be observed in using various methods of data collection and analysis and, in Chapter 2, described the process of reasoning from empirical results to theory, thereby completing the research circle. There is no need to repeat those discussions here. We would, however, like to make two points that may not have come through our sequential presentation as clearly as they should.

The first point is that although we have presented the various data collection techniques separately, they need not be kept separate in the research process. In fact, there are very good reasons for *mixing* methods of data collection in a study. In the first place, different methods can serve different purposes. Researchers may, for example, use focus groups to determine the breadth and nature of people's concerns about a set of political issues, then use survey research to estimate the *distribution* of those same views among the general population. In addition, it is often useful to employ a variety of methods in the data collection stage of a study because of the added confidence *multiple methods of measurement* can give us in the validity of results, as discussed in Chapters 4 and 10. For example, in studying variations in the quality of public services among a city's neighborhoods, one will find it useful to confirm assessments of service quality obtained from survey research by means of aggregate data, official records, interviews with public officials, and the judgments of trained observers. If all these methods of measurement produce a similar ranking of neighborhoods, researchers can feel quite confident that they have accurately measured service quality.

A second point is that empirical research can be exploratory in nature. Rather than using it to test hypotheses derived from explanations, we can use it to provide data to be used in devising explanations in the first place. Each research project generally raises new questions, suggests new explanations, and leads to new research. If you look back at Figure 4.6, you will see a shortcut from *generalization of observed relationships* to *hypotheses* and back to *data analysis*. This shortcut is the result of applying inductive logic in data analysis. It can be an important step in empirical inquiry, for it suggests new data analyses that can allow researchers to refine and elaborate explanations in ways they did not anticipate when designing a project or, even without collecting new data, to test explanations they did not anticipate.

A Checklist for Judging Research

In an evaluation of others' research or in the design of your own, it is often helpful to step back from the details of each stage and try to get an overview of the research, asking whether it meets certain general but clearly stated requirements of sound empirical inquiry. To facilitate your doing this, we have provided, in Figure 22.1, a list of things to look for. The questions are listed in approximately the sequence in which you might expect to encounter different problems in a report of research or in the execution of a project. The rules suggested by these questions are broad, and a project that "checks out" on all these items may still contain subtle or highly technical errors, but if you can answer "yes" to each of the questions in the figure, the research being assessed is probably free of any error that this book has prepared you to identify and exhibits the basics of sound research.

In using the checklist, be aware of three cautions. First, not all questions will apply to any one research project. Exploratory research, for example, will not be designed to test hypotheses, and research based on elite interviews will probably not require a random sample. Second, the questions refer to technical rather than substantive aspects of research. A researcher may do everything correctly and still be investigating a trivial subject. *Valuable research is that which is both technically correct and substantively important.* In judging research, ask whether its proper execution will add useful knowledge to our attempts to understand significant political events. Sometimes, lower levels of technical sophistication are justified by the complexity and magnitude of an important subject. On the whole, the project that adds a little to our knowledge of an important subject is more valuable than a project that adds a lot to our knowledge of a trivial matter. Third, few projects can be free of limitations. For instance, it may be impossible to obtain a representative sample of an entire large population within the resource limits of a given study. It may be necessary to sample only one subgroup (as when a study of American political behavior is conducted with a sample from one city only). Such limitations become errors

Figure 22.1
Checklist

A CHECKLIST FOR EVALUATING EMPIRICAL RESEARCH

☐   1. Is the research question clearly stated? Do we know what the objectives of the research are so that we can assess the overall project? Is the research clearly related to some larger political issue or problem? Is this an important subject to study?

☐   2. Are the units of analysis clearly identified, correctly chosen, and consistently used throughout the project?

☐   3. Are the concepts employed in the research clearly specified and adequately developed? Do the concepts have identifiable referents?

☐   4. Is it clear what explanations are being tested? If a theory is used, is it logically correct? Do the concepts have identifiable empirical referents?

☐   5. Is the theory or explanation consistent with existing literature on the subject? Is there evidence of a thorough literature review? Is the relationship of this research to prior research and larger political issues made clear?

☐   6. Are hypotheses to be tested identified clearly and stated correctly? Do they logically follow from the explanation or theory being examined? Are they empirically testable?

☐   7. If more than one hypothesis is being tested, are the relationships between them specified? Are all hypotheses clearly related to the theory, and their role in testing it made explicit?

☐   8. Are the variables under investigation clearly identified and their status (independent, dependent, intervening, antecedent) specified in the hypotheses?

☐   9. Are variables that might be expected to modify predicted relationships included in the study? (For example, can we expect relationships to hold for both men and women or, in both industrialized and nonindustrialized nations?)

☐ 10. Are operationalizations of concepts stated clearly and measurement procedures specified in sufficient detail that others can replicate them? Have others used these operationalizations?

☐ 11. Are the measures likely to be valid and reliable? Are tests of validity and reliability anticipated? Are threats to validity and reliability recognized and provisions made to control them?

☐ 12. Is the research design clearly stated and appropriate for testing the hypotheses being examined? Are major alternative rival hypotheses recognized and provision made in the research design for examining these hypotheses as alternative explanations? Will the design provide a logically sound basis for causal inferences?

☐ 13. Is the population of interest to the researcher identified clearly? Is the sample used representative of that population? If not, does the researcher recognize the limitations this places on how results can be generalized? Are sampling procedures adequately described?

☐ 14. Is the data collection technique employed (survey research, content analysis, and so forth) appropriate to the study given its units of analysis and the type of information being sought? Are all procedural rules observed that pertain to the particular method of data collection?

☐ 15. Is the data collection fully described? Are outside primary data sources fully identified so others can locate them?

☐ 16. Are coding systems that might affect measurement (such as collapsing various income groups into broad categories or treating certain types of responses as supportive or nonsupportive) fully described and justified?

☐ 17. Is the construction of any indices or scales fully described? Do these summary measures preserve the meaning of the concepts? Do they seem to be unidimensional (to reflect a single underlying concept or pattern)?

(continued)

Figure 22.1
Checklist *(continued)*

A CHECKLIST FOR EVALUATING EMPIRICAL RESEARCH

☐ 18. Have Instruments been pretested?

☐ 19. Have efforts been made to verify results? (For example, have follow-up calls been made to survey respondents, or have alternative sources of aggregate data been sought?)

☐ 20. In presenting the data, are the tables and figures appropriate for illustrating the point they are intended to make? Are they fully discussed in the text and their central significance pointed out? Do they represent the results accurately?

☐ 21. Are tables and figures clearly and completely labeled so that they can be easily interpreted?

☐ 22. Are the interpretations of tables and figures offered correct, or do they suggest a misreading of the data?

☐ 23. Are appropriate descriptive statistics (such as mean and standard deviation) used to summarize the data and supplement tables and figures?

☐ 24. In examining relationships between variables, do the researchers provide evidence on the strength, direction, form, and significance of relationships?

☐ 25. Do the researchers explore the possible effects of antecedent, intervening, and suppressor variables? Do they attempt to control these effects in the data analysis?

☐ 26. Are all statistics used appropriate for the level at which variables are measured, and are they suited to the purpose for which they are used?

☐ 27. Do the data conform to the assumptions (random sampling, normal distribution, and so forth) involved in legitimate application of the statistics used? Have the researchers investigated the degree to which their data fit these assumptions?

☐ 28. Are measures of statistical significance applied only where appropriate and correctly interpreted? Have the researchers avoided confusing statistical significance with substantive significance?

☐ 29. Are major alternative rival hypotheses statistically explored and the results both reported and correctly interpreted?

☐ 30. Is each piece of data analysis clearly related to the major conclusions drawn from the study? Are the interpretations consistent with the data and with the theory or explanation being tested?

    31. Does the research report:

☐   a. contain a precise statement of the purpose of the study?

☐   b. review enough of the relevant literature to demonstrate the contribution of this study?

☐   c. adequately describe the research design, data, and methods used?

☐   d. follow a clear and appropriate organization in presenting findings?

☐   e. state conclusions clearly?

☐ 32. Are the conclusions reached actually warranted by the data presented and the research design used? Does the study make the kind of contribution to the literature the authors claim it does, or have the authors generalized too far beyond the limits of their research?

☐ 33. Have the authors been sensitive to ethical issues raised by the research? Have they satisfactorily resolved these issues?

only when the researcher fails to recognize them and modify accordingly the conclusions drawn from the study.

The checklist can be used to assess others' research as well as to evaluate your own. As a research exercise, you may want to locate an article reporting the results of a research project and evaluate it using the checklist in Figure 22.1, identifying any errors you may find and explaining why they are errors. We have presented the table in a way that makes it easy to photocopy for repeated use.

The last set of standards included in Figure 22.1 for judging research is of a different character from the technical considerations listed there. Research must also be judged for its conformity to ethical standards. What constitutes an ethical or unethical practice is often a matter of personal judgment by researchers, and standards can vary widely. For example, during the Vietnam War, some academics in the United States refused to engage in any research funded by federal agencies they felt shared in responsibility for the war. Others thought that the source of funding for research was irrelevant to the ethical justifiability of projects and judged projects only on their substance. Despite differences of this type, some generally accepted standards of ethical conduct have evolved in all social science disciplines. We present examples in Appendix B. Practicing political scientists should be aware of these professional standards and sensitive to the ethical issues raised by specific research situations.[1]

Conclusion

Armed only with the information contained in this book, you could successfully carry out a very wide range of empirical investigations. You should recognize, however, that this text has only scratched the surface of the huge subject of empirical political research. The dozens of other books listed in our suggestions for further reading should convince you that there is much more to be said and much you cannot learn from this book.

In the process of research, you may discover the importance of the things you do *not* know. Even if you carefully and properly follow every guideline and rule presented in this text, you may find yourself either (1) unable to complete some research projects or (2) producing a set of research results that more experienced social scientists recognize as seriously flawed because you have made errors we did not warn you against. If you follow the suggestions presented in the first five chapters, you should make very few errors in stating hypotheses, operationalizing concepts, searching the literature, or devising a research design. Our chapters on sampling and data management probably provide less complete guides, however, because those processes are both more technical and more closely tied to the situations encountered in individual research projects. Similarly, we have been able to

---

[1] A book that will help you understand ethical questions that sometimes confront researchers is Tom L. Beauchamp et al., eds., *Ethical Issues In Social Science Research* (Baltimore. MD: Johns Hopkins University Press, 1982).

offer you a less than complete guide to the various data collection and data analysis techniques because of the scope and technical nature of these subjects, and you are well-advised to study them further before claiming expertise in empirical analysis. The suggestions for further reading at the ends of chapters provide good *starting places* for acquiring genuine expertise.

We have provided a sound foundation on which you can build your competence as a political scientist. We hope you find that task as exciting and rewarding as we have and that in the future you will agree that getting there was half the fun.

APPENDIX A

Statistical Tables

Table A.1
Random digits

10097	32533	76520	13586	34673	54876	80959	09117	39292	74945
37542	04805	64894	74296	24805	24037	20636	10402	00822	91665
08422	68953	19645	09303	23209	02560	15953	34764	35080	33606
99019	02529	09376	70715	38311	31165	88676	74397	04436	27659
12807	99970	80157	36147	64032	36653	98951	16877	12171	76833
66065	74717	34072	76850	36697	36170	65813	39885	11199	29170
31060	10805	45571	82406	35303	42614	86799	07439	23403	09732
85269	77602	02051	65692	68665	74818	73053	85247	18623	88579
63573	32135	05325	47048	90553	57548	28468	28709	83491	25624
73796	45753	03529	64778	35808	34282	60935	20344	35273	88435
98520	17767	14905	68607	22109	40558	60970	93433	50500	73998
11805	05431	39808	27732	50725	68248	29405	24201	52775	67851
83452	99634	06288	98083	13746	70078	18475	40610	68711	77817
88685	40200	86507	58401	36766	67951	90364	76493	29609	11062
99594	67348	87517	64969	91826	08928	93785	61368	23478	34113
65481	17674	17468	50950	58047	76974	73039	57186	40218	16544
80124	35635	17727	08015	45318	22374	21115	78253	14385	53763
74350	99817	77402	77214	43236	00201	45521	64237	96286	02655
69916	26803	66252	29148	36936	87203	76621	13990	94400	56418
09893	20505	14225	68514	46427	56788	96297	78822	54382	14598
91499	14523	68479	27686	46162	83554	94750	89923	37089	20048
80336	94598	26490	36858	70297	34135	53140	33340	42050	82341
44104	81949	85157	47954	32979	26575	57600	40881	22222	06413
12550	73742	11100	02040	12860	74697	96644	89439	28707	25815
63606	49329	16505	34484	40219	52563	43651	77082	07207	31790
61196	90446	26457	47774	51924	33729	65394	59593	42582	60527
5474	45266	95270	79953	59367	83848	82396	10118	33211	59466
94557	28573	67897	54387	54622	44431	91190	42592	92927	45973
42481	16213	97344	08721	16868	48767	03071	12059	25701	46670
23523	78317	73208	89837	68935	91416	26252	29663	05522	82562
04493	52494	75246	33824	45826	51025	61962	79335	65337	12472
00549	97654	64501	88159	96119	63896	54692	82391	23287	29529
35963	15307	26898	09354	33351	35462	77974	50024	90103	39333
59808	08391	45427	26842	83609	49700	13021	24892	78565	20106
46058	85236	01390	92286	77281	44077	93910	83647	70617	42941

Table A.1
Random digits
(continued)

32179	00597	87379	25241	05567	07007	86743	17157	85394	11838
69234	61406	20117	45204	15956	60000	18743	92423	97118	96338
19565	41430	01758	75379	40419	21585	66674	36806	84962	85207
45155	14938	19476	07246	43667	94543	59047	90033	20826	69541
94864	31994	36168	10851	81553	34888	01540	35456	05014	51176
98086	24826	45240	28404	44999	08896	39094	73407	35441	31880
33185	16232	41941	50949	89435	48581	88695	41994	37548	73043
80951	00406	96382	70774	20151	23387	25016	25298	94624	61171
79752	49140	71961	28296	69861	02591	74852	20539	00387	59579
18633	32537	98145	06571	31010	24674	05455	61427	77938	91936
74029	43902	77557	32270	97790	17119	52527	58021	80814	51748
54178	45611	80993	37143	05335	12969	56127	19255	36040	90324
11664	49883	52079	84827	59381	71539	09973	33440	88461	23356
48324	77928	31249	64710	02295	36870	32307	57546	15020	09994
69074	94138	87637	91976	35584	04401	10518	21615	01848	76938

SOURCE: The RAND Corporation. *A Million Random Digits with 100,000 Normal Deviates* (New York: Free Press, 1966), p. 1. Reprinted with permission

Table A.2
Sample size for sampling attributes at specified levels of precision (in percent with a 95% confidence interval, p = 0.5)*

Population Size	±1%	±2%	±3%	±4%	±5%	±10%
			Sample Size for Precision of			
500	†	†	†	†	222	83
1,000	†	†	†	385	286	91
1,500	†	†	638	441	316	94
2,000	†	†	714	476	333	95
2,500	†	1,250	769	500	345	96
3,000	†	1,364	811	517	353	97
3,500	†	1,458	843	530	359	97
4,000	†	1,538	870	541	364	98
4,500	†	1,607	891	549	367	98
5,000	†	1,667	909	556	370	98
6,000	†	1,765	938	566	375	98
7,000	†	1,842	959	574	378	99
8,000	†	1,905	976	580	381	99
9,000	†	1,957	989	584	383	99
10,000	5,000	2,000	1,000	588	385	99
15,000	6,000	2,143	1,034	600	390	99
20,000	6,667	2,222	1,053	606	392	100
25,000	7,143	2,273	1,064	610	394	100
50,000	8,333	2,381	1,087	617	397	100
100,000	9,091	2,439	1,099	621	398	100
⟶ ∞	10,000	2,500	1,111	625	400	100

SOURCE: Taro Yamane, *Elementary Sampling Theory* (Englewood Cliffs, NJ: Prentice Hall, 1967), p. 398. Adapted and reprinted with permission of the publisher

* Proportion of units in the sample possessing the characteristic being measured; for other values of p, the required sample size will be smaller

† In these cases 50% of the universe in the sample will give more than the required accuracy. Since the formal distribution is a poor approximation of the hypergeometrical distribution when n is more than 50% of N, the formula used in this calculation does not apply.

Table A.3
Sample size for sampling attributes at specified levels of precision (in percent with a 99.7% confidence interval, p = 0.5)*

Population Size	Sample Size for Precision of				
	±1%	**±2%**	**±3%**	**±4%**	**±5%**
500	†	†	†	†	†
1,000	†	†	†	†	474
1,500	†	†	†	726	563
2,000	†	†	†	826	621
2,500	†	†	†	900	662
3,000	†	†	1,364	958	692
3,500	†	†	1,458	1,003	716
4,000	†	†	1,539	1,041	735
4,500	†	†	1,607	1,071	750
5,000	†	†	1,667	1,098	763
6,000	†	2,903	1,765	1,139	783
7,000	†	3,119	1,842	1,171	798
8,000	†	3,303	1,905	1,196	809
9,000	†	3,462	1,957	1,216	818
10,000	†	3,600	2,000	1,233	826
15,000	†	4,091	2,143	1,286	849
20,000	†	4,390	2,222	1,314	861
25,000	11,842	4,592	2,273	1,331	869
50,000	15,517	5,056	2,381	1,368	884
100,000	18,367	5,325	2,439	1,387	892
$\longrightarrow \chi$	22,500	5,625	2,500	1,406	900

SOURCE: Taro Yamane, *Elementary Sampling Theory* (Englewood Cliffs, NJ: Prentice Hall, 1967), p. 399. Adapted and reprinted with permission of the publisher

* Proportion of units in the sample possessing the characteristic being measured; for other values of p, the required sample size will be smaller
† In these cases 50% of the universe in the sample will give more than the required accuracy. Since the formal distribution is a poor approximation of the hypergeometrical distribution when *n* is more than 50% of *N*, the formula used in this calculation does not apply.

Table A.4
Distribution of χ^2

df	.05	.01	.001	df	.05	.01	.001
1	3.841	6.635	10.827	26	38.885	45.642	54.052
2	5.991	9.210	13.815	27	40.113	46.963	55.476
3	7.815	11.345	16.266	28	41.337	48.278	56.893
4	9.488	13.277	18.467	29	42.557	49.588	58.302
5	11.070	15.086	20.515	30	43.773	50.892	59.703
6	12.592	16.812	22.457	32	46.194	53.486	62.487
7	14.067	18.475	24.322	34	48.602	56.061	65.247
8	15.507	20.090	26.125	36	50.999	58.619	67.985
9	16.919	21.666	27.877	38	53.384	61.162	70.703
10	18.307	23.209	29.588	40	55.759	63.691	73.402
11	19.675	24.725	31.264	42	58.124	66.206	76.084
12	21.026	26.217	32.909	44	60.481	68.710	78.750
13	22.362	27.688	34.528	46	62.830	71.201	81.400
14	23.685	29.141	36.123	48	65.171	73.683	84.037
15	24.996	30.578	37.697	50	67.505	76.154	86.661
16	26.296	32.000	39.252	52	69.832	78.616	89.272
17	27.587	33.409	40.790	54	72.153	81.069	91.872
18	28.869	34.805	42.312	56	74.468	83.513	94.461
19	30.144	36.191	43.820	58	76.778	85.950	97.039
20	31.410	37.566	45.315	60	79.082	88.379	99.607
21	32.671	38.932	46.797	62	81.381	90.802	102.166
22	33.924	40.289	48.268	64	83.675	93.217	104.716
23	35.172	41.638	49.728	66	85.965	95.626	107.258
24	36.415	42.980	51.179	68	88.250	98.028	109.791
25	37.652	44.314	52.620	70	90.531	100.425	112.317

SOURCE: From Table IV of Ronald A. Fisher and Frank Yates, *Statistical Tables for Biological, Agricultural and Medical Research*, 6th ed., published by Longman Group, Ltd., London (previously published by Oliver & Boyd, Edinburgh). Reprinted with permission of the authors and the publisher.

Note: For odd values of n between 30 and 70, the mean of the tabular values for $df-1$ and $df+1$ may be taken. For larger values of n, the expression $\sqrt{2x^2} - \sqrt{2df-1}$ may be used as a normal deviate with unit variance, remembering that the probability for x^2 corresponds with that of a single tail of the normal curve.

Table A.5
Values of the correlation coefficient for different levels of significance

df	.1	.05	.01	.001	df	.1	.05	.01	.001
1	.98769	.99692	.999877	.9999988	16	.4000	.4683	.5897	.7084
2	.90000	.95000	.990000	.99900	17	.3887	.4555	.5751	.6932
3	.8054	.878	.9587	.99116	18	.3783	.4438	.5614	.6787
4	.7293	.8114	.91720	.97406	19	.3687	.4329	.5487	.6652
5	.6694	.7545	.8745	.95274	20	.3598	.4227	.5368	.6524
6	.6215	.7067	.8343	.92493	25	.3233	.3809	.4869	.5974
7	.5822	.6664	.7977	.8982	30	.2960	.3494	.4487	.5541
8	.5494	.6319	.7646	.8721	35	.2746	.3246	.4182	.5189
9	.5214	.6021	.7348	.8471	40	.2573	.3044	.3932	.4896
10	.4973	.5760	.7079	.8233	45	.2428	.2875	.3721	.4648
11	.4762	.5529	.6835	.8010	50	.2306	.2732	.3541	.4433
12	.4575	.5324	.6614	.7800	60	.2108	.2500	.3248	.4078
13	.4409	.5139	.6411	.7603	70	.1954	.2319	.3017	.3799
14	.4259	.497	.6226	.7420	80	.1829	.2172	.2830	.3568
15	.4124	.482	.6055	.7246	90	.1726	.2050	.2673	.3375
					100	.1638	.1946	.2540	.3211

SOURCE: From Table VII of Ronald A. Fisher and Frank Yates, *Statistical Tables for Biological, Agricultural and Medical Research*, 6th ed., published by Longman Group, Ltd., London (previously published by Oliver & Boyd, Edinburgh). Reprinted with permission of the authors and the publishers.

Table A.6
Portions of area under the normal curve
(continued on next page)

(A) z	(B) Area between mean and z	(C) Area beyond z	(A) z	(B) Area between mean and z	(C) Area beyond z	(A) z	(B) Area between mean and z	(C) Area beyond z
0.00	.0000	.5000	0.40	.1554	.3446	0.80	.2881	.2119
0.01	.0040	.4960	0.41	.1591	.3409	0.81	.2910	.2090
0.02	.0080	.4920	0.42	.1628	.3372	0.82	.2936	.2061
0.03	.0120	.4880	0.43	.1664	.3336	0.83	.2967	.2033
0.04	.0160	.4840	0.44	.1700	.3300	0.84	.2995	.2005
0.05	.0199	.4801	0.45	.1736	.3264	0.85	.3023	.1977
0.06	.0239	.4761	0.46	.1772	.3228	0.86	.3051	.1949
0.07	.0279	.4721	0.47	.1808	.3192	0.87	.3078	.1922
0.08	.0319	.4681	0.48	.1844	.3156	0.88	.3106	.1894
0.09	.0359	.4641	0.49	.1879	.3121	0.89	.3133	.1867
0.10	.0398	.4602	0.50	.1915	.3085	0.90	.3159	.1841
0.11	.0438	.4562	0.51	.1950	.3050	0.91	.3186	.1814
0.12	.0478	.4522	0.52	.1985	.3015	0.92	.3212	.1788
0.13	.0517	.4483	0.53	.2019	.2981	0.93	.3238	.1788
0.14	.0557	.4443	0.54	.2054	.2946	0.94	.3264	.1736
0.15	.0596	.4404	0.55	.2088	.2912	0.95	.3289	.1711
0.16	.0636	.4364	0.56	.2123	.2877	0.96	.3315	.1685
0.17	.0675	.4325	0.57	.2157	.2843	0.97	.3340	.1660
0.18	.0714	.4286	0.58	.2190	.2810	0.98	.3365	.1635
0.19	.0753	.4247	0.59	.2224	.2776	0.99	.3389	.1611
0.20	.0793	.4207	0.60	.2257	.2743	1.00	.3413	.1587
0.21	.0832	.4168	0.61	.2291	.2709	1.01	.3438	.1562
0.22	.0871	.4129	0.62	.2324	.2676	1.02	.3461	.1539
0.23	.0910	.4090	0.63	.2357	.2643	1.03	.3485	.1515
0.24	.0948	.4052	0.64	.2389	.2611	1.04	.3508	.1492
0.25	.0987	.4013	0.65	.2422	.2578	1.05	.3531	.1469
0.26	.1026	.3974	0.66	.2454	.2546	1.06	.3554	.1446
0.27	.1064	.3936	0.67	.2486	.2514	1.07	.3577	.1423
0.28	.1103	.3897	0.68	.2517	.2483	1.08	.3599	.1401
0.29	.1141	.3859	0.69	.2549	.2451	1.09	.3621	.1379
0.30	.1179	.3821	0.70	.2580	.2420	1.10	.3643	.1357
0.31	.1217	.3783	0.71	.2611	.2389	1.11	.3665	.1335
0.32	.1255	.3745	0.72	.2642	.2358	1.12	.3686	.1314
0.33	.1293	.3707	0.73	.2673	.2327	1.13	.3708	.1292
0.34	.1331	.3669	0.74	.2704	.2296	1.14	.3729	.1271
0.35	.1368	.3632	0.75	.2734	.2266	1.15	.3748	.1251
0.36	.1406	.3594	0.76	.2764	.2236	1.16	.3770	.1230
0.37	.1443	.3557	0.77	.2794	.2206	1.17	.3790	.1210
0.38	.1480	.3520	0.78	.2823	.2177	1.18	.3810	.1190
0.39	.1517	.3483	0.79	.2852	.2148	1.19	.3830	.1170

Table A.6
Portions of area under the normal curve
(continued)

(A) z	(B) Area between mean and z	(C) Area beyond z	(A) z	(B) Area between mean and z	(C) Area beyond z	(A) z	(B) Area between mean and z	(C) Area beyond z
1.20	.3849	.1151	1.60	.4452	.0548	2.00	.4772	.0228
1.21	.3869	.1131	1.61	.4463	.0537	2.01	.4778	.0222
1.22	.3888	.1112	1.62	.4474	.0526	2.02	.4783	.0217
1.23	.3907	.1093	1.63	.4484	.0516	2.03	.4788	.0212
1.24	.3925	.1075	1.64	.4495	.0505	2.04	.4793	.0207
1.25	.3944	.1056	1.65	.4505	.0495	2.05	.4798	.0202
1.26	.3962	.1038	1.66	.4515	.0485	2.06	.4803	.0197
1.27	.3980	.1020	1.67	.4525	.0475	2.07	.4808	.0192
1.28	.3997	.1003	1.68	.4535	.0465	2.08	.4812	.0188
1.29	.4015	.0985	1.69	.4545	.0455	2.09	.4817	.0183
1.30	.4032	.0968	1.70	.4554	.0446	2.10	.4821	.0179
1.31	.4049	.0951	1.71	.4564	.0436	2.11	.4826	.0174
1.32	.4066	.0934	1.72	.4573	.0427	2.12	.4830	.0170
1.33	.4082	.0918	1.73	.4582	.0418	2.13	.4834	.0166
1.34	.4099	.0901	1.74	.4591	.0409	2.14	.4838	.0162
1.35	.4115	.0885	1.75	.4599	.0401	2.15	.4842	.0158
1.36	.4131	.0869	1.76	.4608	.0392	2.16	.4846	.0154
1.37	.4147	.0853	1.77	.4616	.0384	2.17	.4850	.0150
1.38	.4162	.0838	1.78	.4625	.0375	2.18	.4854	.0146
1.39	.4177	.0823	1.79	.4633	.0367	2.19	.4857	.0143
1.40	.4192	.0808	1.80	.4641	.0359	2.20	.4861	.0139
1.41	.4207	.0793	1.81	.4649	.0351	2.21	.4864	.0136
1.42	.4222	.0778	1.82	.4656	.0344	2.22	.4868	.0132
1.43	.4236	.0764	1.83	.4664	.0336	2.23	.4871	.0129
1.44	.4251	.0749	1.84	.4671	.0329	2.24	.4875	.0125
1.45	.4265	.0735	1.85	.4678	.0322	2.25	.4878	.0122
1.46	.4279	.0721	1.86	.4686	.0314	2.26	.4881	.0119
1.47	.4292	.0708	1.87	.4693	.0307	2.27	.4884	.0116
1.48	.4306	.0694	1.88	.4699	.0301	2.28	.4887	.0113
1.49	.4319	.0681	1.89	.4706	.0294	2.29	.4890	.0110
1.50	.4332	.0668	1.90	.4713	.0287	2.30	.4893	.0107
1.51	.4345	.0655	1.91	.4719	.0281	2.31	.4896	.0104
1.52	.4357	.0643	1.92	.4726	.0274	2.32	.4898	.0102
1.53	.4370	.0630	1.93	.4732	.0268	2.33	.4901	.0099
1.54	.4382	.0618	1.94	.4738	.0262	2.34	.4904	.0096
1.55	.4394	.0606	1.95	.4744	.0256	2.35	.4906	.0094
1.56	.4406	.0594	1.96	.4750	.0250	2.36	.4909	.0091
1.57	.4418	.0582	1.97	.4556	.0244	2.37	.4911	.0089
1.58	.4429	.0571	1.98	.4761	.0239	2.38	.4913	.0087
1.59	.4441	.0559	1.99	.4767	.0233	2.39	.4916	.0084

Table A.6
Portions of area under the normal curve
(continued)

(A) z	(B) Area between mean and z	(C) Area beyond z	(A) z	(B) Area between mean and z	(C) Area beyond z	(A) z	(B) Area between mean and z	(C) Area beyond z
2.40	.4918	.0082	2.75	.4970	.0030	3.05	.4989	.0011
2.41	.4920	.0080	2.76	.4971	.0029	3.06	.4989	.0011
2.42	.4922	.0078	2.77	.4972	.0028	3.07	.4989	.0011
2.43	.4925	.0075	2.78	.4973	.0027	3.08	.4990	.0010
2.44	.4927	.0073	2.79	.4974	.0026	3.09	.4990	.0010
2.45	.4929	.0071	2.80	.4974	.0026	3.10	.4990	.0010
2.46	.4931	.0069	2.81	.4975	.0025	3.11	.4991	.0009
2.47	.4932	.0068	2.82	.4976	.0024	3.12	.4991	.0009
2.48	.4934	.0066	2.83	.4977	.0023	3.13	.4991	.0009
2.49	.4936	.0064	2.84	.4977	.0023	3.14	.4992	.0008
2.50	.4938	.0062	2.85	.4978	.0022	3.15	.4992	.0008
2.51	.4940	.0060	2.86	.4979	.0021	3.16	.4992	.0008
2.52	.4941	.0059	2.87	.4979	.0021	3.17	.4992	.0008
2.53	.4943	.0057	2.88	.4980	.0020	3.18	.4993	.0007
2.54	.4945	.0055	2.89	.4981	.0019	3.19	.4993	.0007
2.55	.4946	.0054	2.90	.4981	.0019	3.20	.4993	.0007
2.56	.4948	.0052	2.91	.4982	.0018	3.21	.4993	.0007
2.57	.4949	.0051	2.92	.4982	.0018	3.22	.4994	.0006
2.58	.4951	.0049	2.93	.4983	.0017	3.23	.4994	.0006
2.59	.4952	.0048	2.94	.7984	.0016	3.24	.4994	.0006
2.60	.4953	.0047	2.95	.4984	.0016	3.25	.4994	.0006
2.61	.4955	.0045	2.96	.4985	.0015	3.30	.4995	.0005
2.62	.4956	.0044	2.97	.4985	.0015	3.35	.4996	.0004
2.63	.4957	.0043	2.98	.4986	.0014	3.40	.4997	.0003
2.64	.4959	.0041	2.99	.4986	.0014	3.45	.4997	.0003
2.65	.4960	.0040	3.00	.4987	.0013	3.50	.4998	.0002
2.66	.4961	.0039	3.01	.4987	.0013	3.60	.4998	.0002
2.67	.4962	.0038	3.02	.4987	.0013	3.70	.4999	.0001
2.68	.4963	.0037	3.03	.4988	.0012	3.80	.4999	.0001
2.69	.4964	.0036	3.04	.4988	.0012	3.90	.49995	.00005
						4.00	.49997	.00003
2.70	.4965	.0035						
2.71	.4966	.0034						
2.72	.4967	.0033						
2.73	.4968	.0032						
2.74	.4969	.0031						

SOURCE: Richard P. Runyon and Audrey Haber, *Fundamentals of Behavioral Statistics,* 3d ed. (Reading, MA: Addison-Wesley, 1976), pp. 378–79.

APPENDIX B

ETHICAL CONSIDERATIONS IN EMPIRICAL RESEARCH

The American Political Science Association has adopted a set of "Principles of Professional Conduct." The following rules are excerpted from the section on ethical research practices.[1]

---

1. Openness concerning material support of research is a basic principle of scholarship. . . .

3. In applying for research funds, the individual researcher should:

   3.1 clearly state the reasons for applying for support and not resort to stratagems of ambiguity to make the research more acceptable to a funding agency;

   3.2 indicate clearly the actual amount of time the researcher personally plans to spend on the research;

   3.3 indicate other sources of support of the research, if any; and

   3.4 refuse to accept terms and conditions that the researcher believes will undermine his or her freedom and integrity as a scholar.

4. In conducting research so supported, the individual bears sole responsibility for the procedures, methods, and content of research. The researcher:

   4.1 must avoid any deception or misrepresentation concerning his or her personal involvement or the involvement of respondents or subjects, and must avoid use of research as a cover for intelligence work or for partisan political purposes;

   4.2 must refrain from using his or her professional status to obtain data and research materials for purposes other than scholarship;

---

[1] Reproduced with the permission of the American Political Science Association. The full text of the APSA guidelines is available online at www.apsanet.org/pubs/ethics.cfm.

4.3 with respect to research abroad, should not concurrently accept any additional support from agencies of the government for purposes that cannot be disclosed;

4.4 should carefully comply with the time, reporting, accounting, and other requirements set forth in the project instrument, and cooperate with institutional grant administrators in meeting these requirements; and

4.5 should avoid commingling project funds with personal funds, or funds of one project with those of another.

5. With respect to any public scholarly activity including publication of the results of research, the individual researcher:

5.1 bears sole responsibility for publication;

5.2 should disclose all relevant sources of financial support;

5.3 should indicate any condition imposed by financial sponsors or others on research publication, or other scholarly activities; and

5.4 should conscientiously acknowledge any assistance received in conducting research.

5.5 Authors are obliged to reveal the bases of any of their statements that are challenged specifically, except where confidentiality is involved.

6. Scholars have an ethical obligation to make a full and complete disclosure of all nonconfidential sources involved in their research so that their work can be tested or replicated.

6.1 As citizens they have an obligation to cooperate with grand juries, other law enforcement agencies, and institutional officials.

6.2 Conversely, scholars also have a professional duty not to divulge the identity of confidential sources of information or data developed in the course of research, whether to governmental or nongovernmental officials or bodies, even though in the present state of American law they run the risk of suffering an applicable penalty.

6.3 Scholars must, however, exercise appropriate restraint in making claims as to the confidential nature of their sources, and resolve all reasonable doubts in favor of full disclosure.

7. Political scientists, like all scholars, are expected to practice intellectual honesty and to uphold the scholarly standards of their discipline.

7.1 Plagiarism, the deliberate appropriation of the work of others represented as one's own, not only may constitute a violation of the civil law but represents a serious breach of professional ethics.

The American Sociological Association has also developed a code of ethics to guide scholars as they confront ethical issues in research. Below we have listed some of the items in that code that pertain principally to the relationship between researchers and their subjects. Though the code is written for sociologists, the rules are general enough to apply to all social scientists, and you can read researcher each place the word sociologist appears in the excerpt.[2]

---

1. *Objectivity in Research.* In his research the sociologist must maintain scientific objectivity.

2. *Integrity in Research.* The sociologist should recognize his own limitations and when appropriate, seek more expert assistance or decline to undertake research beyond his competence. He must not misrepresent his own abilities, or the competence of his staff to conduct a particular research project.

3. *Respect of the Research Subject's Rights to Privacy and Dignity.* Every person is entitled to the right of privacy and dignity of treatment. The sociologist must respect these rights.

4. *Protection of Subjects from Personal Harm.* All research should avoid causing personal harm to subjects used in research.

5. *Preservation of Confidentiality of Research Data.* Confidential information provided by a research subject must be treated as such by the sociologist. Even though research information is not a privileged communication under the law, the sociologist must, as far as possible, protect subjects and informants. Any promises made to such persons must be honored. However, provided that he respects the assurances he has given his subjects, the sociologist has no obligation to withhold information of misconduct of individuals or organizations.

   If an informant or other subject should wish, however, he can formally release the researcher of a promise of confidentiality. The provisions of this section apply to all members of research organizations (i.e, interviewers, coders, clerical staff, etc.), and it is the responsibility of the chief investigators to see that they are instructed in the necessity and importance of maintaining the confidentiality of the data. The obligation of the sociologist includes the use and storage of original data to which a subject's name is attached. When requested, the identity of an organization or subject must be adequately disguised in publication.

6. *Presentation of Research Findings.* The sociologist must present his findings honestly and without distortion. There should be no omission of data from a research report which might significantly modify the interpretation of findings.

7. *Misuse of Research Role.* The sociologist must not use his role as a cover to obtain information for other than professional purposes.

8. *Acknowledgment of Research Collaboration and Assistance.* The sociologist must acknowledge the professional contributions or assistance of all persons who collaborated in the research.

---

[2] Excerpted from "Toward a Code of Ethics for Sociologists," *The American Sociologist,* 3 (November 1968), p. 318. Reprinted with the permission of the American Sociological Association. A more contemporary and more extensive version of this code is available online at www.asanet.org/ecoderev.htm. The authors have chosen to reproduce the older formulation here because the most relevant points are more easily identified and interpreted by beginning researchers.

9. *Disclosure of the Sources of Financial Support.* The sociologist must report fully all sources of financial support in his research publications and any special relations to the sponsor that might affect the interpretation of the findings.

10. *Distortion of Findings by Sponsor.* The sociologist is obliged to clarify publicly any distortion by a sponsor or client of the findings of a research project in which he has participated.

11. *Disassociation from Unethical Research Arrangements.* The sociologist must not accept such grants, contracts, or research assignments as appear likely to require violation of the principles above, and must publicly terminate the work or formally disassociate himself from the research if he discovers such a violation and is unable to achieve its correction.

Similarly, the American Association for Public Opinion Research has adopted the following Code of Professional Ethics and Practices.[3]

I. Principles of professional practice in the conduct of our work

A. We shall exercise due care in developing research designs and survey instruments, and in collecting, processing, and analyzing data, taking all reasonable steps to assure the reliability and validity of results.

1. We shall recommend and employ only those tools of analysis which . . . are well suited to the research problem at hand.

2. We shall not select research tools and methods of analysis because of their capacity to yield misleading conclusions.

3. We shall not knowingly make interpretations of research results, nor shall we tacitly permit interpretations that are inconsistent with the data available.

4. We shall not knowingly imply that interpretations should be accorded greater confidence than the data actually warrant.

B. We shall describe our methods and findings accurately and in appropriate detail in all research reports, adhering to the standards for minimal disclosure specified in Section III below. . . .

II. Principles of professional responsibility in our dealings with people

A. The public

1. If we become aware of the appearance in public of serious distortions of our research, we shall publicly disclose what is required to correct these distortions. . . .

---

[3] *Code of Professional Ethics and Practices,* courtesy of the American Association for Public Opinion Research.

D. The respondent

1. We shall strive to avoid the use of practices or methods that may harm, humiliate, or seriously mislead survey respondents.

2. Unless the respondent waives confidentiality for specified uses, we shall hold as privileged and confidential all information that might identify a respondent with his or her responses. We shall also not disclose or use the names of respondents for nonresearch purposes unless the respondents grant us permission to do so.

III. Standard for minimal disclosure

1. Who sponsored the survey, and who conducted it.

2. The exact wording of questions asked, including the text of any preceding instruction or explanation to the interviewer or respondent that might reasonably be expected to affect the response.

3. A definition of the population under study, and a description of the sampling frame used to identify this population.

4. A description of the sample selection procedure, giving a clear indication of the method by which the respondents were selected by the researcher, or whether the respondents were entirely self-selected.

5. Size of sample and, if applicable, completion rates and information on eligibility criteria and screening procedures.

6. A discussion of the precision of the findings, including, if appropriate, estimates of sampling error, and a description of any weighting or estimating procedures used.

7. Which results are based on parts of the sample, rather than on the total sample.

8. Method, location, and dates of data collection.

GLOSSARY

Abstract. a brief statement summarizing the contents of a report

Additive index. a measure created by combining indicators of different aspects of the same concept

Aggregate data. data pertaining to groups of cases or to collectivities

Alternative rival hypothesis. an alternative explanation for obtained results that logically cannot be accurate if the initial hypothesis is accurate

Antecedent variable. a variable that causes variation in the variable that, for purposes of a given hypothesis, is regarded as the independent variable

Applied research. research the primary purpose of which is to examine or resolve particular policy problems

Areal group. a group defined by residence within a particular geographic area

Association. a relationship in which two (or more) variables covary

Assumption. (also *axiom* or *postulate*) an abstract assertion about relationships that serves as a foundation for theoretical reasoning but is not subject to empirical test

Bar chart. a graphic device in which bars are used to represent observations

Basic research. research the primary purpose of which is to develop or test a scientific theory

Beta weight or **beta coefficient.** a standardized partial regression coefficient used to compare the relative effects of independent variables on a dependent variable

Bibliographic sources. systematic listings of publications organized to assist in literature reviews

Bibliography. a compilation of books, articles, and other materials on a given topic

Bilateral bar chart. a two-directional graphic device in which bars are used to represent variation above or below some norm

Bivariate statistics. statistics summarizing the relationship between two variables

Boolean connectors. words such as *and, or,* or *not* that provide linkages among concepts during a computerized literature search

Causal model. a model that graphically specifies a set of relationships between concepts or variables such that change in one or more precedes and gives rise to change in another

Causal relationship. a relationship in which change in one or more concepts or variables leads to or "forces" changes in one or more other concepts or variables

Central tendency (measure of). device for determining the value or score that best represents a set of cases on a given variable

Chaotic models. models of systematic processes that can produce random results

Chi-square (χ^2). a test of the statistical significance of the association between two nominal variables

Closed-ended questions. questions that force respondents to choose an answer from a limited number of options

Cluster sampling. *see* **multistage random area sample**

Codebook. a listing of variables and values indicating how they are coded in a study

Coder. a person who assigns scores to cases or responses, usually with reference to content analysis coded in a study

Codes. numbers assigned to represent different values on variables for purposes of data analysis

Coding. the process of assigning numerical values to represent values on variables

Coding sheet. a structured form for recording data

Coefficient of association. a measure of the degree and direction of association between two variables

Coefficient of determination (R^2). the multiple regression coefficient tells how much of the variance in the values on a dependent variable is "explained" by variance in a *set* of independent variables

Cohort study. a study based on repeated surveys of a specific group (for example, persons born in a given year) at different points in time

Collectively exhaustive. a characteristic of measures by which all cases can be assigned to at least one category

Complex systems. series events in which the underlying mathematical processes determining relationships between variables changes over time posing challenges in mathematical modeling

Computational model. a mathematical model that is specified by nonnumerical algorithms and implemented on a computer

Computer-assisted telephone interviewing (CATI). interviewing using computer display of instrument, usually includes continual calculation of summary statistics

Computer simulation. a mathematical model that is specified by a complex set of dynamic equations and implemented on a computer

Concept. a word or phrase that symbolizes some idea or phenomenon

Concurrent validation. the characteristic of a measure that allows accurate sorting of cases on the basis of related concurrent traits

Confidence interval. an indicator of the accuracy with which a population parameter can be predicted from a sample statistic stated in terms of the range of values above or below the sample statistic the population parameter is likely to fall

Confidence level. an indicator of the likelihood that a sample is representative stated in terms of the probability that a sample statistic is within a given confidence interval of a population parameter

Construct validity. the characteristic of a measure by which it behaves as we would expect on the basis of theory

Content analysis. a technique used in the study of communication-related materials and behaviors

Contingency question. a filtering device used in survey research to ascertain the appropriateness of asking a subsequent question

Contingency table. a tabular presentation summarizing the relationship(s) between two or more variables

Control. in experimental design, to limit the factors influencing a variable under observation; in data analysis, to hold the values of one variable constant while examining the relationship(s) between two or more other variables

Control group. subjects in an experiment not exposed to the independent variable (experimental event)

Controlled time-series design. a research design that uses control groups to assess the impact of an event

Controlling. holding constant the effect of one variable on the relationship between two other variables in order to obtain an accurate measure of that relationship

Convergent validity. a characteristic whereby several measures of a common concept provide essentially the same result

Correlation coefficient (r). the coefficient of association between two interval variables measuring the closeness of fit of data points around the regression line

Covariational relationship. a relationship in which two or more concepts or variables tend to change together for unspecified reasons.

Cross-sectional survey. a survey that compares data from different cases at a single point in time

Data. observations of or information about reality arising from the research process

Data archives. collections of the results of previous research

Data specifications. detailed descriptions of the data that are to be recorded for each case and variable

Data transformation. modification of data to meet the requirements of a particular analysis technique

Deduction. reasoning that moves from abstract statements about general relationships to concrete statements about specific behaviors

Degrees of freedom (*df*). the number of cells in a table or points along a regression line that may be entered without being determined by prior entries

Demographic group. a group defined by some personal characteristic(s) of its members

Dependent variable. a variable whose value changes in response to changes in the value of some other variable

Descriptive research. research concerned primarily with measuring some aspect of reality for its own sake rather than with developing or testing some theory

Direct observation. a technique used primarily in the study of group norms and behaviors

Discriminant validation. a characteristic whereby a measure is valid for one concept alone as opposed to several concepts

Dispersion (measure of). an indicator of variation around the measure of central tendency, that is, an indicator of its representativeness

Dynamic model. a mathematical model that describes the behavior of a process over time

Ecological fallacy. the improper use of aggregate data to draw conclusions about the characteristics of individual cases or groups

Elite interviewing. gathering data through interviews designed to tap the unique knowledge of the respondents

Empirical. pertaining to or characterized by observations or descriptions of reality

Empirically grounded. a type of theory that is based on induction from actual observation

Empirical referent. an observable object or event that corresponds to a concept

Enumerative table. a simple tabular listing of research data

Equivalent measures. indicators that measure the same phenomena in more than one system

Expected utility model. a mathematical model based on the assumption that individuals base decisions on the sum of the payoffs of possible outcomes times their probability of occurring

Experimental design. a research strategy in which the relationship between a given stimulus, event, or other variable and some observable behavior is isolated

Experimental group. subjects exposed to the independent variable (experimental stimulus)

Explanatory research. research that uses observations of reality to test hypotheses and to help identify or develop an understanding of patterns of behavior in the context of a theory

Exploratory research. research designed to discover factors that should be included in theorizing and research on a subject

Ex post facto **experiment.** a research design in which experimental controls are simulated in data analysis

External validity. a form of construct validity demonstrated through the correlation of an indicator with indicators of other concepts to which the original concept should theoretically be related

Face validity. a characteristic of a measure that gives it intuitive appeal

Field experiment. a partial application of experimental design in a real-world setting, as distinct from a laboratory

Field notes. written records made during direct observation

Focus group. a small group used for in-depth study of a subject through directed discussion

Formal model. a model specified in mathematical or some other formal language

Frequency distribution. an ordered count of the number of cases that take on each value of a variable

Frequency distribution control. a procedure by which experimental and control groups can be made equivalent by selection of combinations of subjects with comparable aggregate characteristics

Galton's problem. the task of testing for the effects of diffusion in comparative research

Game theory. a branch of mathematics dealing with the analysis of situations in which outcomes are decided by the joint deliberations of individuals

Gamma (G). a coefficient of association between two ordinal variables

Generalizability. the characteristic that permits the results of research on a limited set of cases to be extended to the population from which those cases are drawn

Going native. the situation in which a researcher involved in participant observation adopts the values and mind-set of those being observed and loses objectivity

Guide. a set of instructions to guide a moderator in conducting a focus group

Guttman scaling. a method of scale creation that provides internal criteria for determining the degree to which a set of items exhibit unidimensionality (measure a single concept)

Histogram. a bar chart showing the distribution of values on a variable

Homogeneity. the degree to which members of a given population are like one another

Hypothesis. a statement predicting the relationship(s) between variables

Independent variable. a variable whose own value changes influence the value of some other variable

In-depth interviewing. a technique for gathering information by interviewing subjects at length while being highly flexible in the structure and content of the questions asked in order to discover unexpected facts

Index construction. combining two or more related indicators into a single, more comprehensive indicator

Indicator. a specific measure of a variable

Indirect causation. the phenomenon by which one variable exerts causal influence on another only by changing the value of other variables that directly affect it

Induction. reasoning that generalizes from what has been observed to what has not—that is, in which an abstract theory is developed from concrete evidence

Inference. reasoning from either observation or a logical system to reach conclusions not already apparent

Informal model. a simplified description of a process or situation using natural language

In-person interview. a survey interview in which the interviewer questions the respondent face-to-face

Instrument. a device or procedure used for taking a measurement

Instrumentation. the specification of steps to take in making observations; the creation of measurement devices

Intercoder reliability. agreement in the values assigned to the same or similar cases by independent observers

Internal validity. a form of construct validity demonstrated by the correlation of several measures of the same concept

Interobserver reliability. the degree to which two or more individuals agree on the details of an event they have observed as part of a research project

Interval measurement. measurement that classifies and rank orders cases so that the distance between cases is known by using a standard unit of measurement

Intervening variable. a variable that influences the effect of an independent variable on a dependent variable

Interview schedule. the questionnaire used with in-person interviews

Judgmental sample. a sample in which specific cases are purposely selected

Key. the explanation of symbols used in a graphic presentation

Key word or **key phrase.** a word or phrase that is meaningfully related to a given concept, used for bibliographic search

Lambda (λ). a coefficient of association between two nominal variables

Level of measurement. the amount of information provided by a set of instruments

Likert scaling. a method of scale creation based on asking respondents to report the degree to which they agree or disagree with a series of statements selected to represent a trait

Line diagram. a graphic device using lines to connect points representing observations so as to suggest trends or other relationships

Linear relationship. a relationship between two variables that can be graphically represented as a straight line

Longitudinal survey. a survey that compares the attributes or behaviors of a given set of cases at different points in time

Mail surveys. surveys conducted by mailing questionnaires to respondents and asking that they complete and return them

Marginals. the frequency distribution as it appears in the row and column totals of a contingency table

Mathematical model. a simplified description of a process or situation, using mathematical language

Mean. a measure of central tendency for interval variables

Measurement. the application of an instrument to count or in some other way quantify observations of reality

Measurement error. inaccuracies in the observation of reality; differences between reality and recorded observations of it

Measurement theory. a statement of why one expects values on an indicator to change when the value of the variable it represents changes

Median. a measure of central tendency for ordinal variables

Method effect. any misleading impact of the particular method used to study a subject on the results of that study

Mode. a measure of central tendency for nominal variables

Model. a simplified representation of reality

Model specification. the process of selecting the variables to be included in a regression model and specifying their relationship to one another

Moderator. the person who directs discussion in focus group and reports on its results

Most-different-systems design. a strategy for comparative research in which characteristics that differ between units of analysis can be ruled out as explanations for others that are shared

Most-similar-systems design. a strategy for comparative research that focuses on units of analysis that are very similar, on the theory that shared characteristics can be held constant when differences between the units are examined

Multicollinearity. the condition in which one or more of the independent variables in a regression equation are perfect linear functions of one or more other independent variables in the equation

Multidimensional. having several facets or elements

Multiple causation. the common situation in the social sciences in which an effect is the result of more than one cause

Multiple indicators. more than one measure of the same variable, especially useful for enhancing the validity of indicators

Multiple regression. a statistical procedure for examining the relationship among a dependent variable and several independent variables

Multiple regression equation. the mathematical equation that represents the conceptual process described by a regression model and is used as a basis for multiple regression analysis

Multiplicative index. a single measure constructed from a combination of measures of different but related concepts

Multistage random area sample. a sample in which geographic units or their analogs rather than individuals are selected for analysis

Multivariate analysis. any statistical analysis examining the relationship between *more than two* variables simultaneously

Multivariate statistics. statistics relating to the relationships among more than two variables

Mutually exclusive. characteristic of measures by which a given case can be assigned to only one category

Negative relationship. the relationship said to exist when corresponding values on two variables change in *opposite* directions

Nominal measurement. measurement that merely classifies cases without regard to rank or distances between cases

Nonexperimental studies. studies in which there is no research design to provide a logical basis for causal inference

Nonrecursive. the term describing a causal model in which at least one variable influences another variable that occurs earlier in the model

Normal distribution. a distribution that is unimodal and symmetrical, with the peak at the center, and in which the mode, median, and mean take on the same value

Normative. pertaining to or characterized by preferences or value judgments

Observation. in science, the application of an instrument to assign values to cases on indicators

Observation point. the time of observation or measurement

Observation schedule. a form facilitating systematic recording of data observations

Obtrusive measure. a measurement that is evident to the research subjects

Obtrusive research. research employing obtrusive measures.

Open-ended questions. questions that allow respondents to answer in their own words

Operational definition. set of observations that represent abstract concepts

Operationalization. the process of designating sets of observations to represent abstract concepts

Optimization model. a mathematical model that is specified by assuming that certain variables in a process or situation are maximized or minimized

Ordinal measurement. measurement that classifies and ranks cases without regard to the distance between them

Pair-comparison scaling. a technique employed in content analysis to measure the intensity of evaluative statements

Panel study. a study that employs the same group of subjects for a series of observations at different points in time

Parameter. any characteristic of a population, as distinct from a characteristic of a sample

Parsimony. the presentation of material in as efficient a manner as possible; simplicity in a theory

Partial regression coefficient. a statistic that indicates the effect of an independent variable on a dependent variable when the effects of all other variables in a model are controlled

Participant observation. a form of direct observation in which the researcher becomes more or less actively involved in the behaviors of the group that is being studied

Path analysis. a statistical technique for assessing the relative influence of variables in a causal model

Periodical indexes. systematic listings of journals and other periodicals used in literature reviews

Pie diagram. a graphic device in which sectored circles are used to represent observations

Pilot study. a small-scale trial of measures and procedures used to identify in advance any weaknesses in the research plan or instrumentation

Population. a set of cases about which one wishes to draw some conclusions

Positive relationship. the relationship said to exist when corresponding values on two variables change in the same direction

Posttest. in an experiment, a measurement taken after the introduction of the experimental event

Pragmatic validation. the process of determining the pragmatic (practical) validity of an indicator

Pragmatic validity. the validity of an indicator as a measure of a concept that is demonstrated by the ability to use it to predict the values of indicators of other concepts

Precision matching. a procedure by which experimental and control groups may be made equivalent through the selection of comparable individuals

Predictive validity. a characteristic of a measure that allows the accurate prediction of future events

Pretest. in an experiment, a measurement taken before the introduction of the experimental event

Prisoners' dilemma game. a mathematical game in which the players achieve a better payoff by cooperating than by double-crossing but in which there is the incentive to double-cross

Proposition. a statement of the relationship between concepts that is logically derived from the assumptions of a theory; a component of a theory

Q-sort. a technique employed in content analysis to measure the intensity of evaluative statements

Qualitative. research based on the researcher's informed understanding of the events under study and not involving statistical comparisons of cases

Qualitative methods. research strategies designed to gather qualitative information, usually in narrative form, in order to describe or understand people and events in their natural setting

Quantile. a measure of position within a distribution

Quantile range. a measure of dispersion for ordinal variables

Quantitative. research based on statistical comparisons of the characteristics of the numerical measurement representing cases being studied

Quasi-experimental design. research in which data analysis techniques or data-gathering strategies are used to approximate the degree of control associated with experimental research

Question branching. ordering survey questions based on responses to earlier questions

Question format. the technique by which survey questions are presented and answered

Questionnaire. a survey instrument intended for use in mailed or self- administered surveys

Quota sample. a sample in which cases are selected to fill a predesignated distribution of attributes

Random errors. nonsystematic measurement errors that render indicators invalid and unreliable as measures of a concept

Randomization. a procedure for selecting cases for study (or for obtaining equivalence in experiments) in which each case in a population, and every combination of cases of a given size, has an equal chance of selection

Random sample. a sample in which cases are selected from a population in accordance with the principle of randomization

Raw data. the product of unstandardized or otherwise unprocessed observations

Reactivity. the circumstance in which persons under study modify their behavior in reaction to the research itself

Recording form. the form used to transfer aggregate data from a source document to machine-readable form

Recursive. the term describing a causal model in which no variable influences any variable that occurs before it in the model and thus contains no "feedback"

Regression line. the line that best summarizes the distribution of data points on a scatter diagram and the slope of which characterizes the relationship in units of change between two internal variables

Regression toward the mean. the natural tendency for extreme values to move toward more typical values over time

Reliability. the consistency with which a measuring instrument allows assignment of values to cases

Representativeness. the degree to which a relatively small number of cases resemble the larger number of cases from which they are drawn

Representative sample. a sample in which all major traits of the population being sampled are present in the same proportion as in the population itself

Research design. the plan of a study that organizes observations in such a way as to establish a sound logical basis for causal inference

Research question. a question identifying the basic information we are seeking in a research project

Respondents. persons who respond to an interview or questionnaire

Sample. a small group of cases drawn from and used to represent some larger group

Sampling error. differences between the attributes of a sample and those of the population from which the sample is drawn

Scale. a series of indicators that can be ordered so as to rank cases according to the degree to which they manifest a concept

Scale score. a single measure of how much a subject has of a given attribute measured by a scale

Scaling. the process of combining several indicators of a given concept into a single complex indicator of that concept

Scatter diagram. a graphic summary of the distribution of cases on two variables, using dots to represent observations

Scheduled interviews. elite or specialized interviews that are guided by an interview schedule specifying the questions to be asked

Scientific research. a method of testing theories and hypotheses by applying certain rules of analysis to the observation and interpretation of reality under strictly delineated circumstances

Screening interview. an interview conducted to select participants for a focus group

Secondary analysis. analysis of data that have been gathered previously, usually by another researcher

Segmented bar chart. a graphic display of data with bars divided into segments to show the distribution of a second characteristic in the population represented by the bar

Solomon two-control-group research design. a variation on the classic experimental design intended to allow researchers to identify any *test effect* present in the experiment

Solomon three-control-group research design. a variation on the classic experimental design intended to allow researchers to identify any influence of *maturation* on the results of an experiment

Specialized interviewing. interviews with respondents who require nonstandard procedures to ensure communication

Spurious relationship. a relationship in which two variables covary but only because of chance or because of the action of some other variable

Standard deviation (s). the measure of dispersion for interval variables

Standarized measures. indicators adjusted so as to allow valid comparisons among units of different sizes in the analysis of aggregate data

Standard score (z). the measure of location in an interval distribution based on standard deviation units about the mean

Standard score of gamma (Z_G). a test of the statistical significance of an association between two ordinal variables

Statistical significance. the likelihood that an association noted between two variables, based on analysis of a sample, might have occurred by chance and might not exist in the larger population

Statistics. numbers that summarize either the distributions of values on or the relationships between or among variables; in sampling, the characteristics of a sample that correspond to the parameters of a population

Stimulus. the independent variable in an experiment

Stratified sampling. a procedure in which subgroups are selected on the basis of one or more shared characteristics and then sampled separately

Structural content analysis. analysis focusing on the format of a communication

Structured observation. direct observation using a prepared schedule or protocol to record data

Subjects. persons who are being studied in a research project

Substantive content analysis. analysis focusing on the meaning of a communication

Summative indicator. a measure of group characteristics created by combining the individual characteristics of group members

Survey research. a technique used in the study of individual attitudes, attributes, or behaviors

Syntality indicator. a measure of some quality or characteristic of a group as a whole

Systematic errors. measurement errors that affect all applications of an instrument and render indicators invalid as measures of a concept

Systematic random sample. a sample in which cases are drawn from a master list by random selection of the first case and application of a selection interval for choosing subsequent cases

Telephone surveys. surveys in which interviews are conducted over the telephone

Test effect. any difference in the pretest and posttest scores of a subject due exclusively to a response to the pretest

Theoretical import. the degree to which a concept plays an important part in a conceptual explanation of an event

Theorizing. the process of stating conceptual explanations for real-world events by asserting systems of relationships among concepts

Theory. a possible explanation for events, often a set of logically related assumptions and propositions

Theory elaboration. the result of theory testing that refines a theory rather than confirming or refuting the theory

Theory testing. an effort to demonstrate the utility of a theory through research

Thurston scaling. a technique of scale construction in which some members of the group being studied are asked to act as "judges" to assign values to items to be used in a scale in order to increase its validity as a measure of some underlying concept

Time-series analysis. a data analysis technique based on regression that seeks to establish causal relationships through temporal ordering

Time-series design. a research design that seeks to establish causal relationships through analysis across time

Trend study. analysis based on a comparison of the same general population (such as persons of voting age in a certain state) at different times

Unit of analysis. the smallest component or element about which generalizations are to be made

Univariate statistics. statistics relating to or describing one variable

Unobtrusive research or **measure.** a measurement that intentionally avoids influencing the behavior of research subjects

Unscheduled. free-form, without a specific format or instrument; said of interviews, observations, etc.

Unscheduled interviews. elite or specialized interviews that are *not* guided by an interview schedule listing questions to be asked

Unstructured observation. direct observation using notes but not a prepared schedule or protocol, to record data

Validation. the process of assessing the degree to which an indicator accurately reflects the concept it is intended to measure

Validity. the extent to which measures correspond to the concepts they are intended to reflect

Value. the characteristic or score of a particular case on a given variable

Variable. a characteristic that takes on different values from one case to another or, for a given case, from one time to another

Variation ratio. the measure of dispersion for nominal variables

Weight. to alter the relative importance of items in an index or cases in a sample; the differential value assigned to a particular item or case to accomplish this

Weighted index. an index in which scores on one variable have been standardized by reference to scores on some other variable in order to facilitate valid comparison of index scores for different cases

Working hypothesis. a statement predicting a relationship between indicators

Zero-sum game. a mathematical game with payoffs such that whatever one player wins, the other must lose

INDEX